CONTROL TOWER CALLING

Nigel Morter

Published by Control Tower Books.
www.controltowernorfolk.uk

Produced and manufactured by Softwood Books

EU Responsible person: Maddy Glenn
Office 2, Wharfside House, Prentice Road, Stowmarket, Suffolk, IP14 1RD
www.softwoodbooks.com
hello@softwoodbooks.com

EU Rep:
Authorised Rep Compliance Ltd., Ground Floor, 71 Lower Baggot Street,
Dublin, D02 P593, Ireland
www.arccompliance.com
info@arccompliance.com

Paperback ISBN: 978-1-7385444-1-7

Dedicated to all those who served at RAF North Creake 1944 to 1945, particularly those who did not return.

Control Tower Calling tells the story of two labours of love. It is lively, people-focussed history of electronic warfare carried out my RAF personnel during the Second World War, together with the way the author and his wife restored the modernist Control Tower. A great read!

Professor Joanna Bourke, Birkbeck University of London

Control Tower Calling is much more than a good read. It is a compelling account of what life was really like on and around an RAF station engaged in most secret work during wartime. Nigel Morter interweaves the remarkable journey he and his wife undertook to restore and repurpose an iconic art deco building with the poignant memories of RAF North Creake veterans. He reinforces their accounts with meticulous research which reveals both inspiring and painful events. There are many books recounting RAF 100 Group's pioneering role in electronic warfare; *Control Tower Calling* refreshingly explains the complex technology and tactics employed in language that ordinary mortals can understand.

Roger Dobson, Chairman RAF 100 (Bomber Support) Group Association

Control Tower Calling is wonderful and has had me laughing out loud and weeping within just a page or two. Thank you, thank you, thank you for bringing RAF North Creake, both now and during the Second World War, so alive for me.

Wendy Neale, Daughter of John Stone, Pilot, RAF North Creake 1944-1945

I applaud the research, and the amount of detail that is packed in. *Control Tower Calling* is very interesting and brought back a lot of memories!

Roy Berrill, Meteorologist, RAF North Creake 1944-1945

If you have not yet read this amazing book, then you jolly well should! This is the story of RAF North Creake through the eyes of the couple who bought the control tower and, whilst being very respectful of its history, have turned it into a delightful and successful B&B.

But the book is so much more than that. Chapters alternate between that story, and the whole wartime story of the airfield, with many, many quotes from people who served there, both air and ground crew. The reader is given a riveting impression of both life on the station and life - and death - in the air on operations.

The author has done his homework very thoroughly and his description of all the aspects of the bomber war is both moving and thought provoking. I rarely read a book from cover to cover but I have this one - I could not put it down.

I have read many books about the reality of life in Bomber Command. For me *Control Tower Calling* is head and shoulders above the rest and I shall certainly read it again and again. My book of the year by a mile!

Dr Steve Bond, Aviation Author

An intimate, revealing and, at times, surprisingly moving account of the domestic life of a wartime airfield and the men and women who served there. A story made even more relevant and lasting by the inner narrative of the Control Tower's long and respectful renovation by the author and his family.

Nigel Morter has achieved a rare and precious thing: a blend of both national and personal histories that focuses on the telling detail, and which wholly avoids the nostalgic impulse and faux-celebratory tone that too many similar accounts succumb to. *Control Tower Calling* is a fitting tribute to the extraordinary times and those extraordinary lives now vanishing all too swiftly behind us in an age increasingly desperate to find meaning, relevance, and reassurance in its own past.

Gary Armitage (Rober Edric), Novelist

ABOUT THE AUTHOR

Nigel Morter runs the Control Tower B&B in North Norfolk with his wife Claire Nugent. From a Labour Movement background, he left school at 16 and became a trade union activist while working for a local authority. After completing a BSc in Environmental Science, he was employed as a Principal Lecturer in Labour & Trade Union Studies teaching graduate and post-graduate programmes. Nigel left HE in 2013 coinciding with a recent move to Norfolk. With unique access to unpublished materials from veterans and their families who approached him with memories, documents and diaries, he felt compelled to document this fascinating story of RAF North Creake before it was lost.

CONTENTS

LIST OF ABBREVIATIONS

ABCA	Army Bureau of Current Affairs
AMWD	Air Ministry Works Directorate
BCHQ	Bomber Command Headquarters
BFP	British Field Products
BSDU	Bomber Support Development Unit
CWG	Co-operative Women's Guild
DROs	Daily Routine Orders
EDP	Eastern Daily Press
Ensa	Entertainments National Service Association
ETA	Central Forecasting Office
FIDO	Fog Investigation and Dispersal Operation or Fog Intensive Dispersal Of
FLO	Flying Control Officer
GCI	Ground Control Interception
HCU	Heavy Conversion Unit
IWGC	Imperial War Graves Commission, now knowns as, Commonwealth War Graves
JPC	Joint Production Committee
LDO	Local Development Order
MRES	Missing Research Enquiry Service
Naafi	Navy, Army and Air Force Institute
NUAW	National Union of Agricultural Workers
NCO	Non-Commissioned Officer

ORB	Operations Record Book
ORBA	Operations Record Book Appendix
OTU	Operational Training Unit
PPU	Peace Pledge Union
PBX	Private Branch Exchange
RAF	Royal Air Force
RAAF	Royal Australian Air Force
RBL	Royal British Legion
RCAF	Royal Canadian Air Force
RCM	Radio Countermeasures
RNZAF	Royal New Zealand Air Force
RASC	Royal Army Service Corp
SROs	Station Daily Orders
SSQ	Station Sick Quarters
SWF	Special Window Force
T&G	Transport & General Workers' Union
TDWC	Temporary Defence Work Committee
TRE	Telecommunications Research Establishment
274MU	274 Maintenance Unit
USAAF	United State Army Air Force
WECo	Walsingham Estate Company
WAAF	Women's Auxiliary Air Force
WRDC	Walsingham Rural District Council

PREFACE

The Control Tower on the former RAF North Creake airfield is a superb example of modernist architecture and the stylistic answer to our Art Deco dreams. From the moment of our discovery of the Control Tower the history of RAF North Creake became an irresistible draw. This book is the result.

Based on extensive primary, unpublished and archival research using a thematic rather than a chronological approach, this book explores the Control Tower story in a parallel narrative: the wartime history of its secret role in jamming German radar through the use of innovative 'Radio Counter Measures'; and the story of our restoration of the building through the joys and challenges, success and heartbreak.

While the book is set in a wider historical context, it is essentially a history of one airfield in Norfolk: it therefore has a European focus and concentrates on the Allied experience of the bombing war, in particular, the Bomber Command war against the German Nazis. The narrative unfolds over 11 chapters, nine of which are followed by a shorter RAF North Creake 'incident report'.

In 1943, at the height of the War, the Bomber Command offensive was laying waste to vast tracts of Europe. As a consequence, the Germans had developed incredibly sophisticated radar systems that allowed them to efficiently track, plot and intercept individual Bomber Command aircraft in the bomber stream. For Allied aircrews this was catastrophic, resulting in, across the war, approaching 50% of RAF aircrew being killed. In one single night, 30/31 March 1944,[1] Bomber Command suffered greater losses than Fighter Command experienced in the entire Battle of Britain.[2]

By the autumn of 1943, the bomber campaign was in crisis as losses reached unsustainable levels. In response, in November 1943, RAF 100 Group was established to co-ordinate effective countermeasures to the German defences; this was the birth of electronic warfare. RAF North Creake, the subject of this book, was one of the stations under their command.

I wish to acknowledge the extensive and generous help of a great many people. This book couldn't have been published without the financial support of our 'crowdfunders'. The book would have been a far less informed work without the generous donation and sharing of documents, photographs and histories pertaining to those stationed here, whether written or in conversations and interviews with families and local people. You are too numerous to list but you will find your contribution in the book and as sources referenced in the endnotes.

I should particularly mention Mike Hines and Mike Hillier for their indefatigable quest for answers to my most detailed questions. Ken Delve, Paul Francis, Jamie Hibberd, who were always at the end of an email. Thanks also to ABN Agri, for the use of their archive, as with the generous assistance of Clovis Meath Baker of Walsingham Estate for the hours spent searching for documents in their archive. Lucy Purvis in the Holkham Estates archive also gave kind help. The same applies to the very helpful staff at the Norfolk Record Office, the City of Norwich Aviation Museum and those at International Bomber Command memorial in Lincoln for the kind gift of materials.

However, I would particularly like to thank John Reid, for being incredibly generous with his time, archive and on the phone when I just didn't get it. There is also Lewis Orchard, who made me believe that he really did enjoy going to the National Archives at Kew, chasing up and photographing all those leads for me. Also Bob Ham for his excellent plan drawings of the Control Tower 'then and now'.

I would also like to thank all the B&B guests that opted for a tour, took an interest and engaged with my thoughts and proclamations on the history of the station and the war generally. You have focused my mind over the last twelve years. It has been a particular privilege to meet and talk to the veterans from RAF North Creake, more in number than we ever hoped or expected: Roy Berrill, David Butler, Vic Flowers, Alan Freegard, Denis Gill, David Graham, Gordon Mercier, Roy Smith. It was a particular joy to have the opportunity to get to know Bernie How so well. We miss him a great deal.

I also owe thanks to all those that read and commented on very early drafts, particularly Tracy King, for her comments, encouragement and advice; my brother Greg, for his very useful help on family matters (pertaining to the book) and more besides. Jamie Keenan at Keenan Design for the fabulous dustcover and Nathan and Maddie at Softwood Books for all their help and guidance in getting this book to the shelf. I can never adequately explain the depths of my gratitude to Mark Risborough (not only for his excellent work on photograph montages), but for saving my work when the computer hard drive corrupted. He got it back when all seemed lost.

Special thanks are saved for Mariane Reeve for her extraordinary work proofreading the manuscript and the marvellous job she did on the diagrams within the book, Emma John for her early, and continued, guidance on the direction of the book, for encouragement, support and enthusiasm. And for writing the blurb on the cover. Mike Mason for his unwavering willingness to comment fairly, sensitively and with great precision and understanding. The book would not have been the same without his help. Finally, to my wife Claire, the first editor, for her remarkably insightful comments, pulling me out of deep rabbit holes that, after chasing research details, I generally found myself down; for forgiving me my very early mornings and long absences; often in the room, but away somewhere else in my head. It's been a lot to put up with and I thank you.

All the views expressed are my own, as are any errors of judgement or fact.

Titles & Terminology

The titles/ranks (hereditary or acquired) of individuals have not been used unless in a direct quote or where the forename is unknown. The term control tower (capitalised when it refers to 'our' control tower) is used rather than watch office. This is a contentious decision for some, particularly veterans of the war, as the term was considered a US imposition. However, as the RAF adopted the title from 1943, after which time RAF North Creake became operational, it seemed the most appropriate. I have also predominantly used the term flying control rather than the postwar term air traffic control.[3]

Photographs

The photographs featured in this book are derived from a number of different sources (acknowledged with the photograph in brackets after the caption). Many have been kindly donated by relatives of the photographer (in the case of Norman Turnbull) or the person or relatives the person featured. In addition, John Reid has generously allowed me to make considerable use of his archive. Unacknowledged images are photographed by either me or Claire.

CHAPTER ONE

ONE BIG RISK IN LIFE WON'T HURT YOU

*One big risk in life won't hurt you, your
fortunes won't dip, friends won't desert you.*

Vic Godard & the Subway Sect (1993) I Can't Stop You.

Claire and I are not, as a rule, risk takers. Not exactly risk averse, more cautious or careful. The very idea of us giving up good careers for the distant prospect of running a B&B in a former military control tower was a nonsense. Particularly when first we'd have to spend a fortune we did not have restoring it. Simply preposterous. Ludicrous.

Nevertheless, it was what we did.

Like so many others fed on a diet rich in *Grand Designs*, we dreamed of undertaking a building project. It wasn't really meant to happen, it was just a pipe dream, something that could occupy you as you stared from a window during meetings at work.

That was, until the morning after our friend Lewis's birthday party in May 2005. As we navigated our way home through the country lanes of Cambridgeshire, just outside Steeple Morden we glimpsed a derelict structure at the side of the road; intrigued, we decided to stop. Located on a former Second World War aerodrome was an operations block, the organisational and administrative hub of a military airfield. We were in love; we took photographs, researched the history of the site, drew plans on the back of beermats and eventually built a reasonably impressive Lego model. It is difficult to explain the passion this building aroused in us; when we first crossed the threshold of that derelict site there was something about the way it felt. Perhaps it was the voluminous scale of the rooms, the way the light filtered in or just the sheer potential that oozed from every brick. But there was something less tangible as well. There is a feeling on derelict airfields that captures you; I think it's best described as the weight of history that hangs so heavy it makes you feel that you can reach out and touch the past. Perhaps it is the imagination, conjuring up distant echoes of the intense activity of the past that then reverberate in the silence and stillness of the present. There is nothing quite as abandoned as a derelict airfield. Whatever the cause, we found it impossible not to be moved.

Many dismissed our love for this building as a mid-life crisis of gargantuan proportions, but the operations block is a wonderful structure that could, potentially, make a splendid home. It is not a conventionally 'pretty' building, having a style humorously described by the playwright Alan Plater as 'secure against aerial bombardment but short on gaiety.'[1] Typically Modernist, the structure's size would compare favourably with an out-of-town main showroom and workshops for a car manufacturer. It was of brick and concrete construction, featuring asymmetric styling, with flat roofs and devoid of any ornament. There were immediate problems with applying the concept of 'home' to this building as there was little recent evidence of where you might source necessities such as water or power. Less prosaically, there was a general atmosphere of austerity derived from an absence of anything of comfort. A postwar attempt to demolish it added to the feeling of neglect; the roof leaked, there were no windows, much of the floor had been dug up, and a combine harvester stood in what would naturally be the sitting room. At some stage, someone had attempted to set a fire in one corner, leaving black smoke scars rising towards the ceiling. On the walls, scrawled in spray paint, were hastily daubed exhortations of love and hate. In short, in need of some work.

Feeling as we did, we knew that there was no alternative but to track down the owner and put in an offer. We wrote to him, he thought about it, we phoned him, he thought some more, and when we finally visited, he said 'no, at least not at the moment'. We held on to that qualification of the word 'no' for some considerable time before we realised that the agony could drag on for years. We then began to look elsewhere. In our search we spent much of our spare time either figuratively crawling around airfields on microfiche or literally crawling around derelict airfields all over East Anglia. Other operation blocks were discovered and we made a couple more offers; both ultimately fruitless.

We continued in this vein for some time. Ultimately, it was a holiday with friends in the Lake District that forced a change. The juxtaposition between the delightful break and my return to work was too much to ignore. The weather was still bright, but I was feeling downcast as I stared from the window of the train on my way home from work. I had been working at London Metropolitan University for nearly 15 years, teaching Labour & Trade Union Studies, a subject I adored, and working with colleagues I greatly valued. I was returning home after a redundancy meeting where three of my colleagues were informed that they were going to be sacked; I was their manager, I considered them friends and I felt really awful. Once home in Welwyn Garden City, I greeted Claire and settled down in sombre mood to check my emails. Sitting in front of my computer, nursing my upset while failing to address my correspondence, I distractedly typed into Google the phrase 'control tower for sale'; as the Control Tower on the former RAF North Creake filled the screen, I, with a voice tremoring with disbelief, called 'Claire, you'd better come and have a look at this'. It was for sale; we would buy it and everything would change.

North Creake is a village four miles east of the former airfield site, which is actually located in Bunkers Hill, Egmere. There was an established pre-war practice of selecting airfield names based upon the parish in which they were situated[2] or a nearby village, but avoiding any names with a phonetic similarity to an existing airfield.[3] This explains why RAF North Creake is not called RAF Bunkers Hill (RAF Biggin Hill, opened 1917), RAF Egmere (RAF Tangmere, opened 1918) or RAF Walsingham (the numerous RAF Somethinghams). Nonetheless, it was always known locally as Egmere 'Drome,[4] a title that occasionally even appeared on official documents,[A] perhaps suggesting some of the confusion that the name caused in this particular case.

From December 1943, in advance of its official opening and while there was still some additional construction work being undertaken, RAF North Creake was occupied by RAF 80 (Signals) Wing.[B] It seems very unlikely, even with Albert Eaton, an aircraft maintenance engineer stationed here between February and March 1944, that any aircraft were involved at this stage.[5] It appears that this period was primarily a 'toughening up regime'[6] in preparation for the opening of the second front. It was arduous, cold and exhausting training, Eric Reedman recalls:

> 'You!', roared one of the instructors, 'The little man there with the glasses, come and stick your bayonet into my chest!' Well, I mean to say that's not cricket is it? Especially if he is unarmed. So I made a feeble attempt as if to charge at him but my heart really wasn't in it. The next thing I knew I found myself on my back, the instructor was holding the rifle, and the bayonet was touching my throat! I still don't know how it had happened.[7]

Peter Giles was also preparing for D-Day on a three-week course at North Creake in the midst of the cold winter months. He recalls, 'snow had fallen, the power had failed, and we ate our meals by the light of two hurricane lamps placed on each table.'[8] He remembers that the course was led by a detachment from the Scots Guards and involved

---

A   Such as the 'Enrolment Form for RAF Personnel' sent to 'Swadling K. at RAF Egmere, North Creake, nr. Wells On Sea, Norfolk' (RAF: 7/5/1944). Ken was killed in action on the 16 June 1944 in the first operational loss from RAF North Creake.

B   RAF 80 (Signals) Wing became an RCM unit in 1940, it was absorbed by the RAF 100 Group on its formation in November 1943 (See Brettingham: 1997).

basic weapons and field training:

> the idea was that we would be able to assist the RAF Regiment in the event of enemy attack ... we practised firing several weapons, including the twin browning anti-aircraft gun on a 'stork' mounting. The guns would rear up in our inexperienced hands, so after a twin stream tracer was seen heading for Walsingham church, the mounting was tied down to the horizontal.[9]

Sid Derry remembers spending his days at RAF North Creake that winter, scrambling around the airfield over muddy ground and through water filled ditches. We met him at an RAF 100 Group reunion in 2012 and asked if he would like to come back to take another look at the place; his response was unequivocal: 'it was the coldest place on earth and I never want to see it again'.[10] We didn't pursue the point.

199 Squadron was the first squadron to be officially based at RAF North Creake. In May 1944, they made their journey from Lakenheath, their previous station, in a motorised convoy (their Stirling aircraft would follow later, after being refitted). Mistakenly believing that the airfield would be located in, or close to North Creake village, they took the main road that led directly there. When, unable to find any trace of an airfield, they asked locals where the aerodrome was, only to be told, 'there's no drome around here'.[11] This unenlightening response resulted in a vehicle returning to Lakenheath for better intelligence.[12] Some time later, when asked to account for their unhelpful approach, the villagers explained (using the local dialect) 'well you never know, they might have bin them there Garmens dressed up'.[13]

Luckily, we were familiar with RAF North Creake having made a visit to the airfield some four or five years earlier, exploring the area in search of an operations block. It was a forlorn hope; research had informed us it was not the 1943 design we favoured, and on the ground, we could find no trace of it.[C] We had missed the Control Tower on

---

C   The remains of the Administrative Site, which contained the operations block, evaded discovery until 2020

that occasion; an easy thing to overlook given it was surrounded by thirty-foot Leyland Cypress, standing like towering sentinels forming an impenetrable screen that would put off all but the most hardened airfield explorers. I think that that was probably the intention.

The night of the web-search Control Tower discovery, we poured over OS maps of North Norfolk with what our son, Cillian, describes as an 'excited Christmassy vibe'; attempting to locate the Control Tower exactly in a chaos of maps and airfield research. Not that we needed much familiarising with the area, as it was only some six miles from Binham, our favourite holiday destination, for the previous 20 years.

The following morning Claire went into work at the University of Hertfordshire, where she was employed as a manager of Graduate Futures, their careers advice service. She was quickly ushered into a meeting where the university were consulting on 'restructuring plans'; anyone who has ever worked for a large corporation or public sector body will know, this phrase is nearly always followed by the news that everyone will need to reapply for their jobs in order to reduce staff numbers. Normally, a gut-churning turn of events. However, compulsory redundancy is generally preceded by voluntary redundancy and, as sad as the restructuring was for her colleagues, this meant that Claire may not just have to leave, they might pay her to do so.

While I was not facing redundancy, the situation with my colleagues had made me feel vulnerable. I had come to work at the university by an unconventional route. I started peripatetic tutoring for the Transport and General Workers' Union (T&G) in 1992, after being made redundant from the ground's maintenance department of Welwyn Hatfield District Council. Redundancy was a fact of life by the 1990s; politicians had been busy persuading us that the period of 'jobs for life' was over. Although it seems to me that this golden age of employment for the working class had been remarkably short-lived, and possibly not even as long as anyone's working life – I suppose, my dad was as close

---

when we were preparing for a fundraising tour of the airfield. It then became obvious that the operations block had long since been demolished.

as you could get – first employed in 1945, he retired in the late 1980s. However, his experience of work would suggest a more complex picture of employment in this supposedly halcyon period. My dad worked as an aircraft inspector at De Havilland's; he was recruited as a trainee inspector to replace the outgoing Government-run wartime scheme of inspectors. By the time I spoke to him about his work in the 1970s, he hated it, felt trapped, but also, paradoxically, vulnerable to redundancy. This threat of redundancy has stained my memory of childhood – it always loomed large as an order of aircraft moved towards completion and would only be stayed at the last moment by a new order. There always seemed to be a new order before any redundancies happened, but close enough to unsettle the workforce. In this way, my dad spent his working life from the late 1960s until he retired due to ill-health in 1987. The factory eventually closed in 1994, plunging Hatfield into a spiral of decline that it took years to recover from, if, indeed, it ever really has. So, by the time I was made redundant in 1992, it just seemed part of life, drilled into us by a political ideology that normalised dismissal.

By British standards I come from a large family. My mum always told me that she wanted two things from a family; a girl and an even number of children, and that my dad wasn't convinced he wanted children at all. They had five boys.[D] As the youngest of the five, I have no recollection of ever wanting for anything, though I was aware that money was always tight. Consequently, I grew up in an atmosphere where taking risks was a luxury you could ill afford; there was security in keeping steady. I vividly remember a period in the late 1970s of overheard discussions of moving to Norfolk. I do not know how far advanced these were, only that the conclusion was that it was best to stay where they were, because they did not feel certain that dad could find work once there. Dad had Type 1 Diabetes and in the 1970s this was

---

D   I am convinced of the veracity of this family tale, although one of my brothers recently told me it was not true; but it's what I remember, it's always amused me and I'm sticking with it. My mum also told me that, throughout her pregnancy, she knew I was a boy and that I was to be called Benjamin. However, shortly after I was born, she looked at me and thought 'Nigel'; it's difficult not to be offended. Enquiring why they chose Nigel, she told me with hilarious honesty, 'I'm unsure; I've never really liked it'.

a 'disability' that he felt, I imagine correctly, limited his employment potential, because of perceived sickness absence; 'best stay where I am', he would say.

Nevertheless, by the standards of the time they had a good deal. Unusually for a couple living on a factory wage, my parents owned their own house, there was a family car, albeit old, and my mum was determined that all her children would look smart whenever they left the house. However, they were careful, never spending money unless they needed to, and only ever replacing things that my dad could not repair. My mum dedicated a great deal of time to the food shopping, finding the cheapest offers in different supermarkets. She made her own bread, not because it was fashionable but because it was cheaper. She adjusted hand-me-downs or made new clothes unless unavoidable. The time of the car's MOT was always a concern, as it would only pass after my dad spent several days lying underneath it effecting repairs. Sometimes the only cost-effective solution was to replace a car that needed too much work; a difficult financial decision to call. In this way our family owned three Hillman Super Minx cars through the 1970s and early 1980s – purchases that had a significant impact on my life, as since being able to drive I have never been without a Super Minx.

Ironically, my parents were ultimately beneficiaries of the much-maligned economics of the 1970s; the mortgage they took out in 1964, a huge financial commitment they could ill afford, was reduced from crippling to piffling by 10 years of high inflation and pay rises. Towards the mid-1980s they were financially secure and my dad bought his first new car.

When it came to careers, my dad's expectations were, unsurprisingly, reasonably low; something, judging from the direction of my early working life, I inherited. The only advice I remember him offering me about employment was, 'don't work in a factory', advice I was happy to heed as I had little intention of doing so. I left school at 16, poorly qualified to do anything. Having wanted for years to be a gardener, I drifted into a Youth Training Scheme on a bedding nursery in Brocket Park near Welwyn Garden City. It was something I quickly came to loathe.

Drifting was to characterise my approach to work for many years to come. I never quite felt confident enough to decide what I should do; I stumbled in a number of ill-considered directions that were insecure and left me perpetually broke. This was coupled with the unfortunate tendency to work in occupations and industries in decline; welcomed by workmates who always seemed to chorus, 'you should have been here 15 years ago, it was great then'. I joined a local authority ground's maintenance department 12 months before Compulsory Competitive Tendering[E] destroyed any joy in it. Becoming active in the Labour Movement, I worked for a trade union, an organisation I was, and remain, passionate about, just as they began to really haemorrhage members. I became an academic around the time of the introduction of student fees and the audit culture of 'measurement and outcomes', a culture that has completely changed the nature of universities for the worse; 'you should have been here 15 years ago; it was great then...'.

Claire was one of eight. Both being the youngest, there are similarities in our experience of growing up, but much that is different. She grew up in rural Ireland and unlike my parents who operated very much as a team (led by my mum, if we are honest), Claire's experience was one of patriarchy. Her father was a well-known and respected member of the community, with all the trappings and limitations that dictates for a child growing up in an area where everyone knows you. He was a man of traditional attitudes and values that did not always, shall we say, chime with Claire's. Having moved from Ireland, Claire was raising a son in London on an incredibly low income and had become adept at stretching the value of the contents of her purse. Living in a council flat in Camden with prospects that did not necessarily look bright, she took the decision to improve her chances by enrolling on

---

E Compulsory Competitive Tendering was part of the Conservative Government's restructuring of the public sector and part of the agenda to 'roll back the State'. All blue-collar local authority direct labour organisations were forced by law to be exposed to the 'market' in order, according to the dogma, to make local authorities more efficient. This efficiency generally meant workers working much harder for less pay and worse conditions.

an access course that would pave the way to a place on a BSc course in Environmental Science at the University of North London.

At Welwyn Hatfield District Council, I had become a Shop Steward and found myself, within a year, the Convenor of the Works. I was in my early 20s and ill-qualified for this role, so I enrolled for education courses with the union. The T&G had a wonderful education department and I discovered that I adored learning; I spent the next couple of years doing as much education as my union facilities agreement would allow. Unwittingly, I found myself advancing in the union, and it was when I started tutoring for them, that I first met the colleagues that were to be in that fateful redundancy meeting some 20 years later. We provided a range of courses for trade unionists to help them understand their role and understand their movement; it was a wonderful programme that I was immensely proud to be a part of. However, trade unions are strange paradoxical beasts, and they showed little compassion when closing the programme, displacing the tutors who were by that time employed by the university. The tendency of trade unions to mimic the worst employment practices of business when they are employers, while simultaneously demanding the best standards for their members at work, troubled me then and continues to trouble me now.

Nevertheless, the trade union movement remains the only effective organisation through which people can ensure a fair deal at work. It can also provide those with little hope of social mobility a route by which they can improve their lot. I was a direct beneficiary of this process; the trade union movement gave me skills, knowledge, confidence and an ability to utilise them that were entirely absent from my life when I left school. An experience that thousands have benefitted from over the history of the Labour Movement. Sadly, an opportunity now open to far fewer people.

The notion of a university degree was first mentioned to me shortly after starting to work with the tutoring team; it was not a proposition I wholly welcomed. Something in my background means I have always had a fear of being seen to fail; indeed I would far prefer to be thought of as lazy but capable than applying myself and not achieving. I found the idea of going to university terrifying, but I was being encouraged by people I respected. I therefore applied for a place and got an interview, where, even without the qualifications to warrant it, I received an unconditional offer. My trouble was, I could think of no plausible reason not to go. So I went.

Claire and I met on my first day at university; I felt on the back foot, given I had been teaching a trade union course and was now a few days late for the start of term. She seemed amazingly organised and armed with a determination to succeed,[F] enviable traits as far as I was concerned. As we became closer over the next few weeks, it became apparent I was an uneasy student and felt undeserving of my place (imposter syndrome, apparently). Claire encouraged and pushed me in equal measure and, by the time I was hooked, I needed to return the favour. In this way we both came through university with good degrees, a strong partnership, but more importantly, with her son Cillian, a family.

By the time I found the Control Tower, Claire and I were in good careers with enviable salaries, a comfortable house in Welwyn Garden City and Cillian, having reached his early 20s, away exploring being a grown-up. Granted, Claire was not a particularly happy university manager and I was feeling vulnerable to redundancy, even with no threat on the horizon, but on paper, we had it all. Nonetheless, after the discovery of the Control Tower, what should have been a pipe dream had become real and achievable; something we had talked of so often that it was overriding any practical concerns. Even though we were yet to see it, emotionally, it was already ours.

In anticipation of a viewing, I had read a little of the history of RAF North Creake; I had bought the invaluable *Action Stations* series on military airfields and the East Anglia edition was now well thumbed. RAF North Creake began life as a dummy or decoy airfield:

F   Claire has always insisted that the only reason she seemed organised was because she had been at the university for three weeks settling her son into the crèche. Even after 30 years, I don't believe a word of it.

In June 1939 it was decided to build both daytime and night dummies for the parent and satellite stations – K for daytime and Q for night. From June 1940 Q sites came into operation ... they were associated with a parent station up to 6 miles away ... 100 Q sites received 350 attacks. As the Luftwaffe became more practised the effectiveness diminished and they were, more or less, abandoned in 1942.[14]

Unlike operational airfields, Q site[G] decoys did not make great demands on land and they could be sited more or less anywhere, regardless of the topography. Their two-man operation involved very few structures as they simply consisted of lights controlled from a shelter with a generator attached for power. The operators used telephones to stay in touch with the parent station (nearby RAF Docking[15]) and they drew attacks by mimicking the lighting layout of runways; they even included a set of head lamps in order to appear like taxiing aircraft.[16] As precarious as this may appear, the impact of Q sites was impressive, with seven out of every ten night attacks hitting decoys rather than the associated operational airfield:

> [although we should be mindful] that a Q site attack could not be automatically chalked up as one deflected from a specific station – but the record is still impressive, both for the volume of bombs which the Luftwaffe had been induced to squander, and the false picture that so many Q site raids were drawing for German intelligence officers.[17]

Whether RAF North Creake induced any attacks, or indeed led to any false impressions for German intelligence, is not recorded. Certainly, there appear to be no reports of air raid activity around the former decoy site during this period. Today, as with so many other decoy sites, there is no known evidence of this Q site remaining on the ground, as all traces were removed during the subsequent building of the bomber

---

G   Although somewhat uncertain, it is assumed that the name of 'Q site' is derived from the Royal Navy 'Q ships'; warships disguised as merchant ships (Dobinson: 2000: 253).

airfield. Examples can be found, often hidden at the edge of farmer's fields; a reasonably well-preserved decoy can be seen on the Warham Marshes on the North Norfolk coast.

Airfield history was a new area of research for me. Many have assumed, because I am passionate about the history of RAF North Creake, that I must have had a life-long interest in the Royal Air Force, probably formed from a background in the armed forces. It does seem somewhat unlikely that someone who had joined CND by the age of 13 and has always erred on the side of peace movements, should harbour any interest in this subject. I cannot deny that I was pleased to learn that the station was closed to operational flying in 1945, meaning that all operations from here took place during the Second World War. This comfortably avoids involvement in the Cold War; a subject about which I am more ambivalent. In my view, one of the greatest contributions that Britain has made to the world, was its stand against fascism in the Second World War, and if there is such a thing as a just war, this was it. Nonetheless, I equally recognise that war is the 'most violent form of organized human conflict,'[18] and is brutal and brutalising. Nevertheless, it was this war that would defeat in Germany and Italy the most pernicious forms of fascism (although it still remained in Spain and arguably Portugal); an action for which Britain would pay a high price. For Britain, the inevitable loss of life that war incurs, while tragically high, did not compare with the catastrophic losses of other nations, but economically, in 1945, Britain was on its knees:

> The British had as many problems, if not more, recovering from victory as the Germans did recovering from defeat … What did Britain get out of the war? Not very much, she lost a very great deal. I suppose, if you look at it positively, she got a moral claim on the world as the nation that had stood against Hitler alone for a year and had provided the moral leadership against the Nazis at a time when everyone else was willing to cave in … The British, I suppose you would have to say, paid the most for victory and got the least out of it[19]

This postwar hardship forced the hand of the new Labour Government, leading it to negotiate a loan, through John Maynard Keynes, from the USA. The terms of this loan led to a great deal of resentment in Britain, as illustrated by a contemporary comment in *The Economist*:

> Our present needs are the direct consequences of the fact that we fought earliest, that we fought longest and that we fought hardest. In moral terms we are the creditors; and for that we shall pay $140 million a year for the rest of the twentieth century. It may be unavoidable; but it is not right.[20]

The war also precipitated a great change in the British landscape; defensive and offensive structures built for the war still haunt the countryside. There had been some wartime resistance to this wave of construction, not in terms of need but in terms of situation. J B Priestley was typical when he wrote, 'there is no reason why time after time they should single out some of the few unspoilt regions in the country, to ruin them for ever'.[21] Reflections upon the scars influenced writing well into the 1950s, with fiction writers such as H E Bates commenting mournfully that:

> this is the country where ... they carved an airfield with bulldozing ruthlessness through every fox-covert and farm and pond and pigsty until nothing but a grey circus, with a perimeter five miles long, a trapeze of radio towers and landing lights, and a herd of black flying-elephants remained.[22]

It is deeply ironic that derelict airfields and some military training grounds are considered vital habitats in wildlife conservation, providing invaluable scrub for rare and declining species.[23] Nonetheless, the popular postwar *Penguin County Guides* noted in 1949 that 'Norfolk was profoundly affected by the war, of which many traces remain; it is said that there was an airfield every nine miles in East Anglia'.[24]

In 1930 there were only two operational RAF stations in Norfolk; at the end of the Second World War there was 37.[25] Each of which gouged and tore at the beautiful landscape. In Egmere (where RAF North Creake would later be located), the first evidence of war arrived just before the decoy airfield in 1940, when the 57th Heavy Newfoundland Regiment of the Royal Artillery were stationed in the fields near Egmere Farm. With two giant Great War vintage 9.2-inch Howitzer guns tasked with guarding against sea invasion from Wells-next-the-Sea or Holkham;[26] invasion never came and they were never used in anger. But there was practise firing. On the first occasion, the blast damaged two Egmere farm cottages so severely that they were abandoned and ultimately demolished. Subsequent practises involved first warning residents in order that they could open their windows and save the glass from blast, but that didn't stop it dislodging the soot in the chimneys and covering the cottage interiors in a coating of black dust. However, there was some advantage to the location of these guns; the residents always felt they'd know of an invasion before anyone else; for if the guns fired and they hadn't been warned to open their windows, the Germans were at the coast. After 16 months, the guns and the Newfoundlanders were moved, not because of any wartime imperative, but as a result of a practise shell narrowly missing a boat in Wells harbour. Locally, it was believed that the probable risk of invasion did not compare with the very real danger from friendly fire.[27]

The silence that returned to the fields of Egmere would be short-lived as construction of the new aerodrome commenced in October 1942.[28] It was built close to the site of the abandoned medieval village of Egmere[H] with its ruined church and views across farmlands and out to the sea beyond; a church that would soon gaze upon heavy bombers stood on dispersals that clipped the abandoned village's furthest reaches. The winds that caressed the crops in the bucolic fields of North Norfolk, very much as they had for generations, would soon be blown by the revving engines of the heavy bombers of Bomber Command. This part of North Norfolk would never be the same again. A scene repeated all over East Anglia and graphically described by Robert Arbib, a visiting American serviceman:

H There are over 150 such abandoned villages in Norfolk (literarynorfolk.co.uk: undated).

As each new field was invaded by our crushing machines, as each new hedgerow was smashed and uprooted and shattered, as each great oak succumbed before axe and dynamite and bulldozer, we felt a pang. For there is nothing quite as final, quite as levelling, as an aerodrome.[29]

The RAF, conscious of its status as the new fighting force, was keen to establish its own character and traditions; a desire it expressed through the design of its aerodromes. In 1920, Hugh Trenchard, the Chief of Staff, spent £13 million of the RAF's £15 million budget on airfields and buildings leading to very heavy criticism from many. Indeed, some were heard to be referring to the RAF as the 'Royal Ground Force'.[30] Undeterred, through the 1930s, he continued to devote 'a surprisingly generous proportion of his budget [one fifth[31]] to the building of solid, elegant stations'[32] in what became known as the 'Expansion Period'.[33] During this period the RAF built a further four stations in Norfolk, so that by September 1939, and the outbreak of the Second World War, there were a total of six operational stations available for the war effort. Nationwide, this building programme resulted in some 100 permanent RAF stations being built before the outbreak of war.[34]

These airfields involved buildings of 'character and uniformity'[35] which were of 'architectural merit',[36] generally in a Neo-Georgian architectural style. The airfield plans were subject to review and approval of the Royal Fine Arts Commission that, along with the Society for the Protection of Rural England, commented on the designs, the sites chosen, and their impact upon the countryside.[37] Expansion Period hangars, for example, were designed to be pleasing with minimal impact upon their surroundings.[38] With the benefit of hindsight, these seem curious priorities for a country so close to total war, but it does explain their impressive bearing.

By the time war was declared, the RAF was organised into five main commands: Bomber, Fighter, Transport, Coastal and Training.[39] The stations of Bomber Command were generally the largest and carried the most personnel (for example RAF North Creake had a total of 3,362 at its peak: 2,951 airmen and 411 WAAFs[40]). This level of staffing reflected the complexity of flying and supporting bombers, in what is characterised as the 'war's single longest continuous battle'.[41] The cost of this continuous battle was high: 55,573 members of aircrew were killed, out of the 125,000 who served (a 44.4% death rate), almost all of whom were officers and NCOs.[I] The losses also reflected the very cosmopolitan nature of RAF Bomber Command, with casualties from all corners of the globe.[J] A further 8,403 were wounded in action and 9,838 became prisoners of war.[42] By 1943, the odds were that only one in six crews would survive their first tour of operations,[43] and the chances of surviving two tours could be as low as one in 40.[K] Put another way, out of any 100 aircrew members, only 24 could expect to survive their first tour of 30 operations;[L] the average number of sorties completed being 14.[44] It is well-recorded that junior officers in the Great War suffered the highest rate of loss proportionately;[45] in Bomber Command in 1943, a navigator would have envied the life expectancy of a second lieutenant in 1916.[46]

The loss rate had to be lower than 4%[47] to stand a favourable chance of seeing the end of a tour and the average nightly loss rate for the war was 2.3%,[48] with the highest loss rate for one night (a raid on Nuremberg 30/31 March 1944) standing at 11.9% (equating to 95 bombers lost[49]). This means that 4.3 Bomber Command aircraft were lost for every day of the war, or 8,953 aircraft lost in total.[50] If your aircraft was hit you had a one in five chance of getting out,[51] and if

---

I   Non-Commissioned Officers (NCOs) have gained their position by promotion through the ranks, whereas Commissioned Officers 'are high ranking officers who have derived their authority from a commission issued by the monarch' (Ex-Mil.co.uk: undated). There may have been a number of different officer ranks on board an aircraft but the pilot was always in charge regardless of rank. Among crews generally, rank meant nothing while at the station as the rank of 'officer' was just a 'method of ensuring better treatment as a POW' (Wainwright: 1978: 127-128).

J   Royal Air Force: 38,462 (69.2%), Royal Canadian Air Force: 9,919 (17.8%), Royal Australian Air Force: 4,050 (7.3%), Royal New Zealand Air Force: 1,679 (3.0%), other Allied air forces: 1,463 (2.7%) (Hastings: 1980: 11).

K   The second tour consisted of 20 operations (Redding: 2005: 117).

L   While a tour is generally considered to consist of 30 operations, Bomber Command actually demanded a certain number of points before a tour was deemed complete (124 in 1944 – 144 in 1945). An operation was worth three points if the target was west of 6 degrees longitude and four points if it was east of 6 degrees longitude (Halpenny: 1982: 9). For crews, the change in what constituted a tour, often mid-way through, led to significant resentment; one airman from RAF North Creake noting in his diary in 1945 '7-hour trip for another damn half' (Thompson: 1945).

you found yourself in the North Sea you had about 30 minutes before hypothermia set in.[52] For aircrew, there were lots of numbers, mostly stacked against them.

In July 1944, in the eastern counties the Regional Commissioner reported that, in the previous six months alone, the emergency services had attended 177 plane crash fires.[53] With a total of 2,500 aircraft believed to have crashed in Norfolk and Suffolk during the Second World War, this was equivalent of at least one a day.[54]

In the cold light of postwar analysis this balance sheet was stark; the costs of Bomber Command's war were eye-wateringly high. For every ton of bombs dropped the cost was £1,[55] and Bomber Command dropped over 900,000 tons on Germany alone; killing between 305,000 and 500,000 German civilians (although these estimates include all Allied bombing, not just Bomber Command).[56] Therefore, in a crude balance sheet assessment, and taking the lower estimate, that is 5.5 German civilian deaths for every aircrew member killed.[57] Such is the tally of war.

Wartime aircrew members, actual or potential, were well aware of the high losses. While some denied they were frightened, suggesting 'a crew which contained one crew member who was afraid jeopardised the safety of the aircraft',[58] most concede they were, at least sometimes scared. As Stephen Wainwright explains:

> We all knew that, statistically speaking, we were breathing borrowed air ... we'd outlived far too many crews not to know ... Had anybody asked, we would have solemnly declared our firm belief that we hadn't a hope in hell's chance of seeing the end of this damn war.[59]

Don Charlwood describes a common sentiment among airmen: 'we were men before a firing squad of erratic marksmen. Kill us tonight or tomorrow night they might; kill us by next month they could scarcely fail to do.'[60] Stephen Wainwright believes that they did not necessarily fear dying, but they did fear pain and feared being taken prisoner of war,[61] and that over the target they were 'silently repeating ... another five minutes and it will be over.'[62] On their bomb run they struggled 'to avoid the urge to flinch and turn aside before reaching their aiming-point';[63] instinctive behaviour that could produce 'creep-back'. That is, dropping bombs just short of the target, setting fires that the subsequent crews may drop just shy of, resulting in the bombed-point creeping back further and further from the intended target. An inevitable temptation, given the experience of being over target:

> the velvet black darkness is broken by the continuous flashes of exploding bombs. Soon a red sore develops in the darkness below. As the city burns the sore spreads, and seems to pulsate with a macabre intensity – in the flames below schools, hospitals, homes and families are being destroyed ... Above the target area, a vast, demented, murderously intent barrage of anti-aircraft fire begins to trawl our aircraft from the sky. They fall like autumn leaves into the inferno below. Some explode in the air, others fall in flames, as numerous searchlights sweep the menacing darkness. These individual lances of white light capture their victims ... from which there is no escape. The captured aircraft, like silver moths, are soon plucked from the sky by the accurate radar-controlled anti-aircraft guns. Two aircraft collide as they leave the target, the flaming wreckage gyrating slowly earthwards. A searchlight almost catches us, its nearness lights up the interior of our aircraft as it sweeps past.[64]

John Wainwright does not consider that fear over target illustrates cowardice, even though most of the aircrew members, given the choice, would have 'turned tail and belted for home ... very few of us were heroes ... we were human beings, and very frightened human beings.'[65] Of course, if you had belted for home before dropping your bomb load on target, the automatic camera illuminated by a photo-flash bomb,[M]

M The photo-flash bomb was so designed that as it fell away from the bomb rack with all the other bombs, a safety pin was automatically withdrawn through being held back by a wire connected to the rack. This then allowed the small propellor on the nose to rotate freely and unscrew itself in the wind caused by its descent.

would capture your retreat and the best you could hope for on your return would be for the operation not to be recorded towards your total; indeed, this was even the case if the bombing was not captured because of a faulty camera.[66]

Some aircrew studiously counted down the number of operations[67] until the end of their tour, hoping they would get through safely. But for many, hope was lost and they believed it pointless 'teasing oneself about the prospect of ultimate safety'.[68] Some, when in a low mood, were rueful about ever having enlisted. Gordon Dennison, who was killed flying from RAF North Creake on 15/16 September 1944,[N] sardonically commented, 'if anybody tells [you] that the Air Force is great, they are just trying to get somebody to enjoy the misery along with them'.[69] Paul Fussell explains that when a crew was gripped with the 'fear of death', ideas of discipline were ineffective, as once they were convinced they would be killed 'everything else was therefore trivial.'[70] And they were often convinced:

> The line between the living and the dead is a very thin line, if you live on the brink of death yourself, it is as if those who have gone before have merely caught an earlier train to the same destination, and whatever that destination is, you will be sharing it soon, since you will almost certainly be catching the next one.[71]

Roland Winfield, a trained medical doctor flying with Bomber Command, postulated that the 'length of time that elapsed before a pilot became aware that operating against the enemy in heavy bombers was a dangerous business ... was directly related to his intelligence and powers of imagination'.[72] He argued that the greater a man's intelligence and the more fertile his imagination the sooner this realisation will occur.[73] Another medically trained member of Bomber Command,

---

When a certain number of turns had been completed, it then fell off completely, allowing a spring to be released, which in turn detonated the flash. All timed so that the flash went off as the rest of the bombs arrived at the ground (Sawyer: 1981: 124-125). 'You had to fly straight and level for about thirty seconds to get the bombing photograph' (Adcock: 2005: 299).

N See 'Missing' below.

Victor Tempest, concurred, suggesting that ideally, a crew needs to possess imagination, but not too much; and be gifted with the intelligence to acquire and impart knowledge, but not so much that he cannot 'go to bed and forget about events of his waking hours'.[74] However, a 1942 report did not limit the impacts to the intelligent and imaginative. It identified three distinct stages of reaction to flying sorties: first, they would be 'raring to go', second, the crews would be 'willing but not volunteering', and third, towards the end of the tour, they would be 'unwilling', but they would not admit this until they were taken off flying or suffered from a breakdown. The author concluded that 'aircrew are placed in a psychologically impossible position and … every pilot without exception will, in the end, develop an anxiety neurosis. It is inexorable and inevitable'.[75] Aircrew had an understanding of this phenomena; they called it the 'twenties'; 'a state of mind that came on after one had completed twenty-one operations'.[76] The primary symptom was 'pilots started to get over-careful',[77] when taking risks was an essential tool in aircrew survival; the timid were frequently killed.[78] Denis Gill, an RAF North Creake air gunner, recognises the symptoms:

> I met an air gunner I trained with. I remember him as a gregarious cheerful character. I was dismayed to see how he had changed. He was obviously under stress, and told me that he was scared about going on operations. He was now very serious and confided in me that he didn't expect to survive his tour of operations. He seemed to have an intuition about his fate. I only hope he was wrong.[79]

Such continuous feelings of anxiety had a profound effect on the lives of aircrew. The routine witnessing of loss, when the crew that shared your billet did not return and beds were 'empty for maybe a week … sort of affects you':[80]

> if we looked ahead (and when we looked ahead) we counted our future in weeks. Calmly. Without melodrama. And, certainly without heroics. The next leave, perhaps; then, if we made it,

we'd take it from there. At Christmas, we considered New Year
... but never Easter.[81]

As a consequence of all this fear and stress, many aircrew members
turned to more superstitious methods of coping; what some refer
to 'pagan or pre-rational modes of thought'.[82] Superstition played an
important role in maintaining crews' morale.[83] No talisman or relic was
too absurd and they came in many guises; lucky coins, pebbles, poems,
letters, buttons, lucky items of clothing (particularly those belonging to
a girlfriend) were either stashed in a pocket or worn, dried flowers, or
in the case of a crew member from RAF North Creake, some needles
from a Scots Pine; souvenirs from a near miss when coming in too low
on a return to the airfield. Then there were numerous soft toys; Murray
Pedan remembers a pilot who preserved his morale by carrying a large
panda and tucking it behind his seat: 'after about 20 trips, the panda's
powers gave out'.[84] Peter Thompson, the son of Wilf Thompson, a
wireless operator who flew from RAF North Creake, relates how Percy
the Penguin flew on all 18 sorties with his father between January and
April 1945:[85]

> made by my mother for my father, for good luck. The crew were
> [sic] going for a raid, they were getting in the aircraft and the
> skipper, Reg Law, asked my father if he had 'Percy the Penguin'
> with him as they were not flying without him. So my father had
> to go back and get him.[86]

Peter still has Percy.

Superstitions arose around an action or inaction, such as 'to
urinate communally on their plane's tail wheel before taking off on
a mission, or sometimes to do the same – as a ritual of thanksgiving
– upon returning';[87] 'superstitious nonsense', John Allison, a Bomber
Command crew member suggests an outsider may think, 'but when
one's life is in the balance night after night, it needs very little to tip the
scales to the side marked fear'.[88] Miles Tripp, an RAF bomb aimer and

novelist describes superstitions surrounding the taking of photographs
of aircrews being unlucky:

> I've heard as much [that it's unlucky], though I don't believe
> in superstitions myself – except for that old hat: I'd never fly
> without that.[89]

A wartime report concerning morale in Bomber Command, by David
Stafford-Clark, was in no doubt about the benefits of such 'superstitious'
reactions to stress. If a crewman who 'flew with his girl-friend's silk
stocking really believed it would protect him, then it would help
preserve his morale'.[90] The need for such things 'under the appalling
stress of combat should surprise no one'.[91]

Concurrent to the rise in superstition there was a decline in
religious observance.[O][92] However, even disbelievers, Mass Observation
found, were 'prompted to prayer by constant danger or worry'.[93]
Nonetheless, war was not easy for organised religions where 'most of
the ten commandments were being broken all day every day'.[94] On
RAF camps, compulsory worship was unpopular, and was frequently
accompanied by 'whistles and catcalls'. And, perhaps with good reason.
John Collins[P] explains, 'the bishops, with sighs of relief, had taken the
opportunity of shunting the "duds and misfits" from their dioceses into
the forces'.[95] Roy Berrill, a meteorologist at RAF North Creake, was
not impressed with some still in the church; he wanted to transfer from
the Baptist church to the Church of England, however, after meeting
with the vicar in Wells-next-the-Sea he concluded, 'he was living in a
different world; didn't seem to know there was an RAF base just up
the road'.[96]

Many found that acceptance of one's fate was the best strategy
and that 'having accepted the worst, it is easy to live for the best and for
the moment'.[97] A former crew member visiting the Control Tower in
2012 described this as a heightened reality; in their downtime they lived

---

O   Although this should not be exaggerated with only about 1 in twenty actually willing to profess atheism
    (Calder: 1969: 478).

P   John Collins was an RAF chaplain during the war and Canon at St Pauls Cathedral from 1948 (Collins:
    1966).

with gay abandon, mostly alcohol induced, and for him, everything was brighter and somehow more urgent.[98] 'We boozed and we laughed; we boozed a little too much and (perhaps) we laughed a lot too much ... but the laughter had little joy attached'.[99] For most, it was just a way of coping. Payday was some compensation, but only a little, particularly given the rates of RAF stipend: 'we spent our pay as soon as we drew it, on the principle that there were no pockets in shrouds'.[100] Michael Renaut, who served as the wing commander of 171 Squadron, described the prevailing attitude at RAF North Creake:

> we lived a very false and hollow life as a result of operational flying, and the tendency was to throw mad mess parties and pub crawls. The spirit of a fellowship amongst men was one fine thing that existed in the face of a common danger. Operational aircrew knew very well that the next trip might be the last and to live a normal life with such knowledge was virtually impossible.[101]

Nonetheless, this was not a universal experience. For some it was always going to happen to someone else:

> Going and coming back [not over target], there was this vague, hard-to-explain feeling of immortality ... it just wasn't going to happen to you ... No matter (as happened sometimes) you could see anything up to three blazing kites going down, at the same time. It wasn't going to happen to you ... Anybody else ... everybody else ... but never you.[102]

Some, in spite of it all, had a 'great time'. It has always surprised me, when veterans visit the Control Tower, the number who maintain 'life hasn't been the same since,'[103] or that 'nothing was ever as exciting again'.[104]

When reaching the end of a tour of 30 operations, crews were offered a breather at an Operational Training Unit (OTU) for around six months, after which they would return to operational flying. It may have been a break from flying sorties, but it was no guarantee of safety as the accident rate at OTUs was appalling. Some courses lost as many as 25% of their trainees before graduation.[Q] There were also other considerations. Airmen had spent 30 operations with a crew that they had become completely reliant upon, they knew each other incredibly well. Most often, intensely close friendships had developed; a bond forged in the heat of (air) battle. If they went to an OTU they would be split up and there was little chance they would ever operate as a crew again. The answer? Volunteer for another tour straight away, that way they would stay together. And many did.

This decision was often difficult to explain to loved ones at home, particularly when it came to a third tour. Victor Tempest describes how, under the scrutiny of an exasperated wife, a crew member justifies himself:

> I will never have to live as closely and intimately with my wife as I will with myself. I go to bed each night with myself and I wake up in the morning to look at myself in the mirror; I must not let that image of myself be something of which I could ever be ashamed because then I could not go on living with myself any longer.[105]

This, Victor Tempest argues, is a 'code' to which airman must adhere; 'it is not only that they cannot do anything that would let themselves down in their own eyes, but they must not let themselves down in the eyes of their comrades'.[106]

If you were lucky enough to survive your time, there were the long-term effects of fighting with Bomber Command. Many members of aircrew struggled with civilian life. Nightmares, flashbacks, survivor's guilt, breakdowns and failed marriages; a myriad of symptoms of post-traumatic stress. Tom Borthwick, a resident of Wells-next-the-Sea, spoke of a vagrant he knew that had been a POW in the war. After an internment of four years he had returned home to discover his wife,

---

Q 5,327 killed, 3,113 injured 1939-45 (Hastings:1980:142-143).

who had been informed of his presumed death, had remarried and now had a child. She told him she didn't want him any longer and sent him away. He stayed drunk because, even 30 years later, when he was sober, he remembered the rejection.[107] Another couple, that had met at RAF North Creake and married during the war, found that on return to civilian life the husband could not cope with domestic living. He left his wife, leaving her to cope with bringing up five children alone.[108] Bernie How, reflecting on his time at RAF North Creake sagely observed 'well it changed people definitely ... I was a different person when I came out of the Air Force to when I joined'.[109]

Michael Renaut serves as a sobering example. Fear, or what he entitled his 'dark suited companion', just couldn't be shaken off when he returned to civilian life. He suffered a nervous breakdown in 1961 caused entirely by his wartime experiences,[110] and in January 1964, at the age of 44, he died. In the forward to Michael Renaut's autobiography, *Terror by Night*, David Young reflects:

> I do not know what was written on the death certificate, but I know what I would have written: 'This man gave the whole of his abundant courage to his Country during six years of war. There was nothing left.'[111]

Why then, when it was well known that losses were high, did young men volunteer? The RAF believed that 'volunteers gave better value than conscripts'[112] and everyone serving in aircrew was a volunteer. But why risk everything, perhaps even your life, to serve with Bomber Command?

Britain had been reluctant to fight another war; the nationally organised Peace Ballot in June 1935 tested public feeling on the matter. It was mistakenly heralded by many as an illustration of the high level of pacifism in Britain.[R] Certainly, there were good reasons for Britain's

---

R   The Peace Ballot was utilised by the Conservative Party leadership to bolster its position on appeasement of the Nazi regime, arguing that there was no appetite for economic or military sanctions against Germany. In fact it showed quite the opposite; the Peace Ballot vote was nearly three to one against the 'absolute' pacifist position (Gracchus: 1944: 19). As Winston Churchill wrote, it 'affirmed a positive and courageous policy [against an aggressor]' (Miliband: 1972: 223).

reluctance to wage another war against Germany; the cost of the Great War, just in terms of casualties, had been appallingly high. The memories of barely a generation earlier were raw; haunting those that had witnessed them. The idea of condemning their sons to a similar fate must have seemed unconscionable. However, close to the end of the decade most conceded the necessity of war against Nazism as the only way of resolving, at this late stage, this particular dispute. Even knowing exactly what that would involve:

> In the last war I remember, as those of my generation do, how young friends, mere boys at college, were made up like parcels and sent off to the front, half-trained second lieutenants, almost chucked into the flames and dead within a few weeks after leaving England ... I think that the men of my generation that were political rather than conscientious objectors to it, were putting up a fight against something they considered senseless. And the more we look back, the more we feel we were right. But we do feel there is a difference in this war ... men who were conscientious objectors in the last war are now leading organizers of victory in the present war.[113]

With the onset of war many volunteered for the forces in advance of conscription; many, particularly anti-fascists, joined up for noble reasons (some being veterans of the struggle against fascism in the Spanish Civil War). However, memories of the Great War hung heavy and 'the 'big words' – duty, honour, country – had a hollow ring'.[114] There would be no patriotic zeal in this war. There was a surge in publication of pamphlets of the 'why we fight' kind,[S] but God's support through the church was deliberately muted; the 'patriotic lexicon'[115] of God, King and Country would not suffice in this 'People's War'.[T] Nonetheless,

---

S For example: Tawney, R. H. (1941) Why Britain Fights; Cole, G. D. H. (1939) War Aims; Morrison, H. (1939) What Are We Fighting For?

T The 'people's war' was a common expression used during and since the war to describe the difference in nature of the Second World War. Tom Wintringham is generally credited with popularising the phrase although its origin is unknown (Calder: 1969: 138). It not only describes that people on the home front were now in the front line, but that war was 'no longer a conflict fought by a warrior caste for the benefit of citizens at home but a people's war that would have to be fought in harmony with the needs and aspirations of the people' (Addison: 1985: 11).

motivations for joining up were complex; some were honourable, for Britain in a time of need; some were to escape lives of poverty and drudgery; some just craved adventure.

With recruits from the Commonwealth, it would be a mistake to confuse pragmatism with wholehearted support for Britain and its Empire. Many servicemen were enlisted from, what were then, British colonies, but they forcefully assert that their enlistment should not be seen as an endorsement of British values. As John Jellicoe Blair was often, as his son recalls, eager to make clear, 'if Britain lost the war we would return to slavery. While we didn't like the British Empire, we certainly didn't want the Nazi Party coming down and running Jamaica for us.'[116] One can imagine similar perspectives towards the British Empire may account for the significant recruitment from Eire, or what is now the Republic of Ireland. However, and perhaps surprisingly, research into the reasons for enlistment from Eire during the Second World War, suggests a myriad of motivations, ranging from 'family tradition, through anti-fascist sentiment, to looking for excitement and glamour, to avoiding trouble with the police.'[117] Gordon Mercier, an air-gunner at RAF North Creake had been working in a munitions factory,[118] a reserved occupation, at his time of enlistment. Nonetheless, he had a personal reason to join-up; a native of Jersey he recalls, 'my dad was missing in France, I wanted to help'.[119]

For many, the collective memory of the Great War and 'getting stuck in the mud',[120] was a significant influence for joining the RAF. For Les King (special operator at RAF North Creake) it was a major consideration when choosing between the forces: 'certainly not the infantry, to experience what my father went through [in the Great War], I couldn't swim, so that ruled out the navy. So it had to be the RAF'.[121] However, many were motivated by more practical considerations. Bernie How, a veteran of RAF North Creake, decided on the RAF, even though his mother was set against him flying,[122] because, all being well, 'you slept in your own bed every night'.[123]

Bernie How, shortly after qualifying as a flight engineer (Bernie How)

The RAF selection boards excluded those unsuitable (on criteria such as health, eyesight and 'background'[124]) and then assigned the suitable to one of two categories: 'PNB, for potential pilots, navigators and air-bombers, who were usually grammar or public school educated, and WEA, future wireless-operators, flight engineers, and air-gunners, which was considered less intellectually demanding (and were also less well paid) trades'.[125]

RAF North Creake veteran Roy Smith wanted to be a navigator rather than a pilot, regardless, the selection board enrolled him as a pilot. Pilot training, a process that often needed two years to complete,[126] took many, Roy Smith included, to countries such as the USA and Canada, where:

one evening, I went out with two or three others, I imagine we had quite a few beers, and I got separated from [them] ... I did not arrive back at the camp until after the permitted time. Knowing that this would be a disciplinary offence, and that I would in all probability be removed from the course, I decided to try and enter the camp by squeezing under the surrounding wire fence. During this operation I heard the sound of a rifle shot, lights were switched on, and I was caught. That was the end of my pilot training and I learnt that I would be sent to Canada on a navigator's course.[127]

Denis Gill, also a veteran of RAF North Creake, at aged 18 volunteered to be a pilot. At the selection board he was told he would have a long wait for pilot training, but if he volunteered for aircrew, it could be arranged quickly. Consequently, he volunteered to be an air-gunner:

a brown envelope came through the letter box addressed to me ... 'What's that?' [my mother] asked. I was all smiles when I told her it was my call up papers. I saw the blood drain from her face. It was obvious this was something she had been dreading ... I took the envelope up to my bedroom that overlooked our back garden. I looked out of the window, and saw my grandfather just below in his yard ... I shouted down to him 'I've got my call up papers!' I expected him to be as happy about this as I was, but as he looked up at me his face was expressionless, then he turned and walked away [he had served in the trenches of the Great War].[128]

After a period of training in the recruit's aircrew trade, they moved towards the final stages of forming an operational aircrew. A critical part of this was 'crewing-up'. In practice, this meant at an OTU all the recruits (of all trades) who had completed training were put in a large room,[129] with the Naafi supplying tea and biscuits,[130] and told to find their own crew mates. This they did through a method of 'natural selection';[131] a seemingly odd concept, but remarkably effective. In a large room, such as a hangar, there were rows of seven seats, each representing a member of aircrew. As crews formed-up they filled the seats.[132] Gordon Mercier remembers some 'stood around like lost sheep [but] the most forward ones soon got stuck in ... in my case it took a little longer'.[133] Bernie How recalls no such difficulty, 'I wasn't very big ... but I was a confident little person you know'.[134] The process has been described both affectionately, as like the 'atmosphere of an old-fashioned teenage dance'[135] and disparagingly, as a 'lot of little dogs sniffing each other'.[136]

Denis Gill circa 1944 (Denis Gill)

Once a crew was formed, it was quite rare for changes to be made,[137] although Denis Gill described his first pilot as 'fucking useless; we soon got rid of him!'[138] Reading his memoirs, one can sympathise with the invective:

numerous landings, that were better described as controlled crashes, in which the instructor often cried out: 'let me have it! – let me have it!' followed by some untactful criticism and choice words. Eventually, after a particularly bad landing, the instructor yelled at our unfortunate pilot: 'Are you trying to fucking well kill us all?' and declared him incapable of properly flying this aircraft.[139]

More usually, it made for tight-knit, self-reliant crews who often became inseparable; they flew together, ate together, socialised together and were billeted together.

There were advantages to Air Force blue uniform, particularly in terms of attractiveness to the opposite sex. Julian Maclaren-Ross observed in London pubs how the 'RAF officers rated tops, being classified in turn by rank and number of decorations; naval officers came second and brown jobs a long way behind'.[140] A theme further explored in Brian Moore's novel, *The Emperor of Ice Cream*, set in Belfast and based on his own wartime experiences just before, and including, the devastating air raids:

> Women over in England are man-starved and hot as coals. When Jimmy and I are covered in Air Force blue, we plan to be bloody great studs up and down the land ... I mean you don't think anyone ever joins up for purely patriotic motives, even the English? ... Fellows join up because they want to leave home, see some excitement, stuff girls, and so on ... This uniform's going to liberate me.[141]

In making plans for our own personal liberation, it had taken an agonising two weeks before we had been able to arrange a viewing of the Control Tower. Leaving Hertfordshire early on a sunny morning in June 2011, we travelled up to Norfolk armed with the knowledge that the Control Tower had been on the market for 16 months without an offer. We had determined our price, and we were determined to stay calm. As we motored on, we were barely able to contain a heady combination of excitement and fear. Even though it was a journey we knew well, we crossed the Norfolk border two hours early, on a trip that takes two and a half hours. The purchase of the Control Tower would be a big step, not as momentous as others had made in their wartime journey to RAF North Creake, but significant nonetheless – 'one big risk in life won't hurt you, your fortunes won't dip, friends won't desert you' – so the man says.

AIR TEST

Halifax NA259

Monday 25 June 1945 was a beautiful sunny day in Norfolk. Many families ventured out to make the best of the weather. With the storm clouds of war lifted over Europe and with the VE Day celebrations hazy memories of more than a month earlier, personnel at RAF North Creake had mostly settled into a new routine. Many had already been redeployed elsewhere in the RAF and some had even been demobbed. The airfield was mostly quiet with few aircraft taking to the skies. At 14:58, Halifax NA259 took off for an air test with four crew members on board:

> Andrew Mill Adams (RAF) Air Gunner, aged 21
> Ian Wilshire Dent (RAAF) Pilot, aged 23
> Raymond Ernest George Seymour (RAF) Flight Engineer, aged 21
> William Way (RAF) Navigator, aged 23

A little over 12 minutes later, it was a burning wreck at the bottom of the cliffs at Cromer.

The crash was witnessed by a number of people,[1] and from these testimonies a reasonably clear impression of the aircraft's last moments can be determined. The first anyone was aware of the Halifax, it was flying in from the sea towards Cromer, quite high up with its tail down as if preparing to make a forced landing in the sea or on the beach. However, it then proceeded inland for a short distance, flying over Cromer before turning back out to sea.

Once over the sea, flying alongside the pier in the direction of the coastguard station, it turned back towards Cromer. Much lower now, but still higher than the cliffs. Its engines were making an 'odd' noise and at least two of the four were issuing thick black smoke. In the sea swimmers witnessed the aircraft flying low enough to clearly see a crew member standing at the door in the fuselage looking down. The swimmers were calling to him to jump; an action he was unlikely to survive, and he either ignored them or did not hear. As far as could be determined by the swimmers the aircraft was high enough to clear the top of the cliffs, but instead hit them just below the coastguard station:

> we were all convinced that he would have missed; he was high enough to miss that cliff … one chap remarked, 'he's dropping', and he hit the cliff … I've relived this, time and time again, and I'm certain he was trying to avoid Cromer … if he'd kept on his straight path, he would have gone right over the centre of Cromer … I think he knew his number was up in any case … if you'd seen the smoke and what was coming out, I wouldn't have thought he'd be airborne for much longer … our impression was, it was deliberate.[2]

From the top of the cliffs the developing scene looked a little different; the aircraft, it appeared, was attempting to make a forced landing on the area of flat ground at the top of the cliffs, but aborted this attempt at the last moment by dropping the aircraft out of sight and into the cliff face. Witnesses from the vantage point of the cliff top had a suspicion as to why this had happened; Frank Nolan was having a cigarette break with his comrades from the 56th (Highland) Medium Regiment R.A., when he saw the plane struggling to lift its tail and:

> my sergeant said run, and we ran for our lives. As we began to move, all of a sudden the pilot must have seen that there were people on the cliff … he knew that if he landed he would kill us all. In that split second he must have decided to crash into the cliffs. He killed himself and his crew to save us.[3]

The impact with the cliffs was colossal and devastating. The aircraft was immediately consumed by fire, leaving people to scatter in all directions in order to escape the exploding petrol tanks and igniting ammunition. This picture of absolute carnage cast an impossible contrast to the scene moments earlier of a community enjoying the delights of the sand and the sea on a fine day in June. If it had been the crew's intention to force a landing on the beach, their change of mind had saved many scores of lives. The front page of the Daily Mirror outlined the devastation the following day, beneath the heroic headline, 'RAF Men go to Death to Save Beach Crowd'.[4] It reported that 'terrified children and their parents flung themselves down among sand castles as a blazing Halifax bomber spluttered above them in the sunlight of Cromer Beach'. All the crew was killed instantly; mercifully, they would have known very little after impact. The only other reported casualties were Sergeant Glendenning of the United States Army Air Force and his British wife, who were both treated in Cromer Hospital after they suffered burns when the bomber crashed 20 yards from where they were sitting[5]. A remarkable, indeed, miraculous escape for those on the beach, allowing the commanding officer of 199 Squadron, Percy Bevington, to offer some words of comfort to Ian Dent's father:

> I can tell you that it appears probable that the aircraft was in trouble whilst flying over Cromer and it was seen to gradually descend as it reached the sea. We are of the opinion that your son had decided to attempt a forced landing on the Cromer Beach but when he saw the crowds of holidaymakers he made a

valiant but unsuccessful attempt to turn the aircraft and fly out to sea. Unfortunately he could not quite turn fast enough and one wing tip hit the cliff side and he crashed on the cliff sands. I have seen a letter in a local paper, from a civilian who was bathing at the time, and the writer is certain that the gallant crew were [sic] trying to avoid serious loss of civilian lives, and in doing so they lost their own.[6]

The author of the letter to which Percy Bevington refers, had felt 'compelled to write'[7] after witnessing the crash. He writes of his 'admiration of the obvious courage and self-sacrifice of the airmen'[8] whom he suggests saved many lives as they 'struggled gamely, gallantly and successfully to keep the plane airborne long enough to clear the crowds'.[9] An 'unselfish action … at the cost of the lives of the crew and leaves us saddened but proud'.[10]

The first fire crew despatched were from Horsham St Faith (now Norwich Airport), who had seen the smoke rising from the fires.[11] It took firemen an hour to quell the flames, having to be lowered down the cliffs on ropes in order to reach the blaze.[12] A schoolgirl returning home to Sheringham from Cromer shortly after the impact, watched the commotion from the bus window as they passed by the scene; my aunt, Sylvia Adams, recalls the struggle the bus had mounting the fire hoses that stretched across the road. Similarly, George Baker, who on his 16th birthday, was working at the Cromer Dairy just across the road from the crash, heard the impact and jumped on his bike to rush to the scene. Unfortunately for George he did not see his father walking down the street as he cut in front of the traffic: 'I was seriously wronged by my dad when I got home',[13] he said. Meeting with a friend at the top of the cliffs he got a bird's eye view of the wreckage, to which his friend's photographs, taken with his box Brownie, testify. They stayed watching for some considerable time. 'For the rest of the day', he said, 'the skies were full of aeroplanes observing the scene'.[14]

Flying in one of those aircraft was Michael Renaut,[15] wing commander of 171 Squadron from RAF North Creake, who subsequently commented in his autobiography, that he was very upset writing, as he remembers it, eight letters of sympathy to relatives.[16] He was not the only person unsure of how many were on board that fatal flight, as it normally took a crew of seven to fly a 'Heavy' four-engine Bomber and, at RAF North Creake, the aircrew numbered eight to each aircraft. The station sick quarters' NCO, John Rees, recollects that the station records indicated that there were five crew on board the aircraft when it crashed, 'but we only recovered four'[17] (note the use of the word 'we', suggesting the SSQ's staff attended the crash site). The bodies were transported to RAF Langham, and later transferred to RAF North Creake.[18] It later transpired that the missing crew member had pulled out of the air test at the last minute for emergency dental work; toothache that undoubtedly saved his life.

This was the last Halifax to be written-off in Bomber Command service.[19] Details given on the Air Ministry Form 78, 'Movement Card'[A], reveal that the aircraft was almost new, having only been delivered to the squadron on 6 May 1945. This was two days before VE Day, and with the consequential sudden shift in RAF priorities, the aircraft had not even been provided with a Squadron code letter.[20] Recording the flight of NA259 on 25 June 1945, the 199 Squadron Operations Record Book (ORB) that records all daily activities of the squadron, relates the events in a remarkably perfunctory manner.

> The only flying carried out was local air tests etc. One aircraft crashed in an air test on the beach at Cromer. The Captain (W/O Dent – AUS. 432360) and crew were [sic] all killed. Aircraft is a total wreck.[21]

The results of initial enquiries recorded on the Air Ministry Report (Form 765[B]) upholds the emerging consensus, with a witness reporting that 'all engines were throttled back and smoke was issuing from the

---

A AM Form 78, 'Movement card' records all movements that an aircraft made from manufacture through allocation to different squadrons, in a similar manner as a logbook would record owners of a motor vehicle.

B The Report Form 765 was normally compiled immediately after an accident and recorded the preliminary findings for accidents that were not attributable to enemy action.

outer engines or mainplanes'. [22] A further witness describes how the aircraft was making an 'unusual sound'.[23] However, the form indicates that as a result of the fire, there was not enough of the aircraft left to make a full technical investigation. Nonetheless, the general conclusions appear to chime closely with Percy Bevington's view that Ian Dent was aiming to make a forced landing on the beach, changing his mind because of the large crowds, but too late to avoid the cliffs.[24]

The official position regarding the causes of the accident is now difficult to determine, as the records of the RAF Board of Inquiry have been lost. However, Air Ministry Form 1180, which records brief details of the Board's conclusions (commonly known as the 'Aircraft Accident Card'), states:

> a/c [aircraft] struck cliff face when low flying from the direction of the sea, a/c turned port but did not avoid cliff. This is considered to be a deliberate case of low flying in which the pilot misjudged his distance from the cliff ... Not believed any technical defect.[25]

Form 1180 further states that the Halifax should not have taken off with a crew of four, implying that this had in some way contributed to the crash. It concludes that disciplinary action should be taken against Flight Lieutenant A W Burley, but it does not define the reason why he should be disciplined; although it seems reasonably safe to assume it is in connection with the aircraft flying short-handed.[C] A crew of a heavy bomber normally had seven members: pilot, flight engineer, navigator, bomb aimer, wireless operator and two air gunners, it is difficult to assert that flying an air test after the war warrants the inclusion of air gunners or a bomb aimer. While one gunner did fly, one imagines this was to operate the radio in the absence of the wireless operator. The critical roles for flying in peacetime – pilot, flight engineer and navigator

---

C   It has been difficult to find out anything about A W Burley. It would seem only one Burley flew from RAF North Creake and he was a pilot with 199 Squadron. He was promoted to the Squadron flight commander and would therefore have had responsibility for this crew. It also seems likely that this was Archibald Walter Burley born in Croydon in 1916. However, whether this is the correct Burley remains speculation (Hillier: 26/2/2024).

– were all on board. After all, throughout the war, the Air Transport Auxiliary, who ferried aircraft for the RAF, routinely flew four-engine bombers of the same and similar types with two crew members.[26]

With the aircraft being virtually new, it is also understandable to conclude that engine failure was unlikely, although not impossible. Despite a number of witnesses claiming to have heard an odd noise and to have seen smoke, this line of enquiry was disregarded. A researcher at the Air Historical Branch reflecting on the disparity between the results of the Board of Inquiry and the consensus of the witnesses suggests, 'pilot error was rather a catch-all term to avoid having to say "we haven't got a clue"... [although] it is strange that the [Board of Inquiry] doesn't seem to have given any credence to the witnesses.'[27] In all probability, it was a result that, it might be hoped, would end any further speculation as to the cause of the crash; it's simpler to blame a dead crew than have an inquiry that reaches an inconclusive verdict. Nonetheless, a sense of injustice regarding the official position persists; an article in 2004 in the regional newspaper, the *Eastern Daily Press*, carried the headline 'Crash Pilot Saved Our Lives',[28] and reported that 'for 60 years pilot error has been blamed for the Halifax's dramatic end ... But now, one man who says his life was saved by the crew's brave action is trying to set the record straight.'[29]

One may wonder why Frank Nolan had waited so long before speaking out; however, as the article explains, he tried to convince the RAF of the pilot's innocence at the time of the crash, 'but the air force were not interested'.[30] Moreover, his approach to the *Eastern Daily Press* was not his first attempt to air his memories of that day. In 1995, obviously haunted by the crash and unable to subsequently find out what happened to the crew, he wrote to Cromer Museum asking, 'if anyone in your office remembers the bomber which crashed into the cliffs near the coastguard station? I often wondered if the pilot was ever decorated for bravery?'[31] Frank Nolan had assumed that the truth would have emerged through the process of official inquiry and imagined that Ian Dent would have been properly recognised for what he had done.

When realising this was not the case his sense of injustice prompted him to speak out. George Baker shares this feeling of injustice, arguing:

> If the plane hadn't crashed into the cliff it would have killed the soldiers and all the coastguards in their station. What the pilot and his crew did deserves to be recognised with a memorial – he shouldn't be blamed for this.[32]

George has for many years tried to get Cromer Council to put up a memorial plaque to the crew, but his attempts to persuade them of the importance of commemorating this event have so far proved unsuccessful.

The pilot, Ian Wilshire Dent, Royal Australian Air Force, who had first joined up with the army and then transferred to flying, was from Strathfield in New South Wales, Australia. He was buried in the Commonwealth War Graves Commission section of the Cambridge City Cemetery. Raymond Ernest George Seymour, Royal Air Force, was the flight engineer, born in Reading in Berkshire in 1924. The only son of Henry and Florence Seymour, his mother died in 1926 and his father survived him by some 30 years. He left his father £183 11s 9d legacy. He was buried at Reading (Henley Road) Cemetery.

Halifax NA259 being cleared away from Cromer Beach (George Baker).

William Way, or Billy as he was known, Royal Air Force, was the navigator on Halifax NA259. Born in 1922 in Morden, Surrey, the son of William and Jeanne. He was buried at Morden Cemetery. Andrew Mill Adams, son of Samuel and Jessie Adams from Davidson's Mains on the north-west of Edinburgh, served with the Royal Air Force as an air gunner. He was buried at Wells-next-the-Sea Cemetery in Norfolk, less than three miles due north of RAF North Creake from where he took off on that fateful day.

CHAPTER TWO

BUILDING MEMORIES

*What has happened in the immemorial
landscape of the English countryside?
Airfields have flayed it bare ... the villainous
requirements of the new age! Over them
drones, day after day, the obscene shape of
the bomber, laying a trail like a filthy slug
upon Constable's and Gainsborough's sky.*

W.G. Hoskins (1955) The Making of the English Landscape.[1]

As we drove deeper into Norfolk our sense of trepidation grew; we had been dreaming of escaping to a new life for so long that, as it started to take tangible form, it was impossible to suppress feelings of nervousness. We would either do it now, while we had the opportunity, or accept that it was never anything more than a pipe dream. However, dreaming was easy and comfortable, but to turn dreams into a reality could, we feared, be a nightmare.

Beyond Fakenham was very familiar holiday territory, although suddenly, we were viewing it through a new lens. Travelling down the 'Dry Road'[A] between Fakenham and Wells-next-the-Sea we

---

A   Local folklore identifies two competing theories claiming to explain the origins of this name; my favourite

began to scour the countryside for evidence of the airfield. A wartime airfield leaves as indelible impression on the landscape as a pen does on paper; it is captured within the nature of the terrain. The scars that the heavy plant left when gouging runways into the traditional farming landscape may, with reclamation by nature, have softened over time, but they are still visible. It is just a question of knowing what to look for.

Norfolk would witness a greater proportion of airfields than almost any other county.[2] It is often stated that this is for topographical reasons. However, Norfolk was actually chosen for the strategic military importance of its proximity to occupied Europe;[3] the topographic suitability of Norfolk was fortuitous, but not the criteria for selection.[4] Indeed, the frequently repeated assertion that Norfolk was a preferred Air Ministry location because of being flat,[B] is misleading as 'the topography is variable'[5] and comprises a range of quite different land forms.[6] Furthermore, the Air Ministry's topographical preferences meant, that while it considered flat land as acceptable,[7] it treated concave land with 'suspicion',[8] but ultimately, it believed 'convex ground is better in every respect.'[9] The top of Bunkers Hill, the site of RAF North Creake, suited these requirements well. It is built on a plateau at the meeting point of hills that rise from all approaches and, although comparatively flat in landscape terms, if anything the land rises a little too steeply. Even after grading, one runway, as old crew members will tell you, lifts a little too much for comfort, when attempting to take off or 'unstick' (as the crews graphically referred to it) a fully laden bomber. Nonetheless, in all other respects, the area on and around the airfield was ideal. It was the careful selection of such locations that ensured that they all share an unmistakable character: this means detecting them within the landscape becomes almost like a sixth sense rather than the assessment of a trained eye. This sense is, of course, honed over years of

---

is that the road passes through no villages and consequently there are no pubs in which to drink – a 'dry' road (Berry: 1989: 83). The second identifies the road as the dry route between Fakenham and Wells as the road through Walsingham was frequently flooded.

B This is a sensitive area for North Norfolk people. The popular reputation of Norfolk as flat can, at least in part, be placed at the door of Noel Coward and his play *Private Lives*; 'very flat, Norfolk'. I have inherited the sensitivity about Norfolk as a 'flat' county and it has now become the point of some hilarity with certain friends who rib me about it. Ironically, the same sensitivity my mum, a native of Sheringham, illustrated when I teased her about 'Norfolk Hills'.

seeking and scratching around old airfield sites. However, once acquired it is never lost, and you can find yourself driving through British countryside, on an unrelated journey, when one of you will remark, 'this looks like an airfield site'; from which point you endeavour to find the 'concrete' evidence needed to confirm your suspicion. Such as it was when approaching RAF North Creake from Fakenham.

We became alerted to the sense of an airfield as the horizon took on the characteristic form. The presence of pillboxes with no obvious purpose (either as a 'stop line' or point of strategic defence) were, we assumed, part of the original airfield defences. Our senses were heightened as we rose towards the plateau where, on the left, a tell-tale track leading to an unknown site had all the hallmarks of wartime concrete. Then, shortly after, signs of airfield architecture began to emerge; 'temporary' half-brick hutting[10] (buttressed four-inch-thick rendered walls; the width of half a brick), Nissen huts, Romney sheds – the type of buildings you will see on every wartime station – this is airfield country.

In 1934 there were 52 aerodromes in the United Kingdom. In 1942 it was estimated that there needed to be some 700,[11] including many to accommodate RAF squadrons displaced as 'the American forces enlarged'.[12] In August 1942, the Air Ministry's Directorate-General of Works devised a standard design for military airfields[13] that fulfilled the needs of all RAF Commands. Known as the 'Class A Standard Operational Airfield',[14] the vast majority of aerodromes built after this time (either new or as extensions) would conform to this design.[15] Planned to address the difficulties that earlier types had revealed, it differed from pre-war stations in a number of important ways. One of the most obvious was the adoption of hard runways rather than grass strips. The Air Ministry had concluded early in the war that the time was fast approaching when the construction of hard runways became inevitable as a result of the increased weight of aircraft, combined with their intensive use from which grass runways took a long time to recover, particularly in poor weather conditions. With the need for a massive expansion in airfield construction, it became obvious that 'suitable grass surfaces could not be provided in the time available'.[16] With the construction of 444[17] military airfields during the Second World War, the UK was often likened to 'an unsinkable aircraft carrier anchored off the coast of Europe'.[18] With this enormous expansion programme, it soon became apparent that it could not be realised while using the pre-war airfield building types. A review of airfield construction established a new system of 'standard building types'[19] that were strictly utility and even austere in character.[20] It is these buildings that give the Class A Standard Operational Airfield such a unique but familiar feel.

Buildings on pre-war airfields were generally concentrated around the airstrips. Consequently, personnel were exposed to significant and unnecessary risk when aerodromes became the inevitable target for Luftwaffe military raids.[21] A system of dispersal was therefore decided upon. This system minimised inconvenience and maximised protection, by centralising the core functions of the airfield in sites located close to the runways (including the airfield site with the control tower, technical site, bomb site and training site), with less critical functions (in terms of flying), being dispersed further away, but in easy walking or cycling distance from the main airfield site. This accounts for the huge area a Second World War military airfield involves. Positioning of these sites was also critical to allow for the utilisation, wherever possible, of the natural features of the landscape. These features, such as, contours of the land, hedges and woods, along with existing clusters of buildings (particularly those on farms), helped to conceal the, on average, 20 discrete sites from aerial observation.[22]

Once the strategic importance of East Anglia was identified, the site selection priorities of topography, soils, transport and existing land use needed to be considered. Of primary importance was topography, followed closely by suitable soil composition and third, was the availability and proximity of adequate transport links. The last consideration, although nevertheless of great importance, was existing land use.[23]

The RAF employed aerial photographic reconnaissance for identifying suitable land.[24] Once identified a 'lands officer' was assigned to survey a potential site, liaising with local surveyors and officials after a particular location had been deemed to be favourable.[25] The process of choosing a site and the commencement of building was remarkably expeditious. From the point of site selection and the associated drawing of rudimentary plans, through consultation, surveying, detailed drawing of all sites and buildings, requisition of land and the appointment of a contractor, a period of no greater than a month should have elapsed. At the busiest point the Air Ministry were overseeing between 20 and 30 airfield schemes concurrently.[26]

Through the introduction of the Emergency Powers (Defence) Act 1939 and subsequent enabling regulations, access to land, for the purpose of assessment, was determined.[27] This legislative provision also gave wide-ranging powers of requisition (and defined compensation for such), allowing for the immediate possession of land and buildings.[28] The Second World War saw 'one of the greatest schemes of requisition[C] ever undertaken',[29] resulting in the requisition of some 272,000 acres of land and 7,421 buildings.[30] At the end of the war the Government held 96,586 non-industrial premises, 220,000,000 square feet of industrial and storage premises and 12,000,000 acres of land, none of it held before 1939.[31] In Norfolk alone, the appetite for land in the construction of Class A airfields was voracious; 23,000 acres of Norfolk's land, almost all of it agricultural and desperately needed for wartime production, were subsumed by airfields.[32] The Air Ministry wrote in 1943:

> In a country the size of Great Britain ... the construction of so large a number of airfields has involved serious encroachments on land formerly available for agriculture and other purposes. It is not possible to express in terms of money what this diversion has involved, but it is considerable.[33]

C   The term requisition is critical as it means to take possession, as distinct from acquisition to take ownership. During the war the 1939 Defence Regulations allowed the Crown to do both (Krusin: 1940: 700). However, it appears, although not certain, that RAF North Creake land was requisitioned, as all documents refer to it in these terms. Compensation was paid and case law established that it should be a 'fair occupation rent' (Krusin: 1940: 706) with further compensation for damage and costs incurred for 'obeying directions' (Krusin: 1940: 706). At Edgar Farm, part of Walsingham Estate, the tenant was paid £32 compensation per year in respect of 32½ acres of land requisitioned for the airfield (Air Ministry Works Directorate: 18/10/1945).

For many landowners, the first they knew of the proposed airfield was when the standard Air Ministry letter dropped on their mat:

> I am directed to inform you that the Air Ministry have decided to construct an aerodrome in the above district and certain land believed to be in your occupation is embraced therein ... Formal notice of requisition will be forwarded to you in due course and a Lands Officer will call upon the occupier and discuss details as to possession and the harvesting of crops. In the meantime, I am to suggest you carry on with normal agricultural operations.[34]

There was an appeal process of sorts, and the Air Ministry attempted to make efforts to address farmers' concerns and even, in some cases,[D] delayed construction to allow for harvesting.[35] Such considerations put challenging demands on those locating appropriate sites for airfield construction. Particularly when difficulties in locating and developing suitable sites grew ever more acute.[36] Ultimately, in the vast proportion of cases, regardless of the relative merits of objections to the siting of an airfield, it would only ever be a question of delay, rather than relocation. The airfield would be built.

Pre-war stations commonly had four intersecting grass strips: with the move to hard runways, it was decided that three were sufficient when sited at 60 degrees to one another. With runway lengths of 2,000 yards for the primary runway (aligned to the prevailing winds wherever possible) and 1,400 yards for two further subsidiary runways, all were 50 yards wide and had a strip of a further 100 yards, cleared at either end, in case of any aircraft overshoots.[37] The runway layout formed a triangle that was encircled by a 50-foot-wide perimeter track (peritrack) which was, on average, three miles long. Around this peritrack were the dispersed stands for parking aircraft; these were to ensure no single

---

D   Such as Old Buckenham, south Norfolk (Nunn: 2019: 94)

concentration of aeroplanes in any one area, to minimise losses during an airfield attack:[E38]

The move to concrete runways was not without a number of challenges. Grass runways allowed for a considerable 'absorption' capacity, where hard runways had none. Therefore, a complete system of surface water removal had to be incorporated from the 75 to 100 acres of paving.[39] This surface water would then be discharged into existing water courses, where capacity allowed, or the water courses would be enlarged.[40] The National Farmers' Union raised concerns about potential damage from water discharge to farmers' field systems, and the Air Ministry recognised the complexity of these concerns:

> In the preparation of our new aerodromes with their large areas of hard runways ... we are faced on almost every site with a problem of effecting satisfactory surface water drainage ... sometimes it is a mere matter of persuading farmers to clean out their ditches but not infrequently it is a matter of arranging for large scale improvements to existing drainage schemes.[41]

Sites that 'would allow for the construction of runways of suitable grade and orientation without extensive earthworks and preparation' were in short supply.[42] Even with this careful selection of suitable sites, construction on such a scale was remarkably resource hungry. The material, labour and plant needs for the construction of a Class A Heavy Bomber Station in 1942-1943 were colossal. On average, runway excavation involved moving 162,000 cubic yards of spoil, the foundations needed 139,000 tons of hardcore (leading to a shortage which was, ironically, resolved by the German blitz of British cities[43]), and the laying of 72,000 tons of concrete for runways and hardstandings.[44] Plant requirements averaged at 90 tipper lorries, 14 bulldozers, six scrapers, seven excavators, four trenchers, 30 dumpers,

---

E   Having first been conceived as a 'frying pan' type (the circle 'pan' where aircraft parked and single track 'handle' leading to the peritrack, that were thought to resemble frying pans from the air). These were soon replaced with the 'spectacle' type design (so called because they resembled a pair of glasses from the air), as these were shown to ease congestion between the stand and peritrack (Halpenny: 1981: 10-11 & Francis: 1996 23).

one concrete paver (800 tons of concrete a day), 15 concrete mixers[45] and consumed 4.5 million bricks.[46] In terms of labour, 'it took seven months from the beginning of construction, with 800 workers continuously employed on the work for an airfield to be brought into use'.[47] However, even working day and night,[48] construction took up to a year and sometimes longer, if poor weather was experienced.[49] Thirteen months in the case of RAF North Creake.[50]

Construction on such a massive scale was difficult to conceal, and the Germans monitored airfield projects, prompting frequent attacks.[51] In an attempt to prevent such attacks, contractors were required to reduce visibility of the works by causing as little disturbance of the ground during construction as possible, and then spraying new concrete with a black bituminous dressing to reduce 'glare'.[52] RAF North Creake did not escape the attentions of the Germans, who attacked in 1942 during construction,[53] reportedly dropping three bombs along the main runway. No one was injured in the attack and the holes were quickly plugged with spoil and concrete by the construction workers. These repairs were rediscovered during the process of runway removal for hardcore in the building of the Kings Lynn bypass in the 1970s; the machine gobbling away the surface came to a sudden halt when it hit the huge concrete plugs used to fill the holes.[54]

Local legend asserts that a garden wall in the nearby village of Wighton was demolished by a bomb intended for the airfield; whether this was the same day as the runway bombing or whether the bomb was actually ever intended for the airfield is now impossible to determine. Indeed, a resident[55] of Wells-next-the-Sea, who remembers the war, maintains the bomber was actually aiming for a radio mast sited in Wighton. Nonetheless, the local legend persists whenever the airfield is raised in conversation at the Wighton pub, the Carpenters Arms.[56] Once operational, there were other incursions over the airfield[F] with John Rees remembering some V1 activity over the airfield.[57] Michael Renaut,

---

F   Whether these incursions were deliberately targeting airfields is a moot point. Locally, the general consensus at the time was that this not infrequent bombing of North Norfolk was caused by Luftwaffe bombers who, unable to locate their UK targets and heading out of UK airspace, unloaded their bombs on seeing the surf line of the coast ahead (Maufe: 22/2/2024).

wing commander of the 171 Squadron at North Creake, recalls that one 'dirty night' in March 1945, while waiting for aircraft to return from an operation there was a radio report of an aircraft on fire approaching. The flare paths were lit in anticipation of an emergency landing, and they ran to the balcony of the Control Tower to gain a better view. They could clearly hear the 'full-throated roar of an aircraft', when suddenly they caught site of what it was; a V1 flying bomb. Having realised it presented no immediate danger, they 'stood and watched; the ghastly thing came down near Kings Lynn'.[58] Michael Renaut explains that this was one of 17 that night, including one that brought down the ceiling in the RAF 100 Group operations room at Bylaugh. However, there is no record of such attacks in March 1945 in studies of V1 activity in Norfolk.[G]

For a resident of the Pink Cottages in Egmere, close to the south of the airfield, an airborne attack came at a very inopportune moment. She was using the outside lavatory in the garden when she heard an aircraft approaching. She realised the airfield was under attack when a bullet shot through one of the roof tiles where she was. The ingress of the bullet expediated lavatorial matters somewhat![59] Bernard Beaumont recalls the same event; while playing indoors he 'heard sharp cracking sounds and then silence as work on building stopped'.[60] Two families of airfield construction workers living on site in caravans near the farmhouse, consequently 'quickly moved out'.[61]

Even when construction was finished, disguising an airfield was a challenging task; the Air Ministry employed artists to advise and trial camouflage methods.[62] They identified that 'regular' shapes used in airfield construction, such as large concrete areas, buildings, roads, railways and water storage made them very conspicuous. Attempts were made to disguise this regularity with nets, ploughing, or with the use of paint, 'disruptive patterning' (in 1942 alone 22,000,000 gallons of camouflage paint was used at a cost of £8,750,000[63]). However, if during an intruder raid a camouflaged building was discovered, the very fact of the camouflage served only to confirm its strategic importance

---

G See Bowyer: 1986 and Bridges: 2023.

and identify it as a priority target. It was primarily for this reason, and the reducing threat of intrusion raids, that, by the spring of 1943, camouflage standards on many stations were relaxed and often even abandoned.[64]

The size of these airfields needs to be appreciated to understand the difficulties of hiding an airfield from the eyes of airborne intruders. With around 3,000 personnel stationed on the average bomber airfield they had to effectively function as a small town. Catering for the needs of work, rest and play involved the construction of some 500 buildings[65] and an area of 600 to 850 acres of land.[66] The work element of Air Force life was focused on the stands, hangars, control tower, flight offices, workshops, stores, and bomb site. Accommodation was mostly in Nissen huts (with sites separated between male and female), personnel could find refreshments in dining halls and Naafis, with entertainment available in the messes, cinema or library. Keeping fit and healthy was encouraged with the inclusion of squash courts, gym, cricket and football pitches. There were also shops, tailors, a Post Office, a church, barbers, a hospital and a mortuary.[67] Training was given in instructional buildings. Fuel for aircraft was, as in the case of RAF North Creake, very often delivered by underground pipeline and stored in petrol tanks – six at 72,000 gallons each – and were, sensibly, sited a considerable distance from any buildings.[68]

Fuel was just one supply consideration for a functioning airfield, water was another. It would be expected that an operational station would use up to 100,000 gallons of water per day,[69] and where reliable supply could not be provided by a local water company, the airfield sank their own bore holes.[70] For RAF North Creake this involved three bore holes drilled to a maximum depth of 106.6 metres.[71] To aid pressure, water was stored in a large high-level water tower, which was then equalised over the site through the use of smaller water tanks, from where water was then pumped where needed for technical, domestic and fire-fighting purposes.[72] With consumption of water comes the associated 'foul' water discharge, and sewage sites were developed for flows of between 15,000-100,000 gallons a day.[73] In a remarkable piece of co-operative planning, districts where the sewage works were likely to be of service in rural development postwar, were sited in consultation with local authorities and in liaison with the Ministry of Health, in a suitable position so they could be put to civil use at the cessation of hostilities.[74] At RAF North Creake things were well-advanced as early as July 1944, with the promulgation by Walsingham Rural District Council,[H] of plans outlining from where they would source water and how they would incorporate the RAF North Creake Sewage Works into their postwar developments.[75]

Electricity was as far as possible obtained from the nearest local supply.[76] During a power cut, such as after an air raid, emergency power could be provided by two huge diesel generators in the standby set house. These could only provide enough power for essential functions (such as the control tower, operations block, runway lighting, and, on longer periods of outage, pumps for water and sewage).[77]

Virtually all UK wartime airfield construction work was carried out by British contractors,[78] on the instruction and supervision of the Air Ministry.[79] Many of the contractors used, such as Laing, Wimpey and Costain, remain familiar today, with the war having established them as dominant building companies. Taylor Woodrow (now Taylor Wimpey) was the primary contractor for RAF North Creake, responsible for the airside in particular, with the buildings built by W O Lawrence.[80] The profits for this work were tightly controlled and there were no fortunes to be made, only reputations. Eight hundred different contracts were issued, using 136 different contractors,[81] who were employing at the 1942 peak, 60,000[82] workers on construction alone. This is the largest building programme in British history,[83] completing, on average, a new airfield every three days.[84]

Labour was an 'intractable problem'[85] for the Air Ministry and, the allotted numbers of workers were never sufficient.[86] Labour imported from Ireland eased the shortage somewhat, and these workers were supplemented by British civilians living near the construction sites.

H It should be noted that Walsingham Rural District Council is a different constituency body than Walsingham Parish Council and the former was abolished in the 1974 boundary changes. In 1944 it consisted of 38 parishes with a population of 17,000 residing in 60 villages (Cotterel: 1944: 19).

These local people were generally under or beyond the age of military service and were receiving 'wages they could have only dreamed of before the war'.[87] John Tuck was under conscription age and lived with his parents in Wells-next-the-Sea when he worked on the building of RAF North Creake. He started on 'general work' before he progressed to plumbing which was where he came into contact with Irish labourers; whom he discovered 'fascinated [him] because of their accents'.[88] He also worked alongside many locals who were employed in a range of activities from mixing cement to skilled trades, many of whom were women. At 17 he joined Tom Grange Haulage in Wells-next-the-Sea, and after a month's training was employed to drive their trucks. Working 12 hours a day, seven days a week,[89] he earned the substantial wage of £12 a week (after overtime), driving 36,000 miles in one year delivering aggregate to airfield sites in North Norfolk including RAF North Creake.[I] This was twice the wage[J] of his father who was an engine driver for the London and North Eastern Railway Company, and a great deal more than when John Tuck found himself in the army at the age of 18.[90] He said that you had to 'watch out for the gangs of women'; he particularly recalls running some women labourers in the back of his truck to Walsingham railway station, where he had been sent to pick up materials. En route, some of the women called for his help; he pulled the truck over, and on mounting the back of the vehicle, he was dragged down as the women tried to relieve him of his trousers. He reflected ruefully that 'Doreen from Burnham Deepdale, laughed about it for years after ... [but he had] never been so terrified in all my life'.[91] This from a man that had spent the rest of the war on active service in the army!

Working on airfield sites was not without industrial conflict, although no employee could resign or be dismissed without the authorisation of the National Service Officer of the district.[92] John

---

I   The weight of this traffic, according to Teddy Maufe, 'ruined the Dry Road', churning such deep furrows at the edges that they influenced the camber of the road well into the 1970s (Maufe: 22/2/2024).

J   Generally, the average weekly wage rose by 80% from October 1938 to July 1945 while cost of living rose by 30%, but the wages for airfield construction were still particularly generous in comparison (Marwick: 1980: 216).

Tuck remembers a time when the Irish labourers threw down their shovels and collectively walked off the job during construction at RAF North Creake.[93] This seems a surprising situation to arise as there was an established system of collective bargaining for those employed on airfield construction. Indeed, terms and conditions were not a matter for the employing contractors but of the national bargaining machinery of the Ministry of Works and were closely regulated.[94] Their strike was in a bid to have London Weighting[K] applied to the site in North Norfolk; an ambitious goal that was ultimately to prove unsuccessful. The strike did not last the afternoon.[95]

Scams were rife. On one occasion, a four-ton tipper lorry paused to be checked in at the sentry point; one sentry, observing the truck from on high, nonchalantly threw his empty cigarette packet on top of the truck's load of aggregate. When the lorry passed the sentry point for the fourth time, each time with a supposedly new load, but still with the cigarette packet resting on top of the aggregate, they challenged the driver. Whether this story is apocryphal is now impossible to establish. If it is, it at least illustrates the prevalence of 'dodges' and, importantly, the level of those involved, as I don't imagine they paid the driver for each load! Notwithstanding, the work was hard and involved long hours. Accidents were all too frequent with 1,359 people killed in construction between 1940 and 1944 (in 1930 to 1934 it was 584).[96] With effectively no civil building works allowed at this time, the only significant construction was on war structures (either defensive or offensive). Therefore, it is difficult not to conclude that these deaths should be considered among our war dead as much as if they had been killed on the front line. Instead, it is near impossible to discover their identities and where they were when they lost their lives. They remain silent victims of the conflict.

Remarkably, the total area of runways, perimeter tracks and hardstandings built in the UK during this period was approximately 36,000 acres or the equivalent of a 30-foot-wide road stretching

---

K   Introduced in 1920, London Weighting is an allowance paid to workers, particularly in the public sector, to reflect the higher cost of living in London and surrounding areas.

for nearly 10,000 miles.[97] When wartime airfield construction had concluded it had involved the carriage and use of some 14,250,000 four-ton lorry loads of basic materials, ballast and cement (excluding materials for buildings). Hundreds of new ballast pits had to be opened and material had to be hauled as much as 50 miles to site.[98] Aggregate for RAF North Creake was carried from a quarry opened in 1942 on the Wiveton Downs, some ten miles away; a huge pit with a circular track that wended its way to the bottom, which took some considerable skill to negotiate the climb out again when loaded with aggregate.[99] Once on site, it was liberally distributed, wherever a hard surface was needed. Even some 80 years later, soil brought in from the pit gives rise to seedlings of broom and gorse in our garden.

Enormous quantities of building materials were transported by rail to small stations nearest the bases under construction,[100] necessitating the development of special sidings[101] alongside the existing rural railways. Which railway station primarily supported RAF North Creake is now unclear, although John Tuck remembers picking up materials from both Wells-on-Sea and Little Walsingham stations during his days as a lorry driver.[102] However, there is little to suggest such sidings at the former railway stations today. During the war, a crisis on the railways necessitated a switch from rail to road. It was then realised that lorries loaded with cement for airfields in East Anglia were returning empty. A scheme was introduced where these returning trucks were filled with potatoes needed in London, thereby minimising transport waste.[103] Whether this scheme applied to North Creake, where the cement was brought in by ship to Wells-next-the-Sea Quay, is undocumented.[104]

Nonetheless, the vast majority of freight moved during the war was transported by rail, with the increase in railway traffic becoming a logistical headache of significant proportions.[105] One only has to consider the growth in freight to realise the organisational difficulties; in 1940, when Britain was constructing much of its defensive infrastructure, the railways carried 717,800 tons of freight. In 1943, at the height of airfield construction the total was 1,513,800 tons.[106]

All this development and organisation came at terrific expense. The construction of RAF North Creake cost, when completed, a total of £666,000 (£331,000 excluding buildings),[107] somewhat below the average for constructing a Class A Heavy Bomber airfield, but still an enormous amount of money in 1943. The programme total (excluding cost of buildings) is estimated at £200,000,000.[108] In 1942, for example, the Air Ministry spent an average of £400,000[L] a day.[109]

It is difficult to comprehend the impacts felt locally from the building an airfield; the activity generated by the construction of these bases, and their regular supply when operational, transformed the daily life of much of rural East Anglia.[110] Many locals in the villages of Great Walsingham and Little Walsingham took in lodgers from the Irish workforce;[111] an unexpected boost to their wartime income. The railways continued to carry high volumes of goods and personnel to the airfields even after construction.[112] Many of the airmen and WAAFs made their way to Little Walsingham when off duty, passing wages across counters in shops, cafes and pubs. Additional income was earned directly from the airfield for Walsingham and Wells residents. Leonard Carver who lived near Egmere Farm at the edge of the airfield, worked as a lorry driver and collected leftovers from RAF North Creake canteens for pig swill. Even his son used to earn pennies bringing abandoned RAF bikes back to the station.[113]

Doreen Leach, who later worked in the Naafi at RAF North Creake, recalls how her mother and father both worked on construction of the airfield; her father as a bricklayer, her mother mixing cement.[114] Similarly, Kitty Skipper recollects how her mother used to cook at RAF North Creake, when the 'Irish were up there building the aerodrome'.[M115] At the age of ten or 11 she used to ride her bicycle up to the airfield after school and standing on 'a box in front of a big old sink' would peel potatoes.[N116] Many more had their services used by

L In 1942 the country's daily expenditure on the war was an estimated £12–14,000,000 (Kohan: 1952: 281).

M While the terms 'aerodrome' and 'airfield' are generally interchangeable, officially the word aerodrome ceased to be used from 1943 (Harrington: 2016: 30).

N Priscilla Meath Baker remembers a cook who worked at RAF North Creake prior to working at Walsingham Abbey. On the first occasion she prepared potatoes, she was so in the habit of cooking for large numbers, that she had peeled a bucket full before she was stopped (Meath Baker: 11/3/2024).

airfield personnel; John Wright remembers accompanying his father, Sammy Wright the Walsingham baker, to deliver bread to RAF North Creake.[117] Gerry Boulter, who had been working as a welder at the motor repair shop 'Massey and Bridges' in Fakenham since leaving school, found his services in demand repairing broken plant.[118]

For many, living close to an airfield, the contrast between their homes and the high technology of an aerodrome must have seemed, at times, incomprehensible. Bernard Beaumont, a child living on the airfield site with construction happening all around him, recalls 'in an area where horses were still in use on farms, the chance to watch and ride massive machines was an experience not to be missed'.[119] The Pink Cottages on the south side of the airfield were old fashioned even by the standards of the time, with outside earth closets, a well for water and oil lamps for lighting. The construction of an airfield with running water, electricity and huge aircraft must have been unimaginable before the fact. Ernest Mallett, living near RAF Little Snoring, a sister station of RAF North Creake, remembers that with no electricity:

> we had no way of hearing the news, in towns there were sirens to indicate raids and lots of people to pass on news and warning but in our tiny village we didn't have this. We had to try and rely on what we observed and heard. We expected raids every night and were thankful when we didn't have one.[120]

Joan Partridge, who as a child in the war, lived in Quarles and recalls the arrival of the bombers; 'when the Stirlings arrived my brother and I, along with the other 4 or 5 children ... went across the fields and peeped through the hedge at these massive aeroplanes – we had never seen an aeroplane on the ground before'.[121] There were also the aircrew and airmen who came with the aircraft; drawn from all corners of the globe with accents never heard before, and probably, for the first time for many, the sight of non-white faces.○ Attending a Heritage Open

---

○ By 1 January 1943, 37% of Bomber Command's pilots were Canadians, Australians and New Zealanders, accompanied by airmen from most of the occupied countries of Western Europe, Poland and Czechoslovakia (Brown: 1990: 1-2). Even countries with small populations had many volunteers, such as the Caribbean,

Days tour at the Control Tower, one former resident of the Egmere Pink Cottages, recalled how she met her future husband on the base, and passed her judgement on its impact locally, 'it was wonderful!'. Many met their spouses in and around the airfield, and it is a constant source of surprise how many of our B&B guests have parents who met at RAF North Creake; their children, who never would have existed without this station, return to pay homage, sometimes arriving with tear-soaked faces.

On that cool June day in 2011, approaching the Control Tower two hours early for our appointment, we could not resist a sneaky drive-by. At the time, we did not realise that the concrete track that serves the Control Tower and its neighbouring houses was a dead end. When we passed the Control Tower, the owners stared out as we stared in. They watched us again, a minute later as we returned a little faster and, I imagine, visibly embarrassed. We drove a 1966 Hillman Super Minx estate; a somewhat conspicuous car, and we became immediately concerned about having now revealed our child-like excitement, and thereby undermined our planned calm negotiating stance. We consequently started concocting justifications for driving by, in the knowledge that any possibility of denying it was not an option. When we arrived at the allotted time, driving our unmistakable car, the owners had the decency not to mention it.

Approaching the Control Tower, for the second time, we drove along the concrete track where cypress trees loomed, starving the area of light and creating a feeling of foreboding.[P] Burrowing rabbits had spilled spoil from their warrens over the track from a bank that was littered with lumps of concrete and remnants of old fences. These fences were held together by a combination of electrical wire and garden hosepipe. Regardless of whether their original purpose was to prevent entry or exit, they had long since been abandoned in favour of a tall wooden fence on the far side of the cypress hedge. All of which cumulated in a

---

from where 6,000 people joined the RAF (caribbeanaircrew-ww2.com).

P   Later it was this very feeling that my dad cited to justify his belief that we had made a mistake in our purchase of the Control Tower.

general feeling of decline and neglect. Pulling up in front of the Control Tower we sat and gazed upon it in silence.

RAF North Creake Control Tower 1945: Norman Turnbull (Control Tower Archive).

Shaped like a squat box (35ft by 33ft 6 inches), it is a two-storey building with a flat roof[Q] with windows on the front elevation that overlooked the airfield. It was built in 9-inch rendered brick, except the front third, which is 13.5 inches thick to provide some protection against blast. The flat roof, balcony and first floor were a poured reinforced concrete slab.

It was built to a standard design (drawing no. 343/43) and closely modelled on its forerunner (drawing no. 12779/41) only with the window sizes on the front elevation reduced to minimise the risk from blast and to facilitate blacking-out.[122] The design was more austere than their predecessors and were the most common of the seven basic control tower types[123] as it was adopted by all RAF Commands.[124] A total of 162 control towers were built to the same specification as RAF

Q A design style adopted after 1937 as a protection against incendiaries and bomb fragmentation (Air Historical Branch: 1956: 30).

North Creake, of these, only a small number survive to the degree of preservation seen at Egmere.[125]

The building looked structurally sound, but the first floor had been clad in cedar shingles above which a shallow pitched roof had been added. While the shingles, when attached, were of high quality, they had now been painted brown and looked very dreary. The roof was a poorly executed structure covered in mineral felt that, if it did not leak already, would not remain watertight for long. The iconic front elevation with its six windows now only sported four, which made the building look awkward. There were soil stacks and grey-water pipes attached to the outside of the building. The postwar alterations made the building remind us a little of a poor imitation of the Swiss chalet that, from memory, appeared on the Alpen cereal adverts.[R] Only this chalet had no mountain views and was cast in the gloomy sun-starved shade of cypress trees. Nonetheless, we felt thrilled; we loved it and we had not even been inside.

The Control Tower had had a mixed career since it fell out of flying control use. The animal feed mill (now ABN Ltd) acquired it from the Air Ministry in the late 1940s, and it passed through many uses: a part-time flat for the director, a storeroom, a mess room for carrot washing staff, but for the longest period, two flats (used as emergency/ temporary accommodation for the mill workers). The mill sold it as a 'house' (actually still two flats) in 1990. It was in 1950 that the central windows were blocked up (and we imagine the cedar shingles appeared); possibly in an understandable attempt to disguise its war use. In the early 1990s the pitched roof was added in order to resolve the problem of leaks and to provide a void for a water tank. While these alterations did nothing for the overall appearance of the Control Tower, they all helped to preserve a building that could now, so easily, be languishing in dereliction like the majority of control towers.

In the late 1930s, the oncoming war prompted a review of airfield building designs, leading towards standardisation and the

---

R   I subsequently looked up vintage Alpen adverts and the building featured looks nothing like the Control Tower when we viewed it, but it is a comparison that people generally recognise.

elimination of superior furnishing and fittings.[126] With the declaration of war and realisation of incurable shortages in raw materials, constraints on design grew ever more severe. As a result they were compelled to subordinate their desire for embellishments to a style of 'strict austerity'.[127] This led the Air Ministry away from the style of Georgian pastiche of the interwar period, that was built to impress and suggest tradition, to a design more purposeful with forms more closely aligned to their function; styles that were more akin to the modern architectural movement. The 1941 design of the Control Tower is very much at the Modernist end of the Art Deco spectrum and reflects this shift. It has a startling resemblance to the 1925 'New Ways' house built in Northampton by German architect Peter Behrens, which is 'generally considered to be the first Modern Movement home in Britain'.[128] This trend was embraced widely across airfield architecture and, indeed, across all wartime building, from tank traps to huts for air raid wardens. A trend that did not escape the notice of The Museum of Modern Art in New York in 1941, when curating the exhibition 'Britain at War'.[S] It was this aesthetic that drew us to airfield architecture, when we drove past the operations block on the former RAF Steeple Morden years earlier.

Claire and I developed our love for Art Deco together. When I moved into her flat, I noticed that Claire had a mirror that complemented a few items I had; a china cabinet (ironically, of an Art Deco style we are now less fond of and we subsequently sold), a mantle clock that was a wedding present to my grandparents in 1927, and a 1950s electric kitchen clock, also from my grandfather (not strictly Deco but inspired by). This is how it starts; slow at first, items from charity shops, Camden Market (we lived just off the High Street, so this was a little too close) and junk shops. Our move to Welwyn Garden City coincided with the growth of eBay, and easy access to car boot sales, meaning it all stepped up a gear. As we honed our knowledge and determined more exactly what we liked, the passion grew.

S   See Wheeler, M. (1941) Britain at War.

There is a back story to this passion in me. I have always been, what Claire would disparagingly call, 'a collector'. This is a term presented in a manner that suggests the need of help rather than encouragement. I have always argued, possibly too emphatically to be convincing, that my love of the 'old' is entirely rational and good for the environment. The truth is, ever since a child I have been drawn to what I would have called 'old stuff', and as I got older this attraction became more discerning and discriminating. Now, it has slipped from a hobby into more of an ideology; I do not like buying new if there are good second-hand versions to be found. This, I would argue, does indeed sit well with environmental philosophy, and certainly prevents any notion of keeping up with fashion. Running a B&B has been a very good discipline, limiting my more ill-considered acquisitions, as we cannot allow the space to become cluttered, detracting from the effect we are trying to create. We therefore now attempt a 'steady-state'[T] philosophy, where we theoretically only allow things into the Control Tower when they are replacing something else, or where a particular need has been identified. This mostly works, on condition it is never applied to art, music or books!

In describing the Control Tower as at the Modernist end of Art Deco, it is to suggest that its design adheres to many of the tenets of the Art Deco style, without embracing the more exuberant flourishes of the Art Deco movement, thereby, arguably, making it more akin to a Modernist structure. Generally, this appears to be a characterisation that most people, with an interest, can envisage and comprehend. Problematically, it actually puts the Control Tower on an erroneous scale of what are separate and, at times, competing movements. However, some do argue that Modernist and Art Deco architectural styles have more in common than their 'respective fans might admit'.[129]

> nearly everyone, even the so-called man in the street, can
> recognise the elements of 'modern architecture' and perhaps
> surmise how it was born – from the marriage between the

T   See Daly & Cobb: 1990.

rational virtues of engineering (logic, function geometry) and the visual virtues of Purism (white planes, pure forms, asymmetrical balance).[130]

Nonetheless, adherents to both movements are still very keen to maintain and articulate the differences. When 20 nations participated in the 1925 'Exposition Internationale des Arts Decoratifs et Industries Modernes' held in Paris[131], it gave a discernible focus to what became known as Art Deco or, as it was known at the time, 'Style Modern'.[U][132]

Art Deco, while inevitably inspired by earlier movements, was mostly a reaction against the pain and filth of the trenches of the Great War, and the poverty and arduousness of most working-class lives. The nature of such lives was only realised, by many, when in close contact with them for the first time in the trenches. Siegfried Sassoon articulates his personal shock at their condition in his semi-autobiographical novel, Memoirs of an Infantry Officer, when the main character, George concludes: 'life, for the majority of the population, is an unlovely struggle against unfair odds, culminating in a cheap funeral'.[133] This new movement expressed, through a burgeoning mood of optimism and escapism, alternative possibilities.[134] However, the return from the Great War, to the land 'fit for heroes' had, for many, turned into a landscape of economic depression and unemployment, and in reality, the 'Style Modern' movement did little, other than express a hope for something else.

The 1925 Exposition is central to understanding the development of Art Deco, with its prescriptive stipulation that everything at the exhibition was to be modern, ensuring the 'maximum of novelty and the minimum of traditional influence'.[135] Nevertheless, the Art Deco movement was not a stylistically coherent movement and it makes little sense to characterise it as such. More sensibly it can be described as 'an evolving network of tendencies and motifs rather than

---

U It was in 1966 that the term Art Deco was lifted by Hillary Gelson from a review in the Times of an exhibition celebrating 'style modern' entitled Musee de Arts Decoratifs (Harwood: 2019: 4). The term was then repeated in Bevis Hillier's 1968 book entitled Art Deco of the 20s and 30s, and again, in November 1970, in an article in Art and Antiques Weekly confirming that by then it had entered common currency (Tinniswood: 2002: 8).

a coherent movement with a leader, a manifesto, and an ideological programme'.[136] Nonetheless, Art Deco can usefully be divided into two categories;[137] the first, as witnessed particularly in France, adorned every available surface with decoration appropriated from a myriad of cultural forms. The second, as seen in the USA and the rest of Europe, a style that embraced a more spare and simple form of design.[138] The latter is more akin to 'Modernism', as Ingrid Cranfield explains:

> The term 'Modernism' designates no particular group of artists or designers, but refers to a general trend away from traditional styles and towards functionalism and economy. The Modernist aesthetic was complemented by ideological strains such as progress, social justice and internationalism. Modernists aimed to produce high quality, practical and appealing products for the mass of the population.[139]

Functionalism is an unavoidable phrase when discussing Modernism, with one architect suggesting that functionalism describes a '"fitness for purpose", which at least sounded sensible if not a little inhuman'.[140] Similarly, Louis Sullivan's phrase 'form follows function' ('an object's purpose should be the prime determinant in its appearance[141]') was borrowed to describe the Modernist 'rational' approach to architecture. This approach incorporated recently developed building materials and techniques of reinforced concrete, steel frames and large sheets of cheap glass and steel windows.[142] The latter, a style element that came to characterise Modernism, was actually adopted as a result of a shortage of wood after the Great War, rather than any aesthetic consideration.[143] Importantly, Modernism adopted the concept of 'total design'; the idea that 'every detail of a decorative scheme – from keyholes to kitchens, rugs and radiators, taps and tiles – was dignified by the designer's attention'.[144] A philosophy it shared with Art Deco.

While Art Deco shared the concept of 'total design' and made use of the same materials and techniques as Modernism, it differed in its greater affinity with decoration. It also embraced other notable materials and processes that are predominantly absent from Modernist buildings, such as, chromium plating, sometimes known as 'staybrite'; glazed terracotta bricks or tiles for ornamenting surfaces and 'Vitrolite' (the opaque coloured glass) for the adornment of bathrooms and walls of many fashionable Art Deco homes.[145]

Appreciation of the Modernist movement was not universal, and detractors were common from within and without. The popular author R T C Rolt published his first book in 1944 (although it was written in the 1930s). *Narrow Boat* is a journey through Britain's canals through which he documents the vanishing way of life of the boatman, and the changing nature of British society; both of which he regrets. His opinion of modern architecture is summed up in his assertion that the 'modern super-cinema style [is a style] of which the eye soon sickens to the point of nausea'.[146] Similarly, John Betjeman, after initial enthusiasm, concluded, in a statement typical of his prose style, that Art Deco was the 'decoration of art school students';[147] a view that chimed with many. Certainly, a glance at any hardware catalogue of the period reveals that the most popular and pervasive style (at least in terms of numbers of products), was the 'country cottage' aesthetic, perhaps, explaining why the reaction to the 1925 Paris Exposition in Britain was reasonably cool. Enthusiasm was limited to a minority often characterised as 'left-wing intellectuals'.[148]

Even for people who aspired to 'something clean and square',[149] many soon discovered that what they really wanted was not 'white-walled austerity',[150] but a building that would reflect their artistic tastes and position in society, without the associated discomfort, however fashionable. Even within the movement criticisms abound, particularly in the early stages where the perceived opulence resulted in Art Deco being viewed as exclusively the preserve of the wealthy.[151] For some, such as the architect James Richards, there was despair at the excesses:

> like all movements that contain something new as well as something important, the modern movement in architecture acquired a following of imitators: vulgarizers who joined up

with the movement only in order to cash in, as it were, on its news value. To this category belong all the makers of jazz-modern shop fronts in chromium plate and glass, and the purveyors of smart angular furniture and all the builders of nasty 'modernistic' villas; people who have no understanding of modern architecture's ideals, but who could not have come into being without it.[152]

However, when it excelled, he believed that 'real modern architecture represents the revival of architecture as an art'.[153] Many Modernists argued that 'high quality and mass production could be complementary',[154] and through the use of such production, modern architecture could be made more available to the ordinary citizen. Indeed, with the depression of the 1930s, the need for economy in style and materials influenced the design character of many buildings in the associated Art Deco style of 'Art Moderne' or 'Streamlined Moderne', particularly with hotels and airports. [155] A style now seen as the very epitome of Art Deco design.

It is commonly argued that the Second World War brought an end to modern architecture, as the 'concentration of energy almost everywhere [was] on destructive rather than constructive planning',[156] and with the introduction of the control of materials through licensing, effectively all building ceased.[157] It is certainly true that licencing placed huge restrictions on building and construction, as all building and civil engineering companies were compelled to register with the Ministry of Works,[158] with licenses introduced in October 1940, aiming:

1. To stop all private building not essential for the war effort or for the upkeep of morale of the civil population
2. To ensure, for the permitted civil building, the most economical use of labour and materials.[159]

From April 1941, building projects over the value of £500 could only be carried out with the permission of Government. This sum was reduced to £100 from 1 January 1942. The Ministry could also dictate material types and the value of materials used (this valuation was regardless of whether the materials were new, second-hand or already owned by the builder).[160] Initially there was considerable evasion of the rules with the courts not seeming 'conspicuously sympathetic'[161] to the aims of the regulations. As a result, the Ministry enforced the rules themselves and evasion markedly reduced.[162] However, not all building stopped, as military construction and war production expanded at an unprecedented rate. As Herbert Read wrote in an introduction to the *1945 Architects' Year Book*:

> For five years we have lived in an economy of expanding war production, and in consequence the manufacture of the commodities normally associated with the designer's function has shrunk to a vanishing point. Naturally a good deal of design talent has gone into the instruments of war, and some day all this material should be surveyed from an aesthetic point of view. We are all conscious of the beauty of some of the fighters and bombers, and all aircraft have details which are well worth consideration from our point of view. Even a bomb may be beautiful.[163]

The same can be said of war-time military architecture but, thus far, the day has not arrived where such a survey has been undertaken, although the movement for such recognition is growing with, for example, publications such as *Streamline Worcestershire*,[164] featuring the control tower at Throckmorton. Nonetheless, generally these 'Nissen huts and other austerity monstrosities',[165] are perceived to be 'militarily functional and devoid of aesthetic merit'.[166] Stephen Nunn contrasts the undeniably elegant airfield buildings of the expansion period 'designed by the likes of Edwin Lutyens and Clough Williams Ellis',[167] with an unfavourable critique of wartime construction:

> conversely, the buildings on airbases constructed during wartime were rapid-build, economically costed and temporary by virtue of their very design and intent. They are the epitome of

form following function, even to the extent of their usefulness being constrained to the duration of the overall strategic objective.[168]

Although he concedes that 'they have found a place in the cultural identity of the local landscape. In common with all other man-made impositions on the land, they are part of the continuing history of the landscape, not anachronistic aberrations'.[169] Despite this concession, he cannot bring himself to believe that they may deserve stylistic regard, asserting that wartime airfield buildings are 'devoid of aesthetic merit'[170] and the very 'epitome of form follows function'[171] (as if this is necessarily an insult!). Nevertheless, I contend, that while pure form follows function is impossible, as we are all products of our cultural influences and such purity of design can only ever be a heady aspiration, Second World War airfield architecture, because of a closer adherence to the ambition of form following function, fulfils more comprehensively the central tenets of Modernism than many proclaimed Modernist buildings. This inevitably results in a strong design aesthetic, that while not to everyone's taste, is a strong aesthetic nonetheless. Indeed, I would further suggest that airfield architecture in many ways contains such innovations in its designs that it could be perceived as bridging the gap between the Modernism of the 1930s and Brutalism,[V] popularised in the 1950s. Far from ending building construction, the Second World War, as with all areas of design, pushed the boundaries during this period. Architects were advising and working with the Air Ministry on the most pioneering structures. It is a pity that, in the process of archiving, the Ministry of Defence saw fit to destroy the minutes of the Air Ministry committee on which architects sat, as we may have been able to glean much regarding their influences and thinking. Unless copies exist elsewhere, this is not to be.

For Claire and I, our shared personal belief in the aesthetic beauty of such architecture brought us to this point, standing before

---

V   The term 'Brutalism' is derived from the French 'Béton brut' (raw concrete) and was coined by the British architects Alison and Peter Smithson. The architecture is generally characterised by rough, unfinished surfaces, heavy-looking materials, straight lines, and small windows (designingbuildings.co.uk).

the Control Tower on the former RAF North Creake airfield. Even disguised in its ugly postwar trappings we could see the beauty. Trembling with anticipation, we knocked at the nasty UPVC front door with all the bravado we could muster.

MISSING

Stirling LJ531 EX-N and Stirling LJ536 EX-P

Francis Brittain is the first name on the RAF North Creake Roll of Honour. Flying his second operation from the airfield and his sixth since becoming operational, he was working with his regular crew as a wireless operator on the night of 16 June 1944. The operation involved flying over the North Sea somewhere mid-point between Sheringham in North Norfolk and Den Helder on the Dutch coast.[1] The aircraft, Stirling LJ531 EX-N, never returned. Nothing has been heard of it since.

The Station Operations Record Book (ORB) simply records that 'one aircraft "N" was missing, nothing being heard from him since Take-Off'.[2] There has been considerable speculation about what could have happened to this aircraft. Certainly it is curious to note that even with two wireless operators on board, no distress signal was sent. The aviation author, John Reid relates; 'this has always been a puzzle to me',[3] as it was standard practice for the wireless operator to 'lock-down' the morse key, particularly when over the North Sea or the Channel. This practice was adopted as it transmits a continuous tone that when picked up by listening posts can be used to locate the crew; thereby greatly increasing their chance of rescue.[4] No air sea rescue, the initiation of which laid with the officer commanding the RAF unit,[5] was launched; normally a matter of procedure when an aircraft was overdue. This, for John Reid, has given rise to suspicions that something unusual happened to this aircraft and, with the absence of verifiable details, inventiveness and speculation has filled the gaps. Such was the speculation, that another aviation author warned him off the subject. Heightening John Reid's suspicions still further, but putting an end to the digging.[6]

The most likely, and perhaps more prosaic, explanation for the loss of Stirling EX-N (LJ531) was that it suffered a sudden and catastrophic event; this would explain the absence of a distress call. It seems reasonable to speculate that, out of sight of any witnesses, it was shot down and crashed in the North Sea after being attacked by a night-fighter. Most probably Unteroffizier Josef Ottrin of the 6./KG 51 who claimed a four-engined bomber in the vicinity around that time.[7] Or, perhaps, as a handwritten note jotted down beside the pilot's name in the unpublished 'sortie records'[8] suggests, 'probably due to collision'. Where the truth lies, we are unlikely to ever know.

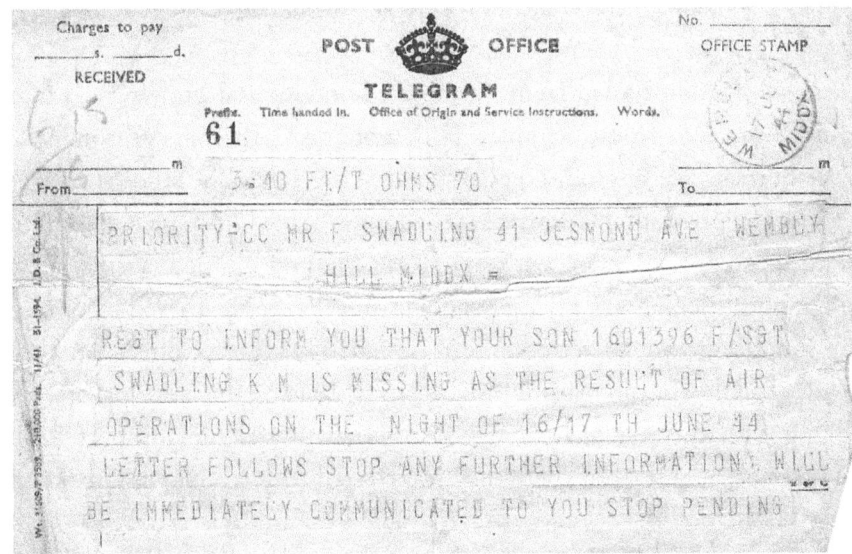

'Missing'. The telegram received by the family of Ken Swadling (Paul Swadling).

When no further news was heard, a standard procedure was initiated. A telegram was sent out the following day to the next of kin of all those on the aircraft, to notify them that their aircraft had failed to return from an operation. The telegram was brutal in its brevity, 'reg[re] t to inform you that your son is missing as a result of air operations'.

For families waiting at home 'missing' was possibly the cruellest word in the English language. Mary MacLeod, writing in a different war, reflected, 'killed is final; wounded means hope and possibilities; prisoner of war implies a reunion in the glad time that peace comes again ... but missing is terrible'.[9] However, for the families of the crew of Stirling LJ531 EX-N, missing is how they would remain.

Those on board were:

Francis Brittain (RAF) Wireless Operator, aged 22
Thomas Wilson Dale (RNZAF) Pilot, aged 25
John Critchley Higginbottom (RAF) Air Gunner, aged 21
William McCreadie Latimer (RAF) Air Gunner, aged 21
Frank Lofthouse (RAF) Special Operator, aged 23
Kenneth Matthew Francis Swadling (RAF) Bomb Aimer, aged 21
John Martin Watts (RAF) Flight Engineer, aged 19
Ronald Joffre Whittleston (RNZAF) Navigator, aged 28

Francis Brittain hailed from Wembley, London, and grew up close to Ken Swadling, from Wembley Hill, London.[10] Thomas Wilson Dale was born in Wellington, New Zealand. After school he studied Law at Victoria University. He worked at the Public Trust Office in Wellington. He enlisted as a pilot with the RNZAF and trained at the New Plymouth Elementary Flying School in July 1942. He arrived in Britain in June 1943 and converted to Stirlings at 1653 Heavy Conversion Unit (HCU), Chedburgh, Suffolk in February 1944. After crewing-up, he, along with the rest of his crew, transferred to 199 Squadron at RAF Lakenheath, and from there they transferred to RAF North Creake in May 1944.[11]

Ronald Joffre Whittleston was also from New Zealand and worked at Shell Lime Products Ltd. He enlisted with the RNZAF at Waipapakauri in May 1942, and was employed on ground duties while awaiting to join aircrew. In November 1942, he commenced his training as a navigator with the Empire Air Training Scheme. He arrived in the UK in July 1943.[12] He left a widow, Frances, in Auckland, New Zealand.[13]

William Latimer, was from Garlieston, Wigtownshire in Scotland;[14] Frank Lofthouse, special operator was from Lupset in Yorkshire; John Critchley Higginbottom, mid-upper gunner of Streatham Hill, London and John Martin Watts, flight engineer, was from Caxton in Cambridgeshire.[15]

Exactly three months later, on 16 September 1944, a second Stirling aircraft failed to return from an operation from RAF North Creake. The aircraft, Stirling EX-P (LJ536), was piloted by Andrew Dempster Heggison. The ORB states, 'the last information on him being at 00:26hrs. when he acknowledged a movement from Group'. According to unpublished 199 Squadron records the aircraft was flying parallel with the Belgian and Dutch coast, on a circuit that would have placed him directly over Den Helder, south of the island of Texel,[16] 'possibly in range of German flak batteries'.[17] It is not unlikely that these guns brought EX-P down, although it is also possible that it suffered catastrophic icing-up as experienced by others that night.[18] However, this is considered less likely as such conditions rarely happen with such speed that no distress call can be sent. Any witnesses were likely to be in the aircraft positioned nearest to EX-P. This aircraft, EX-E, piloted by F/O Lampkin of 199 Squadron, was unaware of the loss until it returned to base.[19] The following day, Stirling EX-B from RAF North Creake together with two Mosquitoes from another unit formed an air sea rescue. Sadly 'without results'.[20] Whatever befell EX-P is likely to remain forever unknown; its secret submerged under the waters of the North Sea. The crew was:

James Duncan Campbell (RCAF) Air Gunner, aged 22
Gordon Joshua 'Billy' Dennison (RCAF) Air Gunner, aged 22
Andrew Dempster Heggison (RAF) Pilot, aged 23
David Thompson Hughes (RAF) Special Operator, aged 28
Murray Kesselman (RCAF) Navigator, aged 21
Lloyd George Langley (RCAF) Bomb Aimer, aged 24
Stanley Cunningham Rennie (RAF) Flight Engineer, aged 20
James Birch Sowden (RAF) Wireless Operator, aged 20

There is scant detail regarding those crew members from the UK: Andrew Heggison came from Aberdeen; James Birch Sowden, wireless operator, from Wirral, Cheshire; David Thompson Hughes, from West Linton, Peeblesshire, Scotland and Stanley Cunningham Rennie hailed from Ayr in Scotland. However, the four further casualties were all members of the Royal Canadian Airforce, about whom, far greater detail is available:[A] Murray Kesselman, was born in Winnipeg to a Russian immigrant father and Canadian mother.[21] After leaving school he was employed by his father as a travelling shoe salesman until 1942, when he enlisted.[22] He applied either as an 'observer or pilot',[23] and RCAF assessments suggested he 'would make good Aircrew material'.[24] The Selection Board, characterised by its frank manner, considered his 'motivation doubtful',[25] and further noted that his 'parents object[ed] to him flying'.[26] The medical officer was even more questioning about his qualities: 'enlisted for patriotic reasons. Was not greatly interested in flying but preferred air force to other services ... does not give the impression of being very aggressive'.[27] It should be noted that Murray Kesselman was Jewish, which may suggest his motivations for enlisting. It may further explain why he doesn't adhere to the stereotypical applicant profile being, perhaps, more motivated by moral or justice imperatives.

In training, Murray Kesselman was considered a 'trainee of average ability and appearance'.[28] He had ambitions to be a pilot, but

---

A   Records of airmen are kept by the British authorities, but access by the public is presently impossible, whereas the Canadian records are accessible.

in interviews it was considered that he 'seems to lack spark'.[29] Indeed, the results from the link trainer[B] indicated that his 'flying ability [was] below average. It was necessary to assist with all landings. Air flying is dangerous ... not safe for further solo. LAC Kesselman has been reselected as a navigator.'[30] He was awarded a navigator's badge on 17 September 1943.[31]

Lloyd George Langley, commonly known as 'Truck'[32] from his pre-enlistment footballing days, resided in Ottawa, Ontario Canada, and was employed as an aircraft inspector.[33] In 1941, on enlisting, the interviewer identified him as a 'good athletic type of young man with fair education and average I.Q. ... confident, alert and anxious to serve. Personality good and character background satisfactory.'[34] With his employer's recommendation he was enlisted in the RCAF and posted to the Inspectors School in Toronto,[35] before remustering for aircrew in 1942.[36]

On the link trainer his aptitude as a pilot was identified in the RCAF's characteristically abrupt language, 'co-ordination and air sense of low average. Tense and erratic on landing'[37] and 'progress appears to have been very slow. Judgement weak'.[38] Regarding his flying abilities, they conclude; 'climbing and medium turns very bad. Approaches badly judged. Flys [sic] into ground. Not pilot material'.[39] Training in navigation suited him much better; 'an extremely hard worker who has mastered his lack of speed and carelessness to become a very reliable, conscientious navigator.'[40] As a bomb aimer, the role he would ultimately adopt, he showed similar aptitude with bomb target tests showing 'steady improvement throughout course ... he is reliable, quite keen, and hard working'.[41]

James Duncan Campbell, from Winnipeg[42] was employed as a grain clerk at Manitoba Poole Elevators,[43] until enlistment in 1942.[44] His training reports noted him as a 'good student. Has sufficient self assurance but could display more initiative. Keen enough and

---

B The Link Trainer was a piece of ground equipment used to make an early assessment of a trainee pilot's aptitude; '[consisting] of a stub fuselage with miniature wings, ailerons, elevator, tailplane and rudder. The controls were connected to electrically driven bellows, and any movement of the controls in the cockpit faithfully reproduced the motions of actual flight ... [the pupil] received his instruction via headphones from an instructor who was seated at a desk nearby (Hammerton: 1943: 24).

occasionally takes the lead.'[45] He was training at the No. 9 Bomb and Gunnery School at the same time as Gordon Dennison, also a gunner on the crew, but as a number of different courses ran concurrently[46] there is nothing to suggest that they met. But it is a possibility.

Gordon Joshua 'Billy'[47] Dennison joined up in January 1941, aged 18.[48] He initially trained as an engine mechanic,[49] before, in January 1943, he remustered as aircrew.[50] When interviewed he gave the impression of 'a likely lad, a little on the slow side, even temperament, active in sports, usual habits. Good service record. Appears earnest in his desire and has good chance of success'.[51] Through the selection process he was rejected as a pilot, something that clearly disappointed him:

> I was up in front of the Selection Board and they figure that my ability to learn isn't up to standard so it is air gunner for me. The officer was quite nice about it though he said that my practical tests were above standard but my theory wasn't so hot … I tried to argue with him but he said that he would give me overnight to think about it, that was last night. So this morning I signed on the dotted line [as a gunner].[52]

On the gunnery course he fared rather better, and the reviewing instructor concluded Gordon as 'a good student. Has sufficient self assurance and displays initiative. Dependable and able to provide good leadership'.[53] Before he left for Britain in January 1944, Gordon Dennison got engaged. [54] It was an engagement that didn't last the strain of separation, and his fiancée called it off shortly before he was killed.[55]

Once through the 'crewing-up' process, and while they underwent further training at the No. 1653 Heavy Conversion Unit in Chedburgh,[56] Gordon's pilot, F/Lt. Fennell was replaced:

> he couldn't land a four engine aircraft so they took him away from us. Now we have a Scotchman [sic] for a pilot, he seems to be a good sort of a fellow. We have only flown two days with him and he seems to be doing OK. With our first pilot we made

some horrible landings it's a wonder the wheels stood up under the strain.[57]

The end of training conferred gratifyingly good results; 'a keen and conscientious A.G. [air gunner] who has worked hard on the course. Should do well on ops'.[58] On 27 July 1944, he was posted to 199 Squadron at RAF North Creake, from where he successfully completed eleven operations.[59] In his last letter home to his parents he seemed settled into a routine; 'to-morrow I will have been here six months, time sure flys [sic] in a way and it is only another four months till Xmas ... well I now have nine trips in and I hope to get over the ten mark before I go on leave.'[60] Gordon achieved his aim with 11 trips completed before his leave; he was lost on his first trip after returning back.[61]

After the initial telegram, a confirmation of the missing status would be sent to families. Officially, it should not arrive more than two or three days after the first telegram. However, longer periods were usual, as the commander in charge of the Air Ministry Casualty Branch, R Burges, considered it better to send a letter late with some news, than a letter promptly with none. Sometimes up to two or three weeks would elapse before confirmation was sent.[62] The family of Gordon Dennison received this letter from RCAF Casualty Officer on 22 September 1944, only five days after the loss. While it lacked concrete news it held out some hope:

> The term 'missing' is used only to indicate that his whereabouts is not immediately known and does not necessarily mean that your son has been killed or wounded. He may have landed in enemy territory and might be a prisoner of war ... Enquiries have been made through the International Red Cross Society and all other appropriate sources and I wish to assure you that any further information received will be communicated to you immediately.[63]

All families of aircrews serving within Bomber Command, regardless of their country of residence or what air force uniform their relative wore, received similar letters (albeit from their own authorities). In letters from the RAF, the British reaffirm their request that the next of kin should resist publicity about the loss. This was in order to prevent the unintentional release of information that may aid the German authorities in their attempts to catch evading airmen. In this first letter received after the initial telegram, the Canadian authorities also cautioned the next of kin about contact with the press. However, they conceded that families could 'release to the Press or Radio the fact that [the aircrew member] is reported missing, but not disclosing the date, place or his unit'.[64] It further outlined that the RCAF could not publicise the loss and also advised that '[names would] not appear in the official casualty list for five weeks'.[65] An Air Ministry leaflet sent out at a similar time, cautioned against the temptation of relatives to listen to German broadcasts for news of their relatives, as it was often rife with misinformation. The leaflet also informed readers that Air Ministry 'official listeners' are scouring German airwaves for reports and news.[66]

A letter from the station or unit of the missing person should be sent within 18-24 hours of the official posting.[67] The Air Ministry's criteria for such letters was insistent that they 'should be signed personally and not relegated to junior officers'.[68] The guidance also outlined that letter should include as much personal detail as possible, but give away 'no information on the circumstances, not even the type or role of the aircraft being flown at the time'.[69] Michael Renaut reflecting on this job in his autobiography revealed:

> the jobs I hated most was writing a letter to bereaved parents and wives when aircraft and crews went missing. I realised how my mother would have felt had she received the fateful letter ... I used to write the letters personally whenever I could but each aircraft meant eight letters and one just hadn't the time to sit and write them all freehand. I hated typewritten letters but on occasions I had no alternative.[70]

It was also believed good practice, although not required officially in regulations, for the station chaplain to write and pass on his sympathies; 'this was a common and much appreciated gesture'.[71]

Relatives were advised of the process for gathering up the effects of missing aircrew. Private effects, under RAF Control,[72] along with inventories, were collected by the 'Committee of Adjustment', and forwarded to the Royal Air Force Central Depository in Colnbrook, Slough, for safe keeping. Bulky items were retained by the station (cars motorcycles, bikes etc.),[73] with cars at RAF North Creake being stored in a field due south of the airfield.[74] Any cash was handed over to the station accountant officer and credited to the airman's account.[75] For those performing the task, such as Joan Hollis at RAF North Creake, it was 'heart rending'.[76] A similar emotion was experienced by those airmen on the camp who witnessed the clearing of lockers.[77] One Committee of Adjustment officer, describes the lengths he went to in protecting the feelings of those at home:

> I go through every single article and piece of paper … according to regulation, all his effects without exception are supposed to be returned, and I could get into hot water … for exercising my discretion. With married men, for example, I burn all the letters they have lying around except those from their wives or family, and if I'm in doubt, I burn. Otherwise you know what can happen: a fellow has a casual fling with some girl he meets on leave and she writes him a letter about the wonderful time she had and so forth. Now if that sort of letter slips through and goes home to his widow, it's a catastrophe; that will absolutely poison her memories and scar her worse than losing her husband. I weed out any troublesome stuff like that very carefully.[78]

However, sympathies waned for the Committee of Adjustment, or the 'ghoul squad',[79] as many airmen referred to it, when they conducted the gruesome task of gathering up any pets and destroying them – to avoid strays – there were 'no exceptions'.[80] 'Needless to say we got round it …

whenever a man got himself a pet he also got a godparent for that pet … in the event of a non-return, the godparent should grab the pet and claim ownership before the Committee of Adjustment arrived'.[81]

Once at the Central Depository the effects were kept until either the airman was found (dead or alive) or his death was presumed (usually, for the purpose of distributing effects, six months from the date the airman was reported missing[82]). With the effects of Prisoners of War, release of the items was allowed with consent of the airman,[83] once it was ascertained who was legally entitled to them.[84] The inventories,[85] supplied with these items, listing some of the pathetic detritus of everyday life, now read as extraordinarily poignant and sad reminders of these tragic losses. No matter how insignificant or worthless, these effects needed to be sorted and catalogued. Therefore, among the items of dress uniform, personal grooming and underwear, you will find listed, a bicycle bell (unserviceable), padlock (without key), pocket mirror (glass cracked)[86] and a loose yale key without a home.[87]

As the day-to-day items of an airman's life waited in a depository in Slough, the families waited anxiously at home for news of their missing loved ones; news that was unforthcoming. In these empty moments the vacuum was often filled with the 'what ifs'. For Murray Kesselman's family, they just wished he had pushed for the leave they'd suggested for Rosh Hashanah (Jewish New Year),[88] leave which would have precluded him from taking part in the operation. Similarly, the family of David Hughes were left wondering, why didn't he go to the camp medic with his sore leg as they'd discussed?[89] These questions remained forever unanswered.

A frequent theme among all family correspondence with the military authorities, was one of growing frustration that no information of any consequence had emerged. The following from the father of James Campbell, writing in January 1945, is typical:

> We feel by this time some five months after our boy disappeared, there can be no good reason why we should not have more information as to the circumstances. All the information we have is that he was sent on a special mission on the night of

Sept. 15th and failed to return. We also received the names of four R.C.A.F. men that were with him, and address [sic] of next of kin. Now we understand that there were six men in that crew as Jim spoke of their being an englishman [sic] and a scotch [sic] man in their crew, and we received a letter from their squadron leader and he was from the R.A.F.

Now we would like to know definitely, was he in an R.A.F. squadron, what was the mission they were sent on, what or where was their destination, how many were there in the crew. Their names, the names and addresses of their next of kin. What kind of plane did they use, and was it equipped with radio.

We are sorry to trouble you people but it would help a lot if we had the answers to these questions … so please do what you can to get this information for us as soon as possible as it is getting harder all the time.[90]

Replies, never evasive, remain sparse on detail:

I am very sorry but I cannot tell you either the nature of the operation or the target. Despite the fact that your son was reported missing several months ago security would be jeopardised if this information was divulged in a letter. I can, however, assure you that the mission was one of very great importance against the enemy. The crew were [sic] flying in a Stirling Heavy Bomber which was one of a large force from this country. Nothing had been heard of one of our aircraft being seen to crash by any of the other crews operating on the same night … I regret very much that the information given is so meagre but I am sure you will understand that we must pay very rigid attention to security in order to minimise future losses.[91]

Even approaches to the Red Cross engender very little:

> We are not permitted to make cable enquiries regarding missing men as they may be evading capture in enemy or enemy-occupied territory and enquiries concerning their whereabouts would only hamper their chances of escape. This does not mean, however, that enquiries regarding them are not being made in various other ways.[92]

By July 1945, even with the end of the war, Lorne Campbell writes 'we have not received any more information of any kind, and surely now, at this late date we may be told more of the mission he was sent on, and the country he was over'.[93] Towards the end of 1945, a further letter from the casualty officer explains the 'aircraft was engaged on Special Support duty in connection with the bombing of the Kiel Canal and mine-laying in the Baltic.' While honest in detail it does not explain what a 'special support duty' involves, which, of course, leads to more speculation. Nonetheless, the letter does seek to make reassurances regarding the official notifications of 'presumption of death',[94] 'that action to presume your son's death was for official purposes only and will not diminish or affect in any way, efforts being made to trace your son'.[95]

A letter from the mother of fellow crew member (Gordon Dennison) in March 1947, describes the difficulty in accepting the fate of their child and the feelings of exasperation at the lack of information:

> It seems very hard to believe that one so young and full of life and loved by all could just disappear with no trace whatsoever. No mark or memorial to mark the spot … If you have the facts on the files in Ottawa I think it no more than right that we should know what they are. I would be very glad to hear from you.[96]

At the bottom of the letter, inscribed by hand, a note reads 'would you investigate and advise [next of kin] if anything further had been heard in this case'. The request elicits the response to the family that, while there was no further news, seeks to assure 'that this [Casualty] service is very thorough and if it is humanly possible I know they will be successful in locating your son's resting place'.[97]

In the face of such, even if understandable, bureaucratic obstruction, one can completely sympathise with families that reverted to more informal networks of support. Families often contacted the next of kin of other crew members that served with their son. Initially, the letters of this informal network contained requests for more information and to keep all informed if any one person is told anything new. However, information received by families was generally derived from official channels and was identical regardless of its source (Air Ministry in the UK, Casualty Office in Canada etc.). But there are snippets that gave clues; the Langley family wrote to the Dennisons in June 1945, explaining what a friend of their son's had told them about the nature of the crew's work:

> [they] were in an operation in support of an attack on Kiel ... almost the complete operation was over the sea ... He doesn't think it looks at all good, especially as they were on secret duty. We have been wondering if we should pass this information on to you or wait for the official word to come through.[98]

The secret nature of their work (the official details of which would not emerge for another 30 years) was further confirmed by the brother of Murray Kesselman, writing to the family of Gordon Dennison:

> they were doing very secretive work. From what we can gather the boys were not on bombing missions, but on very special missions, of which we shall probably never know the details. We believe they have every chance of turning up safe ... I understand that they [flew] at very high altitude and out of range of the anti-aircraft guns, so chances are they had to make a forced landing somewhere and will either be prisoners of war or turn up safe in England ... they were flying a Sterling [sic] Bomber. This type of plane has not been used for bombing raids for a year and a half, but is just used for special work. In

this case, the Air Force will not give out any details as the boys were doing very special work.[99]

The families of those lost on EX-N also built relationships; Paul (Ken Swadling's brother) recalls the family of Thomas Dale staying with them on a visit from New Zealand in 1953; he also remembers his mum and dad becoming very close to the family of Francis Brittain. The close geographical proximity of their houses in London allowed for a strong bond to grow. Hazel, Francis Brittain's mother, had taken the loss of her only son very badly. Paul remembers visits to their house in Kilburn, where his parents would see her at her bedside from where she had seldom risen since the news that her son's aircraft had failed to return.[100] 'They were lovely people', Paul recalls, 'but broken by the loss'. 'However', he adds, 'my parents didn't fare much better and my dad took it particularly badly'.[101] Paul's mother was a native of Germany, his father had met her while serving in the army, and they had married in 1920. One can only imagine the conflicted feelings she felt having a son in Bomber Command fighting against her home country. Paul claims none of it. He asserts that she was a vocal anti-Nazi, and never suffered any prejudice for being German all through the war. 'Unlike me,' he adds, 'at school in the early 1950s'.[102]

Bereavement was not the only hardship that families had to bear, for some losses brought financial hardship as well.[C] In 1946, Mary Campbell enquired to the RCAF Estates Branch as to when she can expect her son's gratuity payment. Clearly in some financial difficulty since the loss of her son, and heightened since she subsequently 'lost [her] husband very suddenly',[103] she hints at the injustice she feels as her son:

C Pay ceases when an airman was reported missing, although allotments and allowances (automatic deductions from pay to a specified recipient) continued for a limited period (Air Ministry: 1943: 1). In the months following a missing report, letters and forms would be sent to relatives from the accounts office at Worcester and any allowances due would be paid. Once death was confirmed, the accounts of the airman would be settled (Hadaway: 2008: 27). If the missing airmen was discovered to be a POW, then the pay was reinstated and the back-pay reimbursed (Air Ministry: 1943: 1). For many this caused continual money worries and for one middle class wife of a missing airman, this meant 'pay gas, coal and leave anything else till next month' (Ryle: 1979: 29).

underwent a double hernia operation in August before enlisting on Dec. 2. He had previously tried to enlist and they told him about his trouble and said the operation would be up to him … His salary was only $68 a month so you may understand how hard it was for him to pay for all operations.[D] We had to help him considerably.[104]

However, financial hardships can be relieved with assistance, but the same cannot be said of the corrosive emotions derived from someone close posted missing in action. The commemoration of the missing commenced shortly after the aircraft failed to return. In 1944, a 199 Squadron flight engineer, Claude 'Ted' Allen, painted a mural of Stirling EX-N on the wall of the 199 Squadron HQ with the simple legend 'EX-N RIP'.[E] Painted using aircraft paint[105] it graphically marked the first loss from RAF North Creake.

In the early 1950s, letters were received explaining that 'due to lack of any information … it must be regretfully accepted and officially recorded that [the airman] does not have a known grave'.[106] The official closure of this process was heartbreaking for families, as there had been no resolution for them. For some without definite proof of death, preferably a body, they 'can nurture false (if not absolutely absurd) hope that the person is still alive'.[107] For many, it is difficult to underestimate the importance of rituals of funerary:

> These rituals and cultural processes surrounding death are some of the most important and prescriptive in almost all societies, closely connected to the psychologically healthy progression of the stages of healing. For this reason the absence of a body owing to loss or destruction can have serious implications.[108]

D On enlisting James Campbell, when asked about any debts, writes on his Attestation Paper: 'I owe my doctor a small sum for an operation for hernia'. Ironically, this operation was undertaken at the insistence of the RCAF before enrolment would be considered (RCAF: 18/11/1942: 1).

E The careful removal of this mural was co-ordinated by John Reid in 1983, and it was subsequently moved to the RAF Museum in Hendon for its continued preservation as a memorial to RAF Bomber Command (Reid: 2014: 219-224). Dedicated by Padre Schofield, with an address by Lance Smith, ex-Squadron Adjutant of 199 Squadron (Harrington: 2012: 54).

However, they are commemorated in other ways. For Murray Kesselman, even though his parents and brother would not talk of the war and their loss, they gifted his nephew his name, Murray.[109] Gordon 'Bill' Dennison has 'Dennison Bay' named after him on Cumberland Lake in Saskatchewan.[110] The middle name of Paul Swadling, who was born not long after the loss of his brother's aircraft, is Frank, in recognition of his parent's close friendship with Charles and Hazel Brittain, and in memory of their only son Francis.[111] Francis also has his picture on his distant cousin's bedroom wall, who dedicatedly keeps his memory alive as one of the eternally 'missing in action'.[112]

The quest for answers never ends. In 1977, at 84 years of age, the mother of John Watts, the flight engineer on EX-N, was still asking people with RAF connections, if they could find out what had happened to her son.[113] For those left to grieve, without answers, the pain never stops.

Claude 'Ted' Allen, captioned 'artist at work' (Allen family).

CHAPTER THREE

MERCURY ON A FORK

Through the obscure glass, we could see the blurred image of someone approaching the front door. We both stiffened a little as the front door opened and we were greeted by the vendor. She welcomed us inside and visibly warmed when she realised how smitten we both were with the building; so much for calm and calculated. Having negotiated the awkward lobby, we were inside a comfortable house with all the hallmarks of domestic life; it felt relaxed with that associated and indefinable sense of 'home' about it. To temper my excitement a little, I tried to apply a practical view to what I was seeing; there were some indications of underlying and, perhaps, expensive problems; the laminate flooring in the hall sunk unnervingly when you put your weight on it, and the utility room door grounded on a long and lifting crack that stretched almost the room's length. But excitement kept beating back practical considerations.

While viewing the upstairs, conversation moved from the general to the more specific, as we began to explain our passion; 'it is derived from the architectural style, but we also have an interest in the history of the period', we confessed. Warming to her role, the vendor began to share some of what she knew. 'Mind the step down', the vendor warned as we crossed the threshold of the Control Room, 'evidence', she said, of the Control Tower's two stages of construction; first to 'support the decoy and then expanded for the bomber station', she told us; 'the bomber station was British and, surprisingly, no bombers had been lost while operational'. In the Control Room, the vendor explained that underneath the laminate floor was oak strip flooring put in when the Control Tower was being built. The 'forward edge,' she said, had 'secret compartments where they would hide documents in case of enemy invasion.'

After a cup of tea, the vendor suggested that we wander around alone. The building was generally in remarkably good order; a symptom of it having been in continuous use since the war. For us, who had seen promise in derelict buildings, a control tower with running water, electricity and with no ingress of rain was paradise. It was after all, already a house. The trickiest elements of planning and conversion had already been overcome; indeed, some of the most difficult decisions about layout – 'should we take out this original Second World War wall, even though it's completely in the way and makes no sense?' – had already been taken. There were some problems beyond those already mentioned: the pitched roof, the UPVC windows, the blocked-up windows at the front, but this seemed small beer. As I sat upstairs in the former control room, Claire looked over at me. 'What do you think?' she asked. 'We have to buy it', I said.

After the viewing, we retired to the pub in nearby Warham. We'd always felt comfortable in the Three Horseshoes and had whiled away many happy hours there when on holiday, and now, in its warm embrace, we felt comfortable enough to discuss next moves. We decided we'd text the vendor directly and ask to see her the following day, have another look and put in a cheeky offer. The following morning, we returned to the Control Tower and, over a cup of tea, had our offer firmly declined. We suggested that we go away, check our finances and come back to her. Before we left, we had another look round, concentrating particularly on the grounds. It's amazing what you miss at first sight. Looking again, we were delighted by the mature native trees in the garden. In particular, there were two magnificent beech trees that were somewhat obscured by the Leyland cypress dotted all around.

Once home in Welwyn Garden City, we phoned the vendor again; nervously and tentatively I made a further offer. '£290,000 is about the best we could stretch to'; the vendor, having clearly had a conversation with her husband to agree tactics, countered, 'the lowest we could go is £295,000'. Having likewise planned for this eventuality, I spluttered 'agreed'. Perhaps unsurprisingly, we felt immediately more invested in the building and its history, and I then felt involved enough to begin to jot down notes of what I'd read, and what we'd heard thus far.

History, particularly oral history, is a slippery thing; it has been said that 'anything processed by memory is fiction',[1] which has a tendency, as Robert Kee suggests, to slip like mercury from a fork.[A][2] Our memories tend to evolve over time to suit our audiences and to suit ourselves. Through repeated telling, we may also edit out details that we believe are tedious; portray ourselves in an unnecessarily bad light; are embarrassing (either for us or for those we don't want to embarrass) or don't entertain. As Mark Thomas reveals about one of his live shows, 'you get a story, give it a polish, and bits of the truth fall off, one night you improvise out a line and it gets a good reaction, the next night it stays in the story and it's suddenly "true"'.[3] And to a lesser or greater extent, we all do it:

> our imperfect memories insensibly formalize the fresh originality of living fact – from whose shape they slowly depart, as machine-made castings depart by degrees from the sharp hand-work of the mould.[4]

Part of the process of writing this narrative was reviewing the things that Claire and I had done since moving here, for what is, after all, very recent history. I was shocked at how much I'd forgotten or

---

A A phrase coined by the British Prime Minister, David Lloyd George when he likened negotiating with the Irish leader, Eamon de Valera, as 'trying to pick up mercury with a fork', to which Eamon de Valera responded, 'why doesn't he use a spoon?' (Kee: 1972: 723).

misremembered, and it was only through the thousands of photographs we have taken that I was able to get an accurate timeline. This difficulty is exacerbated the further one goes back; I can remember with absolute clarity that shortly after passing my driving test, petrol was 82p a gallon. This is not true, when I learnt to drive it had already passed the all-important £1 a gallon mark, what I was remembering was the price of a pint of beer (at the time two things of equal importance!). I would have sworn to the accuracy of this assertion until I looked up relative prices for that time.

I am not suggesting that we intend to mislead; it's just an outcome of the story-telling process, compounded by our tendency to conflate stories with established narratives or with the views of our audience. Anyone who has witnessed an accident or a crime will know how eager the police are to get statements very quickly, ideally before you talk to anyone else, or read any news. Writing in 1971 of his memories of the Normandy landings, Vernon Scannell reflects that they had been 'reduced to a few repeated incoherent images'.[5] The result, he concludes, is that 'I realize that I do not remember it so clearly after all. History remembers it, and I remember it as history.'[6] This problem is intensified when stories pass through generations. Geoff Dyer writes of a family anecdote of his grandfather's enlistment in the Great War; when asked his age he gave the 'wrong' answer and was told by the recruiting sergeant to return in a couple of days, when he would be two years older. A common narrative of Great War recruitment, but Geoff Dyer was convinced of the veracity in this particular case. It was only when he looked at his grandfather's death certificate that he realised that he was 20 at the outbreak of the war.[7] Similarly, at the Control Tower, a guest whose father had served at RAF North Creake, revealed a seemingly painful recollection of his father's reaction to how he had painted the top of a model of a Stirling bomber. His father insisted that their Stirlings at RAF North Creake were never painted in camouflage. I discreetly closed the book I was showing him that clearly illustrated a photograph of a crashed 199 Squadron Stirling with camouflaged wings; although irrefutable, I didn't want to challenge this perception and trespass on his memories. The very real problem is that with time and telling, the accuracy of memories fade. The process of laying-down memories is 'as much about forgetting as it is about remembering'.[8] However, moments of extreme stress, for example, when scared, can work 'powerfully as an agent of sharp perception and vivid recall'.[9] Oliver Lyttelton, Great War veteran and Conservative MP wrote:

> fear and its milder brothers, dread and anticipation, first soften the tablets of memory, so that the impressions which they bring are clearly and deeply cut, and when time cools them off the impressions are fixed like the grooves of a gramophone record, and remain with you as long as your faculties. I have been surprised how accurate my memory has proved about times and places where I was frightened.[10]

J B Priestley maintains that 'what the memory retains is all the reader needs to know',[11] and it is certainly true that very often information gleaned from oral sources can lead to revelations that would have otherwise lain undiscovered. Furthermore, as the aviation historian Ken Delve remarked, the 'worst oral testimony will do is give you a flavour of what it was like and that that, in itself, is extremely useful'.[12]

Many authors rely on diaries and numerous are the examples where they have been surprised, or even appalled, to read what they wrote in their own diaries at the time. Robert Kee, an historian and veteran of the RAF, commented on how he felt on rereading his wartime diaries after 40 years. First, he was surprised at how little was of any help in forming an impression of his days in Bomber Command, 'there's nothing you could really get hold of if you were trying to write a proper historical account of it all'.[13] But worse, he discovered, was his attitude to the war:

> my description appals me now, but the point is it can't have done so at the time ... I see on one bright moonlit night we flew back all the way from the Ruhr at about 100 feet while I fired my machine-gun at almost everything I saw. Does this mean

that we were brutal and callous – real terror bombers as the Germans were even then calling us? It would be a total travesty of the truth to say we were, though a historian might well begin to say so on this evidence.[14]

Letters can be equally misleading. The authors of letters are, necessarily, thinking of the intended recipient. Frequently this results in the more routine and mundane elements of daily life being edited out, but most importantly, in times of stress and danger, the writer may wish to reassure the recipient, 'to hint as little as possible at the real, worrisome circumstance of the writer. No one wrote "Dear Mother, I am scared to death"'.[15] Official letters/memoranda can afford a more accurate representation of a time, but even they, as the 'Winston Churchill minute' after the Dresden firestorm attests, may often be composed with an eye on how one might like to be remembered by future historians. For even though Winston Churchill had wanted the targeting of, if not specifically Dresden, a German city near the Eastern Front, afterward, sensing a change in the public mood, he wrote to the Chiefs of Staff Committee and the Chief of Air on 28 March 1945:

> bombing of German cities simply for the sake of increasing terror, though under other pretexts, should be reviewed ... the destruction of Dresden remains a serious query against the conduct of Allied bombing ... I feel the need for more precise concentration upon military objectives .... rather than on mere acts of terror and wanton destruction, however impressive.[16]

Arthur Harris was furious and responded that he considered the 'allegations of terror bombing an insult'.[17] The official biographers of the Strategic Bomber Offensive were equally scathing when in 1961, they described the minute thus:

> perhaps, among the least felicitous of the Prime Minister's long series of war-time minutes. It appeared to overlook the fact that the Bomber Command attack on Dresden had taken place

not at the end of March, when Germany was obviously facing imminent defeat, but in the middle of February, when the situation had been somewhat less promising and a great deal less clear.[18]

The official historians are generously charitable towards Winston Churchill's motives for penning the Dresden Minute, suggesting 'he was acting on the spur of the moment without due reflection'.[19] However, what seems more likely was that he was acting out of political expedience with an eye on influencing the future narrative of the war. And what better way to influence the future narrative, than by writing it yourself. And he did, with six volumes appearing between 1948-1953 as *The Second World War*. Nonetheless, directly the minute was issued, Charles Portal (Chief of Air Staff) persuaded Winston Churchill to withdraw it and issue one containing less inflammatory language; particularly to omit the word 'terror'.[20]

It is, of course, agreed that there are indisputable facts, such as dates and places and, it is further agreed, that the historian must not get these wrong. However, the concept of 'independent objective facts' in history is a fallacy,[21] and facts can be usefully compared to:

fish swimming about in a vast and sometimes inaccessible ocean; and what the historian catches will depend, partly on chance, but mainly on what part of the ocean he chooses to fish in and what tackle he chooses to use – these two factors being, of course, determined by the kind of fish he wants to catch.[22]

Therefore, while it may not be the intention to write a biased narrative, it is inevitable that an historian will always write from a position, whether consciously or unconsciously, governed by their background, education and beliefs. Indeed, the more an historian is aware of this bias the more they can transcend it.[23]

Narratives involving Arthur Harris, a man who will be permanently associated with the theory and practice of the controversial area-bombing campaign, tend to be coloured by where one is positioned in the 'controversy'. Arthur Harris was appointed commander in chief of Bomber Command on 22 February 1942, and remained in post until four months after the end of the war in Europe.[24] Often described as stubborn, combative, opinionated, a fearsome perfectionist and a fighter,[25] he never retreated from his belief that bombing alone could defeat Germany.[26] The following Arthur Harris quote from 1942, is typical and epitomises the man for both his supporters and detractors:

> We are going to bomb Germany incessantly, and I have no doubt that the day is coming when the United States and ourselves between us will put such a force up in the air that the Germans will scream for mercy ... if I could send up 20,000 bombers to Germany tonight, Germany would not be in the war tomorrow.[27]

In many narratives of the 'bombing war' there is an anecdote commonly used to illustrate Arthur Harris's character, both in support and in attack. Joanna Bourke's book on the Second World War is typical:

> Harris was said to have replied to a policeman who pulled him over for speeding and cautioned him on the grounds that he 'could have killed someone' that 'I kill thousands of people every night'.[28]

Such uses are often proceeded with contextual phrases such as 'Harris was not squeamish about killing civilians; he relished it' (James Parton)[29] or 'racing his Bentley at breakneck speed between High Wycombe and the Air Ministry' (Max Hastings).[30] The same anecdote is used in numerous other sources, sometimes with detail changes but with the central thrust much the same,[B] suiting detractors of 'Butcher Harris', a man they argue relished in the 'mass slaughter of civilians'[31]

Certainly, in his autobiography, Arthur Harris illustrates his awareness of his growing reputation; attempting to redress the balance,

---

B See for example Whiting: 1987: 21, where for some reason he has cited Max Hastings, but changed the Bentley to a 'large American car'.

he suggests that the bomber campaign was 'comparatively humane'. Indeed, he asserts 'for one thing, it saved the flower of our youth of this country and of our Allies from being mown down by the military in the field'.[32] While this assertion is contested by many, it does illustrate that Arthur Harris was troubled enough by the criticism to motivate a reply to his critics. In this light, the speeding anecdote feels a little too 'typical' to ring true. Although Arthur Harris could make use of inappropriate humour, as illustrated by his famous quip that the army would never understand the value of tanks until they could be modified to 'eat hay and shit',[33] could he be so insensitive as to make the death of civilians the butt of his humour? James Pelly-Fry knew and worked closely with Arthur Harris and claims to have heard the speeding anecdote directly from him:

> One night when he [Arthur Harris] was speeding home from London in his Bentley along Western Avenue two police motorcycles raced past him and flagged him down. The conversation was something like this:
>
> Police: 'Good evening, Sir. I have stopped you because you are travelling much too fast. You might kill someone.'
>
> Harris: 'I am on important business. Now that you come to mention it, it's my business to kill people; Germans.'
>
> Police: 'Are you Air Marshall Harris, Sir?'
>
> Harris nodded.
>
> Police: 'That's different Sir! Sorry I stopped you. Please follow us.'
>
> The two motorcyclists now set off at exceedingly brisk pace, so much so that my hero could barely keep up. After telling the story, Bert Harris said with a grin, 'it was the quickest trip I ever made; they must have liked me'.[34]

This impression is entirely different. However, we can't be sure when this book was written, although it was published 50 years after the event. Therefore, we cannot, necessarily, rely on his power of recall (he does, after all, use the phrase 'something like this'), or why he felt motivated to relate it. Possibly he was the original source of the anecdote, he believed it had been misinterpreted, and he was attempting to 'correct' the record and resurrect his friend's reputation; to respond, perhaps, to 'my hero's' (as he called Arthur Harris)[35] critics. Which is the 'truth'? You'll need to judge for yourself.

Narrative pace can often be forced by the obligation to keep the reader entertained. War is often said to be boredom punctuated by short periods of intense activity and terror. History of war tends to focus on the latter; no one is going to give boredom more than a passing reference in an historical narrative. My uncle served as an armourer with the RAF from 1939 to 1945. After training he did not return home for six years.[C] He was posted to countries that had either been or were to become appalling theatres of war; but he witnessed none of it. He always said that he never fired a single shot in anger, and his wartime anecdotes mostly consisted of savouring a wide variety of cuisines in restaurants all over the world – evidenced by his mementos of war – a stash of menus. This is not the stuff of tales of daring do, although I imagine it was an experience of many thousands of men, but, as W Somerset Maugham observes, fact 'is a poor story-teller'.[1] To write a narrative that is interesting, the historian is necessarily selective. As someone reading a draft of this book commented to me, you need to pick and choose what is included, 'otherwise you just have a sequence of events of mixed interest', even if it makes you feel you're fabricating your life story, the 'thing is – that's the job'. However, what governs how a reader understands an historical narrative comes down to which facts the author selects; when returning to the Control Tower on our viewing day, we must exercise caution over what we've been told of its history.

With the exceptions of having been a decoy and RAF bomber airfield, none of the other stories of RAF North Creake we were told

---

C My dad always reflected upon this time with sadness. Dad was ten years old when his brother left and they were very close. When he returned, Dad was 16, and he no longer knew his brother. It was a gulf they never overcame; another sideshow of war. I don't really remember meeting my uncle but my mum used to talk with great amusement about the time he visited in the 1960s. Being unfamiliar with us as a family but knowing there were five boys, he bought us all gifts. Slabs of toffee you broke with a hammer – I was four months old!

on our first viewing of the Control Tower were accurate. RAF North Creake's role in the Second World War is shrouded in secrecy as a result of its involvement with, what was then called, Radio Counter Measures,[D] and now known as 'Electronic Warfare', with every element of its development during the war being 'most secret'.[E] The constraining effect this has on undertaking any research into its history is immense, as it is often concealed and challenging to unravel. The details of the purpose of this airfield only really emerged in the 1970s, being as it was covered by the 30-year rule.[F] Further releases came with the 50-year rule and I have been assured there is still more to come under the 100-year rule. This means, of course, that in the absence of written evidence, what emerges is oral history and myth; some of which we heard on our first viewing. What we can be certain of is that the step on the first floor at the entrance to the Control Room is nothing to do with it being built in two halves; one when it was a decoy station and the other when it went fully operational. The real, and less exciting, explanation is that after the war, when the mill took on the Control Tower, they rewired it and, as the walls are so hard, they ran the conduit on top of the existing solid concrete floor and simply laid a new screed over it to cover it up, resulting in a step. When we took the later screed up, we found the 'concrete' evidence. The secret hiding places were simply access hatches for the control desk wiring that ran under the oak floor in the Control Room (only in this room was the reinforced concrete floor fitted with a wooden floor on top). As for the comforting lack of losses, the records tell us that 18 aircraft were struck off charge – 11 of which were 'fail to returns' – and 73 aircrew members died. A reasonably high price for one airfield and 11 months of war, but that was the nature of the bombing campaign.

D   This term was coined by Edward Addison of RAF 80 (Signals) Wing and latterly Air Officer Commanding RAF 100 Group (Streetly: 1978: 14).

E   'Most secret' was Britain's highest level of secrecy, the US term 'top secret' is now generally used.

F   According to official Government documents, the 30-year rule 'governs the point at which records of lasting historical value are normally transferred to the National Archives and made available to the public'. This has now been reduced to 20 years giving 'a better balance between openness, affordability and the protection of information which, if released prematurely, could harm good government and be contrary to the public interest' (Ministry of Justice: 26/2/2010).

From the mid-1920s British prospects in any future aerial war seemed bleak, with British politicians and military leaders struggling to develop a coherent defensive strategy against aerial bombardment. The Air Staff predicted a collapse in civilian morale in the inevitable conflict as there was 'no possible defence against this sort of attack'.[36] Indeed, in the Prime Minister, Stanley Baldwin's, infamous speech of 10 November 1932, he mournfully proclaimed:

> I think it is as well for the man in the street to realize that there is no power on earth that can protect him from being bombed. Whatever people may tell him, the bomber will always get through ... The only defence is in offence, which means that you have to kill more women and children more quickly than the enemy if you want to save yourselves.'[37]

In the mid-1930s the consequences of aerial attack were becoming ever more apparent. When in 1937, as part of the fascist coup against the democratically elected government of Spain, aircraft of the Condor Legion (the Luftwaffe in all but name)[38] attacked Guernica, British statisticians collated figures revealing losses that could be expected in similar attacks on Britain. It was confidently predicted that in any future war with Germany, Adolf Hitler would bomb Britain immediately after the declaration of hostilities, and continue for a period of 60 days, leading to the deaths of around 600,000 people.[39] However, the first air raid casualties of the war were some six months later in March 1940, when the Luftwaffe attacked a minor target in Orkney, injuring a few civilians.[40]

Nonetheless, in anticipation of devastating bombardments, Franklin Roosevelt appealed to the belligerents to renounce the bombing of civilians.[41] The British government agreed to target only military objectives and outlined in 1940, that any 'attack must be made with reasonable care to avoid undue loss of civil life in the vicinity of the target'.[42] Indeed, in the House of Commons, the British Prime Minister, Neville Chamberlain announced, 'whatever be the lengths others may go, His Majesty's Government will never resort to the deliberate attack on women and children, and other civilians for purposes of mere terrorism'.[43]

However, by May 1940, Bomber Command military targets included civilian industrial/infrastructure that, it was perceived, aided the war effort (power stations and blast furnaces etc.).[44] The war cabinet's support for this change of emphasis relied on public anger in response to Luftwaffe outrages in the low countries. Since, it asserted, 'any hopes that the Germans might apply a code of morals in the West different from that which Poland had experienced in the East, were quickly shattered by the mass bombing of Rotterdam',[45] and now, the 'gloves were off'.[46] Here began Bomber Command's strategic air offensive against Germany. Legitimised by perceptions of Nazi immorality in warfare, it was also, the 'sole means at Britain's disposal for attacking the heart of the enemy'.[47] The new Prime Minister, Winston Churchill, now elevated Bomber Command to primacy and personally ensured that the bomber offensive, 'would consume the lion's share of Britain's industrial resources'.[48] By July 1940, he was unequivocally stating his position in a minute to William 'Max' Beaverbrook (Minister of Aircraft Production):

> when I look round and see how we can win the war I see that there is only one sure path. We have no Continental army which can defeat the German military power. The blockade is broken and Hitler has Asia and probably Africa to draw from. Should he be repulsed here or not try invasion, he will recoil eastward, and we have nothing to stop him. But there is one thing that will bring him back and bring him down, and that is an enormously devastating, exterminating attack by very heavy bombers from this country upon the Nazi homeland. We must be able to overwhelm them by this means, without which I do not see a way through.[49]

On the night of the 24/25 August 1940, and with the Battle of Britain still raging, German aircrews mistakenly bombed central London.[50] Against the advice of the Air Staff, the British War Cabinet immediately sanctioned a reprisal attack on Berlin for the following night. Involving some 80 aircraft,[51] three of which were lost, [52] it was not a successful raid. With Berlin covered by a blanket of cloud[53] and with Bomber Command being dogged by problems of accuracy, little damage was caused and there were no serious civilian casualties.[54] The majority of the bombs fell on land around Berlin, leading RAF bomber crews to quip that they 'made a major assault on German agriculture'.[55]

Nonetheless, the action had infuriated Adolf Hitler who 'declared he would rub out'[56] British towns and cities with fire:

> I want fires everywhere. Thousands of them! Then they'll unite in one gigantic area conflagration. Goering has the right idea. Explosive bombs don't work, but it can be done with incendiary bombs – total destruction of London![57]

And so began the London Blitz, during which, on the rooftop of the Air Ministry building, the future head of Bomber Command, Arthur Harris, watched London burn. He later noted in his autobiography that this was the sole time during the war that he felt vengeful, and compelled to utter his now infamous words, 'well, they are sowing the wind.'[58] However, any notion of a strategic bombing campaign was hampered by the primary problem that, As Garro Jones MP explained in the House of Commons:

> we know that these heavy bombers cannot operate except from extreme altitudes or by night. In the former case they cannot hit their targets; in the latter case they cannot find their targets and have not found them … As far as direct hits on specified industrial targets by high-flying aircraft by night are concerned, we might as well send the long-distance bombers to the moon.[59]

The move to night-time flying in December 1940,[60] had made operations much safer, but the targets proved more difficult to find and to hit. The

Butt Report of 1941,[G] studied the accuracy of Allied bombing; it results were a shock. Of those recorded as 'attacking the target',[61] only 30% of bombers reached within five miles of the aiming point (within the 75 square mile area surrounding target),[62] and of those only one in three bombed within three miles of the target.[63] Over Germany the results were even worse, with only one in four being within three miles of target,[64] but over the Ruhr it dropped to one in ten.[65]

In response to the report, and through a cunning policy sleight of hand, the RAF changed the emphasis of the bombing campaign. The tacticians argued that while the target point remained military/industrial, the inevitable hits beyond the target would strike workers' houses, shops, cinemas and cafes as a consequence of their close proximity to the target. As unfortunate as this was, the destruction of what the workers owned and enjoyed would, in what Max Hastings suggests was a view born of prejudice that massively underestimated the resilience of workers,[66] cause a colossal drop in industrial output as their morale collapsed. Charles Portal asserted that this effectively meant that 'every hit would be of value'; a position wholeheartedly supported by Winston Churchill.[67] Therefore the weakening of morale, that is, 'the will of the German people to continue the war', had become the central focus of the bombing campaign. However, this change of emphasis in bombing policy was not openly declared, and the Air Ministry would continue to argue that it was pursuing legitimate industrial targets only.

This outlook was adopted by the majority of RAF senior officers, most of whom 'understood perfectly well that this meant killing civilians'.[68] This led to the Air Ministry and Bomber Command finally abandoning its 'futile efforts to hit precise targets',[69] and instead concentrating on urban area-bombing. Nonetheless, even with a change in emphasis, the bombing offensive was still difficult to justify. Winston Churchill, while still vocally supportive of the bombing strategy, no longer believed that bombing alone could win the war.[70] Moreover, the cost, in terms of lost crews remained stubbornly high. From August

---

G   David Miles Bensusan-Butt, an economist and member of the War Cabinet secretariat examined over 600 photographs taken by night bombers flown between June and July 1941 and analysed the results (Webster & Frankland: 1961: 178).

1941, the RAF lost one bomber for every ten tons of bombs dropped.[71] The bomber offensive of 1940-1941, 'killed more of the R.A.F. than German civilians'.[72] However, given the small size of the offensive, total losses were 'negligible and the effect on the German war potential was equally negligible'.[73] Reflecting upon this, on 13 November 1941, the bombing campaign was suspended.[74]

14 February 1942, saw the recommencement of the bombing campaign under a new directive. 'Precision bombing' was no longer the ambition; the defeat of German morale, particularly that of industrial workers, through 'area-bombing' was now the primary objective.[75] On 28/29 March 1942, Bomber Command mounted an attack on Lubeck. This sought to send the highest numbers of bombers possible in the shortest conceivable time to the target, thereby, overwhelming German defences and its fire-fighting capabilities.[76] From Bomber Command's perspective, it was a great success;[77] when success was measured in acres of devastation per acre of built-up area attacked.[78] Further raids suggested more success for Bomber Command, at Rostock (23 to 27 April 1942), the Nazi propagandist Joseph Goebbels declared that 'community life there is practically at an end'.[79] Winston Churchill appeared pleased:

> You will remember how the German propaganda films, seeking to terrorize neutral countries and glorying in devastating violence, were wont to show rows of great German bombers being loaded up with bombs, then flying in the air in battle array, then casting down showers of bombs upon the defenceless towns and villages below, choking them in smoke and flame ... Though the mills of God grind slowly, yet they grind exceedingly small. And for my part I hail it as an example of sublime and poetic justice that those who have loosed these horrors upon mankind shall now in their own homes and persons feel the shattering strokes of retributive justice.[80]

Through this 'retributive justice' the Allies would demoralise the

German population. The thesis of demoralisation was underpinned by the publication in 1942, of the 'Cherwell Memorandum'. German born Frederick Lindemann (Lord Cherwell), Winston Churchill's Scientific Adviser, was informed by the research of John Bernal and Solly Zuckerman on the bombing of Hull and Birmingham. Contrary to Frederick Lindemann's reading of their research, John Bernal and Solly Zuckerman's analysis had led them to conclude that there was no evidence of panic in either Hull or Birmingham as a result of the bombing.[81] However, Frederick Lindemann saw it differently, and he drew different conclusions, around which, the bombing campaign was formed:

> careful analysis of the effects of raids on Birmingham, Hull and elsewhere have shown that, on the average, one ton of bombs dropped on a built-up area demolishes 20-40 dwellings and turns 100-200 people out of house and home.
>
> We know from our experience that we can count on nearly 14 operational sorties per bomber produced. The average lift of the bombers we are going to produce over the next fifteen months will be about three tons. It follows that each of these bombers will in its lifetime drop about forty tons of bombs. If these are dropped on built-up areas they will make 4,000-8,000 people homeless ... Investigation seems to show that having one's house demolished is most damaging to morale. People seem to mind it more than having their friends or even relatives killed.[82]

Frederick Lindemann believed that there was little doubt that such 'de-housing' raids, as they were euphemistically called, 'would break the spirit of the people'.[83] Many welcomed his analysis and found his calculations simple, clear and convincing, although some were not so convinced:

> It had been generally assumed that aerial bombardment would quickly shatter popular morale, causing deep civilian

reactions... The progress of this war has tended to indicate that this expectation was unfounded.[84]

Nonetheless, Frederick Lindemann won the day and the area-bombing campaign intensified. Shortly after, Arthur Harris was appointed to the commander in chief of Bomber Command. Although not the architect of the area bombing policy, he was convinced of its veracity and pursued it with vigour and determination. On 30/31 May 1942, he mounted his most audacious raid so far; called Operation Millenium, it was waged against Cologne and was the first raid involving 1,000 bombers. After receiving approval from Winston Churchill and Charles Portal he begged the assistance of Training Command and Coastal Command, in order to reach this arbitrary number of bombers.[85] On the night, a final total of 1,047 aircraft flew, and 898 claimed to have bombed the city,[86] dropping 1,455 tons of bombs.[87] The tail-gunners on aircraft returning from the raid claimed that they could see the glow of fires for 100 miles after target.[88] Between 469 and 486 people were killed on the ground, 5,027 were listed as injured and 45,132 were 'de-housed'.[89] Forty-one aircraft[90] were lost. Winston Churchill was jubilant, despatching a telegram to Arthur Harris immediately:

> I congratulate you and the whole of Bomber Command upon the remarkable feat of organization which enabled you to despatch over a thousand bombers to the Cologne area in a single night and without confusion to concentrate their action over the target in so short a time as one hour and a half. This proof of the growing power of the British bomber force is also the herald of what Germany will receive, city by city, from now on.[91]

Nonetheless, in spite of the rhetoric Winston Churchill's position on bombing was evolving. While he no longer believed that the bombing campaign could alone win the war, he did believe it was a way of softening-up Germany for the invasion of Europe by the Allies:

both [America and Britain] recognized that aerial bombardment was the key to victory. The bombing created a 'second front', it helped the USSR, and diverted Axis resources from the production of bombers to anti-aircraft guns and fighter planes.[92]

With the German invasion of the USSR on 22 June 1941, Winston Churchill announced his unreserved solidarity with Russia that same evening,[93] although there was little Britain could do to assist their new ally.[94] From the point of their entry into the war the Soviet Union would, for the most part, have to contend with fighting four-fifths of the German army.[95] While Winston Churchill understood what was being borne by the Soviet Union,[96] and despite pressures he was under from both Joseph Stalin[97] and some British citizens,[98] he was opposed to the quick deployment of ground troops in Europe. Haunted by memories of the Great War and concerned about catastrophic British losses, he feared that an early invasion could potentially mire British troops in the mud of Northern France for months, if not years. Winston Churchill wanted to stave-off a ground assault on Europe until Germany had been exhausted by the exertions of war,[99] and he was fully aware that it was the Soviets who were paying the price for this strategy.[100]

In late 1941, with the Japanese attack on Pearl Harbour and the German declaration of war on the USA, Winston Churchill thought it imperative to dissuade Franklin Roosevelt from any impetuous action on Europe.[101] At a conference between Winston Churchill and Franklin Roosevelt (22 December 1941 - 14 January 1942), Franklin Roosevelt proclaimed his commitment to creating a second front in 1942.[102] Through gradual persuasion, Winston Churchill convinced him that invasion that early was impossible,[103] and, with all options considered, the only effective support for the USSR would be through North Africa, although this may delay the invasion of Europe still further.[104]

While the US was softening to this position, Winston Churchill felt stung by the accusations of inaction and attacks of 'bad faith, weakness and cowardice'[105] from Joseph Stalin. He therefore suggested a meeting with Joseph Stalin to outline Britain's continued commitment to the war, and to dissuade him from any temptation to seek a negotiated peace with the Nazis.[106] They met at the Kremlin (12 August 1942[107]), where Joseph Stalin immediately accused the Allies of being afraid of the Germans and fearful of taking risks. However, eventually, Joseph Stalin became persuaded of the merit of Operation Torch (invasion through North Africa), if it could secure the defeat of Erwin Rommel and speed up the withdrawal of Italy from the war. Nonetheless, what Joseph Stalin found most attractive was the British promising to 'pay our way',[108] with an intensified bombing campaign of Germany. An air offensive that would shatter the morale of the German people.[109] With the thought of this, 'Stalin came to life'.[110]

The Allies were due to meet at Casablanca in January 1943, but, with the urgency of the fighting at Stalingrad, Joseph Stalin could not attend. Therefore Winston Churchill and Franklin Roosevelt met alone. The participants agreed that the greatest chance of a successful invasion of Europe would be through the weakening of German resolve by an aerial assault on German targets.[111] The bombing campaign was therefore a high priority. The instruction for Bomber Command was clear:

> your primary aim will be the progressive destruction and dislocation of the German military, industrial and economic system, and the undermining of the morale of the German people to a point where their capacity for armed resistance is fatally weakened.[112]

Arthur Harris saw Casablanca as a mandate to continue with the area-bombing campaign, thereby condemning bomber crews to an intensified level of operations, with all the associated losses for the crews above and the civilians below. These objectives were also reflected in the aims of Charles Portal for 1943 and 1944, with his ambition to drop 1.25 million tons of bombs on Germany (killing an estimated 900,000 people and seriously injuring another one million), destroy the enemy's industrial and transportation infrastructure, and make 25 million people homeless.[113] In pursuit of this aim, in 1943 alone, the bombing levels achieved were five times that of 1942.[114]

Carl Spaatz, commander of the USAAF in Europe, concurred with Arthur Harris's view that Germany could be defeated by airborne attacks alone.[115] However, he did not approve of area-bombing, as he believed that while civilian casualties arising from 'precision bombing'[H] were acceptable, the 'deliberate mass slaughter of civilians was not'.[116] As a consequence the USAAF took away from Casablanca very a different aim: that of the bombing of strategic industrial targets.[117]

The Bomber Command attack on Hamburg, over the course of ten nights between 24 July and 3 August 1943, would prove pivotal in the area bombing offensive. The RAF completed a total of 3,091 sorties, dropping 10,000 tons of bombs. The now infamous Hamburg firestorm occurred as a result of the bombing on the night of the 27/28 July 1943. It was not deliberate. The firestorm was an unexpected result of very concentrated bombing, unusually high temperatures (30 degrees centigrade at 6pm) and low levels of rain, resulting in unusually low humidity. About half-way through the raid the fires in the city began to join together, drawing oxygen from the surrounding air; suddenly the city was engulfed in one huge conflagration, with air being drawn into it with the force of a storm. It raged for around three hours and only subsided when all combustible material had been exhausted.[118] It killed over 18,000 people (only 280 were killed in the factory district).[119] The city was devastated over the ten nights and an estimated 40,000 people died (31,647 confirmed deaths of which 15,802 could be identified.[120]), most of whom suffocated when oxygen was drawn out of their basement shelters. In the immediate aftermath, 1,200,000 left the city fearing further raids.[121] Murray Pedan, although describing an attack on Kassel, describes vividly the impact of an aerial assault, and even though there was no firestorm, the horrendous scene of devastation is very apparent:

H Max Hastings argues that in the winter of 1943/44 the Americans were effectively area-bombing as the Norden sight proved useless (Hastings: 1980: 269).

Already the city was a scene of savage destruction and garish beauty combined. In a hundred places huge cargoes of incendiaries were just flaring into life, the brilliant glare of their magnesium and phosphorous contents radiating the breathtaking beauty of gigantic handfuls of cascading diamonds on a black velvet backdrop. As we began our bomb run toward the clustered TI's, which shimmered in rich red splendour, vicious shock waves from the high explosives raining down rippled and tore across the heart of the city creating an effect like bursting bubbles in boiling porridge, and the thousands of spreading smaller fires began merging into a giant unquenchable conflagration ... Sam [navigator] took one glance out the window at the maelstrom of bursting coloured torrents of fire pulsing with angry black flak puff ... he had seen enough, and never again did he ask to look at another target.[122]

From a Bomber Command perspective, the Hamburg raid was a huge success: it destroyed morale, with a wide range of voices within the political and military leadership of Germany heard to say, 'the war is lost'. Adolf Hitler, on hearing the details of the attack, and for the only known time in the war, conceded it might be necessary to sue for peace.[123] It denied factory workers their work, homes and often their families, and it turned many civilians openly against the Nazi party.[124] For Albert Speer, the German Minister of Armaments and War production, it was a catastrophe:

Hamburg had put the fear of God into me. At the meeting of Central Planning on 29 July, I pointed out if the air raids continue on at the present scale, within three months we shall be relieved of a number of questions we are at present discussing. We shall simply be coasting downhill, smoothly and relatively swiftly ... Three days later I informed Hitler that armaments production was collapsing and threw in the final warning that a series of attacks of this sort, extended to six more major cities, would bring Germany's armaments production to a total halt. 'You'll straighten all that out again', he merely said. In fact he was right.[125]

A great deal of research went in to discovering how to maximise the effectiveness of an air raid. At the Building Research Establishment they created mock-ups of typical German buildings, with German furniture, to enable researchers to make informed decisions when calculating incendiaries needed for effective raids.[126] The bombers were loaded with a combination of one-third high explosive to two-thirds incendiaries; the blast from the high explosives would remove windows and doors, allowing the fires from the incendiaries to readily spread.[127] Moreover, the high explosives also left craters in the roads inhibiting the movement of fire-fighters and thereby their ability to extinguish fires.[128] Bombing accuracy had also greatly improved, with target markers dropped by 8 Group 'Pathfinders'[I] marking the aiming point, with radar developments making it easier to find the target,[J] and the introduction of the master bomber on the night of the 21/22 June 1943, controlling the raid from above.[129] The master bomber controlled the attack while circling the target, drawing the bombers into the aiming point by radio transmitted exhortations; 'the whole time you were on the bombing run the master bomber was talking to you … "Bomb to the left of indicator. Bomb to the right of indicator. Bomb forward. Bomb forward. Take it more forward"'.[130] All these developments helped the accuracy of bombing dramatically. However, the air-dropped bomb still remained a blunt tool; Murray Pedan explains why:

> It was not too difficult to keep the wings almost perfectly level, and the fuselage almost perfectly level fore and aft, and the air speed indicator almost dead on the predetermined figure, and the rate of climb indicator almost perfectly centered [sic], and

---

I   Formed in 1942, the role of the Pathfinders was to 'guide squadrons of the main force to the target, which they had marked with coloured flares and target indicators' (Falconer: 1998: 10).

J   Primary among these came in October 1941, with the development of H2S; a radar that scanned the ground ahead of the aircraft and replicated 'strong indications' of the surface back to the aircraft on a cathode-ray screen (Rowe: 1948: 116) enabling accurate target-finding even through cloud.

the altimeter almost exactly of the footage prescribed; but the margins between all those almosts and perfection seemed to interact in geometric progression to invalidate the bomb aimer's setting and produce discouragingly large errors in the point of impact.[131]

As blunt as it was it had now become a well-rehearsed strategy on the path to Dresden; the very name of which has become synonymous with the horrors of area-bombing. Although Dresden was already on a list of cities to be bombed,[132] the raid was at the behest of Winston Churchill,[133] in order to support the Russian General Antonov,[K] in his request for bombing support on the Eastern Front as:

> Dresden was an important junction, they didn't want reinforcements coming over from the Western front and from Norway, from Italy and so on; and similarly on the following day … Antonov very clearly said, '[we want] the Dresden railway junction bombed because we are afraid the Germans are putting up a resistance, a last stand as it were'. And we agreed to this.[134]

For crews, at the time, it was just another job. On the night of 13 February 1945, 804 aircraft took off from airfields in the east of England, and hit Dresden in two phases with a three-hour gap in-between. They dropped 1,478 tons of high explosive and 1,182 tons of incendiaries.[135] A third wave of 311 USAAF bombers attacked the city the following day.[136] It is still uncertain how many were killed in the resulting firestorm, as the city was thronged by refugees fleeing the Eastern Front. However, most modern estimates put the figure at between 25,000 and 40,000 dead.[137] Estimates vary wildly but furnished with data from the former Soviet Union this is now thought to be the 'fairest estimate'.[138]

K   It would also, speculation suggests, serve as a warning to the Soviet Union of the awesome power of Bomber Command, should they be harbouring any postwar expansionist plans; part of a strategy of pre-emptive 'intimidation against Russia' (Taylor:2005:433).

The reaction to the raid in Britain was both instant and damning; coursing through the corridors of Whitehall, through the Air Ministry and on to Parliament where Richard Stokes MP, while praising aircrew for their 'great loyalty, devotion, courage and determination',[139] gave a scathing verdict of Bomber Command tactics.[140] The cries of outrage may in some way explain Winston Churchill's Dresden minute, but not excuse it.

Notwithstanding changing public opinion, the bombing continued, indeed, intensified. During the first four months of 1945, in 36 major operations over 181,000 tons of bombs, or around one fifth of the aggregate for the entire war, were dropped by Bomber Command aircraft,[141] of which 608 were lost.[142]

Aircrew had no control and no influence over the direction of bombing strategy, where they were sent or whether they dropped bombs. They had, for a myriad of motivations, bought in to the life of bomber crew and often they paid a very high price, frequently with their lives. For the residents of the bombed German cities, it would be terrifying and devastating. For the bombed and the bombers alike, their life, while lived, was inescapable.

* * *

Buying a house is an odd thing; you have to invest enough emotionally to see you through all the protracted nonsense of the process, but not so much that you'll be devastated if it falls through. We were on the back foot; our house was not even on the market, and while it was loved and cared for, we'd never quite finished it; those nagging little jobs at the end of a substantial makeover that never seem to be prioritised over meeting friends for a drink or squeezing in that weekend break that we so obviously deserved. They were now urgent and they all got done. 'This will sell in no time', the estate agent confidently predicted, and then, silence. A little knot began to tighten in our stomachs. After eight days Amy arrived for an arranged viewing, she walked around asking sensible questions and caressing fittings; she liked it, we could tell.

On the bus, travelling to the university the following morning my phone rang; we had an offer and the advice was, although lower than we wanted, we should accept. I phoned Claire and we concluded it would work and we should accept the offer. It was ten days since the house went on the market, and with one viewing and no other interest, we'd sold it – the knot slackened – a little.

The next few weeks, leading into months, dragged by; we wanted to move in August to coincide with the university quiet time, but it was not to be. We were then plagued by delays from estate agents, solicitors, and holidays. The Norfolk estate agent called about progress as there was someone else interested in the Control Tower. Although concurrently panicked and sceptical the knot tightened; I phoned the vendor and she said they weren't interested in anyone else's offer;[L] the knot slackened. More delays, searches and environmental reports (I wrote a scathing response to the one for our house. It wasn't exactly why I'd done a BSc in Environmental Science, but it all helps). With hope rather than certainty, we started to pack up our things. A brief escape at a friend, Lou's, 40th birthday party, allowed us to relax a little. However, we reduced the benefit of the break by clutching the estate agent's particulars of our 'crazy' purchase. Friends were very interested to see it, some were genuinely very supportive, while others, in spite of their encouraging words, had doubtful looks. We'd taken along a photograph of Debach control tower to illustrate how it should look; I'm not sure it helped.

When back home, we foolishly went ahead and bought a new front door for the Control Tower (of classic 1930s design) and in September, on the condition they kept it for another month, we bought a 1930s three-piece suite. 'We could always re-sell them on eBay.' We eventually exchanged in the third week of September; we set a provisional moving date of Monday 3 October 2011. Packing started in

---

L   There was indeed a second potential buyer – I caught up with him at our opening event in June 2014. He was, in fact, a former work colleague and friend, Mike Ward, who I'd known for 20 years; he lived in Norfolk and wanted a 'bigger place'. He ultimately decided that it was too much work. The main comment he made was that he 'would have kept the sheds!'.

earnest. Our anxious rescue cat, Isis[M], suspecting something was wrong (nothing good ever comes from packing bags or boxes) began to show terrible symptoms of stress. Two days before we were due to move, she began continually throwing up. We took her to the vet the next day and he recommended an injection, but he was not confident it would work. Thankfully it did; until the drive up.

By midday we'd arrived at the Control Tower and with warning signs duly pasted on a bedroom door, left the cat pacing her 'safe' zone. Shortly after, the removal lorry arrived.

By 9.00pm they'd unpacked the lorry. We waved off the removal men and closed the front door. We were finally alone in our new home. Walking through to the kitchen, the sudden silence heightened a sense of unfamiliarity, exacerbating existing but contradictory emotions of excitement and trepidation. But here we were, we'd done it. The bed was made, the essentials unpacked and Isis, having explored the house, was sitting next to us on some packing boxes, purring. We had a beer and the knot unravelled.

M Isis was named by our son, Cillian, after the Egyptian goddess.

FEWER THAN FIVE MINUTES FROM BASE

Stirling LJ518 EX-K

September 1944 had been mostly cool and unsettled, with the middle of the month particularly wet, with some parts of the UK experiencing three times the average rainfall.[1] On the night of 25 September 1944, the weather showed little improvement. Main Force[A] had been stood down and Bomber Command was only set to fly minor operations.[2] However, 199 Squadron and 171 Squadron at RAF North Creake, as part of Bomber Support, were detailed for sorties.

Six Stirlings of 199 Squadron and six Stirlings of 171 Squadron[3] commenced take-off at 18:53.[4] All took off, although two aircraft returned early; 171 Squadron 6Y-E and 199 Squadron EX-X, both with navigational problems. For those continuing, weather conditions were 'very unfavourable'.[5] While most completed their operation successfully, some were 'seriously affected by adverse weather conditions, and it would appear that aircraft were often considerably

---

A Main Force was the title given to Bomber Command squadrons that fulfilled the Commands primary function of waging the bomber offensive. Their role was to drop the bombs.

off the route ordered'.[6] All aircraft had returned safely to base by 01:43,[7] with the exception of Stirling LJ518 EX-K. The North Creake Operations Record Book states, 'one aircraft of No. 199 Squadron 'K' crashed at Melton Constable on return. No survivors'. The 199 Squadron ORB outlines that it had been the sixth aircraft airborne when it took off at 19:02,[8] and that it 'crashed in bad weather near Saxthorpe, Norfolk and the crew was killed instantaneously. The aircraft is a total wreck'.[9] Tragically, the aircraft crashed in a direct line with runway three, fewer than five minutes' flying time from RAF North Creake. The crew had only arrived at their first operational station, RAF North Creake, on 11 September 1944.[10] On board were:

Len Barham (RAF) Special Operator, aged 29
Francis Chatwin (RAF) Pilot, aged 27
Colin Henderson (RNZF) Bomb Aimer, aged 25
Ambrose Loveland (RAF) Flight Engineer, aged 31
John Naylor (RAF) Air Gunner, aged 36
Pyrs Roberts (RAF) Air Gunner, aged 19
Robert Saddler (RAF) Wireless Operator, aged 22
Richard Savage (RAAF) Navigator, aged 22

Stirling LJ518 EX-K, while making its approach to RAF North Creake, descended through low cloud and struck the top of a large oak tree[11] located on a hill.[12] An 18-year-old eyewitness cycling home at 21:45, described how he 'heard a low flying aircraft, I looked to my right and saw a plane hit some trees'.[13] The aircraft then applied power on all engines and pulled up steeply, then stalled and 'plunged to the ground taking off part of the hedge on the road to Edgefield'.[14] It completely disintegrated on impact, bursting into flames and spreading wreckage over some considerable distance, blocking a minor road.[15] It was an appalling scene:

By the time I reached it, it was a mass of flames and bullets were exploding, I was there for a while until RAF and USAAF crash crews turned up, as I left they were arguing over whether it was an English or American plane, I left them to it and made my way home. On my way home I spotted a Perspex plane window lying in the lane, I picked it up and took it back to the crash crews and from this it was determined that it was in fact a Stirling.

The medical officer and nursing orderly from RAF North Creake proceeded to the scene of the crash.[16] The Stirling had crashed some 100 yards north of the B1354, Saxthorpe to Briston Road, near Locks Farm.[17]

The last line of the ORB for RAF North Creake, for the night and early morning of the 25/26 September, records that the 'Station Concert Party gave a final show "Sailing Along" to a good audience'.[18] To modern eyes, it may seem a little unfeeling, or even callous, to report such an event at the very time fire crews, ambulances and rescue parties had been despatched to the crash site. However, the role of the ORB was to record activities on the station, and when in the hands of a conscientious author, they recorded a wide range of duties, tasks and social events that would otherwise have been lost.[B] Moreover, while in this case it is probably unlikely that the station personnel at the show had any idea that a crash had occurred, it is uncertain that it would have altered their actions if they had. On an operational station one could not always afford to be in tune with emotions, as a pilot on another station recalls, 'you didn't have all that much feeling about people dying or getting killed. But you didn't know all the crews so when one went missing you didn't notice it unless they happened to be friends of yours'.[19] This was not, of course a universal approach, but

---

B   Operation Record Books (ORBs) are an invaluable resource to an airfield historian; however, they do vary in quality immensely. Generally, each station had at least two; one for the station and one for the squadron. If a procrastinator was appointed to the task, one that considers the role a chore, they may have only completed it when it was due to be signed off by the station commander. This may have meant having to catch-up on days, sometimes weeks of entries, with the consequential problems of detailed recollection (Delve: 2/6/2017). With RAF North Creake, there are three ORBs, one for the station and one for each squadron. The 199 Squadron varies in quality enormously, initially very short on detail and often inaccurate, it improves greatly as the months pass (one assumes as the result of a change of scribe), the 171 Squadron ORB is better and reasonably consistent and the station ORB is very informative and was clearly written by someone who took the task seriously.

for many it was a method of coping; at least until you had completed operational flying.

At the site, an eyewitness[20] mentions both RAF (presumably from RAF Oulton as that was approximately a mile away), and USAAF in attendance (other postwar accounts report a Civil Defence crew also attending[21]). It was normal procedure, when the police had been alerted to an air crash by local residents, that they would report it to the Air Ministry,[22] and that the nearest RAF station, in keeping with their responsibilities,[23] would send firefighting and rescue crews to assist. John Rees, the flight sergeant in charge of the RAF North Creake station sick quarters also attended;[24] but nothing could be done to save the eight on board. The priority, once it became obvious it was no longer a rescue operation, was to dowse the fires and recover the dead. The bodies were removed by personnel from RAF Oulton and remained in Oulton overnight. They were transported to RAF North Creake on 26 September 1944.[25]

The emotional needs of the bereaved were always of high consideration for the RAF, both for the relatives but also for the morale of fellow RAF personnel.[26] The importance of the 'swift identification of bodies, knowledge of the means of death, and reassurance both that death had been swift and painless'[27] in comforting the bereaved, was always understood by the RAF authorities. Grief understandably threw up raw emotions, and one RAF station adjutant, Edgar Reeks, remembers a 'letter from one of the parents accusing the RAF of robbing their son of his wristwatch, which had been a 21st birthday present that he would never have parted with. My job was to tell parents that all we could find of the six bodies was two pounds of flesh which had to be divided between six coffins'.[28]

It was not unusual that they 'could only find pieces';[29] the forces experienced by aircrew in a high-speed impact made the task of their recovery a harrowing one. With the stipulation that for 'proof of death' ... 7lbs (3kg) was needed to 'establish a body',[30] they did what they could. However, sometimes 'even small fragments of spine or skull, without which life could not be sustained, were often deemed sufficient.'

In these cases, while no document appears to exist adopting it as 'official' policy,[31] weighted, full-sized sealed coffins were used.[32] Raised to the appropriate weight of a body, sometimes using sandbags or even sacks of potatoes,[33] they gave grieving families the impression that the whole body had been recovered.[34] A fighter pilot in the Battle of Britain, Dennis Noble, was killed on 30 August 1940, in Hove, Sussex. Records show that the salvage team had 'removed all of Dennis's remains',[35] when in fact, practically all had been left in the aircraft. A situation that was either as a consequence of pressure of time or as a result of the incumbent dangers associated with removing a body from a crash site. When the aircraft was excavated in 1996, the almost complete body was found within the Spitfire.[36] Misleading the relatives as to what had been removed may seem hard to countenance now, however it was done with the best intentions at the time, particularly important when it is realised that many churches would not consider a funeral without a body.[37] Accordingly, the notion of an open coffin at a funeral was out of the question. Michael Renaut recalls a funeral from before he was at RAF North Creake, where a difficult situation arose regarding the fiancée of a dead pilot:

> The young girl asked me if she could put her wedding-dress in the coffin and she particularly wanted to do it personally. I told her it was best to remember him as he was and not to look at the ghastly mess in the coffin but she insisted and was crying desperately … I knew that there were only sandbags … and charred flesh in the coffin and I simply didn't know how to dissuade her. I eventually asked the station padre to come to my aid and he finally managed to quieten her and persuade her to let us do it.[38]

Achieving the right balance between the provision of information to bereaved families and protecting them from the unexpurgated truth of aerial warfare, was to plunge another airman into very hot water. After a very high-impact crash of a Stirling bomber returning from operations, George Wright, the Adjutant at RAF Chedburgh, wanted to prevent the agony of uncertainty of a 'missing' telegram for the mother of one of the casualties. When only six bodies out of the seven on board could be positively accounted for, he conducted his own enquiries into the possibility of someone surviving the impact of such a crash. Satisfied when informed that no-one could have survived, he authorised the signal to say, 'killed in action'. Subsequently, the airman turned up having been thrown clear of the maelstrom at the point of impact. His mother was, of course, delighted, but having buried what the Air Ministry had sent her, she was furious at what she saw as Air Ministry bureaucratic incompetence. The officer, having shown what he perceived as a kindness, 'got hell from Group, and hell from Bomber Command; hell from the papers, and hell from the people who read the papers'.[39]

There were no such dilemmas at the Stirling LJ518 crash site. The bodies had been removed and with death confirmed, Norman Bray, the RAF North Creake station commander, issued the death certificates to the local authority.[40] As a result of the aircraft's 'designation on the most secret list',[41] a thorough search of the crash site was conducted to ensure the removal of all secret equipment from the wreckage. The RAF 43 'Salvage and Repair'[42] Group were responsible for organising the clearing of crash sites. The Group was divided into geographical units and in North Norfolk this role fell to the RAF 54 Maintenance Unit.[43] Each geographical area had its own particular salvage recovery challenges, with access to mountainous or coastal mudflats causing particular difficulties for lifting equipment and vehicles.[44] In flatter areas, such as the crash site of Stirling LJ518 EX-K, recovery was technically easier, but with its own specific complications. In open pasture, a wide area could be littered with numerous hazards.[45] Therefore, particular attention had to be paid to the recovery of every metal scrap in order to protect cattle from ingesting fragments and causing damage to their internal organs.[46]

At the time of the crash, the RAF 54 (Salvage and Repair) Maintenance Unit was operated from a site on Trumpington Road,

Cambridge.[47] Equipped with large transporters and lifting plant,[48] the unit usually consisted of eight personnel (a sergeant, two corporals, four crew, specialising in either airframes or aeroengines, and a driver).[49] On site, the severity of the impact would be determined and categorised into one of the following:

Category A (aircraft repairable on site by station/unit personnel)
Category B (repairable but not on site and only by MU
      repair unit)
Category C (aircraft repairable on site but not by unit personnel
      and would involve specialist engineers, usually
      from a Maintenance Unit)
Category E (beyond repair and only salvageable for spare parts
      or, as a salvage engineer put it, a 'sweep up'[50] job)

It should be noted that generally, with a crash such as this, only categories B to E would apply.

The purpose of the unit was to clear the crash site and preserve any usable or repairable parts. In the case of Category B and C, the aircraft needed to be carefully dismantled so it could be returned to the central depot, 'overhauled, and put back into service'.[51] For a four-engine bomber the process of dismantling could take up to five days, for smaller, two engine types, perhaps three.[52] At the central depot, each wreck was carefully examined and major sections, such as fuselages, that could be used, had any damaged components removed and replaced by parts from other crashed aircraft that had suffered damage in a different way. This process was known as 'cannibalisation'.[53] However, Stirling LJ518 was beyond repair and less care would be needed dismantling it.[54] Once at the central depot, the aircraft would be marked '"R to P" (Reduce to Produce)'[55] and then stripped down to its usable constituent components;[56] even the most 'hopeless-looking pile of metal scraped from some field'[57] could yield at least 20% useful parts. Indeed, there appeared to be some parts which always survived undamaged however catastrophic the impact.[58] These components were then either supplied to MU repair sections around the country or sold back to the aircraft manufacturers for reuse on new machines, thus saving precious wartime man-hours.[59]

There were no reports of the crash the following day in the local papers. This was not unusual but there certainly was no mandatory ban on reporting air crashes. With the crash involving an aircraft from RAF North Creake performing secret duties, the press was probably asked not to report on the story.[60] There was good co-operation between the wartime newspapers and the authorities, with the press commonly looking for an official comment on any news item. However, if a government ministry, or representative of the armed forces suggested a story shouldn't be reported, the press would generally comply without recourse to official sanctions.[61]

For the crew's family members, the process of notification would commence and instruction would be sought regarding the families' wishes for the internment of their loved-ones' mortal remains.[62] Families of an airman who lost his life on British soil could leave it to his unit to organise a funeral, with an RAF chaplain conducting the service at a cemetery close to the station.[63] Alternatively, families could claim the body for burial at their local cemetery; the RAF would arrange to transport the body with appropriate respect (regulations stated no open, freight, or cattle cars[64]) to their home town.[65] A representative of the RAF unit or the station where the aircrew member had served would, if possible, 'accompany the body and attend the funeral'.[66] The lost aircrew's units were also 'strongly encouraged to provide flowers or a wreath',[67] although the cost of these would have to be raised by the station personnel, as they could not be purchased with public funds.[68] In policy guidance in 1943, the Air Ministry was quick to remind its staff that the treatment of dead RAF personnel when regarding burials and funerals had 'a marked effect on public morale'.[69] As a consequence, bodies of airmen were consistently treated with reverence and respect in preparation for, and during, the burial.[70]

Costs of these arrangements were broadly met by the RAF. At a funeral close to the RAF station, the RAF chaplain and all services were laid on at no charge, and two travel warrants would be provided for family members to attend.[71] For 'other ranks' a free coffin and plot would be provided; however, the families of officers would have to pay.[72] This option was usually adopted for Allied or Dominion personnel. In a funeral local to the home of the deceased, all costs would be met by the RAF.[73] There were also further allowances for the cost of the plot and coffin.[74]

Around the time of the funeral, the Imperial War Graves Commission (IWGC) would write to the family to explain the process of internment and outline the IWGC's responsibility for the care of the grave.[75] They would arrange for the temporary marking of the grave with a wooden cross and subsequently organise for the permanent marking of the grave with a headstone. Upon this headstone, if the family wished, would be a personal inscription.[76] At the Beddgelert New Cemetery in North Wales, the headstone of Pyrs Owen Roberts, mid-upper gunner of Stirling LJ518 reads, 'he flew the skies but not for fame to safeguard us it was his aim',[77] in memory of his ultimate sacrifice.

Francis Reginald Chatwin, pilot, from Birmingham and married to Phyllis Chatwin from Bolton, was cremated at the Birmingham Municipal Crematorium. Ambrose William Loveland, flight engineer, from Surrey and married to Marguerite Loveland of Shirley, Croydon, Surrey, was buried in the West Wickham (St John the Baptist) Churchyard. John William Naylor, rear gunner, was married to Ena Naylor, of Southall, Middlesex and was buried in the Gedney Hill (Holy Trinity) Churchyard. Richard Thomas Percival Savage, navigator of Tivoli Hill, Queensland, Australia who is, along with Colin Silkirk Henderson, buried in Cambridge City Cemetery (known locally as the Newmarket Road Cemetery[78]).[79]

Colin Selkirk Henderson was born in Dunedin New Zealand. After school he was employed as a clerk at Meredith and Coy (indentors and manufacturers) Dunedin, and as a machinist at Coulls Somerville and Wilkie (a publishing and stationery firm) Dunedin. He enlisted with RNZAF in May 1942. His initial training commenced at Rotorua in July 1942 and then in Canada under the Empire Air Training

Scheme. Trained as a bomb aimer, he left for the UK in October 1943. After further training he transferred to 1657 HCU Stradishall, Suffolk and converted to Stirlings.[80]

The local Sussex paper (*Hastings and St. Leonards Observer*[81]) covered the funeral of Robert Campbell Saddler, wireless operator and only son of Archie and Mabel Saddler, that took place on Monday 2 October 1944. He had been a member of office staff at the *Observer* for three years before enlisting.[82] The service was conducted by J Morgan, at Christ Church, Blacklands, in Hastings and the mourners included his parents, sisters and many friends.[83] The interment took place at the Borough Cemetery with six RAF sergeants acting as bearers, with three volleys being fired over the grave by an RAF firing party. Three 'beautiful floral tributes'[84] from the 'officer commanding and officers; the warrant officers and senior N.C.O.s; and the corporals and other ranks of his squadron'.[85]

Leonard Alfred Barham, the special operator on Stirling LJ518, who should not have been with this crew but was flying as a 'spare bod',[86] was from Cawston, Norfolk, a village located only five miles from the crash site and where he now rests in the local church cemetery. At his funeral aircrew from his squadron were guard of honour.[87] He was survived by his parents, two brothers and a sister (Henry Arthur Barham, Edward John Barham and Iris Kathleen Barham).[88] One cannot help but speculate whether on the night of the crash they heard the impact or saw the glow of flames in the night sky. Did the inevitable rumours surrounding the crash reach them before the official notification, and did they, subsequently, visit the site to pay homage to their lost son, or did they always determinedly avoid it?

Leonard Barham's niece, Rosemary Bower, stayed living locally.[89] After the excavation of the crash site in the late 1990s, Rosemary and her family attended a special unveiling ceremony at Flixton Aviation Museum in Suffolk, of an exhibition cabinet dedicated to the crew,[90] including some of Leonard's personal effects.[91] Reflecting upon the death of her uncle, she commented that these were 'young men who were not the fearless heroes (as I saw them in childhood) but frightened young boys who were all the braver for continuing with their horrid task'.[92] The crash, Leonard's niece and the museum display were featured in the 2000 Discovery Wings Television documentary *Plane Clothed Detective*.[93]

Stirling LJ518 EX-K was the third aircraft to fail to return to RAF North Creake. An eyewitness, even though only three or four years old at the time, still 'vividly remembers the crash'.[94] He pauses for thought whenever he passes the site of the, still surviving, oak tree that the aircraft first struck on that fateful night.[95]

CHAPTER FOUR

FIRES WERE STARTED

Stirring from sleep in a very familiar bed, I opened my eyes to an unfamiliar room. Once over the surprise, the memories of the previous day returned. I focused on the room and its gaudily-decorated walls and my mind turned to the parting words of Oscar Wilde; 'my wallpaper and I are fighting a duel to the death. One or the other of us has to go'. Buying this place, I thought, was just the beginning.

We set about making a more thorough exploration of the house and garden (it would take literally years to reach all the corners such was the overgrown nature of it). But for the moment, we were content with familiarising ourselves with what was in easy reach. The joy of moving to a new house in a new area is that feeling of discovery. The downside is not knowing anyone or where best to buy things. We thought we knew Norfolk reasonably well, but it's different knowing where they serve a good pint and where you can buy a ¾ inch tap washer.

On the second day of being in the Control Tower, our eBay-purchased Art Deco sofa arrived. Delivered by Mark Balderstone; someone we had followed up from an advert in the *Wells Quay*, a local free magazine. Mark would become our go-to man for the movement of almost anything, and there was plenty to move. Among the most troubling were the original Art Deco bathroom suites. We knew the style we wanted but they were not common. I placed a saved search on eBay, and with each suite of the correct typed listed, we made a bid. Over the next few months eBay purchases would take Mark and I around the country. Mark is physically very strong, always willing to have a go, and particularly good at spatial interpretation; if you need to get something around a corner and into a tight space, he could tell you where to place it. An invaluable skill when faced with an extremely heavy bath, on the first floor of a delightful Arts and Crafts house, with a delicate staircase lined with thin spindles and an awkward turn.

Before leaving Welwyn Garden City I had struck a deal. We knew someone who needed cedar shingles, and we agreed, if he helped us remove them, that he could have those on the Control Tower free of charge. For us, in a similar way as a dog claims a lamppost, we would be publicly proclaiming 'we're here and we mean business!'. He arrived the first Saturday after our move and, although he decided the shingles were of no use to him, he very generously stayed and helped remove all the ones we could reach from the balcony; just under half the total. The job then had to be finished by Paul Bishop, a local builder, with a cherry picker one cold and damp December day. It made the statement we wanted, and we thought it was a great improvement. In truth, it made the Control Tower look derelict and that's how it looked for the next two years. However, we did have an almost inexhaustible supply of kindling.

We had no idea where to go next, so we started with the garden. Something I was far more comfortable with, as the Control Tower works filled me with trepidation. Initially we embarked upon uncoordinated tidying, in a bid to establish how the land lay before we started landscaping for real. Some time later, friends, Danielle and Jonathan, came to stay with us. Walking around the garden Danielle, a professional garden designer, commented on how wise it was to establish the garden before commencing works on the house. I silently took the compliment. She is, of course, correct, and for many reasons, but primarily there is huge value in living in a house for a while to understand what might work before making irreversible decisions.

However, in this case, she was mistaking 'reluctance' for 'strategy'; the truth is, I didn't know what on earth I was doing in the house, but I was comfortable in the garden. Similarly, another friend, Pam, asked, 'how do you know in what order to do things?', assuming that we did; we didn't. We just nibbled away at the edges until we made inroads, and once there were inroads, we followed them. This is not to suggest we were entirely without strategy or plans. We knew what we broadly wanted to achieve, and the Art Deco style finish and furniture was never in doubt. Indeed, we were foresighted enough that shortly after moving we began the search for the aforementioned bathroom suites (as these would define the size of the B&B bedroom ensuites), the reclaimed parquet flooring for downstairs, and bi-folding doors for the living room (a frantic eBay bid on New Year's Eve while in the pub with friends and little signal). We knew if we didn't prioritise their acquisition, they had the potential to severely delay the build. However, with these considerations to one side, it is fair to say, we commenced work outside from a position of apprehension, not a grand plan.

Soon after the move a neighbour, Ian Foreman, passing by, welcomed us to the community. We had been a little concerned about the reception we would receive from local people; outsiders moving here from 'that London'. We need not have worried. We were welcomed, and the harder we worked the more they took to us.[A] At our first meeting Ian told me 'I nearly bought the Control Tower in 1990'; it was to become a familiar refrain that we would hear repeatedly from different people. Ian worked as an electrical engineer at the animal feed mill based in the south hangar. His skills and contacts would play an important part in our restoration.

Within a couple of weeks, I was asking Ian about two original Nissen huts alongside the Dry Road, that were to be demolished. I was commenting that we'd really like to build one to garage my Rootes cars, and Ian said, 'I'll see what I can do'.

A Ironically, the only people that appeared unhappy about us moving to Norfolk were neighbours that moved here after us from outside the county who, imagining a rural idyll, were angry that we wanted to run a B&B business.

In October 2011, we hosted our first friends' weekend at the Control Tower. Fearful our enthusiasm would not be contagious and worried that the actuality of the building would confirm their doubts regarding our sanity, we didn't canvas views. Today, asking them retrospectively what they thought, the most they will generally commit is 'we thought it was a lot of work'. We imagine the conversations in the cars on the way home embraced somewhat starker terms. One weekend when winter had taken hold and temperatures plummeted to -12, Howard and Marianne, friends from Welwyn Garden City, visited. We'd cleaned up as best we could and both bathed. Emptying the water out we realised it wasn't draining, in panic we baled it into the lavatory, but that also wouldn't drain. We discovered there was an ice plug in the pipes running on the outside of the wall. I looked at Claire and said, 'they're going to think we're fucking mad!' Generously, they never passed comment, probably because we had other lavatories. However, on this October weekend the temperature was higher. At midnight, walking back towards the house after beer and food around a bonfire, we were both grabbed by Lewis. Having always been clear about his support for our move he said, 'look, against the night sky, you can see what it'll look like when it's done'. He was right, in the dark and with lights in the windows, the pitched roof disappeared and we got the first glimpse of what it might be.

Rob and Greg, two of my brothers, visited and pushed us to start properly. Greg, a gardener by trade, had brought his chainsaw and felled the first cypress trees. Rob toured the place asking about plans. As sketchy as they were, I did my best to explain our agenda. He expressed surprise at my naivety, voicing his concern that we could never achieve what I planned in the garden, let alone the house, on the budget we had. I didn't admit it, but I was deeply concerned he was right.

Just in the garden, there was so much to do; there was about a third of an acre of postwar concrete where a previous owner had run a wood yard. There was a plethora of sheds in which he cut, dried and stored his wood, and there was also a grime-covered portable office. Then there was rubbish everywhere; stacked up in sheds and littered around the garden. It would seem, rather than deal with it, previous occupants had put it to one side or buried it in a hole. Weekly, I would wander around the garden collecting litter, generally two bags each time and put them in the dustbin. With more time, I would separate 'lumber' into usable, recyclable and rubbish. We got to know the local scrapmen very well on their monthly trip to the Control Tower. One particular hole, the 'pit of peril',[B] an ancient marl or chalk pit, was now piled up with domestic, garden and building rubbish. Then there were the trees, an estimated 160 of them encircling the whole plot. This, an overgrown cypress hedge, had reached some 30 feet in height, with additional cypress planted within the plot.

First, I needed to find out what I could do. I phoned the planning officer and then the conservation officer; both of whom were extremely helpful. The planning officer seemed surprised that I would seek his view on whether he would approve of us making a 1942 RAF control tower look like a 1942 control tower again. The conservation officer simply observed that there were no TPOs (tree preservation orders) 'up there', we could do what we wanted. This surprised me as there are two magnificent beech trees and possibly the best example of a field maple I have ever seen. However, they were somewhat hidden by the cypress. This all meant we could get on.

We cleared out sheds, listed both the Portakabin[C] and the log-burning boiler (located in the air raid shelter) on eBay. The portable office sold, but for less than we hoped, but it was good to see it go. The boiler, 'of unknown condition', we hoped would reach a little more than scrap value. While sluggish to start, it ended in a bidding frenzy that was accompanied by squeals of delight from Claire. It raised approaching £1,000, money that would pay for a considerable amount of our initial groundworks.

B   For any Gerry Anderson fans, this is a homage to the *Thunderbirds* episode of the same name.

C   Portakabin is a trade name that has become synonymous with all potable site offices. However, if you list a non-portakabin as a Portakabin on eBay it will be removed after a complaint from the company. Luckily for us, before the listing was deleted someone had already contacted us and they ultimately bought it. I wonder if Hoover do the same.

Ian returned with news of the Nissen huts. He had negotiated, once the asbestos cladding had been removed, that he'd help me take them down and I would just need to pay the scrap value. Once agreed, Ian had recovered any original feature he could find before the stripping commenced, including a bench lamp and the original weapons door from the armoury. On a wet evening in November 2011, we set about dismantling it. It was now I began to become infected by the concept of conserving, not only the memory of the history, but physical artifacts as well.

We leant the remnants of the huts against the air raid shelter, including the Crittall windows with broken panes of glass. I looked at it and wondered how I would ever rebuild it from this assorted pile of scrap. But we did, with help, some from trades and some from friends and family. When Claire's sister came over from Ireland for a holiday, they helped us clad one side of the 60-foot building in tin. Retrospectively, this was a mistake. A summer storm with high winds caught the side like a sail. Worried, I went out to have a look; it was moving alarmingly against the ground fixings with each gust, flexing and creaking with the occasional pronounced groan. All I could do was walk away and hope the welds would hold. They did. By September 2012, completely clad in new tin, it was finished enough to bring my Super Minx Convertible home. Within a year it would have power, water, an equipped workshop and it would have the original windows repaired installed and glazed.

In the run up to our first Christmas at the Control Tower in 2011, unbeknown to us, Lewis had been making visits to the National Archives in Kew. He was researching the Station Operations Record Book (ORB) for RAF North Creake. We did not know of the existence of such a thing, but Lewis had done his research. The RAF North Creake ORB is peppered with the most amazing detail, as the airman who wrote it up every night must have really taken to his job. It is an invaluable document.

For a Christmas present, beginning on the 17 December 2011, Lewis sent us RAF North Creake activity instalments every night, until Christmas day, in what he called 'a North Creake Xmas', with vignettes from other days from 1944-1945. It was these nightly instalments, read in our bedroom (the former control room), that, more than anything else, made us realise the importance of what we'd taken on; it made the history very immediate, it almost felt touchable.

RAF North Creake with the Control Tower middle left, shortly after opening 1944 (John Reid Collection).

RAF North Creake was signed-off as complete on 1 November 1943.[1] It was passed to Bomber Command 3 Group on 23 November,[2] but was quickly transferred to RAF 100 Group on 7 December.[3] On 31 December 1943, it was declared fully complete and ready for operations.[4] However, the Air Ministry needed to identify airfields that it could develop into super heavy bomber stations, with longer runways. These would accommodate the larger bombers that were being developed at the time.[5] Therefore, RAF North Creake was immediately placed on 'Care and Maintenance', pending a decision.[6] For David Maufe, who had learnt of the plans from Holkham Estate (from whom he rented the farmland that surrounded the airfield) the news was deeply unsettling as he would lose an even greater proportion of his land to these extensions. However, he had no option but to continue farming until the outcome was known.[7] On the airfield site itself, RAF 80 (signals) Wing (part of the RAF 100 Group) had moved in, utilising it as a training ground between January and April 1944.[8]

Ultimately, with Lakenheath and Marham undergoing development as super heavy bomber stations,[9] and with the increased demand for capacity in the run-up to D-Day,[10] the extensions to the runways at North Creake were postponed.[D] It subsequently opened on 1 April 1944[11] and was then transferred to 199 Squadron on 25 April.[12] A station flight was formed with a Tiger Moth (replaced by an Oxford in June) becoming the first aircraft stationed at North Creake.[E13] Personnel of 199 Squadron and the RAF 2842 Squadron[14] RAF Regiment (for airfield defence) steadily began to arrive from mid-April. On 1 May 1944, RAF North Creake was officially declared open,[15] with the station warrant officer, M Stones, signing for the RAF buildings.[16] The ORB then began to record all activities, including the details of settling-in and 'beautifying' the station ... especially in regard to the gardens'.[17]

We continued the process of 'beautifying' assisted by the unexpected help of the son-in-law of our neighbour Ann. He had just become self-employed, he had a chainsaw certificate, plenty of experience and, importantly from our perspective, charged an hourly rate we could afford. Things started moving forward apace. We felled the unwanted trees, dug up the butts with hired diggers and burnt both (other than the logs that, once seasoned, we could burn inside). Generally progress was good, but not everything ran smoothly. The septic tank, that had been hidden by years of weeds, made its position clear when I drove the tracked digger over the corner of it. I stared in dismayed surprise as the concrete cover folded in. We discovered later

---

D   If North Creake had been converted to a super heavy bomber base, it would have almost certainly survived beyond the war and could even still be in use today (Delve: 2005: 172).

E   Most stations had a station flight where officers who were flying trained could 'keep their hand in'. They were also used for ferrying airfield personnel around or picking-up abandoned aircrews from places such as RAF Woodbridge Emergency Landing Ground (Delve: 24/1/2023).

that this was the last of three covers to collapse into the tank, somewhat limiting its capacity. Paul Bishop saved me the job of climbing into the tank and retrieving the broken concrete by lassoing every bit out from above, Wild West style, with a well-placed rope. The very definition of a cowboy builder perhaps?! As nasty as such jobs were, our spirits were lifted daily by skeins of pink footed geese on their way to roost, a magical sound that now still takes me back to the early days of our time at the Control Tower.

Our neighbour Ian continued with his regular drop-ins and was now frequently joined by Paul and Julie, more neighbours from further down the track, who always walked their dogs after work. Chatting about the works became a daily routine, and all had advice and skills to offer. Friendships were forged.

I had always prided myself, particularly as my mum was a native of Sheringham, that I could understand the Norfolk dialect. I was wrong and had never properly appreciated the allowances that are made for 'outsiders'. It is a beautiful accent; soft, gentle and often quietly spoken. I remember vividly talking with Ian and Paul for about ten minutes and realising I had understood a fraction of what was said. Appealing for some leniency, Ian informed me, 'well bor, you're a local now an' you're gewin ta hev ta larn'. A remark I found both complimentary and slightly ominous.

Through the whole process of clearing trees, Claire and I returned to a more primitive and basic lifestyle, engendered by the process of building and maintaining fires; fires that were started almost daily. This retreat to an atavistic existence meant that most of our waking day was spent setting, feeding and, come the evenings drinking ale in front of the huge bonfires. While we felt warm in the glow of the flames, our back halves, without realising it, were very cold and our extremities were becoming susceptible to temperature-derived complaints. Our ears particularly suffered chilblains, causing the skin to blister and flake. We were rather jolted from this simple way of life when Cillian came to visit; 'what the fuck is going on with your ears?', he exclaimed, somewhat horrified. It was at this point we decided that, perhaps, we needed to get out more.

We had started visiting James Beck Auctions in Fakenham, for the very real reason that there was much we needed for our project. But also, incidentally perhaps, because I love auctions and they appeal to my collecting gene. A gene I publicly very much deny having. What the auction did do, other than provide us with much that was useful and a great deal that wasn't, was plug us into a local community; a community bond that was cemented by lunch at the pub on the way home. The first time we entered the Bull in Walsingham, the landlord, Nelly, came over to us, shook our hands, and said 'I recognise you from the auction; you've moved into the Control Tower. Welcome to the Bull'. It was a realisation of how small and knowing the community we had moved into was. The pub became our favourite regular and we lost many hours in its warm, friendly glow.

While we met many locals in places such as the Bull, who knew North Creake intimately, we still maintained some hope, but little real expectation, of meeting a veteran of the station. In 2014, we were invited to an event organised by the Stirling Society (dedicated to the memory of the Stirling Bomber). At first, we thought we were mistaken when we heard this chap say he'd served at RAF North Creake; for a start he didn't look old enough. Explaining that we lived in the Control Tower, we quickly hatched a plan for Bernie How to visit after the event. When he first arrived, he seemed reluctant to discuss the war, preferring to concentrate on the nature of our building works. However, he was clutching a journal,[18] within which was a picture of his crashed Stirling. This was Bernie's war story, and our way in.

In September 1944, on his 29th operation, Bernie was on the runway in Stirling LJ569 EX-C. Approaching take-off speed (between 80 and 100mph) the starboard wheel hit some debris. The tyre burst, the undercarriage collapsed and the aircraft came down.[19] The wing was torn off as it made contact with the ground, the fuel tanks in the wings ruptured spraying fuel everywhere. Eventually, the aircraft came to rest in a cloud of debris and a mist of fuel. I asked Bernie how it felt to be in such a crash; he considered the question momentarily and then concluded, 'very noisy'.[20] This was a typical Bernie understatement. As help raced towards them, the aircraft crew, recovering from shock, made a quick assessment of injuries. Apart from cuts and bruises, only the pilot, Ernie Harker, had any significant injuries.[F21] They scrambled out as best they could and ran from the aircraft, believing it might explode at any moment.[22] The journal Bernie was holding states that the aircraft was, 'not surprisingly ... fit only for the scrap heap',[23] and looking at the photographs it's easy to see why. However, the aircraft was in fact repaired and flew again.[24] I wonder if they showed the new crew the photographs.

Bernie How's crashed Stirling LJ569 EX-C, September 1944 (John Reid Collection).

Bernie officially completed 40 operations (equivalent to one and a half tours) all with 199 Squadron (his logbook actually outlines 43[25]). 'You got used to it', he told us. 'The first one was a bit nervous, if you like, but you got used to it'.[26] He started his tour at Lakenheath and transferred to RAF North Creake when it opened. On 10 April 1945[27] he flew his last operation. Having dropped their bomb load, rather than observing the general practice of flying a wide arc in order to avoid the following bombers, his pilot turned directly back into the bomber stream. 'He must have panicked', Bernie said. They spent a

---

F He was admitted to sick quarters with lacerations of the left eye and a fracture of the left ankle. He was transferred to RAF Hospital, Ely on 18 September, 1944 (RAF North Creake: September 1944: ORB).

harrowing period avoiding collisions with the oncoming bombers; 'how we didn't hit one I just don't know. We were meeting other aircraft above and below us. I saw lots of aircraft and they must have seen us as well'.[28] He told how they sat in silence on the way back to base. 'We was dead quiet. No one hardly spoke'.[29] When it emerged at the debrief, the commanding officer simply told them, 'that was your last op'.[30] Bernie said, 'I've always wondered if he grounded us because he knew how exhausted we were, and how unlikely we were to survive another sortie'.[31] Characteristically, Bernie held no malice towards his pilot for endangering them, simply recognising that they were all exhausted and that they all made mistakes.[32]

Through the course of the eight years we knew Bernie, he helped us understand aircrew life in a way we could have never achieved without his experience. We would ask him general questions and we'd ask him very specific ones; most of which he answered but often, he'd look at us and just say, 'it was a long time ago'.

Bernie How (middle of back row) with his crew beside Halifax RG389 EX-H (Brian How).

Bernie, as a flight engineer, was responsible for the running and safety (in terms of mechanics) of the aircraft. He monitored fuel, engine oil pressure and temperatures. He advised when an engine needed shutting down and tried to keep the engines alive in their arduous work.[33] He was constantly switching between fuel tanks and pumping fuel, when needed, to ensure even distribution of the petrol between the 14 tanks.[34]

The role of the flight engineer had been introduced in 1942, in recognition of the growing complexity of bombers.[35] On a flight they barely got to sit down; Bernie explains 'you could just have a seat but mainly you was up and down looking at the engines'.[36] They had a myriad of checks and duties connected with the aircraft's serviceability before and after take-off. Each of which they recorded on their log-sheets.[37]

Alongside the adoption of the flight engineer role, there were other crew changes. Rather than an observer there were now two separate roles: the navigator and bomb-aimer. The wireless operator remained and there were two gunners; the mid-upper and the rear gunner.[38]

It was said that it took a pilot to fly an aeroplane to Germany, an engineer to look after it, a wireless operator to maintain the link between base and target, a navigator to find the destination, a bomb-aimer to place the cargo accurately, and two gunners to protect the plane and their fellows.[39]

There was a constant 'chatter' between crew members on the intercom. Interestingly, regardless of how friendly the crews were with one another on the ground, while in the air they used only their titles; 'it was always "pilot to navigator", "wireless operator to bomb aimer" etc.'.[40]

The skipper was asking the flight engineer if all the engines were ok. He was asking the wireless operator if he still had contact with his wireless. And the bomb aimer used to sit next to him. … [The navigator] had a curtain all round him and he was giving the skipper instructions of a course to fly … The flight engineer and the navigator were doing most of the talking and the skipper was asking questions and everybody else was in their own thoughts.[41]

Bernie would never hear of any greater importance being applied to any member of the crew; 'we were all vital to the aircraft's successful operation'.[42] This is a sentiment commonly held by bomber crews:

> one of the compensations for the evil and horror of war, is the relationship between members of a flying crew. For eight hours or more seven men in each monster bomber will be isolated from all we understand as civilisation. Miles up in the air they will battle the wind and storm, lightning and ice, pitting every resource of science against the deadly resources of science seeking to destroy them. They will expose themselves deliberately to what must seem at times like certain death, caught in the fantastic contradiction of knowledge that can be used at the same time to save and to annihilate.[43]

Appreciation of each other's role was aided by some interchangeability between them in an emergency. Although never formalised, the flight engineer might operate as a stand-by gunner 'if anything happened to the gunners'.[44] Also, he might take over flying the aircraft, if, as in the case of Jack Hawksworth, a flight engineer flying out of North Creake, the pilot needed the lavatory.[45] Pilots did have their own lavatorial arrangements but most often, if needed, he would use the chemical Elsan[G] lavatory. Murray Pedan explains why:

> up front, alongside the pilot, a funnel hung on a clip. Running from the funnel was a tube that led discreetly to the great outdoors. Theoretically, and theoretically only, if a pilot's need to relieve himself reached serious proportions he could use

---

G In a Halifax, the Elsan lavatory was, on a 'small curtained off area on a raised platform, close to the port entrance door and mid upper gunner's station. It was not flushable but used blue coloured chemical tablets whose fragrance permeated the whole length of the fuselage. Everyone did their best to go before flight and would only use the facility in a dire emergency' (Church: undated.).

the funnel, without discomfort and without leaving his seat. In practice, when such an emergency arose, remedial action was not all that easy; in fact, obtaining relief was a humbling process. After one had disposed of the first layer by undoing a bulky flying suit, the problem of avoiding the entangling tapes of the Mae West and unfastening buried fly buttons with cold fingers remained. When the blast of cold air from the cockpit suddenly penetrated to the target area, indicating that one had been successful thus far, the major problem remained, namely, finding the object of the search, which invariably contracted in the chilly surroundings to a size approximating that of a light switch, and somehow training it over the folds of clothing to the edge of the funnel. Even with this feat accomplished, accuracy at critically high nozzle pressures was not impressive (I attempted the feat twice during the early stages of my tour, then concluded that dying of a burst bladder was ever so much easier and less humiliating).[46]

The flight engineer was also responsible for loading the colours for the day in the Very pistol located in the roof.[47] This was in case of attack from friendly anti-aircraft guns; the colours of the day were to assure anyone concerned that the aircraft was indeed friendly. Roy Smith, a navigator who also transferred from Lakenheath to North Creake, describes an incident in February 1944,[48] where, subjected to anti-aircraft fire over London, their wireless operator 'fired off the colours of the day to no avail', it must have been hairy, given that, as a precaution, the fight engineer opened the escape hatch:

> our mid-upper gunner bent down from his turret to see what was going on and seeing the hatch was open, switched on his intercom to contact the pilot. However, when bending down he must have pulled his intercom plug slightly out of the socket, so there was no connection to other crew members. Having seen

the open hatch and being unable to communicate with anyone, he assumed that we had all jumped, and quickly followed suit.[49]

They completed their operation without their mid-upper gunner.[50]

Friendly fire was not only an issue limited to the ground. As an air-gunner, correctly identifying a friendly aircraft could be extremely challenging and there is no doubt that some losses resulted from mistaken identity:

> The truth was, of course, that some of our rear gunners were getting a bit twitchy, and before waiting to make positive identification would hose off at shadowy aircraft behind them and pump off streams of ammunition ... it is hard to condemn them, but they should have known the difference between a four-engined bomber and a twin-engined fighter even on a dark night.[51]

But it was difficult, particularly when not all friendly aircraft were four-engine bombers; as Denis Gill, a gunner with 199 Squadron at North Creake recalls, 'I didn't fire on him ... he wasn't directly behind me ... and because of that I thought could it be a Mosquito? ... I'm quite good at recco, but it was so dark I couldn't really make out and I thought Christ I don't want to shoot down a bloody Mosquito.[52] Tom Sawyer, a Main Stream bomber pilot, recognises that aircrew were injured and aircraft were damaged by friendly fire, but 'God only knows how many were actually shot down'.[53] The German night-fighter ace, Heinz-Wolfgang Schnaufer,[H] witnessed the outcome of mistaken identity, as he held back from an attack and watched while two Lancasters shot each other down.[54]

Friendly fire wasn't limited to bullets either. For Stirlings particularly, the risk of being bombed from above was a constant worry. The Stirling regularly flew at a ceiling height of around 12,000 feet, with Lancasters and Halifaxes some 8,000 feet above. These bombers at

---

H Heinz-Wolfgang Schnaufer had 121 kills to his name, he survived the war only to die in a road accident in France in 1950.

20,000 feet were 'busily dropping bombs around, past, and occasionally through'[55] the Stirlings below.

The navigator provided the pilot with a compass course to fly and the pilot constantly updated him with height and airspeed for his calculations. The navigator was surrounded by:

> about twenty-five maps, two or three charts on which to plot his course, and a log sheet in which all occurrences on the trip are meticulously recorded … [he also] carries a computer, with which he calculates the track and direction of the wind, the last word in sextants, and a planisphere from which to obtain the direction of the stars.[56]

Once in the air 'the first task was to obtain a fix (ground position) and from this calculate the forward course for the flight',[57] a process from mid-1942, that most often used the navigational aid Gee.[I] The bomb-aimer's job was to calculate the correct point to release the bombload. This involved almost two minutes flying straight and level over target.[58] It was a tense moment for the whole crew, but for the bomb-aimer in a Lancaster bomber, there were other considerations:

> there wasn't sufficient space in which to sit so I lay … to my left was the bombsight computer box which was connected by two drives to the sighting head which was about eighteen inches away from my nose. The front turret was directly in front of, and above, the sighting head and it contained two Browning .303 machine-guns. To my right, and within reach of my hand, was the pre-selector box on which the order of releasing the bombs could be set.[59]

I   Gee was a navigational aid that came into service in Bomber Command in March 1942, utilising signals from three ground stations (one 'master' and two 'slaves'); the position of the aircraft was determined by the time difference between the receipt of these signals in the aircraft. Although not accurate enough for 'blind-bombing', its introduction saw an immediate improvement in bombing accuracy up to a maximum range of 300-400 miles. It remained in use for the rest of the war (see Cockburn: 1945: 60 and Redding: 2005: 59-60).

Generally, the bomb-aimer did not open the bomb doors until the last practical moment, 'as soon as I did, a draught got going – not for me but for the rest of them! The navigator was holding on to his maps – that was the testing time!'[60] For the period of the bomb-run, the bomb-aimer took over the aircraft, 'steady. Steady. Steady. Left. Steady. Right. Steady. Steady. Left. Right. Bombs gone,' and the plane 'would go wumph ... it would be up in the air, when the bombs were released'.[61] 'Bomb doors closed!',[62] he would cry and the whole crew felt a sense of relief.[63] Either side of the bomb-run the bomb aimer used to commonly 'sit in the number two [pilot] seat'.[64]

The wireless operator received all messages to, and transmitted all messages from, the aircraft. Given that on most operations radio silence was practiced, the wireless operator's role could be limited. He therefore assisted other crew members, particularly the gunners, in their duties and helped in any minor emergencies that occurred.[65] The gunners could return the favour, having been taught to transmit Morse code.[66] Importantly, if the aircraft was in distress, he would transmit positional signals allowing for the aircraft's last position to be located. If they were forced to ditch in the sea, he remained at his post transmitting signals. Once ditched, if there was time and if he were able, he removed equipment from the aircraft to allow for continued transmissions from the dinghy.[67] Out of all the crew members, being the furthest from the escape hatch, it was the wireless operator that had the worst chance of survival.[68]

Once ten miles out to sea and not within five miles of any 'surface craft, wreck or buoy',[69] and as long as visibility was over five miles and the aircraft above 1,000 feet,[70] the gunners tested their guns. These restrictions, stated in the RAF North Creake guidelines for gunners, avoided any accidental hits.[71] Gordon Mercier, a mid-upper gunner at North Creake, explains, 'we [used to] fire down at the sea ... to test our guns ... the skipper said, "Are we ok navigator to test the guns?" And the navigator said, "Yes." And I said, "No. ... I can see land in front of me. Down there. I can see land".[72] The navigator had made a miscalculation and placed the aircraft over the sea when in fact they were still over land.[73] Gordon further explains his advantage, 'I had the best view of anybody in the aircraft. I was sitting on the top ... the view was fantastic because in daylight you could see for miles and miles and miles'.[74] Vic Polichek was awed by the view from his rear turret in the dark; 'from the target area, I could see the flames for many miles. It was very interesting when flying over the front line areas, one could see the many cannon flashes, and machine gun tracers flashing in many directions. Much like fireworks and no admission price to see it'.[75] For some, in these moments, they felt the joy of flying in spite of the known risks.[76]

Leaving the English coast around Dungeness (Judith Errington).

The primary role of gunners was to fend off attacks; 'Jack' Philipson, a pilot with 171 Squadron at RAF North Creake, would always announce 'it's a clear night tonight keep a good watch out – keep those turrets weaving gunners, that's what keep[s] you alive'.[77] Views on being a gunner vary, perhaps according to which gunner position you were. Gordon Mercier describing his role in the mid-upper turret explains, 'it was very satisfying being a gunner. You felt as though you were doing a good job'.[78] It is instructive contrasting this opinion with the one he espouses in relation to the rear gun turret, 'I only flew once as rear gunner and I hated it'.[79] Denis Gill believes, '[air gunners] were superfluous … in night flying … I just sat there and waited to be killed. There's no way you can … shoot down a night fighter'.[80] His scepticism is well-founded; British bombers were grossly under-armed, being equipped with .303 (7.7mm) machine guns with a range of 600 yards, and derisorily called 'pea-shooters' by many; 'we were using those things from the Western Front in the First World War … they've got a range of next to nothing'.[81] The aiming of these .303 guns was problematic also; 'due to the vibration in a rear turret, bullets did not, as many imagine, go in a straight line, but at a range of 6,000 feet could end up anywhere within a 100 feet diameter circle!'.[82] The decision to arm bombers with .303 machine guns had received no analysis of what it took to bring down a modern aircraft.[83] The alternative armament, the US .5 (12.7mm) machine guns, were much better, and while there was a willingness to equip RAF bombers with these, there were none available as the American manufacturers needed them for their own bombers.[84] Heinz-Wolfgang Schnaufer conceded that British bombers equipped with these would certainly have worried them.[85] The German night-fighters were commonly armed with ten or 20mm cannon with an effective range of 1,000 yards.[86]

Nevertheless, contrary to Denis Gill's view, night-fighters were shot down. In April 1945, an outward bound 171 Squadron bomber sighted a FW190 at 300 yards. An evasive manoeuvre was immediately enacted while the rear gunner opened fire. 'Strikes were seen immediately in engine and cockpit.' The fighter followed them through their evasive manoeuvres but at 200 yards the mid-upper gunner was also able to fire, noticing 'strikes in engine and port side of fuselage'. The fighter, still on the starboard side, was seen to be on fire and breaking away gradually in 'something like an uncontrolled shallow dive. Indicating the possibility that the pilot was hit'. The bomb-aimer witnessed the fighter hit the ground and explode.[87] Arthur Adcock, an RAF North Creake wireless operator describes another encounter:

> This particular night I had a quick contact on my radar ... enough for Charles (the pilot) to corkscrew to starboard just at the time the night fighter opened fire on us. We were hit, the cannon shell blowing away our bomb bays and some of our rear fuselage belly and, as we were dropping, the night fighter, now above us, was clearly visible against a moonlit sky. Our gunners fired a 2 to 3 second burst from all eight guns right into him and the aircraft, a ME410, exploded with a huge flash. I saw the bright flash quite clearly from my small window, but the gunners reported seeing large pieces flying in all directions, then nothing – no parachutes were seen, so the crew of two had died. The night fighter must have been stalking us for some time, but our part of the action lasted only about 30 seconds, so apart from the initial shock, I had no time to feel fear during the action, that came later when I had time to think how close we had come to being shot out of the sky.[88]

Even without a well-organised foe making every attempt to kill you, there are the more prosaic and routine dangers of flying. Flight was still relatively new in 1939, and even with the rapid development of aircraft technology, the reliability of aircraft was a significant factor in losses. There were myriad problems associated with four-engine bombers in the war years: electrical, hydraulic and mechanical. The following experience from a North Creake wireless operator is typical:

> Flying in Halifax 'B' they returned barely an hour into the mission when Gee 'burnt out'. In the same plane on January 28,

1945, they aborted the sortie 30 mins in, when the hydraulics failed, and again on March 21 after the same problem occurred after being airborne for 40 minutes.[89]

In the summer months, engines would overheat causing fuel pressure warning lights to blink; 'all the flight engineer could do was silently pray'.[90] Failing engines were almost routine to aircrew; I have not met a crew member yet that couldn't tell you of a number of occasions with engine troubles. Even though reasonably frequent, failing engines could spell serious difficulties:

> He [Stirling flight engineer] quite frequently told the pilot he was shutting an engine down ... and then later on he told them he'd restarted it ... I think during our tour he [shut down engines] about ten times ... he shut down two at one time and we were losing height all the time and he managed to get them back.[91]

Bernie How explains, 'we came home on three engines ... a few times ... overheating or ... wasn't powerful enough and the pilot ... would say, "Bernie something's wrong with the inner starboard. It's not pulling". Then we had a chat about it ... [and we would] feather it[J] ... No doubt that was done hundreds of times in different aircraft'.[92] If the propellor would not feather it caused it to 'windmill'. This produced considerable drag which slowed progress and spent extra fuel; 'pulling an aeroplane through the sky with an engine windmilling is much the same as pushing a stalled car while leaving it in gear'.[93]

If the engine that had failed controlled the electrics which operated the undercarriage, then that meant the undercarriage had to be hand cranked. An arduous task on the Stirling with its huge undercarriage; '4 of us – 2 at each side – working at maximum speed,

---

J   Feathering is practiced when an engine fails and needs to be shut down. The propeller presents a large, flat surface to the airstream and can act as a windmill which causes high drag since the propeller is free to turn. This 'windmilling' can also further damage the engine. This can be minimised by rotating the blades until they are edgewise to the flight direction, known as 'feathering'. Thereby, greatly reducing the drag (Commercial Aviation Safety Team: undated: 4).

changing with our partner every 30 – 60 seconds. We took 3 minutes to lock each undercarriage in the down position'.94

On other occasions the engine failure was caused by fire or resulted in fire. A perilous situation as the flames could compromise the main spar, connecting the wings to the aircraft, in minutes.95 Roy Smith suffered such a circumstance and '[the pilot] instructed all crew members to assemble at the escape hatch and to be prepared to jump when instructed. In the meantime he had put the plane into a steep dive and managed to blow out the flames. Had he been unable to do this, he would not have escaped from the aircraft alive'.96

Some problems had simple causes but could result in dangerous situations. Gordon Mercier, remembers, 'I had to get out of my turret and close the [main entrance] door which had come open ... me being small I could hardly reach and the skipper said, "Don't forget to put your parachute on in case you fall out" ... And twice that happened'.97 Bernie How experienced the same problem, 'you had to be careful as the air pressure could drag you into the Atlantic ... it was a bit frightening'.98 Denis Gill recalls that the 'sliding door of my rear turret often jammed shut, and I had to call up our engineer to open them from the outside. There was always the hope that if we were in trouble one could bail out, and I was convinced that if the order to bail out was given, I would find my turret doors had jammed'.99 Conversely, a logbook entry from Brodie Reid identifies flying back to base with the bomb doors stuck open,100 with the consequential drag and unnecessary use of fuel. However precarious these tales sound, these are the stories of those that made it back to tell them. There are the unknown thousands that did not.

And then there was the weather. Weather affected the safety of crews in many ways. Sometimes, it just simply betrayed them. Each minute an aeroengine ran it produced one gallon of water as steam. This normally dispersed, however, on a cold night it formed into 'long white condensation trails of vapour'.101 The German night-fighters could follow these trails and estimate the distance, the density of the stream and the 'true direction'102 of the bombers ahead.

Then there was St. Elmos' fire; caused by atmospheric electricity, it could cause a 'bright phosphorescent radiance',103 which could gather at the leading edges of the wings or around the tips of propellor blades. Frequently accompanied by 'dreadful turbulence', it could cause the loss of aircraft.104

But worst of all was the cold; generally, it can be assumed that for every thousand feet of ascent there will be one to two degrees lost in temperature.[105] During the winter of 1944/45 temperatures of minus 50° were recorded at heights of 20,000 feet over Germany.[106] There was a rudimentary heating system in the bombers but as Arthur Adcock remembers, it 'was ineffectual and the object of much abuse by aircrews … the cold was numbing and almost unbearable'.[107] For the gunners, and particularly the rear gunner, the cold was a constant foe; 'the turrets were cold, or I should say damned cold'.[108] And, as Jim Feasey recalls, 'I can remember … ice on my oxygen mask and tube which had to be broken up every few minutes';[109] critical, if the supply of oxygen was to be preserved. There were a number of other reasons why the oxygen supply might fail: a kink in the tube or a technical fault in the system, but for gunners, icing up was the most common. Rear gunners could suffer a lonely death from anoxia[K] as the effects are not easily recognised and a victim was often reliant on the intervention of a fellow crew member. However, isolated in the rear turret, it was difficult for other crew members to realise there was a problem:[110]

> during a long flight, moisture and saliva (even vomit in the case of secret suffers of air-sickness) trickled into the thin, corrugated, rubber tube feeding the mask. This froze in extreme temperatures forming a deposit that eventually blocked the tube.[111]

Anoxia has a number of stages. Without oxygen at 20,000 feet there is a feeling of mild elation, 'not dissimilar to that experienced after one

---

K Anoxia is when the brain or body completely loses its oxygen supply. The situation for aircrew could, perhaps, more accurately be described as hypoxia, the insufficient supply of oxygen. However, the term anoxia is generally used in aviation literature and I have continued in the same manner.

or two well-mixed gin and vermouth'.[112] The feeling will increase the longer that one is deprived of oxygen, then drowsiness will set in, which will be followed by unconsciousness and then death. With intervention, a person can make a speedy recovery, but without, at 30,000 feet, 'one is very likely to be dead within fifteen minutes'.[113]

There was cold weather equipment provided; 'super electric suits and gloves',[114] although they did on occasions fail, or partially fail, meaning only part of your body was warm when the rest was very cold.[115] Also there was the famous Bomber jacket, extra-long johns; vests, which were 'very warm … they came up to your neck and everything'.[116] Fleecy boots; four pairs of gloves, the closest to the skin being silk, 'so that if you had to do anything with the guns you took the three pairs off and just left the silk glove … if you touched the guns with your [bare] fingers [they] stuck to the guns … it was so cold it would fetch the skin off'.[117] While the mid-upper gunner position was warmer than that of the rear gunner, as soon as he turned his gun forward, he was exposed to the wind that whistled 'through the holes where the guns are and you absolutely froze … I can remember my eyebrows froze [and my] eyelids froze'.[118]

Temperatures of minus 50° also had a severe impact on the aircraft; 'the oil went into lumps and aircrew could hear the engine rumbling'.[119] More serious still was icing-up, which normally took the form of a 'sort of hoar frost appearing on the leading edges of the wings and the front of the cockpit canopy and front turret'… but was usually thrown off by the pulsating membranes along the wings and did not collect on the airscrews.[120] The majority of aircrews experienced this at some stage. Jim Feasey, a gunner at North Creake, explains a typical situation, '[we] climbed through solid cloud to 20,000 feet, icing up all the way, at one stage Jack thought he was going to lose control. We all got ready to get out but we broke into the clear and went on'.[121] Sometimes it could be even more harrowing, with ice deposits altering the profile of the wing and causing drag, 'great chunks of ice' could get thrown off the propellers and they would thump 'ominously against the sides'.[122] Les King of 171 Squadron at North Creake remembers a perilous time with great clarity:

> On the night of the 28th January 1945 snow had fallen heavily during the morning accompanied by strong gales and all personnel at North Creake were put to work clearing runways for them to become operational. We took off in Halifax LK868 to climb to 12,000 ft only to become badly iced up and lose control. We finished up levelling out at 1,500 ft with Joe Brogan and the flight engineer, F/S Len Ley ... fighting together to pull the stick back and so fly straight and level.[123]

With a struggle they managed to land safely. With luck, the aircraft cleared the ice cloud, and the ice would melt; with luck that is.

With snow there was poor visibility; Ken Chapman, also of 171 Squadron recalls, one morning 'the weather was atrocious ... [we] were rather shaken when we flew past a church steeple at about 150 ft, and then had to struggle to miss the huge water tower at North Creake'.[124] Similarly, Denis Gill remembers flying as the temporary replacement gunner and returning to North Creake in heavy snow and strong winds:

> our pilot made three attempts to land, and finally succeeded with a hard landing on his third try ... like all pilots of his [young] age, his experience of flying our large four engine Stirling was minimal. As he joined us, his first words were 'sorry I didn't get it down the first time'. Unknown to him, at that point in time, he was my hero![125]

These experiences changed the crew's attitude toward some cloud formations, the 'contemplation of having to fly through towering cumulonimbus clouds in winter, knowing full well that they would be loaded with ice particles ... sometimes created more anxiety among the crews than the bombing operation itself'.[126]

Nevertheless, for the bombers, the primary foe remained the German defences. In the early part of the Second World War, it was generally believed that 'the risk from anti-aircraft defences would be slight [and] that the bombers ... would generally be able to evade fighter attack'. However, it soon became apparent that neither of these assumptions were true.[127]

The Luftwaffe initially had a force of nearly one million well-trained men employed on anti-aircraft guns; 'probably more effective in hindering enemy air operations and shooting down or damaging enemy bombers ... than any other anti-aircraft organisation in Europe'.[128] They were generally equipped with versatile 88mm cannon 'flak' guns, that sent up shells that left a characteristic black cloud hanging in the sky.[129] These projectiles, fired at extraordinary rapidity, exploded sending out 'jagged metal fragments that tore through nearby aircraft'.[130] The explosions were accompanied by a distinctive smell that hung in the aircraft[131] and reminded some of 'Guy Fawkes night after the fireworks'.[132] The bombers were often first harassed by flak from flak ships anchored just off the enemy coast.[133] However, it was over target where a 'vast, demented, murderously intent barrage [began] to trawl our aircraft from the sky'.[134] The projectiles that missed made a sound 'reminiscent of overhanging branches scraping the roof of a double decker bus'[135] as the shrapnel pieces cleaved the air; 'absolutely hundreds, hundreds of bursts of flak ... And nearly always at the right height as well.'[136] Jack Philipson, a pilot with 171 Squadron remembers a lucky escape, flying towards target he noticed the 'odd burst of flak ahead and to port. Then Bang!, Bang!, Bang!, Bang! By the second Bang! I had the aircraft into a steep starboard turn of 90 degrees, followed by another to port and climbing back on course fast ... Nobody was hurt'.[137] Frequently they hit their targets, and airmen regularly witnessed fellow crews 'fall like autumn leaves into the inferno below',[138] leaving them to wonder whether they would be next.[139] 'Lancasters tended to be on fire wingtip to wingtip falling down almost like a leaf, Halifaxes ... tended to spin down'.[140]

The sky above target was filled with beams of arching searchlights waiting to land on a quarry. The radar-controlled 'Master' searchlight had a distinctly blueish colour and would suddenly swing on to a bomber and hold it, whatever evasive manoeuvre was tried. Once captured in the light of the Master's beam, the other searchlights associated with it, would be switched on and 'cone' the aircraft, leaving the Master free to continue searching for other victims.[141] Once coned, as Denis Gill recalls 'the captured aircraft, like silver moths, are soon plucked from the sky by the accurate radar-controlled anti-aircraft guns':[142]

> [The Halifax] bucked with the force of the explosion, and folded amidships right underneath the H2S blister but kept coming forward on an even keel. The two outer engines then literally pulled themselves out of the main plane and fell away forward in a gradual sinking movement. The crew then started to bale out, the rear gunner from his turret, two from the upper escape hatch, then two more from under the nose. Gradually the Halifax lost height and started to disintegrate, with the outer wing sections going first. The port inner engine then burst into flames trailing black smoke and balls of fire. Everything seemed to happen in slow motion, and the whole spectacle had a peculiarly macabre fascination. The debris surrounding the Halifax looked just like a wall diagram of a sectionalised bomber as it fell slowly from view.[143]

Some aircraft were peppered but survived, and the war souvenirs of many airmen include a lump of shrapnel from a 'near miss'. Such a piece had holed John Panton's father's wireless set.[144] As a wireless operator from RAF North Creake, his logbook simply states for 19 October 1944, 'holed by flak'.[145]

After the abandonment of daylight bombing and formation flying by Bomber Command, they subsequently flew at night as a stream of independently navigated aircraft. Early on, this had proved a reasonably successful tactic.[146] Before July 1940, there had been no German specialist night-fighter organisation until Hermann Goering, the head of the Luftwaffe, ordered Josef Kammhuber to establish one.[147]

Through most of 1941, Germany developed its 'Ground Control of Interception' system, which they were confident, at full strength, would defeat Bomber Command's flying technique.[148]

Completed by autumn 1941 and known as the Kammhuber Line, the new German defensive system was organised into a series of overlapping boxes in a chain 'along the length of the European coast, from North Germany to Belgium, and [also] around the most important German cities'.[149] Each box was equipped with three radar sets; one radar called Freya and the further two known as Würzburgs.[150] Between the three sets a very good impression of any raid could be constructed quite early on.[151] During 1941 the British realised that their aircraft were 'under observation well inland in the south and east of England, as soon as they gained reasonable height'.[152] As a consequence, the enemy was able to establish early warnings of impending attacks, and could prepare their night-fighters well in advance to intercept the stream as soon 'as it arrived overland'.[153] Bomber Command, knowing of the Luftwaffe's ability to plot bomber streams, adopted tactics to foil the German plotters, such as dog-legging (making sudden changes to the route being flown). This was 'supposed to weave us through the heavily defended bits. It was also meant to fox fighters'.[154] However, the Luftwaffe were soon able to counter such stratagems.[155]

Each early-warning Freya radar, located (with two associated Würzburgs) in every defensive box, was the first to pick up incoming bombers. It would then direct one of the Würzburgs to the bomber's position. The second Würzburg would then begin to track the German night-fighter that was to make the pursuit. As the bomber approached, the ground controller would direct the fighter towards the position of interception on his 'Seeburg Table'.[156] On the glass top of the Seeburg Table, 'the bomber and fighter were shown as spots of coloured light, red for the bomber and blue for the fighter'.[157] The first Würzburg which was tracking the bomber, would now direct three searchlights towards its quarry. If they successfully located it, a succession of searchlights would light up, illuminating the bomber's progress across the box. This would allow the night-fighter to establish visual contact with it.[158] In

1942, the night-fighter's ability to locate the bomber was further aided by the introduction of the aircraft borne Lichtenstein radar, obvious by its 'mess of aerials'[159] on the aircraft nose. This radar could home in on a bomber from an effective distance of two miles down to a minimum of 200 yards.[160]

There were, however, limitations to the German interception system; ground reflections made it difficult to track aircraft below 6,000 feet. Also, interceptions had to be completed quickly as the aircraft soon passed out of Würzburg range.[161] Moreover, each defensive box could only engage a single bomber at any one time, and this engagement, which would usually last around ten minutes, left an unguarded gap in the defences.[162] Therefore, if the bombers flew 'in a tight mass all would pass through unscathed bar the one or two unfortunates upon whom the German fighter controllers focused their attention'.[163] This technique, adopted by Bomber Command, effectively saturated the Kammhuber line with huge numbers of bombers, thereby overwhelming the defences.[164]

With the steady development of the bomber offensive, German radar equipment was correspondingly updated. Würzburg was redesigned as Giant Würzburg with the reflector dish size doubling, 'allowing it to detect aircraft 40 miles away'.[165] The ultimate in German radar design, introduced in 1942, was 'Wassermann'. This could give the height, range and bearing of an aircraft 175 miles away:[166] 'this was the finest early warning radar to be introduced by either side in the Second World War'.[167] By 1943 the system worked extraordinarily well; the following description of an interception on the night of 22 June is typical:

> The Freya early-warning radar had detected a large force of R.A.F. bombers crossing the North Sea. Schnaufer was ordered to box code-named 'Meise', fifteen miles north-east of Brussels. The R.A.F. target for that night was Krefeld, in the Ruhr, and the route should have passed well to the east of 'Meise', but at 1.20 a.m. Schnaufer was informed by radio of a lone bomber

– far off course – approaching the box from the west. On the ground, the men of 13/211 signals company manning 'Meise' were already tracking Schnaufer's Messerschmitt with one Giant Würzburg radar; now the other swung round and began sweeping the night sky, looking for the raider. The hand-over Freya early-warning system went without a hitch, and by 1.26 a.m. the flight path followed by the unsuspecting British crew was already appearing on a series of co-ordinates on the fighter-control's grid, and as a red spot of light went across the frosted screen of 'Meise's' Seeburg table. Second-Lieutenant Kuhnel, the fighter-control officer of the 'Meise' signals company, guided Schnaufer over the radio-telephone into position ... Schnaufer's orders were to fly straight towards the bomber then, Just before the two aircraft crossed, turn through a half circle; the night-fighter slid round neatly on the tail of the bomber – a perfect interception. In the rear of the Messerschmitt Second Lieutenant Baro, the radar operator, observed a small hump of light rise up from the flickering base line of his screen: an enemy aircraft, range 2,700 yards. No need for further instructions from ground, unless things went wrong. Baro passed Schnaufer a running commentary on the bomber's position until 1.30 a.m. when [it was engaged and shot down[L]].[168]

The German defence system was further supplemented in July 1943, when a new night-fighting strategy was introduced to complement the existing systems. Developed and tested by Hajo Hermann, it used single-engine day-fighters 'freelance', relying on their Lichtenstein airborne radar to find bombers.[169] The hunt was further aided by searchlights that 'can hold their target sufficiently long even in hazy weather ... that means the conditions of interception are similar to that of daylight'.[170]

L   Stirling BK712 of 218 Squadron flying out of Downham Market, had eight on board all of whom were killed: W.G. Shillinglaw, RAAF, A R Helvard (from Denmark), R P Goward, P D McArdle, T R Lunn, D J Ashby-Peckham RNAF, A E Gurney, E D Hart. They are buried at Langdorp churchyard (rafcommands. com: undated(a)).

All fighters allocated to this system assembled in the vicinity of radio beacons when the bomber formation was approaching. They would then launch 'en masse' into the bomber stream where 'they would pursue the bombers until the limit of their endurance'.[171] And they were as 'tenacious as bulldogs ... [and] antagonists of formidable skill and courage'.[172] The new tactic was given the code name 'Wild Boar', and for a while caused a significant rise in losses for the RAF. Even on a dark night, once the stream was intercepted, a fighter could make visual contact with an average of one to three bombers; and with increased visibility, this could be anything up to 25.[173]

In the summer of 1943, an ingenious new weapon was fitted to the night-fighter; 'Schrage music' (jazz music).[174] This was a pair of upward-firing 20mm cannon set at an angle of 60 degrees directly behind the pilot's cockpit.[175] The method favoured with this new weapon was to approach completely unseen from below the bomber (a notorious blind spot), and then fire a short burst into the wings and fuselage. It was almost invariably lethal.[176] Heinz-Wolfgang Schnaufer estimated that by the end of the war 50% of attacks involved the upward firing gun.[177]

For bomber crews, their best hope of avoiding such an attack was to see it coming. There were two devices that aimed to alert aircrew to the approach of a night-fighter: Boozer and Monica. Boozer signalled a red warning light on the pilot's panel when a night-fighter radar had locked on, but it frequently gave false signals.[178] Monica gave an audible 'clicking' alarm in the crew members' headphones when a night-fighter was approaching from the rear. The clicks increased as the range closed. However, it could not differentiate between friendly and enemy aircraft and would, therefore, also frequently sound a false alarm.[179] Moreover, and more unfortunately, the German Flensburg radar fitted in the night-fighters could home in on the Monica signals; leading to Monica's withdrawal from service.[M][180] This essentially left the

M Derek Jackson of Fighter Command conducted extensive research into the radar equipment on a captured Junkers 88 in July 1944. In a number of tests he trialled the onboard German Flensburg radar against the Monica, commonly fitted to Main Force bombers. He discovered that the Flensburg radar could track Monica from over 130 miles away. Even when 71 Lancasters all used their Monica equipment, he could still

most reliable early warning system for the bombers being the eyes of the gunners. Consequently, while on an operation, and particularly when over occupied Europe, they constantly scanned the skies looking for approaching fighters. An exhausting exercise.

On seeing a night-fighter, even when out of range, a gunner would often open-up with his guns. While this may promote an early attack,[N] often the night-fighter would break from the bomber and look for another target, unwilling to risk an attack if their approach was known, or hold back and wait, coming in again for another attack in about five minutes.[181] John Wainwright, a tail-gunner who survived the war, observes 'no air-gunner I ever met was wildly keen on killing German fighter pilots. All we wanted 'em to do was piss off. And 9,000 [bullets] a minute – plus the fact that he could actually see one in every four – usually had the desired effect'.[182] An experience of the crew of 199 Squadron EX-X, flying in October 1944, seems to confirm this view. Attacked by a 'twin-engined fighter', the rear gunner shot 200 rounds at it, 'as soon as gunner opened fire it broke away. No claim'.[183]

Nevertheless, the most frequently practiced response to a night-fighter approach was the 'corkscrew'. This allowed a night-fighter an unmolested approach until within range of the bomber's guns. Sitting 'tight, experiencing the feeling of the condemned man awaiting the tread of the executioner in the corridor'.[184] Then, at perhaps 600 yards, taking a sudden, violent evasive manoeuvre involving the aircraft diving fiercely in the direction of the approaching night-fighter. The night-fighter would be forced to peel away, and at this point the gunners, particularly the mid-upper gunner, had a chance. Jim Feasey remembers, '[we] got in a long burst at it, my four guns jammed due

---

isolate and track one bomber. It became clear; the use of Monica was perilous. 'Harris took characteristically decisive action ... he ordered the immediate removal of the tail-warning radar from all aircraft in his command' (Price: 1967: 214-215).

N Particularly in the case of new night-fighter pilots who lacked the confidence of finding another target and were consumed by a 'keenness for a kill' (Redding: 2005: 278).

to the ammunition belt twisting, luckily, the fighter dropped away and we saw no more of it'.[185] For the bomber, the aim of the dive was to lose 1,000 feet in six seconds,[186] before suddenly steeply climbing. 199 Squadron pilot Jeff Reidy describes how when approached by a night-fighter he, 'toppled all the gyro instruments chucking the aircraft around the sky'.[187] The aircraft would rattle terribly as speeds quickly increased[188] 'causing parachute packs, navigation instruments, and all the other loose gear to fly wildly about the aircraft'.[189] It was like being on 'a merry go round. You were thrown this way and that way',[190] only with an uncertain outcome.

The more violent the corkscrew, starting with a really steep dive and turn, the more difficult it was for a night-fighter to follow and 'usually most successful';[191] a corkscrewing bomber was an extremely difficult target.[192] Night-fighter pilot Heinz-Wolfgang Schnaufer believes it was the mid-upper gunner who warranted most respect, as he was at closest range to the fighter and was given a 'good chance to fire'.[193] However, he does suggest that it was possible to stay underneath a corkscrewing bomber as long as the manoeuvre was not too violent. They could then attack when the bomber changed direction; 'usually at the top'.[194] He had personally shot three bombers down with his upward-firing guns mid-corkscrew.[195] Moreover, he believes a corkscrewing Halifax was an easier target than the Lancaster, but the Lancaster caught fire more easily.[196] For the crew, 'if they were lucky they evaded the night-fighter, if they were very lucky their aircraft stayed in one piece'.[197] Bombers were not designed to withstand this kind of punishment, and while many did, some suffered catastrophic failure of the aircraft structure, particularly if the aircraft was 'war-weary' or had been damaged in the combat.

If the crew had spotted the night-fighter, the corkscrew was their best chance of getting away. However, Heinz-Wolfgang Schnaufer had personally attacked between 20 and 30 bombers, and 'of these only 10% saw him at a range of approximately 150 to 200 meters and corkscrewed before he could open fire'.[198] And even when attacked 40% of aircraft did not fire or manoeuvre.[199]

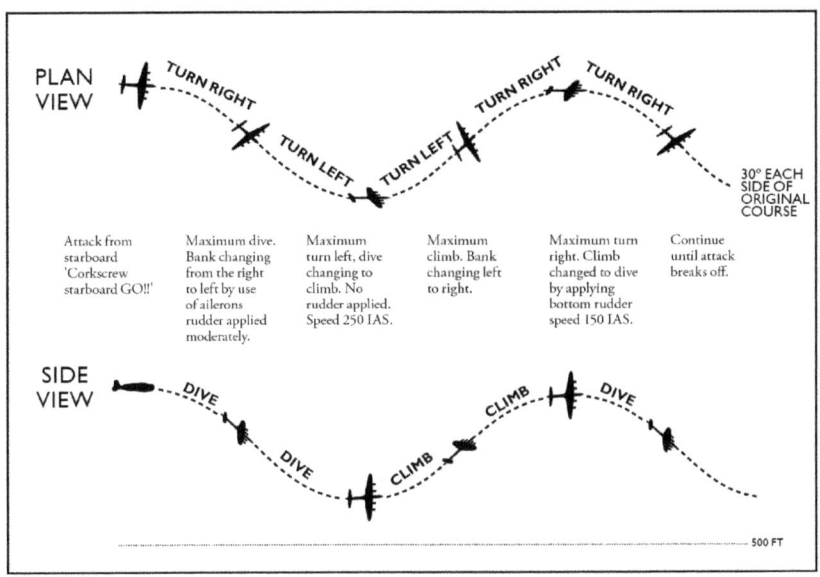

The Corkscrew Manoeuvre

Further risks accompanied the corkscrew manoeuvre. Sudden and violent changes in position could often lead to collisions with other aircraft in the bomber stream. Additionally, such manoeuvres would move an aircraft some considerable distance very quickly. Often a period of disorientation would follow for the navigator. If a fix was not determined in haste, a crew could quickly find themselves lost. Being lost was dangerous:

> you've been flying for hours between two layers of cloud, one above you, one below, you are out of petrol, you are probably out of ammunition, you are shot to pieces, you are on one and a half engines, and you know full well that you are not going to get home, and you are calling, 'Mayday,' 'Mayday,' distress signal, on your radio telephone and you repeat this thing like some death dirge into the darkness.[200]

For the bombers this was an unequal battle. The German defences were resulting in an increasingly heavy toll on Bomber Command. In 1943,

2,225 Bomber Command aircraft went missing on night operations; German night-fighters claimed 1,816 of these. A further 5,177 aircraft were damaged with some 14,000 aircrew killed.[201] However, there was a chink in the armour; their defences had a weakness. The Kammhuber defence system, to be effective, relied entirely upon the Lichtenstein, Freya and Giant Würzburg radars, and upon the communications between the night-fighter pilot and the ground controller.[202] All of these were vulnerable to interference. Bomber Command had a plan.

* * *

In 2012, we were starting to piece together the story of RAF North Creake and the bombing war. Often the stories were surprising and were learnt when we were least expecting them; arriving in the cars of passing strangers.

A remarkable discovery was made by Claire, literally, in our own back yard. Tidying up after the removal of 600 tons of concrete from the postwar yard, I was in a digger and Claire was doing detail work; mainly litter-picking the surface. I saw her throwing what looked like rubbish into a bucket. She then stopped, looked more closely, smiled and turned to look at me, clutching the find. What she had found the British had codenamed 'Window'; strips of aluminium foil that had been used to confound radar. How it had survived so long in the ground is a question we have pondered a great deal. We can only assume that it had lain in a building and it was swept out just before the concrete was laid, and thereby preserved in the dry soil underneath. Why they would have retained it for so long is also a moot point. It could have been accidental or, more likely, deliberate, for as we learnt subsequently it had many domestic uses from wedding day confetti to decorations for festivities. Len Bartram, a local child in the war remembers, 'for Christmas 1944, with other local lads, taking Window from the storage compound at RAF Foulsham and using it to make decorations'.[203] He further recalls:

I had a collection of many different types, from three foot long pieces to boxes of tiny strips like confetti and rolls with a tiny parachute attached. This last sort rattled in the wind and was used for scaring birds from our garden.[204]

He was not alone in collecting Window. Ernie Mallet from Great Snoring recalls 'waking up and seeing rolls of silver paper covering the countryside and hanging in trees; some rolled up and some loose like streamers, I collected some and had a roll … I don't know where the silver paper came from or why it was there, but it was a sight to behold'.[O][205] However, for Bomber Command, the use of Window was far more critical.

The concept of jamming radar had been mooted as early as the late 1930s. In June 1937, Reginald Jones[P] had been impressed by the 'sensitivity of radar … [it] could detect a single length of wire one-half a wavelength long … at a range of twenty miles'.[206] Reflecting upon this ability he related his views to Frederick Lindemann regarding the vulnerability of radar. All one needed do was 'sow a field of dipoles over the North Sea and the radar screens would be full of echoes. Trying to detect an aircraft through this would be like trying to see through a smokescreen'.[207] To which Frederick Lindemann replied, 'that's a good idea – I will get Winston to raise it'. [208]

Radar is a system that reports the position of aircraft through the detection of their radio echoes. In order to prevent any enemy using these echoes to track or intercept Allied forces they must be neutralised. Reginald Jones identified that this could be done in two ways: 'by persuading him that you are either (a) where you are not, or (b) not where you are… the art of spoof lies in so colouring his appreciation … that he comes to a false conclusion'.[209] This false conclusion was predicated upon the sowing of spoof echoes from spurious reflectors:

O Ernie gave the Window to his sister, Pam, to pass onto us at the Control Tower (Mallett: undated).

P Professor Reginald V. Jones was a physicist and a Scientific Officer for the Air Ministry before the war, rising to the post of Assistant Director of Intelligence in 1941. He was appointed to the Director in 1946; a role he performed until 1952 (Foot: 19/12/1997).

> If a reflector is made of a simple wire or strip of metal of length equal to half the wavelength used by the radar station, it resonates to the incoming radio waves and re-radiates them to such effect that … a few hundred such strips or wires would reflect as much energy as a whole Lancaster bomber.[210]

On 3 December 1941, the Radio Counter Measure Board of the Telecommunications Research Establishment (TRE) discussed the possibility that metallised paper may be effective against enemy radar.[211] However, it was not until 1942 that any serious research was undertaken. Trials by Joan Curran (the only female scientist at TRE) under the direction of Robert Cockburn (head of TRE) began to determine, 'the shape that would produce the largest radar echo for the lightest amount of foil'.[212] Copper foil was initially used, but ultimately she discovered a simple oblong cut from aluminium foil gave the best results.[213] By March 1942, after testing Window against all British types of radar, Joan Curran reported that satisfactory results could be achieved with 'in no way excessive'[214] use of resources. Indeed, an initial (1942) 'qualitative examination of the potentialities of Window [identified it as] almost certainly the most powerful single countermeasure'.[215] Robert Cockburn needed a code name for this new initiative, a codename that did not bear any relationship to the reflector use or design. Reputedly, he called on Albert Rowe, the superintendent of TRE, who looked around the room and said, 'why not call it something like window?' And Window it became.[216]

The form finally favoured was a strip about 25 centimetres long and between one and two centimetres wide.[217] One hundred and sixteen pieces equalled a small aircraft on a radar screen[218] and 2,000 strips together in a packet, tied with an elastic band, (and costing fourpence each[219]) were enough to give an echo similar to a heavy bomber.[220] The rate of fall was estimated at 300 feet per minute[221] and Joan Curran reported that the effect would last about 15 minutes, if the bundle was released at about 10,000 feet.[222] Ten such reflector 'clouds over one mile would saturate the radar screen and make it virtually impossible to pick out echoes from aircraft in the area'.[223] This would mean an estimated 400 tons of Window – about 1,000 million strips - would be required per month.[224] The material, gathered in packets, each weighing approximately one pound, was jettisoned from the aircraft, generally down the flare chute, at the rate of about one a minute. This would 'produce an enveloping cloud of spurious echoes'[225] generating the 'radar equivalent of a smoke-screen, through which succeeding aircraft could fly'.[226]

The importance of this research was quickly realised by Bomber Command and on 4 April 1942, they ruled that they should start using Window.[227] However, while testing had revealed that it suited its purpose against German radar extremely well, unfortunately it also identified that it was equally effective against British radar. Alarm bells were sounded.[228] Suggestions of concealment as propaganda leaflets[229] did little to quell concerns that the Germans would soon realise the purpose of the foil and simply replicate it and use it against the British home defences.[230] Potentially, if the fear of Herbert Morrison, Ministry of Home Security, was realised, it could lead to a new wave of bombing against Britain.[231] Particularly as Britain had not yet gained the strategic initiative in the war.[232] Consequently, further trials were demanded. Meanwhile, the Vanesta company[Q] had received an order for Window, to be delivered in time for the 1,000-bomber raid on Cologne. However, before it could be deployed, Bomber Command conceded an indefinite postponement in the use of Window.[233] Frederick Lindemann asked Derek Jackson (Fighter Command's chief radar officer) to undertake trials[R] from RAF Coltishall in Norfolk.[234] These concluded that the use of Window should be prohibited until the RAF had discovered an

---

Q   This was not an exclusive contract, with at least the Sun Engraving Co Ltd also being involved in the production of Window although, interestingly, they believed they were the 'only firm producing Window for the Air Ministry', which they initially called 'Mixture'; a title used in correspondence thereafter (Greenhill & Valentine: undated: 1-3).

R   Ironically, at the same time Derek Jackson was running his trials with Window, the Germans were working on their version called 'Duppel' (Price: 1967: 120). Named after the Berlin suburb where it was first developed, it was tested over the Baltic against German radar sets (Jones: 1978: 299), it produced similar results to Window. As soon as Hermann Goering heard about it, he 'imposed a strict ban on the matter being pursued any further ... the chief of signals, General Wolfgang Martini, had to hide the files deep in his safe, and even the mention of the word "Duppel" became a punishable offence' (Bekker: 1967: 311-312).

antidote.[235] Derek Jackson could not countenance the use of Window, and he subsequently argued that the loss of airborne radar was not worth the one in every 1,000 bombers it would save.[236] While these figures were hotly contested, with Arthur Harris asserting that there was 'a good possibility of saving one-third of our losses on German targets by using this counter-measure',[237] he did not push hard for Window's introduction until April 1943. His biographer, Henry Probert, suggests that he had been holding off, 'partly because of pressure from Fighter Command and partly because of the influence of Herbert Morrison. Harris and Morrison, who was a great supporter of Bomber Command … saw quite a lot of each other'.[238]

By April 1943, the movement to sanction the use of Window was gaining momentum. Charles Portal now declared that he was 'unalarmed by the copy-cat use of Window' as many aircraft had new equipment that was unaffected by it, and besides, with the victory at Stalingrad the tide of the war had changed unequivocally against the Germans.[239] Nonetheless, at a conference held on 2 April, Bomber Command was once again refused permission, but this time as a result of Royal Navy objections that cited the impact on their sea-borne radar. A moratorium on its use was sanctioned until after the invasion of Sicily.[240]

By June, opposition was crumbling. At a meeting on the 23 June, Robert Watson-Watt again outlined the damage to our own night defences,[S] but Leigh Mallory, the head of Fighter Command, countered that even though he was responsible for the defence of Britain, the priority should now be 'saving the casualties in Bomber Command'.[241] Moreover, Frederick Lindemann, who had, up until now, opposed the introduction of Window, outlined that on balance he felt the time was fast approaching when it should be used.[242] At a final conference on 15 July 1943, with objections regarding German retaliation still being raised by Herbert Morrison, Charles Portal responded that the German bomber force was 'weak, badly trained and over-extended'.[243]

S   Reginald Jones later remarked that Robert Watson-Watt's attitude to Window was 'rather like that of the British officer in *The Bridge Over the River Kwai* – any idea that radar might be put out of action distressed him, even if it was German radar' (Scott: 1993: 40).

Winston Churchill stated that he was personally prepared to take the responsibility,[T] and as a result Herbert Morrison withdrew his objections.[244] Winston Churchill famously then exclaimed, 'let us open the Window!'.[245]

Arthur Harris had hoped that the first operational use of Window would be at 'exactly one minute past midnight' on the sanctioned date, but he was thwarted by the weather. [246] Instead he had to wait for a further 24 hours and the night of 24 July 1943; the first night of the week-long assault on Hamburg with its consequential firestorm. Huge 'fires were started'[U] resulting in a massive conflagration in the raid codenamed Operation Gomorrah: the name was significant, 'Gomorrah was one of the 'cities of the plain', along with Sodom, destroyed with fire as punishment for its citizens' misdeeds'.[247]

In preparation for the raid, other than the usual cargo of bombs and incendiaries, groundcrews found themselves loading huge numbers of small packets on to the aircraft which they erroneously believed to be leaflets. In fact, these contained millions of strips of Window.[248] The crews were briefed in the afternoon and through a statement issued by Bomber Command Headquarters were informed:

> Tonight you are going to use a new and simple countermeasure, 'Window', to protect yourselves against the German defence system. 'Window' consists of dropping packets of metal strips which produce almost the same reactions on R.D.F.[V] as do your aircraft. The German defences will, therefore, become confused and you should stand a good chance of getting through unscathed while their attention is wasted on the packets of 'Window'.[249]

T   The delay in use of Window is the 'subject of considerable controversy' as, it is suggested, it caused an unnecessary loss of bombers which could have been prevented. However, Robert Cockburn believes the delay allowed for 'improved methods of production' and large stocks to be built up and gave the RAF time to become thoroughly familiar with the technique. Earlier use would have meant an early change of night-fighter techniques by the Luftwaffe that could have been disastrous for Bomber Command (Cockburn: 1945: 56).

U   'Fires were started' was a familiar wartime phrase that was subsequently used as the title of a popular 1943 documentary style feature-film about the Blitz on Britain. Written and directed by Humphrey Jennings of the Crown Film Unit (Aldgate & Richards: 1986: 220).

V   Radio Direction Finding, latterly known as radar.

The briefing emphasised that the benefit was a communal one, and that rather than the effect of each bundle dropped it was the cumulative effect that would protect them.[250] The crews were enthusiastic about the claims for Window,[251] and became convinced that it would 'turn the odds dramatically' in their favour.[W252]

The 791 bombers crossed the eastern coast of England in a stream 200 miles long and 20 miles wide.[253] They then converged at 'Position A' (290 miles from England and 80 miles from Germany). Commonly, but not exclusively, it was the bomb-aimer that made their way to the hatch, window or flare chute (whichever was being used[X]), armed with a torch and a stop-watch.[254] At the rear of the fuselage the 'Window' bundles were stacked waiting.[255] In order to maximise disruption of the enemy radar, one packet had to be dropped each minute.[256] The operator needed to open the packets, remove the elastic band that held the strips inside together, and then thrust the whole bundle out into the slipstream, which then scattered it far and wide.[257] On some occasions a stopwatch or hat, mistakenly went out with the Window.[258] After reaching 'Position A', all the bombers were on the same course but at varying altitudes from 15,000 to 18,000 feet.[259] At this height, the temperature was minus 20 degrees Centigrade,[260] causing great discomfort for the crew member responsible for discharging the Window. A task that was also hampered by 'an oxygen lead, intercom connections, darkness and the general difficulty of physical exertion at high altitudes'.[261] The first packet was dropped from a Lancaster five minutes after it left 'Position A' and all subsequent aircraft on reaching the same point, followed suit.[262] One wireless operator remembers 'watching a steady stream of these little strips streaming past me and disappearing into the darkness over the main spar ... [like] a shoal of

---

W The crews were better informed about Window than one might suppose. Reginald Jones had been busy building up support for the measure: 'with a little subterfuge, Jones managed to get approval for a couple of his men to visit most of the Bomber Command airfields in a hectic fortnight prior to the day of the fist planned use and brief the crews on the use of Window and its potential effect' (Pheasant: 2003: unpaginated).

X Later on in the war, the bomb-aimer would use a specifically designed chute in the nose of the aircraft to despatch Window (Longmate: 1983: 264).

river fish darting along in murky water.'[263] That night they would drop 40 tons of Window or 92 million separate strips.[264]

Back in Britain, Reginald Jones had chosen to visit a listening station at Kingsdown, Kent.[Y][265] He was delighted at the chaos that he heard. The listeners could hear that the German controllers were estimating, rather than the 791 aircraft airborne, a force of 11,000 bombers.[266] The German night-fighter crews were circling their appointed radio beacons, awaiting instructions from ground control that would lead them to their first interception. However, the controllers could not help, 'soon the ether was thick with confused appeals and exclamations: "it is impossible – too many hostiles" ... "I cannot control you." "Try without your ground control"'.[267] Another Luftwaffe control officer describes the chaos: 'it was just like trying to find a glass marble in a barrel of peas'.[268] Frustrated German night-fighters were following their radar to a mass of echoes only to discover a cloud of Window and 'not a single machine in sight':[269]

> We heard one controller get fixed on a packet of this stuff ... and telling it to waggle its wings and so forth[Z] ... when another controller saw extra aircraft appearing where only one had been before, he burst into indignation over the radio, 'The English bombers are propagating themselves,' and then we heard a quite different voice taking command and I wondered whether it might be Goering himself and it turned out it was.[270]

Even the searchlights were affected. Usually bolt upright before rapidly tilting over to trap some unsuspecting bomber, they were now sweeping blindly over the sky in the vain hope of a target.[271] By this stage, all seven night-fighter boxes responsible for the defence of Hamburg were out of action.[272] Josef Kammhuber later declared, 'the whole defence

---

Y   This was an RAF 'Y' Service station, staffed by the Department of Air Intelligence and was responsible for listening to Luftwaffe air traffic transmissions (Johnson: 1978: 13). Made up of a chain of wireless-intercept stations reaching across Britain, they logged all transmissions heard (Harrington: 2018: 200).

Z   Used as a method of radar fighter identification; making a right-left waggle ('Rolfe-Lise') caused the 'radar echo to wax and wane' (Jones: 1978: 301).

system was blinded at one stroke'.[273]

From the aircraft Bomber Command despatched, only 12 had failed to return; a loss rate of 1.5% compared with 6.1% for the six previous attacks on Hamburg. It is arguable that Window, on this one raid, saved between 70 and 80 aircraft.[274] However, if you strayed from the bomber stream dropping Window effectively 'advertised' your position,[275] with the highest bombers having the least protection. Some flying as high as 23,000 feet were attacked by night-fighters as they could be seen on the Würzburg screens.[276]

With the first use of Window 'the whole elaborate system of GCI (Ground Control of Interception] was destroyed'.[277] Robert Cockburn later said it was 'completely shattered and never fully recovered'.[278] This view is contested by Max Hastings who has argued that 'only once, at Hamburg, had the debut of Window provided the momentary tactical advantage'.[279] However, a general consensus seems to be that the lower loss rate was maintained 'throughout the early winter'.[280] Indeed, Bomber Command estimated that the use of Window saved 200 aircraft in the first two months.[281] Although, as Robert Cockburn concedes, 'by the beginning of 1944, the loss rate was again tending to rise'.[282] Edward Addison concurs that 'the Germans never completely recovered from the effects of 'Window',[283] although he also recognises that after the initial surprise German fighter control began to readjust their methods in order to minimise the chaos caused.[284] The response was faster than the Allies had hoped.[285]

On a return to Hamburg on 28 July 1943, the tactics of night-fighters had changed. The Luftwaffe were now using a system with much looser control of the night-fighters when Window was being used. Rather than airborne AI systems the Luftwaffe were making much greater use of Zahme Sau (Tame Boar), tactics that had a much greater reliance on running commentary from ground controllers to find bomber contacts.[286] However, losses remained remarkably low.[287]

Subsequently, even though there was no counter to Window, Bomber Command losses were beginning to rise alarmingly, as 1943 became 1944.[288] The Germans had become used to differentiating between the real and the spurious returns by 'filtering out the relative speeds'.[289]

With Claire's Window discovery carefully placed inside for safekeeping, the garden works continued. An Easter gardening party saw much achieved. With hospitality provided by us, cake provided by Amanda Foreman (Ian's wife) and labour by unsuspecting friends.

Paul Bishop offered to help to dig a trench to run power to the Speech Broadcast Building and then harrowed the ground after. The concrete was replaced with an orchard and a meadow and the whole garden was re-landscaped. We raked and seeded the meadow in the hot June of 2012. The weather broke the day after and the torrential rain resulted in much seed being washed from our meadow. It germinated sometime later; a couple of miles closer to Wells than originally intended.

It was our intention to garden naturally. I have always been opposed to the use of chemicals in domestic gardens and we now embraced wildflower planting for the benefit of us, our future guests and for local wildlife. With the absence of chemical inputs, either through principle or neglect (we're unsure which), for the previous decade, and with the introduction of wildflowers, the burst of wildlife was extraordinary. However, with wildflower gardening, as my brother Greg pointed out, 'edges are critical'. Without sharp edges it quickly looks like neglect. We planned for sharp edges around the Control Tower to reflect the formality of its design with one 'formal' bed of cultivars adjacent to it. However, it didn't seem to matter how well we planned, we always seemed to put the enormous pile of seasoning logs in the wrong place, which we then had to move on a number of occasions. Ten years later we have just finished burning them, and their tiny 'remnants' pile serves as a useful beetle bank. We continued with the garden, as time allowed, over the next couple of years, tackling the enormous number of nettles through thorough digging. Brambles proved somewhat more challenging and still reappear today. We continued to plant more trees and by the run-up to our opening had far exceeded the number we had felled. However, generally, we left the garden to 'mature', as we moved inside.

ABANDONED NEAR PARIS

171 Squadron Halifax NA108 6Y-V

On the night of 26/27 November 1944, 270 Lancasters and eight Mosquitoes of 5 Group were detailed to bomb Munich. Bomber Command subsequently claimed it was an accurate raid in good visibility,[A] causing extensive damage, particularly to the railway targets.[1] Stirlings and Halifaxes from RAF North Creake supported the operation with seven aircraft detailed for sorties.[2] However, one failed to take off due to 'engine trouble'[3] and three returned early with equipment failure.[4] Two aircraft completed their operation successfully, but 171 Squadron Halifax NA108 6Y-V, 'did not return and is reported missing'.[5] This was the first aircraft loss for 171 Squadron[6] and the first Halifax Bomber to be lost from RAF North Creake.[7] The crew was:

J C Allan (RAF) Rear Gunner
Robert Francis Allen (RAF) Pilot

A Interestingly, the North Creake Operations Book notes that the weather experienced by the North Creake crews, as reported at the de-briefing, was '10/10 Strato Cumulus with cloud tops reaching up to 20,000 feet'.

Alexander Christison (RAF) Flight Engineer
S W Cook (RAF) Special Operator
J Fyfe (RAF) Mid-Upper Gunner
Lester Michael Keen (RNZAF) Navigator
Arthur Joseph Stephen (Steve) Scanlan (RNZAF) Wireless
Operator
Lionel Benjamin Sydney Simmonds (RAF) Bomb Aimer

Arriving on 1 October 1944, the crew had been an early posting to the 171 Squadron after it had been reformed at RAF North Creake.[8] Once settled, they had been allocated a special operator (S W Cook) who operated the radar equipment contained within the aircraft.[9] Their first operation from RAF North Creake was on 20 November.[10]

Halifax NA108 6Y-V had been delivered new to RAF North Creake some time after 27 September 1944.[11] It made its maiden, and only, sortie on this raid. [12] It states in the 171 Operations Record Book that it was believed the Halifax had 'landed' in France,[13] when it had in fact 'crashed' in France at Donnemarie-Dontilly,[14] a town near Paris. The aircraft had been plagued with difficulties during the flight, including failure of 'some of the navigational instruments',[15] severe icing[16] and running critically low on fuel.[17] Its last moments are vividly described in the account of Alexander Christison, the flight engineer on the aircraft:

> we came to the decision that we had not enough fuel to get back to England ... The weather was really appalling and we could not see the ground nor the stars above [as] we were in solid cloud. We then decided to land at a drome given to us at the briefing so flew there and called them up but got no reply (later we learnt they had no facilities for night flying at all). By this time our fuel was really low.[18]

The crew had to choose between the illusion of security in the aircraft, hoping to land before the tanks ran dry, or jumping out and confronting an unknown fate in a country they could not see. They baled out. Fortunately, having made this decision, all the crew landed safely with no reported injuries.[19] Halifax NA108 6Y-V flew on until crashing 'in open fields'[20] destroying the aircraft[21] with wreckage scattered over a wide area.[22] Alexander Christison recalls how, having baled out:

> I landed in the middle of a ploughed field which was very damp and muddy, it was dark and pouring with rain. I hadn't the vaguest idea where I was, I found my torch in my Mae West and with the aid of its light made my way to a canal and walked along its bank till I came to a cart track which eventually led to a road. On hearing a cock crow to my right I turned toward the sound and after three quarters of an hour I reached a farm on the outskirts of a village, but the gates were locked. I could see a light shining in a window so I shouted, the gate was opened by a woman who took me into the house.[23]

It's difficult to imagine how it felt to land, alone, in a country you didn't know where they spoke a language you didn't understand, unsure how you would be received by the locals.[B] However, this was November 1944, and Alexander Christison had landed in Montigny, a town near Paris, in an area that had been liberated by the Allies in the previous three months. He continues:

> She gave me some coffee and a roll and butter whilst I dried myself by the fire. The door opened and a man came in holding an automatic pistol keeping me covered he was not convinced that I was RAF but when I produced a packet of Woodbines and offered him one he realised I must be British. Drinks were

---

B   Should one come down in hostile territory, the escape kit included a photograph that could be used for producing forged documents. John Wainwright describes the process: 'one evening we were told not to shave until further notice. Two mornings later, we were admitted one at a time. We were told to take off our tunics and ties we were given the choice of an assortment of tattered ties, scruffy civilian jackets and (if we cared) ill-fitting capes. Then we were posed and photographed ... we were each given three copies of our own photograph and told to keep them safe ... those photographs had to go with us on every operational flight. In the event of something nasty happening, the undercover boys and girls in occupied Europe, could provide all the forged documents needed to get us through a normal police check-up' (Wainwright: 1978: 59).

produced and it was smiles all round. I was then escorted to another house where a woman spoke a fair amount of English. After more drinks and coffee and much discussion it was decided to drive me ... to Donnemarie, where there was a police station, and a telephone.[24]

Once at the police station Alexander Christison was reunited with six of his crew mates who were already there. Shortly thereafter, they were joined by their pilot; 'we were naturally delighted to see each other especially as there were no injuries'.[25] The crew was now in receipt of the best of French hospitality, and they were 'plied ... with food and drink all of which they [their hosts] could ill afford to give'.[26] With the French military contacted, they were relocated to Provins where signals were sent advising of their safety. They then retired to the officers' mess for another meal. It was now 3.30pm on Monday 27 November. After a medical at a military hospital in Provins, they were put to bed, but were woken at 7pm for dinner and an evening in the town.[27]

On Tuesday 28 November, they received breakfast in bed and a 'stream of visitors'[28] shaking them by the hand and wishing them luck.[29] Before they could shower, a lorry arrived to transport them to Le Bourget, but not before collecting their parachutes and lunching in a local restaurant. Having arrived in Le Bourget, they again dined, walked around the town, bought English cigarettes and had a few drinks.[30] The following morning they reported to an RAF medical officer for a check-up. Alexander Christison recalls that they were finally 'issued with a razor and toothbrush [and were] at long last ... able to make ourselves respectable again'.[31]

A Dakota flight returned the crew to England. Landing at Croydon at 1:30pm on Wednesday 29 November, they were then directed to the receiving centre at St. John's Wood.[32] Alexander Christison remembers, 'we were then issued with new uniforms to replace our torn and muddy ones, suitably attired we went to the pub for a celebratory drink [and] then to bed'.[33] On Thursday 30 November they were once again debriefed and given another medical. The Air Ministry informed the crew that they would be entitled to seven days 'survivors leave',[34] and issued them with rail passes for the journey to North Cheadle.[C] Travelling by train on 1 December, they arrived back at North Creake at 4:30pm. The following day (2 December), they were once again debriefed and as Alexander Christion later recalled, 'given four days leave!'.[35] This 'privilege[D] leave', running from 4 December to 7 December 1944, is confirmed in the 171 Squadron ORB.[36]

After his return, Alexander Christison wrote to the manufacturers of Woodbine cigarettes outlining his experiences in France. He explained how the cigarettes had changed the attitude of the French resistance as 'no German would have Woodbines'. As a consequence he received 200 Woodbine cigarettes from the company[E] concerned.[37]

On 15 December 1944, the crew flew their first operational flight since the crash. The make-up of the original seven-man crew was unaltered, however, the special operator, S W Cook, transferred to an instructor's role at RAF North Creake (the reason for this is not stated). His position was replaced by Gordon Stanley Jevons on all but five of the crew's subsequent 26 operations, before they completed their tour on 24 April 1945.[38] With the end of the war in Europe the crew inevitably disbanded and all had been posted from RAF North Creake by July 1945. Only the pilot, Robert Allen, remaining on flying duties.[39]

Lester Keen, the navigator, from Hokitika, New Zealand was employed as a welder postwar and in 1947 married Joyce Homes in Paddington, London.[40] He died in 1980 in Bishop's Stortford, Hertfordshire, age 60.[41] Lionel Simmonds, the bomb aimer, returned to London after the war and married Magdalena Katona in Marylebone in 1963.[42] He died in Barnet, Middlesex, on 30 December 2002, aged 80.[43]

C   It is unclear whether 'North Cheadle' is a typographical error and should actually read North Creake. This would make sense as they clearly travelled back to North Creake the day after. However, this is complicated by the fact that 'Cheadle' was the site of a 'Y' listening station and may possibly also be the location of some of the MI9 interrogations of returning aircrew. Nonetheless, an error seems most likely.

D   Privilege leave, so called as in wartime there was officially 'no formal right to leave'. 61 days maximum privilege leave a year and maximum 48 hours of weekend leave a month. Non-flying personnel received 7 days leave every three months (Hawton: 1944: 148).

E   The veracity of this particular tale is a little in question as part of the process of preparing for operations was to hand-in anything that would identify aircrew should they have to bale out. One suspects that British cigarettes would have aroused suspicion and would have to have been surrendered before take-off, although this is not certain.

The wireless operator, Arthur 'Steve' Scanlan returned to his birthplace of Gisborne, New Zealand, after the war. He worked as a builder and died on 9 January 2011, aged 90.[44] The replacement special operator, Gordon Jevons, spent his last years in Torbay, Devon, having moved from his native Warwickshire.[45] He died in 1990 at the age of 70.[46]

Both J Fyfe (mid-upper gunner) and J C Allan (rear gunner) were promoted to flight sergeant on 19 December 1944.[47] The pilot, Robert Allen received a promotion to flying officer on 2 August 1945. Alexander Christison (flight engineer) was promoted to flight sergeant on 17 April 1945.[48] Nothing further is known of these four men after they ceased flying.

CHAPTER FIVE

TALKING, NOT LECTURING

On 31 August 2013, I ceased to be a lecturer at London Metropolitan University. The following day I was booked to give a talk on the RAF 100 Group at an event organised by the National Trust at Blickling Hall, North Norfolk. I had been asked to do it as there 'was no one else'. Not a ringing endorsement, but given my level of knowledge of the subject, a reasonable assessment. I was now unemployed or, strictly speaking, self-employed; nonetheless, this was the first time I had been without a job in some considerable time. It made me nervous.

The roots of my redundancy stretched deep into the earliest days of my teaching. Unsurprisingly, Labour & Trade Union Studies was, for some people in positions of influence, a subject that they wanted removed from any publicly-funded syllabus. However, more surprisingly, there were even some at the university that felt the same, but for different reasons. A colleague would always proclaim how much he wanted our department to close, so that we all could be made redundant and get on with other things. I always countered this argument with the fact that I thought we did important work and, from a selfish point of view, I really needed the money. He partially got his wish, but they came for me. Apparently, my university school had to implement financial savings and they considered the most effective action was to 'delete' all 11 of the Principal Lecturer posts, being as they were the highest paid. It wasn't certain, but 'if I was a betting man, I wouldn't put any money on you being here in three months', I was told.

These cold winds of reality had arrived in the spring, not long after the severe winter storms in Norfolk had abated; storms that had wreaked havoc over our already badly scarred project. We hadn't considered the level of windbreak the cypress trees had afforded our garden. In high winds the sheds, in which I kept two of my classic cars, demonstrated how time-ravaged they'd become. While Claire was on the telephone, discussing a new mortgage, I was at the window, nervously listening. With shock, I noticed the winds were lifting the corrugated steel roof of the shed, along with its nine-inch-thick support posts, into the air. It was a scene of chaos; other items stored in the shed for 'safe keeping' had fallen on the Humber. The car itself was pushed down against its springs as one of the support posts of the shed was repeatedly being lifted and dropped on the top corner of the wing and bonnet. From where I was standing it looked like a write-off. Claire, having come off the phone now called the police as we were worried that the shed's 60-foot-long roof would flip over onto the road. I went to Ian Foreman for help. Shortly thereafter, he arrived with a digger and, while he supported the roof, I extracted the cars. He then flattened the shed with the front bucket to prevent the wind from catching it. A policeman arrived and asked what was wrong. We explained the situation and that we'd now got it under control and he said, 'just as well, we've got trees coming down everywhere'.

On inspection, our Hillman was unscathed, and the Humber had come through the onslaught with remarkably little damage. The wind actually did us a favour as the cost of repair to the Humber was reasonably low, and it resolved the problem of how we were going to demolish the sheds in their dangerously close proximity to the road. Over the next two days we cleared up the mess.

At work I met with my manager. We discussed my situation and he explained his limited room for manoeuvre. Ultimately it was agreed that my post would be deleted and I would be demoted to a senior lecturer (on protected pay) and the position would be reviewed in a year. I had a stay of execution, helped by protests from students and trade union general secretaries. This was a huge relief as recent work had made the Control Tower look the worst it had ever looked. It would have been massively devalued if we had been forced to sell.

While we had another year, the threat of redundancy had brought our situation into sharp relief. Our plan to restore the Control Tower back to its original iconic modernist look, was now in jeopardy, as it involved major (and expensive) work. On the outside we needed to remove the pitched roof, put back windows, re-render, move all the extraneous services and repaint. Inside, there was an absence of heating: it needed plumbing, replastering walls, new floors and ceilings (in the majority of rooms), new bathrooms (all reclaimed), new electrics and a good deal of reconfiguring. But the redundancy threat made us rethink, and we couldn't quite see a way through it.

A visit from a former colleague of Claire's allowed us to explore our options with fresh eyes. Her reaction was unexpected, simple and sorely needed, 'well you'd better just get on with it', she said. So we did. The priority now was to make it a functioning house and B&B. The work on our ultimate aim of the 'modernist icon' would have to be over a longer timescale. This was about survival. There was still plenty to do and it needed cash. Howard and Marianne visited armed with a roll of brown paper. Confused, we enquired, 'why?'. 'Business planning', we were told. In what turned out to be an incredibly useful exercise, Claire and I spilled out all our plans for replacing our lost income. They were many, unformulated and disparate. 'You can't do all this, it's not possible' we were told. So a strategy was formed. First, we would put our classic cars to work in private wedding car hire and 'Wedding Wheels-next-the-Sea'[A] was born. In the coming months it

---

A Wedding Wheels-next-the-Sea ran for four years, providing cars to around 80 weddings. Although most often a pleasure, it was a surprisingly stressful occupation. There is so much pressure on marrying couples to have the 'perfect' day, that any glitch can seem disastrous. This is a source of worry when you're relying on 50-year-old mechanical technology; while in the driving seat, you find yourself alarmed at every unusual sound and every unfamiliar smell.

would help a little towards the costs of the Control Tower renovations. More importantly, it would help us understand how to start, promote and maintain a business.

In March 2012, against Claire's advice, I had a brief flirtation with working on the Control Tower. I removed a false landing at the bottom of the stairs, and removed the tongue and groove boarding that lined the walls running up the stairs. She was right, it now looked awful and would take considerable effort to make good. In May 2012, it became more determined than a brief flirtation. We booked-in Steve Leader, a builder and friend (we met during our time holidaying in Norfolk), and in advance of his arrival, we removed the horrendous and unmatched arches that had been put in over the two doorways into the living room. This was very gratifying but was a solid commitment to the building project. With Steve, we then opened the aperture to receive our eBay-purchased 1930s bi-folding doors. Now armed with the taste for change, we set about removing three postwar walls around the house. We succeeded only in making the inside of the house match the look of dereliction on the outside. A situation that caused Claire's visiting four-year-old nephew to comment 'why have you ruined your house?'

At some point during the wall demolition something went in my eye. It wasn't painful, but it was irritating and all attempts to remove it failed. My mum's long-term advice of 'sleep is what you need' didn't work either. In the morning, looking in the mirror, I could see a circle of rust surrounding a shard of cold chisel sticking out of my pupil. I went to the hospital and they poked, pulled and got something out. However, they were unsure it was enough; I would need an appointment with the eye clinic the following day. Right-enough, there was more; he had to drill it out with an oscillating drill-head. A peculiar but not uninteresting process.

On the outside of the Control Tower, the steps to the roof were being removed. Stephen Lake, a local metal worker, had taken on the job, and with the help of Paul Bishop, who had a machine on-site, the steps came down. I discussed with Steve what was salvageable and he assured me he could re-use the treads. In historical terms, these were the most important part; airmen's feet had used them. Concurrently, Paul was fitting the bulk LPG tank. In advance of the hole for the tank being excavated, he had used his cable avoidance tool locator (CAT) to detect buried wires; he had called me over to discuss the results. The sensor on the machine was going mad. I then realised that where we were due to place the tank was the most direct route from the Control Tower switch room (which originally contained all the switch gear for the runway lights) to the runways. We had to dig regardless but dig carefully. I went back to landscaping and before long I heard the digger go quiet, I looked up and saw Paul walking towards me; 'you better have a look' he said. Words you don't ever want to hear. I walked back with him and in the trench were three glazed four-inch pipes; the top one had been shattered by the bucket and inside was packed with rubber-encased copper wires. Ian Foreman walked past and soon jumped down the hole; 'they're dead' he said. With further discussion we concluded we'd hit the main run of runway lights. No harm done.

The same month, my eldest brother Rob, a very skilled carpenter, arrived to fit a new (reclaimed) front door. He also insisted upon resetting our front step. When we removed the shuttering a month later, we were overjoyed. And then Dad had a stroke.

The effects of the stroke had not been too bad but they were causing him difficulties. He needed rehabilitation and it was decided he should stay with us. I had, particularly since becoming an adult, been very close to my dad, but this period would strain our relationship. Dad wanted, understandably, to go home and live independently. The doctors told us that for this to happen he needed to work hard at his rehabilitation. A programme was set up for him (the Norfolk services for the elderly were magnificent), nurses came daily and physiotherapists came once a week to get him to move. We encouraged, nagged and cajoled him into exercising. We grew frustrated, he grew resentful and resistant. He would tell us he was feeling too tired, but we were told it was all part of the effects of the stroke. At no point did he tell us how ill he was feeling. In fact, he was suffering from undiagnosed chest infections. These would grow worse and within a year they would kill him.

My grief at his loss, and I missed him terribly, was mixed with awful feelings of guilt. I dwelled on thoughts of how we could have enjoyed those last weeks together, rather than nagging him to exercise. It still bothers me ten years later.

Guilt is a terribly corrosive thing, and I was no stranger to its effects. Before Claire and I were married, while holidaying on the North Norfolk coast, I was approaching a corner on the coast road when a motorcycle came round the bend on our side of the road. With no options for avoiding a collision other than braking hard, he hit my car with immense force. The inquest recorded that he died instantly. This instant changed many people's lives. Predominantly for the motorcyclist, for he lost his life, but there were also those that were just passing and tried to help, those in the emergency services that had to deal with the impacts and practicalities of such an event. Then there are those for whom it will last much longer. Those who will hold him in their memory and who will go through a whole gamut of emotions before a kind of healing begins. For me, and I can only speak for me, I felt awful.

It is irrelevant whether this feeling is reasonable; everybody, including the police and the coroner told me there was nothing I could have done, and nothing to feel guilty about. But he died against my car; I felt it through the brake pedal and the steering column. I couldn't sleep, I couldn't work. I would rise to temper quickly and be reduced to tears in a moment. Was it normal to feel like this after such an event? I could find no one who knew, no one who had experienced it. The doctor offered pills; I didn't take them.

If I felt like this after such a relatively small event, how could airmen possibly cope after what they'd been through? How did they relate these experiences to their domestic lives and how did they manage to just 'get on with it'? Many, of course, didn't cope, but these cases were by far and away the minority, and there are remarkably few reports of problems with (undefined) post-traumatic stress. Many suggest that we now live in an age where we've gone 'soft'. Certainly, in Britain, we are, thankfully, now more generally remote from violent death. The process of death has become institutionalised, ritualised, sanitised and hidden by euphemisms. Perhaps this is part of it. After the war there was a collective understanding of loss and violent death. If you had served and experienced awful things there were many others around you that had experienced the same; a nod of acknowledgement followed by the words, 'so you were there too'? And perhaps this helped, a shared understanding. For me, this offers a better explanation than 'going soft'. In my recovery, help arrived from a student on one of my courses; he asked me what was wrong as I didn't seem the same. He had been through similar, 'it will take you five years', he said 'it did me'. My response was normal and proportionate, it seemed. But it changed both Claire and I, and was, I suspect, a significant contributing factor towards wanting something else. A desire that ultimately led us to the Control Tower.

Work continued on the build. We started by repairing the floors. Conduit from long-abandoned electric cable had pushed up the asphalt, the cause of the springiness in the hall floor. It also caused the long crack in the floor in the utility room that we saw when first viewing the Control Tower in 2011. Ultimately a simple and inexpensive repair. In October 2012, the steps to the roof returned; they looked fantastic. The first job wholly completed. They were also fitted just in time for the arrival of the asphalt roofers.

Duncan Patey is a very skilled asphalter and we were very lucky to find him. He set about removing the pitched roof and were halfway through as the weekend and high winds arrived. As we left for a weekend away, Cillian arrived with his friends to look after the house; we expressed our hope that the roof would stay in place. It did. I'm not someone that subscribes to the idea that 'youngsters are bloody useless'; generally my ideas chime with the French proverb, 'if only the old people had the understanding and the young people had the chance'.[1] However, my natural inclinations were challenged when, after we returned, I was approached by one of Cillian's friends in bare feet bemoaning the temperature in the house (to be fair there was no heating). It was all I could do to suppress repeating one of my dad's tropes, 'if you're cold, put some bloody socks on' (although he was generally referring to a jumper; I always wore socks). Cillian now ruefully reflects, 'the Control Tower wasn't windtight; it was cold, draughty. I loved it but they were city-dwelling folk; they didn't like the cold or walking, just wanted to sit around – they hated it from start to finish!'

Before the roof was stripped, we had been advised to have a 'tin hat', that is, a scaffolding cover to protect the building from the weather. The cost was an extra £10,000; money we could ill afford. We decided to take a chance with the weather. The roofing work now moved on apace, the second half of the pitched roof was removed and all the old asphalt was stripped off revealing an ammo boot footprint in the concrete; judging from its position, it looked like a worker's trademark. Now left with a heap of unusable roofing timbers (we'd salvaged what we could), we gathered with neighbours in the garden on 5 November for a bonfire party. It was a great night until rain cut the festivities short. Claire and I returned inside. In our bedroom we found a multitude of drips emerging from the ceiling. We quickly gathered all the pots and saucepans we could and caught many of the drips. Sleep that night was accompanied by the cacophony of an orchestra of ill-tuned water drops.

The following day, the asphalting commenced. A debate ensued as to whether the roof had originally had gutters or hoppers. Duncan Patey, who had previously repaired Thorpe Abbots control tower, maintained it should be gutters, particularly as the upstands at the edge of the roof were often loose and looked like an afterthought. I preferred the hoppers and it was agreed that we go with the existing arrangements. The wisdom of this decision was revealed when, as a result of an article in the local paper, I received a phone call from Diana Parsons. Diana claimed a relative had taken wartime photographs of our control tower and airfield; 'would you like them?'. I was decidedly sceptical as I had always been told that no wartime photographs would exist of North Creake Control Tower, as control tower photographs were generally rare, but on a secret station, 'not a chance'. We were astonished when a couple of days later the most fantastic photographs arrived. Neatly mounted and annotated in pages of an album by the photographer, Norman Turnbull. Norman had been an airfield controller at RAF North Creake and a keen photographer. Aside from the pleasure of seeing pictures of the airfield when it was operational, the detail of the Control Tower, both inside and out, was incredible and confirmed our decision to go with hoppers as the right one. There they were on the side of the building in 1945.

Norman Turnbull, airfield controller, RAF North Creake (Control Tower Archive).

We always preferred to use local trades recommended by people we knew. An exception to this rule was the use of a large local plumbing firm. We considered the job complex and wished for the guarantee and security that a larger firm affords; it was a mistake. Luckily, the plumber allocated to the job, Aaron Buckie, was young but very good (this was the first job he worked on independently). The firm itself was difficult to work with. At the point of pricing we had shown the company the actual sanitary ware we wished to use and where we wished to put it. We also made clear that we wanted no plumbing runs fixed to the exterior of the building. Once the plumbing work commenced, with the exception of Aaron, they were constantly trying to convince us to do the reverse, and complained about the difficulties arising from the use of 'second-hand stuff'. One particular row saw us having to cut the four-inch holes in the floor for the soil pipes ourselves, a job we assumed was in the price. You could understand their reluctance; the building is difficult to work on and the plumbers had nick-named it the 'tool-eater', in honour of the amount of drill bits and, at times, drills they burnt out. Being blast-proof, everything is harder and takes much longer than expected. For example, cutting through a wall for access to an ensuite, would generally be expected to involve a couple of hours' work; angle-grinding down both sides and knocking out the bricks. However, this interior wall was 13½ inches thick and once cut, the heavy sledgehammer just bounced off, leaving barely any impression at all. It eventually took two days of hard labour to break it through brick by brick. So reluctance was understandable, and each 4-inch soil pipe hole took half a day to cut. Nonetheless, our experience was not good.

In November 2012, we were still hopeful that the plumbing would be complete for Christmas. The plumbers were at this stage working in every room and, inevitably, creating mess everywhere. It's extraordinary that mess and dirt always come as a surprise even when the sound of angle-grinders is a constant companion. Claire and I had held on to the naïve belief that we could maintain a 'safe zone' in the Control Tower; a space where we could retreat and be clean. When we entered this space one day to find a plumber cutting through the wall engulfed in a cloud of dust, we finally conceded that we had to accept the experience of stepping out of bed onto gritty floors.

Things were moving apace; the roof had been finished and reclaimed quarry tiles underneath the Rayburn became the first finished floor surface. With the promise of friends arriving the day following Boxing Day, we concentrated on preparations to make the Control Tower as comfortable as possible. Radiators went in, the boiler went on the wall and the rudiments of the reclaimed kitchen were fitted. Now, for the first time in three months, we had hot running water. The ensuite for our room quickly followed, but as Christmas approached, it soon became apparent that this would be the only working bathroom when our group of friends arrived. The day the trades departed for Christmas, we were left with a house in a state of disarray with five days, including Christmas, in which to get it straight. Late on Christmas Eve we were still clearing piles of brick rubble from a bedroom where internal cupboards had been knocked out. At 10pm we put up the Christmas tree. On Christmas Day we'd been invited to a private dinner at the Bull in Walsingham. Nelly, the landlord, was a perfect host. For the first time in what seemed an age, we were wearing good clothes and talking to people with only a passing interest in the Control Tower; it was a tonic. Boxing Day, we were back to it, stripping out a bathroom that needed to become a bedroom the following day. Soil pipes were pushed away from the outside of the building and the holes were roughly filled with concrete to protect Pam from the winter north-easterlies that hit that elevation. We had done enough. Just about. And we could take some days off in the company of friends.

* * *

In 1940, Robert Cockburn began research into jamming equipment at the Telecommunications Research Establishment (TRE). In the same year, the RAF 80 (Signals) Wing was formed to provide intelligence on enemy radar systems with Edward Addison appointed to take charge.[2] The initial work on radio countermeasures (RCM) was purely defensive, involving the jamming of German offensive radar in conjunction with Fighter Command.[3] Offensive use of RCM was rejected as such activity would compromise the bombers, who operated in absolute radio silence to avoid German detection.[4]

By February 1942, the British had achieved a fairly complete picture of German radar operations.[5] It was becoming increasingly obvious that in order to stem Bomber Command losses, something would need to be done about German radar defences.[6] Consequently, the efforts of TRE were directed towards the 'problem of neutralising the enemy's extensive night defences'.[7]

Shiver, a RCM device that jammed German frequencies of radar, marked the official end of 'radio silence'[8] and the beginning of Bomber Command's acceptance of jamming.[9] In October 1942, Bomber Command called for the development of RCM equipment against Freya and Würzburg; signalling the start of Bomber Command's RCM war.[10] The introduction of more countermeasures followed, however, they lacked 'any effective co-ordination of effort'.[11] In late 1943, Bomber Command demanded 'a unit equipped to undermine the enemy's use of his electronic devices'.[12]

At a meeting on 29 September 1943, involving the Air Ministry, Bomber Command, Fighter Command, the US Eighth Air Force and TRE,[13] it was quickly settled that this new unit should have sole responsibility for (1) the control of countermeasures; (2) their operational employment; (3) collating intelligence relating to such measures; (4) examining the results of their use; (5) learning from such results so the countermeasures can be deployed to 'maximum effect'.[14]

In order to achieve the independence of thought needed to develop effective countermeasures, it was seen as important that the functions of radar development and RCM development should be separated. It was impossible to expect 'someone who has put all their effort into researching and developing something to apply the same effort in its destruction'.[15]

Edward Addison[16] was persuaded to lead the new RAF 100 Group on the proviso that the 'new formation would be large enough to handle its brief'.[17] TRE initially suggested that Fighter Command might be best suited to hold jurisdiction over the new Group, as they could enhance existing relationships and technical experience. This assertion was refuted by Robert Saundby (Deputy at Bomber Command) as Fighter Command's experience related to defence rather than offence.[18] Ira Eaker (USAAF) concurred, stating that he 'hoped the time would come when we should be able to seek out the enemy instead of trying to avoid him'.[19] However, Fighter Command resisted ideas of transfer of their squadrons.[20] Arthur Harris intervened, insisting that Fighter Command's 'Serrate' and Intruder squadrons should be transferred into Bomber Command.[21] He further proposed that 'they should be formed into a Group whose specific role would be to conduct co-ordinated offensive action in support of the bomber offensive against the German night defence system'.[22]

Moreover, Arthur Harris complained that Fighter Command 'were contemplating a much more leisurely process of rearrangement than we consider acceptable … it seems as if … the formation of the new Group is a matter of comparatively low priority'.[23] Norman Bottomley (Deputy Chief of Air Staff) observed that while at the outset radio devices were entirely the preserve of Fighter Command, they had now been developed for the offensive and 'it would therefore be a mistake to tie the development of radio counter-measures to Fighter Command'.[24] It was finally agreed,[25] and Fighter Command conceded squadrons on condition that they remained available for defensive work.[26] Equipped with Mosquitoes,[B] the squadrons were transferred. However, many aircraft were in a poor state[27] and they subsequently suffered mechanical problems, early returns and inevitably losses.[28] Nonetheless, with fighter squadrons and bomber squadrons operating within the same group for the first time, Edward Addison noted that they had formed a 'strange conglomeration'.[29] Michael Renaut, who would later command 171 Squadron at RAF North Creake, believed that the work of the bomber squadrons within the Group was always compromised by much of the leadership being from Fighter Command. While there is no suggestion that the best interests of RAF 100 Group were at stake, he does pinpoint that:

> they hadn't much clue when it came to knowing about bombing-up a Halifax. They were inclined to change the bombload half an hour before take-off and wonder why it took so long! The fighter outlook was permanently present and they

---

B   The Mosquito was a twin-engined fighter-bomber that came into service in July 1941. An incredibly versatile and fast aircraft, it was made entirely of wood by de Havilland Aircraft Company in Hatfield, Hertfordshire (Turner: 1979: 41).

regarded the Halifax much as a Mosquito when it came to refuelling and bombing-up.[30]

RAF 100 Group, 'a novel, highly specialised unit employing skilled scientific and service personnel'[31] and squadron of both fighters and bombers, was established on 23 November 1943.[32] What unified these disparate squadrons was their role in Bomber Support and, in the majority of cases, their interaction with radar technology. With 'Confound and Destroy [as] a compelling motto',[33] RAF 100 Group night-fighters were flying with the bomber stream 'destroying' night-fighters, while the heavy bomber squadrons were left to 'confound' German radar.

All RAF 100 Group stations were located in the 'bulge' on the east of England in North Norfolk,[34] chosen 'for reasons of remoteness as its activities were highly classified'.[35] At its height in 1944, it had 14 operational squadrons.[36] First were the fighter squadrons that arrived at West Raynham and Great Massingham on 3 December 1943, they were then followed by Foulsham, Oulton, North Creake (all three with heavy bombers) and Little Snoring, and Swannington (Mosquitoes); the latter five were all allocated to the Group on 7 December 1943.[37]

The Group utilised a myriad of approaches, ranging from tracking radar, through the interception of signals, to jamming radar out altogether. Measures such as Corona,[C] introduced on 22 October 1943, caused immense confusion and anger from the German controllers. After practise, 100 Group personnel could intercept German ground controllers' communications and broadcast music or Adolf Hitler's speeches across the airwaves.[38] Famously, a Corona interception instructed 'all German nightfighters to land because of the danger of fog'. They did.[39]

On the jamming side, RAF 100 Group would initially suffer from the need for haste and problems of delay. Delays were caused

---

C Corona utilised four stations with ground jamming platforms that made it possible to issue real-time verbal communications to the German night-fighters and controllers. The misinformation was mainly limited to operational instructions as false information about bombers was considered 'too dangerous'. Evidence of its success was provided by the Germans themselves in the form of 'frayed tempers' of both controllers and night-fighter pilots heard by the 'Y' Service listening in (Harris: 1995: 137).

by a lack of suitable four-engine aircraft for the role.[40] Eventually Ira Eaker (USAAF) intervened to ensure the provision of enough of the US Boeing B-17s, arguing that the US Forces would benefit as much as the British from this initiative.[41] Conversely, in the haste to equip the new Group with appropriate RCM equipment, apparatus was built hurriedly, 'inevitably at the expense of sound design'.[42] Consequently, RAF 100 Group had no functioning jamming squadron until April 1944,[43] the same year that a sufficient margin could be built up to allow adequate time for proper design of the RCM equipment.[44] Nonetheless, by the time these squadrons were operational the Group was using such an array of RCM techniques,[D] that they had brought chaos to German night-fighter communications.[45] As the Luftwaffe General Josef Kammhuber commented, they were 'always setting the Luftwaffe Night Fighter Command new problems to solve'.[46] Indeed, as another Luftwaffe General, Erhard Milch observed, 'I am beginning to think that we are sitting out on a limb and the British are sawing that limb off'.[47]

With special operators and banks of secret electronic equipment on the aircraft, the crews flying on 100 Group heavy bombers understood that they were doing something different. However, 'it was so secret, they didn't even tell us what it was all about, how the equipment we were carrying might help; yet we were the ones putting our lives on the line every time we went out on operations'.[48] And lives *were* being put on the line; the Air Ministry had expected high losses from these operations, indeed the 100 Group commanders 'had assumed at the outset that the casualties among the crews in the Bomber Support role would be even higher than those in Main Force'.[49]

* * *

Before arriving at an operational station, aircrews and groundcrews had been through a long process of preparation. Most of the training

---

D See Brettingham: 2002 or Streetly: 1978 for excellent discussions of these techniques.

involved learning a role, whether pilot, flight engineer, meteorologist, map clerk, radar mechanic or all the other multiple vital roles on an RAF bomber station. However, not all the training was welcome:

> [as a gunner] I was shown how to bayonet the enemy, shoot with a rifle and a revolver, and throw a grenade. How this related to being an aircrew rear gunner I still do not know. In a similar way, how the hydraulic system that operated the rear gun turret was explained in great detail. But if it went wrong in flight, there was nothing at all that I could do about it, so that must be seen as a waste of time.[50]

The training of aircrew was expensive, averaging at £10,000 per man: as Arthur Harris dryly observed, 'enough to send ten men to Oxford or Cambridge for three years'.[51] Other than the role that the crew member performed, it covered the theory of parachuting, though, to the relief of crews, this did not include a jump.[52] It also included preparing for a crash landing in water (ditching) – jumping in the sea in full kit and manhandling a dinghy.[53] After, of course, they were taught to swim.[54]

They were also taught how to evade capture behind enemy lines. This generally involved taking aircrew, when dark, to a remote part of the country with no food or money and telling them to return to camp on their wits alone.[55] And use their wits they did. Bert Berry, who served at North Creake as a wireless operator, remembers walking along the railway line as an expedient way to return to base. This had the 'bonus of an old sack full of discarded lumps of steam coal, gleaned from the track-bed ballast and providing a welcome boost to the meagre RAF allocation'.[56] Gordon Mercier, later a gunner at North Creake recalls:

> we went to a café and said, 'have you got any scraps that you want to throw away because we're in the Air Force and we're trying to escape and they've given us no money' ... 'Of course you can. Come in'. We had a meal. A proper meal. We did that twice ... [then] we went to the bus driver and said, 'Look, I'm ever so sorry. We're in the RAF and we've been told that we've

got to get back to camp without any money. Is there any chance you can let us on the bus?' He said, 'Course you can.' And he dropped us at the gate … And that was our experience of learning how to escape.[57]

Not all new arrivals were new to flying. In the case of RAF North Creake most of the personnel were transferred on 1 May 1944, when 199 Squadron became an RAF 100 Group jamming squadron.[58] They arrived with their servicing echelon, No. 9199, but no aircraft.[59] Typical was Roy Smith, a navigator, who transferred mid-first tour.[60] Once he had completed this tour, he immediately volunteered for another 'because there was a shortage of experienced crews', and rather than this second tour consisting of the normal 20 operations, it was reduced to 15; 'in retrospect, it probably was not a wise decision as the war would have been virtually over by the time we were due to recommence operations'.[61]

All airmen and WAAFs had to follow the same procedure of 'booking-in' on arriving or leaving an operational station, even for the day. However, this was a more complex process when first posted to a station. On arrival airfield personnel reported to the guardroom and then to the orderly room in the station headquarters where billets were allocated.[62] The accommodation was spartan on wartime stations. It was commonly in Nissen huts with the beds arranged along both sides of the hut.[63] These huts were generally too cold or too hot, although for about two weeks of the year, the 'perfect temperature'.[64] The beds were provided with mattresses in three squares, known as 'biscuits'.[65] A shelf ran the full length of the hut above the beds on which was kept greatcoats, 'best blue' uniform etc. The rest of the kit was stored in a locked kitbag alongside the bed.[66] Occupants tended to prefer the corner beds as the beds nearest the central stove generally became seats.[67] A common practice was to keep the allocated coal for the stove stored underneath a bed to stop it being 'thieved' from outside.[68] Huts contained little furniture apart from the odd table and wooden chairs.[69]

Once settled, it was time to complete the 'New Arrival Chit', which involved acquiring signatures from different sections on the camp.[70] Such as, station sick quarters (where you would be given a FFI – Freedom from Infection – inspection to identify any infectious diseases);[71] pay accounts to register your arrival; the padre; the sports store; the catering officers etc. This process would normally take a day or two and was perceived as good for station orientation.[72] Also, private bicycles needed to be registered at the guardroom, as did cameras (it being an offence to use one without permission in the form of a permit).[73] Finally, airfield personnel reported to the orderly room with the 'New Arrival Chit' for duty.[74] Phyllis Willmott felt frustrated by the procedure:

> I could see that, when I was posted, it was important that I should hand my bicycle back to the section of the camp from which I had taken it on my arrival. I could also see that a visit to the sick bay to check that one had not brought in nits was perhaps unavoidable, that ration books had to be collected or handed in, and blankets too. What was less comprehensible to me was having to trail round the camp getting appropriate signatures from the many others, such as the electrical stores or transport section, listed on the page-long chit that had to be completed.[75]

Phyllis had arrived at RAF North Creake at the beginning of May 1944, having travelled to Norfolk by train:

> The slow train seemed to halt at Walsingham station. Neither Jean nor I could make out from the instructions on our travel warrants whether we had to get out at this station or the next one called Wells-next-the-Sea. After exchanging a few sharp words with Jean, I decided I was going to get off here at Walsingham and Jean, grumbling at my hasty decision, followed ... we should have stayed on the train. It did not matter much. The porter at the station phoned through to the camp and all we

had to do was wait half an hour for transport to arrive to fetch us, so we sat on our kitbags outside in the sunshine, our tennis rackets and gas masks piled up beside us.[76]

Travelling uphill from the railway station to the airfield 'through green, winding lanes, we could see that the countryside here was pretty'.[77] After the settling into the camp they reported for duty at the meteorological office in the Control Tower:

> We were greeted on our arrival at the Met Office by the senior forecaster ... he was tall and dark, with a strongly cut chin, and he wore spectacles with tortoise-shell type rims. With his open brown eyes, his face wore a look that was either serious or puzzled. We were to find out that he was not so much a serious man as a thoughtful and intelligent one who was more often amused than puzzled, even though his solemn expression often concealed the fact. His assistant forecaster ... was younger, a boyish creature with reddish hair and a pale skin who was amiable enough but not much interested in either the work or the life on the camp.[78]

Some personnel had been at the camp for some time, such as Vic Flowers who was posted to North Creake in March 1944, more than a month before it achieved full operational status. Once the station was operational, he would become the sergeant in charge of station signals.[79] But most arrived either just before, as with John Rees, Medical NCO,[80] or more likely with 199 Squadron in May 1944. Betty Price, who met her future husband while serving as a WAAF with him at Lakenheath recalls; 'my husband was with 199 Squadron ... he was an electrician. I was ... on the same camp and worked in the station armoury office'. She remembers it was 'a bit of an upheaval when we all had to move to North Creake'.[81] At the end of May 1944, it was recorded that 'on the whole ... North Creake is settling down very well despite the seemingly inevitable hold-ups due to incomplete building and the presence of contractors'.[82]

Vic Polichek at the rear turret of his Halifax (Jayne Jennings).

Once 199 Squadron was settled, new personnel arrived as and when other staff were posted away or as replacement crews. Vic Polichek, a rear gunner with 199 Squadron remembers arriving at RAF North Creake on 23 February 1945, 'very late, tired of course, but were welcomed with a serving of steaks, most uncommon'.[83] Keith Thompson, a navigator, arrived at North Creake on 12 February 1945; he wrote up the highlights of his first two days in his diary:

> [On the train] … carried on to March, K's Lynn then Heacham & Wells, Rotten b's charged us 5/3 cash for bikes. Transport to [airfield] Station. Had dinner in Mess. Collected blankets & sheets & went to billets.[84] … [Tuesday 13 Feb] 'Got chit & went round with it in pouring rain. Lecture on Flying Control … Cycled to Wells … Saw *Fanny by Gaslight*. Got tight on Port in the Mess. Bob tight on whisky'.[85]

All 199 Squadron's Stirling bombers were transferred to other units within the RAF before leaving RAF Lakenheath.[86] Nevertheless, they remained on Stirlings, as their size and manoeuvrability made them the 'most suitable platform for offensive jamming operations'.[87]

Keith Thompson (front row on the right) with his crew (John Reid Collection).

The 199 Squadron long-standing motto 'Let Tyrants Tremble', pleasing both in construction and sentiment, applied equally to their new role. They transferred with their existing commander Norman Bray,[E] who immediately assumed the role of station commander and was replaced by Percy Bevington. Percy Bevington was an unusual appointment as squadron commander, as he was not a pilot but a navigator.[88] Ten days after 199 Squadron's arrival at North Creake, their new Stirling bombers began to arrive.[89]

E   Norman Bray was better known as Little 'Nan' Bray as his initials were N.A.N. and his height 5 feet 4 inches (Renaut: 1982: 155). He was very popular and well-liked by all ranks. He once put himself on fatigues because he was late for PE. While serving at RAF North Creake, he lived in a Church House, Walsingham with his wife and children (Meath Baker 12/3/2024). He was killed in July 1953, flying a Gloster Meteor (an early jet), at Leuchars in Scotland when, immediately after taking off, his cockpit canopy opened, upsetting the airflow of the aircraft and causing a spin. The aircraft 'stalled and dived into ground alongside Leuchars railway station where a train was standing' (aviation-safety.net). Michael Renaut recalls, 'Little Bray was a man of intense energy and he certainly kept me busy as a squadron commander, what with training and conferences and visits to Group Headquarters ... he was a ball of fire, not frightfully competent as a station commander, but he had *everyone* organised ... like a human dynamo [he] worked me to the bone' (Renaut: 1982: 155).

Percy 'Bev' Bevington Squadron Commander 199 Squadron (Russ Bevington).

The Stirling bomber was the first four-engine aircraft to become operational with Bomber Command. It was perceived as being 'capable of giving tangible expression to the Air Staff's beliefs in strategic bombing',[90] and delivering, in Winston Churchill's words, 'the shattering stroke of retributive justice'[91] against the enemy. For many crews it was a delightful aircraft. Jeff Reidy, an Australian pilot at RAF North Creake, captures a typical sentiment, 'I liked the Stirling very much, when we finished the tour, we didn't want to go on Halifaxes; we wanted to stay on Stirlings'.[92]

Nonetheless, official RAF historians referred to the Stirling as 'a disappointment'.[93] While many pilots were ferociously loyal to the aircraft,[94] its shortcomings were always understandably prominent. As Michael Renaut, the wing commander of 171 Squadron at RAF North Creake explains:

> The Short Bros Stirling ... never succeeded as a bomber because its ceiling height with a bomb load was pathetically low. I only discovered the reason when I spoke to their Chief Test Pilot after the war. This was because several feet had to be trimmed off the wingspan after the design of the prototype in order to get it into a standard RAF hangar! Thus a certain amount of

necessary 'lift' was sacrificed because the Air Ministry would not (or could not) alter the hangar entrance width. How we ever won the war with such master planners I just do not know![95]

This assessment of the aircraft is widely repeated and there is certainly no question that the Stirling was an aircraft with limitations. When in flight, although commonly complimented for its handling, the maximum service height was very restricted, leaving it within the reasonably easy reach of German flak and anti-aircraft guns. As a consequence Stirling losses became disproportionate to that of the Lancaster, when the latter came into regular service.[F] The cause of this limited ceiling height was down to the relatively narrow wingspan of the Stirling, the width of which is commonly blamed on (as with Michael Renaut), the Air Ministry's requirement that it should fit into a standard hangar. However, in a 1936 Air Ministry design specification (B12/36) sent out to all interested aircraft manufacturers, it explicitly states that the wings 'should not exceed a span of 100ft.'[96] This specification also requires a large bomb capacity (maximum 14,000lbs) and a cruising speed of 230mph at 15,000 feet.[97]

The most common RAF hangar, at the time, had a span of 152 feet and a maximum door span of 126 feet,[98] contradicting the assertion that the 100 feet limit was in order to fit into a 'standard RAF hangar'. So how did this fallacy arise? The first reference to it was in 1942, when the leading aviation journal *Flight* stated that 'the wing span was limited by the Air Ministry to 100 feet – from considerations of hangar space, one presumes.'[99] What is surprising and, perhaps, disappointing, is that the postwar Air Historical Branch's *Pre-War Evolution of Bomber Command 1917-1939*,[100] repeated this fallacy. This led to an almost universal acceptance of this baseless 'fact'. Subsequently, aviation authors began inserting the word 'standard' before RAF hangar.[101] Why or how this emerged is unclear. The wingspan limit was actually the result of analysis by the Air Ministry where:

F   For comparative losses by aircraft see Middlebrook & Everitt: 1985: 707.

RAF Steeple Morden operations block 2004 (Control Tower Archive).

RAF North Creake Control Tower in 1973 (Alan Wood).

The Stirling mural painted by Claude 'Ted' Allen before it was removed to the RAF Museum in Hendon (John Reid Collection).

The sergeants' mess as painted by Claude 'Ted' Allen; the artist responsible for most of the nose art on the aircraft at RAF North Creake.

The Control Tower on our viewing day, June 2011 (Control Tower Archive).

Contemplating a change of life; 'we have to buy it' (Control Tower Archive).

The view towards the Control Tower from the yard on the viewing day, June 2011. The top of the Control Tower can just be seen above the portable site office (Control Tower Archive).

No turning back. Our first weekend at the Control Tower sees Claire channelling 'Rosie the Riveter; 'we can do it!'. October 2011 (Control Tower Archive).

Leyland cypress trees that dwarfed the Control Tower and cast it into shade are felled, October 2011 (Control Tower Archive).

Fires are started, October 2011 (Control Tower Archive).

Large plant invades the Control Tower grounds and removes the postwar yard, March 2012 (Control Tower Archive).

A major discovery: RAF North Creake 'Window' under the postwar yard, March 2012 (Control Tower Archive).

'It's all ahead of ya, like a wheelbarra'. Claire working in the 'garden', March 2012; note the pile of Leyland cypress logs in the background (Control Tower Archive).

Runway powerlines uncovered when excavating the hole for the gas tank, April 2012 (Control Tower Archive).

The works move indoors. Claire beams with delight as she removes the twin arches between the hall and living room, May 2012 (Control Tower Archive).

Demolishing postwar amendments to the Control Tower layout. We would grow used to rubble underfoot, May 2012 (Control Tower Archive).

The steps to the roof return in preparation for the removal of the pitched roof, October 2012 (Control Tower Archive).

the prime consideration ... was to balance weight against the need for higher performance (speed, range & load). At the time of design in 1936/37, the RAF (including the bomber stations) were operating at home off grass strips ... continuing to do so into the early war years. The simplest way of ensuring ease of ground handling and operations on grass or other natural surfaces in poor conditions: keep the weight down by restricting wingspan.[102]

199 Squadron Stirling LJ514 EX-B 'Bear' (as it was known) with nose art by Claude 'Ted' Allen featuring a bear holding a beer bottle. A pint jug of beer denotes each operation (beer is pronounced 'bear' in Norfolk). This was a record-breaking Stirling having completed 74 operations (John Reid Collection).

This is not to say that the design of the Stirling was not detrimentally impacted by these decisions, but to lay all the blame at the door of the Air Ministry seems churlish as the specification was described before the Stirling was conceived and was not adapted to fit with it.

Trials at Martlesham Heath in Suffolk concluded that the wingspan led to take-off and landing runs being excessively long.[103] This ultimately led to a redesign of the undercarriage. The designers found that by increasing its length they were able to add three degrees to the ground angle and thereby increase lift, shorten take-offs and reduce landing distances.[104] However, it did make the undercarriage vulnerable to collapse and caused a problematic tendency to swing:

> Stirling's pronounced tendency to swing sharply to starboard on take-off ... if one opened the throttles evenly, the swing would put the aircraft off the runway in a few seconds, long before it achieved enough speed to give rudder control. The answer to the problems was to stagger the throttles, opening both starboard throttles substantially in advance of the port side pair.[105]

Detail of Stirling the LJ514 EX-B nose art (John Reid Collection).

It took a high degree of skill and care to coax the Stirling into the air and it foxed many pilots. Geoff Parnell, an air-gunner with 214 Squadron summed-up the feeling of many, 'the bloody thing wouldn't fly'.[106] A sentiment shared by Arthur Harris and expressed forcefully when he was in discussion with officials from the Ministry of Aircraft Production; 'It's murder, plain murder to send my young men out to die in an aircraft like that'.[107] Nevertheless, many crews had great affection for it. '[The Stirling] was a beautiful aircraft ... once up there. A beautiful aircraft to fly.'[108] Many concluded 'it served us so well'.[109] Certainly, its robust structure withstood remarkable punishment, 'being riveted, [it] could have great chunks knocked out of [it] and still keep going', asserted Arthur Clarke, a navigator who served with 199 Squadron.[110]

By 1944, the Stirlings were being steadily withdrawn from front-line Bomber Command service. 199 Squadron at RAF North Creake became the last Bomber Command squadron to fly them operationally,[111] with Stirling LJ516 EX-H being the last to fly an operational sortie, leaving on 14 March 1945. Taking off with a crew of eight, among whom, were two Squadron leaders, including Michael Docherty Squadron Navigator Leader, and the squadron commander,[112] Percy 'Bev' Bevington, wanting to say goodbye.

On 8 September 1944, RAF 171 Squadron was formed, becoming part of RAF 100 Group's jamming provision and the second squadron to be based at RAF North Creake.[113] Having existed earlier in the war as a reconnaissance unit,[114] it was now reformed as a bomber squadron from the detached 199 Squadron 'C' Flight and a 'trawl' of Main Force Bomber Command squadrons for crews.[115] They commenced flying duties on 15 September 1944.[116] Initially equipped with Stirlings transferred from 199 Squadron,[117] they quickly converted to the Handley Page Halifax having completed only 87 sorties in 22 operations on Stirlings.[118] Michael Renaut, the newly appointed commanding officer of 171 Squadron, was not happy about some of the crews posted into his squadron from the Bomber Command trawl:

> Fourteen Halifax crews had been posted to me from 4 Group and, with few exceptions, I thought they were pretty awful. Evidently all squadrons in 4 Group had been asked to allocate one crew to 100 Group, 171 Squadron, and my guess was that this had enabled their squadron commanders to get rid of their unwanted garbage ... [I] demanded an interview with the AOC ... I put my cards on the table and said that I considered I had

been sent a load of poor crews and asked him to personally make a few changes. He reluctantly agreed and certain crews were removed from my squadron and better replacements sent.[119]

Gordon Mercier (IBCC Digital Archive).

Jim Feasey remembers how his pilot, Jack Philipson, saw a notice while they were at a Heavy Conversion Unit in Cambridgeshire. It was 'asking for crews for special duties in No. 100 Group so we volunteered thinking it might be supply dropping to the resistance'.[120] Initially with 199 Squadron, they were the first crew to transfer to 171 Squadron.[121] Their first six operations were on Stirlings, 'on our fourth trip we survived an attack by a ME210 fighter … my 4 guns jamming in the process'.[122] Another gunner, Gordon Mercier, recalls his transfer to 171 Squadron:

we did five trips at Snaith ... and the CO called us in the office and sat us down and said, 'You're posted'. ... I can remember the skipper saying, 'what have we done wrong?' He said, 'You've done nothing wrong ... you're the most experienced crew and we've been told to choose the most experienced crew to send them to a new squadron being formed called 171 Squadron in Norfolk.[123]

Ken Chapman didn't volunteer; he was recruited without his knowledge.[124] While on leave, an appeal went up for volunteers for special duties; no one stepped forward being worried what 'special duties' might involve. When Ken Chapman returned from leave, he discovered lots had been drawn and he, and one other, were being transferred to 171 Squadron.[125]

Ernie Hughes was serving at a training unit between tours. He and his friend, Bob Ledicott, both flight engineers, were often 'downing the odd pint'[126] and bemoaning their 'routine jobs',[127] wishing for a return to operational flying:

It was when Bob was on leave that a notice came out asking for volunteers to serve in a new squadron being formed for special duties. This is our chance, I thought, and went to the C.O.s office. He was pleased at my offer to go, but couldn't tell me anything about the new squadron.[128]

Ernie Hughes also informed the CO that 'Flight Sergeant Ledicott would also wish to go, Sir, but he is on leave at the moment'. So his name was also included for transfer. When Bob returned and Ernie Hughes greeted him with the good news, 'Bob nearly exploded "You idiot!" he shouted among a torrent of unkind words. "I've just got engaged"'. But their transfer to 171 was settled and they arrived in December 1944.[129]

The motto for the new squadron was *Per dolum defendimus* – 'we defend by confusion' or 'confound the enemy'.[130] The choice of motto, and indeed the motif associated with it, is an interesting one. Unusually, the correspondence between Michael Renaut and

J D Heaton-Armstrong (with responsibility for RAF Heraldry at the Chester Herald), has survived. The first approach was made by Michael Renaut in September 1944, requesting a squadron badge. His initial enquiry was cautious stating, 'I am not at liberty to discuss the role of the Squadron, as it is engaged on work of a most secret nature. I would suggest, however, a shield or Hermes, with flashes of lightning, as the Squadron is engaged on work of a Signals nature'.[131]

In response, JD Heaton-Armstrong suggests 'if something generally symbolic of signals will meet your wishes ... Hermes and the head of Hermes have already been taken for badges, but there is no demi Hermes holding, or in front of, lightning. Would you like this?'[132] Having received a positive reaction from Michael Renaut, a sketch was then sent for his approval. While very positive about the sketch, discussions continued with Michael Renaut ultimately suggesting an alternative idea:

> Since writing to you previously I have given considerable thought to this matter and submit another suggestion, for which a sketch is enclosed. In the centre is a black German Eagle with black cross on a white background on its white breast. Bars in silver confront the Eagle.[133]

Michael Renaut, apologised for the inconvenience, explained that the new idea 'depicts more clearly the type of work upon which we are engaged'.[134] The Chester Herald appeared unruffled, responded 'would not your latest suggestion be best symbolized by placing a portcullis in front of an eagle displayed? I do not know whether your functions are stopping the Hun eagle as much as interfering with his messages, so that it is difficult for me to judge how far the suggestions are appropriate'.[135] Surprised by this remarkably prescient interpretation of the Squadron's work, Michael Renaut agreed the 'portcullis would perhaps be even more suitable. It is essential that the portcullis be silver. I cannot give Squadron details but can go as far as to say that confounding the enemy and denying him his prey symbolises our type of work' (the insistence on silver reflected the Squadron role in Window operations). [136]

Michael Renaut then suggested a motto; 'we bar thee from thy prey'.[137] J D Heaton-Armstrong was unimpressed: 'I am not taken with the motto as it stands. It seems rather long and more of a statement of fact than a motto. Perhaps you can give it further thought.'[138] Michael Renaut, who then consulted his Squadron leaders finally conceded, 'I am afraid that all efforts by the Squadron to suggest a motto have failed, and I am wondering if it would be possible for you to think of something?'[139] With the war nearly at an end, Michael Renaut was rather less guarded with his words and continued: 'the motto we want should convey the intention of confounding the enemy defences and so preventing his interception of our attacking aircraft'.[140] J D Heaton-Armstrong responded, 'would the Latin for "confound the enemy" do for your motto?'.[141] This was agreed. However, it was now 18 April 1945, and the war was almost over. Indeed, the very day the badge was sent for official sanction[142] was the day on which 171 Squadron was disbanded (27 July 1945). The Squadron badges have since been produced despite this.[143]

On 21 October 1944, the first two of the new Halifax IIIs (NA674 and NA107) were delivered to 171 Squadron.[G] They went directly to work, flying operations the same day.[144] 171 Squadron crews, new to the Halifax, were sent to a Conversion Unit to familiarise themselves with the aircraft, mostly at 1659 Conversion Unit (HCU) at Topcliffe.[145] Generally scheduled to be a combination of classroom sessions with 14 hours of day and night flying, conversion took around a fortnight to complete.[146] But not always.[147] In October 1944, Jack Philipson went to 1659 HCU, Topcliffe for conversion: 'we got copies of the Pilot's Notes before going up there from North Creake. Seven days in and out (9.55 hours flying) and you were a Halifax crew'.[148]

All crews completed conversion training in November 1944.[149] The equipment modifications on the Halifaxes, needed for their new role, were found to be a rather larger job than anticipated.[150] Consequently, it would be the end of November before all 20 Halifax

---

G Both these aircraft were subsequently lost (see Appendix one).

IIIs had been delivered to the Squadron.[151] The transition from Stirlings to Halifaxes for groundcrew was reasonably straight-forward, as engines and the RCM were the same.[152]

199 Squadron Halifax RG388 EX-S at RAF North Creake 1945 (John Reid Collection).

The Halifax, a staple of Bomber Command operations from 10 March 1941,[153] is often mistaken for the better-known Lancaster with which it shares a twin tail. Not well regarded when first introduced, it rapidly gained the reputation of being grossly underpowered and, more worryingly 'a killer'.[154] The rudder design could frequently promote fatal 'rudder stall' at low speeds, particularly when attempting the corkscrew manoeuvre when it often caused 'an uncontrollable (and unrecoverable) dive.' [155] Subsequent modifications eliminated the problems and the Halifax became an excellent aircraft,[156] much liked by crews.[157] Particularly, when fitted with four Bristol Hercules engines as the performance was greatly improved;[158] as Jack Philipson observed, 'the Halifax rattled and bounced but it was fast'.[159] Indeed, the Halifax could reach speeds of 215mph at 20,000 feet and at lower heights 280mph could be achieved.[160] Jack Philipson remembers:

> After dropping the bombs and turning for home instead of throttling back a little I would just touch the elevator trim. Slowly the speed would build up, so after a quarter of an hour or so you could be up to 180 m.p.h. (faster if you got under

10,000 feet). We used to catch up the Main Force Lancs (who flew at 150-160mph) on the way home.[161]

Pete Thompson's father, Wilf Thompson, a wireless operator at RAF North Creake, would often relate the story of a fellow North Creake crew who were out on a test flight. On seeing a Lancaster they drew up alongside it waving at the crew. The pilot of the Halifax then feathered one of his engines and pulled away, leaving the Lancaster in, metaphorically speaking, its dust.[162] Certainly, hyperbole is at play here, but it has the ring of truth, and one is inevitably reminded of young men in performance cars at traffic lights today.

199 Squadron began its conversion to the Halifax in February 1945, with their first operation on this type being on the 21 February.[163] The process of conversion was completed during March, 'having severely restricted its activities during February'.[164] Bernie How, reflecting on his conversion to the Halifax commented:

> I think it was lighter [than the Stirling] and it was probably a little bit more compact. Yeah. It was a lovely aircraft ... I loved the Stirling and I think the whole crew did. Probably when we was taken off, I wouldn't say it was tears but we were disappointed that we weren't going to fly a Stirling anymore but the Halifax was good.[165]

* * *

By mid-2012, I was beginning to grow in confidence about my grasp of the history of the station. Few books discussed it in any detail, but I was starting to piece together the nuggets of information I was finding, into a reasonably coherent picture. My knowledge was boosted by events such as a visit from the Airfield Research Group. And informed by meeting locals such as Tony Nelson (with his huge scratch-built

Stirling bomber)[H] and Teddy Mauffe, whose family had moved to the area just before the war and had regular visits from RAF North Creake personnel. Our burgeoning presence on social media was also generating much interest in our project. It would often engender visits from interested parties, Stephen Squires among them. Stephen would be a constant source of support through the build and beyond. Initially, he wanted to metal detect our garden; we were happy for him to do so and he turned up much that was interesting, including a bomb fuse!

Meanwhile the works continued, the kitchen was removed and sold on eBay, the plumbers had returned and the electrics were progressing beyond first fixes. We had been very lucky when Ian Foreman had introduced us to his electrician friend, Stephen White, who had arrived and assessed our electrics. He pointed out that the building was still essentially functioning as two separate flats with separate consumer boards. He then proceeded to rip out the electrics leading to our downstairs lavatory as he couldn't, in good conscience, leave us using them. Steve made us feel safe and confident. He would tell us when our desired use of reclaimed fittings did not comply with safety regulations, and he would make them fit when he was confident they did. He never made us feel foolish for wanting to preserve an airfield fitting, such as when I wanted to fit a wall-mounted Anglepoise over a kitchen unit as 'it was from the armoury in North Creake'. It was rewired and wired into the circuit. He even started to arrive, unannounced, with switches and fittings he'd removed from other houses and thought might be useful to us.

On 31 August 2013, I was made redundant. The redundancy payment, although not generous for 15 years' service, would be useful. On Sunday 1 September, the start of a new academic year, I gave the talk at Blickling Hall on behalf of the RAF 100 Group Association on the subject of the role of the RAF 100 Group in the Second World War. I was talking, not lecturing. It was, in the short term, unpaid and insecure. A fine summary of how I felt about my life. I walked in

---

H Tony Nelson has been a keen supporter of the Control Tower project, bringing along his Stirling Bomber model (which forms part of his Norfolk Model Air Force) to open days and painting an incredibly detailed plan of the Airfield Site for our living room wall.

front of the small group assembled to hear me speak. I opened the box I was carrying that contained the Window that Claire had found in our garden. I then began to explain what it was, and for what purpose it was used.

Since the early foundation meetings of the RAF 100 Group, it had been decided that it would take responsibility for the offensive use of Window.[166] This offensive use fell to the 'heavy' squadrons within the Group. Through experimentation at TRE, it had been discovered that a small force of aircraft 'Windowing' with precision at a high rate – one bundle every two or three seconds – could simulate the approach of a much larger bomber force.[167] This 'spoof' would almost always precede the appearance of the Main Force. Its presence would lead the enemy to believe that the spoof was in fact the main attack. Forcing the German controllers to commit fighters to intercept it, [168] and thereby, placing the night-fighters on the 'wrong foot, and unable to get back to intercept the bomber stream when the error had been detected.'[169] With the introduction of this new method of confounding the German defences, the Special Window Force (SWF) was born.

On the night of 14/15 July 1944, the SWF flew its first sortie made up of available aircraft from the Group's heavy squadrons.[1170] Jack Philipson remembers getting into his aircraft and being 'greeted by this great stack of brown paper parcels holding Window'.[171] The method adopted for the jettisoning Window involved up to 24 heavy bombers flying in two lines. Each line, or row, had 12 aircraft with 2¼ miles between them. The second line of bombers would be 30 miles behind the first.[172] Each bomber jettisoned one bundle of Window every two seconds[173] (in contrast, Main Force crews usually dropped one bundle every two minutes[174]). In this way the formation would sow a radar echo-reflector the size of a bomber stream of some 500 aircraft.[175] The enemy would see on his radar a large force of aircraft approaching, whose head would suddenly divide into several prongs, each of which

---

I   RAF 100 Group had no dedicated force for Window operations, the Special Window Force was made up of 'heavies' from 100 Group bomber squadrons that could be diverted from other RCM roles on any particular night (see, RAF 100 Group: October 1944: ORB: 2).

pointed at a vital objective. He now had to guess which of these prongs constituted the real menace.[176]

The maiden Halifax SWF operation was on the night of 21 October 1944.[177] 171 Squadron Halifaxes took-off but were quickly recalled as the weather was deteriorating:[178]

> It would appear, however, that one of the aircraft had failed to receive the recall signal and had pressed on to the target where it was erroneously plotted by the Hun controllers as a force of some thirty heavy bombers approaching the Reich – a successful if unintended start for the Squadron![179]

The 171 Squadron ORB records that 'after two aircraft had got airborne, the operation was cancelled. One of the Halifaxes had even reached its target before the recall message had been received'.[180] On the same or a similar occasion, Bert Berry, the wireless operator[181] on Halifax NA107 6Y-T,[182] remembers that after refuelling at Manston in Kent and grabbing 'a bite to eat from the Church Army mobile canteen'[183] they took off:

> It appears that all of the No. 100 Group's Heavies had been instructed to land at Manston, so things were pretty chaotic. Eventually, we got airborne again and the second stage of the operation was under way. Having completed our mission and a further four hours of flying, we were on the return journey home. It was only then that I picked up our aircraft call sign on W/T and the message 'return to base'. As we were already doing that, we wondered what on earth was going on.[184]

At the de-briefing they discovered that they were the only aircraft to complete the operation. It would appear they were 'out of range of the radio transmission when the "ops cancelled" broadcast was made'.[185] The following day the reports from Intelligence revealed that this solitary aircraft had been reported as a 'considerable bomber stream, with German fighter stations alerted for action'.[186]

These false impressions could last up to an hour after the spoofing aircraft had passed. While under the effects of Window, 'any estimate of the number of enemy aircraft present could be arrived at only by guesswork'.[187] This important, but 'a mite arm-aching'[188] work, came at the cost of exhausting crews. Jack Philipson, a pilot with 171 Squadron, recalls that the usual load of Window was 1,600lbs, sometimes carried with '3,500lbs of bombs ... extra fuel in case we had to stay out longer ... an SO [special operator], 12 jamming sets [and] a cathode oscilloscope to read the wavelength of the signals we jammed'.[189] The flight engineer would use the front chute to dispense 'N' type Window against the Würzburg radar at the rate of 12 bundles per minute, and the special operator would use the rear chute dispensing 'S' type ('about a meter and a half long and 1½ inches wide') at the rate of 36 bundles a minute.[190] Harry Freegard explains that it came in unglued cardboard boxes that were stacked along the fuselage; some were reels, three in each box which 'initially had a silk parachute but later changed to paper'.[191] Once thrown out of the aircraft, they hit the slipstream, dismantling the box and causing the reels to unwind into a long streamer of Window.[192] Don Prutton, Windowing with 233 Squadron at RAF Oulton, had a more relaxed approach to the quantities launched through the chute:

> In practice we knelt or sat on the floor surrounded by the mountain of bundles and when the navigator gave the word the plane started weaving gently and we started pushing the stuff out fast. When the time came to increase the rate we just went even faster but whether it was correct or not we never knew.[193]

Robert Cockburn, the director of TRE, recognised that 'dispensing Window was very unpopular with operators'[194] and it's not difficult to understand why, when some months, the heavy squadrons of 100 Group were dropping more than 200 tons of Window.[195] On one occasion in March 1945, a 'poor crew had to throw out – by hand – nearly two tons of Window.'[196] A contemporary 100 Group report playfully illustrates that 200 tons of Window, 'if all strips were laid end to end … would go round the world three times',[197] or as it further explains, be equal to an area 'of several hundred thousand Group Captains' carpets!'[198] This was why, Robert Cockburn concluded 'the development of an automatic dispensing machine[J] receive[ed] much attention'.[199]

Aside from the crews' discomfort, the effects of Window could be dramatic. Raids in December 1944 illustrated that 'very large number[s] of fighters reacted to a simple Feint force … [forcing] controllers to make hasty and ill-conceived decisions'.[200] However, the success of a Window spoof was reliant on the skill of pilots and navigators, to ensure that their aircraft were always in the correct position at the right time. Sometimes their abilities came in for criticism, as illustrated by a memo from a particularly officious observer at 100 Group HQ:

> The aircraft are spread on a front of about 60 miles instead of 10 miles … so far off track that they might just as well have stayed on the ground … the instances quoted are specific ones but every plot shows a number of aircraft whose track keeping and/or time keeping, is defective. The full effect of the small

---

J Charles Joseph Merryfull, born in Adelong New South Wales, during the latter months of 1944 devised and made, along with others (Fred Nieman, Ted Cattell (Nieman: 6/4/2021)), an automatic Window dispenser while serving as a pilot with 199 Squadron at RAF North Creake. Vic Flowers remembers '[it] was a masterpiece of welded mild steel and moving parts' (Brettingham: 2002: 283). In February 1945, Joe Merryfull was detached to command the newly formed Window Research Section of the Bomber Support Development Unit at RAF Swanton Morely (RAF 100 Group: ORB: February 1945). While results were encouraging, 'no entirely satisfactory design became available for use' (Cockburn: 1945: 58) and testing continued. There is doubt as to whether a dispenser entered service before the end of the war, although there is some unconfirmed evidence that 199 Squadron were equipped with them (Streetly: 1978: 105). On 8 July 1945, Mosquito PZ178 with Joe Merryfull and Francis Grady on board took off from the Swanton Morely to test an adaptation of the machine (warmemorialsregister.nsw.gov.au). 'At 1018, debris from the Mosquito fell near the Norfolk village of Docking, some 14 miles northeast of King's Lynn' (aviationmuseumwa.org.au). The aircraft had suffered a catastrophic structural failure and had plunged to the ground. A subsequent report into the accident concluded that:
> the port 'Window' tank had detached, due to failure of its attachment beam. As the tank fell away, it is believed it struck the tailplane and caused the Mosquito to dive out of control. Instinctively, it is thought, the pilot pulled back on the control column imposing severe 'g' forces on the starboard wing, which then broke off (aviationmuseumwa.org.au).
> Francis Grady was buried in his hometown of St Helens in Lancashire and Charles Merryfull is interred at Cambridge City Cemetery. Before enlisting Charles Merryfull had purchased land in Peakhurst, Australia and with his untimely death his parents constructed a house in his honour named 'Stirling' in commemoration of their son's career with the RAAF and the aircraft he flew (warmemorialsregister.nsw.gov. au).

> Window force cannot be realised if a percentage of aircraft do
> not perform efficiently ... a copy of plots should be sent to each
> station and they should be required to investigate and report
> to this Headquarters on the reasons for those navigational
> failures'.[201]

Interestingly, the reply is not so forthright and suggests that the 'accuracy of navigation has certainly improved' and identifies examples of 'particularly good one[s]'.[202] And there were many good examples. A contemporary report illustrates that on the night of the 14/15 October 1944, when over 100 aircraft attacked Duisburg and 200 aircraft attacked Brunswick, it was assumed that the Duisburg force would escape with light losses but Brunswick force would be at serious risk. Consequently, a Window spoof was organised in the hope of drawing away some night-fighters. The results were 'beyond expectation',[203] as it 'diverted the enemy's attention away from the Brunswick force almost entirely'.[204] Similarly, on 6 November 1944, in an attack against Gravenhorst and Koblenz, a spoof to Gelsenkirchen caused five Gruppen to become airborne out of a total of seven that took off that night.[205]

From August 1944, RAF 100 Group adopted the tactic of 'conditioning'. This was where RCM would be flown but without an accompanying attack. The purpose of this approach was to 'keep the enemy night fighter organisation out of bed'[206] by forcing the Luftwaffe into a state of alertness. This would have two benefits. Immediately, it would waste enemy resources, but second, familiarity would induce a feeling of complacency about Allied activity, leaving the enemy vulnerable to attacks when they were off-guard.[K][207] Another change of tactics saw intruder Mosquitoes accompanying the SWF during October 1944. This was in order to add to the effect of the spoof, but then to take advantage of enemy reactions to the SWF and attack Luftwaffe

---

K Such a raid was ordered against Bremen on 18 August 1944 after a series of spoofs the previous nights (Streetly: 1978: 63).

night-fighters.[208] On two nights in December 1944, this tactic caused more Luftwaffe night-fighters to be shot down than bombers.[209]

By November 1944, such constantly-changing tactics had led the Luftwaffe to fly 'virtual standing patrols' after repeated attacks in the Ruhr area. To counter this the SWF employed a technique called 'saturation Windowing'.[210] This involved Windowing over the whole Ruhr in order to 'blind the enemy as to a specific target'. This tactic was later employed on nights when the Main Force was not flying, just to confuse the enemy, frequently forcing them to respond when there were no operations.[211] This kept the Luftwaffe flying, exhausted their pilots and wasted precious Axis resources.[212] These measures achieved such levels of success that in February 1945, an instruction was received at RAF North Creake, that future stand-downs would only be considered as a result of adverse weather conditions that rendered flying impossible.[213] Such conditions had hampered operations in January 1945, when snow had prevented North Creake crews from flying, and it had not 'been possible to harass the enemy to the extent one would have liked'.[214] But such weather was rare.

The Halifax, with its improved speed, lift and ceiling height, made the dropping of bombs, as well as Window, a possibility for the first time.[215] 171 Squadron began bombing operations from February 1945, with 199 Squadron, once converted to Halifaxes, quickly following their lead:[216]

> this new departure was met with great enthusiasm among the crews, as they felt – and rightly so – that they were now hitting the Hun – if only in a limited way, instead of flying over his territory and protecting the main force – indeed a most important job, but one which does not give the same feeling of satisfaction as that of destroying enemy installations.[217]

Indeed such was the success of this development that Edward Addison requested further aircraft for the 171 & 199 Squadrons to 'exploit this method of distracting the Hun by bombing a 'feint' target not far removed from the route, or from the real target'.[218] He argued that with bombing included within their repertoire, the Group would cause a 'sting' as well as a 'buzz'[219] if:

> it were possible for these aircraft, or some of them, to drop an appreciable load of bombs at the end of their penetration, the Hun's attention would be held for a considerably longer period that if the sorties were entirely sterile.[220]

Consequently, March 1945 saw 171 Squadron's greatest effort; it was the 'highest ever seen in the history of 100 Group',[221] with Edward Addison commenting that they had been generally 'able to marshal sufficient aircraft for the purpose of diversions … by dint of "flogging" our squadrons somewhat mercilessly'.[222] As a result, crews at RAF North Creake were flying operationally far more regularly than their Main Force equivalents. This regularity, and the practice of flying in weather that would most frequently have grounded Main Force aircraft, spurred Norman Bray, North Creake's station commander to comment at a briefing in early 1945:

> Main Force has been stood down due to bad weather, but we fly, gentlemen, even when the sparrows are walking.[223]

It was arduous work.

We were no stranger to arduous work ourselves; we were working on the Control Tower every spare hour. Daytime progress was inevitably hampered by the frequent questions from the builders on-site. And there were many trades, including sparks, plumbers and carpenters. Therefore, for us, the most productive time was late into the evening. Works were continuing in every room and my redundancy money was slipping through my fingers like the proverbial sand. To arrest the decline in our finances, Claire and I decided to share a part-time job at the Three Horseshoes in Warham. Having known Iain Salmon, the landlord, for years, he was happy for us to choose which one of us was on shift as long as one of us was there. It helped a little.

Of more help was Claire's consultancy work (setting up a website and online learning materials) and the income from Wedding Wheels-next-the-Sea. However, none of this was sufficiently lucrative to allow us to complete the build.

Nonetheless, we continued with the work in the optimistic belief that it would 'come good'. Insulated plasterboard went up and was plastered and the plumbing continued. On the outside, Steve repaired the render as effectively as he could (re-rendering was out of the question financially[L]). Claire and I were run ragged trying to complete jobs either just ahead or just after the trades. In preparation for the approaching December, I set about fitting new fire surrounds and backs to the existing chimney breasts. I had attempted to repair the bedroom fireplace shortly after we moved in, when we realised how expensive the electric heating was to run. I realised, having ripped-out a huge built-in headboard, that the chimney breast needed significant rebuilding and repair. I consequently retreated, only to return to it in stages throughout the build. The living room fire surround and back (a 1930s single piece) would be straightforward, I assumed. However, it was too tall for the hole, and I had to replace the lintol higher up and repair the chimney breast. In time for the cold, we lit fires and in the long evenings reflected on money woes. However, just as concern was really taking hold, I received notice of the inheritance from my dad. It was a lot more than we expected.

Being the wise and sensible people we'd become, we set about deciding how to spend it all. Things that had been impossible dreams, suddenly became possibilities. We researched replica Crittall metal windows; the quotes were frightening, with one representative telling us it was the highest domestic quote he'd ever given. I laughed, he looked at me sternly and said, 'oh but I'm serious'. All the prices were, more or less, on a par. We chose our favourite supplier and ordered them.

Now all seemed possible. We set a date for, what was now becoming, an ambitious opening event. It would be the weekend of

---

L   This is never acceptable as water always finds a way through repairs and we struggled with the ingress of water until we had the whole building re-rendered just before, and between, Covid lockdowns.

the 70th Anniversary of D-Day; the first operation from RAF North Creake. It was more than six months away; loads of time.

The works went up a gear. Alan 'Streaky' Bacon, who had moved into our workshop rent-free in exchange for flooring it and building shelves, was now our resident carpenter, and he was set to work on various jobs beyond my carpentry skills level. He was joined by Tom 'the bike' Hodges, another carpenter who came to help lay the reclaimed parquet flooring. This was a job I'd done before in our previous house, but by February 2014 we had realised that six months wasn't long at all, and we needed help. Gardeners, painters and labourers followed. Our bank account began to show the strain.

Design had always been something that came reasonably easy to Claire and me. We could always see in our mind's eye what it was that we were trying to achieve. Planning it out, generally, revealed that we both had very similar ideas in our heads. This process was often aided by alcohol. I'm sure this would not be regarded as advisable by the Chief Medical Officer, but luckily this was before they reduced the levels of 'safe drinking'. We found it beneficial to use a beer or two as a reward for a good day's work; it also had the advantage of promoting imagination. There was a point of diminishing returns and when too much beer was consumed, often our imaginative ideas did not survive the scrutiny of the cold light of day. Nonetheless, some of our most inspired ideas emerged this way. However, they always meant extra work; no idea ever seemed to save time, such as deciding to move a bedroom wall to make room for a dressing table, or blocking up a door in the utility room so we could build a larder. It was always more work. But with worthwhile results.

Late in February 2014, the windows arrived and the second wave of chaos ensued. The days generally began with a slice of toast grabbed between arriving trades; eaten on any clear foot of surface that could be found, among piles of rubbish and detritus. We were now running to get ahead of the window installers. The first window was installed in the living room. It looked fantastic and we were struggling to contain our excitement. We then started to knock out the middle windows on the front elevation. These were blocked up in 1950, when the Control Tower first became a home, they had done it well. Eventually a hole appeared, and progress was made but with the installers waiting. When complete, we moved downstairs to open-up the second window, now with practise it went quicker; just in time for the installers to offer the new window up. Something was wrong. The window was too big for the hole. Not by a matter of adjustment, but by over a foot. Claire and I had made a significant error; we had assumed that the window in the middle upstairs was the same size as the window downstairs and ordered it as such. It wasn't. The installers suggested we get another one made, but that was incredibly expensive and, more importantly, the delay would take us beyond our opening date. Instead we would open up the hole. This presented problems as the lintol above the previous window was enormous (cast in situ) and the only way to get it out was to break it up. This would leave the building above unsupported. I sought advice and through discussion and observation, we worked out that there was support along the entire length of the front elevation, just below the balcony. So if the worst came to the worst, we would only lose a few courses of bricks. We went ahead and, in spite of huge forces being applied to that lintol, nothing above moved. Testament to the building's strength. The replacement lintol proved hard to source and eventually Mark Balderstone (with the van) was co-opted to pick one up from Norwich. Grant (plasterer and brick layer) was due to arrive that evening to replaster the window reveals; we begged him to put in the new lintol for us. He took on the job with relish, and at 9pm all was done and we were sharing beers of thanks. However, this was Friday evening, before the May Day Bank Holiday; the installers wouldn't be back until Tuesday, and we only had a sheet of polythene to protect us from the weather and to keep us secure. We went to the scarecrow festival in Wighton anyway.

May had arrived far faster than we had hoped. Our 'D-Day' was approaching worryingly quickly and there was still so much to do. Seventy years earlier things were just as busy. The RAF 100 Group had acquired RAF North Creake to home one of their jamming squadrons.[224] Equipped with jammers code-named 'Mandrel', their first use would be on 5 June 1944, in support of D-Day.[225]

NOTHING HEARD
SINCE TAKE-OFF

Halifax NA674 6Y-Q & Halifax NA111 6Y-Y

Just short of two months after commencing operations from RAF North Creake, 171 Squadron suffered its second failure to return.[1] On the 9 December 1944, six Halifaxes took off; all were airborne within 15 minutes.[2] Halifax NA674 6Y-Q was the last to take off at 17:35.[3] The estimated time of return was around 22:45,[4] but the 171 Squadron ORB records, 'one aircraft is missing, and up to midnight, no message has been received'.[5] The crew was:

> Stanley Albert Brown (RAF) Bomb Aimer, aged 22
> Thomas Anthony Victor Brown (RAF) Navigator, aged 21
> John James Villiers Higgins (RAF) Air-Gunner, aged 39
> John Herbert Hinton (RAF) Special Operator, aged 19
> John Kirkpatrick (RAF) Flight Engineer, aged 25
> Stanley James Moore (RAAF) Wireless Operator, aged 21
> Trevor Sutherland Powe (RAAF) Pilot, aged 21
> Henry Stanton (RAF) Air-Gunner, aged 20

Shortly after 'missing' had been recorded in the station ORB, Michael Renaut (commander of 171 Squadron) sat down to write the eight condolence letters.[A] Thus starting a process of communication that would go on for years.

First to reach the families were the telegrams. One such telegram, addressed to John Powe (Trevor Powe's father[B]) informed him that 'Trevor Sutherland Powe is missing as a result of air operations',[6] expressing 'sincere sympathy in your anxiety'.[7] Little more was received until April 1945, when the Royal Australian Air Force Casualty Section wrote that enquiries with the International Red Cross Committee have produced, 'no further news of your son'.[8] John Powe replied expressing his regret at the lack of news, and asked, with the end of war in Europe, any information of his son's operational 'exploits would be greatly appreciated'.[9] The Casualty Section responded, seeking to reassure the family that 'this Department will not relax its efforts to secure any evidence regarding the circumstances of the loss of his aircraft'.[10] Moreover, an official enquiry had been raised with the Missing, Research and Enquiry Service (MRES), but, they warned, 'its task will be prolonged and difficult'.[11]

On 18 September 1945, Trevor Powe, along with the rest of the crew, were presumed dead.[12]

MRES was the ultimate expression of the need to address missing aircrew. At the end of the war almost 42,000 aircrew were missing 'without trace' and their families, along with the wider public, wanted answers. MRES was an attempt at a co-ordinated response. Consequently, it:

A For the family of Trevor Powe, who lived in Sydney, Australia, the letter from Michael Renaut written on 10 December 1944 would not be received until 3 February 1945. Trevor also had a friend, Helen Stevens, in Sydney, that he wished to be informed should anything happen to him. She must have been important, perhaps his lover and donor of the lock of hair found among his personal effects? (naa.gov.au: undated).

B A copy of this and all other correspondence was also sent to Helen Stevens and both continued to be informed until the last communication from the Casualty Section was sent out in 1948 (naa.gov.au: undated).

took the search to the battlefields, and systematically scoured millions of square miles to account individually for and bury their list of missing men and women. Unlike anything that had gone before, they began with a list of every known missing person, and as they were found, they were ticked off.[C13]

On 2 December 1945, John Powe writes to the Casualty Section in a tone of thinly veiled fury. He had a copy of a report, received via an unnamed relative of a crew member. Quoting at length, he outlined where the aircraft crashed and where the crew members are buried and that more information would follow as it was discovered.[14] He signs off; 'I cannot understand why we have not had the same information passed on to us here'.[15] The RAAF Casualty Section were now clearly in a difficult position, and they attempted to pull their lines of information together. In defence of the Casualty Section, it does appear inappropriate that the author of the original report shared this information before the investigation was closed,[16] suggesting, perhaps, that someone connected with the investigation had a personal interest in the case. However, the RAAF Casualty Section were certainly on the back foot, and their reply of 1 January 1946 was an attempt to make up ground. Quoting from a signal 'recently received',[D17] they state:

[MRES] was instructed to ascertain from the German citizen any fact concerning the seven unknown members, and otherwise secure any evidence concerning the burial place and identity of your late son and his comrades. The signal concluded with reference to a letter dated the 23rd October, 1945, which has not yet been received by this Department. It is desired to assure you that it was not intended to withhold the above details from you but, as the information was inconclusive and moreover, as some correspondence dated October were still

---

C   Constituted on 26 July 1945 (Spark: 2010: 186) it calculated that 41,881 aircrew had gone missing over Europe during the war. By 1950, 23,881 had been discovered, and another 9,281 were now formally 'lost at sea' which left 8,719 unaccounted for (Hadaway: 2008: 7).

D   Actually received on the 5 December 1945 (RAAF Overseas HQ: 5/12/1945: unpaginated).

arriving late in December, it was considered that the missing letter may have given more detailed information.[18]

The casualty officer now also addressed the request for information on the nature of the operation that night. Even, perhaps, revealing a little more than he should: '[they] were engaged on an anti-radar operation … using equipment with which to render the enemy radar inefficient and so enable the main attacking bomber force to remain undetected for as long as possible'.[19] In the meantime, the Casualty Section were in communication with RAAF Overseas HQ, regarding the missing letter, demanding a replacement 'copy urgently'[20] as it was 'not, repeat, not received'.[21] It subsequently arrived on 11 January. They wrote to John Powe informing him that they were in receipt of the missing correspondence and 'as anticipated, the text conveyed the information' as outlined in John Powe's earlier letter.[22] The story of the crash and what happened to the crew then emerges.

On 9 December 1944, Halifax NA674 6Y-Q was on a bomber support operation, Windowing in the direction of Koblenz.[23] At around 20.00 hours, the aircraft flew over a German spotting position near Lutzerath. Shortly after, the Halifax was hit by an anti-aircraft gun barrage, 'caught fire and burned violently',[24] crashing at Kennfus, 12km SW of Cochem.[25]

On 19 April 1945, a patrol of the 671st Field Artillery Battalion of the United States Army,[26] came upon men working on the Halifax wreck. The officer, having seen the condition of the aircraft, reported that 'the end was quick and there was no prolonged suffering by any of the men in the plane'.[27] Subsequent investigation revealed that an aluminium tag, taken from the wreckage, identified the aircraft as Halifax NA674.[28]

On 12 September 1946, I Clowes of MRES, visited Herr Bambusch[E], the Burgermeister,[F] in Lutzerath. During an interview, he

---

E The Burgermeister is cited in this document with two alternative spellings of his surname; Bambusch and Hambusch. Another document (Sturch: 19/10/1945: unpaginated) has an additional alternative spelling; 'Hambuch'. It is now difficult to determine which is correct, but the one chosen for this text is the most frequently used.

F Burgermeister literally translates as 'town master' and would be similar to a British mayor.

determined that once the aircraft had stopped burning, the Wehrmacht had taken charge and 'four very badly burned bodies were extracted from the remains'.[29] They were buried without coffins at Lutzerath Cemetery. The Germans knew 'or guessed'[30] that there were seven bodies in the aircraft, but heavy snow prevented them from recovering them all.[31]

The Burgermeister argued, that because of bad weather, he was prevented from giving instruction to remove the remaining bodies until 20 April 1945.[32] Two further bodies and 'the remains of a third'[33] were subsequently recovered from the wreckage. It was during this recovery that they were witnessed by the US patrol.[G] These remains were also buried at Latzerath Cemetery, close to the other four.[34] A Catholic priest conducted the ceremony.[35] However, Herr Bambusch was unable to say in 'what order these airmen were buried',[36] and had no idea of their names, as the documents and possessions were taken by the Wehrmacht.[37]

MRES then paid a visit to Herr Schnieder, the Burgermeister of Urschmitt, seven kilometers from Lutzerath. It was discovered that in the second week of December 1944, 'an English flyer had been found in a tree in a field near the village. Apparently, his parachute had opened too late and he had broken his neck'.[38] He was buried in a sack on 15 December 1944 by the Wehrmacht, in Urschmitt Cemetery. The grave was 'marked with a single cross bearing the following inscription, 'Heir ruht ein Englischer Soldat.'[39] This 'English Soldier' was identified as RAF air gunner, Henry Stanton.[40]

The MRES team reached the decision that the only means of identifying the seven airmen buried at Lutzerath Cemetery was to organise an exhumation on 2 March 1948.[41] Although the report does not confirm that the only airman buried in a separate grave at Lutzerath is Thomas Brown,[42] it seems accepted as they concentrated on the identities of the six remaining airmen.[43] Trevor Powe and Stanley Moore were buried independently, but with a shared marker cross. Their identity was confirmed by their Australian battle dress, however,

G Although the dates are a day out and do not entirely correspond.

it was 'impossible to say which is which'.[44] The remaining four airmen were in a collective grave, with two coffins, one of which contained the remains of three crew members.[45] None of these four airmen could be separately identified.[46]

All eight were reinterred at Rheinberg War Cemetery. Henry Stanton and Thomas Brown separately, Trevor Powe and Stanley Moore together, and Stanley Brown, John Higgins, John Hinton and John Kirkpatrick in a collective grave.[47] Individual headstones mark the spot.

Stanley Brown, the bomb aimer on Halifax NA674 6Y-Q, was from Mile End, London.[48] His epitaph simply reads, 'at rest'.[49] Stanley Brown arrived with his crew at RAF North Creake on 1 October 1944. Before arriving in Norfolk, they had crewed-up at RAF Moreton-in-Marsh, Gloucestershire, and initially served with 158 Squadron at RAF Lisset, Yorkshire.[50] Very little is known of the navigator, Thomas Brown, born in Stretford, Lancashire.[51] Similarly, little is recorded of John Higgins, but at 39, he was old by aircrew standards.[52]

John Hinton from Walthamstow, London,[53] the special operator, was from a family of tobacconists.[54] John Hinton had been a member of the Air Training Corps before joining up.[55] One of four children, his sister Doreen,[H] while 'prone to exaggeration and flamboyancy',[56] would later comment that John 'had gone down with HMS Hood!'[57] Jo Burt, who remembers his aunt saying this, wonders if 'perhaps, it was too painful a memory for her. I am not aware that it was ever mentioned again'.[58]

The flight engineer, John Kirkpatrick, was a stand-in for Frederick Swatton, the regular flight engineer who was absent for an unknown reason.[59] From Belfast, John Kirkpatrick, had transferred to 171 Squadron from No. 42 Base at RAF Marston Moor in Yorkshire.[60] Before arriving at North Creake he was awarded the Distinguished

---

H Doreen Hinton, better known as Pip Hinton, married into a family of performers and achieved fame in her own right, particularly on the children's television programme *Crackerjack*. Pip's nephew, Jo Burt, is a guitarist who played, among many others, with Black Sabbath. Pip's sons are, actor, David Burt and director and producer, Michael Burt (Neely: 21/10/2020).

I Jeff Neely, a relative by marriage, believes that Doreen Hinton may 'have conflated an event or two'. A Cousin of John Hinton (special operator on 6Y-Q), Robert Hinton served with the Royal Navy and was lost on HMS Veteran, along with the entire crew, when it was sunk by a German U-Boat on 26 September 1942 (Neely: 21/10/2020).

Flying Cross in recognition of gallantry and devotion to duty in the execution of air operations.[61] His epitaph reads, 'we mourn our loss'.[62] Frank Swatton, who should have been the flight engineer on the night, survived the war.[63]

The wireless operator Stanley Moore was from New South Wales, Australia. Before enlisting he had completed years one and two of a degree at the University of Sydney Faculty of Economics.[64] His epitaph reads, 'dearly loved son of Richard and Doris Moore of Sydney'.[65] In February 1945, two months after Stanley Moore's death, his father, Richard Moore, nominated John Stanton (Harold Stanton's father) to receive Stanley's bicycle.[66] Next-of-kin living outside of Britain were advised of the difficulties of storage and the impracticalities of sending such articles overseas.[67] Such items would be held for three months after aircrew were posted missing. If they remained missing beyond this time, the articles were sold and the proceeds passed onto the next-of-kin.[68] Alternatively, the relative could nominate someone to receive the item. In this case John Stanton was the benefactor.[69]

Fellow countryman and pilot, Trevor Powe, not only shared his home nation with Stanley Moore, but also his hometown; living in the 'adjoining suburbs of Willoughby and Chatswood on the lower North Shore of Sydney'.[70] With less than eight months separating their ages, it does not seem unlikely that they knew each other.[71] Trevor Powe enlisted on 20 June 1942, arriving, after pilot's training, in Britain on 31 July 1943.[72] His epitaph reads, 'our dearest possession – his memory'.[73]

Air gunner Henry 'Geordie' Stanton was born in Gateshead, County Durham.[74] He is commemorated on the Guide Post War Memorial, Choppington;[75] an honour he shares with Sidney Stuart, a flight engineer, who was killed on the night of 7/8 March 1945, on Halifax NA111 6Y-Y, also of 171 Squadron. It was the fourth aircraft of this squadron to fail to return;[76] 'nothing being heard after take off'[77].

The Station ORB describes the night of 7/8 March 1945 thus:

Three Stirlings and ten Halifaxes of 199 Squadron and two Halifax of 171 squadron were detailed to form a Mandrel

Screen – and ten Halifax of 171 Squadron for a combined Window/Mandrel/Bombing Patrol. All took off. Three Stirlings and eleven Halifax completed their Mandrel patrols, jamming from 19:25 to 21:40 hours at 17,500/15,000 feet … nine Halifax completed the combined patrol discharging Window and jamming from 20:10 to 21:06 hours at 20,000 feet down to 12,000 feet. Bombs were dropped on Munster. 199 'Y' returned early with artificial horizon u/s. 171 'H' landed at Abingdon. 171 'Y' missing.[78]

The crew was posted to 171 Squadron on 1 October 1944, having been transferred from No. 51 Squadron at RAF Snaith, Yorkshire.[79] The special operator was Donald Biggar, who was allocated to the crew shortly after their arrival at RAF North Creake. Donald Biggar had been posted from 214 Squadron at RAF Oulton in Norfolk on 18 October.[80] They flew their first operation together on 5 December 1944, and were detailed to fly regularly from then on. 7 March 1945 was their 17th operation.[81] The Main Force targeted Dessau, Hemmingsted and Harburg with 171 Squadron supporting the raid to Dessau as part of the Special Window Force. They also operated Mandrel and dropped a bomb load on Munster.[82] The aircraft was attacked and shot down by a German night-fighter, believed to be either Oblt Hans-Heinrich Breitfeld 9/NJG5 or Oblt Rehkate III/NJG5.[83] The Halifax crashed at Langschede south-east of Dortmund.[84] Once again, for the unsuspecting families at home, telegrams were despatched. Those on board the aircraft were:

Neville Percy Baker (RAF) Air Gunner, aged 22
Donald Charlton Biggar (RAF) Special Operator, aged 24
Harold Alexander Coutts (RCAF) Bomb Aimer, aged 31
Alexander Wightman Ferme (RAF) Mid-Upper Gunner, aged 24
Sidney Stuart (RAF) Flight Engineer, aged 20
John Michael Stone (RAF) Pilot, aged 22
Kenneth George Thomas (RCAF) Navigator, aged 21
John Wyatt (RAF) Wireless Operator, aged 23

The April 1945 RAF 100 Group 'Operations' report, announces, in typically wartime language, some good news:

> flight Lieutenant Stone had been reported as safe. His wife was the first person to receive the news. Stone eventually arrived back at the Unit and was barely recognisable. He had been captured by the Huns who had removed his hair in one fell swoop and it was obvious that he had been given only very scant food rations. Stone had a good tale to relate on his treatment by the Huns, and this information must have proved very useful to the Air Ministry, by whom he was interrogated on arriving in this country.[85]

John Stone, the only survivor, believed he was 'protected by the armour plating of his seat and seat back'.[86] He was seriously injured, shattering his knees either in escaping the aircraft or on hitting the ground.[87] Knowing evasion was impossible with such injuries, he crawled to a farmhouse. After knocking at the door he was let in by a German citizen who gave him water and let him rest on his sofa. He phoned the authorities and while he waited for their arrival, he let John sleep in his own bed as he was clearly in pain (having to bend his knees on the sofa).[88]

The Gestapo picked him up and took him off to the central depot at Frankfurt,[J] where he was questioned. During this period of interrogation, he spent time in solitary confinement, was brutally beaten and given very little to eat or drink.[89] It would seem the Gestapo were suspicious as John was wearing his dress uniform under his flying kit.[90] The only reason he was wearing his best blue was because of the speed with which he was needed to stand-in for a pilot who had been taken ill.[91] After a week he was moved to a Stalagluft near the Baltic.[92] However, liberation arrived quickly. After the camp was heavily

---

J Aircrew brought down anywhere in Europe were first taken to the Central German Interrogation centre at Frankfurt-am-Main. While they were asked many questions, some of which were 'cleverly disguised or suggestive', they were only required to give their Name, Rank and Number. 'Those who were kept there longer than a day or two could reckon they were being useful to the Hun!' If not, you were quickly transferred to an aircrew prisoner of war camp or 'Stalagluft' (Renaut:1982:162).

bombed, taking advantage of the chaos, he simply walked out with a fellow RAF officer.[93] Unchallenged, he stole a bike en route to aid his escape, and 'in just a few miles the two pilots ran into the advancing American Forces'.[94]

He was repatriated to Britain on 3 April 1945.[95] He was interrogated by MI9,[K] an experience that deeply affected him as he did not feel believed. His son Jonathan Stone, muses 'when a pilot is the only survivor in the loss of an aircraft, of course there must be questions asked. Perhaps it is in the nature of "debriefing" that those doing the questioning are rather accusatory in their manner'.[96] The written outcome of this debriefing makes harrowing reading:

> We were proceeding on a course of approximately 350° on the last leg to the target. At 7½ minutes before zero hour, the Navigator F/O Thomas informed me over the intercom that we were ½ minute behind schedule and that we had 8 minutes to go. A minute later, we were attacked by fighter without previous warning from either of the gunners. My first order to put on parachutes was issued immediately. There was no acknowledgement from any of the crew. The F/E [flight engineer] then informed me that P/O [Port Outer] engine was on fire – intercom very faint. I acknowledged and feathered. A/C [aircraft] at this time was in steep spiral to port, which I was not able to control properly, as the rudder controls had been affected. I asked the B/A [bomb aimer], F/O H.A. Coutts to come up and help me hold the aileron control while I tried to put the fire out. He answered immediately 'OK Skipper, coming up' and appeared in the hatch way between my cockpit and the nose. Meanwhile, the P/O had feathered itself, and by holding the aileron control fully to starboard, I was able to get the plane out of the spiral. Immediately we were on an even

K   The Directorate of Military Intelligence (MI9) was responsible for supporting resistance groups and 'for encouraging Service personnel to escape or evade capture'. All were debriefed on their return to the UK and any useful information derived from such interviews was passed on to those responsible for tracing lost aircrew (Hudson: 2020: 127-128).

254

keel, and whilst the B/A was just climbing the steps from the nose, we received a second burst – approximately 30 seconds after the first. The rudder controls were completely severed, and A/C again veered slightly to port despite full opposite aileron. I immediately gave the order to bale out. No acknowledgements, although the intercom was still faintly serviceable as I could hear my own voice in my headphones. B/A disappeared from hatchway – I heard a bang in the nose and a cold rush of air, as though the front escape hatch had been opened, reached me. It might, however, have been a shattering of the B/A's Perspex vision panel. 20 seconds after I had given the order to bale out, the aileron control was snatched from my hand and the A/C turned over on its back and began to descend rapidly in an inverted spin. 10 seconds after inversion one of the 500 lb. bombs exploded and I was blown clear through the dinghy escape hatch above my head. A great number of 2 ft square sections of A/C accompanied or passed me in my descent. I saw no sign of any other parachutes in the limited area of my vision.[97]

At a subsequent meeting at RAF North Creake in 1945, Michael Renaut records that when he met John Stone again, 'he looked perfectly fit except for the shaven head!'[L98]

The news of John's survival was passed on to families impatient for information on their loved ones. For Joyce Thomas, the wife of Kenneth Thomas (navigator), it was the first tangible news since John Stone had been posted 'missing'. Joyce and Thomas met in Bournemouth, Hampshire, after Kenneth's posting to the UK with the RCAF.[99] They were married on 27 May 1944.[100] J Harris (Canadian Casualty Branch) explains to Joyce Thomas, that this news provides no 'definitive information concerning the fate of your husband',[101] and

L   Michael Renaut outlines this event in some detail in his autobiography claiming he had been to their wedding 'only a few weeks before' and that he was in contact with his wife and was the first to report John Stone's survival to his wife by letter (Renaut: 1982: 161). Both of these of are contradicted by the family. It seems likely that he is either conflating events or he is being inventive with his narrative.

while this news from John Stone's statement 'may prove of little comfort to you, it is considered you would wish to be informed'.[102] This news must have been particularly devastating for Joyce as she was now six months pregnant[103] (Joyce's daughter Janis[M104] was born in November 1945). However, the Canadian Casualty Branch wished to assure Joyce that 'investigation is continuing on all such cases of missing personnel'[105] by MRES, although they caution, 'this is a work of great magnitude, investigations being of necessity a lengthy process'.[106] Joyce Thomas was paid a gratuity payment based upon the service career of her husband, Kenneth Thomas, of 949 days (504 of which were overseas [from Canada]). It amounted to C$551.74.[107]

The subsequent report by MRES identified that the crew members were all buried separately. It is unclear from the report how many were identified when buried, but the report states that Sidney Stuart was in a marked grave. However, through the exhumations, he was subsequently discovered to be buried in another grave. As well as Sidney Stuart, Harold Coutts, Neville Baker, Alexander Ferme and Kenneth Thomas[N] were all positively identified. This was either through their names stamped onto their clothing or by identity tags. This left Donald Biggar and John Wyatt. The investigator, J Friend, felt comfortable identifying Donald Biggar from his 'officer type shirt' as he was the only remaining person of sufficient rank to warrant such a shirt. The last remaining body was therefore presumed to be John Wyatt. He concludes, 'subject to your approval I will issue instructions to have all crosses correctly inscribed'.[108] The crew was reinterred at the Reichswald Forest War Cemetery, Germany, 6 May 1947.[109]

Neville Baker, the air gunner on Halifax NA111 6Y-Y was from Portsmouth.[110] Little else is recorded of his life. Similarly, Donald Biggar from Dalbeattie, Kirkcudbrightshire, Scotland, has very little detail remaining.[111]

M   There is some suggestion that Joyce and Janis Thomas moved to Canada postwar, to join Kenneth Thomas's parents (Toronto Star: 16/11/1945).

N   The detailed description of the exhumation of Kenneth Thomas still exists: 'Description of Body: complete smashed & burnt. Height: Cannot be determined. Fingers & Hands: None. Identity Discs: None. Remarks: Eraser in pocket' (RAF: 6/5/1947).

Harold Coutts, bomb aimer, was from Alberta, Canada.[112] Before enlisting in June 1942, for the dangerous occupation of aircrew, he was employed, with macabre irony, as a life insurance salesman.[113] On 6 August 1941, he married Gloria Hendricks in Alberta and on 14 March 1944, their son David Coutts was born.[114] At initial training in Canada, he was described as 'definitely suitable … a good worker who is very dependable. He is capable of shouldering responsibility and is popular with his fellows'.[115] His bomb training evaluated him as an 'average bomb aimer',[116] although, more positively, the trainer suggested that his 'pinpointing ability in air work showed steady improvement. His ground studies work consistently good. He is quiet, cheerful and industrious'. However, questions were raised regarding his motivation. On enlisting, the medical officer described Harold Coutts as seeming 'to have ability but a lack of motivation and enthusiasm do not make him a good prospect'.[117] This is surprising as the medical officer had also described him as 'alert [and] well-mannered'.[118] Moreover, he discussed with Harold Coutts the problem of his finger on his left hand that 'cannot be extended' and remarked, 'he is willing to have finger amputated if it interferes with flying'.[119] A surprising willingness for someone who lacks motivation. Nonetheless, he achieved his Air Bombers Badge on 17 September 1943,[120] and on 30 October, he arrived in Britain.[121] Once in Britain, his motivation is again questioned, 'bombing results only just satisfactory. General air work could be greatly improved – he does not work hard enough on his own initiative. With greater application he could reach a much higher standard'.[122] However, he successfully progressed to aircrew.[123]

Little is known of Alexander Ferme, mid-upper gunner other than he was born in Broxburn, West Lothian, Scotland. There is also nothing further recorded of John Wyatt, wireless operator.

The news of the only survivor of the crash, John Stone, was relayed to his wife, Joanna, on 1 April 1945 when her father-in-law telephoned:

'John's safe' ... that is all I heard, could not speak at all, my mother took over the telephone whilst I stood in a complete daze. After about half an hour I recovered my voice and the rejoicing began, what rejoicing indeed.[124]

John's words to Joanna when phoning home for the first time were, 'hullo darling, sorry I'm a bit late'.[125] While one might expect John Stone's return to relieve any anxiety in his wife, Joanna instead ached with concern; 'my poor darling with all his hair shaved off and supporting himself on two sticks but ALIVE'.[126]

John Michael Stone was the sixth of seven children. Born in Ealing in December 1922, his first job was as a clerk with Dennis's Motor Company in Guildford. His daughter, Wendy Neale is unsure why he enlisted with the RAF, but thinks 'the uniform had something to do with it, and quite probably, the glamour'.[127] He met Joanna while serving 'as she was in the WAAF ... [she] outranked him at the time, which pleased her hugely'.[128] They married in January 1944, 'in a very low-key ceremony ... their honeymoon was two days in a hotel in Morecombe Bay. No money at that time for anything more'.[129] They had their daughter, Wendy in December 1944,[130] the same month that John flew his first sortie from RAF North Creake.[131] John Stone survived the war and had a son, Michael, in 1946. Very sadly Michael died on 22 November 1950 from pneumonia, during an operation to clear a misdiagnosed blockage.[132]

On demobilisation, he worked in his father's shipping and finance company. However, John's war experiences profoundly affected him; he suffered from nightmares and would wake up screaming.[133] Illustrating all the hallmarks of survivor's guilt, he used alcohol as a coping mechanism; an addiction that would plague him until the age of 65.[134] Poor sleeping, nightmares, drinking and relationship breakdowns, all classic symptoms of what would now be diagnosed as post-traumatic stress disorder, and in addition, with the death of a child; 'Dad's drinking increased, Mummy was in and out of mental hospitals – and also drank rather heavily'.[135] 'Thankfully', Wendy reflects, 'I had the support of wonderful grandparents and aunt and uncles on both sides of the family'.[136] At the time of Michael's death, Joanna was enacting divorce proceedings.[137] For John, it was the end of the first of four marriages.[138] His job involved a move to South Africa, where he met his second wife with whom he had a further two children; Jonathan and Kim.[139] He then moved to Australia where he met his third wife, Lynette, with whom he had three children (Peter, Penny and Nicholas).[O]

And so the ripples of one night in March 1944 reach through the generations.

O John did achieve a major ambition; he became an actor. On moving to Australia in the early 1970s, he featured in a couple of films, notably the *Killing of Angel Street* (1981). He also did a stint on the *Benny Hill Australia* show and episodes of *Home and Away* (Neale: 6/2/2024).

CHAPTER SIX

D-DAY

We were far from finishing the renovation of the Control Tower, but we were busy publicising the date of our opening event. Posters had been produced some time earlier and they were now posted widely around the area and on all social media platforms. 70 years earlier, Allied military leaders were endeavouring to keep their plans secret. Operation Overlord, the invasion of Europe, more commonly known as D-Day,[1] was now in its final planning stages. Long tracts of the south of England resembled a vast military camp and, with uncharacteristic humour, Dwight D Eisenhower, supreme commander of the invasion, remarked, 'only the great number of barrage balloons floating constantly in British skies kept the islands from sinking under the waves':[2]

> the landings were, for once, meticulously prepared … The French beaches had been surveyed. Vast forces had been accumulated: 1200 fighting ships against 15 German destroyers, 10,000 aircraft against 500 German, 4126 landing craft and 864 transport ships. There were tanks with flails to clear minefields, amphibian tanks, tanks to destroy concrete, tanks that laid their own carpets, tanks for bridging dikes. There were two artificial harbours, called Mulberries, to be towed across the Channel.[3]

The Nazis had been bombarded with contradictory intelligence regarding the invasion since 1943. German High Command was fed a sequence of spurious agents' reports in preparation for the invasion.[4] The Germans had assumed that they had many agents in England, but most the British had 'turned around'.[5] They were now feeding back Allied misinformation regarding the landing sites of the impending invasion. This subterfuge, it was hoped, would persuade the Germans that the landings were planned for Pas de Calais.[6]

It was impossible to disguise the heavy build-up of armaments and troops on the British side of the Channel. It was therefore decided that decoy military camps, airfields, munition dumps etc. should be established to give the impression of an invasion force-in-waiting in the south-east of England.[7] German reconnaissance aircraft were then allowed to operate over Kent, but no further west.[8] Also, in the knowledge that the Nazis collated bombing statistics and analysed the trends, the Allies ensured that two targets were selected to be attacked around Calais for every target selected in Normandy,[9] reinforcing the perception that Pas de Calais was the Allied choice for the landings. Furthermore, a fictitious Fourth Army HQ was established in Scotland that involved considerable wireless traffic. This was an attempt to convince the Germans that an alternative invasion force would also head for Norway.[10]

To reduce losses at the beachheads, Solly Zuckerman, as Scientific Director of the British Bombing Survey Unit, devised a strategy where both Bomber Command and US bombers would be used to target German supply lines in France and Belgium. This would hinder the reinforcing and resupplying of the front lines.[11] This plan was initially unpopular with both the USAAF and Bomber Command, Arthur Harris stridently condemning it in a memorandum:

> It is clear that the best and indeed only efficient support which Bomber Command can give Overlord is the intensification of attacks on suitable industrial centres in Germany. If we attempt to substitute for this process attacks on gun emplacements,

beach defences, communications or dumps in occupied territories, we shall commit the irremediable error of diverting our best weapon … to tasks which it cannot effectively carry out. Though this might give a specious appearance of 'supporting' the army, in reality it would be the greatest disservice we could do them.[12]

Winston Churchill and his advisor, Frederick Lindeman, were also in opposition to the plan. Winston Churchill suggested it would cause the 'butchering of French civilians before the invasion had even started',[13] and Frederick Lindeman added that any damage caused, could be easily repaired.[14] However, when Winston Churchill's appeal to Franklin Roosevelt to abandon the strategy was over-ruled, the matter was pressed no further[15] and the opposing voices ceased. Once decided, Arthur Harris put his full weight into the campaign and, attempted 'to avoid heavy civilian casualties',[16] he demonstrated that Bomber Command could indeed conduct a precision bombing campaign.[17] Solly Zuckerman concluded that to this end, Arthur Harris had done 'all that could have been asked for'.[18] The strategy was an objective success, with nearly all the bridges over the Seine and most over the Loire destroyed.[19] The French railways, that had run 100 enemy supply trains a day, barely managed 32 by May 1944.[20] On 3 June 1944, the Reichsbahn (German National Railway) published a report considering whether it was worthwhile attempting to repair the railway infrastructure at all.[21] Subsequently, in his 1947 autobiography *Bomber Offensive*, Arthur Harris appears to tacitly concede that his doubts about the strategy had been unfounded, even citing the view of German officials opining its great success.[22]

However, it was not just a question of German supply lines. Protecting the coast of occupied Europe from invasion was the formidable wall of 92 German radar sites.[23] Therefore, in advance of the invasion, the RAF flew nearly 2,000 sorties against these sites and 'succeeded in putting out of action all but sixteen'.[24] Some of these 16, located north of the river Seine, had been deliberately left unharmed, in order to pick up and report diversion fleets. These diversions, codenamed 'Glimmer' and 'Taxable', were to play a critical role on D-Day.[25]

Robert Cockburn of the Telecommunications Research Establishment (TRE) had been experimenting with methods of generating two 'phantom fleets' as decoys from the true invasion force.[26] Joan Curran,[A] also at TRE, had developed a decoy technique that involved aircraft flying in rectangular orbits over a 16-mile square area at 3,000 feet, dropping Window while also creeping forward at a speed of eight knots. In this manner, it would be possible to produce a feint on German radar, resembling a large fleet of ships.[27] This would give an impression of an invasion force heading towards Pas de Calais.[28] Concerns were raised about this strategy that Robert Cockburn felt compelled to answer:

> imagine the scene: a frightened under-trained young conscript radar operator sees the 'ghost fleet' on his screen and reports it to his headquarters as the long-expected enemy invasion force; so do his colleagues at other radar stations along the coast. Soon there appears a nice broad arrow on the situation map at the headquarters; the 'ghost fleet' is now a military fact. If aircraft were then to fly into the area and report it clear of ships, would their reports be believed? Probably not ... once a broad arrow representing an enemy attack appears on the situation map at a military headquarters, it is a military fact and it takes a lot to remove it.[29]

However, there was still a good chance that any remaining and functioning German radar station might detect the real invasion force. To prevent this, radio countermeasures (RCM) were going to be essential. Discussions had been ongoing since the Autumn of 1942,[30] about what form this might take. It wasn't until six months before the invasion that any 'definite' decisions were made',[31] including for the use

---

A   Joan Curran, who had conducted the initial Window trials in 1942, did the mathematical calculations for this extraordinary spoof (Price: 1967: 202).

of Mandrel.

Mandrel, first introduced in 1941,[32] was ground-based and was used to 'push back the long-range radar cover'[33] emanating from occupied Europe. These German early-warning radars operated on restricted frequency bands and were relatively easy to jam.[34] However, with developing British jamming techniques, the Germans began using wider frequency bands on their radars. These required more sophisticated jammers, with much greater power to jam them.[35] When RAF 80 Wing was formed in 1941, it was given the responsibility for all radar jamming, and it quickly began experimenting with airborne Mandrel.[36] Initially successful when mounted in Fighter Command aircraft, it was the crudest form of jamming.[37] It created visible interference on the German radar screen that prevented the operators from determining what was before them. While it certainly caused some nuisance, with German ground controllers at times finding it 'nearly impossible to control the night-fighters',[38] it didn't incapacitate the Freya system.[39] The initial Mandrel 'shock' passed as German operators became used to the jamming and could ameliorate its worst effects. Consequently, Mandrel was withdrawn from the bomber force.[40] However, with the formation of the RAF 100 Group, greater potential for Mandrel was identified. It was discovered that aircraft, working in combination, could link their jamming capacity and thereby form a protective screen behind which forces could be hidden.[41] The development became, for the Allies, a critical part of the RCM discussions and plans for D-Day.

* * *

By May 2014, discussions and plans concerning our opening were well advanced. We had wanted the event to have a period feel, so we had asked Lewis, a keen period dancer, for contacts in the DJ world (I have none in this period of music, my tastes concentrating, although not exclusively, on music emerging some 30 years later). He put us in touch with Ralph Sayers, the Swinging Detective, and arrangements were made. So visitors could embrace the vintage style, we also arranged for

Hair Raid Shelter to join us, performing 1940s makeovers. We involved the Little Vintage Lover Fair, a series of regular local fairs, who would run a sale in the Nissen hut. On the catering side, we approached local producers, one such being Beeston Brewery, who brewed Stirling beer, that featured a picture of the mural of the first Stirling lost from RAF North Creake on the bottle; a perfect fit.

We had decided early on to have two separate events. The first would be for veterans of RAF North Creake and their families. The second, would be the official opening. It was therefore decided that we would invite the veterans around for afternoon tea, the day before we held our opening event. As the veterans had already attended, we wanted someone else from the story of the Control Tower to cut the ribbon at our official opening. Luckily, we had heard of such a person that we thought might fit the bill.

We had attended an event run by the film society, Screen-next-the-Sea in Wells-next-the-Sea. It was a showing of Ken Loach's *Angels' Share* with an associated whisky tasting. In conversation beforehand, I was told that Peter Melchett had lived in the Control Tower after the war; I had never heard this before, and even though he lived locally, I was sceptical.

Peter Melchett was a bit of a legend in our house. When Claire and I were studying Environmental Science at university, one of our lecturers, and now a very good friend, Mike Mason, had based a lecture on Peter Melchett. Focusing on his work as Executive Director of Greenpeace UK (1989-2000[42]) the lecture scrutinised the dumping of the Brent Spar oil platform at sea, a highly controversial topic at the time. Intrigued and impressed by Peter Melchett's work, we kept abreast of his endeavours with interest and when, in 1999, he led a group of protesters who destroyed a trial crop of genetically modified maize at Walnut Tree Farm at Lyng, Norfolk, we were fascinated. Peter Melchett, along with a further 27 Greenpeace activists was arrested. At the subsequent trial in September 2000, at Norwich Crown Court, they were all acquitted by the jury, who sympathised with their defence that they were 'acting to prevent pollen from the genetically-modified maize from polluting neighbouring organic crops and gardens'.[43] From our perspective, he was the ideal man to cut the ribbon.

Further enquiry revealed that he had indeed lived in the Control Tower as a child. When Peter Melchett was born his family had lost much of its wealth and his father had started a grass-drying business in the south hangar at North Creake (the forerunner of ABN, the mill that still operates there today).[44] The family stayed in cottages on the North Norfolk coast, that were seasonally rented out as holiday homes. Peter Melchett remembers:

> [it] was great fun, particularly in the summer when the holiday homes were occupied by holidaymakers and we went to live in a flat in a disused control tower in the middle of an airfield … of course, I thought this was amazing, living in a flat in a control tower on an airfield with this huge factory all around, [with] machines and fascinating smells … [It] must have been a complete nightmare for my parents.[45]

Indeed, when we pressed Peter for memories of this time, he went away and asked his mother:

> I think she pretty much managed to wipe all the memories she had left, [and remembers] only that it was extremely cold … [and] me, in my highchair, refusing to eat anything … the other thing she remembers is the flat roof and my determination that I was going to throw myself off it at the first opportunity.[46]

Nonetheless, Peter's recollections were that he had a 'very happy childhood and … a very privileged childhood'.[B]

B   Peter had been schooled at Eton, but took the decision, along with his partner Cassandra Wedd, not to send his own children as 'I certainly think it is wrong to have private education, people buying themselves out of the system'. This approach to privilege he also applied to his hereditary peerage and both he and Cassandra decided that they wouldn't get married 'so that he wouldn't pass on the peerage' (BBC: 2018: Last Word), insisting that inherited privilege 'shouldn't be perpetuated' (BBC: 2000: Desert Island Discs). With his father's untimely death, he became a peer at 25, taking the Labour whip (BBC: 2000: Desert Island Discs). He was appointed by Harold Wilson as Junior Minister for the Environment and later to Northern Ireland (BBC: 2018: Last Word), where he was the first Minister 'who'd been willing to listen to Punk Rock, let alone like some of it' (he chose *Alternative Ulster* by the Stiff Little Fingers as one of his tracks on *Desert*

On 6 April 2014, we sent him a letter and after a softening-up preamble, we asked if he'd consider cutting the ribbon at our opening. We suggested, 'it would be a rather nice completing of the circle in terms of the residential part of the Tower's history'. We received a quick response happily agreeing to cutting the ribbon, and expressing that it was 'quite a surprise to hear that the Control Tower still stands and is in use. I do (just) remember living there'. So it was true, and it hadn't just been the whisky talking.

Things were beginning to fall into place, and now all we had to do was finish the build.

When we first set the date for our opening, we also booked a 'recover from the build' holiday the month before the opening date; so confident were we that we had enough time to complete the works. We were hopelessly naïve. In early May 2014, we could no longer count the time we had left in months, but only in weeks. We looked at what we had left to do, and started 'chucking labour at it'. It would no longer be possible to complete all the work without more help. This had a significant impact on the budget, with the weekly pay day being something that we had to prepare for during the previous seven days: withdrawing our cash limit every day. Never has so much money passed through my hands so quickly. Afterwards, we would all retire to the Bull in Walsingham for a debrief over a couple, or so, pints. For a while, we felt like we were a significant part of the local economy.

The build now moved on apace; around us were plumbers finishing some first, but mostly second, fixing; window fitters, finishing up; a carpenter, fitting kitchen cabinets;[C] gardeners appeared for the

---

Island Discs). He led an official inquiry into pop festivals, subsequently resisting calls to ban free festivals and leading to legislation that Michael Eavis, the founder of Glastonbury Festival, credited with the event's long-lasting success (Guardian: 3/9/2018). His last act in the House of Lords 'was to vote for the Bill to abolish hereditary peerage' (BBC: 2018: Last Word). Sadly he died aged only 70 in 2018. In a moving moment, I heard his obituary on Radio 4's *Last Word* while working in the Nissen hut; using excerpts from *Desert Island Discs*, he talked with considerable affection about the Control Tower. It was quite a surprise to stumble across this programme while out doing DIY. I found out much of the detail about his life while researching this book. It was a delight to meet him; I feel sad that I didn't know him.

C   We had purchased a metal 1960s kitchen off eBay for £62. These units had been supplemented by laboratory units placed back-to-back to form a peninsula, and a kitchen cabinet kindly donated by Dave Carr, a former MA student, on a visit; 'Nige', he said, I want you to have this'. This was unified with the laboratory units by using the same chrome handles (I had a ready supply that I had salvaged from Hillman Super Minx interiors over the years). Tom made an additional unit out of old wardrobes to match the metal

first time, laying patios and driving chaos further towards the edges of the garden. There were metal fabricators on the balcony, plasterers, tilers (this was actually Tom Hodges, a carpenter, but now desperation had turned him into the man to go to when anything needed doing; constantly moving him around jobs as urgency dictated – it must have been infuriating for him; he appeared stoic). Claire and I bridged the gaps between jobs, doing what needed doing and organising what came next. In spite of all the chaos, there were moments of intense pleasure, punctuating the slog; the sheer joy of seeing the six windows on the front elevation emerge from behind their plastic protection, made both Claire and I tearful. It was coming together. I was finishing the layout for the Board Room ensuite, laying a concrete plinth on which the bath would stand and, in-between, trying to move our bedroom (the Control Room) forward. We still believed, or hoped, it would all be finished. This illusion was shattered when we attempted to put the Board Room bath in place, and the weight of it carved gouges into the 'gone off' but still 'green' concrete. With a wobbling bath, we reluctantly gave up on completing the Board Room in time. I would now concentrate on the Control Room.

Working on the structure of the Control Room's built-in wardrobes, I realised there was no way the work would be far enough advanced for the plasterers to finish-up before we went away. Reluctantly, we decided to delay the holiday until I'd completed the work. With the delayed departure, we left for our shortened holiday and made our way to Herefordshire. We left behind a vast array of trades, beavering away under the watchful eye of Tom.

Seventy years earlier, the demands of Operation Overlord had required all aircrew leave to be cancelled.

In early May 1944, 199 Squadron's brand new Stirlings were yet to arrive;[47] they were still at 'TFU' (TRE's Flying Unit) in Defford, Worcestershire,[48] being fitted with Mandrel equipment:[49]

---

units and all were finished off in aqua blue paint with new Formica tops; we thought it looked splendid!

the fitting of such a squadron at short notice required some ingenuity. T.R.E. prepared an appreciation of the technical requirements and the plan was finalised at the end of March ... The drawing office at Defford completed the prototype installation details within a month and S.I.U. [Signals Installation Unit] fitted out twelve aircraft within six weeks. This considerable achievement was the result of intensive effort by all concerned.[50]

Mandrel III had been developed to cover the wide dispersal of frequencies being used by the German long-range early-warning radars at that time.[51] On the 10 May 1944, the first fully-equipped Stirling arrived at North Creake.[52] Aircraft then followed in twos and threes for the rest of May,[53] from both Defford and the Bomber Support Development Unit (BSDU)[D] at Foulsham, Norfolk.[54]

Mandrel's operation required an extra member of crew called the special operator, who 'was trained to operate the complex radar equipment on board'.[55] A bank of up to eight Mandrel transmitters was positioned 'between the wing spars'[56] on each aircraft. These aircraft were also fitted with additional alternators in order to 'cope with the electrical load'.[57] A training course of three weeks[58] was provided for special operators at RAF North Creake shortly after their arrival.[59] No-one was permitted to ask the special operator details of the equipment or for what it was used; not even fellow crew members.[60] Indeed, 'anyone found guilty of such was subject to immediate Court Martial'.[E61] Jack Philipson remembers, 'we were only told what we needed to know to do the job and were not allowed to discuss our work, not even amongst ourselves'.[62] While crews most often bonded through the crewing-up and training process, the special operators were allocated to them

---

D   In April 1944, the BSDU was founded at RAF Foulsham to 'handle the development and trials of new equipment and tactics pertinent to the Group', a role that had previously been undertaken by the Fighter Interception Unit at Ford (Streetly:1978:43).

E   Vic Flowers remembers that 'security was very strict' (Brettingham: 2002: 282). Indeed, so concerned were the authorities about breaches of security that when William Bolton was killed on 2 May 1945 (see 'Dove Over Europe' below), his wife was summoned to the Air Ministry and warned not to divulge anything she might know of her husband's duties (Rees: 2003: 94).

without discussion or consultation. This often caused a divide in the crew, if not deepfelt resentment. The special operators themselves, were encouraged to be aloof or prickly, to make the maintenance of their secret easier, particularly avoiding social contact with their crew.[63] A detail that the son of a navigator from North Creake said, 'made perfect sense; my dad always said he was difficult'.[64] Bernie How, flight engineer with 199 Squadron, commented simply, 'we didn't mix with them'.[65] One rear gunner, stationed at North Creake, Harry Freegard, claimed that he didn't even know there was a special operator in his crew, as he 'always arrived separately' after he was in his turret.[66]

Once supplied with aircraft, the Squadron underwent intensive training for its new role.[67] The purpose of the Mandrel Screen was to form a '20,000 foot electronic curtain [that] completely blocked the probing beams of the Freyas'.[68] This caused the monitors of the German ground controllers to 'yield nothing but a deluge of "snow"'.[69] The function of this deluge on D-Day was, as Arthur Harris wrote in his postwar despatch, 'to cover the assault forces by jamming all the coastal radar in the Channel area'.[70] Achieving this aim required the Squadron to fly in a tightly co-ordinated manner, to ensure that no interruptions to the screen were experienced. Initially, this was attempted by 'visual' formation, but this proved impossible in poor visibility.[71] Therefore, the navigation leader at RAF North Creake, Michael Docherty, devised a method of 'station keeping' (maintaining correct position) known as the Racecourse Pattern.[72] An impression of the critical precision of this station keeping, is indicated by an instruction to aircrew that, 'watches are synchronised to exact second, as late as possible before take-off'.[73]

The Racecourse Pattern was a circuit formed around a Gee navigational fix, perpendicular to the enemy coast. Known as a 'jamming centre', two aircraft adopted this pattern, starting at opposite ends of the circuit.[74] The sides of the Racecourse Pattern were ten miles long, with the aircraft doing a turn at each end to maintain it. The complete circuit had to take exactly ten minutes to complete[75] (unless adjusting for wind[76]). This would ensure, even in bad weather, that the aircraft remained in the correct position in relation to one another.

Flying of this nature required a very high standard of piloting and navigation.[77]

The special operator would sweep the long-range frequencies, listening for enemy signals, while the Mandrel equipment was in the 'receive' position. When instructed, or at a given time, he tuned into the same frequency and turned his equipment to the 'transmit' position. It then transmitted a 'noise-modulated jamming signal'.[78] When this equipment was used en masse, and backed up by ground stations in the UK, it effectively produced a solid screen of interference that the German early-warning radar could not penetrate, hence the term 'Mandrel Screen'.[79]

RAF 199 Squadron was held in readiness at RAF North Creake for the Normandy invasion.[80] The planned delivery of 'puzzling

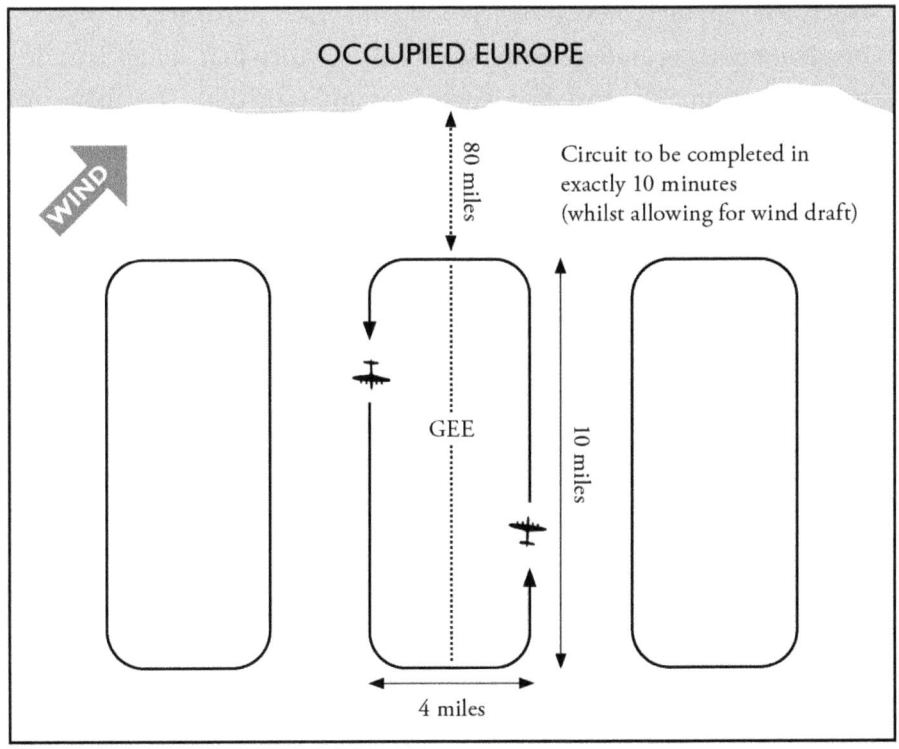

Mandrel Screen: The Racecourse Pattern

surprises upon the Germans'[81] required considered measures to prevent 'disclosing [them] prematurely to the enemy'.[82] This meant no operational use of the equipment in advance of its deployment on D-Day. If successful, Mandrel would constitute 'a serious breach in the German early warning system'.[83]

From 1 to 4 June 1944, training continued.[84] Frank Hancock recalls he and Ray Varley were ordered 'by a flight sergeant … to get some black and white paint from the stores to paint the invasion recognition strips on the wings and fuselage. We were almost put on a charge for arguing that we only needed white paint'.[85] However, mostly the preparations were thoroughly considered. On 4 June, Ken Hartley was enjoying a film at the cinema in Wells-next-the-Sea, when the film suddenly stopped, and the house lights came on; 'several RAF police entered the cinema and ordered all military personnel to return to their bases, whereupon scores of soldiers and airmen left hurriedly'. However, on that night, operations were scrubbed. 'Twenty-four hours later it was "on" again. What we had worked for and waited for was about to happen.'[86] This time, personnel at the cinema were 'surprised to see a scrawled message appear on the screen asking them to return to base at once'.[87]

For Phyllis Willmott, a WAAF meteorologist recovering from illness in the RAF North Creake station sick quarters, the news of D-Day came from a colleague:

> Jean came in to see me and told me … in a conspiratorial whisper – because Philip had ordered it must not be mentioned outside the office – she reported that there was to be 'something big on tonight'. From these few whispered words I knew that what we had all been expecting was now imminent.[88]

John Wright, the son of Walsingham baker 'Sunny' Wright, remembers trying to deliver bread to RAF North Creake with his father and being turned away; 'the next day the big news was that we had invaded France'.[89] On the airfield site, groundcrew hurriedly, but meticulously, prepared the aircraft for their support for the invasion of Europe. Murray

Pedan, stationed at another RAF 100 Group airfield, recalls that, at the briefing, 'just before the curtains were parted to reveal the greatest secret of the war,'[90] aircrew, although they were all seasoned airmen, sat with heightened anticipation with, 'quickened pulse and respiration'.[91] He suggests they 'would probably have provided a medical man with the material for an interesting paper on the effects of excitement, anticipation and intense curiosity, combined with the normal stress associated with flying on operations'.[92] At the same moment at RAF North Creake, TRE was giving assistance with the Mandrel equipment until the 'last few moments before the actual operation'.[93]

On 5 June 1944, at 21:40 hours, take-off commenced at RAF North Creake. One hundred and forty-four aircrew in 19 aircraft[94] took off, 16 aircraft detailed for Mandrel Screen and three aircraft in reserve. The 16 all took off within 15 minutes and steadily climbed to a cruising height of 12,000 feet on their first operation from RAF North Creake.[95] The Mandrel Screen was set to be flown between Littlehampton and Portland Bill,[96] at a height of 18,000 feet.[97] To ensure the successful operation of the Screen, once in position, the 16 were divided between eight jamming centres, spaced no further than ten miles apart (the beam width of the enemy early-warning radar).[98] To economise on the number of aircraft used, the aircraft were kept as far back from the coast as possible. If jamming at 30 miles from the coast, the aircraft requirement would be 30 (15 jamming centres to cover a 150-mile front). If it was flown at 100 miles back from the coast, this requirement would be reduced to ten aircraft (five jamming centres).[99] On D-Day, it was decided to fly 70-80 miles back, therefore requiring 16 aircraft in eight jamming centres,[100] resulting, it was hoped, in the coastal radars from Cherbourg to Le Harve being jammed.[101]

The two spoof forces (Glimmer and Taxable) left at a similar time as the main invasion force, in order to maximise confusion. Glimmer involved RAF 617 Squadron bombers and Taxable, RAF 218 Squadron bombers, both dropping their Window in the box formations.[102] A separate 'ghost' bomber force of RAF 101 Squadron Lancasters and Flying Fortresses of RAF 214 Squadron, flew along the line of the Somme,[103] acting as a diversion. German ground controllers, consequently, ordered all available aircraft to intercept these bombers, however, once they entered the fog of jamming, it became impossible to communicate with them. One Lancaster was intercepted and shot down; the crew survived.[104]

Concurrently, the Royal Navy were busy emitting a literal 'smokescreen'.[105] They were also producing a metaphorical one, with motor launches towing balloons, codenamed 'Filbert'. These were '29-foot-long naval balloons with a nine-foot-diameter radar reflector built inside its envelope'.[106] These simulated a radar echo of a 10,000-ton ship.[107] In addition the navy also had over 200 escort ships carrying jamming transmitters:

> and all were switched on. There was nothing subtle about this, the final trick in the Allies' radio-counter-measure repertoire. It blinded the defenders as cruelly and effectively as pepper thrown in their eyes.[108]

199 Squadron Mandrel aircraft arrived in position at 23:30 hours on 5 June 1944. As soon as the Mandrel equipment was turned to transmit, a large impenetrable screen of interference, that denied a view of everything behind, appeared on the German radar screens. The German operators were now alerted to something 'big' happening.[109] To distract them from the significance of this interference, RAF 199 Squadron aircraft were joined by four further bombers of the USAAF 803rd Squadron,[F] based with RAF 100 Group at RAF Oulton in North Norfolk.[110] These American Boeing B17 aircraft flew four jamming centres with just one aircraft in each.[111] This formation was flown to hide

---

F   In the spring of 1942 the US established 'Radio Research Laboratories' at Harvard, to 'concentrate entirely on RCM projects'. It worked closely with TRE and provided for the USAAF the same support as TRE gave the RAF. Britain also gained considerably from RRL's work (Cockburn: 1945: 8). The first equipment produced by the US organisation was heavily influenced by British design and thought (Harrington: 2016: 20). USAAF 803rd Squadron served with the RAF 100 Group in 'all but name' (Streetly: 1978: 43). Initially based at RAF Sculthorpe and then RAF Oulton with RAF 214 Squadron, they did night-time operations with Bomber Command (Streetly: 1978: 78-79). By the end of January 1945, they had virtually stopped their work with Bomber Command (Streetly: 1978: 81). Max Hastings commented that it was a remarkable triumph for British technology; 'until the end of the war the Americans were almost totally dependent on British electronic devices to wage their own air offensive' (Hastings: 1980: 189).

the spoof fleets heading for Pas de Calais, but with only one aircraft in each jamming centre it was an ineffective screen. This deliberately weak screen meant that, while appearing to conceal the 'phantom invasion force', they were actually allowing the Germans to 'see through the chinks in the blanket jamming'.[112] The Allies hoped these tantalising glimpses, which the Germans would believe they were not meant to see, would confirm their erroneous belief that the direction of the invasion was towards Pas de Calais.[113] A cunning application of psychology.

In the first minutes of 6 June 1944, a bombardment of beach defences signalled the start of the attack. Simultaneously, the huge force was busy crossing the Channel.[114] At dawn 1,136 RAF Bomber Command aircraft bombed and eliminated ten of the most important coastal batteries in the Seine Bay. Within the first 24 hours, Allied forces flew 14,674 sorties and dropped 10,395 tons of bombs.[115] Meanwhile, over Normandy, heavy transport planes were continually unloading 'their human cargoes.'[116]

At this time, the Mandrel Screen Stirlings of 199 Squadron had made an unwelcome discovery. As soon as the special operator had turned the equipment to transmit, the Gee signal, on which the navigators were relying, disappeared. Mandrel jammed it out.[117] One 199 Squadron navigator managed 'purely on visual contact'.[118] However, this was unreliable and most navigators reverted to 'dead reckoning'[119] and astral navigation.[G120] Despite these challenges, the integrity of the screen remained until some, after flying for an average of over eight hours,[121] were forced to leave as a result of critical fuel levels.[122] Alan Wood describes what he saw on his flight that night from RAF North Creake:

G With dead reckoning navigation, sometimes maps could be used but it was in most cases too cloudy and the terrain had to be very distinctive to achieve positive recognition from 12-15,000 feet. Fixes were often confirmed by other crew members who were in a better position to see lakes, rivers and railways that usually provided the best fixes (Smith: undated: 6). When other methods were unavailable, the navigator used astral navigation, as Roy Smith, a navigator from RAF North Creake explains: [Dead Reckoning by the stars] 'was tedious and meant unplugging one's I.C. [intercom] and oxygen, struggling along the fuselage to the astrodome, reconnecting the equipment, taking 30 shots with a bubble sextant (this was done automatically over a two minute period which averaged out 30 readings). Having done this, one endeavoured to work out a position from data contained in the Air Almanac, plot this on the chart, calculate the new wind velocity, and a new course to the next specified position. One tried to do this within a period of six minutes but certainly not more than ten minutes. Even in these relatively slow aircraft 10 minutes covered 30 miles, and anything longer could mean getting too far off track before correcting course' (Smith: undated: 6).

We saw quite a lot of the boats going out, and when we were going round and round we saw the Navy bombarding the beaches ... [on return was the] incredible sight of these thousands, literally, thousands of boats, cheek by jowl, almost touching, going across the Channel to the invasion beaches.[123]

* * *

The holiday in Craswall, Herefordshire was a real tonic. Not that it was a complete escape, as we still had merchandise to design and order; but it was a break from the frenetic activity of the Control Tower. Some months before, I had a nasty episode when I breathed in spores from mould growing on some oak strip flooring. It had developed a reaction in my lungs that gave me bad asthma-like symptoms. I was given steroids to clear it up but without knowing the cause. I subsequently discovered the cause about a month later, when moving the same boards I came down with the identical symptoms. On holiday, my breathing hadn't fully recovered. This limited my walking capacity and forced upon us a more sedentary break than we would otherwise have considered. It did us good; the weather was fine, we ate well, drank a little and chatted a lot.

On our return we discovered that work had progressed well in our absence. The balcony asphalting was now complete, as was the patio and the air raid shelter was painted. We employed the help of a decorator, 'Pete-the-Paint',[H] as June hove into sight. By early June things were frantic (but planned). The floor finishers came in and polished the concrete stairs. I hired a digger and completed the last of the outside works, before tons of shingle arrived to top-dress the drive to the Nissen hut and the new car park. The digger was then replaced by a road-roller

---

H   There is still a great fondness in Norfolk for nicknames and many of the trades we used were primarily known by their nickname: London-Pete, Alan-Streaky-Bacon, Tom-the-Bike-Hodges etc., often as with Tom-the-Bike and Pete-the-Paint, rather than a pun on their name, it follows a characteristic that's notable. Tom is always seen on a pushbike getting around, and Pete is a decorator. The latter is a corruption, probably unknown to most other than Pete himself, of Peter-the-Painter; an early twentieth century Russian anarchist and artist (hence painter) who was funding revolution through criminal activity in the East End of London and reputedly died in the 'Siege of Sidney Street' in 1911 (Rogers: 1981).

to compact the gravel. Meanwhile painting continued, skirting went on and the original oak floorboards in our bedroom were repaired by Streaky. The floor finishers returned to strip, sand, wax and polish the parquet floors (with only just enough time for the wax to harden before our event). Their endeavours eliminated the peculiarly abstract pattern of gym stripes on the randomly-laid parquet blocks, reminders of its former existence as a school floor. With most of the ground floor being polished, furniture was scattered all around; mostly outside. Luckily the weather held. With Friday, the time left fell to critically low levels; Streaky, the carpenter, parted with the words 'see you Monday'; failing to grasp the hallmarks of a passing deadline. We retired to the pub, leaving behind a house in disarray.

A couple of pints in, and unable to put off the moment any longer, we returned to the Control Tower to an evening of putting things straight. During the afternoon, help and a new injection of energy had arrived in the form of Cillian and a number of friends. On opening the front door for Michelle, she looked in and said, 'it is tomorrow?'. Then hurried away to rustle up more help from her husband, Michael. Surplus stuff was piled in the workshop and in an out-building. The garage end of the Nissen hut was swept in preparation for the Little Vintage Lovers Fair.[I] We had done as much as we could for the evening, we'd have to finish off the following day; the start of our D-Day anniversary weekend.

On the morning of Saturday 7 June 2014, the veterans' arrival time was getting ever nearer and we still had some outstanding jobs. We had been hopeful that this would just involve some final cleaning and catering preparation. However, Tom was back grouting the tiles in the kitchen and I was still fitting kitchen worktops. Our neighbour, Paul Upton, arrived to help, and he busied himself putting up blinds and hanging my dad's clocking-in clock.[J] Others helped make up beds,

---

I   We had planned to have the floor painted and had even bought the paint, but deadlines had defeated us. It would be further eight years before we eventually did it.

J   This was a retirement present for my dad, who clocked-in all his life. A good friend thought it would be amusing to buy him a clocking-in clock so he wouldn't miss it. The friend, Pete Petersen, was a security advisor at a Schweppes factory, from where the clock came. I thought it very funny, I'm reasonably certain my dad did.

making the rooms look presentable. The generosity of friends through this process was astounding. A mite humbling.

Next, I rushed out to cut the grass while Claire continued to ready the house. Generally, the garden looked far better than we could have hoped; the oxeye daisies in the meadow were in full bloom and nodded in the light breeze, as if approving of the early summer sun. Unexpectedly, while cutting the grass, a huge storm burst; I was completely soaked finishing the job. Just as I abandoned the mower in the air raid shelter a car pulled up; our first guest, the son of a veteran and two hours early. I welcomed him as best I could and tried not to look flustered (I'm not sure I succeeded). Dripping from the rain, I made some polite excuses and went to get ready. Claire settled him in as she busied herself around him cleaning. Thankfully, with the arrival of Lewis and the awakening of Cillian, came more help.

At 2pm veterans began to arrive. With their arrival the sun returned. David Butler, rear gunner; Denis Gill, rear gunner; Bernie How, flight engineer; Philip Burkinshaw, paratrooper; Percy the Penguin (a soft-toy veteran of 16 raids) and their families. A good result for D-Day plus 70.

It was the most extraordinary afternoon. From arrival, the age seemed to fall away from these men. They chatted excitedly around the table, swapping stories and trying to work out if they'd ever been the 'spare bod' on someone else's plane. Brian How, Bernie's son, commented after, 'I've never heard any of these stories before'. We climbed to the roof with the veterans commentating all the way, explaining how things were and what they understood of that time. We learnt so much about the place we had chosen to live. At the end of the afternoon, Philip Burkinshaw, while thanking Claire and I for a lovely afternoon, parted with the words 'thank you for keeping our memory alive'. It had never occurred to me that it would mean as much to them, as it did to us. I was floored, I looked at Claire who had welled up and beyond her Stephen Squires was in tears.

Without much time to reflect we continued with our preparations for the following day. Claire attempted to make open day direction signs on the computer, but found her brain no longer worked. Instead, we gave up and spent an enjoyable evening sorting merchandise and anticipating the next day. Later, we even managed to sleep.

Early, stall holders and helpers began to arrive. Feeling refreshed and excited about the day ahead, we busied ourselves with final preparations. Debbie Crane, who was providing tea and cake arrived and set up; Hair Raid Shelter did the same. Claire was their first customer, but what was meant to be a relaxing interval, turned into an inescapable period of constant questions. However, during the inevitable lull immediately before an event, Claire and I escaped to the roof; from here we achieved a commanding view of the festive preparations. With nerves beginning to rise, we pondered, will people come? We were just in the process of talking ourselves into a full-scale worry, when we became aware the traffic on the Dry Road had changed in tone. It was slowing up. And then we saw it. They were coming; more than we ever imagined.

It was a wonderfully busy afternoon, bathed in glorious sunshine. The vintage fair was thronged with people. Lewis, who had volunteered to cover my stall, did a marvellous job of clearing our tat. From the vantage point of the balcony, I watched an old kitchen dresser that we no longer needed, bob off above head height down the drive, I presumed sold.

Peter Melchett, before cutting the ribbon, did us proud with memories of the Control Tower and kind words about the quality of the restoration.[124] Rather than people leaving quickly they stayed. Some listened and danced to the 1940s music, while others sat on rugs and deckchairs and enjoyed afternoon tea. This all made for a fabulous backdrop for Chris Richmond's online video documentary,[K] and for when ITV News arrived for an interview with Claire and me. The tours were very popular and oversubscribed. We sadly had to turn people away from the tours, including the family of Ted Allen (who painted

---

K Chris Richmond, who was a part-time filmmaker, had been documenting progress on the restoration of the Control Tower since October 2012. Shortly after our opening, he released the film online at *Norfolk Uncovered*. He certainly captured the chaos of transformation and it caused interest at the time and many guests still arrive having watched it now.

the mural of the lost Stirling). However, Claire gave them a quick private tour.

The bar was Cillian's domain, from where he could look up from the speech broadcast building and 'see people dancing on the lawn ... everyone was gushing their hearts out'. For me, it was a welcome respite from the busyness around. The Stirling Beer, provided free of charge by Beeston Brewery, proved popular, and the income raised was the foundation of our fund for the still yet unborn memorial campaign.[L] At one point, sitting in the bar enjoying a pint, I passed comment on the wall-mounted wartime photographs of the Control Tower to someone that was scrutinising them. He pointed at a young boy in the photograph, someone we'd been hoping to identify, and said, 'that's me'.[M] He then produced a landscape version of the photograph from his wallet. I delighted in filling-in the circumstances of the photograph with him.

Roy Gibson (small boy) with his parents Malcolm and Ivy, from Walsingham, and LAC Harrison: Norman Turnbull (Control Tower Archive).

L   The campaign was formed and began in earnest in 2016 (see Chapter 11).

M   This was Roy Gibson. In the busyness of the event I failed to take his details. However, when giving a talk in 2023 to the Fakenham Men's Probus, he made himself known in the audience.

As people drifted away, we gathered with neighbours and friends to finish the beer. The day ended with a heavy shower that initiated a timely halt; we retreated inside and had a reasonably early night. The following morning was dry and bright. I walked around the garden collecting litter (of which there was very little), and cutting down, the once celebratory and now deflated, balloons. In two weeks we would open for business, but first, a little time off.

Seventy years earlier, there was no option for time off; the invasion of Europe had just begun with, by the evening of 6 June 1944, 156,000[125] troops landed on the Normandy beaches. For those troops, the journey to Berlin was all ahead of them. It would be long, arduous and result in thousands of casualties.

All aircraft had returned safely to RAF North Creake with only Stirling EX-B reporting problems and landing at RAF Langham.[126] LJ565 EX-Q took off at 21:40 hours, but returned to base at 22:41. The 199 Sortie records record a problem with 'radar', but nothing more specific.[127] Whatever caused the return, EX-Q took off again at 01:07 hours and completed the operation safely.[128] The following day a signal was received from RAF 100 Group Headquarters:

> You did famously last night …. The next few days will necessarily be the critical period of this operation. Calls upon you may be heavy and the weather may not be easy. I know that you will do your damnedest to meet all assignments with the efficiency and determination which has characterised the whole of your share of Overlord to date.[129]

For Phyllis Willmott, 'lying in [bed] all washed out, and with my temperature still wobbling up and down, I could have wept. It was just my luck to be in the sick-bay on D-Day'.[130] Also feeling sick, but to the back teeth, was William Betts, who would later be 199 Squadron leader.[131] He had wanted to fly, but, as he wrote in his logbook, he was in 'control of marshalling at takeoff; worse luck'.[132] However, each member of aircrew and groundcrew, regardless of task they performed, made a vital contribution to the success of the operation.

It is of course difficult to determine exactly what contribution these deception measures made to the successful invasion of Normandy. Arthur Harris commented after the war, that the work undertaken by 100 Group during the invasion was of 'paramount importance'.[133] He further noted in *Bomber Offensive*, 'the enemy, it appears, was completely taken in by our bogus convoys and convinced that the main assault was to be in Pas de Calais',[134] and it is significant that the Nazis did not seriously deviate from their belief that Pas de Calais was the location of the main invasion until July 1944,[135] a whole month after the landings at Normandy. Postwar it was recognised that 'considerable confusion was caused to the German early warning system',[136] and that without their jamming support the 'fight to secure the beachhead in Normandy would certainly have been far bloodier'.[137] In the event, with post-operation analysis suggesting that the 'Mandrel Screen was at least 95% effective',[138] only one German radar station actually caught a glimpse of the armada approaching Normandy. However, such was the general level of confusion that its warning went unheeded:[139]

> the seaborne and airborne landings took place with negligible losses and a full measure of tactical surprise was obtained. The general slowness of the enemy's reactions on land to the invasion of Normandy was almost certainly due to lack of a clear appreciation of the situation.[140]

At RAF North Creake, apart from D-Day, the use of Mandrel was being limited as it badly affected navy and army communications.[141] Crews, though at times detailed for operations, did not fly any sorties and their time was mostly occupied with training.[142] By mid-June 1944, in the face of mounting losses, the reticence to use Mandrel had dissolved. Flying operationally resumed once again on 16 June 1944, this operation also involved RAF North Creake's first aircraft loss of the war.[N143]

N See the chapter 'Missing' above.

The Racecourse Pattern continued as the method of maintaining station,[144] but with an amendment. The crews would now 'slightly shorten its down leg and make the following up leg correspondingly longer. This initiated a shift in the position of the circuit'[145] and thereby caused the pattern to 'creep' forward.[146] The navigational difficulties experienced formerly in 'maintaining station', were now exacerbated by this development; they would be a constant headache until the end of the war, being regularly raised in RAF 100 Group's Operations reports.[147] Nonetheless, the crews were busy; during August 1944 alone, the Group put up Mandrel Screens on 16 different occasions.[148]

Mandrel jamming received a boost in September 1944, with the formation of 171 Squadron; North Creake's second jamming unit.[149] By October 1944, both Squadrons were regularly flying Mandrel operations.[150] On 6 October 1944, 16 Stirlings (12 of 199 Squadron and four of 171 Squadron) flew a Mandrel Screen[151] supporting twin attacks on Dortmund and Bremen.[152] Reginald Jones, Assistant Director of Intelligence MI6, recalls the night:

> the German early warning radar was jammed by a screen of 100 Group aircraft operating their 'Mandrel' jammers; as a result the nightfighters were only able to attack after our bombers had been over the target for ten minutes. Similarly, the Dortmund force flew low over France and turned north and climbed towards the Ruhr again screened by 'Mandrel' aircraft ... the result was confusion to the defences, and General Schmid reacted with castigatory diatribe to the whole German nightfighter organization: 'I am astonished that in spite of pains, admonitions, and orders throughout the whole year, I have not succeeded in bringing the Jagd Divisionen [German Fighter Division] at least to the point of being able to distinguish in what strength and in what direction the enemy is approaching'.[153]

The success continued, and during December 1944, with targets commonly 'in or near the Ruhr',[154] Mandrel proved effective in 'denying to the enemy controllers early warning in time to move fighters from adjacent areas to the target area'.[155] Notwithstanding determined efforts to do so, the German defences had very little success in intercepting the Main Force bombers.[156] In spite of this success, the Stirling aircraft, used by both North Creake squadrons, had begun to display their limitations. Struggling to maintain the higher altitudes required,[157] they were also incurring difficulties when flying in adverse weather conditions, often with Mandrel jamming out navigational aids.[158] Many of these problems would be overcome with the introduction of the Halifax bomber from October 1944.[159]

The new Halifaxes were fitted with Mandrel equipment at St Athan,[160] with conversion completed for both squadrons by March 1945.[161] The advantage of Halifaxes was they could comfortably jam at 18,000 feet, and could Window at 22,000 feet.[162] The latter became particularly important as a result of the operational requirements of the Special Window Force (SWF) formed on 14 July 1944.[163] The SWF was born from the 'realisation of the potential of combining Mandrel and Window'.[164] Robert Cockburn at TRE had always made clear that Window should only ever be considered as a supplement to electronic RCM, as its effects are only useful in the immediate area where jettisoned,[165] producing 'general noise, in order to fill the gaps in the electrical jamming'.[166] Now, with the Allies making steady progress in occupied Europe and punching a 'gigantic hole in the radar chain',[167] the SWF spoof operations, in combination with Mandrel, were returning excellent results. They were significantly reducing the time any Bomber Command raid could be plotted by the German controllers.[168] However, by the end of July 1944, shortages in the supply of Window had led to conservation measures by the RAF.[169] Personnel were warned to take care 'in handling the stocks available to prevent wastage',[170] as it would 'be some time before stocks [were] plentiful',[171] even with production being 'stepped-up'.[172] Nonetheless, July was a good month for 199 Squadron:

Out of the 31 days we have been standing by on 29 occasions and have actually operated 15 times. A total of 222 aircraft took off, 220 of which completed successful sorties. All these sorties were completed and the accompanying air tests carried out without a single accident or incident of any description. This accomplishment for a two flight heavy squadron reflects very well on the hard work put in by, and efficiency of, both ground and aircrews and is certainly cause for much gratification.[173]

Nonetheless, by the end of August 1944, operations were being curtailed by this shortage.[174] Eventually, with Window stocks at sustainable levels, Windowing stepped-up unrestricted by anything other than the weather.

In August 1944, 199 Squadron and USAAF 803rd Squadron, were being regularly joined by a 'half-dozen Mandrel B-17 aircraft of RAF 214 Squadron'. Operating the Mandrel Screen on 16 nights during the month, they discovered that, not only did the screen hide the bomber stream but its presence 'attracted enemy fighters into the area being affected'.[175] The RAF 100 Group decided to utilise this phenomenon as a further enhancement of its spoof operations. In addition, August also saw the introduction of the technique of 'Mandrel breakdown'.[176] That is, simulating a breakdown in the Mandrel Screen by turning off some Mandrel jammers and thereby allowing the German controllers to glimpse the SWF, and to assess the size of the illusionary force and mount a defence against it.[177] Within a couple of months, the RAF 100 Group had grown significantly more confident about the success of such operations, and reported, in language typical of the war:

Mandrel Screen, Window Spoof and Communications Jamming have been operated on all nights major operations took place ... The enemy has given no indication of being better able than he was to deal with these countermeasures, and, in fact, November has seen some of their greatest successes, and, it is believed his greatest frustrations so far ... The radio countermeasures operations will grow and develop and the Hun's frustration will further increase. Exhaustion and attrition will have their effect ... the lot of the German night-fighter is one that must be already rife with anxiety and apprehension; no longer is it the envy of all the Luftwaffe. Its unpopularity will grow.[178]

The SWF continued to confound German controllers, causing 'great upset',[179] as 1944 turned into 1945. On 28 January 1945, aircraft from RAF North Creake mounted their longest Mandrel penetration into Europe with the screen almost at Stuttgart. In consequence, navigators experienced much weaker Gee signals that the Mandrel equipment almost obliterated.[180] Deep penetrations also caused the return of an old problem; the enemy were possibly viewing bombers behind the protection of the Mandrel Screen, as the screen reached east of The Hague (still in enemy hands). 'This was overcome by increasing the length of the Screen and bending back the more northern stations to smother sightings from Holland'.[181] In February 1945, there was some suggestion that the enemy was beginning to counter the worst effects of Mandrel, but this appeared unfounded as by March they seemed 'to have little success in looking behind it', and the screen was successfully operated on 20 nights.[182]

By this time, the bombing raid had become a well-organised and complicated entity; no longer was it just a question of a stream of bombers, taking off from numerous bases, and converging on a single target. For example, on 20 March 1945, Bomber Command detailed two primary targets; first, 235 Lancasters and Mosquitoes set out for a synthetic oil refinery in Bohlen near Leipzig and, second, at Hemmingstedt, in Schleswig-Holstein, 166 Lancasters were to bomb an oil field.[183] There was also an earlier 'nuisance' raid on Berlin involving 35 Mosquitoes.[184] With the heavy bombers crossing the Channel 'the complications for the German radar operators began'.[185] At 02:05 hours 14 aircraft from 171 and 199 Squadrons turned their Mandrel equipment to transmit, forming a Screen of 80 miles across Northern

France,[186] 'blanketing all Freyas' [sic] screens with snow'.[187] This resulted in German Fighter Control being unable to determine anything on which to base assessments of the size or direction of that night's raid. Indeed, they were 'unable to tell whether there were operations pending' at all.[188] Shortly after crossing the coast of France, the Bohlen force, hidden by the Mandrel Screen, split into two streams with 41 Lancasters breaking away and heading off to the north-east.[189] Meanwhile, two fighter squadrons from the RAF 100 Group (23 Squadron and 515 Squadron) harassed enemy night-fighters at their bases, 'orbiting for hours on end, dropping clusters of incendiaries and firing at anything that moved'.[190]

Also flying that night, on a parallel course to the Main Force, was a decoy of 64 Halifaxes and Lancasters from Operational Training Units.[191] They were followed by German ground controllers, who were attempting to predict the target and preparing to move night-fighters accordingly. On almost reaching the German border at Strasbourg, they simply turned, and went home.[192] At the same time, the two streams heading towards Bohlen burst through the Mandrel Screen.[193] The larger force was proceeded by four Halifaxes of 171 Squadron and seven Liberators of RAF 223 Squadron, 'laying out a dense cloud of "Window" which effectively hid the bombers following them'.[194]

At this point it was still impossible for the German fighter controllers to determine the size of the force, or where the target would be. Indeed, as the bombers crossed into Germany, Major Ruppel of the Central Rhine Defence Area, 'seriously under-estimated the strength of the two approaching formations'.[195] Eighty-nine Luftwaffe night-fighters had now been scrambled to intercept the bomber stream, and they were currently orbiting beacons awaiting instructions, while German controllers waited for the situation to become clear.[196] Unwilling to come to a conclusion precipitately and risk an error, the controller waited 'precious minutes ... to make a valid assessment of the threat'.[197] Concluding the attack was heading for Kassel, the controller ordered all aircraft, with the exception of one squadron, in the direction of the city (the remaining squadron he directed to protect Frankfurt).[198] Initially it appeared that he had made the correct assessment as target markers and bombs, typical of the opening of an attack, began to fall on the city. But this was part of the illusion which was then further heightened as 171 Squadron Halifaxes and 223 Squadron Liberators brought the Window feint right up to Kassel.[199] The German night-fighters continued to wait over Kassel for some 20 minutes after the feint had begun, shooting down one 100 Group Liberator that consequently crashed killing all but one of the crew.[200] The German controller, after 20 minutes, realised he had been tricked. He ordered his force eastwards chasing the bombers, believing that Leipzig, the nearest city to Bohlen, was the probable target.[201] However, it was too late, as the bombers were within 30 miles of Bohlen.[202]

Not even at this point did the deceptions relent. The larger bomber force, that was heading for the refinery, once again, split in two.[203] As target markers fell upon Bohlen, more target markers were being dropped on Leuna, some 20 miles to the north-west. Here, two Halifaxes of 199 Squadron accompanied by four flying fortresses of 214 Squadron, were laying a second Window trail away from the main Bohlen force. Then, together with 12 Lancasters, 'they marked out Leuna as if for a full-scale attack',[204] thereby, making the spoof far more convincing and drawing away night-fighters from the Main Force bombers at Bohlen.[205]

The RAF 100 Group report of the night simply concluded, 'the bomber losses would have undoubtably have been much heavier without the Feints'.[206] A total of 675 sorties were flown that night. Thirteen aircraft (1.9%) were lost.[207] For Bomber Command, it was a very successful raid.

March 1945 proved a very busy month for both squadrons. Mandrel Screen was in operation on 20 nights, with 123 sorties completed by 199 Squadron and 144 sorties by 171 Squadron.[208] The airfield also managed to average 'the highest number of hours flown per aircraft' in the Group,[209] and 199 Squadron, at 1,380 operational hours flown, recording the greatest total of any of the 100 Group Squadrons.[210] It had been realised since the Mandrel Screen's early use for D-Day, that its use would, in itself, constitute a timely warning of an impending attack, given that it was always established 'some hours before our main force was due to reach its objective'.[211]

> to overcome this disadvantage, the screen was frequently deployed at times when the rest of Bomber Command had the night off. The presence of the screen, therefore, might or might not herald the approach of our main forces; and the enemy, on the grounds both of morale and economy of fuel, eventually became loath to put his fighter into the air as soon as he heard the screen take up its position.[212]

With frequent repetition of the tactic it was hoped that it would 'invalidate the presence of jamming as evidence of the approach of a raid'.[213] Edward Addison called this tactic 'conditioning'.[214] It could also be used to good effect with Window, and the RAF 100 Group, 'mounted Mandrel screens and Window spoof operations almost every night, regardless of whether there were real bombing operations'.[215] The RAF 100 Group monthly Operations reports give many examples:

> all heavy squadrons of the Group have completed sorties with the [Special Window] force which operated in November [1944] on 28 occasions. In 8 instances the Window Force operated independently (backed by a Mandrel Screen) in the absence of any major attack by Bomber Command, in order to force the enemy to fly. A particularly successful operation of this kind was carried out on the night 10/11th November when the Window spoof force operated twice during the night, being taken for a genuine bombing force on the second occasion, with consequent heavy fighter re-action.[216]

In this way, the 'enemy's defences would be alerted and his fighters flown unnecessarily',[217] maintaining 'steady pressure on the already over-extended and strained German defence organisation with its dwindling fuel reserves'.[218] Inevitably the Luftwaffe controllers became suspicious but 'their suspicion tended to delay their reaction to actual Bomber Command attacks, often until it was too late'.[219]

While the squadrons at North Creake primarily used only two countermeasures (Mandrel and Window),[O] there also appears reasonably frequent use of Monica, although it was not strictly an RCM, being developed as an early-warning device and fitted to British Main Force bombers in 1943.[220] It alerted the crew of the presence of nearby aircraft through the use of an audible signal. However, through the use of an onboard device, 'Flensburg', the German night-fighters had been able to track Monica signals from some very considerable distance and used them to home in on bombers. Once this was realised, Monica was withdrawn from service.[221]

It was subsequently fitted to North Creake bombers with the sole intention of attracting night-fighters to their aircraft, thereby, drawing them away from the Main Force bombers.[222] With such tactics, it is little wonder that it was expected, unbeknown to the crews, that 'these spoof formations would suffer heavily'.[223] Indeed, one RAF 100 Group pilot ruefully observed that, 'we were usually all too successful,

---

O There is some suggestion that other special operations were carried out from RAF North Creake, particularly those assisting the SOE. It would make operational sense, as heightened levels of security at RAF North Creake were already in place and it would be reasonably straightforward to alter aircraft routes (particularly those of the Windowers). In conversation, veterans have mentioned to me that there were occasions when they took-off with nine on board and they came back with eight, and there have even been suggestions that there was a Lysander based at RAF North Creake for such special work. 199 Squadron had undertaken special duties from RAF Lakenheath and it would be unremarkable that they continued with similar operations here. However, this also raises the possibility that the memories of such operations are a conflation of wartime experiences. Nonetheless, more precisely, Christopher Nieman recalls that his father, Fred (a fluent German speaker), who served as groundcrew at RAF North Creake, flew SOE operations 'but wouldn't talk about it' (Nieman: 6/4/2021). Describing him as a 'complex, secretive man', he states that 'some aspects of his wartime service don't add up. He was basically trained as an engine fitter and to my knowledge was never officially used as aircrew, [although] he seemed to regularly be on the planes' (Nieman: 6/4/2021). Moreover, Christopher explains that his mother had once been told by a senior RAF officer 'that both he and her had been checked and security cleared even before he was called up. She was also told, that if he was killed on active duty, she would receive a Wing Commander's widow's pension. Very strange for groundcrew!' (Nieman: 6/4/2021).

Teddy Maufe, from Branthill Farm, recalls a family legend where his father, David, working the fields near the Control Tower, witnessed someone dressed up in a stripy shirt and beret, looking like a caricature of a Frenchman with everything but the onions around his neck. A week or so later, in the company of RAF North Creake guests, he humorously suggested, 'if they drop him in France he'll be shot!' He was firmly admonished and cautioned 'you never saw that' (Maufe: 22/3/2024) leaving him feeling very foolish. Although such feelings didn't prevent him from happily relating the story in social settings postwar (Maufe: 22/3/2024).

Nevertheless, despite these stories, it should be noted that even with significant enquiry, no documents have been discovered to confirm the use of RAF North Creake in special operations, and without such documentary evidence special duties of this nature remain speculation. But the stories are sufficient to acknowledge that such work was more than a possibility.

from our point of view, in drawing large numbers of enemy fighters into our immediate area'.[224] Michael Renaut remembers a night late on in the war when night-fighters were very successfully drawn to the decoy stream. 'On 14th April I briefed my crews for operations on Berlin [Potsdam] and the Main Force were to attack a target close to hand. We carried bombs this time and about two tons of 'window' so it looked like being a warm trip.'[225] Jim Feasey takes up the story:

> I volunteered for a trip with our CO, W/C Mike Renaut DFC, as his regular mid-upper gunner was sick ... Our SO [special operator], F/S McDonald, was jamming with his Mandrel sets and we were dropping tons of Window ... Nearing Berlin our own Halifax broke off and, whilst we were on our own, we dropped a small number of bombs on the barracks at Potsdam ... Over Potsdam we were coned by several searchlights. Mike dived and weaved but there were so many to try to evade. Nothing hit us and there was no flak which was usually an indication that there were fighters about. We had two fighter attacks from behind and Mike saw two fighter attacks develop from head on. He 'yawed' [deviated from the horizontal line of flight] the aircraft and the cannon fire swept under the wing. The WOP [wireless operator], 'Rusty' Willis, who had opened his curtain to see what was going on, said, 'Blow that', or words to that effect, and promptly closed his curtain again! I tried to do something by calling out directions to dive but Mike was doing what he thought was best. I could see a fighter high up above but that was all I could see as I was blinded by the lights. After about 15 minutes we managed to fly out of it all ...We were short of fuel and we had to land at Manston, in Kent, and spend the rest of the night there. We returned to North Creake in the morning.[226]

Officially the raid on Potsdam was recorded as 'little more than a "fringe" target'.[227] Michael Renaut recalls the raid:

my mouth went dry at the first attack and I literally felt my hair standing on end during the excitement in the target area. The strange thing was that although I was scared out of my wits. I managed to remain calm and hoped that my skill as a bomber pilot would out-manoeuvre the comparatively inexperienced night fighter pilots on my tail.[228]

Michael Renaut believed he was for the 'chop' that night.[229] Edward Addison, leading the RAF 100 Group commented, 'they had to draw upon them the wrath of the defenders so that the real bombers could go unscathed'.[230] A contemporary RAF 100 Group report concurred:

small forces of these heavy aircraft have been sticking out their necks … trying to persuade the enemy that they are the real bomber forces and that the bomber force is the feint force. They have gone out by themselves; they have broken away from the main force. They have dropped flares, target indicators and incendiaries on small targets in order to attract to themselves the enemy fighters.[231]

In the event, losses were not as great as feared, and averaged at a similar rate as Bomber Command generally.[232] The lower than expected losses were, perhaps, a result of the low density concentrations of aircraft flying on these operations, or that they were possibly benefitting from protection afforded by the very equipment they were using.[233] What is certain, is that the disruption they caused to German night defences was of a significant benefit to Bomber Command bombers, as recorded at a German Air Ministry conference on 5 January 1945:

today the night-fighter achieves nothing. The reason for this lies in the enemy's jamming operations, which completely blot out ground and airborne search equipment. All other reasons are secondary.[234]

By the end of the war more than ten out of every 100 aircraft on a raid, rather than being part of the Main Force, were in a Bomber Support role.[235] For RAF North Creake, this all began with D-Day in June 1944. The crews were informed that Mandrel operations were vital, but no crew members, other than the special operator, knew what it actually did. If they pushed at a debriefing to find out if they were doing it right, generally the response was 'oh we'll let you know if you should have done otherwise'.[236] Bernie How, reflecting on his role on D-Day commented:

> we just hoped we were doing a good job; you'd never really know. We probably did.[237]

And they did.

OPERATION GISELA

On 3 March 1945, the 2,000[th] night of the war, RAF Bomber
Command sent two large forces of bombers to Germany; 234 aircraft
attacked the synthetic oil plant at Kamen and a further 222 aircraft
bombed an aqueduct on the Dortmund-Ems canal at Ladbergen. RAF
100 Group despatched 61 aircraft flying radio countermeasures (RCM)
sorties in support of the Main Force.[1]

RAF North Creake contributed to the RCM effort by operating
a creeping Mandrel Screen to protect the forces attacking Kamen and
Ladbergen.[2] Take-off commenced at 18:23 hours[3] and involved four
Stirlings and five Halifaxes from 199 Squadron, along with seven
Halifaxes of 171 Squadron.[4] The Screen was formed at 15,000 feet,
from 20:45 hours to 21:30 hours: jamming from Antwerp in Belgium,
to Aachen in Germany, obscuring the approach of the bombers from
German radar. The Screen then moved further east and jammed from
22:20 hours until 22:45 hours; 'all the Mandrelleros[A] carried out
their missions'.[5]

Three Halifaxes of 171 Squadron were detailed for combined
Window and Mandrel operations. One aircraft failed to take off, and

---

A 'Mandrelleros' was the collective noun used in the squadron and station ORBs for aircraft flying with
   Mandrel jammers on board.

the reserve (Halifax NA109 6Y-S), took off in its place, only to return early with instrument failure.[B6] Halifax NA105 6Y-N also returned early 'with port outer u/s'.[7] The remaining Halifax (LK874 6Y-C, piloted by Peter Jennings[C]) carried out his Window patrol successfully, 'discharging his load from 21:20 to 22:10 hours'[8] and jamming on the outward journey and again on the homeward.[9] This lone 171 Squadron Halifax was joined by six aircraft from 214 Squadron and two from 223 Squadron, forming the Special Window Force that night.[10] Operating in the direction of the Ruhr area, they caused some confusion but attracted few night-fighters. With the operation 'completed successfully',[11] the aircraft turned for home. However, 'at 00:06 hours, the station [was] warned of intruders'.[12] RAF North Creake would shortly feel the wrath of Operation Gisela.

On account of an edict issued by Adolf Hitler in 1941, that 'the place to shoot bombers down was over Germany, not over England',[13] there had been very few Luftwaffe fighter incursions over Britain; regardless of the potential effectiveness of this strategy for the Nazis.[14] However, during 1944, military intelligence was suggesting that attitudes were changing in Germany. It was believed that plans were being developed to 'employ a night-fighter intruder force, of some strength, against our returning bombers while they were landing at their bases and therefore at their most vulnerable'.[15] Such a threat was realised on the night of the 3 to 4 March 1945; 'Operation Gisela'. The origins of this scheme lay with Heinz-Wolfgang Schnaufer, a top scoring night-fighter pilot, and it was originally scheduled for the end of February 1945:

> but details of the plan were obtained and the British made it known by broadcasting the contemporary hit tune 'I Dance with Gisela tonight' on the Allied propaganda station 'Soldatensender Calais'. Gisela had therefore been postponed until the British relaxed their vigilance.[16]

B   This aircraft took off at 19:04 and returned 20:11 (Hines: 2022: 95). It was piloted by Brodie Reid whose logbook states 'DNCO instruments u/s' (Reid: 1945: Flying Logbook: RAF Form 1767).

C   Peter Jennings would lose his life on air operations on the 16/17 April 1945 (see 'Mid-Air Collision below).

Intruders had been active on several nights in early 1945 and 'more than once had successfully infiltrated the returning bomber stream'.[17] Dietrich Peltz (Luftwaffe General) committed 142 night-fighters to the operation, far too few to commit a serious blow to RAF Bomber Command.[18] Flying as low as 30 metres to avoid detection on British radar,[19] Arnold Doring of 10/NJG3 recalls:

> we are heading for the peninsula of Flamborough Head, our sector to penetrate the British mainland. This is the same route that the returning bombers belonging to British 100 Bomber Group are taking, in the area NW of Hull. We are ordered to keep absolute radio silence, the Tommy should not notice anything. Neither are we allowed to engage any Viermots [four-engined bombers] in combat over the North Sea, as we must succeed in totally surprising them.[20]

Arthur Harris argued that the diversion of aircraft was the best 'means employed to overcome this threat'.[21] Accordingly, a plan was established for 'the systematic diversion of the aircraft from any threatened bases to other airfields to the west and south-west'.[22] A simple one-word code: 'scram', would be given by the duty flying control officers (FCOs) in the control tower to enact the diversion strategy. Crews would be pre-briefed each day as to the diversion arrangements; 'Central Flying Control had no easy task ... finding alternative airfields for up to 1,500 aircraft on every night on which the bomber force operated'.[D23]

FCOs were required to remain at their posts during a raid, whereas all other staff took cover.[24] During the 'scram' process, vigilance was required to avoid 'the transmission of any message which might be of value to the enemy'.[25] An air raid warning red signal, mounted on the highest point of the control tower was 'illuminated [to] indicate the presence of enemy aircraft in the vicinity'.[26] In addition, a single master blackout switch was fitted for use in an intruder emergency, this

---

D Diversions from and to RAF North Creake were frequent for numerous reasons such as: lighting failure (January 1945); weather (unsurprising in January 1945, but there were also diversions in months such as June 1944); and runways blocked by crashed aircraft – for example in August 1944 (North Creake ORB: 1944-1945).

would extinguish all the airfield lighting and hide the aerodrome from easy view.[27]

Just after midnight on 4 March 1945, the intruders claimed their first victim; Mosquito MM640 of 169 Squadron based at West Raynham, killing both airmen on board. Over the next two hours a further 21 aircraft would be destroyed, with at least a further 20 being damaged.[E28] The RAF were caught off guard with the low-flying tactics of the German night-fighters allowing for no early warning:

> I crossed in somewhere between the Wash and the Humber. As we approached the coast I opened up and climbed higher, and we found ourselves among the returning bombers. We could see them on our radar. The unpleasant aspect of the affair was that there were lots of searchlights on the coast. Just after we had crossed the coast I looked down obliquely and I saw a row of searchlights sweeping the sky, and then we saw a number of searchlights standing still and pointing directly upwards, possibly an approach lane to an airfield. I flew through them, and I came to an airfield. There was a Lancaster on the circuit, and the airfield lighting was on. I let down my wheels and flaps to slow myself down to his speed, and shot him down.[29]

The intruder activity wasn't just limited to targeting bombers, as 27 airfields experienced strafing attacks.[30] At RAF North Creake, the alert for intruders was received at 00:06 hours,[31] the 'scram' notice was immediately broadcast, diverting aircraft to Weston Zoyland[32] in Somerset. However, for one aircraft in the circuit, preparing to land, the call came too late.

At 00:20 hours 171 Squadron Halifax NA673 6Y-P, piloted by W A Short, was fired on by an unseen aircraft at long range, as it circled waiting to land.[33] The rear gunner, K B Fuller, spotted a second approach on the port side, the pilot took an immediate evasive

---

E   There is some disparity in the numbers of RAF aircraft lost in this intruder operation. Martin Middlebrook claims 20 aircraft shot down by intruders (Middlebrook: 1985: 674) whereas Bowman claims 24 aircraft (13 Halifaxes, nine Lancasters, one Mosquito and one B-17 (Bowman: 2015: 126).

'corkscrew' manoeuvre to port.[34] Around 50 rounds were fired from approximately 600 feet, but passed above the aircraft, between the mid-upper gunner's position and the rear turret.[35] A further burst of fire was received from astern and above; the rear gunner fired a short burst in the direction of the tracer bullets and the enemy aircraft immediately ceased firing. W A Short undertook another 'wild corkscrew' as 6Y-P came under a third attack, this time from the starboard (as observed by the rear gunner, bomb aimer and special operator). The Halifax corkscrewed starboard with tracers passing below.[36] All the attacks took place within a 15-minute timeframe, the visibility was down to 4,000 yards due to ground mist,[37] which possibly explains why no strikes were received.[38] The gunner took some retaliatory action but was restrained by the 'fact that other friendly aircraft [were] in close vicinity'.[39]

The response from the ground was limited, perhaps owing to the reduction in the strength of the RAF Regiment protecting the airfield in July 1944;[40] 'five Bofors Flights were posted to stations on the south coast to strengthen the anti-aircraft cover against flying bombs'[41] and the personnel of the four Hispano Flights were also posted. The anti-aircraft 'defence of the station [was] now entirely in the hands of the station personnel'.[42] At RAF North Creake, like all other RAF bomber stations, the intruders met no resistance[43] when 'they shot up the airfield. Fortunately nobody was hurt, nobody was killed and they disappeared and they never came again'.[44] Halifax NA673 6Y-P eventually landed at RAF North Creake at 01:30 hours, presumably after returning from Weston Zoyland.[45]

Concurrently, having successfully completed their operation, 171 Squadron Halifax NA107 6Y-T, was fewer than 40 miles from base.[46] Flying on automatic pilot[47] at 3,000 feet south-west of Norwich,[48] it was rapidly approaching the airfield. The Halifax had taken off from RAF North Creake on 3 March 1945 at 18:38:[49] on board were:

Walter 'Wally' Braithwaite (RAF) Bomb Aimer
Norman George Errington (RAF) Wireless Operator
W. G. Hayden (RAF), Special Operator

Horace 'Harry' Laking (RAF) Fight Engineer
Percy Clifford Proctor[F] (RAF) Pilot
George David Alfred Richards (RAF) Mid-Upper Gunner
Eric Vane Stephenson (RAF) Rear Gunner
Daniel Thomas Twinn (RAF) Navigator

They had first flown together on an operation from RAF North Creake on 28 February in Halifax NA109 6Y-S, having been posted to 171 Squadron on 13 February. All the crew members were experienced airmen with George Richards, in particular, having already completed 25 sorties, comprising of 144 hours flying.[50] The special operator, W G Hayden, was posted to RAF North Creake on 21 January 1945, and subsequently, joined Percy Proctor's crew.[51]

Tonight, Norman Errington, the wireless operator, had just received the 'scram message' and was in the process of passing it to Percy Proctor, the pilot, when he exclaimed 'good God Norman, don't you know what just happened?' To which Norman replied, 'I have a jolly good idea.'[G][52] What they had realised was they were now under attack from the Ju88 of Kurt Fladrich,[H] of III/NJG4:[53]

> cannon shells came whizzing right through the aircraft in a head-on attack. A burst of fire hit the starboard side of the aircraft, set fire to the wing and inner engine, shot away the leading edge of the wing, damaged the elevator and caused an explosion in the flight engineer's department. Squadron Leader Proctor the pilot, gave the order to bale out as the Halifax was becoming uncontrollable.[54]

The Halifax was claimed destroyed at 00:33 hours.[55] The 171 Squadron

---

F   There seem to be two variant spellings of his name: Proctor and Procter, while Procter is used frequently, I have opted for Proctor, as this is the spelling that appears in official documents (ORBs, London Gazette etc as well as some secondary/internet sources). But mistakes can be made in official documents and I accept it may be wrong.

G   One imagines the language in reality was somewhat more colourful!

H   This was Fladrich's 15th and last claim (Parry: 1987: 131). He survived the war and died in January 1995 (luftkrieg1939-45.dk).

ORB simply records, 'aircraft was shot down by an enemy intruder, but all the crew baled out safely'.[56] However, the Halifax had dropped to 1,000[57] feet, barely affording the crew enough time for their parachutes to open. Nevertheless, having baled out, all eight landed safely in and around Knettishall.[58] Halifax NA107 6Y-T, burning furiously and losing height, crashed at Walnut Tree Farm, South Lopham, five miles north-north-west of Diss, Norfolk.[59]

Of the eight on board, seven landed around Knettishall Airfield,[60] 'the first swing of the parachute brought [Percy Proctor] in quick contact with the ground and he lay unconscious for over an hour …When he regained some sensibility … [He felt] himself all over for missing or broken limbs,'[61] though injured, everything was thankfully there. Also injured were Wally Braithwaite (bomb aimer), George Richards (air gunner) and Eric Stephenson (air gunner).[62] Harry Laking (flight engineer) 'apparently under the impression that there was no hope of survival and anxious to save time and money in transportation, glided into a cemetery!'.[63]

It appears that the injuries sustained by Walter Braithwaite were minor as he, together with Eric Stevenson had returned to RAF North Creake by 14 March 1945, along with Harry Laking, who had burnt his wrist.[64] George Richards (mid-upper gunner) sustained a broken ankle[65] when he reportedly landed on a petrol bowser.[66] He was admitted to RAF Hospital Ely on 5 March 1945. Discharged from hospital on 14 March 1945, he was granted sick leave until 29 March 1945.[67] Percy Proctor's specific injuries are unknown, but as he was also admitted to Ely hospital, discharged on 14 March and then granted sick leave until 29 March,[68] they were presumably of some significance.

As a result of the 'scram' message, one 199 Squadron aircraft[I] and five 171 Squadron aircraft were diverted to Weston Zoyland,[69] all of whom had either been in the circuit at the time, or approaching the airfield.

I   Halifax RG381 EX-Q, piloted by C T King returned to RAF North Creake a little over seven hours after taking off (Hines: 2022: 48).

At RAF North Creake in the early hours of 4 March 1945, things were becoming calmer. While the incident had resulted in no loss of life at the station, it did make people twitchy. Gordon Mercier recalls that there was 'no procedure other than to keep my eyes open ... you could be fired on as you were landing ... you had to keep your eyes open right until the moment you landed'.[70]

Other airfields along the east coast were not so fortunate. Of a total of 785 sorties flown, eight aircraft were lost over Germany (and one over the sea),[71] and intruders destroyed up to a further 23 bombers and one Mosquito, with more than 20 other aircraft damaged over Britain.[72] The Mosquito and five of the bombers crashed in Norfolk,[73] all of them from RAF 100 Group stations.[74]

However, the Germans also sustained losses, for eight fighters failed to return, nine more crashed with the loss of three crews and a further 11 sustained landing damage.[75] Three of the night-fighters had been shot down over Britain, becoming the last Luftwaffe losses sustained over the UK during the Second World War:[76]

> a lot of my comrades were killed that night. A lot had to make emergency landings or bale out because they ran out of petrol ... The losses we had on Gisela were mainly due to bad weather and petrol shortage, and there were scarcely any from enemy action.[77]

Percy Proctor's crew had thankfully survived the attack.

The crew flew its first operation after Operation Gisela on 8 April 1945, although the rear gunner Eric Stephenson was replaced by R K Stone (posted from 277 Squadron on 19 March). The crew then underwent a number of personnel changes before their last operation on 23 April 1945 (W Hayden, special operator, and Norman Errington, wireless operator, were both replaced).[78] The end of the war in Europe sees Walter Braithwaite posted to Air Sea Rescue, Norman Errington at 1332 Conversion Unit at RAF Riccall, Yorkshire and Percy Proctor, who had been appointed 171 Squadron's 'B' Flight commander and subsequently acting Squadron Leader, posted to the RAF 100 Group HQ. The special operator, W G Hayden was attached to No. 14 Radio School,[79] although, nothing further is known of his postwar life. George Richards was discharged from the RAF in 1946. Horace Laking remained with 171 Squadron until 4 July 1945, and later served with the RAF in India before being discharged on 26 July 1946.[80] Eric Stephenson remained with the RAF until he retired in October 1961.[81]

Little is known of the postwar career of Daniel Twinn, other than that he was still in the RAF when his name appeared on the manifest of a ship arriving in Southampton from Cape Town, South Africa, in 1947. He was married in 1952 and had two children. He died at the age of 63 in Thurrock, Essex. Horace Laking lived to the fine age of 90 and died in December 2012, in Harthill, Yorkshire.

Before joining the RAF, Eric Stephenson had married Irene Ranshaw in 1938 in Durham. They had two children, a daughter born just before the war, and a son born just after. Percy Proctor married Mabel Shepherd in Wandsworth, London, 20 days after the end of the war in Europe. He died in Dover, Kent, in July 1991, aged 79. Walter Braithwaite married Margaret Moon in Leeds in 1947. They had three children and he died in Bristol, Gloucestershire, in December 2017 at the age of 95. Norman George Errington joined the RAF in 1942, the same year he married Florence Reeve. He died at Kings Lynn, Norfolk, in November 1984, aged 69. George Richards later worked for some time as a coal miner, he died in September 1989, at Bishop's Stortford, Hertfordshire, aged 77.[82]

At RAF North Creake on the morning of 4 March 1945, the RAF scribe was completing the Operations Record Book for the station. After recording the loss of Halifax NA107 6Y-T, he thought it fit to mention another loss experienced at the station. The last paragraph reports, for 3 March 1945, 'the Rugby Match played between the station XV and R.A.F Langham resulted in a win for our opponent, the score being 9–22'.[83]

CHAPTER SEVEN

PLANNING AHEAD

With all the momentum of the opening behind us, it was time to think about planning ahead and developing the B&B business. But first we needed a little time to recover from the stresses of the build. We also needed another cat. Very sadly, Isis had died in January, and a house just isn't a home without a cat.

I had inherited a prejudice from my father – the best cats are female short-haired tabbies – I wouldn't entertain the thought of anything else. I found the perfect candidate in a rescue centre in west Norfolk. I phoned up, only to be told she was already reserved, 'but we do have a beautiful black-and-white cat'. Stumbling, embarrassed, as I didn't want to reveal my prejudices, the receptionist lost no time sinking in the emotional claws of a sad story; 'we found her under a hedge, very sad and abandoned, she had a badly damaged eye, which we've had to remove'. 'Oh', I said. 'We then discovered she was pregnant and she's currently nursing four kittens.' 'I see', I said. 'She has a wonderfully gentle nature, loves being held.' 'Ah', I said. 'But no one wants to adopt black-and-white cats and with the fact she only has one eye...' We adopted the black-and-white cat. And one of her kittens.

There is nothing unique about our feelings regarding keeping pets, and when RAF North Creake was operational, the personnel stationed here felt much the same. There were numerous cats and dogs on site and even a mascot goat called 'Wingco', whose billet was the dispersal near Egmere farm; 'when not smuggled aloft by crewmen, Wingco took great delight in leaving the dispersal point and making for the farmhouse where he would devour every flower in sight, then appear at the French windows, mouth stuffed with flower heads, demanding more to eat.'[1] In spite of the high affection with which this goat was held, he was put on a charge after gaining access to the map room and dining on the maps of Europe.[2] It's not recorded what Helen Storrar, the map clerk, felt about Wingco after that, although she was fond of animals and had a dog named 'Snogger', who was born at Lakenheath and accompanied her to every station until she was demobbed.[3]

As our cats, Window and Mandrel, settled-in, we waited for bookings. We had had a few guests booked in but, as to be expected in the first couple of months of business, bookings were sparse. When planning our B&B we'd always had a very clear vision; it was going to be our ideal B&B: it would be vegetarian (as we are both vegetarian and couldn't consider anything else); it would be furnished with original Art Deco furniture to complement the building and fittings; it would have no outside entertainment – no TVs and no piped music. TVs, we believe, kill conversation and the possibility of other entertainments (we would provide plenty of books, jigsaws and board games). And music generally divides opinion along lines of personal taste. Therefore, we decided our rooms would be quiet, apart from the ticking of clocks and, hopefully, the babble of conversation. Now with time to reflect, we were wondering if we'd developed a B&B that only two people would want to stay in. And they owned it.

We did have one very regular guest, our son, Cillian. At our opening he told us how much he'd like to get away from Hertfordshire and he wondered if he could join us at the Control Tower. The thought was delightful, but we were concerned about the reality. We get on extremely well as a family, but we all have very strong ideas about what we like and what we don't, and these don't always coincide. The only way this could work was to make the chalet in some way habitable. The chalet is a wooden lodge in the grounds of the Control Tower, built in the 1990s by a previous owner for use as accommodation; since we had moved in, we had used it for storage. We all agreed that Cillian and I would work on it together and he would stay in the Control Tower until it was habitable enough for him to move in. With hindsight, this agreement was probably more readily endorsed by me than Cillian, and when he found a job and a group of friends, understandably, his desire to help reduced. This led to friction, and he ended up moving to an unacceptably incomplete chalet, just so we could all have our own space again. It wasn't too long before he moved to Wells-next-the-Sea; a decision from which we all derived comfort. The equilibrium of our relationship was restored.

The Control Tower B&B is an unapologetically niche offering, and certainly not everyone's 'cup of tea', but we believed, though the audience to which it appeals would be smaller, it would be very dedicated and loyal. So how do we reach them? We tried advertising and we had produced some leaflets, but neither seemed to bring much business; just wasted money. Even when placed in related destinations (RAF museums etc.) or appropriate journals, the guests who booked in never seemed to have discovered us through the leaflets or advertising. Indeed, of the couple of thousand leaflets produced, I'm only aware of one person motivated to book. He picked it up at RAF East Kirkby, Lincolnshire, in around 2015 and kept it to one side and eventually booked in in August 2023. Hardly a successful promotional strategy.

What really did penetrate was feature articles, both locally and nationally. The *Eastern Daily Press*, from their first article in 2012 onwards, had been very supportive, as had local television and radio (running outside broadcasts from the Control Tower). This all increased the 'chatter' locally. National specialist interest magazines, such as *Flypast* and *Vintage Life*, really helped and we saw guests arrive as a consequence, as we did by being included in holiday features in national newspapers. It's the advantage of living in an unusual building with a fascinating history; you can achieve such coverage.[A] There is something

---

A An unforeseen outcome of press attention is unexpected arrivals through the post. Many people sent us

about two people giving up sensible careers in a bid to change their lives by taking on the restoration of an old building and using that building for their B&B business, that is pretty irresistible to the media. Then there is the war angle. And both combined and, with the merest suggestion of slight eccentricity, makes for media gold! Interestingly, it is almost impossible to predict what coverage will achieve good results. We thought articles in very specific journals, such as aviation-related or vegetarian magazines would bring good returns. But no. Whereas a small article about touring East Anglia in the newsletter of the Institute of Advanced Motorists (conveniently edited by a guest), brought us more than any other single article.[B] Nonetheless, what was most successful was social media (which luckily Claire is very good at) and then, ultimately, word of mouth. We are now blessed with many regular and loyal guests.

Ironically, while we wouldn't consider having TVs in the B&B, we were considering renting out the Control Tower as a location for filming. The BBC filmed a section of *James Martin: Home Comforts,* as they needed a retro kitchen. However, the income isn't terrific compensation for the disturbance and it conflicted with the needs of guests. We had an enquiry for another TV series where we were asked to accommodate a couple of presenters who were touring East Anglia. This sounded ideal. But when scouts visited, it became clear they wanted a filming location at the price of B&B rooms, which made us a little grumpy. Ultimately, they turned us down in favour of a glamping site anyway. We were gutted, no pun intended, when we heard it was *Gone Fishing* with Paul Whitehouse and Bob Mortimer. Although I subsequently read in an interview, that Bob Mortimer would never stay in a place without a TV!

historical information as a result of seeing us 'in the paper', some even contained RAF North Creake artifacts, such as the Norman Turnbull photographs, programmes for entertainment, a military police notebook and so on. We were even sent a painting of the Control Tower by Howard de Monfort who was inspired by the picture in *the Times*. Howard was a retired architect who we discovered, when he came to stay, had designed the new shrine development in Walsingham.

B Three weeks before the manuscript for this book was handed over to the publishers an article by Emma John appeared in *the Times* Saturday travel section (24/2/2024). Featuring only the Control Tower, it has produced far more bookings than any other coverage we've received.

With neither of us coming from a hospitality background, hosting was a little daunting. Consequently, we dipped our toes in by instituting a 'stay for a donation' scheme during the build. This scheme meant guests could stay in our ongoing project and pay us what they felt we were worth. This was very useful in terms of raising our profile; it also gained us some very loyal guests, but mostly it taught us a huge amount about the job. While hosting guests for the first time had been terribly nerve-wracking, we discovered that we really enjoyed sharing our home. This was a relief, because up until that point, we didn't know if we would. The shifts at the Three Horseshoes pub in Warham had also taught us a great deal. Not only that drunk people are not funny when you are sober, but also what people expect from a host. Particularly, the art of knowing when someone wants your attention and when they would rather be left alone. From my perspective, it was a big change from lecturing; where people have to listen to you as their grades depend upon it. Whereas it is perfectly acceptable to have no interest in a host whatsoever. An ego-bruising lesson to learn!

Hosting events was also useful in raising our profile and they achieved good media support. Our first foray was with Heritage Open Days; organised by English Heritage (now Historic England), they are a weekend of special events where the public can view historic properties free of charge, that are not normally accessible. Holding our first event in September 2013, it was well attended and received a lot of attention. As much as it raised our profile locally, it also allowed us to meet many people with a connection to the Control Tower who furnished us with the most fascinating detail. We hosted more Heritage Open Days over the next couple of years and other events besides. Sadly, they also drew unwanted attention. A new neighbour who bought a second home in what he hoped would be a rural idyl was disappointed to discover a new B&B nearby. Over the coming months and years he tried ever more wearisome ways of obstructing us.

He was undoubtably unhappy about us, but from our perspective it was infuriating. He initially questioned the legitimacy of our business claiming there was a 'no business' covenant in the deeds.

The deeds he referred to were never registered and our deeds said no such thing. We did our best to ignore him. However, the open days made him apoplectic. He wrote us an awful letter which ultimately forced us into action. Although we really enjoyed open days, they did create a lot of work and reduced our income; we therefore decided we would no longer host such events. However, retreat was not the answer, so we decided to deal with his accusations by becoming very transparently legitimate. I phoned the council and checked our legal position, I even raised the spectre of business rates as we were opening a fourth room, something we'd been advised wouldn't affect us. As a result we became partially business-rated.[C] We then approached our local councillor, who was leader of the council at the time, and asked him to mediate. He went to see our neighbour. We've had no contact since.[D] While, politically, I am a considerable distance from our local councillor (and he knew it), he did an excellent job.

The thing about living in an historic building is that public curiosity goes with the territory. If attention makes you unhappy, it seems a curious building to buy. However, for the time being, we would have to content ourselves with outlining the history, eight guests at a time. Nonetheless, we would still keep finding ways to tell people about the Control Tower.

Unusually located outside the perimeter track,[4] the Control Tower at RAF North Creake is on an artificially elevated position in front of runway number two. Given its primary function was the control of take-offs and landings, both day and night, it is surprising that it was so distant from the main runway. However, at the time of its construction, Bomber Command was already committed to night-time operations and with them, the associated challenges of operating in

---

C   Our neighbour ultimately did us a favour. He made us evaluate what was important and critical for business survival and led us to drop some of the more elaborate plans for exhibition spaces and such. While the move to business rates was irritating at the time, during Covid it triggered quick and automatic grants that actually meant we survived a very difficult time. An irony that was not lost on us.

D   It was not the end completely. During Covid he decided to ignore the 'stay at home' instruction and visited his house. While it was annoying no one here did anything about it. That is, until he stayed overnight. He was then reported to the police, who paid him a visit, instructed him to return home and not to come back. He automatically assumed that we had reported him (we didn't) and told the police that we were still taking in guests. Therefore, we also received a visit. It was obvious to everyone, that it wasn't true and the police soon left.

RAF North Creake airfield controller's caravan with rainbow:
Norman Turnbull (Control Tower Archive).

The functions of the airfield controller were 'to assist, by visual means, in the control of aircraft taxying, taking off, and landing'.[8] For this purpose, he was equipped with two signal lamps (one red and one green), a Very[E] pistol with red cartridges only, binoculars and a direct telephone line to the Control Tower.[9] Brian Martin, working at a control tower in Oxfordshire in 1946, remembers that the phonelines 'were always being cut by the grass-cutting machines'.[10] The Air Ministry had at their disposal, approximately 3,000 cylindrical unit gang-mowers for towing behind a tractor.[11] Whether they were used at RAF North Creake, where sheep apparently grazed,[F] is not recorded.

The airfield controller supervised local air traffic by refusing permission to land to aircraft where there was a danger of collision, on instructions of the FCO,[12] or when the path of the incoming aircraft

---

E Very is now the more common variant spelling of Verey.

F Early on in the build, a man paid an unexpected visit. As a 15-year-old shepherd when North Creake was operational, he grazed his sheep on and around the airfield. This seemed a remarkable revelation; surely aircraft and sheep do not mix? I have never been able to corroborate this information and in my distracted state caused by early days and late nights on the build, I did not take the former shepherd's details to follow-up.

was obstructed.[13] He could also refuse permission to take off, if to do so would obstruct an aircraft approaching to land or take off.[14]

The only wartime access to the Control Tower was on the rear elevation (east facing). Since 1945, a further three doorways on the ground floor have been added. Directly inside, a corridor leads straight towards the front of the building. During the war, the concrete floor would have been covered with linoleum, with walls of green coloured render to waist-height and off-white distemper above. Today, the walls are of a single colour with parquet flooring throughout the ground floor (with the exception of the lavatory, kitchen and utility room; all tiled). During the war there were three doorways on the left of this corridor as you entered the Control Tower. The first door was for the teleprinters; these were a reasonably secure form of communication that worked on GPO telephone lines and were operated in a manner similar to typing.[15] Unusually, North Creake Control Tower had a larger teleprinter room than was normal, containing at least two teleprinters (two was standard with one being connected to the Defence Teleprinter Network'[16] and the second being dedicated to the meteorological section to send and receive forecasting data from RAF 100 Group HQ). Roy Berrill, a meteorologist in the meteorological office at RAF North Creake, remembers the teleprinters 'would clatter away the whole damn time'.[17] This wasn't their only complaint about the meteorological office (situated next door through the second door on the left). Phyllis Willmott, a meteorological WAAF at RAF North Creake, remembers arriving at the Control Tower and seeing that the view from the window, 'looked on a few scrubby bushes, not the airfield. I was disappointed that we would [have no] ... panoramic view of the airfield, or of the weather ... especially when there was flying or when thunderstorms and lightning tore open the skies'.[18] With this and with the 'charting bench' position lost to the extension of the teleprinter room, the meteorological section decamped to the watch office at the end of the corridor. Postwar, the teleprinter room and meteorological office were knocked into one and served a number of different functions including office, lavatories and a mess room, but it now functions as the guest living room and breakfast room for our B&B.

The watch office (an obsolete title as it had no air traffic control function), is structurally the same today as it was in 1945, but is now our private kitchen and sitting/dining room. Other than the plaster to the walls and the reclaimed flooring, it feels similar. Postwar, the central window was blocked up and a dividing wall built across the middle. The wall is now demolished and the window has returned, although it is double the height of the original. The pyrotechnic cupboard at the south end, contained signalling flares and rockets; being obviously volatile, they were protected by a heavy steel door and had a sacrificial window that would have vented the blast. The window is blocked up and our cooker now stands in place of the cupboard.

During the war the Control Tower was heated electrically due to the sensitivity of equipment to dust[19] emitted from coke stoves and was 'relatively warm'.[20] The open fires were put in postwar and the reclaimed surrounds added by us. Sue Yarham, who lived in the Control Tower in the 1980s, remembers that the open fires, supplemented by paraffin heaters generated condensation that dripped off the ceiling and landed on her face while she tried to sleep. For some reason, she still adored the place.[21] The warm and dry meteorologists in the watch office did not hold the attractions of the Control Tower in such high regard.

Every three hours, the meteorologists would draw up a map for the local area. Every six hours this was supplemented by a map for the British Isles, and every 12 hours would be drawn the largest map of the sequence, which included the Atlantic Ocean and parts of Europe.[22] It was a difficult task and one that was, technologically, in its infancy. Consequently, poor meteorology, particularly in the early part of the war, led to many aircraft losses.[23] Roy Berrill readily concedes 'weather forecasting at that time was pretty crude',[24] particularly at RAF North Creake when it came to 'the wretched North Sea Stratus'[25] or sea frets:

you knew the fret was sitting out there on the North Sea, but you couldn't forecast when the heck it was coming in. And so it was quite possible that when the aircraft came back, the fret would suddenly come in and the aircraft couldn't land.[26]

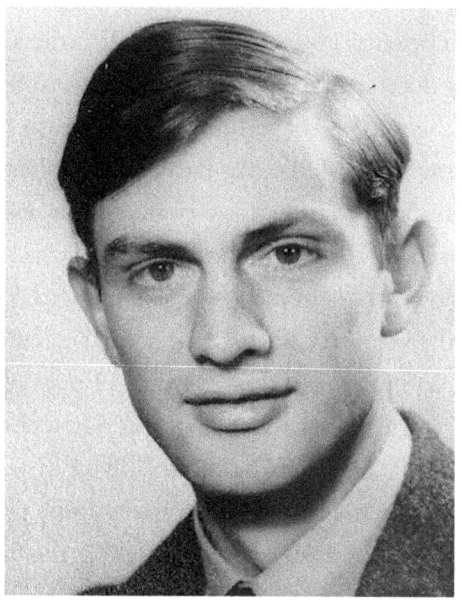

Roy Berrill, RAF North Creake Meteorologist (Roy Berrill).

He continues, that generally, 'accuracy was pretty hopeless',[27] as the aircraft were flying at heights of between 10,000 and 20,000 feet, 'whereas forecasting during the war was done at 2,000 feet'.[28] This was further compounded as aircraft entered the jet stream; 'we didn't know anything about what it did, or how it worked':[29]

> we had an ... instrument, it was on a pole and it was like a garden rake but with the prongs sticking upwards ... [used] to estimate what the height of cloud was in the jet stream ... you had to time it between each of the prongs and then you had to calculate how fast the jet stream was ... it was a ridiculous arrangement because you were looking at cloud from anything from 30-35,000 feet.[30]

As inaccurate as this sounds, from this weather forecasts were drawn. 'It's amazing really, how well we did do ... considering the limited amount of information.'[31] And, indeed, huge advances were made in the discipline of meteorology during the war.

Detailed weather information was fed to ETA (the code name for the Central Forecasting Office[32] in Dunstable[33]) from a number of sources in Britain and further afield; weather ships recorded conditions in the Atlantic and meteorological flights flew over Europe,[34] recording wind height and speed, barometric pressure, humidity, temperature[35] and icing-up conditions.[36] The meteorologist's own local forecasting at each station, also contributed critical data towards the overall picture:

> one of my duties as a 'Met girl' was to go outside every ten minutes to the hour every hour to take readings of barometric pressure, temperature and rainfall, as well as to assess visibility, wind direction and force and type and amount of cloud. All over the country at several hundred stations WAAFs like me (and, on some naval stations, Wrens) were following the same procedure at exactly the same time each hour of the day and night.[37]

The equipment the WAAFs used was contained in a white louvred box known as a Stevenson Screen, placed on the outside of the Control Tower.[38] For wind speed there was an anemometer, but for wind direction they could simply turn until the wind hit both ears equally; the wind being in the direction where the nose points.[39] A subjective assessment of visibility was also made by checking how far they could see across the airfield; a difficult process at night in the blackout with 10/10 (complete) cloud cover.[40] Judging cloud cover could also be difficult due to the reflection of the orange lights from the Control Tower,[41] although this assessment could be aided by use of one of the airfield 'Sandra' searchlights.[42] During the day, cloud height could be assessed by releasing a red balloon, which ascended at approximately 300 feet per minute, and timing how long before it entered cloud.[43]

Phyllis Willmott was not enamoured with having to 'fumble through dense fog to find the instrument box, or to go out in the darkness when the owls were screeching or, worst of all, to find a crowd of rats scuffling ... [it] was no fun'.[44] On return to the safety of the Control Tower, all the weather data was recorded[45] and sent to RAF 100 Group Headquarters by teleprinter.[46] Complete forecasts of Britain and Europe were then returned to all airfield meteorological sections by the same method;[47] this process happened, once an hour, 24 hours a day.[48] Roy Berrill recalls the information returned was very reliable[49] and once received 'your met. assistant, who was usually a WAAF[G], would interpret [it] and plot it on your map'.[50]

When no operations were scheduled, the meteorological section still had to function in the same way.[51] Roy Berrill claims he still did his full shifts, but he and his WAAF assistant took it in turns to rest.[52] However, Phyllis Willmott remembers it otherwise; 'when the flying stopped, so did almost everything else, leaving the Met WAAF on duty feeling very much alone in the vast and eerie emptiness of the darkened airfield. The forecaster went home to his bed, while upstairs in the Control Tower the one or two left on duty in case of emergency tucked down to sleep'.[53]

Roy Berrill explains that as one of the three meteorological officers, he worked a three-day shift pattern: day one, 13:00–22:00 hours; day two, 08:00–13:00 hours with a second shift commencing at 2:00–08:00 hours, and with day three free.[54] The meteorological WAAFs shared 'this awful three watch system'[55] which was always subject to change as a result of staff shortages due to illness or leave:

> at present I'm working rather hard as one girl is on leave now which means we work morning and evening one day, and afternoon and night the next. We do have the third day to rest, but as we really have to work, or at least, keep awake all night long, it really is necessary to sleep a good part of that day.[56]

G   All the meteorological assistants in the UK were women. The male equivalents went overseas. There were a number of WAAF officer forecasters later on in the war but they remained few (Spear: iwm: 1/10/22).

However, Phyllis, while on shift, resisted the temptation to 'while away the minutes in comfortless, senseless dozes',[57] choosing instead to keep herself occupied. Nevertheless, if she did succumb to the temptation, between the watch office and the meteorological office was the duty pilot's rest room. The duty pilot was a redundant role on stations where a flying control organisation was established.[58] This room, which now functions as our utility room, was originally accessed from the corridor, but a new connecting door between the watch office and the duty pilot's rest room was punched through postwar and the original door subsequently bricked up. During the war it was exclusively used by the meteorological staff[59] and contained a bed and a picnic stove;[60] 'very often we didn't have breakfast, we used to make toast in the met office'.[61] The bread for the toast was part of the rations provided for shift work:

> this usually consisted of a loaf, a lot of butter or margarine, perhaps a great hunk of cheese or something like that. Pots of jam, tins of cocoa, always used to give us lots of cocoa, we would have preferred tea on night duty to keep us awake, but they would issue us with cocoa and it used to pile up in the cupboard. Nobody used it.[62]

A small perk of the shift system along with not having to attend morning and church parades[63] (an advantage shared with the FCOs, who were also excused 'orderly duties'[64]). At North Creake, these supplies were supplemented by Phyllis' colleague with her 'cajoling charms'.[65] She somehow managed to negotiate not just rations from the cookhouse but also ration book coupons, that she used to 'obtain treats for us, such as chops from the butcher's shop in Walsingham'.[66] The presence of hot drinks and food also made the meteorological staff more widely popular, attracting visitors from beyond the staff of the Control Tower as it became 'a popular place, not only for weather predictions … but for the attractions of cups of coffee and tea, and the company that went with them'.[67]

For the meteorological WAAFs, the work didn't just involve weather recording as there were numerous other tasks they had to perform, including cleaning and polishing the floor, a 'hateful job, but it must be done'.[68] In a letter to a friend Phyllis Willmott complains, 'my hands are filthy ... as I have been busy changing ribbons, cleaning out the food cupboard, dustbins, sweeping etc. Now of course, I am all behind with my work'.[69] On some night shifts, between weather observations and when there were no operations to keep her alert, Phyllis drank coffee, wrote letters[H] and read books to occupy her time and to 'fight off dozing'.[70] She read a wide range of titles (limited only by what was in the station library). These included Anthony Bertram's book on *Design* which she describes as giving 'an amazingly enlightening view of modern architecture. I began by finding I disagree very much with some of the author's views, and ended by thinking perhaps there was a great deal in them after all.'[71] She also discusses Virginia Wolf's *A Home of One's Own*,[72] which she tracked down even though 'books like everything are now difficult to find – at least the ones one particularly wants'.[73]

Phyllis Willmott's time as a meteorological WAAF also afforded her the opportunity to fly, something that would have been almost unknown for a woman of her class before the war. Even though it was strictly forbidden to give joyrides to WAAFs, Phyllis and her meteorological colleague with the help of a couple of aircrew friends, persuaded a pilot, William Hancock, to take them up on an air test early in 1945.[74] While unimpressed with the comfort that the Stirling bomber provided, she found the experience a 'wonderfully exciting one'.[75]

to see England lying maplike below, to scud along the tops of cloud was, at that time, not an everyday occurrence for anyone

---

H   Luckily some of these letters survive and contain remarkable detail of everyday life on an airfield. Phyllis Willmott (nee Noble) became an academic postwar and wrote four autobiographies. *Coming of Age in Wartime* (1988), charts her development from a bank clerk to a free-thinking independent woman. Her letters through this period catalogue this development and often identify the books she reads and the impact they have on her. A deeply beneficial if unintended consequence of the war. Phyllis Willmott left her archive to Churchill College Cambridge from where it is publicly accessible.

other than aircrew. The noise was dreadful and I quickly became quite deaf. This deafness served me well when Adam [Alan Wood – navigator] decided to tease me by getting Daisy [William Hancock – pilot] to feather two of the four engines. As Adam gleefully pointed to starboard, where the propellers were no longer turning, I wondered what the message was that he was mouthing to me and why he seemed so amused. Not wanting to appear stupid, I nodded my head and smiled back. As he was asking whether I would like to see us flying on only *one* engine, this made me seem pretty cool and much impressed Adam.[76]

She described the experience in a letter to her friend Peg in March 1945; 'I had the sensation of surf-riding, for the cloud sort of bellowed forward as we seemed to skid along the tops!'.[77] Quite a contrast to the fixed terrain of the Control Tower.

Phyllis returns to earth: 199 Squadron LJ565 EX-Q. From left to right, Ben Rigs, Alan Wood, William Hancock, Oly Pask, Phyllis Willmott and Pamela Moran (John Reid Collection).

Opposite what was the meteorological office door, was a flag cupboard[1] and two lavatories (one for officers and one for other ranks). How rigidly this was enforced is not recorded; it somehow seems out of step with the 'people's war'. Interestingly, there was no demarcation between women's and men's lavatories, and as there are no other facilities close by, one presumes both sexes used the Control Tower lavatories. Indeed, Beryl Spear, stationed elsewhere, remembers that as ablution facilities on dispersed sites could be somewhat basic, housed 'in great stone huts with taps all down the middle with horrible old bowls to wash in ... [and] quite often in the morning there wasn't any hot water ... very often we'd get dressed and go down to the met. office and wash'.[78] One lavatory remains in a similar position, but the other, along with the flag cupboard, was removed postwar. The space is now a hallway for the new front door (an opening made when the Control Tower became two flats). In this hallway stands an artifacts cabinet containing garden finds, purchases and donations all pertaining to RAF North Creake. On top of this is a framed photograph of a young man in RAF uniform; a subject of some intrigue for guests, it is my dad at the start of his National Service in 1947. Now gazing permanently upon a comfortable domestic space, it is sad to reflect that he never got to see the Control Tower finished, although unlike my mum, he did at least see the direction of travel.

My mum died in 2015, two days short of her 80th birthday and seven months after we'd opened. She had been ill for some time with a form of dementia that had robbed her of her voice for the seven years prior to her death. Such is the indignity of this awful disease; it steadily stripped her of sparkling intelligence, wit, joy and dignity. She had grown up in Sheringham on the North Norfolk coast and left home for London, at her father's behest, when she was 16. Born in 1935, she was four years old at the declaration of war. Her father, Donald Blyth, had been too young to fight in the Great War and too old in the Second World War; a fact he always regretted. He volunteered to be a firewatcher, in the hope that it would place him in the 'thick of it', and

---

1   Contained signal flags associated with the signals mast (Francis: 9/2/2024).

there is some suggestion he used to catch the train from Sheringham to London to do this (although this is unsubstantiated). My mum's earliest memories of wartime Norfolk were of shortages, skies dark with noisy bombers and beaches full of barbed wire. My aunt, Sylvia, used to tell a compelling tale of when they were bombed out of their house in Barford Road, Sheringham, when a sea mine, dropped by parachute, exploded at the front of their house. They were all in; my grandfather in the living room (at the front), my grandmother in the kitchen at the back and the children at the front in an upstairs bedroom. My grandmother, being some distance away was unhurt, my grandfather was saved by the robust 1930s sofa in which he was sitting, and my mum and her brother were saved by Sylvia forcing them to the floor when she recognised the sound of a falling bomb. The house was too severely damaged to live in, so they moved in with my great grandparents, also in Sheringham. This experience goes some way to explain my mum's fear of thunder, a fear later compounded when her school was hit by a thunderbolt.

Dad grew up in Welwyn in rural Hertfordshire, having moved out of North London in 1935 at around the age of five. My grandad, Eugene Morter, who was always a great influence on me, took his family out of London when he was unable to find work because of his constant labour organising.[J] He had managed to persuade a building society, in spite of being unemployed, to lend him some money to build two houses; one to live in and one to sell. He was a phenomenal negotiator.

Born in 1899, he did an apprenticeship as a wheelwright and finished as pneumatic tyres scaled up production. He was old enough to serve in the Great War, but his reserved occupation in the aircraft industry (both London-based at Aircraft Manufacturing Co in Edgware and Fredk Sage in Grays Inn Road) and ill health (partial blindness) kept him from the armed forces. His last exemption appeal hearing failed in July 1918.[79] However, he never served with the armed forces, so what happened subsequently is unclear.

J   My grandfather was a fervent advocate of trade unionism and wherever he was employed he would 'organise the unorganised', that is, recruit people into the union and build an active trade union organisation within the workplace. This made him very unpopular with employers and, consequently, he could find no-one willing to employ him within a reasonable area of where he lived.

After the move to Hertfordshire, he got a job building flats beside the A1 in Hatfield. I remember him telling me it was the most dangerous site he'd ever worked on. Consequently, the workers struck for improved safety. While on the picket line, a fellow worker mentioned to my grandad that they were looking for coachbuilders across the road at de Havilland. He started work there in around 1936 and stayed there until he retired in the 1960s. During the war, having been elected as a shop steward, he was on the Joint Production Committee (JPC)[K] and he was at work when the factory was bombed in October 1940, killing 21 workers and injuring 70 others.[80] My dad, who was at school that day, remembered the lone Ju88 aircraft flying over the school on its way to bomb the factory. The rumours of the attack reached Welwyn before my grandad returned from work. Despite such events, Dad always talked fondly of the war; viewed from the relative safety of mid-Hertfordshire, it seemed exciting. He was obsessed by aircraft, he watched them, drew them and made award-winning models of them.[L] And when one accidently jettisoned a fuel drop-tank, he made a sledge from it. He only used it once, 'it was terrifyingly fast', he said.

Like so many others of their generation, my mum and dad met at a dance. My dad persuaded my mum to take a job a de Havilland Propellors, where she worked describing the lift and drag of propellors through diagrams based upon information provided by on-site experts.[M] They were married in 1957 and I came along, the last of five boys, ten years later. I always got on extremely well with my parents with only a few notable points of friction when growing up. One continual source of irritation for my mum, was attending parent's evenings to be told, 'he's very bright but won't apply himself'. The truth was I disliked school intensely, I was very happy with the social side, but the work I

K   In February 1942 the Government signed an agreement to set up JPCs for all engineering firms with more than 150 workers. As well as benefits for production, the Government thought they might neutralise militant trade unionists. It is estimated that JPCs and their equivalents covered more than 3.5 million workers (Calder: 1969: 398).

L   Although strictly true, as the model did win an award; it was awarded first prize at Welwyn Village Fete.

M   I don't remember Mum ever talking about her work at de Havilland propellors and only through writing this book did I realise this absence in my knowledge. Luckily, I had contact details of Ann Petersen, a former work colleague, who could fill in the gaps. It is curious to reflect that I knew much of my dad's working life and so little of my mum's.

found, at best, unstimulating, preferring to choose my own direction of study. Mum always used to laugh when relating that I came out after my first day and said, 'I don't like it', and I never changed my mind. I always got on with my teachers, possibly too well, as it allowed me to get away with doing very little, with one teacher passing the comment that, 'you're the only pupil I've known that never leaves school with any books'. The inevitable consequence was, that although I was entered for ten O levels, I passed two; geography and pottery (and the latter was a CSE).

Rather like my grandad, who my dad said could get in a political row waiting for a bus, I was always politically vocal. This probably marked me out as different at school.[N] Mum argued that I always had an opinion on everything. She would frequently tell of a day I spent with her and my dad and, while in a shop at Beaulieu Motor Museum, she picked up, what looked like, a piece of branch, behind which was a beautiful picture of a glorious house plant. I said to her, 'if you buy that, you're nothing but a gullible tourist'. She bought it and, of course, it grew, wonderfully. Subsequently, the plant was always known as the 'gullible tourist'; I still don't know its botanical name, but I have its offspring growing rapaciously in our guest living room; a verdant symbol of my folly.

The predictable regret arising from my poor performance at school, coincided inevitably with the greatest period of friction with my parents, as I battled with my own sense of frustration and fear about my future. Mum pointed to an advert in the local paper for grounds maintenance staff at the local authority and persuaded me to apply. It was one of those milestone decisions that eventually brought me to the Control Tower. I now have no regrets about the pathways that led here, but I equally realise, my dad could very easily be looking out upon something far less comfortable from behind that glass frame.

In the hall is also the door for the Switch Room. During the war, this room, and this room alone, was accessed externally through

---

N   Some years after I left school, I was stewarding on a TUC march in the pouring rain and a teacher with whom I shared similar views (but not a love for maths), came up to me unseen, grabbed me by the arm, pointed and said, 'I knew it!' Then walked away grinning.

a doorway on the north elevation of the Control Tower. The doorway from the hall was knocked through when this room became a kitchen. Now our office/study, the Switch Room was solely for use by electrical engineers and was where the power supply entered the Control Tower; power not just for the building but for distribution for much around, including, for example, the runway lights.

Runway lighting had come a long way since the beginning of the war:

> A primitive form of flare-path, composed of small, battery-fed electric lamps laid out on the grass by hand, and supplemented in poor visibility by paraffin flares of the road-mender variety and a massive and clumsy floodlight, constituted the only lighting system at most airfields in the first year of the war.[81]

In 1944, a pilot of a heavy bomber returning from an operation at night would have a whole network of lighting to support him. By May 1944, 75% of Bomber Command airfields, North Creake included, were equipped with an advanced system of airfield lighting known as Drem[O] Mark II.[82] A returning pilot would first see 'Sandra', a 'searchlight directed vertically from the airfield site'.[83] Shortly after, an outer asymmetric circle of lighting that surrounded the airfield (with an approximately 12-mile circumference and involving between 50 and 60 lights) would come into sight. Following this ring of lights, the pilot would be guided to the 'lead-in string' lamps that formed a smooth curve of lighting that led from the outer circle to the main airfield funnel lights.[84P] These in turn, would guide the pilot to the runway in use.[85] At RAF North Creake, one such light lit up Branthill Farm farmhouse. David Maufe, the farmer, came to visit the station commander to ask if it could be moved as it made him feel vulnerable to intruder attack. He was told by Norman Bray the importance of that light for morale, as it

---

O Originally developed at RAF Drem, a Fighter Command station in Scotland under the command of 'Batchy' Atcherly (rafdrem.co.uk).

P To see a fully comprehensive account of all airfield lighting, development and function see Air Historical Branch: 1956: 514-581.

lit up a symbol of the England the crews were fighting for. He didn't ask again.

Just before the runway, the pilot would pass the angle of approach indicator,[86] showing, on a vertical plane, three colours; 'an approach at the correct height the pilot would see a green light, if he were too high he would see yellow, if too low he would see red'.[87] The runway itself was illuminated with sodium 'flare path' lamps every 100 yards along both sides of the runway (closer if there was a bump in the runway). The aim was for the pilot to always have four in view.[88] In poor visibility these were often supplemented by additional 'portable' flarepath lighting; 'the portable sodium flarepath was an essential provision to increase the range of visibility over which it was possible to continue to operate aircraft'.[89] It involved six horizontal sodium tubes (standard street light fittings) placed on the ground and pointed upwards.[90] This was not fitted at all RAF stations, but one suspects, given the conditions in which squadrons were expected to operate at North Creake, it was installed here. Around the point of touchdown, the aircraft would pass the 'crossbar' (seven light fittings, 25 feet apart, reaching across the runway and into the prepared grass surface either side).[91] This was placed at 800 yards before the end of the concrete runway 'to warn pilots of the extent of the runway still available ... and to mark the last safe point of touchdown'.[92]

On clearing the runway, the aircraft would follow the perimeter track back to their dispersal by use of taxi-track lighting (amber on the outside, blue on the inside),[93] spaced at 150 yards apart but much closer on bends.[94] All lighting circuits were repeated on an illuminated mimic diagram located in the Control Room. From this, airfield lighting could be controlled and the location of faults identified[95] (excluding flarepath lamps, as these were checked by regular inspections).[Q96] The infrastructure to support such a comprehensive system of lighting was immense:

Q This was part of an airfield inspection that needed to be conducted 'at least twice daily ... for this purpose a car or light van is to be available at the control tower permanently for the exclusive use of the Flying Control Section' (Air Council: undated: 68).

the installation of Mark II airfield lighting was a task of considerable magnitude involving route lengths of approximately 30 miles of overhead lines and 22 miles of underground cabling for each station ... Altogether over twelve thousand miles of overhead line installations were carried out in the United Kingdom ... involving the erection of about half a million poles and over 9,000 miles of trenching or ducting ... during the war period.[97]

Access to the first floor of the Control Tower is via the stairs on the right as one enters the building. When we moved in, these stairs were carpeted and the exterior wall of the stairway was lined with tongue and groove boarding up to waist height. We subsequently removed the carpet to discover oak capping on the steps and risers. Underneath this were beautiful concrete steps with rounded edges. These are now polished and the walls plastered.

With a turn on the landing and then rising up two more steps, straight ahead is the Signals Room. The staff stationed here were responsible for signals both coming in and going out, at varying levels of secrecy (the 'most urgent' messages were sent as signals, using the teleprinter either in 'plain' or 'cipher'. The degrees of priority were: Most Immediate, Emergency, Immediate, Important).[98] Signals staff were also responsible for the flimsies, containing the various codes, frequencies etc. used by aircrew on operations and printed on rice paper. The details on the flimsies were highly secret and being on rice paper, edible; Doris Acres, who worked in Signals at RAF Newmarket, remembers that she had 'a deal of sympathy for any airman shot down and having to dine off these papers, for whilst the paper itself may have been palatable, the printer's ink looked thick, black and decidedly unpleasant'.[99] The Signals Room is smaller than it was during the war, as two bathrooms now occupy a blockwork partitioned-off section within it. Across the corridor from the Signals Room is the Controller's Rest Room, provided with, we believe, a desk, tunic cupboard and daybed where the duty flying controller could take 'a nap when there was no flying in progress'.[100] The ensuite is, of course, a recent innovation.

Continuing along the corridor and dropping down the step you enter the former Control Room at the west elevation of the first floor. The Control Room was designed with floorboards mounted on battens (now complemented by the same pattern boards throughout the first floor), and at RAF North Creake, in what seems an incredibly extravagant use of materials, these are made of oak. The floorboards are stamped underneath with the legend 'Harris Mills, made in the USA', and were probably imported in 1943 under the terms of the lend-lease agreement – a debt the UK Government only managed to repay in 2006.[101] Such extravagance seems uncharacteristically wasteful of the Air Ministry as there appears no good reason for its installation. The only possible use, other than aesthetics and warmth, is to provide a void in which there is a defined culvert at the leading edge for control room cabling. Vic Flowers, RAF North Creake station signals section, remembers using this to install 'a new operational channel'[102] in the Control Tower. This was required to run through the building and up to an aerial on the roof.[103] Notwithstanding, it does make a beautiful floor with a wonderfully readable history in every mark, scar and hole (drilled for cables to run to the control desks).

The control desks ran almost the length of the Control Room and faced towards the airfield site for the purpose of air traffic control. During the war the area of jurisdiction of flying control was generally considered to extend 3,000 yards beyond the airfield perimeter and 20,000 feet above it.[104] Operating throughout the day and night,[105] the flying control organisation was responsible for the control and safety of aircraft and crews during the period between departure (from dispersals) and at the time of their return.[106]

Before 1942 there was no unified system of air traffic control in Britain.[107] However, with increasing air traffic and thereby growing levels of accidents[R] it was decided to institute a universal system of

R A total of 1,451 aircraft were either written off or damaged as a result of airfield accidents during the latter half of 1941 (Smith: 1981: 26).

flying control. In March 1942, a conference of all RAF Commands agreed that:

> the full control of local aircraft traffic at airfields [should be] placed firmly in the hands of the Flying Control Officers, and ... detailed regulations for local air traffic and a standardized landing procedure, [should be developed] based on the best points of various Group schemes'.[108]

The Control Room: Norman Turnbull (Control Tower Archive).

Regulations followed in June 1942 with the hope that this would 'ensure a steady and orderly flow of aircraft from air to ground'.[109] Nonetheless, it was recognised that one set of regulations would not be the answer for the whole myriad of airfield conditions and, therefore, the possibility was allowed for 'deviations to suit local requirements'.[110] The regulations provided an excellent basis for handling air traffic with a 'degree of safety and efficiency which could never have been attained without [them]'.[111] Consequently the annual aircraft damage rate (not attributable to enemy action) per 10,000 hours flying, fell from 44 in 1942, to 23 in 1943, to 15 in 1944, and during the four months of 1945 to eight.[112] By the end of the war a total of 2,700 FCOs and staff were employed in Bomber Command.[113]

Although there was a senior flying control officer at each station, the routine operation of the flying control system was the sole responsibility of the FCO on duty.[114] This involved the despatching of aircraft as required; the safety of aircraft in direct communication with the station (day and night); and giving pilots assistance with navigation or weather information as and when they required it,[115] or when in distress. The seriousness of this 'lost or in distress'[116] assistance was assessed by the FCO on duty and would generally fit into one of four categories:[117] (1) distress: the aircraft is in vital need of immediate assistance and must land without delay; (2) emergency: the aircraft is in very urgent need of assistance and in immediate danger, but can possibly continue in flight if assistance is promptly given; (3) difficulty: the aircraft is in urgent need of assistance but is in no immediate danger and can carry on with its authorised flight if assistance is given and (4) uncertainty: the aircraft is in need of re-assurance, but is in no immediate danger and intends to carry on with its authorised flight.[118]

During operations, airfields with two squadrons, such as North Creake, could clear aircraft for take-off as rapidly as every forty-five seconds.[119] A Mosquito pilot with RAF 100 Group observed, 'this was no stunt, but a miracle of organisation and drill which happened regularly'.[120] The need to then land aircraft quickly on their return, because of their vulnerability to intruder attack,[121] was equally critical. At the beginning of 1942, the average rate of landing was one aircraft every six minutes, meaning, landing two entire squadrons would occupy, 'between three and four hours'.[122] Arthur Harris pinpointed the problem in his postwar despatch:

> the force which was envisaged would create a density of air traffic in the night sky around the base areas far in excess of anything previously experienced, and the safe landing of

such a considerable number of aircraft, returning virtually simultaneously to their closely-packed airfields in the dark, with only a narrow margin of petrol endurance, was in itself a problem of the first magnitude[123]

Before the end of the war, the landing time for an aircraft was routinely reduced to under two minutes. This was only made possible by good team-work and mutual confidence between pilot and control officers.[124] At RAF North Creake, on a night of maximum effort, up to 40 aircraft could be landed in as little as 90 minutes.[125] With the close proximity of airfields to one another and with as many as 5,000 daily aircraft movements over East Anglia,[126] the job of a wartime controller could be a challenging one.

When assistance was requested by an aircraft,[S] it was the duty of the FCO to offer it 'swiftly and intelligently'.[127] The manner in which requests for assistance were made, most often denoted the urgency of the appeal. A call of 'Mayday'[T] meant an aircraft was in distress and needed an immediate priority landing, whereas a 'darkie call'[U] was a request for assistance by a lost aircraft. This service utilised low power transmitters and receivers on 24-hour watch at the Control Tower and in the airfield controller's caravan.[128] Radio transmissions were permanently tuned-in to the Bomber Command frequency and on loudspeaker for this purpose.[129] The calls would only be heard in a ten-mile radius[130] of the lost aircraft. The airfield was then permitted to give the name of the airfield in 'clear' (uncoded) language, thereby giving the lost pilot an idea of his position. If he needed further assistance the FCO could consult the map in the control room and give him a course to steer.[131] If

S   An aircraft in distress and requiring a priority landing had three alternative ways to communicate with the control tower. First, they could call on R/T, if not working or unavailable they could, second, make a series of short flashes on their Navigational or Aldis Lamp and, third, fire a white Very flare. Response from the control tower to visual signals (rather than radio) was despatched using a Aldis lamp or Very pistol coloured flare: Green: you may land, Red: wait and try again, White: you may not land – go away (Smith: 1981: 29).

T   Mayday is a phonetic corruption of the French 'm'aide', in English 'help me' (Skan: 1990: 26).

U   I have used this spelling deliberately out of hope rather than expectation, as it can mean 'to appear dark, indistinct' (Collins English Dictionary: 1994: 403) and makes sense in this context. However it is a variant spelling of the more commonly used, in RAF literature (including official documents), 'Darky' which is an unquestionably racist term. One hopes that the latter spelling arose from a mistake or ignorance, but I fear that this is not the case and actually reveals the appalling prevalence of unacceptable attitudes at the time.

the aircraft was experiencing difficulties of a technical nature, the FCO, before offering advice, would seek, whenever possible, advice from the technical officer or from a pilot experienced in that particular type of aircraft.[132]

Aside from these critical roles, much of what the FCOs did was routine. Shifts were 'organised around meal-times' in the same manner as those of the meteorologists and similarly if 'one of the three airfield controllers went on leave or reported sick, the others were expected to cover for him'.[133]

When reporting for duty the duty FCO took on the responsibilities for supervising a number of staff in the Control Tower and those performing flying control duties elsewhere on the airfield, including airfield controllers, look-out personnel, flare path personnel, fire tender and ambulance parties and radio telephone operators. [134] They also had to maintain a formal record of 'all items of interest, telephone calls, assistance given to aircraft, visits … etc.'.[135]

The day watch was busy with aircraft doing 'circuits and bumps (practise take-offs and landings), air tests and visiting aircraft, etc.'[136] Visiting pilots generally reported to the control tower immediately after their aircraft had been parked.[137] Regardless of what shift or how busy it was, the duty FCO was not permitted to 'leave the precincts of the flying control office during their tour of duty, unless properly relieved'. [138] Where a shortage of staff existed, exception was made for 'meals when the weather is fine and no flying is in progress'.[139] Although, he still needed to keep the 'Group Flying Control or Sector Controller and the station telephone exchange informed of his whereabouts'.[140] FCOs were forbidden from flying on operational sorties unless authorised by Group Headquarters, although they were encouraged 'to fly as frequently as possible on non-operational flights'.[141]

FCOs also needed to inform the station and squadron commanders of the state of serviceability of the airfield and advise on the latest weather.[142] To fulfil the latter, FCOs maintained close liaison with meteorological staff who advised them hourly on weather conditions,[143] 'to ensure that any necessary change of flare path or runway ... [was] carried out expeditiously'.[144] Of course, in very poor weather conditions aircraft would not fly. This decision was not in the gift of a meteorological officer, but a Group level decision made after consultation.[145] If the weather closed-in unexpectedly while the aircraft were out on operations, there were two options: first, at North Creake,[V] they could employ a procedure for 'cloud breaking'. This involved regulating the number of aircraft in the circuit over the station and reducing the rate of landing to six aircraft every ten minutes to avoid congestion and the chance of collision. Aircraft outside this circuit adopted a racecourse pattern and awaited permission to enter the circuit. Gradual descent, authorised by the Control Tower was then made to 400 feet, at which height, aircraft should be in contact with airfield lighting and able to make a normal landing.[146]

Second, and frequently used if poor weather was expected before the time of return, was establishing arrangements for aircraft diversions to airfields with better weather prospects.[147] Weather forecasts would often indicate requirements for 'the diversion of considerable numbers of aircraft to airfields in other parts of the country'.[148] In the first years of the war diverting aircraft was a 'hazardous enterprise to be avoided if at all possible'.[149] With no co-ordinated ground organisation and a lack of harmonisation of flying control procedures,[150] operations were not 'undertaken unless there was a good prospect of the aircraft returning to their own bases'.[151]

By February 1942, with the necessary machinery in place for the 'orderly diversion of aircraft on a large scale'[152] and with the standardisation of landing procedures, diversions began to be considered 'as the normal means of overcoming otherwise awkward situations'.[153] This normalisation peaked with the publication in 1944 of the *Bomber Command Diversion Schedule*. Carried in every aircraft, it gave details of all bomber-compatible airfields in Britain. This meant that diversions could be instituted easily 'without the need for transmitting information of a cumbersome nature and of assistance to the enemy'.[154]

V   This procedure was developed by the North Creake meteorological section in conjunction with the navigation section officer.

It then became routine to establish provisional diversion arrangements for aircraft before their return to base where doubts about the weather existed, 'instead of waiting ... until landing had become impossible and diversion essential'.[155] Indeed, it became good practice, if necessary, to have diversion arrangements for the whole bomber force before take-off, so that crews could be briefed of the details beforehand.[156]

A frequent cause of diversion was fog. If fog unexpectedly settled over a wide area when the aircraft were out, this could easily result in very few airfields being available on which to land. In order to minimise the potential for disaster from such a scenario, the Air Ministry introduced FIDO.[W] Trialled in 1942, it used petrol pumped at high pressure through perforated piping alongside runways; when vaporised it was ignited, to literally burn the fog off.[157] Burning 65,000 gallons of petrol for every hour in use,[158] the first successful operational landing with the aid of FIDO was 19 November 1943.[159] Before the end of the war in Europe, 2,500 successful FIDO landings had been made that 'would have been impossible or highly dangerous otherwise'.[160] A 1944 memo sent to all squadrons flying with RAF 100 Group, offered guidance for landing on FIDO equipped runways:

> the instrument panel and cockpit lights must be turned up bright before the approach is made since the glare from 'FIDO' dazzles the pilot and thus prevents him from seeing the instruments at their normal dimness ... [and the] aircraft will be brought in 5 to 10 miles an hour faster than normally since they will have to traverse the air disturbance caused by the first FIDO cross bar jets.[161]

It is difficult to imagine what it must have been like to land on a FIDO runway; one assumes there must have been conflicting emotions of relief, at suddenly being able to see the ground, mixed with the fear of flying over flames and then having to land between two raging

---

W FIDO initially meant Fog Investigation and Dispersal Operation, but by 1944 Fog, Intensive Dispersal Of became a more common definition, but most commonly it was just FIDO (Francis: 1993: 125).

infernos. Particularly if your wings and petrol tanks had been holed over target. Gordon Mercier, a mid-upper gunner remembers, 'we did land on the FIDO twice which was a very, very strange and frightening procedure ... it was like diving into hell'.[162] A flying control officer at RAF Marham in Norfolk, recalls the moment the burners were lit:

> the resultant effect had to be seen to be believed – the double line of flaming jets coupled with the roaring noise ... the first night we lit up, we had telephone calls from as far away as Peterborough to know if we were on fire ... the whole idea was not to provide light in the fog, but that the heat generated would cause the fog to lift. It did just that, and if you watched you could see it happening, creating a tunnel in the fog into which an aircraft could safely land.[163]

Eventually FIDO was installed at 15 airfields (11 of which were Bomber Command),[164] with the nearest to RAF North Creake being RAF Foulsham, another RAF 100 Group station.[165]

Accidents on wartime airfields were by no means unusual, and RAF North Creake can be seen as reasonably typical of an operational bomber station. John Rees, the flight sergeant in charge of the sick quarters at North Creake remarks, 'I was always involved in the unpleasant side of crashes and accidents both on and off the Station'.[166] A total of 18[167] aircraft were 'struck off charge'[X] in the 11 months RAF North Creake was operational. Five when taking off or landing.[168] However, this figure only includes those that were recorded and the total is not necessarily complete. For example, Steve Bond and Richard Forder discuss an aircraft from RAF North Creake that crashed at RAF Oulton on the 17/18 January 1945, causing enough chaos to involve diverting orbiting aircraft to RAF Foulsham.[169] This aircraft could not have been 'struck off charge' as it would have been recorded. Therefore it must have been repaired. Nevertheless, there is no mention of such an incident in either the Station ORB or the Squadron ORBs. Similarly

---

X   See appendix one

no record exists of when Vic Polichek experienced brake failure when landing at RAF North Creake, crashing through a fence and landing nose down in a ditch. Still in the tail turret, he 'jokingly said ... I almost had to use my parachute to exit the aircraft'.[170]

Near misses were also reasonably common. Vic Polichek recalls another occasion when just before take-off, one 'starboard engine failed, causing the bomber to veer off the runway resulting in a ground loop,[Y] barely missing two bombers'.[171] And the night of 7 March 1945,[172] when Jack Philipson barely got airborne. The main runway was being repaired[173] and they had to 'take off overloaded on the short runway (1400 yards) running up hill with only a 5mph wind,[174] heading to the right side of the Control Tower and the offices',[175] which they scarcely missed:

> it was the only time I though[t] we were not going to make it. Usually as soon as we're airborne it's up undercart and at 200ft back to 2,600RPM ... off with the flaps and away we go. But this time, she seemed sluggish and we were getting close to the end when 110mph came up I kept full power on until we were well away from the airfield.[176]

In an accident involving 171 Squadron Halifax NA694 6Y-H, the Station ORB reports that it 'crashed on landing at base his undercarriage being u/s',[177] but, interestingly, this is not cited as the reason the following aircraft were diverted, instead it blames bad weather.[178] Curiously, the 171 Squadron ORB does not mention the incident at all, only reporting 'three diverted to Woodbridge'.[179]

Woodbridge was a purpose-built Emergency Runway. With every operation producing its 'crop of damaged aircraft and injured crews',[180] something needed to be done to improve their chances of survival once they were back over the UK, but in distress. In 1941,

---

Y   This usually occurred to tail-draggers (Stirlings included) and was caused by a sudden tip to one side with the result of a wing digging into the ground followed, if moving fast enough, by a cartwheel. Sometimes the aircraft could spin round on its axis in a horizontal plane and it's possible this would equate to a ground loop terminology being used (Reid: 16/3/2023).

Emergency Runways were born.[181] Consisting of one runway 3,000 yards by 250 yards,[182] they were substantially larger than a standard 'Class A' airfield, allowing for the concurrent landing of aircraft in emergencies. Eventually three emergency runways were built along the east of England at Carnaby, Woodbridge, and Manston. They were 'equipped with every conceivable facility to assist such aircraft to as safe a landing as possible'. [183] Coming into operation during the winter of 1943/44, they were used by 11,250 aircraft before the end of the war.[184]

At RAF North Creake, on the 4 December 1944, pieces of 6Y-H were littered along the main runway. At 21:23 hours, the bomber had approached on three engines and then on touchdown 'the port wing inadvertently dropped and the aircraft landed heavily'.[185] There were no injuries, [186] but the brand-new Halifax on its first operation from RAF North Creake[187] was wrecked and subsequently struck off charge.[188] Making this a very 'expensive trip'.[189] The pilot, Jack Philipson, recalls the night:

> after returning from a bombing and Window operation on Kassal. Halfway home the port inner engine tachometer went 'off the clock'. The engine was OK so I thought it was instrument failure. About 25 minutes from home I noticed orange flicks coming out of the exhaust of the same engine … [the] temperature went up, the oil pressure went down, so I feathered the engine.
>
> When we got near to base I told them we had an engine 'out' and asked the flight engineer to go back and de-isolate the flaps and 'take out' the undercarriage 'up' locks for landing … the flight engineer returned to tell me that he had carried out his checks and everything was OK.
>
> I came downwind, eased the trim on the rudder and aileron, eased the power of the starboard inner engine and opened both outer engines a little to take off a little load on the rudder stick. I selected undercarriage 'down' and instead of two reds going to two yellows for undercarriage movement I

got two reds, two yellows and two greens. 'Lights up the creek,' I thought, so I closed all throttles to see if the horn would blow on the crosswind leg.

Neither the bomb-aimer or myself could see if the undercarriage was down. It was cloudy, dark, and there was a crosswind. We both agreed it must be OK, horn OK, lock out, lights up. We could not think of a reason for it not to be. After selecting 'up' and 'down' three more times in we went.

Looking back I remember vaguely feeling the tail wheel touch down, then we settled on the belly, the propellor blades clicking as they hit and folded back and we sailed off the runway and across the grass to the middle of the field. After the aircraft stopped I turned off the magneto switches the horn started to blast. 'Too late' was the cry! One new aircraft 'wiped out' after sixteen hours![190]

When visiting the UK in 1986, Jack Philipson met up with his bomb aimer, Norman Harrington, who quietly told him, 'when they lifted her up they found a 500lb bomb hung-up underneath! It must have been a smooth belly landing!'[Z] [191] Hung-up bombs, even with the wheels down, were, because of the high chance of detonation, the 'most tense of emergencies'.[192]

The following day, further expense was incurred when 199 Squadron Stirling LJ567 EX-X, one of those diverted to Woodbridge the night before, 'struck a four-foot high wall'[193] (sometimes cited as a pillbox[194]) coming in to land. With a damaged undercarriage, it was forced to return to Woodbridge to make a wheels-up landing.[195] Once again, there were no injuries to the crew but the aircraft was deemed beyond economic repair.[196]

When a crash occurred 'on, or in the vicinity of the airfield', there was an established procedure to follow. An ambulance and fire

---

Z   While hung-up bombs were not infrequent, there is no documentary evidence to support 6Y-H having carried a bombload on the night it crashed. Bomb targets did not commence from RAF North Creake until February 1945 and although it is not impossible that an earlier bombing sortie took place, there is no mention of it in the ORB. We should therefore conclude that it was unlikely.

tender were despatched immediately and the spare fire tender called-up. Flying control then informed the medical officer, station commander and squadron commander concerned. Reports of crashes outside the vicinity of the airfield or when an aircraft was overdue,[AA] were referred to the station commander.[197] At this point and when it was believed to be missing over the sea, the station commander ordered an air/sea rescue and then informed Air Ministry F.C.4 (Ops.).[AB] Similarly, if an aircraft was believed to have crashed reasonably near the base, searches were organised by the police duty officer with RAF Units often called upon to assist.[198] Otherwise, it was reported to Air Ministry F.C.4 (Ops.) who would then take responsibility for it, co-ordinating reports, all known information and, when believed the aircraft had crashed within Britain, organising searches.[199]

During this time there would be studious activity, but sombre mood, in the control room. In the war the control room, taking up more than half of the first floor of the Control Tower, was much bigger than the impression one derives today. Postwar walls were built to divide up the room to provide an additional two bedrooms. We removed one of these postwar walls and amended another to allow for the return of the central window, but also allowing us to add an ensuite for the Control Room bedroom and keep one additional bedroom (the Board Room; so called as the operations board was mounted on the south facing wall). The balcony that reaches around the front elevation (west facing) was originally accessed through two doors at either end of the control room. Today only one, on the south elevation, remains. The balcony leads round to the steps to the roof, which was used as a viewing deck during the war. The view from the roof is remarkable, in the winter when the trees are denuded of leaves, the sea is easily visible across the northern horizon. In the foreground are the two hangars (still extant), to the east is the Technical Site (much of which remains). In what is now our garden there would have been a building directly behind the

---

AA An aircraft became overdue when the pilot had not reported to the FCO at the airfield of destination 'within one hour after the estimated time of arrival' (Air Council: undated: 48).

AB Air Ministry F.C.4 was a branch of the Directorate of Flying Control and Rescue, responsible for, among other things, overdue aircraft (Air Ministry: undated: 4).

east elevation. Its purpose is unknown. To the north was the fire tender shelter, demolished after the war. Just beyond stood, and still stands, the Stanton air raid shelter, and unlike most shelters of this sort, it was never banked up with soil. Built of pre-cast concrete sections at the Stanton Iron Works in Nottingham,[200] it sheltered 50 people during a raid and was for the use of personnel in and around the Control Tower.[AC] This did not include FCOs, who were required to remain on duty.[201]

Flight Officer Faulkner (left) and LAC Harrison (right) look out over the runways: Norman Turnbull (Control Tower Archive).

At the end of what is now our garden is the Speech Broadcast Building. This building housed the amplifier equipment that transmitted station broadcasts on the 'Tannoy' system.[202] First introduced in early 1940, 'its purpose was to enable operational instructions to be passed clearly, rapidly and simultaneously to personnel'.[203] With microphones placed at the main 'operational centres' (operations block, control tower and battle headquarters[AD]), the Speech Broadcast Building was

---

AC Stanton Iron Works company (situated on Littlewell Lane, New Stanton, south of Ilkeston, Derbyshire) in the 1930s began to produce a wide range of concrete products and with the outbreak of the Second World War Government contracts followed. 'The new plant was therefore adapted for the manufacture of concrete air-raid shelters, to begin with supplying upwards of 1,000 tons per week to the Air Ministry and over 110,000 tons during the war' (Flinders & Corns: 2019: 87-89).

AD There is some considerable debate as to whether a Battle Headquarters was ever built at RAF North Creake

generally situated centrally between the microphone points in order to keep the length of microphone circuits to a minimum.[204] The amplified signal reached around the airfield (including dispersed sites),[205] with an average requirement of 150 speakers.[206] It was heated by thermostatically controlled electric heaters to protect the amplifying equipment which was designed for instantaneous operation and was permanently connected to the electricity supply.[207] Today, still heated electrically, it functions as our garden room. A place for guests to sit in all weathers and view the Control Tower.

To the south of the Control Tower are our neighbours, located in houses developed from the former squadron headquarters and flight offices. To the west, beyond our rebuilt Nissen hut, are the runways. Today the Airfield Site is dominated by the eco-power generation sector with a 120-acre solar farm generating electricity for the National Grid and an anaerobic digester producing biogas from primary agricultural products. Both initiatives entered the planning cycle shortly after we moved here, and by mid-2012 we were immersed in battling plans that by late 2012 also included a local authority sponsored Local Development Order (LDO).[AE] These three plans combined threatened to swamp the Control Tower and destroy much of the surviving fabric of the airfield. The solar panels were planned to come right up to the perimeter track behind the Control Tower, but it was the LDO that involved, on paper at least, some of the most worrying proposals. Not only did it propose the demolition of the 'ugly Technical Site', it contained powers of compulsory purchase across the area that included our Control Tower and our neighbours' houses. Needing to exercise sufficient opposition, along with our neighbours, we mounted a campaign. What really irked Claire and me was that this did not only threaten our home and our livelihood, but it held the history of the airfield in total disregard; something that ran completely contrary to everything we had hoped

---

although they were present 'at all major airfields' (Innes: 1995: 40) of this period. They were partially underground with, usually, three rooms and a hydraulic turret from which you could view an attack and direct operations against it. A potential site of such a building can be viewed on some contemporary photographs, but there is no further evidence of its existence.

AE LDOs provide permitted development rights for specified types of development in defined locations. They are flexible and locally determined and can allow for accelerated development (local.gov.uk).

to achieve. In a meeting with the architects of the LDO, in the face of great resistance from the local authority representatives, we put our case fervently. An air of hostility reigned until I pointed out that their risk assessment of the project, outlined in the planning documents, did not detail the risks associated with having residents in the middle of the LDO. Indeed, they weren't even mentioned. In the first concession, our properties were removed from the plans. Further concessions followed including the local listing of the Technical Site which would be 'conserved and enhanced'. Such were the concessions, that by the time of the final planning hearing, I went on the radio stating that I broadly approved of the plan as it would bring much needed skilled jobs to the area. Although in all honesty, I was still sad that the character of the area would change. Ultimately, the LDO didn't proceed. It was going to need significant local authority seed money and with a change of political flavour at North Norfolk District Council. The plans were quietly sidelined (although officially still live).

The solar park presented greater oppositional difficulties as the arguments in favour were better rehearsed (and were conflicting for Claire and me, as we support environmental power generation). Ultimately, it came down to the developer's disregard for the history of the airfield; one representative was heard to say, regarding other solar park developments on airfields, 'no one usually cares'. Our very public campaign won some concessions. At the last moment, I made an appeal to the planning committee hearing, that the panels should be pulled back from our border in order to preserve the relationship between the Control Tower and the number two runway. This request was granted and it was enough to win our support. On reflection, the development has been far less intrusive than first feared and it now protects the layout of the runways from further development for some considerable time. By which point, we hope, there will be more consideration shown for the history of this site.

However, with the anaerobic digester we grossly miscalculated the impact. Having viewed the planning documents we considered the impact on us and the airfield, although making questionable environmental claims, would be limited. We were wrong, and it is this development that has caused more nuisance than any other with, I would argue, small, if any, environmental benefit.[AF]

With all this worry it was, at times, hard to maintain the enthusiasm to persist with the build. Everyday irritations disproportionately rattled me. On one particular day I was acting as a banksman to an HGV driver who, blindly following his satnav, had mistakenly come up our lane (a constant source of irritation). After seeing him out onto the main road, I became aware of another driver attempting to catch my attention and I thought 'what now!'. As the driver leaned across the passenger seat towards the open window, he said, 'I just wanted to say I think you're doing a brilliant job of the Control Tower', and then pulled away. I was stunned and almost tearful. I went back in and told Claire; it lifted us both more than I can express. The driver was Mark Risborough and subsequently, Mark's mum bought him a voucher to stay and he and his wife, Claire, would become friends who would contribute profoundly to the memorial project.

Through it all we did still manage to continue with the build. Beyond our opening, the restoration of the Control Tower continued behind the scenes. Opportunities were grabbed when it was quieter but were constrained by the pressing arrival of the next guests, meaning, there was never enough time to recover from the disruption any reasonably large works would involve. Therefore, larger jobs had to wait, and instead, there were a lot of completing jobs (kitchen cabinets, glazed and painted, utility room cupboards), garden work, furniture jobs I could do in the workshop (bookcase for upstairs vestibule, study bookcase) and planning ahead for the bigger jobs we could do during longer periods off-duty.

The meteorological WAAFs coming off shift, had to get chits from the administration office for early or late meals.[208] The last meal at the Naafi 'went on to about 6. It involved a sort of cooked tea ..., and bread and butter and jam[AG] or something like that'.[209] Phyllis

---

AF See Monbiot: 14/3/2014.

AG It seems probable that bread and jam was a reasonably common way of filling-up during the war. With bread unrationed and, if one had access to fruit, jam could be easily homemade (even without much sugar). When I was a child and growing fast, I made constant requests of 'can I have a bowl of cereal?', regardless

Willmott 'sometimes popped into the cookhouse for breakfast ... after night duty, but Jean was so pernickety about what she ate that she hardly went there'.[210] For the FCOs coming off duty there was the 'operational eggs'.[211] This caused numerous 'envious glances' from all the other ground staff officers eating their beans on toast, glances that were sometimes accompanied by 'a few good humoured but snide comments'.[212] A repast and a brief respite before the next operation. At Bomber Command Headquarters they were planning ahead. But for the moment it was downtime and one could push the thought away. Until the next shift. And who knows what that will bring?

---

of the time of day (victims as we were to the advertising of breakfast cereals in the 1970s). My mum would normally relent, but dad, if he was in earshot, would always say 'if you're hungry, have some bread and jam'. This made it seem like a punishment, rather than, as I now recognise, a delicious treat.

'FRIENDLY FIRE'

Nine Stirlings of 199 Squadron and four Halifax of 171 Squadron were detailed to provide a Mandrel Screen[1] in support of raids on Leuna, Osnabruck and Giessen.[2] Forty-two Mosquitoes also flew separate 'diversionary and nuisance'[3] raids on Berlin, Schwerte and Hanau.[4] 6 December 1944 was a cold night and most aircraft suffered severe icing, with Stirling LJ617 EX-E returning after 45 minutes because of the severity of the weather conditions.[5] Diverted to Emergency Landing Runway at RAF Manston in Kent, it returned later the same night to RAF North Creake, landing at 22:38 hours.[6] Another 199 Squadron Stirling, LJ559 EX-Q, piloted by Jack Thurlow, left the Mandrel Screen early, presumably, due to the prevailing weather conditions, or perhaps due to a shortage of petrol,[A] and set a course for Britain. While flying at 16,000 feet, the Stirling suddenly, and unexpectedly, fell into a steep dive.[7] Jack Thurlow fought to regain control (in all probability with the assistance of other crew members, as control would be extremely heavy and difficult to regain). Dropping 14,000 feet and reaching speeds of 450mph, they battled with the bomber as it headed ever closer to the ground. Finally, at just 2,000 feet, they managed to regain control and set the aircraft on an even keel once again. To pull this Stirling

---

A   As was the case with 171 Squadron Halifax NA112 6Y-L (North Creake ORB: December 1944).

out of such a steep dive was an extraordinary feat, and one assumes, unexpected. The realisation that they might just survive the night, must have filled the air in the bomber with a tangible and heady sense of relief. Diverted to RAF Manston, they landed at 21:00 hours. Exhausted but safe.

It was believed that severe icing caused this nearly catastrophic dive.[8] Once on the ground, an inspection identified the Stirling as Category 'B' (beyond repair on site). However, on further inspection it was discovered that the Stirling was suffering from severe over-stressing of the airframe[9] and re-categorised as 'E'. It was finally struck off charge on 10 February 1945.[10]

The pilot of Stirling LJ559 EX-Q, Jack Alvin Thurlow, or Tiny as he was generally known, was an impressive man, standing at 6' 3"[11] with a well-built athletic frame.[12] So much so that he caused some concern at his enlistment with the medical officer noting, regarding his weight, 'can reduce'.[13] At his interviews for the Royal Canadian Air Force, he was found to be confident, easy, with an upright carriage and dress that was neat, conservative and clean. He spoke with a clear voice and was alert and sincere.[14] His references described him as 'thoroughly honest, willing, accurate and reliable'[15] with 'a splendid character'.[16] His air force interviews concluded that, he was a pleasant personality, a gentleman,[17] who, at the end of hostilities, wanted 'to Stay in RCAF'.[18] He was 'anxious to fly as a pilot'[19] and it was believed, he 'should do well'.[20]

Born on 25 April 1918, in Woodstock, Ontario, Canada,[21] he worked as an oil refinery pipe fitter at Imperial Oil Co.[22] immediately before enlisting in June 1941.[23] At training he was found to be:

> an average Bolingbroke [aircraft] pilot. Approaches tend to be too flat, and leaves too much to be done close to the ground – i.e. flaps down, then trim, then throttles, consequently landings were rough and not consistent. Air work good.[24]

He was awarded his pilot flying badge on 5 June 1942.[25] He served at a number of stations before being posted to the 199 Squadron on 13 November 1944.[26] He flew his first operation from RAF North Creake as a co-pilot on 25 November 1944, and finally flew with his own crew on 30 November 1944.[27]

Roy Berrill, a meteorologist in the Control Tower, recalls that he didn't know Jack Thurlow very well, but he used to meet him 'socially in the mess'.[28] A 'very nice chap, very friendly'.[29] On one occasion he asked him if he could go up in a Stirling for a test flight; 'by all means', Jack said, 'come and have a look at what it's like flying these damn things':[30]

> anyway, I went up with him circling round and round … he misjudged his height and he hit the deck with a heck of a bang. He cursed like mad. Anyway, he went out that night and he never came back.[B31]

His body was never found.[32]

Jack 'Tiny' Thurlow (Bomber Command Museum of Canada).

B   Roy had never discovered the fate of Jack Thurlow and his crew until we were able to tell him during an interview nearly 80 years after the event.

That night, 5 March 1945, both squadrons were supporting raids on Chemnitz and Bohlen.[33] The RAF North Creake Operations Record Book describes it thus:

> four Stirlings and two Halifax of No. 199 Squadron and six Halifax of No. 171 Squadron were detailed to form a Mandrel Screen with six Halifax of 199 Squadron and two Halifax of 171 Squadron to participate in a Window/bombing patrol. All took off. Three Stirlings and eight Halifax completed their Mandrel patrols, jamming from 18:50 to 22:00 hours at 15,000/18,000 feet ... Eight Halifax completed their Window/bombing patrol discharging Window from 19:31 to 20:57 hours at 18,000 feet descending to 11,000. Bombs were dropped on Mannheim and Worms. 199/'E' was reported shot down by A.A. near Thionville.[34]

Jack Thurlow's aircraft had indeed been hit by anti-aircraft fire, not so unusual, but Thionville was liberated by the Allies in November 1944. The anti-aircraft fire was friendly[C] and the damage caused was catastrophic. Struck by a 90-millimetre shell, the plane had lost two of its engines and had a hole ripped through its fuselage.[35] The aircraft tilted violently to port.[36] Ronald Noon-Ward climbed to his astrodome from where he could see the wing; there was a hole approximately six inches in diameter in it. 'Fire was shooting through it. The wing was aflame!'[37] Jack Thurlow ordered the crew to bale out.[38] It is commonly written,[D] that the crew, other than Jack Thurlow, baled out of the crippled Stirling. The reality, taken from the 'stand-in' mid upper gunner Fenning's statement, seems somewhat different:

C Richard Townshend Bickers (1994: 1) writes 'friendly fire means being shot at or bombed by one's own side. It is a fatuous term, detested by all, but it serves because everyone understands its meaning. A less injudicious term is fratricide. It is inexact because it means the killing of one's brother, but it is reasonable to extend it to brothers-in-arms. What about sororicide, however since so many women serve? ... the most logical term is amicide, the killing of friends'. For the purposes of this chapter, I have chosen to use friendly fire, recognising all its linguistic limitations.

D Confusion is compounded by the 199 Squadron ORB stating that 'the rest of the crew escaped by parachute', suggesting a more orderly escape than was the reality.

at approximately 20:30 hours [we] were in the vicinity of Thionville, and I personally had verified the height with the captain at 18,000 feet a matter of two or three minutes previously; we were just above 10/10 cloud.

Everything was running smoothly and our first intimation that we were under fire was when the starboard outer engine and mainplane were hit with what appeared to me [a] burst of heavy anti-aircraft fire. The starboard outer burst into flames and a large hole was also made in the centre of the mainplane between the outer and inner engines. The captain immediately ordered 'bale out'.

I vacated my turret, donned my parachute, retained helmet … and made for the rear hatch. The Special W/Op was immediately in front of me and the rear gunner was coming from his turret and dropping on his knees preparatory to opening the hatch. I plugged in the intercom at the hatch in order to advise the Captain that three had gone out of rear exit. Immediately on plugging in I heard the Captain say 'quick give me my chute' almost simultaneously a tremendous explosion occurred behind me and I opened my eyes to find I was descending and that my parachute was open. I should mention that there was a very pronounced smell of petrol inside the aircraft.

I have since verified with the Bomb Aimer and he confirms that he got as far as getting his hands on the Captain's parachute when the explosion took place; this [means] the Captain did not have his parachute on.

On landing (quite comfortably and safely) I discarded my chute and harness etc., and proceeded on foot to 'find the lay of the land'. I fortunately found eventually that I was on friendly territory approximately 15 miles in front of the German lines and proceeded in company with two French soldiers to the nearest hospital.

I have further verified with the remaining six survivors that nobody escaped out of the hatches – all were blown out when the aircraft exploded and disintegrated in mid-air … On 9.3.45 I explored the vicinity where the aircraft crashed in company with two other American officers to satisfy myself that there was no secret equipment undestroyed (I took some petrol in a can as a safeguard) but the aircraft had landed all over the countryside in the midst of a large wood spreading over a tremendous area and it was impossible to find everything although over two hours were spent searching. I was told by an M.P. that the aircraft burned for four hours on crashing to the ground.[39]

Ronald Noon-Ward's recollections reinforce this version of the events. In preparation for evacuating the aircraft he had removed his helmet and oxygen mask and clipped his parachute to his harness. He then climbed over the main-spar and headed for the rear of the plane. Progress was impeded by the unintentional deployment of the mid-upper gunner's parachute inside the plane,[E] and smoke had reduced the visibility.[40] Ronald Noon-Ward remembers that he was just preparing to jump when:

I suddenly feel a severe stinging sensation in my face then a tremendous pain in the groin, as if someone very large and very strong had kneed me, and the third sensation is absolute silence. Then I realize that I am floating to earth … the aircraft had exploded. I cannot believe my situation. It is a clear moonlit night above, heavy cloud below, no aircraft and no other parachutes in sight. My main thought is, my God, am I the only survivor? Nobody at home is going to believe this.[41]

Seven of the crew had been exceedingly lucky to have donned their parachutes in the short period between being attacked and the aircraft

---

E   Interestingly, this is omitted from the mid-upper gunner's statement above.

exploding (estimated at around 20 seconds[42]). They were also lucky that they survived their subsequent expulsion from the aircraft, albeit all injured.[43] Jack Thurlow, being unable to reach for his parachute in time, presumably, because he had been occupied until the last moment keeping the aircraft under some control, was not so lucky. The surviving crew members were:

A Plumtree (RAF) Flight Engineer
Ronald Gordon Noon-Ward (RCAF) Navigator
E A Evans (RAF) Bomb Aimer
A A Twaddle (RNZAF) Wireless Operator
T R Nichols (RCAF) Special Operator
F Fenning (RAF) Mid-Upper Gunner
W J Phillips (RAF) Rear Gunner

It has been impossible to discover much detail of six of the survivors; only information regarding Ronald Noon-Ward's escape seems to have survived. After landing with his parachute, and once sufficiently recovered, Ronald Noon-Ward headed towards a light in the distance. His sight was impeded 'by a flap of skin from his forehead which had torn loose and was slipping over his eyes'.[44] Walking over a level field he called for help, but no one responded. He therefore continued making his way towards the light. As he neared the light he shouted once again but there was still no response. Eventually he reached the edge of the field and was confronted by a steep embankment. At the top of the bank he could just work out men standing there with guns but was relieved to discover they were Americans. He once more asked for help and they replied that they 'would be happy to help him once he had got out of the mine field'.[45] Ronald Noon-Ward scrambled up the bank from where he was assisted on his way to large a building. It was heated by a fire and the pain from his burns forced him back outside. When medical assistance arrived, his flying suit was cut off and he was given a shot of morphine. He was offered a cigarette, which he accepted, but after inhaling he removed it from his mouth and it took part of his lips away with it.[46] He was taken to No. 106 Evacuation Hospital in Thionville, France on 5 March 1945, and then on to No.130 American Base Hospital on 7 March 1945. The next day he was repatriated to the UK and taken to Basingstoke Neurological and Plastic Surgery Hospital. From here he was transferred to The Queen Victoria Hospital in East Grinstead where he underwent two operations to the burns on his face and hands. He thus became a member of McIndoe's Guinea Pig Club,[F47] where Ross Tilley decides he will need some 'trimming up'.[G48]

LJ617 EX-E, was the last Bomber Command Stirling lost in operations over occupied Europe.[49] This particular Stirling was delivered new to 199 Squadron on 30 August 1944,[50] it had operated with 171 Squadron, flying 20 sorties as 6Y-P, and later 6Y-K, prior to moving to 199 Squadron, where it flew a further 27 missions as EX-E;[51] 'a remarkably fine achievement'.[52] It had been shot down by American anti-aircraft fire, in, a sadly, all too frequent occurrence. Numerous are the incidents described by crews of being fired upon by friendly anti-aircraft batteries, particularly over London,[53] where the 'jittery Army gunners always cut loose at you':[54]

> the main cause of such fatal errors is simple fear. The planes must not be allowed to get too close, and hence you fire at a distance too great for positive identification. The planes might be the enemy; in fact, they are quite likely to be.[55]

These errors can be exacerbated by poor weather conditions and the weather at the time was up to 10/10[ths] cloud cover, which the Stirling was just above.[56] However, aircraft recognition was also a significant problem and misidentification of aircraft was common; 'being shot at by friendly coastal batteries became as unremarkable as skidding on a banana skin or a hangover after a heavy night in the mess':[57]

F   649 patients were treated at East Grinstead often with pioneering reconstructive plastic surgery by Archibald McIndoe. Because of the innovative nature of this surgery, the patients were colloquially known as the 'Guinea Pigs' (http://rafbf.org).

G   Ronald Noon-Ward died at home in St. Thomas, Ontario, Canada in April 2014 (Guinea Pig Club Archive).

the last eighteen months of the war saw the worst errors of judgement caused by idiocy, incompetence or total loss of self-control; as well as pardonable accidents that resulted from a breakdown in communication caused by enemy action ... some American squadrons had evidently not ... learned to identify even the most frequently seen British aircraft.[58]

These erroneous actions were not just executed by the Americans; friendly fire was a symptom of warfare on all sides of the conflict, and by all armed forces. Jack Philipson, a pilot at RAF North Creake recalls flying to Charleroi only to be shot at by 'our own guns which, fortunately, fell short of our height'. [59] Ruefully he reflects, 'the RAF were supposed to notify army intelligence of all flight movements, particularly at night. Somewhere there had been a breakdown in communication'.[60] Richard Townshend Bickers, writing in the mid-1990s, appeared somewhat intolerant of why such situations may arise (a surprising occurrence given he has first-hand experience of warfare in the Second World War):

> people guilty of causing accidents through carelessness are apt to attribute them to hallucinations – anything but an admission of their own obtuseness or inefficiency. It is odd how young men whom their Squadron Medical Officers rate as sound in body and mind, and who have never flirted with the supernatural or suffered from a visual aberration, see things that aren't there[61]

However, there was no doubt about the feeling of remorse the incident engendered among the personnel of the American anti-aircraft battery, when it was realised what had happened, and there was no suggestion of them 'flirting with the supernatural' in order to explain the circumstances. F Fenning, the mid-upper gunner on Jack Thurlow's aircraft, relates in his debrief statement how:

the following day, Lt. Col. Sam C. Russell of the 38th A.A.A. Brigade, A.P.O. 403, U.S.A. called at the hospital and expressed to me his deepest sympathy with the crew at what he termed 'a regrettable accident which should have never taken place'.[62]

The saddest element of all, is that it is probable that Jack Thurlow would have survived the incident if he had managed to don his parachute. In a two-page letter of condolence to his next of kin, Percy Bevington, the commander of 199 Squadron, explains that 'Tiny stayed at his station' keeping control and was therefore 'unable to put on his parachute before the explosion took place'.[63] He further states that he believes that pilots flying within Bomber Command 'need to be equipped with a parachute that can be permanently worn'. [H64] Norman Bray, RAF North Creake station commander, concurred, insisting that if this style of parachute had been adopted, Jack Thurlow 'would have been saved'.[65]

He was just 26 when he was killed,[66] and with no further trace of him he was presumed dead on 24 October 1945.[67]

Jack Thurlow is recognised on the Woodstock cenotaph in Canada.[68] However, for some, such as Jack's relative by marriage, Janet Cassells-Jancetic, memorials do not capture the whole story. It is more personal; it is about 'who he was and what he meant to people',[69] particularly for his mother, who she relates 'never got to bury her son, … she never knew where he was … Sometimes you need to sit back and appreciate what your ancestors have done'. [70]

H   While there were some supplies of the US back-type parachute and some, such as Vic Polichek, equipped with it (Polichek: 3/2/1998), the British quick release type was found in tests to be 'superior'. Production started in February 1945 and priority was requested for 100 Group Squadrons (RAF 100 Group ORB: February 1945). Whether this happened is not recorded.

CHAPTER EIGHT

NEVER ENOUGH SLEEP

By mid-summer 2014, we were getting more guests and becoming more accustomed to running a B&B, although every arrival still made us nervous. Starting a hospitality business is an extraordinarily steep learning curve; in the beginning it was usually only two guests at a time and we probably overdid the hosting. We certainly couldn't have maintained that level of input. Then there were the logistical considerations; the first time we had four guests staying, all wanting different eggs, the order of preparation was a minefield. But this just needed practise.

An unexpected delight of the Control Tower B&B is the calibre of our guests; there is something about the building that attracts the sort of guest we want to meet. It is a distinct advantage that the building is a destination rather than just rented rooms. They come for the Control Tower, fall in love with North Norfolk and, thankfully, keep coming back.

What really surprised us on the Venn diagram of guest interests, is the large intersection between vegetarianism and Art Deco. There is also a remarkable level of couples where one enthuses about wartime history and the other loves deco; both being delighted to have found us. Although on one occasion a guest arrived with her new boyfriend from whom she was successfully keeping her passion for wartime airfields quiet; she had to sneak down separately and 'eeeek!' at us. We're a safe space for obsessives.

Though it has become a humorous B&B mantra 'don't mention the war', generally little time passes after a guest arrives before it crops up. So much so that it became evident that guests, and people in the local area, would appreciate a history tour. This was something we never expected to do when we envisaged our business, but with my growing obsession and the apparent appetite for it, we started. They have proved very popular and what is wonderful, is that on the tours, the history is also provided by the guests; relatives with the stories of their families, documents, artifacts and then, most fantastically, the veterans themselves. The surprise of receiving out of the blue a letter or email from a veteran because they've heard what we're doing, has been marvellous. It has also been a boon to my research.

By now, the Control Tower had become our home, but also, and not for the first time, a workplace. For a while British Field Products had operated an office from the Control Tower when running the mill next door, but, of course, the primary period of activity, had been for the war effort. At that time the Control Tower, as with the whole airfield site, was a hive of activity. Take, for example, 9-10 September 1944. A reasonably typical 24 hours at RAF North Creake.

On 9 September 1944, an intelligence officer at RAF North Creake, Robert Darracott,[A1] based in the operations block, starts the day by studying the previous night's reconnaissance photographs. These are interpreted, assessed and measured against the aims of the operation.[2] In the operations room, taking up the whole of one of the walls is the operations board, which the watchkeepers[B] are busy wiping clean. The paperwork relating to last night's raid has been tidied away and 'Form Y', outlining the results for the operation, has been completed and

---

A   Robert Darracott, formerly a navigator, he was promoted to intelligence officer on his arrival at RAF North Creake (Hillier: 14/2/2024).

B   Watchkeepers in operations blocks in the early years of the war, were employed at the rank of airwoman but the role had, by this point of the war, achieved the status of sergeant, with duties including responsibility for keeping the operations board up-to-date and broadcasting, by Tannoy, information such as briefing, meal and blackout times (Ford: 1992: 19). They also staffed telephones and pushed the scramble button to receive orders from Group HQ (Hall: 1985: 47).

sent to RAF 100 Group HQ at Bylaugh in North Norfolk, for onward transmission to Bomber Command Headquarters (BCHQ).[3]

The intelligence officers are also required to outline to RAF 100 Group HQ the number of serviceable aircraft and the available crews to fly them.[4] This information is forwarded to BCHQ for possible inclusion in tonight's operation.[5] At around 10:00 hours[6] the RAF 100 Group holds a conference using the GPO 'Privacy System',[7] more commonly known as the scrambler.[8] Led by Edward Addison, it involves all the commanding officers at stations within the Group,[9] including Norman Bray of RAF North Creake. This conference discusses the purpose of the night's operation, the type of countermeasures being performed, the numbers of aircraft required, routes, timing, bomb loads and weather.[10] The watchkeeper writes down faithfully the whole broadcast and later this detail is confirmed by teleprinter.[11] This information is then continually updated throughout the morning.[12]

The crews to be listed on each of the squadron's battle orders are sent by teleprinter, along with the codename[C] for the target.[13] It is now 'all stations go'.[14] The intelligence section provides the requisite information necessary for a successful operation:[15] details of previous attacks, relevant maps,[D] outlines of the 'type of target, the reason for its importance, the exact aiming point, the route there and back with a description of all known enemy defences'.[16]

Aircrew and aircraft are chalked up on the station operations board, with the estimated time of departure, time over target (H-Hour) and estimated time of return.[17] Norman Bray finalises details of the flarepath, marshalling points, any airfield obstructions and direction of the wind, all of which will be displayed in the Control Tower.[18] The meteorological section is being constantly updated throughout the day to allow for the preparation of the latest and most accurate weather

---

C   Bomber Command used codenames for targets which were published in a secret document locked in a safe for use by intelligence officers. Named after fish they were devised by Robert Saundby; a keen angler (Ford: 1992: 21).

D   The map clerk was 'responsible for ordering and maintaining all maps needed to cover all operational territory – which meant the whole of Europe'. As a result of the requirement of the map clerk to provide a 'full set of maps to cover the entire route issued to every navigator and bomb aimer', they were generally one of the first to know the identity of the target and route for that night (Hall: 1985: 56).

forecast possible for the briefing.[19] The meteorological assistants, such as Phyllis Willmott, are producing synoptic charts and visual aids to assist at that briefing.[20] These are updated as further, more reliable information, is received from ETA (the code name for the Central Forecasting Office in Dunstable[21]).[E22]

Elsewhere, the RAF North Creake navigation officer, in advance of the briefing, is providing the route for the bombers for tonight's operation.[23] He also works out, governed by the desired time over target,[24] the time the aircraft must leave the airfield in order to successfully complete their sorties. It is important that this is defined expeditiously as all other operational timings are dictated by it. These details are then communicated to the engineering officers, particularly the flight engineer leaders, and the petrol load is then decided upon.[25]

Also informed are the cookhouses for the sergeants' and officers' messes, that will have to prepare rations for the trip as well as meals at the correct time before take-off and after landing. The station sick quarters prepares the ambulances and their crews are readied; the fire officer does the same. The Control Tower is then given advance warning of the time at which to stop all non-operational flying.[26]

Aircrews rise from their slumber well after all others on the station and then have a 'leisurely breakfast'.[27] Stephen Wainwright, based on a bomber station in Lincolnshire, recalls:

> reveille was a word unknown to operational aircrew in Bomber Command. If you wanted breakfast you had to be in the mess before nine o'clock ... they were good breakfasts too. Shelled eggs and real bacon, served on linen-covered tables by a W.A.A.F. waitress ... then to the mess bar. Not for booze but to find an armchair, pick up a newspaper, read what brand of garbage the Ministry of Information was feeding to the public ... and listen to Lord Haw Haw. That bastard! As often as not he knew that night's target before we did.[28]

E   Meteorologists would forecast the weather for an area of Europe without any particular knowledge of the target in advance of the briefing, 'we were just told the information that we had to give the crews' (Berrill: 27/6/2021).

By 11:00 hours, aircrew would normally be found playing cricket or lounging on the grass by the flight offices, waiting to find out whether operations were scheduled for that night.[29] If they were, groundcrews would begin the process of preparing the aircraft immediately.[30]

The servicing echelons for the squadrons at RAF North Creake are Numbers 9199 (for 199 Squadron) and 9171 (for the 171)[31] and are responsible for carrying out daily inspections on all aircraft.[32] Highly regarded on RAF stations, they work on aircraft 'all hours and all weathers'.[33] Close bonds were often formed between groundcrews and aircrews. Bernie How remembers that he got to know them well and would often speak to them on his days off; 'you'd have little talks in the engineers' section. The chief man ... would talk to you or you could ask him questions. Probably pass an hour that way. Mainly operational stuff.'[34]

As a constituent part of the 18 ground engineers and 12 flight maintenance staff involved in keeping each bomber serviceable,[35] the instrument section conducts daily inspections: minor and major. That is, varying from a simple visual check and cleaning to a major inspection when 'an aircraft [will] be out of service whilst comprehensive testing [takes] place'.[36] If any faulty instruments have been reported 'these [have] to be dealt with first, in case they [turn] out to be long jobs'.[37] Then every instrument is checked and set as necessary.[38] The oxygen and nitrogen bottles are then topped up. If the Special Window Force is operating, Window will be loaded on the aircraft at this time.[39]

Aircrew always preferred to use the same aircraft. A large degree of superstition could be attached to a particular aircraft, and it was the cause of some considerable anxiety if a crew was allocated the 'wrong' one.[40] Several factors influenced whether it was possible to use the same aircraft including, the 'rank of the pilot and his degree of assertiveness, the seniority of the crew, the availability of the aircraft – and the importance the Captain attached to the issue'.[41] But Leonard Cheshire felt the notion of 'ownership' was critical:

we each owned our own aircraft and, almost more important still, our own groundcrew, both of whom we looked upon as part of ourselves and which only under dire necessity would we lend to anyone else. Proportionately, as these ties of mutual understanding and confidence developed, one flew to greater effect, was the more likely to survive damage or injury and serve out one's time in the squadron with more peace of mind.[42]

For Ted Cattell, RAAF pilot at RAF North Creake, he would not have anyone other than Fred Nieman 'touching his engines!'.[43] If a bomber was 'struck off charge', telling a groundcrew that 'their' aircraft, 'for she was theirs as much as ours',[44] was very difficult; 'I could see that the loss of the aeroplane that they had looked after so conscientiously affected them deeply'.[45] Groundcrew mechanics 'literally had the lives of aircrew in their hands',[46] reliant, as they were, on their thoroughness as to 'whether the planes were going to stay in the air or fall out of the sky'.[47] A responsibility they took seriously, but in good humour, as a groundcrew motto reveals, 'difficulties quickly overcome, miracles take a little longer; the Latin translation of this being – "ubendum – wemendum"'.[48]

Groundcrews, unlike aircrew, 'were not glamourised in verse and news-print',[49] and they had to contend with all weathers. In the heat of the summer, climbing into an aircraft, the metal skin 'could be very hot to one's hands',[50] but it was the cold that was the hardest. The winter of 1944-1945, with icy cold winds blowing off the North Sea, was particularly severe. Servicing engines on trestle stands at around 20 feet, 'it was a frequent thing for a chap to slip on the greasy main plane and roll off and fall on the concrete hard-standing beneath'.[51] Irene Storer, who worked in instruments maintenance and repair at Downham Market, Norfolk, describes how on one occasion she was determined to stay warm; 'I had on a shirt, cardigan, battledress, boiler suit and a greatcoat. So, wearing five pairs of sleeves, I attempted to climb up into the aircraft, only to find that I could not lift my arms!'.[52] Dick Hughes, who also worked as an instrument 'basher' at RAF North

Creake, developed the practice of blowing down the air speed indicator tube to ensure it was clear. One bitterly cold day, as his lips contacted the metal tube, he suffered instant frostbite, scarring him for life.[53]

Servicing a Stirling at RAF North Creake (Chris Nieman).

Aircrew and other airfield personnel sympathised with the plight of groundcrew. Roy Berrill working in the 'relatively warm'[54] Control Tower commented, 'the maintenance was always done in the open air and the poor devils that had to service the aircraft, must have been frozen stiff ... how they managed it, I don't know ... But there you are'.[55] And it was work that went on 'round the clock'. However, there were, according to Bill Pride, an engine mechanic at Bardney, Lincolnshire, some small compensations:

> there were no parades and there was no particular time that you started work. That depended really on the serviceability of

the aircraft for which you were responsible. There was really no discipline. Nobody bothered about anybody's hair being too long or anybody's buttons not being clean, or anybody's boots. The only people that interfered with this were the headquarters staff and the man responsible for station discipline – the notorious Station Warrant Officer, who on several occasions held up the chaps and told them all they were on a charge for having long hair and dirty boots and all the rest of it. This sort of thing was later quashed by the senior officers of the flight who said that they couldn't spare their men to be doing jankers.[F56]

Some discipline was essential for the safe functioning of the station and it's understandable that M E Putors, was Confined to Camp for 14 days by Norman Bray, when he was discovered 'smoking in Stirling aircraft LJ577', contrary to flight orders.[57] And others were reprimanded with 14 days 'Confinement to Camp' for 'damaging by neglect ... Halifax aircraft NA105 and NA112 whilst moving Halifax NA105'.[58] Then there was the occasion when a member of airfield personnel 'fail[ed] to prepare Halifax aircraft LK874 for operations in that he took no action to ensure that the aircraft was refuelled prior to time of take off'.[59] Harold 'Frank' Sant, a mechanic at North Creake, had a run-in with his head of section: 'if the engine packed-up they used to be able to ... feather the propellor[G] so it didn't cause windmilling. Apparently, I'd forgotten to do something and he said he'd have my guts for garters if I did it again. Very unfriendly'.[60] After seeing the Air Sea Rescue launches from the quay at Wells-next-the-Sea, he applied, was accepted and re-mustered.[61]

F   A breach of 'King's Rules and Regulations' resulted in being put on a charge (or fizzer as airmen called it). Recorded on Form 252 Charge Sheet and heard by the commanding officer (or deputy) accompanied by discipline NCO, Flight Sergeant Denman at RAF North Creake (Hartley: undated). Minor offences usually received a couple of days 'confined to camp' and known as 'Jankers'. This meant guardroom parades, twice a day, for full kit inspection (Ford: 1992: 11).

G   The term 'airscrew' rather than propellor is often seen in contemporary literature. The Air Ministry put a stop to the use of the term after a signal requesting six airscrews resulted in the delivery of six aircrews (Skan: 1990: 21).

Groundcrews take a break at RAF North Creake:
Norman Turnbull (Control Tower Archive).

On the operations board details of aircraft serial numbers, code letters and pilot names of those crews taking part tonight have been completed. The 'order of battle', a 'Roneoed sheet of cheap foolscap',[62] with the crew names of those taking part is now produced. [63] It will be posted (normally somewhere between 11:00 or 11:30 hours[64]) detailing the times of the pre-operation meal, pre-briefing, main briefing and transport to aircraft.[65] Since discovering that they are flying tonight, few could relax.[66] Arthur Adcock, a wireless operator at RAF North Creake, recalls 'no matter how many operations you had completed, that feeling of fear when you saw your name on the Battle Orders, never diminished'.[67] Geoff Parnell, stationed elsewhere, concurs it:

> [makes] you feel as if someone has hit you in the stomach. After that you live through the day in a comatose state, you are neither really alive or dead ... you wander around waiting subconsciously to go there [and] get it over and get back.[68]

'We're flying tonight lads', was generally the phrase used by Gordon

Mercier's skipper,[69] that heralded the news of an impending operation. Some were anxious at such news, others ambivalent, but a few, such as Gordon Dennison, an air gunner with 199 Squadron, appeared to welcome it. Writing home he states, 'well I am on a squadron now and don't mind it at all, I have six trips in now but have a long ways to go before I get to … 50'.[70] But for the majority it was a difficult time: 'the gnawing, aching, nibbling fear is like a sort of rumble of thunder in the pit of the stomach, yet there are so many hours to go … everyone feels it'.[71] For many the more operations that one completed the worse it got:

> I was beginning to find that the strain of operational flying had a pronounced cumulative effect. Each time I found myself on the battle order the ordeal of waiting – an ordeal punctuated by the ritual of air test, briefing, and flying meal – seemed intensified, the muscles of the abdomen hardening until they felt like the extended ribs of a miniature umbrella. The tension would ease briefly as we finally got started and raced down the runway on take off, then it returned with redoubled force as we approached hostile territory, to reign supreme and worsen progressively as the trip wore on.[72]

With some, the strain was obvious to all, as Denis Gill, a RAF North Creake air gunner, recalls; 'every morning Andy was very quiet. If there was an operation on he ate his meal in silence. If there was no operation his demeanour would change and he would become cheerful and talkative'.[73] However, it was not only those who were taking part that felt the strain, there were those married to aircrew members that had decided to lodge close to the station. Worry was a feature for them every time an aircraft left at night. The close proximity of spouses was generally discouraged, but there were few hard and fast rules regarding husbands living out of camp with wives.[74] Nevertheless, the strain was obviously compounded by the knowledge that their morning goodbye, might be their last:

if a soldier goes off to fight the war for some time there is a formal farewell with a great deal of feeling, and both he and his family know that the occasion is not likely to repeat itself ever, and that although it is possible that the soldier will not come back, the strain of the parting has to be endured but once. With an airman 'living out' the matter was totally different; in no farewell ever were emotions allowed to come to the surface at all, but uncertainty prevailed all the time ... she could not know if she heard aircraft going out and then coming back where he was, and for several hours on end she had to undergo tremendous suspense. She could not telephone the aerodrome because there was a security ban, as always when operations were on, and because of course there would have been chaos if every wife were to have telephoned every time aircraft went out and came back.[75]

Michael Renaut, wing commander of 171 Squadron, explains that he and his wife, Yvonne, used to use a simple code to keep her informed of the night's schedule, 'I used to ring her up and say that I was "busy" (this meant that my squadron was operating but I wasn't flying myself) but if I said I was "very, very busy" that meant I was flying on operations myself and she would know not to expect me back until the early hours of the morning'.[76] Yvonne Renaut describes how worry was always a constant companion, but they would never admit it to each other; 'we were both putting on an act the whole time'.[77] As a consequence she never realised how frightened he was, 'he always put on such a brave façade. Always, laughing and looking happy'.[78]

By mid-morning aircrews 'were shaved, spruced and at our respective [aircraft]. Sharing fags and tea with the ground crew'.[79] The armourers would be there, often WAAFs, whose job it was to strip and clean Browning guns, and 'belt' the bullets ready to feed into the bomb turrets.[80] The tail turret guns had many feet of ammunition tracks that lay along the side of the fuselage; these had to be checked thoroughly for any possible ammunition belt stoppages as 'stoppages could be fatal to a crew'.[81] Gordon Mercier describes how it was 'one of our jobs on the ground to calibrate the guns so that it didn't hit any part of the aircraft ... when it was revolving ... it stopped the guns from firing ... Because you could hit the front of the aircraft quite easily ... And you could hit the tail quite easily as well'.[82] The Browning .303s were then 'harmonised to produce a tight grouping of rounds at a given range'.[83] Tested against firing butts on the ground, they were adjusted, typically (although not universally) at 400 yards.[84]

All aircraft tests had to be completed by a certain time so that any problems could be reported to Squadron or Engineering Wing for repairs (they were entered on 'Form 700 Servicing Record'[85]). Although, some groundcrew left the tests as late as possible, when the inside of the aircraft was less busy. Ken Derbyshire remembers from his time with 199 Squadron:

> there were so many trades trying to get up and down the aisle of the fuselage, what with the bulkheads and the turrets and their bullet tracks etc., I decided I would let some of this die down before retesting ... there came a period before take-off when engine testing had stopped and the dispersal became strangely quiet – crews were at briefing and most of the others had retreated to the flight hut – that was the moment I chose to do my particular task.[86]

Once all checks were complete, aircrews would then decide whether they needed a flight test; alternatively, their flight engineer could perform a ground test on the peri-track.[87] Denis Gill remembers an occasion at RAF North Creake during a test 'when the engines of the plane were at full throttle ... one of the propellors flew off and hurtled across the field fortunately missing everyone'.[88] Normally, depending on time of take-off, all air tests would need to be completed before lunch. The more meticulous and prepared a crew, the better the chances are of survival.[89]

If the aircrew and groundcrew are satisfied that the aircraft is serviceable then the arming and refuelling can commence on the dispersals. A heavy bomber would consume approximately a gallon of fuel per mile,[90] therefore an average trip to Germany would burn around 2,000 gallons per aircraft.[91] It was delivered by tankers filled up at the airfield's bulk tanks. These tankers needed to be earthed through ground stakes otherwise static from the aircraft could cause a spark 'with disastrous results'.[92] While refuelling, groundcrew electricians are checking that the accumulators on the aircraft are all fully charged. Radar mechanics are fitting the radar equipment with appropriate detonators, so that in the advent of a crash over enemy territory, the equipment can be destroyed, thus preventing it from falling into enemy hands.[93] The radar section at RAF North Creake was a very cohesive unit and many of the radar mechanics, such as Howard Gray, recall their time with great affection:

> some of my best memories of the radar section relate to the corporals upon whom we relied so heavily. With such support, along with that of the sergeants, it made the job so much more manageable. I recall one older corporal, a former radio man in civvy street, who had not had a radar course but was able to repair a special trainer when nobody else could.[94]

After lunch, many crews try to pass the time by sleeping, but many never succeed.[95] The contrast between the calm English countryside of the present, contrasted with thoughts of being over the target causes such anxiety that, for many, it makes it impossible to rest. Some airmen attempt, in advance of the briefing, to guess the target identity by working out the fuel load and type of bombs being prepared.[96] The Tannoy then announces the time of briefing for aircrew.[97]

Some aircrew attended a specialist briefing before the main briefing.[98] Wireless operators and Vic Flowers, sergeant in charge of signals, attend one, although Vic 'had to leave when times and frequencies were discussed for the RCM work'.[99] At this meeting the wireless operators collect their 'goodies bags' from a WAAF in the signals section which contained pliers, screwdriver, flimsies, Q Codes, log and torch.[100] Flight engineers and navigators would also each have a meeting in their respective sections.[101]

Twelve aircrews file into the briefing room; ten to fly, two in reserve.[102] An armed Service Policeman guards the door,[103] the station is locked down and no one is allowed on or off.[104] 'It was said that in the early days [of the war] there was one occasion when somehow the name of the night's target got around the village and the whole operation had to be cancelled. Perhaps just a story.'[105] True or not, precautions are now taken with, for example, the Dry Road being closed, the airfield telephone boxes being chained shut[106] and the door of the briefing room Nissen hut[107] locked.[108]

In the general briefing room the crews gather at separate trestle tables[109] waiting for the briefing room map, that was covered by a curtain,[110] to reveal its secret. All the crews rise as the commanding officers enter the room,[111] the squadron commander welcomes the aircrews and the roll of captains is called.[112] Then, with use of the traditional phrase, 'gentlemen, the target tonight is ...',[113] the curtain is drawn back and the wing commander announces the target as Monchengladbach, about 250 miles as the crow flies.[114] It is not a deep penetration, but if it were a 'rigorously defended hotspot', there would be gasps from even 'the toughest character',[115] followed by a collective groan from the assembled crews,[116] accompanied by:

> extremely rude comments from the crews who had been to the target before, but Groupie would attempt to calm the situation by making some witty remark such as 'don't worry too much chaps, the last time I was there it was guarded by two men and a dog', which provoked even more obscene remarks.[117]

However, tonight it's not too bad. The 1:500,000 scale[118] map has red tape indicating the route to be taken.[119] It has cellophane pinned to it with notable features (such as heavily defended areas) marked in a Chinagraph pencil.[120] The bombers do not fly a direct route to target but dogleg; a course 'that changes direction several times, to keep the enemy night-fighter controllers guessing as to which target has been chosen'.[121]

To any casual observer, there is a confusing array of emotions on display at the briefing. Even seasoned flyers would not want to display overtly 'windy'[122] sentiments; secret feelings, not to be shared. Denis Gill explains for some, such feelings could be impossible to conceal; 'none of us were very happy. I was sitting between Andy and Mitch, a mid-upper gunner, and Mitch nudged me and said "look at Andy". I did so and Andy's pale features were white, white as a sheet'.[123] Only a fool would not feel apprehensive in this situation and the real courage is the strength that keeps you going in spite of your fears. These supressed but warring emotions are what gives the briefing an unreal feeling:

> the familiar atmosphere unlike that I ever saw filmed or described. It was only possible to understand the mixture of barbarism and sensibility, inanity and cunning, cowardice and courage which ran through members of an Air Force squadron in varying degrees if you had it inside as well. And then you had neither the wish nor the time to think about it self-consciously at all. Before a trip it was necessary to develop a shell of indifference so that the conflicting emotions inside you might be kept out of the way and I suppose it was this that outsiders took for calm and nonchalance or determination and praised accordingly.[124]

The wing commander then indicates the aiming point on the map, outlines the size of the Main Force (113 Lancasters and 24 Mosquitoes[125]), the time the attack commences (H-Hour) and the time from which they commence the Mandrel Screen jamming (01:15 and cease at 05:45 hours.[126]). Then the Intelligence Officer explains the reasons for the attack (from a briefing sent from BCHQ[127]), such as the targeting of factories of military production, railway locomotive works, transport hubs, assistance to ground forces. He then explains how the RAF 100 Group jamming and diversion operations should misdirect the German defences. He also advises the route to adopt, what defences to expect, their location and how best to avoid them.[128]

Ernie Hughes, flight engineer with 171 Squadron, describes how inevitably a 'glamour' slide breaks the tension: 'strange how photos of pin-ups got mixed up with pictures of the "target for tonight"[H] … this brief aside always met with loud cheers'.[129] Then the Navigation Officer advises the crews of the take-off times and anything special to note en route. Also he outlines any wind changes to note since their specialist sectional briefing.[130] Next, the Meteorological Officer, using a diagram to illustrate,[131] describes the expected weather conditions at all stages of the trip. Roy Berrill suggests that 'everyone listened to the briefing intently until the met. report, then they went to sleep',[132] even though it contained critical information regarding 'winds so that aircraft could maintain position without drifting away'.[133] Essential for the effective operation of Mandrel. The aircrews could be an unappreciative audience:

> the met bloke said a few words … more often than not they were the same few words. It was going to be bloody cold, it was going to be bloody cloudy and it was going to be bloody windy. He found scores of ways of saying it, but that's what it boiled down to.[134]

Reflecting upon it nearly 80 years later, Roy Berrill, suggests this was 'fair comment'.[135] He remembers the barracking, but doesn't think it was undeserved, 'we were learning a lot and there was a lot we didn't know'.[136] The meteorologist's position could be further undermined by being unable to reflect any sudden change in weather; even if the accuracy of the forecast could be challenged by simply looking out the window, 'we were only allowed to tell them the official forecast'.[137] Roy Berrill recalls one particular occasion at RAF North Creake where the official forecast stated 'it was going to be just cloudy'. But shortly before the briefing the colleague from whom Roy was taking over shift,

---

H   Roy Berrill has no memory of pin-ups appearing (Berrill: 25/3/2023).

pointed out, 'you better notice this, there's a thunderstorm in South Lincolnshire'. Shortly after the briefing, 'they got off, got themselves ready to go ... and suddenly this thunderstorm came slap bang on top of us ... the most enormous Cumulonimbus' ... half an hour later the whole operation was cancelled ... It was the most amazing mess the Group people had ever made'.[138] However, it was Roy that had to face 'the howls of derision'[139] at the next briefing.

The wing commander then rises again and gives detailed tactics of the operation, order of take-off, further details of countermeasures and details of the return trip.[140] The briefing also includes a presentation from the Flying Control Officer[141] who outlines what conditions to expect on the return to the station.[142] Last, Norman Bray, the station commander, stands and gives a few words of encouragement and motivation to the crews. Stephen Wainwright, a rear gunner at another bomber station describes[143] how he could never remember the meeting reaching a conclusion, they 'repeated themselves a few times, then petered out ... that was OK by us ... we been told "what" and "when". We all reserved the right to decide the final "how"'.[144]

The doors of the briefing room were unlocked and the crews began to meander out. Always the last to emerge were the navigators, as they had to complete 'a flight plan so that if they were killed the crew would have something to get them back'.[145] Left on their tables in the briefing room, under the guard of the Service Police, they will be collected in a 'large canvas bag'[146] which the navigator then collects from the navigation section before the raid. Other than the flight plans, this bag also includes log sheets (Form 441) navigation tables, the Dalton Computer and the necessary charts and flimsies for the raid.[147]

From before the briefing the armourers had begun preparing, fusing, delivering and loading the bombers with the specified bombload. This process can take over five hours and they are still not complete when the aircrew emerge from their briefing.[148] Madeline Morgan remembers 'we were searched before entering the Bomb Dump for matches or cigarettes or anything that might be inflammable, and the bomb trolleys we had to drive were also searched'.[149] Victor

Tempest, a medical officer from another bomber station, marvelled at the organisation of bombing-up and reflected upon the cosmopolitan nature of the bombing campaign:

> it was an instruction to see an English W.A.A.F. drive a load of American manufactured 'death' laid on the trolleys by an Australian ground crew to a Canadian-built Lancaster, flown by New Zealanders and serviced by men from any country who wished to serve the Allied cause. This sight could be seen. It is not a fantasy and it made for a unity of purpose which spelt victory. It was not a fairy story; it was an everyday occurrence.[150]

Handling bombs and servicing heavy aircraft accounted for 330 killed and 759 injured among groundcrew. Another 1,040 died from other, so called, natural causes. Arthur Harris explains what this means:

> many fit young people ... contracted illnesses by working all hours of the day and night in a state of exhaustion ... in the open, rain, blow or snow, in daylight and through darkness, hour after hour ... on wartime aerodromes where ... accommodation .... offered every kind of discomfort ... [and] it was often impossible to even get dry clothes to change into.[151]

After the briefing the aircrews file in for their 'ritual egg and bacon'.[152] Often referred to as the last supper as 'it was for a lot of guys'.[153] Gordon Mercier remembers 'sometimes there was chips but we always had bacon and eggs. And big portions as well'.[154] Even bigger if your crewmate didn't fancy his, as Keith Thompson, navigator on his second tour with 199 Squadron writes in his diary, '4 eggs, my two & Joe's'.[155] The pre-op meal could be 'a noisily good-humoured affair ... it was one way of staving off that empty feeling of anticipation in one's stomach'.[156] It was certainly a mixed blessing for some with 'a number of people rolling food around in their mouth with no appetite whatsoever'.[157] Others recollect the WAAFs who served them with a good deal of affection and they are particularly appreciative of their sensitivity: 'those that served us in the sergeants' mess, [with] their tart (no pun intended) replies to our criticisms of the quality of the food provided, but silence with a smile when we queued for our egg and chips before operations'.[1158]

The aircrews then reassemble in the crew room[159] to hand in all the items one was prohibited from taking when flying operationally; 'you had to empty your pockets so that you'd got nothing to identify yourself with at all ... we were told to clear everything out. Especially bus tickets ... Anything that could identify you or your squadron ... like postcards from the family with your address on'.[160] A WAAF from another bomber intelligence section recalled the canvas bag, one for each crew, for the 'collection and safe keeping of each man's private possessions, papers etc.'. This could be a 'rather "chokey" task at times, when someone would say "if I don't come back ... you have this"'.[161] Also in attendance would be either Peter Gorrie, or Robert Dyke, the North Creake medical officers,[162] giving out caffeine tablets (wakey-wakey pills) for those who want them, as well as aspirin and any other medicine required.[J][163] These wakey-wakey pills are in fact Benzedrine (an amphetamine) to be used in an emergency.[164] Often referred to as a Benny,[165] aircrew frequently kept them 'tucked away in [their] pocket'.[166] Phyllis Willmott, meteorological WAAF, suggests their use in letter to her friend as a solution to her tiredness, 'I really must see you [Peg], and I could easily take some waki-waki [sic] pills and skip bed for just one day'.[167]

Then a 'cigarette and a gentle wander ... to get geared up'.[168] 'Geared-up' was aircrew shorthand for the issuing of all necessary provisions for the operation, this included a sweet ration (barley sugars, Fry's Chocolate Creams, Crunchie bars and three or four bars of Cadbury's Dairy Milk[169]), chewing gum, a vacuum flask containing hot drink,[170] and an orange,[171] all of 'which you distributed in your

---

I   Priscilla Meath Baker remembers a cook they employed at Walsingham Abbey had left her employment at the airfield as a result of the mental strain of aircrew not returning after an operation (Meath Baker: 11/3/2024).

J   The RAF were the first to carry injections of morphine in the air contained in a one-dose disposable syringe (Tubunic Ampoule), 'only to be used over the target on seriously wounded aircrew to ease severe pain'. Sealed with red sealing wax in the first-aid haversack, if the seal was found to be broken after return a report had to be written up (Hall: 1985: 128).

pockets'.[172] Often crew members 'used to keep the chewing gum and give the sweets to the girl who drove the crew truck'.[173] An escape kit was also issued,[174] prepared afresh for each raid.[175] It was known as 'Pandora' and was 'only to be opened if the aircraft was forced down or one had to bail out'.[176] It contained a 'big map of Europe on silk',[177] and a compass, often disguised as a tobacco smoker's pipe; the evader 'just broke it open and the compass was inside the barrel of the pipe'.[178] Also included were Horlicks tablets, water purifying tablets, relevant currencies, and a hacksaw blade (stowed away inside its handle).[179] All enclosed in a small plastic box, which doubled up as an effective flask[180] and 'just slipped into your … breast pocket'.[181] In March 1945, a memo was issued at North Creake reminding crews of the importance of returning these Pandoras to the intelligence section after operations. Michael Renaut insisted the failure to do so was in 'the vast majority of cases … sheer carelessness and neglect of duty …. any future cases … will result in the individual concerned losing the 48 hours privilege pass usually allowed with the periodical crew leave'.[182]

Last, of course, is all the bulky flying gear. Air gunners don electronically heated 'Irvine suits',[183] the rest of the crew generally wear thick roll-neck sweaters under their battledress, three pairs of gloves (silk, woollen and gauntlet), a belt with a revolver (and six rounds), and flying boots.[184] They then check their oxygen masks on 'a test rig'[185] and the WAAFs from the parachute section issue each crew member with their own parachute,[K] harness and life jacket (known as a Mae West[L]). Generally supplied with the parachute was the hackneyed joke 'if it doesn't open bring it back'.[186] The tradition in many squadrons was that any aircrew member paid five shillings to the parachute store WAAF, if a parachute was accidently opened (five shillings being more than a day's pay).[187] Arthur Adcock recalls, 'I always took the [parachute] given to me without any qualms but some people insisted on refusing the

---

K   When allocated a parachute, 'no matter where you went it was your responsibility to get it back' (How: 8/3/2017).

L   So called as when inflated they supposedly took on the shape of the voluptuous Hollywood actress of the same name. To operate one pulled a toggle and it inflated automatically, Gordon Mercier remembers that if you inflated too early you would not 'have been able to get out of your turret'. The air could be topped-up manually, by blowing in through a tube on the side (Bartlett: 23/11/2021).

first one and accepting the second, much to the annoyance of the Cpl in charge, who did not or would not understand the superstitions that some crews had'.[188]

Now, with a little over an hour from take-off, they move to the assembly area to await transport to the dispersals.[189] By this point of the war, transport was most often in the form of crew buses driven by WAAFs, 'especially designed for the job, no longer requiring the undignified scramble to get into the back of an open lorry'.[190] On board were usually two or three crews, who are dropped, in turn, at their aircraft.[191] It was between now and take-off that operations were often scrubbed.

Aircrews hated a 'scrub' as they felt that they were now emotionally prepared and 'over the worst';[192] as Ernie Hughes pointed out, a paradoxical 'fear of reprieve'.[193] Tom Sawyer, a pilot for Bomber Command, believes the responsibility for the final decision as to whether to send the bomber force 'must have been an awesome weight on the shoulders of [Arthur Harris] the C-in-C.'.[194] However, when 'sometimes we had even got into our aircraft and started up the engines before cancellation came through',[195] it was highly frustrating and worried the nerves, 'having got keyed-up and ready to go, it was galling to suddenly "let go" as it were, knowing that tomorrow you would have to go through the whole process again'.[196] Sometimes it was just one aircraft that didn't take off, as in when Denis Gill and Andy Croxall, regulars with Harold Sturrock, were due to fly as 'stand-ins' with another crew; 'Sturrock suddenly roared up in a jeep and said ... "get in you're not going"'.[197] From where he derived the authority to make such a decision Denis and Andy never found out.[198] The crew had a reputation for 'not getting on and being at odds with one another (proving not all those who were in conflict together formed strong camaraderie!)'.[199] Indeed, on this particular operation an argument had broken out between the navigator and pilot. Denis recalled, 'Andy said to me: "I am convinced we are going to die on this operation!" But ... he always thought he would not survive any of the operations we went on'.[200] While one imagines it was a great relief to get out of this particular sortie, Denis

Gill reflects that if he had been the squadron commander, he would not have let Harold Sturrock dictate who flew and who did not.[201]

However, most commonly the reasons for a 'scrub' were more mundane, as Gordon Dennison wrote in a letter home, 'we have had it for today it is storming, cold & wet. We are suppose [sic] to fly to-nite [sic] but the weather stopped us'.[202] Likewise, Keith Thompson recorded in his diary on several occasions, 'battle order scrubbed at the last minute'.[203] Or at one point, 'Battle Order. Briefing 2:30 … On, off, reserve, & then on again! Got off OK'.[204]

The armourers also dreaded the announcement 'operations scrubbed'. As this involves 'debombing' and another five hours work.[205] As Leslie Hay, a pilot of 49 Squadron perceptively observed, 'all [the work] had to be undone when the bombers couldn't take off. We went to bed or somewhere whenever we could, but the ground crew couldn't do that'.[206] For aircrew, perhaps it was the release of that emotional preparedness that caused some of the more boisterous behaviour seen at RAF stations, as a pilot with Bomber Command reflected, 'perhaps this is why those spontaneous parties would erupt sometimes when the "ops scrubbed" came through at the last moment'.[207]

It wasn't just a total scrub that created extra work for groundcrews. Late notice of change of target could involve altering the bombload or, if it was a shorter distance, removing some of the fuel from the aircraft's tanks; 'an unpopular task'.[208] Even with a single change of aircraft due, perhaps, to a mechanical fault, the whole line back to BCHQ would have to be informed, operations boards corrected and a new aircraft prepared with the requisite fuel, bombs, and target-confirming camera.[209]

In the Control Tower, as take-off time approaches, there is a hive of activity. Norman Bray, the station commander, squadron leaders and flight commanders, engineering officers, etc., if not detailed to fly, would position themselves in the control room.[210] In the station sick quarters there are three people on duty; one crash orderly, one standby and one WAAF.[211] The crash ambulance (three regular drivers – Jock Gillies, Roy Copus and WAAF A C W Holland[212]), along with the fire tender,[213] are at Flying Control 30 minutes before take-off. They remain on duty for the period aircraft are in the air; 'it was a cold business during the winter because we had no extra cold weather clothing'.[214]

Preparing for an operation on dispersals: Vic Polichek
touching the propellor tip (Jayne Jennings).

In the gathering twilight or in full darkness, the aircrew are greeted by the groundcrew standing at dispersal 'with a grin and the words: "all's well"'.[215] They are 'fussing over the aircraft, polishing the cockpit windows and turrets as a speck of oil on the turrets could, in the dark, be mistaken for a fighter'.[216] Equipment is stowed on board, the turrets are traversed and guns elevated and depressed.[217] The wireless operator checks his fuses and generator readings to satisfy himself that everything is serviceable,[218] and the pilot checks that everyone can hear and can be heard over the intercom.[219] With approximately one hour to go before take-off the flight engineer carries out an external inspection of the aircraft.[220] This involves a check for damage starting at the nose through to the back of the bomber. Inside the aircraft, fuel gauges and panel readings are checked.[221] Then the pilot and flight engineer start each engine in turn and all engines are warmed to a minimum temperature, leaving the pilot to run through a series of engine and mechanical checks from the cockpit.[222] The rest of the crew climb inside and check their sections. If they are considered to be satisfactory, the pilot signs 'Form 700' indicating that the aircraft is serviceable.[223] After this the petrol bowsers arrive to top up the fuel tanks.[224] Now the aircraft is ready and, inside or outside, the crew wait for a signal flare from the Control Tower; red indicates that the operation is scrubbed green that they should to prepare to taxi.[225] Some enjoy 'a last smoke and chat',[226] others, sit on the grass or play football.[227] Often, while they await take-off, the squadron commander, flight commander, engineers and the medical officer appear at the dispersals, offering last minute advice.[228] Arthur Adcock recalls at RAF North Creake, 'trucks arriving with hot coffee and sandwiches to drink and eat at the dispersal and to fill our Thermos flasks with coffee to drink during the flight ... then ... we would form a semi-circle and have our final pee on the port wheel, to the amusement of the groundcrew and the scampering off in all directions of any WAAFs present!'.[229]

Vic Polichek (far right) with his crew, waiting for the signal to board the aircraft (Jayne Jennings).

Eventually, a green flare from flying control signals that it is time to board the aircraft.[230] On board they are greeted by the 'sickly smell of dope mingled with fainter vomit, glycol, rexine, grease and metal. This conglomerate smell was foreign [to the] nostrils'.[231] Arthur Adcock describes how, once in the aircraft, he 'could physically feel the last half-hour's laughing and bravado draining away from me, being replaced by a clammy, slightly nauseous feeling. I tried, without much success, to project my mind forward to the end of the mission'.[232] At RAF North Creake there is a set procedure for take-off involving eight stages, to allow for 'smooth running and avoidance of accidents and confusion'.[233] With some amendment by crews to suit their own purposes, it generally followed a similar pattern: the flight engineer is always last in, stamping his 'foot on the door to ensure it's safely locked'.[234] He reports to the pilot; 'engineer to pilot; rear hatch closed and secured. OK to taxi'.[235] Now is the last opportunity for any final issues can be resolved. 'The word "fuck" [comes] over the intercom. It [is] our pilot's voice. Our W/O [wireless operator] … [asks] what was wrong. "I've left my 'chute behind", [is] the terse reply. "Not to worry", said Andy our W/O, "I'll get one sent out to us". "Forget it" was the reply he got, and on that operation, our pilot [flew], without a parachute!'.[M236]

Aircraft are scheduled to leave their dispersal in a prearranged order or on receipt of instructions from the flying control officer.[237] The pilot signals to the groundcrew to slip chocks 'by flickering at least 3 times on the Downward Indent Light'.[238] The voice of the wireless operator is heard making a test call to the Control Tower[239] as the 'ground crew signal "chocks away" by waving a torch side to side'.[240] With navigation lights switched on,[241] the lumbering machines trundle noisily down the peritrack towards the runway, except on one occasion when pilot, Harold Sturrock, who was 'an excellent pilot and handled our Stirling aircraft as if it was a big toy',[242] was making good pace moving towards the runway when the wing commander's admonishing voice came across the radio from the Control Tower, 'Flight Lieutenant Sturrock, that's a perimeter track you are on, not a fucking racing track. Slow your aircraft down!'.[243]

The aircraft are now in a queue, some are turning sideways into the wind to prevent the air-cooled engines overheating while they are stationary. In turn, the aircraft taxi to the marshalling point where an airman is stationed to guide pilots and prevent collisions.[244] In the bombers 'the bomb-aimer sits alongside the pilot to assist in the take-off, adjusting the throttles and monitoring the instrument readings.

M Denis Gill does not define in his written memoire on what date this event occurred.

The navigator and wireless operator look out of the side windows at the small groups of people huddled to watch the aircraft off.[245] Among them are the groundcrew,[246] the padre,[247] and a small group of WAAFs (who try to never miss a take-off and hopefully a return).[248] At the perimeter fence there is usually 'a group of civvies'[249] including Bernard Beaumont, sitting upon the rubble of his former home watching in readiness for take-off.[250] On occasions the Earl and Countess of Leicester pay a visit to the airfield to watch the evening take off with their daughters.[251] But not tonight.

At the end of the runway the navigator and wireless operator move to the floor with their backs to the main spar and their hands behind their heads to cushion against any jolts. The two gunners sit with their backs to the rear spar.[252] The first aircraft, Stirling LJ516 EX-H, piloted by Ernie Harker, and for one night, co-piloted by F/S Walford, is given the green light by the airfield controller.[253] The co-pilot opens the throttles and for a moment the aircraft strains against its brakes.[254] With final permission given with a steady green Aldis lamp signal,[255] the brakes are released and the aircraft rapidly accelerates along the runway. Engines now screaming in maximum boost (a sound still remembered by some in Wells[256]) with the throttles pushed 'through the gate',[257] the aircraft battles its own weight and the rise on the runway to get airborne. Arthur Adcock remembers, 'everyone in the aircraft would be particularly tense at that time; it was always a hazardous few minutes getting a fully loaded aircraft airborne'.[258] At 00:36[259] the runway controller flashes a white light along the fuselage as the aircraft passes him, lifting into the air, he records the aircraft details[N] and the exact time of take-off. These details are then telephoned through on a fixed line to the Control Tower where the Control Room WAAFs mark them up on their board, as they do with each subsequent aircraft.[260] This information they also forward on to the station operations block, where their watchkeepers keep their operations board up to date minute

---

N Each aircraft in a squadron was allotted a distinguishing letter which was to be used on all occasions to identify the aircraft (Air Council: undated: 76).

by minute.[261] It is then further relayed to RAF 100 Group HQ so they can do the same.[262]

Four more aircraft pass in quick succession, LJ562 EX-V at 00:37, LJ514 EX-B at 00:39, LJ510 EX-A at 00:43 and LJ536 EX-P at 00:44.[263] With the engines on a maximum power climb the aircraft rise slowly into the air, circling round as they gain height.[264] 10,000 feet takes 12 minutes and 20,000 takes 35 minutes;[265] 'all this was in the hours of darkness, generally their [people of Wells] sleeping time. I never knew the population to complain and they were always very hospitable towards us'.[266] Those living around the airfield recall the fading noise of the aircraft, as they slowly climbed further from earshot and disappeared into the night.[267] A short distance away the motor transport section driver sits on shift in the ambulance near the runway, hoping for the best, but on occasions seeing the worst.[268]

At 00:47, LJ578 EX-S is commencing its fifth sortie with its present crew,[269] and with its throttles wide open, it is just lifting off near the intersection with the number two runway.[270] The pilot stalls the aircraft twice as he struggles to get it airborne. The first time, when they were about 15 feet above ground and they return back down with a heavy drop. The second time, when at greater height, on their return to the ground, the undercarriage collapses on contact with the runway,[271] causing, as Geoff Mitchell, the mid-upper gunner explains, the aircraft to 'swing'.[272] Denis Gill, the rear gunner adds more detail:

> our 30-ton aircraft carried on for some distance on its fuselage, tearing off all four engines. One, near the fuselage was embedded into the soil, with a prop blade at 45 degrees to the ground, our aircraft slid sideways into it, and it cut through the fuselage where I was sitting like a tin opener! Luckily the aircraft hit something and I was thrown sideways, just as the prop tip sliced through the place where my head had been resting.[273]

Flames rip through the central section of the aircraft as the 2,300 gallons of high-octane fuel begin to ignite.[274] Neither of the gunners can see forward as their view was obscured by the incandescent light from the flames contrasting with the darkness elsewhere in the aircraft. Consequently, 'those of us in the rear … thought that the front of the aircraft had bought it, and those in front thought we had had it in the back'.[275] It is imperative that they escaped the aircraft before the fuel tanks explode. Denis Gill attempts to get out but recalls 'it was pitch black and my foot slipped and got caught in the structure of the Stirling. I kept trying to pull it out and I thought oh sod that … I pulled my foot out the boot and got out of the aircraft'.[276] Both gunners manage to escape and run from the wreckage:[277]

> I stopped near our aircraft concerned about the crew in the cockpit area. Flames from the fuel were about ten feet high on each side of the fuselage. Then I saw the top escape hatch open, the six other crew members ran down the top of the fuselage between the flames, over the top turret, on to the tail plane, and joined me and the other gunner to watch our aircraft being consumed by flames. The mid-upper turret's twin Browning guns were pointing down and sideways, about 10 degrees to the fuselage, in line with where we were standing. The heat triggered the guns off, and tracer bullets were flying just over our heads![278]

Roy Berrill, who occasionally went to the control room for take-off, to listen to the conversations between the airfield controller and the Control Tower, remembers the Stirling 'crashed and burst into flames … detonating machine guns over the area'.[279] However, the 199 Squadron records no mention of this incident in the Operations Record Book (ORB).[280] The North Creake ORB states unsentimentally, 'aircraft 'S' (F/L Wood) swung on take-off, crashed and burnt out. All the crew got out safely'.[281]

Even if you walk, or more likely, run from a crash, you are required to see the medical officer for an examination; 'the inspection varied considerably in scope and thoroughness, depending on what had happened and how busy the doctor was'.[282] Geoff Mitchell[O] recalls that on that night 'luck was with us and we survived.' [283] As was the practice, they were all sent on immediate seven days crash leave, Geoff would have preferred to get straight back in an aircraft and fly again, but that was not the way.[284] Denis Gill remembers the following day he attempted to acquire replacement boots from the equipment store,[P] but an unsympathetic 'officer in charge, sitting behind a desk, clearly did not believe that I had tried hard enough to salvage my flying boots, and implied that I had panicked'.[285] The pilot who was unable to control the Stirling was returned to Training Command and restricted to two-engine aircraft; he survived the war.[286] Roy Berrill remembers that they cleared the runway quickly, but he is not sure how long wreckage remained on the airfield site.[287] Even with aircraft flying over enemy territory with a foe trying very hard to kill them, the moment of take-off and landing were still disproportionately dangerous in comparison to any other moment of flight.

At 00:49, a mere two minutes after LJ578 EX-S failed to take off, LJ518 takes to the air; there was no possibility of delaying the operation. A further four aircraft subsequently take off, the last being LJ542 EX-G, the replacement for LJ578 EX-S,[288] after which the runway lights are extinguished.[289] Now an eerie silence falls over the aerodrome. The WAAF watchkeepers, in the RAF North Creake operations block, staff the telephones and keep a log of all conversations.[290] The WAAF signal section wireless operators listen-out for aircrew transmissions and also log them.[291] In the Control Tower, FCOs and RT operators sit in front of the large uncurtained windows.[292] They drink tea or cocoa and talk (reading is difficult in this subdued light),[293] while they wait, eager for news of the progress of the operation.

Sometimes, aircraft leaving the airfield circuit took an initial unauthorised diversion before adopting the officially recognised route. Nan and Dickie Thomas had got married since meeting in the RAF, consequently they had an arrangement that Dickie would phone Nan

---

O   Geoff Mitchell's cap and tunic hang on display in the Control Tower, kindly donated by his children.

P   Where theoretically, anything from 'a corkscrew to a coffin' can be provided (Hawton: 1944: 143).

at a certain time at a phone box outside the Crown Hotel in Skegness (where Nan was billeted):

> on one particular evening … I was expecting a call as he had been on 'ops' the previous night, so I was waiting outside the box when a bloody great Halifax came down the road flashing its lights and waggling its wings! I got the message that he would not be ringing me at that time! I presumed he had been out on an exercise, so I rang the Officers Mess a few hours later, only to be told he was not available. That meant only one thing – he was on 'ops' again! I learnt later that he had not dared to waggle his wings any more as he had a load of bombs on board!![294]

Subsequently, Nan moved to a billet some three miles from RAF North Creake, 'our digs were right in line with the main runway, so when Dickie took off, whether on an air test or on "ops", he could hold the nose down a little longer and come right over the house. I used to stand in the garden and wave goodbye with a tea towel'.

In the RAF North Creake airfield controller's caravan, the motor transport section staff, stationed nearby (in case of flarepath lamp failure), have 'a good "fry-up" towards midnight',[295] helping them to stay warm while they wait for the aircraft to return. The duty nurse stationed in the sick quarters, is with an ambulance driver and a male orderly. In charge of all the wards she sits alert, waiting for the telephone that is linked to flying control to ring. She would be the first to receive the message; 'prepare for landing – to commence in [such and such] minutes'. [296] Meaning that an aircraft is in trouble and is returning early. The ambulance driver and orderly would be despatched to the end of the runway and she would quickly move to the crash theatre and prepare for incoming patients.[297] She hopes the call won't come.

In the WAAF sites, some of the personnel are awake, waiting for an agreed signal from their lover indicating a safe return, such as, with Jean's fiancé, Bert Berry, making a low pass over the Naafi Site.[298]

Yvonne Renaut remembers, 'I'd wait for the planes to go out and I'd stupidly lay awake trying to count them in, as a lot of wives did … very silly thing to do'.[299] Her husband, Michael Renaut, attempted to dissuade her from such a practice, 'it was such an unreliable method of assessing losses that I persuaded her to give up the idea and sleep. This silly business of counting the bombers on the returning circuit was entirely unreliable … some planes circuited three or four times before landing'.[300]

RAF North Creake Motor Transport Section May 1945 (John Reid Collection).

Two aircraft disappearing from view: Norman Turnbull; his original caption reads 'who will return?' (Control Tower Archive).

In the Control Tower, alongside the FCOs and flying control WAAFs, the station commander, squadron commander, medical officer and flight commanders also wait.[301] Roy Berrill, the meteorologist similarly waits, but downstairs in the meteorological office.[302] On occasions, an aircraft would need to return early with technical trouble and ask for permission to land, having frequently had to first 'stooge to waste petrol'[303] before making their return. Tonight two aircraft are forced to return early, aircraft EX-K and EX-V. EX-V, 'owing to port outer engines becoming unserviceable due to coring'.[Q304] But otherwise the Control Tower just keeps a listening watch.[305]

As the estimated time of return approaches, some 'go out onto the balcony to listen for the first sounds of the returning aircraft.'[306] With the aircraft approaching, suddenly the silence in the Control Tower is broken by the voice of a pilot R L Todd, captain of the first aircraft (Stirling LJ562 EX-V) requesting landing instructions on the radio telephone and played through the loudspeaker. Almost immediately, the air is full of voices asking for their turn to land or height at which to circle. They are stacked 'at 500 feet intervals and circle the airfield at their allotted heights'.[307] Instructions are given via RT as the emphasis is now on the speed of landing rather than security. To keep abreast the FCO has a 'board with lines of hooks upon which to hang discs painted with the aircraft identification letters. The horizontal lines on the board represent 500 feet in height'.[308] As aircraft land, the other bombers are instructed to drop 500 feet 'until the last has landed'.[309] Priority is given to aircraft that are short of petrol, badly damaged or have wounded on board.[310] If a pilot indicates by RT that he must land immediately, the FCO informs the airfield controller and instructs any aircraft which have already received permission to land to await further instruction.[311]

There will be a surge of activity logging each aircraft on the operations board as it lands; 'one R/T operator did the talking and one the logging – it would have been impossible to talk and write at the same time. Sometimes with 20 or more aircraft circling overhead ... we

---

Q 'Failure on both engines ... the cause of this failure was given as "coring" – something to do with fuel restriction and cooling problems, apparently this could happen with the Hercules engines' (Shelley: 14/5/2009).

were working at a furious pace'.[312] If a North Creake bomber lands at another airfield,[R] the Control Tower will receive the details from Group HQ immediately.[313] The board would be updated accordingly and the information passed on. If the time passes when the fuel on a late return is exhausted, then, and only then, as dawn begins to light the sky, is the word 'missing' written against that aircraft's letter on the operations board.[314] Thankfully not tonight.

RAF North Creake Halifax G – George, just before touch-down after a raid: Norman Turnbull (Control Tower Archive).

The last aircraft in, Stirling LJ510 EX-A, touches down at 06:23 (it took-off at 00:43). Aircraft, having landed, taxi to the end of the runway before turning off to their dispersals.[315] At their dispersals, engines would be silenced, a 'silence broken only by the whirr of gyroscopes slowly running down'.[316] Once out of their aircraft there was a sense of joy:

> I have never experienced a sensation of relief quite so intoxicatingly satisfying as what I felt as I climbed out the

---

R   All operational stations were required to keep twenty to thirty free beds for such diversions (Sawyer: 1981: 134).

rear door and stepped onto the lovely, wonderful, marvellous, fabulous, solid old concrete of that good old dispersal.[317]

On the crew bus taking them back from dispersals some felt it was 'worth doing an operational trip just for the joy of showing off quietly to the W.A.A.F. driver'.[318] But for most they sat silently in their emotional and physical exhaustion. However, before retiring there was the debrief; 'only a quarter of an hour at the most',[319] but it had to be done:

> no matter how tired the crew, the attendance at debrief was mandatory. Beyond helping in the assessment of the raid's general effectiveness, a well-conducted debrief revealed many specific details while the crews' experiences were still fresh in their minds. The information sought ranged from new developments in German defences and tactics to the accuracy of the weather forecast.[320]

In the interrogation room, all those that had taken part in the briefing, the squadron commander, navigation officer, signals officer, meteorological officer, gunnery officer, etc. wait for reports of the operation. Also in attendance is the padre, not for any religious reasons, but in the role of unofficial counsellor.[321] Gradually, the aircrews drift in:

> there was scant similarity between the figures around me and the Brylcream-ad airmen on the recruiting posters ... seven hours of sweating concentration in a snug flying helmet had left everyone's hair plastered to his head like wet fur. Bleary eyes, and faces etched with the imprint of oxygen masks and the weariness spawned of acute tension and lack of sleep, complemented the sagging posture and occasional sighing exhalation of cigarette smoke to present a picture of men wrung out like dish rags – men who had had enough adventure to do them for a bit.[322]

On entry they help themselves to a cup of tea or coffee laced with rum,[323] 'which tasted terrible but worked therapeutic miracles',[324] particularly as a 'potent allayer of nerves especially after a dodgy experience in the air'.[325] Almost all drank it, even the staff that hadn't been flying,[326] and if there was some left over, the ambulance and fire tender crews had it.[327]

The subsequent report on the operation of the 9/10 September 1944 on Monchengladbach, described it as, a 'devastating raid on the centre of this target without loss'.[328] The intelligence that informed this conclusion was derived from, among other sources, debriefings, led by intelligence staff,[329] including Robert Darracott.[330] These debriefings involve questions on dinghy sightings, distress signals, enemy shipping etc. These come first so that any details can be passed on for 'onward transmission and action'[331] and will inform searches for any missing crews. Ultimately, if they remained missing, the information was invaluable for the work of the Missing Research Section towards the end of the war and beyond.[332] The crews are then questioned about details of the target: its identification, the weather in the target area (detailed on Form RAF 2330, Weather Observations by Aircraft Crew[333]). The crew also report on bombing details (time, height, magnetic heading) with the bomb aimer's description of results. Also, details of enemy defences, damage to their aircraft, etc. are detailed. Finally, the pilot gives his personal report. Archie Hall, a WAAF in Intelligence at RAF Mildenhall, recalls that she always 'had the greatest admiration for their patience in sitting and answering when all they wanted was their fried eggs and their beds'.[334]

All the debriefing reports are gathered in, analysed and sent to Group HQ; 'they contain the impressions of tired men – men who have flown for hours over enemy territory or over the sea, men whose bodies have been subjected to the strain of high altitudes and perhaps abrupt descents, men who have often had even more gruelling experiences'.[335] At Group HQs these reports are very carefully studied[336] and forwarded to Bomber Command where the intelligence branch sort out the corn from the chaff and an accurate picture of the night emerges. 'From this it was possible to correct our estimations of their flak batteries, determine how many night-fighters had been bagged, corroborate and confirm "unusual events". If several crews reported the same "hallucination" at the same time and in the same place, some credence usually attached to their reports.'[337]

Not all recollections of the debrief are negative; Tom Sawyer recalls the 'warmth and comradeship of the debriefing session ... the good-humoured banter and line-shooting as we all settled down together'.

After the debriefing the aircrews tuck into their eggs and bacon; a post-operation reward insisted upon by the commander-in-chief and kept for the whole war, even though both ingredients were becoming scarce.[338] 'It could have been anything from midnight to 8 o'clock in the morning but the meal was there'.[339] The crews then retire to bed physically exhausted and emotionally spent. Denis Gill recalls in the particularly bitter winter of 1944/45 when:

> hard frost covered the ground and snowflakes began to fall. We entered our billet quietly to not disturb the other sleeping aircrew. The last glowing embers in the billet stove were losing out to the cold air. I warmed my hands around the still warm stove pipe. Threw my great coat over my bed, pulled off my flying boots that we all kept on, and like the others, got into bed fully clothed.[340]

Experiencing similar temperatures, Dennis Smallwood, special operator with 171 Squadron, recalls 'it was not unusual to wear one's flying kit and RAF greatcoat over pyjamas. Seaboot stockings were also a great asset to comfort. I remember Geoff Homer ... our skipper, bringing in an electric fire which he would place between his knees under the blankets. You should have seen the rising steam! He used to say, "when the steam turns to smoke wake me in a hurry!"' [341]

Murray Pedan, flying out of another RAF 100 Group station, RAF Oulton, recalls a Canadian gunner's nightmares that involved him being back in his aircraft and under fire. He would frequently wake up in terror, often waking the rest of the crew up in the process: 'so frequently did he experience these nightmares that every night, as he punched his pillow and settled himself for sleep, he would sigh jokingly to the rest of us: "well, chocks away."'[342] For many, as Stephen Wainwright, a rear gunner with Bomber Command relates, sleep would not come, 'unless they'd wept'.[343] For others, it was all part of the aircrew routine; 'the homecomings, the landings, debriefings, the long-delayed meals, the longer-delayed sleep'.[344] While this chapter reflects one night's effort, the whole process was repeated night, after night, after night. There was never enough sleep.[345]

* * *

Our lives don't compare in any way to what RAF personnel went through on this station in the war. If we could relate to any element of the veteran's wartime experience, it would be the exhaustion. We hadn't expected it. Running a B&B, if the life suits you, is a wonderful occupation. However, when you start out, you don't know what to expect or how to plan for what you don't know. Consequently, and necessarily, we took all bookings that came to us. This resulted in us having, in our first real summer, an eight-week period without any days off. This may not sound too arduous, but guests are in your house and may want something at any point of the day. Therefore, you are never really off duty and the sleep you do get is never as restful as the sleep when you are in your house alone.

We did all our own laundry, housekeeping, building maintenance, garden maintenance and continued to work on unfinished elements of the build. It was naive and it was unsustainable; there are not enough hours in the day. We learnt, we needed to build in 'leave' or, at least, some stand-down from duty. There was never enough sleep.

MID-AIR COLLISION

The crew of Halifax LK874 6Y-C had good reason to be growing in confidence; they were well into their tour, the Allies had air superiority and the Nazis were in wholesale retreat. They had every chance of seeing their tour through to the end. Peter Jennings had a particularly good reason to feel optimistic, his fiancée was coming over to the UK and they were getting married.[1] David and Ann Maufe, who farmed close to the airfield at Branthill Farm, had become very close to Peter and were to host his wedding reception and had booked a room for them at the Black Lion Hotel in Walsingham for their wedding night.[2]

Everything to live for.

Norman Ashton, a flight engineer, flying with 156 Squadron, recalls:

> I was asked by Group to take some colour film of the proceedings. On the way to target I missed a scoop when I couldn't grab the cine-camera fast enough to get a few shots of a collision between two Lancs, which caught fire and plunged to earth in flames.[3]

A still from the film shows the immediate aftermath of the collision between Lancaster PB403 (156 Squadron) and Halifax LK874 6Y-C on 17 April 1945 (Norman Ashton mistook the 171 Squadron Halifax for a Lancaster). All 15 aircrew were killed. On board the Halifax were:

The immediate aftermath of the collision between Halifax LK874 6Y-C and Lancaster PB403 from Norman Ashton's footage (unattributed).

Robert Allen Brown (RCAF) Bomb Aimer, aged 22
Eric George Draper (RAF) Special Operator, aged 20
Frank Dyson (RAF) Rear Gunner, aged 31
Peter Sinclair Jennings (RNZAF) Pilot, aged 23
Clifford Thomas Jones (RAF) Navigator, aged 30
George Vaugham Knowler (RAF) Flight Engineer, aged 23
Royston Sperling (RAF) Air Gunner, aged 19
Albert Storey (RAF) Wireless Operator, aged 19

On Lancaster PB403 were:

Frederick John Cuthill (RAF) Flight Engineer
Herbert William Elliott (RCAF) Air Gunner, aged 22
John Jamieson (RAF) Pilot

Francis William O'Reilly (RAF) Navigator, aged 22
Frederick Lewis Ponting (RAF) Bomb Aimer, aged 34
Douglas Ellwood Smith (RAF) Wireless Operator, aged 20
Eric Wilson (RAF) Air Gunner, aged 21

The operation for the 16/17 April 1945 involved attacks on railway yards in both Pilsen and Schwandorf (subsequently reported as accurate with severe damage).[4] The RAF North Creake ORB records that:

> twenty three Halifax were detailed – eleven of 199 Squadron with four of 171 for a Mandrel/Window/bombing patrol to Prague; and eight of 171 Squadron to support main force in attack on Schwandorf. All took off ... 171/'C' is missing.[5]

The 171 Squadron ORB states 'one failed to return – nothing having been heard since take off'. It would be some time before the news of the collision would reach RAF North Creake.

Some aircrew feared collisions 'more than enemy action'.[6] And with good reason:

> one of the great sights was to see the hundreds of bombers silhouetted in the sky, mainly on our outward leg, with the sunset behind us. The beauty dwindled and soon it was dark and a case of survival, due to the darkness.[7]

Denis Gill, an air gunner with 199 Squadron, suggests with hundreds of aircraft converging on defined 'turning points',[8] in darkness, without navigation lights, some aircraft will be in the wrong position; 'some will turn ... too early, and some will turn a bit late'.[9] With bombers above, below and beside you, collisions became inevitable.[10] You could not always see them, but you were constantly aware of their presence, 'once in a while our plane would buffet a bit from the slipstream of a bomber ahead of us, or perhaps one could see the exhausts of others'.[11] Denis Gill describes one particularly harrowing experience:

> I turned the rear gun turret to starboard, and saw the large shape of a Halifax bomber heading straight for the side of our own aircraft out of the darkness! It seemed to be exactly on our own level, but ... we seemed to be hit from above by a giant sledge hammer that actually pushed our aircraft down so hard, that my immediate thought, was that the wings must break ... how the Halifax missed us, seemed like an act of providence, and the tips of its propellers must have missed the top of our Stirling fuselage, not by feet, but by inches![12]

Gordon Mercier, also serving with 171 Squadron at North Creake, remembers:

> you had to keep your eyes open ... that was the most important job ... all of a sudden you'd realise there was a bomber sitting just on top of you and you'd got to get out of that without hitting him. And we had that several times.[13]

Keith Rankin, aircrew with 199 Squadron at Lakenheath, recalls a trip where a Lancaster was heading straight for their Stirling; '[the bomb aimer] instructed our pilot to dive and before I could say anything there was a blinding flash about a hundred feet behind us as two Lancasters ran into each other'.[14] He reflects, 'I often wonder why there were not more mid-air collisions with so many bombers in a confined area'.[15] Nonetheless, it was quite unusual to witness such collisions; aircrew generally only observed the consequential explosion, and explosions could have multiple causes. Moreover, to capture a collision on film, even if it is only its direct aftermath, is incredibly rare. Normally, the fate of an aircraft would be unknown, 'possibly due to collision'.

Such is the speculation regarding Halifax NA687 6Y-A on the night 6 January 1945.

Bomber Command had detailed 482 aircraft to fly operations, targeting the railway networks of Hanau and Neus. Considerable damage was caused to the railways but bombs also hit the surrounding areas causing thousands of buildings to be destroyed with the loss of some 129 lives. The raids were supported by RCM sorties by the RAF 100 Group including a spoof raid to Kassel involving the Special Window Force.[16] Halifax NA687 6Y-A was involved in a bomber support operation when it crashed.[17] The RAF North Creake ORB records:

> ten Stirlings of No. 199 Squadron ... and four Halifax of No. 171 Squadron were detailed to provide a Mandrel Screen and three Halifax ... to discharge Window ... All took off ... two Halifax of No. 171 Squadron ... discharged Window between 18:35 hours and 19:16 hours ... 171/'A' is missing, nothing being heard of him after take off.

A footnote at the bottom of the entry adds further details; '171/'A' Halifax NA687 crashed at Ambly (Namur) approx 8km ESE of Rochfort France. All crew lost'. Those on board were:

Alfred Charles Cheese (RAF) Bomb Aimer, aged 23
Geoffrey Cox (RAF) Pilot, aged 23
Frederick Edwin Thomas Davy (RAF) Special Operator, aged 20
Stanley Reeves Fenwick (RAF) Flight Engineer, aged 20
Charles David Craven Farlie (RAF) Air Gunner, aged 23
Ronald Maden (RAF) Navigator, aged 23
Albert Edward Meekings (RAF) Wireless Operator, aged 20
Charles Donald Mison (RCAF) Mid-Upper Gunner, aged 22

Bomber Command Operational Research Section[A] assessed the loss of NA687 and concluded 'probably collision with MZ469'.[18] Halifax MZ469 Z5-N was also an RAF 100 Group aircraft with eight aircrew

---

A Bomber Command Operational Research Section was responsible for much quantitative research with Bomber Command. Based at BCHQ it had, by early 1942, been arranged into three sections: 'Research into success of Night Operations; Research into losses in Night Operations; Research into Day Operations.' Later it became responsible for the production of the extremely important *Bomber Command Quarterly Review* and the *Bomber Command Raid Reports*. Radar and radar countermeasures were also added to its research remit (Wakeman: 2020: 10-11).

on board. It flew with RAF 462 Squadron from Foulsham and was part of the Special Window Force on 6 January 1945.[19] Piloted by Mervin Walter Rohrlach (RAAF), aged 26, also on board were:

> Eric Gordon Baker (RAF) Air Gunner, aged 19
> Joseph David Beardsmore (RAF) Flight Engineer, aged 21
> Douglas Henry Lawrence (RAAF) Wireless Operator
> Leslie Gordon Marshal Mannell (RAAF) Special Operator, aged 31
> John Scaife Sanderson (RAF) Navigator, aged 22
> Norman Stanley Scott (RAF) Bomb Aimer, aged 21
> Vivian Claude Topham (RAF) Air Gunner, aged 19

Both bombers crashed near Hargimont, Belgium. 171 Squadron Halifax NA687 6Y-A, came down between Hargimont and Ambly at 'La Mouchonnière' and Halifax MZ469 crashed at 'A l'épine' at the boundary of Hargimont and Harsin.[20] Two bombers crashing at the same time, at almost the same place seems 'rather exceptional',[21] however, no other crews reported witnessing a collision.[22] German fighter flares were reported by other 100 Group crews in the Hargimont/Ambly area at 18:35 and 18:40 hours[23] (Halifax MZ469 crashed at 17:30 hours[24]). Luftwaffe night-fighters made claims for four Halifaxes[25] that night, but precise details are unknown,[26] therefore the possibility of both aircraft being lost to enemy action remains.[27] Nonetheless, a collision seems the most compelling explanation, particularly as no flak was reported in the area by returning 462 Squadron crews and there were no Luftwaffe fighter claims that 'correlate with the almost simultaneous loss of two aircraft at that time and place'.[28]

There are also first-hand accounts. One crew member of 462 Squadron Halifax MZ469 survived the crash. Douglas Lawrence, the wireless operator, writing postwar, records that there were no fighters, no anti-aircraft fire and no searchlight activity in the area before the crash.[29] He remembers that it was a 'routine flight until, over Belgium, our bomber received an enormous impact, causing extensive damage and loss of control of the aircraft'.[30] In the formal debrief statement following repatriation in July 1945,[31] he states 'I was dropping 'Window. The next thing I knew there was a large hole opposite W/OPs. position and the aircraft was out of control'.[32] On impact, Douglas Lawrence had passed out.[33] When he regained consciousness, he remembers looking around and seeing 'a great hole in the nose … in the place where the navigator and bomb aimer worked. They had disappeared'. There was another hole in the side of the aircraft opposite the wireless operator's position, and just forward of the starboard engines:[34]

> I reached out and clipped on my parachute which was lying on the floor next to the big hole by the starboard engine. What happened next is a bit of a blur, because one moment I was standing by this big hole in front of the engine, and the next I was floating down to earth. I have no recollection of actually jumping or of pulling the rip-cord, but I do remember looking up and seeing … this beautiful, large white canopy against the black sky. What a sight.[35]

Douglas Lawrence believes he was blown out when the aircraft exploded[36] and that he saw his bomber crashing below him:[37]

> falling was a delightful feeling … a sense of being suspended above the moonlit earth, and it really looked beautiful, until I saw the explosion below me, as our aircraft hit the ground.[38]

According to eyewitnesses, the aircraft did not explode mid-air but remained reasonably intact with the pilot struggling to circle and lose height before attempting an emergency landing, suggesting he was able to maintain some level of control.[39] One engine had 'become detached'[40] and it would seem at least one other engine was not working[41] and the aircraft crashed 'in a hedge between two corn fields'[42] in deep snow.[43] Gérard Marlaire, who saw the wreckage shortly after, wrote that the aircraft was mainly intact and only the cockpit and one wing were burnt out.[44] Therefore, it could not have been Douglas Lawrence's aircraft, as he had reasonably assumed, that he saw burning as he descended in his parachute. It seems likely that it was in fact, Halifax, NA687 6Y-A, from RAF North Creake that had suffered 'catastrophic damage'[45] from the impact with Douglas Lawrence's Halifax, causing an uncontrollable descent, explosion and fire on contact with the ground.

Douglas had no idea what to expect once his feet touched the ground. 'My landing was in a large open area, covered in snow and with a few large rocky outcrops.'[46] On landing, he could see what he thought was his Halifax, 'a burning, crackling wreck about half a mile away',[47] He buried his parachute in the deep snow,[48] and with small cuts on his forehead and ear and feeling 'shaky and dazed'[49] he realised that there was:

> heavy gunfire in three directions, north, west and south, and I thought this was all about five to ten miles away at the most, so I determined that I had landed behind enemy lines ... I headed east. Not far across the field was a roadway, and on reaching the edge I heard a vehicle approaching. I hid behind a small bush. The car was carrying three upright German officers, driven by their chauffeur. It passed within ten feet of me. Soon all was quiet again, so I decided to follow along the side of the road for a little. I rounded a corner and walked smack into a German soldier who was guarding a command post, and was immediately apprehended ... so ended freedom.[50]

He reflects that in the first few days after his capture, he was 'living in a state of shock and confusion, with having been knocked unconscious',[51] the parachute fall, followed by the 'mental impact of being classified as a prisoner of war, and then the realization that your friends are all dead ... The mind can, after a while, become a bit out of tune with what is happening'.[B52] Back at his station, RAF Foulsham, on 7 January 1945,

---

B   Douglas Lawrence was held in a number of camps before he was liberated by the US Army on 29 April 1945. He writes of his experience subsequent to being captured, 'after marching about 60 miles through snow, with insufficient food and water, 3 American Airmen, myself and about 200 American and British personnel (army) were brought to Euskirchen to a disused schoolroom ... I was then brought into this room, which was lit by 2 candles, and questioned by the one German and on refusing to answer his questions I was knocked around by two more, who were standing one on each side of me. I was kicked and

his Senior Squadron Radio Officer, Max Barkla, wrote in his diary, 'lost Rohrlach's crew last night. W/Op was Curly Lawrence, a nice lad of boyish appearance ... only kids – or perhaps I'm getting old'.[53]

On the crash site of 462 Squadron Halifax MZ469, the Germans would not let Gerard Marlaire (a 23-year-old local resident and later a priest[54]) secure the aircraft. However, the liberating Allied forces were pushing forward and on 14 January 1945, the US 7 Parachute Battalion discovered the crashed Halifax along with four bodies of airmen. The following day the battalion padre buried them next to the wreckage of the bomber.[55] On 5 February 1945, Gerard Marlaire informed 16 Air Formation Signals of a charred corpse still in the aircraft. It was subsequently removed and buried next to the four bodies discovered earlier.[56] Gerard Marlaire also informed the authorities that two further bodies had been found when the snow retreated, approximately half a mile from the crash site.[57] He stated, in spite of three appeals, he had been forbidden by the Americans to 'touch or remove the bodies for fear they might have been booby-trapped by the retreating Germans'.[58] It was decided that since 'the bodies were being ravaged by birds',[59] they should now remove them for burial.[60] They were recovered by personnel from the 16 Air Force Signals and buried at the British Military Cemetery at Hotton on 7 February 1945.[61] They were later identified as John Sanderson and Norman Scott; both were stationed in the front of the aircraft and were, in all probability, knocked out by the impact 'perhaps unconscious, and thus not able to deploy their parachutes'.[62] The body of Leslie Mannell was buried by the local population at the same cemetery.[63] The five corpses buried beside the crashed aircraft were exhumed on the instruction of the investigating officer of the 151 Repair Unit and reinterred on the 21 February 1945, at Hotton Military cemetery alongside their crewmates.[64] The report by D H Everitt, submitted on 24 February 1945, concludes that 'there is no news about the eight[h] member of the crew',[65] still presumed to be

---

knocked unconscious twice. As I still refused to answer the questions asked they threatened to shoot me, and kicked me towards the door. I was led down the street to an old barn where the other 200 men were sleeping and there allowed to sleep' (462squadron.com).

missing. It would be more than two months before Douglas Lawrence's parents received a telegram stating; 'pleased to inform you that your son Flight Sergeant Douglas Henry Lawrence has been liberated by the Allied Armies and is now safe in the United Kingdom'.[66] The debris of 462 Squadron Halifax MZ469 remained for some time on the fields of Hargimont, with children seen playing in the damaged cockpit.[67] Even when John Sanderson's brother visited more than two years later some wreckage remained, 'and much anti-radar silver-paper strips'.[68]

At the crash site of 171 Squadron Halifax NA687, they were struggling to account for all the aircrew. An American Graves Registration Unit had removed five bodies, which were then buried at Ambly Communal Cemetery,[69] Namur, approximately 14km from Marche, and only 5.6km from Hargimont. With the snow retreating, a further two bodies were found by civilians of the village of Ambly and buried at the Communal Cemetery on 28 January 1945.[70] These bodies were exhumed by the 151 Repair Unit investigating the crash, but they were only able to determine that one had been an air gunner. An identity card belonging to Alfred Cheese, was given to this investigation unit by a resident who also informed them that his body had been taken by the Graves Registration Unit and buried at the US Military cemetery at Henri Chappelle.[71] The families of the missing airmen were kept informed:

> as the crew comprised of eight members, seven of whom only were accounted for ... it was impossible to determine the identity of the five un-named until the finding of the eighth member. In these unhappy circumstances a special enquiry was made of the Royal Air Force Missing Research and Enquiry Service to pursue investigations in the area of the crash.[72]

On 3 July 1945, the families were informed that the eighth member had been found by a French civilian and had subsequently been identified as Frederick Davy.[73] As a result 'the necessary steps for the formal presumption ... [of] death will be taken shortly'.[74]

An official request to move the three bodies at Ambly Communal Cemetery and reinter them at the US Military Cemetery at Henri Chappelle alongside their crewmates was submitted. Unfortunately, this cemetery had been closed. Therefore a request was submitted to the US Graves Authorities that sought permission to dis-inter the five crew members buried there and rebury them at Ambly Communal Cemetery. This request was granted, and on 13 April 1946, the five graves were exhumed:[75]

> in grave No. 107 (marked unknown) was found pieces of R.A.F. officer's shirt and pieces of under-pants bearing [a] laundry mark ... only small pieces of the body were left and these were unrecognisable as they were badly charred. Grave No. 110 (marked unknown) contained pieces of O.R. [other ranks] R.A.F. shirt and a name inside neck Faulat Bellfas?
>
> We then took these five bodies to Ambly Communal Cemetery for reburial.
>
> We exhumed the unknown there and found an R.A.F. Battle Dress with F/O [Flight Officer] braid and the name R. Maden on an R.A.F. Officer's shirt collar. This left two of the crew unidentified but as one was an officer and the other was an N.C.O., it was decided to assume the one with the pieces of R.A.F. Officer's shirt as F/LT Cox and the other with the R.A.F. other ranks shirt as SGT. Fenwick.[76]

Thus the 'missing' case was closed and the names submitted for headstones.

Of the eight killed on Halifax NA687 on 7 January 1945, little is recorded of five of them. Geoffrey Cox, pilot, was the son of William and Emily Cox of Oxhey near Watford, Hertfordshire; Frederick Edwin Thomas Davy, special operator, son of Frederick and Ellen Davy of East Ham, Newham, London; Charles David Craven Farlie, air gunner, son of Charles and Phillis Farlie of Farnborough, Hampshire; Stanley Reeves Fenwick, flight engineer, son of Harold and Ethel Fenwick of Giffnock, Renfrewshire, Scotland and Albert Edward Meekings, wireless operator, son of Albert and Rosalea Meekings from Leicester.

Alfred Cheese, bomb aimer, was married to Georgette Cheese, of Marylebone, London, who visited his grave in Belgium in 1948.[77] He was born and educated in Bethnal Green and his family moved to Wealdstone, Harrow in around 1936, when his father took up employment with Kodak. Alfred Cheese worked in the printing trade at the HMSO in Wealdstone where he met Georgette, who was working there as a secretary. They were married on 30 January 1943. Alfred's RAF operational career started in August 1943, when he joined 199 Squadron at Lakenheath, before transferring to RAF North Creake as a member of 199 Squadron 'C' Flight, which became the nucleus of the reformed 171 Squadron in September 1944.[78]

Ronald Maden, navigator from Accrington, Lancashire, joined up in February 1942. He was with 199 Squadron at Lakenheath before moving to RAF North Creake and was transferred to 171 Squadron in September 1944. The son of Jacob and Annie Maden, he was one of four sons. Tragically, Jacob was no stranger to the worst of war, having been shot and injured on the first day of the battle of the Somme. He had also lost another son, John (Jack), in 1943, to air operations with Bomber Command.[79] His eldest son, Harry, survived the war, serving with the army, and Clifford, his youngest, was, thankfully, too young to fight.[80]

Charles Mison, mid-upper gunner, from Ottawa, Ontario, served with the Royal Canadian Air Force. At the time of his enlistment he worked as an aircraft fitter at Ottawa Car & Aircraft Ltd.[81] He was the only son of Charles and Laura Mison. Living at home, he identified 'model aircraft' as a hobby and smoked moderately and drank socially.[82] The selection process treated him brutally, suggesting that he possessed a 'questionable amount of determination and courage'[83] and 'does not impress … gives impression of being forced to join-up'.[84] Once training began in Canada, the air gunner reports, state that he 'requires more than ordinary instruction but worked hard. Appears uncertain of himself at times and tries to bluff'.[85] By the time his training in Canada concluded, his reports hadn't improved; 'on several charges and a bad example for his course. Copes in the air although slack. Very slovenly and dull looking and doesn't know what discipline means'.[86] However, things changed when he arrived in Britain, 'this student has good knowledge of guns and turrets. Keen, he was a little on the slow side at first but has improved a great deal while on the course'.[87] By the time his death had been confirmed and headstones were being erected, the Canadian authorities couldn't praise him enough:

> it is a privilege to have the opportunity of sending you the Operational Wings and Certificate … I realise there is little which may be said or done to lessen your sorrow, but it is my hope that these 'Wings' indicative of operations against the enemy, will be a treasured memento of a young life offered on the altar of freedom in defence of his Home and Country.[88]

The Medical Record Card for Charles Mison records that his 'plane crashed over enemy territory', that he died of 'multiple injuries' and was 'identified by personal belongings'.[89] For Charles Mison, along with his crewmates, despite subsequent evidence that makes the collision thesis seem reasonably compelling, officially, the cause of the accident on 6 January 1945, 'was never established'.[90] However, with the loss on 16/17 April 1945, with film footage of the actual collision and witness testimonies regarding where and when the accident happened, the last moments of Halifax LK874 6Y-C are in no doubt.

When questioned by a MRES investigation team visiting Murlenbach in January 1947, following reports that 15 airmen were buried there,[91] the local Burgomaster [mayor], Heinrich Thewes, reported that two four engine bombers had collided in mid-air over the village.[92] Other witnesses also gave critical information regarding the collision. Otto Lehfeld, a forester who lived near the crash site, was quite certain that the aircraft had crashed at 02:00 on 17 April 1945.[93] He showed the investigators to the scene of each crash. Both aircraft were unidentifiable, the first was about three kilometres south-west of

Murlenbach in the middle of a wood,[94] there were several unexploded bombs around the wreckage and[95] 'the aircraft had plunged into a hill and exploded. Enough remained to identify it as British but that was all'.[96] The second aircraft had crashed at about three kilometres west of Murlenbach, the bodies had disintegrated and there was no possibility of survival,[97] 'as [the aircraft] had exploded over a swamp, pieces being scattered in all directions'.[98]

At the crash site on the hill, Otto Lehfeld had found a ring (inscribed with initials), a watch and a book,[99] which were identified as belonging to Robert Brown (of 171 Squadron Halifax). As a result the families were informed that all crew members were being reclassified 'missing believed killed',[100] although, 'due to the severe nature of the crash, it was not possible to establish the identity of any of the other members of either crew involved'.[101] Nonetheless, in view of the fact that no other aircraft crashed in the area at that time (other than Lancaster PB403 and Halifax LK874), 'there can be little doubt … that the remains of the two crews are buried at Murlenbach'.[102] Theodor Meyer had carried the bodies to the grave, he stated 'that the remains were very small and were buried in five small boxes'[103] at the side of the road by German civilians, under the direction of American soldiers.[104] The MRES, on the basis of the information discovered, requested that the case be closed.[105] Subsequently, both crews were reinterred in Rheinberg British Military Cemetery.[106]

Ann and David Maufe ran Branthill Farm, a mile north of RAF North Creake, where the pilot of Halifax LK874, Peter Jennings, was a regular visitor. David had volunteered to entertain aircrew with leave passes who were at a loose end. A number of aircrew used to visit, 'sometimes, just for a beer and a bit to eat, sometimes for the night'.[107] They had 'huge warmth'[108] for Peter and had been looking forward to his upcoming wedding.[109] Instead they were comforting his fiancée, who had arrived from North America expecting wedding celebrations, only to be informed of the tragic news.[110] After Peter's death, Ann and David adopted his Old English Sheepdog, Bungle,[111] as Peter's fiancée could not take him back home on the ship. Ann and David found Bungle a great comfort and he lived with them until well into the 1950s.[112] Peter had obviously made an arrangement with someone, that if he went missing, Bungle should be taken to Branthill Farm, 'as airmen from North Creake brought him down soon after he went missing'.[113]

Ann and David had planned to ask Peter to be godfather to their next child (Gina, born 23 April 1945) but, as they were aware of superstitions surrounding the adoption of such commitments by aircrew, they didn't want to ask before the end of hostilities.[114] Ann and David were absolutely devastated by Peter Jenning's death.[115]

Peter Sinclair Jennings was born in Hong Kong in 1921 but returned to New Zealand at an early age. After school he was employed at the Department of Industry and Commerce. He enlisted in November 1942 and after initial training he was sent to Canada under the Empire Air Training Scheme. After he was awarded his flying badge, he was posted to No. 2 Instructor's School, Vulcan, Alberta as a staff pilot. He arrived in the UK in November 1943, and after converting to Halifaxes at 1658 HCU Riccall Yorkshire, he was posted to 171 Squadron North Creake on 3 December 1944.[116]

Clifford Jones, navigator, was born in Salford, Manchester in 1915, two years before his father, Arthur Jones, was killed fighting in Mesopotamia during the Great War. Clifford worked as a plumber before enlistment and was married Betty Alcock in Stoke-on-Trent in 1942; they did not have any children.[117] Betty subsequently married again and had two children[118] one of whom, Jane, remembers, 'we offered to take Mum but she refused, it was part of her life she would never talk about. I only found out when I found a wedding photo at about nine'.[119]

Little is recorded of most of the other crew members. Frank Dyson, rear gunner, was married to Hilda Dyson of Nafferton, Yorkshire; George Knowler, flight engineer, was married to Nora Knowler of Hounslow Middlesex; Royston Sperling, air gunner, was the son of Leslie and Sybil Sperling; Albert Storey, wireless operator; there are no further details known, and Eric Draper, special operator, was the son of George and Hilda Draper of Carrington, Nottingham.[120]

Robert Brown, bomb aimer, RCAF, had completed 913 days' service on 17 April 1945, with 366 being overseas.[121] Hailing from Lanark County Ontario, he was formerly a logger; when enlisting he was 'ambitious to be a pilot, however, [he was] willing to serve where best suited in aircrew'.[122] In training, he was described as 'young with plenty of dash ... his application throughout the course has been good and the results achieved ... satisfactory. He should mature with training and seems to possess the ability to make a success of his aircrew training'.[123] However, piloting was not his forte; 'this pilot lacks the ability to judge height and admits he can't tell how high up he is. Continually flys [sic] into the ground, co-ordination poor in turns. Training to be discontinued as pilot'.[124] He fared better as a bomb aimer working 'conscientiously with good all round results'.[125] He was posted to 171 Squadron at RAF North Creake on 30 December 1944,[126] where he survived less than five months as an operational bomb aimer.

The loss of his aircraft triggers for him the gathering of his things and those of his crewmates, and the drawing up of an inventory to be sent to the Central Depository in Slough. For Robert Brown however, there are other complications for the grieving family to address; there was a Morris 8 (JF7583) on the station. Robert bought the car off another RAF North Creake crew member, N I Noel, but he didn't have the full £45 asking price. So Eric Draper wrote out a cheque in full payment for the car and Robert Brown wrote a cheque for Eric for £25 (thereby still owing him £20).[127] The cheque for £25 was still uncashed at the time of the collision. In reconciling the estate, a decision was reached between all parties[128] that the uncashed cheque would be returned to the family of Robert Brown, and the family of Eric Draper would collect the car from RAF North Creake.[129] Similarly, there was an anomaly over a bicycle belonging to Robert Brown which the Central Depository tried to resolve.[130] However, by April 1946, BCHQ wanted to move on. They responded to enquiries regarding the missing bicycle with the terse reply that 'all of the personnel at R.A.F. Station North Creake have now been changed, it is considered that no useful purpose can be served by referring this matter to that station'; they further argued, 'it is not unlikely that he disposed of [the bicycle] in some manner before he was missing from operations'.[131] No resolution is recorded in the archives.

Such are the tragically pathetic loose ends of any loss.

CHAPTER NINE

STAND-DOWN

*There was not flying every night,
but I would say we only had about
three nights off in any fortnight.*

John Rees, Senior NCO RAF North Creake Station Sick Quarters, 1944-1945.1

When no operations were ordered, the station was not idle and many critical functions continued; groundcrews still worked on aircraft, and aircraft still flew. There were also the 'communal chores to be done',[2] many chores were completed 'on the basis of volunteering for what one liked best – or disliked least'.[3] For many, quiet nights were spent 'sewing and darning',[4] although, if beyond repair, uniform clothing could be exchanged at the Clothing Parades.[5] Polishing buttons was still a mainstay of slack times. Even with the introduction of plastic buttons on much of the uniform (to save brass),[6] the task hadn't been rendered entirely redundant. The daily ritual of polishing boots, to ensure an 'unnatural gloss'[7] finish on the toes, was an involved skill. A technique that Henry Park, a bomb aimer at RAF North Creake, passed on to his children, who, postwar, would polish their 'shoes to perfection each weekend'.[8]

Washing oneself, using the RAF two-chain shower; 'one chain for cold and one chain for hot',[9] was unpleasant. A more palatable solution for many was not to bathe until they went home on leave.[10] Therefore many practiced spot-washing at a basin, complicated by an absence of sink plugs forcing personnel to carry their own.[11] However, problems with washing could be more fundamental; Jack Sinclair recalls a 'broken-down water supply' in the height of the 1944 summer heat,[12] and Phyllis Willmott complains in November 1944, 'we haven't had any water in the baths, basins, or lavatories in the billets throughout camp, since the day before yesterday morning! Really disgraceful'.[13]

The provision of food was more reliable and unaffected by stand-downs. There were three messes on site: officers', sergeants' and airmen's. The messes provided meals in two or three sittings of 80 people per day.[14] The catering officer, Lionel Playfoot, was mentioned in despatches as outstanding, 'whose good work has materially contributed to the well-being of all ranks of the station'.[15] Some ranks disagreed; in the airmen's mess where 'other ranks', who arrived equipped with 'irons' (knife, spoon, and fork)[16] described the food as swill.[A17] Whereas, in the officers' mess they could expect laid tables,[18] polished cutlery, napkins, waitresses and outstanding food.[19] In the sergeants' mess, there was less ceremony than the officers' mess and the quality of the food was not as good, but a good deal better than the airmen's mess; 'Good on the whole'.[20]

While airfield personnel, particularly aircrew, were somewhat protected from the constraints of rationing, some shortages in supply could still arise. However, these could often be mitigated with the help of local people, such as Albert Bambridge, a farmer from North Creake village, who used to supply the airfield with meat and eggs.[21] Moreover, senior officers often felt the need to supplement this supply still further. Michael Renaut, armed with a rifle, was fond of taking out his Hillman and shooting six brace of partridges and a couple of brace of pheasants;[22] although, he concedes, 'it wasn't exactly good sportsmanship'.[23] On

---

A   David Graham, a radar mechanic at RAF North Creake 1944-1945, and voice of Parker and Brains in the 1960s TV series *Thunderbirds*, was particularly vociferous about this when he came to visit the Control Tower in April 2019.

one occasion, having decided to host a dinner party for the Earl and Countess of Leicester, Michael Renaut persuaded a reluctant Norman Bray, that he should poach some of the Earl's own pheasants for dinner. Michael Renaut recalls the night:

> the four of us sat down to a glorious meal; the chef had done bread sauce, game chips, bacon and all the trimmings and we scrounged some tinned fruit salad and some cheese to follow. We bought a bottle of wine at the local pub and altogether we put on a fine banquet ... halfway through the meal Lord Leicester, with a twinkle in his eye said, 'remarkably devoid of shot these birds, Michael!'.[24]

Another supplement to the mess table was hare, shot on the airfield by the light from headlamps; 'it wasn't easy shooting from a moving car but it was grand sport and our best night we bagged fourteen hares'.[25] Thankfully hares are still found on the former aerodrome, but the airmen shooting them are not!

If poaching wasn't your game, another option was to eat at the Navy, Army and Air Force Institute (Naafi). The Naafi was a state-owned not for profit company;[26] officially a civilian organisation, it provided services to the armed forces.[27] At the RAF North Creake Naafi, Jean Berry was primarily responsible for the 'Wagon', as it was affectionately known, delivering sandwiches, tea, and tray-baked cakes out to those working on dispersals. The tray-bakes were 'cut into profitable portions ... [with] any left-over portions ... taken to the Naafi kitchens where they would be crumbled and sandwiched between two layers of sweetened pastry to be cooked and re-emerge as Nelson cake ready for resale'.[28] Doreen Leach also worked in the RAF North Creake Naafi alongside her sister. At the age of 15, Doreen used to cycle up from Wells every day, regardless of the weather (unless there was very bad snow, in which case they were collected).[29] Initially sent by the Wells Labour Exchange they 'worked hard for very bad pay', washing dishes, cleaning floors and serving mostly groundcrews, whom she described, with a smile, as 'very cheeky'.[30] Beryl Spear, stationed at RAF

100 Group HQ, remembers the Naafi affectionately as a 'social place' with hot pies and lots of music.[31] Phyllis Willmott also recalls that the Naafi 'was good and therefore popular and well used ... [we] spent many merry hours ... arguing about politics ... teas[ing] me about my supposed socialism.[32]

Phyllis modestly asserts that one explanation for their popularity was as 'non-smokers we were always willing to swap our cigarette allowance for sweet coupons'.[33] This informal bartering system troubled the authorities and in January 1945, a new 'ticket' system was introduced for all RAF and WAAF, 'of the rank of corporal and below',[34] to prevent abuse of the system when obtaining their rations.[35]

Many decided to take food preparation into their own hands, with ambitions ranging from toast cooked against the stove in a Nissen hut,[36] to Canadians defeathering an acquired chicken by nailing it to a pole and burning off the feathers with 'lighted newspaper torches. What a mess and smell that created!'.[37] The radar section took it to another level, regularly travelling to Wells-next-the-Sea and buying mackerel directly from the fishermen for the 'price of a bob or two'.[38] When back in the radar section they would:

> butter the rolls [bought earlier from a local shop], prepare the mackerel ready for grilling on the stove which would be banked up ready for the purpose, and [with a] firkin of beer purchased from the NAAFI canteen earlier in the day ... sat round the fire and ate our 'sumptuous' repast.[39]

Stand-down or not, breakfast heralded the commencement of daily duties for many. The Commanding Officer, Norman Bray, issued both daily routine orders (DROs) and station routine orders (SROs). Compiled and typed onto wax stencils for duplicating,[40] they included names of those rostered for orderly duties,[41] as well as such things as blackout times,[42] awards, mentions in despatches, training schedules and general notices.[43] All such orders were pinned to notice boards daily together with personal occurrence reports (details of personnel sickness and leave).[44] Examples of rostered duties include the station orderly duty, involving the inspection of accommodation sites for cleanliness and order, and the checking at meal times for 'any complaints'.[45] The WAAF orderly officer had similar responsibilities for the WAAF sites and also, at around 22:00-23:00 hours, checking on the billets to see if 'all the good WAAFs were tucked up in their beds'.[46] Phyllis Willmott remembers that 'it was always possible to creep in across the fields'[47] and sneak in undetected:

> there was a good deal of such coming and going during the night. One girl in our hut regularly set her alarm for 3.30a.m. so she could get up and go out to meet her love when he returned from 'ops'.[48]

Every other Friday there was a pay parade to attend.[49] It was the job of the pay clerk to calculate the sum (to the nearest two shillings[50]) based upon notice of any promotion, detention, re-classification, or other events which might vary the pay entitlement.[51] The calculations were worked out the day before and entered into ledgers in pencil (inked in when paid out at the parade[B]). On the morning of the pay parade, the accounts officer (with escort), collected the cash from the bank; several thousand pounds in notes and two-bob bits.[52] At the parade, personnel were called forward:[53]

> three or four people with the pay officer with cash in front of them. You never give your full number, always the last three, he'd shout, 'Airman How', you'd say, 'Yes sir, 804'. Then you'd draw your pounds and shillings. Whatever it was. Once you got to aircrew, you were paid in the bank.[54]

Permanently primed for an alert was the station sick quarters (SSQ), with 12 beds for RAF and six for WAAF personnel (plus two isolation rooms with a bed in each).[55] For the Senior Medical Officer, Peter Gorrie, and the second in command, Robert Dyke,[56] the work was

---

B   There was also a Daily Casual Pay Parade for those going on leave, postings, night shift or such reason for not attending main parade (Ford:1992:11).

mainly routine, including medical examinations, vaccinations[57] and dentistry (performed by Ralph Syder). This could all be scheduled. Less predictable was illness; the sick parades would attend to the minor ailments, but there were always admissions for the more seriously unwell. Phyllis Willmott recalls her bout in the SSQ:

> the Medical Officer, who had been for many years in the peacetime RAF (and so had little experience of treating women), was inclined to believe I had appendicitis. I managed to persuade him I hadn't because I didn't want to be sent off to hospital. His junior, who had more experience of treating women, was not so easy to convince. 'Why have you burnt a mark on your right side with a hot-water bottle if you have no pain there?' he asked. He was rightly resentful when his senior, dismissing his opinion, said he would not send me to hospital if he could help it – and went on to call me soothingly his 'problem WAAF'.[58]

It was appendicitis, and when on leave in London it reemerged; she collapsed with 'rampantly generalized peritonitis' from which she nearly died.[59] Another member of airfield personnel was not so lucky having only recently returned from leave;[60] fitter armourer, James Lightfoot, was found unconscious in his billet on the morning of 5 February 1945.[C] He was appraised at the SSQ and placed on the 'dangerously ill list'.[61] In the only air evacuation from RAF North Creake, he was flown to RAF Witchford, from where an ambulance took him to RAF Hospital, Ely; 'the patient died a few hours after admission'.[D62]

The SSQ also had a fully-equipped crash room ready for emergencies.[63] Even with no scheduled flying, an aircraft in distress could require the skills of the SSQ at any moment. On 29 July 1944, six

---

C The Station ORB erroneously states the date as the 6 February 1945, whereas the appendices to the 171 Squadron ORB correctly lists the date as 5 February 1945. Further research identifies that James Lightfoot died of a cerebral haemorrhage. He was 31 and married to Elsa Eleanor of West Hartlepool (rafcommands. com).

D James Lightfoot was buried at Stanton Grange cemetery in Hartlepool on 10 February 1945 with full military honours. F/O Sampson represented RAF North Creake at the funeral with floral tributes from the 'Commanding Officer, officers and other ranks, N.C.O.s, and airmen' (Hartlepool Mail: 12/2/1945).

Flying Fortresses of the USAAF, made an emergency landing at RAF North Creake. Bernard Beaumont, a teenager working on adjacent farmland, watched aircrew climb down from the aircraft, dazed and injured, and a truck take away the dead body of a crewman to the mortuary.[64] Flying a daylight operation to Merseburg, Germany,[65] it had been hit by flak. Having lost two engines and burning ferociously, with the bombardier, Tommy Gumaer, mortally wounded,[66] the aircraft turned back. The crew battled with the fires[67] while also administering first aid to Tommy Gumaer.[68] Unable to return safely to its base in Polebrook, Northamptonshire, it was diverted to the airfield.[69] However, by the time it landed, Tommy Gumaer was dead.[70] He was 20 years old.[71]

Two other crew members were slightly injured[72] and were treated at the SSQ.[73] The aircraft were taken to the reserve dispersals in front of the east hangar (clearly visible from the Dry Road).[74] A local resident remembers that 'they stood there for weeks; one of them was so badly shot up that I was shocked that it made it back'. The aircraft, in spite of the damage, was repaired by a mobile unit from the USAAF,[75] and returned to flying on 6 October 1944.[76]

Stand-downs were often forced on account of poor weather, and training could usefully be instituted to fill the time. The winter of 1944/45 was particularly cold, particularly at RAF North Creake; 'one of the coldest postings I ever had',[77] leading to:

> a shortage of coal, so we had to scrounge for wooden items to burn in our very small heater, located in the center [sic] of the Nissen hut. Some coal was on hand to be used for essential purposes such as the hospital and messes. The wood soon became scarce and one really had to look everywhere and anywhere to find some.[78]

Roy Berrill recalls the Nissen huts being freezing cold;[79] the stove was 'red hot at night, you woke up in the morning to have a wash, too bad, the water was frozen'.[80] Helen Storrar, the map clerk, also recalls the water was rationed due to the water tower freezing up; 'we had to take our washing on the boot lorry to the YMCA in Norwich'.[81] From the 8 to 12 January 1945, the squadrons were stood down due to snow with many set on clearing runways.[82] On 29 January, blizzards caused 'drifts up to 11 feet deep, making use of the airfield impossible':[83]

> driving snow swept over the Station during the night, and snow penetrated through every crevice, covering the inside of many huts on the Station. In fact, on the following day, when the thaw commenced, hardly a hut or office on the station escaped some flooding.[84]

Flooding could be a problem in other seasons; just before midnight on 30 June 1944, the Orderly Officer was telephoned and asked to visit the WAAF site, where heavy rain had caused an invasion of thousands of earwigs and beetles. 'The W.A.A.F. asked to be allowed to evacuate, which application was refused and peremptory action with shovels, soon ridded the hut of the hordes of insects.'[85] The heavy rain caused flooding in the accounts section and accounts books and ledgers had to be hung out on the lines to dry. It emerged that 'a large proportion of the buildings on the station are far from weather-proof'.[86] If such weather made flying impossible, Norman Bray often instructed 'maximum training',[87] in the form of 'lectures and instructional films'.[88]

Training was an ever-present feature of life on an operational airfield. With a dedicated site, it covered a wide range of topics, including practical exercises on emergency procedures for flying controllers and synthetic training for bomb aimers and gunners; and training on radars.[89] There was also a flight simulator (Link Trainer) operated by Peter Black;[90] it was 'absolutely basic but you could fly a hypothetical route'.[91] These were supplemented by lectures on subjects including 'Windowing and Spoofing'[92] and evading capture by Anthony Reynolds.[E93] There were also discussion groups on topical

---

E Anthony Reynolds was shot down over Germany on 10 July 1943, and successfully evaded capture. His pilot was killed and five other crewmen were captured; he was the only evader.

issues and current affairs,[F94] such as that by Squadron Leader Mackay (Bomber Command's Woman Medical Officer) who gave a lecture on 'sex hygiene' during April 1945,[95] as venereal disease was a significant problem, with Bomber Command said to have 'the highest rate of venereal disease in the RAF'.[G96]

Training was also required for flying, to keep wits sharp and to make familiar any new techniques or innovations. Keith Thompson wrote in his diary on 6 March 1945; 'stand down but we are on fighter affiliation.[H] Kite U/S after messing about'.[97] Ken Chapman, a pilot with 171 Squadron, was practising air-to-sea firing on a ship[I] about a mile offshore over Brancaster Bay.[98] Flying over the beach 'suddenly the nose of the aircraft was covered with sand and water, I never did find out what caused it but I think I had set off an acoustic mine on the beach'.[99] There was no damage, but the airman sitting in the nose was badly shaken.[100]

Roy Mitchell, practising on the same wreck with another crew, was preparing to fire all eight guns at 200 rounds a minute, when one of the crew noticed movement and shouted, 'there's somebody on the damn thing!'. A figure was then seen running away across the sand. Roy, being Brancaster born, recognised him:

> I went into the pub in Brancaster Staithe that night ... I said to this chap, 'what were you doing on that ship today?' and he said, 'Roy, it's like this. They came here and scuttled it and the sailors went away leaving practically everything on the ship ... they only took the compass.' I told him, 'Well, it's by absolute

---

F   The army had a comprehensive current affairs programme publishing its own pamphlets through the 'Army Bureau of Current Affairs' (ABCA) (see Mackenzie: 1992). The RAF considered themselves too busy to run such a programme but they did receive the ABCA pamphlets. Norman Bray held a conference in August 1944 regarding the arrangements 'for Discussion Groups on the station' (RAF North Creake: 1944: ORB). The ORB does not outline any topics, but from the evidence of RAF Woodbridge during the same period, topics included: What is the Future of India?; Is Progress an Illusion?; and the Future Possibilities of Spain after the War (RAF Woodbridge: 1944: ORB).

G   The incidence of VD in 1942 Britain was 70% up on that of 1939. New Defence Regulation (Reg 33B) introduced in November 1942 allowed 'in carefully defined circumstances' for compulsory treatment of sufferers (Laird: 1943: 34-35).

H   Fighter affiliation involved flying mock interceptions with fighter aircraft in order to practise interception evasion techniques (Pedan: 1979: 461).

I   The ship was anchored by the navy and sunk by the RAF who used it for target practise (Maufe: 22/2/2024).

sheer luck that you weren't cut in half' ... he was horrified! He never went near that ship again, or, if he did, he made sure there were no aircraft about![101]

As a result of all these expected, and, at times unexpected aircraft movements, Flying Control were required to perform their duties regardless of stand-downs.[102] On 17 April 1945, at approximately 16:30 hours,[103] Halifax PN169 of 171 Squadron was taking off for an air test. The pilot, Johnny Butler, experienced an engine cut out,[104] causing the Halifax to swing violently off the runway and towards the two T2 hangars.[105] Ken Chapman, a pilot with another 171 Squadron crew, was alongside Johnny for the air test:[106]

> I filled my battledress with buns from the NAAFI wagon and sat in the second pilot's seat. Unfortunately we swung on take off and shot across the airfield and demolished an airmen's toilet ... it would usually be full of groundcrew having a quick smoke but fortunately ... they had completed their work and had pushed off early leaving the toilets empty.
>
> We hit two huge trees which stopped us dead. The aircraft, plus 2,000 gallons of high-octane fuel blew-up immediately. The other side of the trees was the MT Section and fuel dump so the trees did us some good! Johnny tried to get out of the escape hatch but his 'chute was stuck in the opening, I pushed him out and he disappeared.[107]

On hitting the ground, the pilot, Clive John 'Johnny' Butler, fell back into the flames and sustained life-threatening burns, while Ken Chapman fell forward, away from the flames, breaking an ankle.[108] The MT Officer raced over and pulled the pilot away.[109] There were two further injuries to the wireless operator, G R Henderson, and the flight engineer, A Hill, although the nature of the injuries were 'not specified'.[110] The Station ORB records the incident thus:

a Halifax aircraft piloted by F/Lt. Butler, swung off the runway and crashed on the Fakenham Road bursting into flames. The pilot was severely burned, and was transferred to R.A.F. Hospital, Ely, being placed on the dangerously ill list. F/Lt. Chapman, another member of the crew, sustained an injury to his leg, and he was transferred to R.A.F. Hospital, Ely.[111]

Before arriving at Ely, the ambulance initially took them to Kings Lynn. Ken Chapman recalls, 'Johnny's face was charred black and he kept asking for a gun to shoot himself. At Kings Lynn, they took one look at him and said he was too bad for them. He asked me to stay with him and so we went all the way to Ely Hospital'.[112] Johnny Butler was lucky to survive. Michael Renaut went to see him in the early stages of his recovery and was shocked by the burns, 'when I visited him in hospital in the burns ward, his face was almost unrecognisable',[113] he had 'lost his fingers and ears and was in a bad way'.[114] Both Johnny Butler and Ken Chapman were still in hospital at the end of the war.[115]

Johnny was transferred to East Grinstead and became 'one of Sir Archibald McIndoe's longest serving patients',[116] receiving skin grafts for new eyelids, nose and eyebrows.[117] After leaving East Grinstead, he married Olive, read History at Manchester and joined Manchester Educational Authority, teaching history. He died on 16 November 1989 aged 69. His obituary in the Guinea Pig Club magazine described how they will 'miss John's cheery disposition'.[118]

Visiting the site in the 1970s, John Rees noted, 'the tree now dead was still there'.[119]

* * *

As an active RAF station between 1944 and 1945, RAF North Creake, like all stations of this period, it was a conglomeration of races, creeds and cultures, drawn from throughout the world and from every facet of society. What might seem a recipe for friction actually garnered an atmosphere of reasonable congeniality and harmony. Classes interacted in a way seldom experienced in peacetime, challenging preconceptions, but also identifying difference.

One of the most obvious distinctions were accents, and different use of the same language. Many middle and upper class personnel arriving on camps were shocked at the casual use of expletives; a bomb aimer with Bomber Command describes how an airman, discarding a worn-out article, expresses his distaste; 'the [f]ucking [f]ucker's [f]ucking well [f]ucked'.[120] The witness explains, that with continuous exposure to such language it soon 'went by unnoticed',[121] indeed it wasn't long before he himself had 'adopted this method of expression'.[122] For some, this was not a paucity in a speaker's level of self-expression, but a creative approach to language; one to be cherished along with the men using it.[123] Jack Harris, from the radar section at RAF North Creake, recalls with affection, Des Bingham 'gazing at the screen of a radar set, occasionally thumping the box with a clenched fist and making remarks about its pro-creative abilities'.[124]

While this mixing of classes may not have been the 'great leveller'[J] that many suppose, it did challenge some of the worst prejudices. Arthur Baldwin,[K] having experienced the great generosity of those he had formerly considered below him, reflects 'upon all the silver spoons in the well-born mouths, such as his own ... [and] the social fortitude of the poor'.[125] He noted differences between the way groundcrew (frequently working class) and officers were treated, concluding that 'perhaps there are in effect two R.A.F.s: the air one and the ground one. Apparently there can be little wrong with the former; but as for the latter, Heaven help the lowly airman'.[126] These distinctions were reinforced with petty regulations including those allowing an officer to leave the camp at will, whereas other ranks were only permitted to leave at certain times and only after booking-out, and booking back

---

J   The 'Air Ministry never lost their conviction that gentlemen made the best aircrew'. Class prejudice was evident from the recruitment stage with bias unashamedly apparent. Sending memoranda with assertions such as 'there are indications in a number of directions that we are not getting a reasonable percentage of the young men of the middle and upper classes who are the backbone of this country, when they leave the public schools' (Hastings: 1980: 215).

K   Arthur Baldwin, the son of Stanley Baldwin, the British Prime Minister, enlisted as a private in the RAF to test the theory that it was a meritocracy. He, of course, didn't advance and eventually took a commission under pressure from the Air Ministry (and doubtless his father).

in again on their return.[127] Nonetheless, there was a prevalent belief that among bomber aircrew there was equality, reinforced by the notion that no role on an aircraft was of greater importance than any other.[128] However, this well-used trope concealed a less palatable class division, with gunners frequently referred to as the 'manual workers',[129] whereas the pilot was the 'gentlemen up front'.[130] These distinctions were not just apparent in the air, they existed on the ground, where officers had partitioned rooms and had help from WAAF batwomen who tidied their billets and made their beds,[131] whereas:

> we lived in unlined Nissen huts … after landing from a sortie you had to get into a very cold and damp bed and try and catch up with some sleep. Sometimes you tried to light a fire in a very small and inadequate stove but usually abandoned the effort because of wet sticks and very wet and poor fuel.[132]

Add to the mix, the cosmopolitan nature of RAF stations, and one could expect friction. However, the reality was somewhat different; Bernie How's crew was reasonably typical, made up of three from Canada, two from London and two from Suffolk (he fails to mention the special operator),[133] all getting on famously.[134] Relations between the different nationalities on the camp seemed reasonably harmonious, and there are no reports of any difficulties emerging or punishments meted out.[135] Anecdotal evidence from crew members generally indicates good relations between them, regardless of nationality or race. The only gripe that ever surfaces appears to be one of pay, and Bernie How's remarks on the subject seem reasonably typical:

> [Canadians] got more money than we did … you'd pull their leg every now and again and they'd say 'hard luck' … we done all right. Then it was good money. But they got more. Same with Australians, New Zealanders whatever.[136]

Similar to Bernie, Gordon Dennison, who would be killed alongside his crew in September 1944,[L] flew with five Canadians, an Englishman and a Scotsman ('seems to be a good sort of fellow but I have a job understanding his language').[137] Crews frequently involved men from New Zealand, Australia, occupied European states (particularly Poland and France), as well as personnel from India, Africa and the Caribbean.[M] There is no indication at RAF North Creake of personnel from France, Poland or India, but there are references to personnel from the Caribbean and South Africa. Visibility of personnel from regions such as the Caribbean, would often be obscured if their country had no separate air force as the recruits would, more than likely, join the RAF, and disappear behind a British uniform. This is particularly true if they were groundcrew. For example, of the 7,000 Caribbean volunteers recruited throughout the war, 6,560 were groundcrew,[138] with their full details only being recorded on their personnel files, which remain, sadly, unavailable.

Vivian Hutchinson Cooper was born in Annotto Bay, Jamaica. His pilot, Dickie Thomas, was mustered to drop supplies to Tito's resistance in Yugoslavia. However, 'with Viv being black, it was called off just before inoculations as it would have caused difficulties with the Americans particularly with Viv being an officer'.[139] Therefore, in order to keep the crew together and rather than face race discrimination they were posted to 171 Squadron at RAF North Creake.[140] Discrimination against those from non-white backgrounds was not just an issue for the US authorities; such prejudice was also evident in Air Ministry circles. Indeed, anyone of a non-British background was generally considered less than ideal for aircrew, with a 1942 Air Ministry memorandum highlighting with distaste the 'growing proportion of Colonials in Bomber Command'.[141] Moreover, Arthur Harris argued that the 'English made the best aircrew because they had the strongest sense of discipline'.[142] However, such concerns were not to be expressed at airfield level, and the Air Ministry issued a confidential memorandum in June 1944, stating:

L See the chapter 'Missing' above.

M In May 1945, there were approximately 17,500 Commonwealth recruits in the RAF, 'in a variety of roles'. A further 25,000 served with the Royal Indian Air Force (Bourne: 2012: 10).

all ranks should clearly understand that there is no colour bar in the Royal Air Force ... any instant of discrimination on grounds of colour by white officers or airmen or any attitude of hostility towards personnel of non-European descent should be immediately and severely checked.[143]

In reality, close proximity eroded much preexisting prejudicial thinking and such personnel were most often considered vital members of closely bonded crews.[144] Vivian Cooper became an architect after the war and, having married Joan Hadaway from Surrey in 1945[N], they then moved location many times. As a consequence, Dickie Thomas sadly reflected, 'the only one we have lost touch with is Viv, the Jamaican – our last known address was Ghana'.[145] Vivian died in Nigeria in 1992 and as with most veterans, he died without recording his experiences. However, his experience was unlike most who served at RAF North Creake, but it is now, sadly, forever absent from the record.

Citizens of the Republic of Ireland are, for the same reasons as recruits from Jamaica, difficult to identify. While workers openly left Ireland to work on British construction projects, they were forbidden from joining the British military forces as this would compromise Ireland's neutrality.[146] However, a report in 1945 produced by the Admiralty, War Office and Air Ministry, put the number of Irish citizens serving with the armed forces at 42,665, of those 11,050 were serving with the RAF.[147] A year later total numbers were downgraded to 38,000 with 'no explanation'.[148] However, there is speculation that, for reasons of political palatability, the numbers may have been equalised with those of Northern Ireland, who without conscription,[149] had reasonably low recruitment figures for a region of the UK.[150]

It is evident that there was Irish representation at RAF North Creake. On 2 May 1945, William Mackay, a flight engineer with 199

N   Joan had previously been married to Gordon Hadaway in August 1940, also in the RAF he was killed in May 1941. Vivian and Joan had four children two born in the UK (Ian, Surrey, 1946 and Keith, Glamorganshire, 1947) and two abroad (David, 1954 and Margaret 1955).

Squadron was killed in a raid over Kiel.° Very little is known of his background, other than he was from Glenageary, Co. Dublin and that he received a Degree from Trinity College.[151] With Trinity College's 'Anglo-Irish and Unionist tradition,'[152] it can, perhaps, be deduced that this was the probable motivation for joining up.

Harry Freegard, a UK-born rear gunner, was in a crew consisting of Canadians with the exception of himself and the pilot, E J Hurrell, from the USA. E J Hurrell crossed the border into Canada and joined the RCAF after realising in early 1941, that the USSAF was not a guaranteed route into flying. After Adolf Hitler's declaration of war on the USA in December 1941, the USSAF was keen that any US citizens serving with other air forces should transfer to the USAAF. E J Hurrell refused to transfer until he had finished his tour with Bomber Command and, in spite of significant pressure, stuck to his guns and remained at RAF North Creake until the end of the war.[153]

For those recruited abroad, arriving in Britain could be a culture shock. Gordon Dennison, from Canada, describes in his letters home; 'I had my first taste of [beer] last night and I don't like it at all',[154] then there was the money, 'this English money is getting me down … it just doesn't make sense'.[155] But most vehemence was saved for the weather:

> boy is it ever cold over here and damp you are never warm from the time you get up in the morning until you go back to bed … But I guess I will get use [sic] to it in time, the joke around here is that summer came last year on a Wednesday but this year they think it will be on a Sunday.[156]

He continues, 'it sure is lazy weather … I often wondered what gave Englishmen the lack of ambition and I believe that it's this weather'.[157] However, when it brightens up, he sees things a little differently; 'the weather here has been grand of late and the evenings are so quiet and still it sure is beautiful … everything is so green'.[158] Such weather, if it coincided with a stand-down, would send 'all who could swimming,

---

O See 'Dove Over Europe' below.

playing tennis and otherwise taking advantage of the sunshine'.[159] Although, in stand-downs, many chose to spend time 'lounging'[160] on their bed or in the messes reading newspapers and books.[161] Or, they occupied themselves writing and reading letters. While phone calls were possible from phone boxes on site, letters were perennially popular.[162] Letter writing was prolific and personnel persisted even when conditions were not ideal; 'the lights in the camp have fused to-night so I am using a cycle lamp to write this'.[163]

Royal Mail worked reasonably well throughout the war,[164] although there were always concerns about how long mail took to arrive, leaving service personnel, particularly when waiting for letters from abroad, unsure whether the cause was unreliable relatives or an unreliable mail service. 'Two months since received letters from home',[165] Gordon Dennison writes, 'letters from Canada have taken from 5 March to 22 March but letters home are taking 6 days!'.[166]

Once settled into the station, Keith Thompson, a navigator at RAF North Creake, wrote regularly to both his mother and fiancée, Avice.[167] He wrote letters almost every day with responses received, at least initially, just as frequently (in March for example he wrote to Avice 17 times and she to him 19 times). He was incredibly impatient for letters and when none arrive for a couple of days, his frustration was capitalised in his diary; 20 March 1945, 'NO MAIL!!', the phrase repeated when nothing arrives in the second post.[168] He wrote what he refers to as a 'STINKING LETTER TO AVICE' (22 March)[169] presumably when he felt their correspondence was not frequent enough. She replied to 'THE'[170] letter on 27 March. Their engagement did not last demobilisation.[171]

In what must be the first time in warfare, the military personnel often felt less at risk than the civilians. For those with relatives in major British cities, the worry could be insufferable; Phyllis Willmott wrote in August 1944, as the V1s and V2s were striking London, '[it's] unfair that up here seems all so safe and remote from war, whilst home is having such hell'.[172] As a consequence she can't resist repeatedly phoning home to check on the safety of her parents. Until her father sets her straight:

'you don't want to keep ringing up like this. It's a waste of money.' From Dad this was an order to stop worrying; and somewhat irrationally, and even though the air attacks continued relentlessly ... [his] intervention succeeded in relieving the worst of my anxiety.[173]

Phyllis was not alone in her worry; Beryl Spear working at RAF 100 Group HQ recalls, 'you rang up home and found out they were all right, but you didn't know they were going to be all right the next minute'.[174] Nonetheless, the greatest fear remained with those at home, concerned for the safety of their loved ones on operations. Joan Calvert, whose job it was to censor airmen's letters,[175] recalls how, 'at times it was heart breaking',[176] but for the relatives, after receipt of that most feared telegram, what status did that 'last letter home' assume? And what of its final salutation that may be read after news of their death? For Ron Maden, killed on 6 January 1945,[P] it was the simple words, 'well must close now, hoping you are OK. Cheerio, Ron'.[177] The very last goodbye.

* * *

Before we opened, and while we were still restoring the Control Tower, we adopted a very geographically-focused way of life, seldom leaving the confines of the Control Tower if we didn't need to. We happily satisfied ourselves with things that needed to be done and embraced simple pleasures.

Fires played a considerable role in our time off, where we sat watching the flames and planning next stages. We drank beer around the fire and we drank whisky to plan; probably a little too much, but we were working hard and it was our reward. Inside we'd avidly watch *Grand Designs*, perhaps for the hope of inspiration, or more probably to identify with those not having an easy time; happy in the knowledge that it usually turned out well. We'd taken out all the aerial sockets in the house, as they were in every room and such devotion to television

---

P   See 'Mid-Air Collision' above.

depressed us. Consequently, we watched TV on our worn-out laptop with poor Wi-Fi that caused regular buffering and the computer to overheat during the adverts; it all added to the atmosphere. We probably could have listened to more music, read more books and watched more films; but these things were still packed away in boxes, protecting them from the filth of a chaotic house renovation. However, in the first year or so, we were contentedly occupied with the project; making our own entertainment.

During the war, while some felt that, because of the airfield's remoteness, there was no access to quality entertainment,[178] others believed the opposite; that because of its isolation, everything was provided for.[179] In all messes, alcohol was available and readily consumed. The officers' mess bar was opened on 18 June 1944, and the first of a series of regular dances was held with over '250 people present'.[180] Guests were often invited and the local GP commented postwar that he used to spend a lot of time on the airfield as 'there was never a shortage of whisky'.[181] Primarily though, this was where officers 'socialised, and boy, did some of them socialise too! If there was no operation most of them were drunk by evening'.[182] Michael Renaut, as president of the Officers' Mess Committee,[183] was keen to organise parties:

> we flew a Halifax over to France and brought back fresh lobsters and champagne and I organised one room in the mess to be a miniature casino! We discovered that someone in the airmen's mess had been a professional croupier in peace-time so we ... made him in charge of the gambling department! Bray and I thought that we'd make enough on the roulette table to pay for the party (about £600) but we hadn't reckoned on this so-called croupier; as the evening wore on he accepted drinks right and left and finished up tight as a coot paying everybody and falling off the back of his stool.[184]

After the party one of the guests, Silvia Combe,[Q] could not find her car and was worried about how this might look if it reached the newspapers (car use was severely restricted in wartime Britain); luckily it had 'been borrowed by a drunken airman',[185] who had, presumably, been drinking in another mess. Most aircrew members would go to the sergeants' mess in the evening 'for a shandy or two when not on ops',[186] although, unlike in the officers' mess, junior officers were not allowed to spend more than £5 a month on drink at the bar.[187] Still a reasonable amount given a sergeant navigator was on £3, 3s 6d per week in 1943.[188]

Sunday nights were open nights, with WAAFs and Naafi personnel invited along.[189] The mess featured an ante room to the dining hall with a bar, piano and small stage.[R] On the blackout boards was painted a parody version of the phonetic alphabet; 'in the manner of "A for Orses" ..."C for yourself" ... and "Q for beer".[190] The latter was a reference to Joe Brogan's crew,[191] with a reputation 'for being a "boozy" lot'.[192]

Parties were a regular feature of mess life, either spontaneous or planned. On 8 July 1944, Ensa[S] 'gave a first class show [and] afterwards in a most sporting manner, joined in an impromptu dance in the Officers' Mess'.[193] Or organised; [28 June 1944] 'the W.A.A.F Birthday Celebrations were held on the Station ... a dance given by the W.A.A.F. was held from 20.00hrs. till midnight and a good time was had by all'.[194] With dancing being such an important feature of the social milieu, dancing classes, led by LAC Sumpter,[195] were offered on the station twice a week.[196]

Dances at RAF North Creake most often involved those invited from outside the station. Jessie Grimes, who was billeted with the land girls at Longlands on Holkham Estate, describes one particular night:

Q Silvia Combe, was the Daughter of Thomas Coke, (Earl of Leicester). Michael Renaut had made friends with both daughters, Silvia and Mary Harvey, 'both of whom were very attractive and charming girls'. The senior officers attended 'endless parties at their home' and dinners at Holkham Hall; 'Earl and Countess of Leicester ... were a delightful and most hospitable couple' and the daughters were 'such good fun and such good company' (Renaut:1982: 149-150).

R Claude Allen, who painted most, if not all, the nose art on the aircraft, also painted a picture of the sergeant's mess featuring one of his paintings on the wall. The picture still exists and his family were kind enough to give us a high quality print of it (see plate ?).

S Ensa (Entertainments National Service Association), was effectively the entertainments branch of Naafi (Miller: 1971: 74).

a [airfield crew] bus was arranged to collect us and girls from several villages around. We had an extra late pass that night. After the dance was over, we all piled into the bus ready to return to our hostel, but unfortunately for us, 'planes were returning from a mission over Germany and the bus was required to bring the airmen back to their billets. So we all had to get out and go back into the hall ... we tried to ring our hostel to explain why we would be late but we couldn't get through ... eventually the bus returned ... the village girls were taken home first and we were nearly last. It must have been well after 2 am when the bus stopped outside our hostel ... A very annoyed deputy matron came and let us in, and although we tried to explain, she wouldn't listen. We all went off to bed in disgrace! ... needless to say we didn't go to Egmere again.[197]

Dances were not the only entertainment on site. Cinema had become an increasing important aspect of British life, and the war had seen a colossal increase in cinema attendance from an estimated 19 million attendees a week in 1939, to over 30 million in 1945.[198] Proportionately, it was no different on the airfield, with some attending twice a day.[199] Any absence of the cinema was keenly felt, as Keith Thompson reflects, 'Sunday 1 April 1945: 'Blowing like billio [sic; should read Billy-O]. No lights so no cinema'.[200] The films shown at the camp cinema were provided by Ensa, initially, rather irregularly, but from 18 December 1944, 'every night, with a change of programme twice a week'.[201] For those who preferred audio rather than visual, there was the Station Music Circle. Holding its inaugural meeting on 6 August 1944, playing gramophone records, it presented programmes 'of light classics'.[202] With increasing popularity,[203] it settled in the information room[204] in the Naafi Block,[205] meeting weekly until the end of the war.[206]

Entertainment was not just restricted to the recorded, there were also live shows, most frequently in the airmans' dining hall.[207] Mostly, these shows were performed, as regularly as once a week, by Ensa.[208] Bernard Beaumont, a local schoolboy, had managed to acquire passes for Ensa shows and films.[209] On occasions when he forgot his pass, he still managed to persuade the orderly officer that 'he had a right to be there'.[210] The shows covered a wide spectrum of entertainment; variety, comedy, plays, classical recitals, ballet, big-band swing and sing-along.[211] Plays included, *Thunder Rock*,[212] a 1939 play by Robert Audrey and a 1942 film starring Michael Redgrave; *Round About213* by J B Priestley and *Acacia Avenue214* by Mabel and Denis Constanduros. The Conesford Players, a theatre company from Norwich, produced Noel Coward's *Private Lives* to a large audience;[215] a contentious choice given his assertions that Norfolk is 'very flat'.

RAF stations did, at times, attract big names. These included Blanche Coleman's Ladies Orchestra[216] and Tommy Kinsman and his Band,[217] both very popular bands playing ballroom music; the RAF Gang Show,[218] formed by Ralph Reader, singer, dancer and choreographer,[T] and even a performance by the world-renowned Kyasht Ballet.[219] A Station Concert Party also put on productions throughout their time at RAF North Creake, both on the camp and in the local area.[220] One of their productions, *Candlelight Vanities*, includes an unknown Eric Sykes, performing a 'potted pantomime', titled *Little Cock-Cinder Boots*, where he plays Fairy Slapanfondlit! One assumes this is the same Eric Sykes who would later find fame. We are not certain he was stationed at RAF North Creake,[U] but it does seem likely. Another well-received Station Concert Party production was *Drawn from Life;* 'a very fine performance … a most original show … with admirable thoroughness'.[221]

To improve fitness, sport was encouraged on the station with fixtures announced on the DROs.[222] Facilities on site included a brick-built gym, squash courts, and football, rugby and cricket pitches; surprising on what was a 'temporary' airfield. As the station geared-up operationally, an active programme of sports and fitness was arranged[223]

T The RAF Gang Show was the services' equivalent to Ensa recruited from the ranks of the RAF; on condition they were not aircrew or skilled engineers. Concerned about welfare, particularly on remote, RAF camps, the RAF Gang Show had a dual role, to boost morale and to report back on any rising discontent. Both Peter Sellars and Dick Emery served with the RAF Gang Show (Brownswood: 2019: unpaginated).

U Generally, a Station Concert Party involved members from the units on the station concerned (groundcrew or aircrew), but not exclusively. Occasionally, personnel from nearby stations may join (Delve: 7/2/2024).

by the Sports Officer.[224] Football and cricket matches were played regularly on and around RAF North Creake, with an inter-sectional football tournament among the RAF trades including squadron armoury, electrical and instruments section, RAF Regiment Bofors, and RAF Regiment Hispanos.[V][225] The ultimate winners were the Hispanos who won shortly before the RAF Regiments were disbanded to serve on other fronts.[226]

Games were also played against other RAF stations and local football teams.[227] The teams from the area included Walsingham Football Club (who the RAF North Creake team beat 11-0)[228] and even Norwich City. Such matches would generally attract quite a crowd.[229] Bernie How was a keen footballer and, in his own words 'was useful'. As a lifelong Ipswich fan, the result of ten goals to Norwich City and one to RAF North Creake[230] must have been particularly galling. Bernie never mentioned the Norwich City match, but he did regale us with tales of another game:

> we played this army team … 'you know who you're opposite and who you'll be meeting in the field?' I said, 'no.' 'It's Dickie Dawson', he was at Wolverhampton Wanderers of course. He toyed with us.[231]

The greatest rivalry was saved for the other local RAF stations. RAF Docking, Foulsham, Little Snoring and Great Massingham were all competed against with mixed results.[232] There was also an active cricket team, generally playing against outside teams, including one from the village of Egmere,[233] but, once again, the main opponents were other RAF stations.[234] There were also rugby, hockey, badminton and netball tournaments;[235] with every week a number of sporting fixtures scheduled.[236] RAF North Creake even hosted a sports day in July 1944,[237] with 'an enthusiastic crowd [that] watched the events for which there were plenty of entries'. 199 Squadron team scored the most

---

V Both Bofors (or sometimes spelt Beaufors) and the Hispanos were anti-aircraft guns used by the RAF Regiment in airfield defence and embraced as team names.

points with Harold Sturrock being awarded overall champion.[238] Phyllis Willmott, wrote in a letter to a friend that she 'only entered one race, the long jump, and no prizes: a fine mess I made of that, making a flying headlong crash into the sand having tripped over the springboard'.[239]

With such entertainment and distraction provided some have suggested that 'it reads like a holiday camp, pity about the war!'.[240] Indeed, they did even provide a rest camp in the pine woods near the lifeboat station[241] at Wells-next-the-Sea, for:

> personnel from the [RAF 100 Group] Stations with the most packed sleeping accommodation ... various camps and sites were inspected from the point of view of sanitation and hygiene and general suitability, and the finally selected site was at High Cape, on the coastal site just west of Wells-on-Sea.[242]

Interestingly, no member of airfield personnel with a record of having malaria was allowed to go,[243] as there was concern that a saltwater malaria-carrying mosquito was breeding there.[244] It was inspected, but no breeding colonies were found.[245] Nonetheless, the camp proved unpopular and did not last long.[246]

While accepting the need for a rest camp, there could be no collective time off for all airfield personnel. Even with notable public holidays, the operational requirements made the collective celebration of religious or cultural festivals almost impossible. One partial exception was Christmas 1944. Plans were made for an extensive programme of Christmas celebrations ('subject to operational commitments')[247] which would commence on Christmas Eve.[248] Aircrews were detailed for operations that evening with the last aircraft landing back on the station at 21:10 hours.[249] In their absence, celebrations had already begun with *Once Upon a Time*, starring Cary Grant, showing in the cinema in the afternoon, followed by a 'concert by the Station Concert party'.[250] The Station Glee Singers, who had been touring villages to raise funds for the Wells Cottage Hospital,[251] returned to lead carol singing 'at 22:30 hours in Institute'.[252]

In the printed programme of events, Norman Bray thanked everyone for their endeavours:

> You have all worked very well indeed and your efforts are sincerely and gratefully appreciated. I hope it will make your Christmas all the more enjoyable to know that you have been instrumental in saving the lives of thousands of our gallant crews, and that there is many a household in Britain and the Empire whose present joy would have been turned to sorrow but for the work you have done.[253]

On Christmas Day both squadrons were officially stood down, and the day started with a parade and carol service followed by a comic football match, 'Officers v. Sergeants'.[254] The latter were 'soundly beaten'.[255] Throughout the day there were sporting competitions, but the main event was the cycling derby.[256] Participants cycled once around the perimeter track, starting and finishing at the Control Tower.[257] Only unmodified service bicycles were to be used, and winning participants would receive prizes of cash and beer.[258] A member of 171 Squadron groundcrew came first; his name is not recorded.[259] There was also a WAAF bicycle race, 'same conditions but shorter route'; the winner is also not recorded.[260]

Christmas dinner was served in the airmen's mess and 'in accordance with usual Royal Air Force custom, about 100 Officers and senior N.C.O.s carried out the good work of serving Christmas dinner to the airmen and airwomen'.[261] Officers relieved all airmen and airwomen on duty watch for the duration of the meal.[262] For Phyllis Willmott, her shift in meteorology started at 16:00 hours, but with no flying, the 'Control Tower was quiet'.[263] However, personnel sending best wishes and poems around on the teleprinters, may have proved a distraction.[264] Between 20:30 and 01:00 hours there was a Christmas party for all ranks and guests,[W] where Father Christmas delivered

---

W It seems likely that this was the occasion that mischievous personnel at RAF North Creake attempted to get John Gurney of Walsingham Abbey drunk. He seldom had a drink and they were unsuccessful (Meath Baker: 11/3/2024).

'everything but a Whisky and Soda'. It also promised 'free refreshments (except beer!)'.[265] 'A grand time was had by all.'[266]

On Boxing Day, there were further sports played and the station commander and officers entertained groundcrew NCOs in the officers' mess 'in appreciation of their loyal and good work'.[267] Norman Bray also visited Ely RAF hospital with gifts for RAF North Creake personnel. In the evening there was a 'Liberty run'[X] to Kings Lynn and Fakenham until 00:30 hours and a 'whist drive and social in the Institute for RAF and WAAF corporals and below; relatives and friends invited'.[268] All ranks were also encouraged to pass on Christmas greetings onto the Naafi staff; 'though few in number they have done their best to maintain the service in the face of many difficulties, not least the grave shortage of staff'.[269]

Festivities continued throughout the Christmas week, including an Ensa show, dances and a farewell 'to our poultry farm!'[270] However, operations were detailed for the last three nights of the year, although 'the lads returned from operations in time to join the station New Year's Eve Party'.[271] Ron Maden wrote home that it 'was very good considering the circumstances'.[272] Six days later he was killed in operations over Germany.[273]

> Goodbye, Nineteen Forty Four,
> We don't want you any more,
> But we'll work like bees inside a hive
> To end the War in 'Forty Five'. [274]

Christmas and New Year has always been an important time in our calendar. Not for any religious reason, but because it is a time for pause and reflection. Before we moved to Norfolk, we always had large Christmas parties. Alas, the parties were no longer possible as it was too far for our friends to come just before Christmas, but they came for New Year's Eve.

X The Liberty run was a transport service provided for airfield personnel.

Our initial Christmases in the Control Tower were brief affairs, the needs of the project limiting our ability to celebrate. We did decorate, but not until Christmas Eve. Before we opened the B&B we were drawn to local celebrations; the Wells Christmas Tide being a particular highlight, where Father Christmas sails straight in from Lapland, accompanied by dancing snowmen/women; who could want for more? Unless it is Christmas drinks in Walsingham; a spectacular and unexpected evening of storming good fun. On the day itself, we would walk to the pub with Cillian and push the project from our minds, mostly.

After the B&B opened, we needed to plan social time more. With Christmas and New Year an option for paying guests, we started celebrating our Christmas on the twelfth night. We also reintroduced our Christmas party, but mostly for local friends. Some friends from further afield did make it, but generally it was too far and too remote.

While RAF North Creake was reasonably remote, there were relatively large towns around. Kings Lynn is approximately 20 miles, Norwich similar, and the smaller towns of Fakenham (eight miles) Wells-next-the Sea (three miles), with the villages of Walsingham (2.5 miles) and North Creake (3.5 miles). Liberty transport was often provided to the larger towns:

> for dances and pubs; bout all there was really. They used to have dances there quite regular … [Dances were good?] as they go, yeah. Never hardly went to Norwich, it was a bit too far.[275]

Better-off personnel often owned cars, and then these distances were nothing. Keith Thompson bought a car for £35[Y] which subsequently 'burnt 2 qts. of oil'[276] in one short journey. When he did use it, with tyres so hard to come by, he inevitably suffered punctures, indeed between buying his car in March 1945, and leaving RAF North Creake in June 1945, he experienced 18 flat tyres; with two on one day.[277] Another crew managed to buy an 'Austin 7 for £10 between us'.[278] However, it

---

Y   As a navigator, Keith Thompson would have been paid around £5 a week (Hammerton: 1943: 13).

appeared the vehicle was a disappointment, as it was 'difficult to get all crew in at once'.[279]

If a car was not an option, a bicycle was the best opportunity for independent transport. For Phyllis Willmott, immediately after arriving at RAF North Creake, the 'priority … was getting bicycles'.[280] Vic Polichek, like many others, had brought a bicycle with him, which he had purchased new while stationed in Scotland; 'sadly someone stole it while I was on the squadron. Never did locate it so I suppose an R.A.F. chap took it home to his family'.[281] Gordon Dennison wrote explaining the advantages of a bicycle; 'it will save me a lot of walking',[282] he continues, 'our whole crew has one now except for one and I imagine he will be having one soon'.[283]

The bicycle represented freedom: the ability to get around independently and during stand-downs to get a break from the camp. Many spent their free time cycling as there was 'not much else around',[284] and touring the 'area on my RAF bicycle'[285] seemed like a good option; setting 'off in the afternoon on a ride down the hill to explore what the village of Walsingham had to offer':[286]

Vic Polichek on his bicycle (second from left) with his crew (Jayne Jennings).

free-wheeling all the way down to Little Walsingham on those rare 'days off' having sometimes stayed in bed until nine o'clock – a rare luxury! Having a late breakfast at a little café there, bacon and egg (a *real* egg). I can't remember how much it cost but in those dark days it seemed a meal fit for a king. [287]

Eating seemed to feature a good deal in airfield life. Wilf Thompson recalls, that when 'passing Holkham Hall Estate, they would nip over the wall and fill their tunics with apples',[288] or more legitimately, personnel would visit a café and have 'baked beans and wartime dried egg as we read the papers, discussed last night's "op" and wondered about tonight's'.[289] Alternatively, in Walsingham, there was 'tea in a quaint old cottage with leaded windows, where bowls of marigolds and cowslips on the tables brightened the gloom of low ceilings and heavy beams'.[290]

Within easy walking distance of the Airfield Site was Quarles Farm where William and Anne Hudson (Quarles tenant farmers) used to hold tennis parties to which RAF North Creake personnel 'were invited for a bit of relaxation. It was a beautiful grass court'.[291] Otherwise, from the perimeter track, 'you could free-wheel'[292] into Wells-next-the-Sea. Stand-downs afforded you the opportunity, 'in fine weather … [to] cycle along the causeway by the little harbour and laze in the sun on the sand-dunes and beaches',[293] but it was 'a good slog coming back'.[294]

While some were off exploring the area and seeing the sights, others preferred the cinema in Wells or Fakenham, although in Fakenham, seats could be difficult to obtain:

the place was always full of Italian prisoners of war. Memory spotlights without pride, the night that some of us brave boys in blue fortified at a nearby hostelry, then marched into that cinema to turf out the Italians. As I remember, they went without argument. Not so the theatre management. They made a rare old stink. As the saying goes there was 'trouble back at the camp'.[295]

There were also dances at Holkham Hall,[296] cultural entertainment with artists including Lionel Tertis, the violist,[297] or even parties for officers hosted by Dr Scott, the GP in Wells in his 'pleasant Georgian house'.[298] However, the most frequent reason for mounting a bike, was to get to the pub. Ken Hartley remembers:

> there were not many occasions at North Creake when the lads in the radar section could go out en masse for a booze-up … [when] the whole squadron was put on stand-down … several of us … would all cycle down to Wells on our battered service bikes, park them outside the Edinburgh and go to our normal upstairs room. There the mild and bitter would flow, sent up, several flagons at a time, on the 'dumb waiter' … on these rare occasions, having saved up our pennies, we would let ourselves go and have a very enjoyable night.[299]

The 'fishermen type pubs'[300] in Wells were popular, with the Crown supposedly out of bounds[301] to all but officers. Indeed, Michael Renaut's wife was lodging at the Crown and remembers his crew 'joining them, and everybody being so happy and jolly'.[302] Wilf Thompson's crew favoured 'the Hero' pub in Burnham Overy Staithe 'for a few beers',[303] although it was too far for most, who preferred the pubs in Little Walsingham[304] or, as with the staff of the SSQ, the 'Half Moon at Great Walsingham which was small, friendly and rather scruffy'.[305] However, most frequently airmen would visit the Black Swan in North Creake, or as it was affectionately known, the Mucky Duck.[306] On asking Bernie How, why, he answered with a twinkle in his eye, 'the land girls were stationed next door'. And so they were. With the high demands on labour, too few from Norfolk had volunteered to work on farms, therefore the county became an importer of young women.[307] At North Creake village, a hostel for over 100 land girls[308] had been established in the Shooting Box, next to the Mucky Duck;[309] '[the pub] was always crowded. Land girls and the RAF ... just ordinary beer, you wouldn't get any of the better beer, just the cheap stuff. Always seemed plenty'.[310]

Aircrew tended to have few friendships outside their crew[311] and were most often a strong cohesive unit:

> Johnny wouldn't come out; he wasn't a drinking man ... But the rest of us were quite together yeah ... [the wireless operator] he could drink, he could drink more than me. Harry his name was ... him, me, the mid-upper gunner, the bomb aimer, he liked a few pints.[312]

There were exceptions; if your roots were local the same bond may not exist, as you might often prefer the comforts of home, to the company of your crew. Roy Mitchell, an air gunner in 171 Squadron, from Brancaster (six miles from the base), lived 'unofficially' at home:

> I didn't know the other fellows as I should have done as I wasn't on the Station that much ... I used to get up in the morning, whether I had been flying or not, and have my breakfast and go down to the pub for a game of cards. I'd go up to Creake and say to the pilot, 'anything on?' and he would say if we were going to be operational, or we might be doing an air test ... I would be there when I was needed and had a bed allocated to me in the billet ... but I only used it when there was a short break between jobs.[313]

For most aircrew, and similarly for some on the ground, lifelong friendships were made, both inside and outside the camp. Norman Turnbull, an airfield controller, became friendly with a family in Walsingham and frequently visited them until his death in 1985. Roy Gibson, the son in the family, still talks very fondly of him today.[314] Eric Nicholas from Penrith in Cumbria, remembers seeing someone he knew from his hometown in the canteen soon after arriving at RAF North Creake. He had met Frank Newall at school, but after meeting up at the airfield they became lifelong friends.[315] For others, it was not the case. Roy Berrill, in meteorology, explains, 'you met so many people and you don't stay long enough to make proper friends ... we'd all got a job to do, and we got on with it'.[316] He did meet aircrew in the mess, although, as he recounted in 2022:

> I didn't get close ... because they came and went. I was more interested with my colleagues in the Met. Office and the Air Traffic Control because they were more relevant as far as I was concerned ... I did know one or two of the ground crew, the maintenance people ... but I have no contact with them – not now.[317]

He does remember the operator of the link trainer, Peter Black: he had a car and they would tour Norfolk; 'he came to my wedding but never saw him again'.[318] Nonetheless, aircrew generally 'drank, womanized and often went on leave together'.[319] For Bernie How's crew, womanising led to a minor division:

> [the rear gunner] he'd go out, he had a girl in Walsingham so he was occupied ... he was already married in Canada ... he was a scammer.[320]

The heightened emotions of war led to what became known as 'war aphrodisia',[321] understandably as 'we were young and could die tomorrow'.[322] Phyllis Willmott observed; 'unfettered youth added to the upheavals of war made a flammable mixture'.[323] And she wasn't immune to its effects, with a 'local boyfriend ... nothing in it of course!'.[324] However, she subsequently developed a 'soft spot for [a] particular pilot',[325] which rapidly became more serious:

> Adam had a black Ford. We drove around the countryside, got out of it to dally in woods, haystacks or sand-dunes and, parked for hours on the edge of the WAAF site, made love inside it until all hours of the night.[326]

Ultimately, the relationship ended with Phyllis heartbroken; they'd been thrown together by war, but were not suited; as she, an 'aspiring intellectual ... [and he] pretend[ing] not to be intelligent simply to avoid serious discussion'.[327]

Sex was a frequent compensation for the stress of aircrew life[328] and RAF North Creake was a typical wartime station. Paul Berry's mother, Jean Berry, always recounted that her Naafi dormitory included:

> the abundant 'Smudge' Smith who was a popular feature of airfield life. Jean's bed in the hut was close to a window and it fell to her to open it at all hours to allow Smudge to return from her night-time liaisons ... one story suggested Smudge and a hapless airman had to abandon their tryst rather quickly one evening, and the next morning a corset was found blowing in the breeze across one of the main runways.[329]

'Loose morals' were viewed as 'destructive of discipline',[330] however, marriage, the 'obvious alternative to casual relationships, was discouraged'.[331] Even so, many marriages did arise from friendships made on airfields, marriages which have lasted the course; Jean and Albert Berry, having met at RAF North Creake, were married in 1946. Betty Price married Bill in August 1944, while stationed on the airfield:

> a great number from the aerodrome came to the wedding, the ceremony was held in the parish church at Wells-on-Sea. Our best man was Reggie Arrowsmith, known as 'Digby' and another electrician, a big fellow called 'Spud' Murphy gave me away.[332]

Given that 'today's wife could so easily become tomorrow's widow',[333] many agonised over marriage proposals. The morals of a WAAF in Phyllis Willmott's hut, with thick make-up and hair teased into a high pile on which 'her cap would hardly fit',[334] were viewed with suspicion by her hut mates. But they were wrong; she was actually struggling with conflicted emotions. Should she:

Nigel starts to lay the kitchen floor in prepartion for the Rayburn and installation of the heating system (Control Tower Archive).

Chaos in the Control Tower. The spare room filled with furniture and bathroom suites, November 2012 (Control Tower Archive).

Nigel reinstating the doorway to the Control Room and laying reclaimed floorboards, May 2013 (Control Tower Archive).

With the roof finished and render patched, our son Cillian and his friends hold a a painting party, June 2013 (Control Tower Archive).

*Re-opening the middle windows on the front elevation of the
Control Tower, April 2014 (Control Tower Archive).*

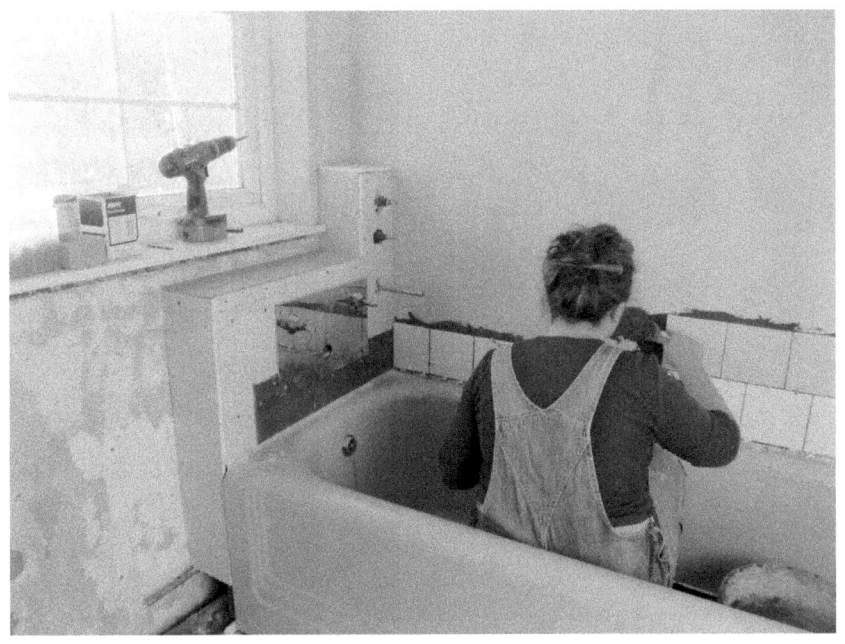

*Claire commences tiling in the Signals Room en suite with
plumbing works ongoing (Control Tower Archive).*

Breakfast in the midst of chaos. Grabbing some toast while windows are fitted and rubble is removed, April 2013 (Control Tower Archive).

Cillian ponders the distance still to go when erecting the scaffold tower (Control Tower Archive).

A rare day off in the convertible on a trip with friends to the Wighton Scarecrow Festival (Howard Partridge: Control Tower Archive).

*Scrubbed-up and ready (enough) to open the B&B, June 2014
(Paul Macro Photography: Control Tower Archive).*

*The Control Tower with the hedge and garden starting to
mature, August 2022 (Control Tower Archive).*

Guest living room November 2023 (Steven Adams Photography: Control Tower Archive).

Stirling Suite annex en suite bathroom November 2023 (Steven Adams Photography: Control Tower Archive).

Signals Room November 2023 (Steven Adams Photography: Control Tower Archive).

View towards the Control Tower from the site of the postwar concrete yard November 2023 (Steven Adams Photography: Control Tower Archive).

RAF North Creake memorial site November 2021 (Paul Macro Photography: Control Tower Archive).

Dedication Day for the memorial with Bernie How, Flight Engineer 199 Squadron RAF North Creake, 5 June 2022 (Steven Adams Photography: Control Tower Archive).

against her own sense of propriety, be willing to go further with her fellow, who claimed that she should because he wanted to marry her, 'I don't want to end up like Doris' ... Doris was a girl who had recently been quietly discharged when she was found to be pregnant.[335]

Wartime promotes a prevalence of such heightened emotions, particularly when fuelled by alcohol. This often led to poor judgement and reduced standards of behaviour. Punishments fill the pages of the casualty lists; G H Cathcart received a severe reprimand for 'refusing to produce his identification card on demand, using obscene language to a Warrant Officer [and] being insolent';[336] F/S Gold forfeited three day's pay for failing to obey an order having been stood down:

> he was told he could proceed out of camp and to return at 09:30 on the 25/1/44. This he failed to do ... absent 3 days 3 hours ... wearing W.O. badges and cap (Field Service) prior to effective date of promotion.[Z337]

These incidents bear all the hallmarks of alcohol-induced antics. Similarly, Phyllis Willmott writes home that 'we have had some trouble here over WAAFs getting drunk. This had led to one Queen Bee stopping any dances on camp. To me that seems a queer method of keep[ing] girls on the straight and narrow path'.[338] Drink-fuelled trouble wasn't just confined to camp:

> complaints have been received concerning the rowdiness of R.A.F. and W.A.A.F. personnel when leaving local village dance halls. The station commander feels sure that this disturbance is caused by the few and that the majority of personnel are content to enjoy themselves without annoying others. He requests all

---

Z   Officially, members of military personnel were not deserters until absent for more than 21 days (Hawton: 1944: 148). At the end of the war there were an estimated 20,000 deserters at large, with no ration cards 'dependant for food and clothing either on private charity or by breaking the law' (Keesings: 1947: 8392). In 1950 the figure was 7,000-8,000; between 2,000-3,000 of whom had deserted during the war (Keesings: 1950: 10,760).

decent-minded personnel to help him maintain order at outside functions and thus save him from being compelled to put these places out of bounds.[339]

After a few drinks even getting home could prove problematic, as personnel would 'mount [their] bikes and wobble back to camp'.[340] The unfamiliar countryside, darkness and fog could all play havoc with the sense of direction. Vic Polichek recalls the evening he cycled 15 miles with his crew for a liaison with four women, who worked in a nearby factory:

> going over was just fine for it was daylight ... After a pleasant evening and about midnight, Bill and I proceeded down the road for base, of course fog had set in so naturally we became disorientated ... about 2 or 3 hours later, standing at a cross road intersection, wondering which road to take ... a distant sound came closer and closer, turning out to be an airman on a cycle. Anxiously we asked if by chance he was heading for North Creake air base. Follow me, he said, and happily we did. Boy what a relief.[341]

On another occasion Vic Polichek and his flight engineer, Bill Whitworth, had been at the Mucky Duck:

> [we] started cycling down the street when we heard a voice calling, 'oye there, oye there, stop!!!' It was the local bobby of course. I swerved to go around him however Bill ran right into him, right between the legs. Needless to say Bill received a good dressing down ... from a distance I could hear some harsh words being said. I am sure that bobby had an uncomfortable sleep that night.[342]

Denis Smallwood recalls 'pedalling like mad with no lights showing, the local policeman used to shout, "where are your lights?" to which came the chorus reply, next to our livers'.[AA][343] Despite such flippancy, the police were a constant source of concern for returning airfield personnel. Phyllis Willmott wrote home 'I am on a summons for riding my cycle without lights ... it really is a trifle worrying for I am certainly in for a hell of a lecture from the WAAF C.O. ... and if by some real bad luck it is discovered that on the night of the crime, I had not even booked out, I really am in the soup'.[344] Similarly, Ken Hartley recalls:

> there was a whole crowd of us, aircrew as well as groundcrew, officers as well as sergeants and other ranks. I don't think anyone had lights on his bike – you just didn't bother in those days ... batteries were not easy to find in wartime and they also cost money ... suddenly shadowy figures pounced on us from behind the roadside bushes! Being rather befuddled at the time we didn't at first realise who they were. Then it dawned on us that the shadowy figures were coppers, some in uniform, some in plain clothes. Those ... who were lucky pedalled furiously and were able to escape their clutches. Others like me were stopped, had our names and numbers taken, and several days later were summoned to appear at the court in Little Walsingham ... [and] fined five shillings for riding a bicycle without lights.[345]

* * *

Initially, nights out were a rare occasion for us. When we did go out it was in the daytime, task shopping and mostly for building materials. We allowed ourselves James Beck auctions in Fakenham on a Thursday, ostensibly for the purpose of picking up cheap furniture for the project. It was true in part, but mostly it was for the break. On the way home we'd stop at the Bull for egg and chips, we began to get to know people and to make friends. James Beck Auctions had furnished us with many vintage bikes,[AB] a good few of which were pre-war for that 'authentic'

AA 'Lights and livers' is a butchery term to describe offal. Lights refers to lungs.

AB We had a plan to offer vintage bikes for hire, but this proved too complicated to enact, and out of around the 35 vintage bikes we had, we now have four exclusively for our own use.

period ride to the pub, or to the Real Ale Shop for four pints of beer to lubricate the build. It was these visits that allowed a friendship to grow with Teddy and Sally Maufe of Branthill Farm (the location of the Real Ale Shop), whose family moved-in in 1936. This populated our conversations with plenty of tales of RAF North Creake's war. With Teddy we went to a wonderful beer tasting at the Jolly Sailors in Brancaster, jointly hosted by Mark of Beeston Brewery, who would later produce our memorial beer; *Drink to Remember*.

As a break from the Control Tower, pubs began to feature more commonly, first we walked west, involving the Lord Nelson in Burnham Thorpe, but generally, our travels started to take us east, to familiar holiday haunts of the Three Horseshoes, the Carpenters Arms and the Chequers in Binham, where we'd sit out front and watch the swifts whirl around the summertime skies. However, the new favourite was the Bull in Walsingham. Full of local characters (and useful trades!), we spent many happy evenings there. The night-time walks back, whether in winter or summer, were also special. Having received Norman Turnbull's photographs of the surrounding area as well as the airfield itself, we began to realise how little had changed since the war.

Nights out with neighbours began to expand more generally into their social groups and we became socially busier. The initial promise of close friendships with this group faded with time. Who can say why a friendship fades? But they did. Nonetheless, we remain companionable.

In the build-up to opening, for the purposes of our social media profile as well as directly for our guests, began the critical process of learning more about the area. Wedding Wheels recces helped, taking us to places we wouldn't have considered, or didn't know about. We also found ourselves, often aided by visiting friends, on the Norfolk tourist trail; seal trips, boats out of Wells quay and walking around the spectacular snowdrops at Walsingham Abbey. We revisited our favourite holidaying haunts of Warham Camp, Binham Priory and so on. Walks on beaches always featured, and Norfolk has some spectacular beaches, but we also explored inland, finding quiet off-road routes through green lanes and holloways.

Opening kept us entertained with the coming and going of guests, many of whom, over time, became friends. Sometimes, after a busy weekend and with a night off, we'd buy a couple of pints at the Chequers to switch off and then purchase some treats from Trevor's shop in Binham, come home, light the fire and watch a favourite film, such as *A Matter of Life and Death*, thereby reclaiming our hearthside.

With the build mostly having come to an end and with the business settling in, we began once again to crave cultural experiences. We'd enjoyed the film festivals promoted by Screen-next-the-Sea in Wells and we'd even sampled comedy in the dazzling lights of Norwich, but what we really needed was music. More specifically, our favourite bands. We had visited London on gig trips to see bands such as the Flaming Stars and Vic Godard & the Subway Sect, but with the opening of the B&B, it was difficult to get away. The last gig we went to in London was to see one of our favourite bands. In the weeks leading up to it, I had noticed the name 'Phil Wilson' on our booking calendar but didn't think it could be *the* Phil Wilson of the same legendary 1980s band, the June Brides whom we were due to see the following weekend. But it was. A pity I gave him my cold, just before his 100 Club gig. I can testify, from personal experience, it didn't spoil the night.

His visit set a train of thought in motion, leading to us tentatively arranging gigs in Norfolk for bands we like (and have access to) which may, in time become a feature of the Control Tower offering. The first, in November 2023, featured Pete Astor performing alongside Neil Scott at our inaugural 'Stand-Down' gig. It was an extraordinarily wonderful night. As joyous as such initiatives are, they still create considerable and inescapable work. Similar to essential duty shifts on a wartime airfield, a live-in hospitality business means there is never truly time-off unless you take leave.

Leave promised a complete escape from camp; physically if not emotionally. Aircrew received more leave than groundcrew,[346] but, those ground staff on shifts could attach rest days to their leave and extend their period away:[347]

in spite of difficulties of travelling throughout the war, it seems astonishing ... how much time and energy people, including me, spent moving up and down the country ... [Hitch-hiking] was not really so easy ... and, although I did hitch-hike home from there on occasions when I had time to spare but could not get a travel pass, I normally travelled to North Creake by train. Typically of the times, this had meant first taking a train on the branch line to Norwich – which sometimes would take two hours to cover the thirty miles![348]

Vivian Cooper (on right with an oar) with his crew on leave in Cambridge (Judith Errington).

Roy Berrill recalls going on leave to see his fiancée in Ilford Essex.[349] 'At that time there was a railway that went right through to Wells',[350] where you could catch a train to Kings Lynn and from there a connection to London.[351] Passenger services took second place to the movement of troops or equipment needed for the war effort, so timetables were often disrupted,[352] and the journey of 100 miles to London could often take 'five good, slow, hours'.[353] Roy didn't go home very often:[354]

> on one particular day the train got about a mile out of Wells-on-Sea and got stuck in a snow drift … so we all had to get out and plough through the snow alongside the railway line on foot.[355]

Similarly, Phyllis Willmott remembers; 'I caught a train to London in the late afternoon, expecting to arrive at Liverpool Street early that evening and be home … before bedtime'.[356] However, as a result of bad snow:

> I spent the whole night in the unheated train, which started and stopped with infuriating uncertainty and pulled into London terminus at dawn the next day … I counted myself lucky to have had a seat and also – as I was travelling with Desmond from the Met Office (who was in fact longing to get home to his fiancée) – to have someone to snuggle up to when trying to doze and keep warm through a very cold night.[357]

Others didn't need to rely on trains, for instance Bernie How's Canadian navigator, Johnny Russell, had a car; 'on the way to London he would take me to my parent's house, have a drink and a bite to eat and then pick me up again on his way back through'.[358]

We'd maintained some holidays throughout the build: visits to Craswall in the Black Mountains or Lindisfarne in Northumberland, were a much-needed respite from the chaos. However, as the business developed, we could neither afford the time away nor spare the expense. We did make one trip to Lincolnshire, a county we love, and while we had a lovely time walking and seeking out antique shops, it did occur to us, it was something we could do from home in Norfolk. And for five years, between bookings, that is what we did.

Recently, with the business more established, we've felt the need to roam again. We have now had some delightful holidays in our favourite UK haunts. Getting away makes it easier to relax, although you always have to stay on top of bookings. And even when you're in a restaurant in the remote foothills of the Brecon Beacons, there is always a reminder, when a fellow diner from the next table asks, 'aren't you from the Control Tower?'. Luckily, we adore it.

A DOVE OVER EUROPE

'ADOLF?? DEAD?? …
BERLIN TAKEN !!!!'.[1]

On the morning of 2 May 1945, the newspapers proclaimed the death of Adolf Hitler. All over Britain celebrations were being held. In a Norfolk pub they had pinned-up the newspaper front page and, all night, revellers raised their glass to it.[2] At RAF North Creake, while spirits must have been high, there was no time to celebrate. Operations were on.

There had been no Main Force bombing sorties since 26/27 April 1945, 'and most squadrons thought that their war in Europe was over'.[3] However, Allied intelligence suggested that the Germans were planning to reinforce troops in Norway and were amassing forces in the Baltic Ports, especially at Kiel,[4] in order to mount a last stand.[5] Fighting in Norway would be difficult and the Allies were keen that this should be avoided. Accordingly, 'to prevent further loss of life and prevent a continuation of the war in Norway',[6] it was decided to bomb Kiel harbour. Main Force would not be detailed for this operation, instead it would be maximum effort for the RAF 8 Group (Pathfinders) and RAF 100 Group.[7]

There were four elements to the raid, utilising a total of 293 aircraft.[8] The force of bombers would first attack airfields in the Kiel area,[9] followed by a further three raids on Kiel, Schleswig and a decoy to the North Frisian Islands at Flensburg. [10] The bombing at Kiel (the primary target) was set to commence at 23:00 hours, with a second wave attacking exactly an hour later.[11]

It was to be a record night for RAF 100 Group with 82 heavies taking part.[12] At RAF North Creake, 39 Halifaxes, drawn from both squadrons, were detailed for operations (38 flying, one in reserve[13]); 'by far and away the largest number of aircraft and crews placed on the Battle Orders since moving to North Creake'.[14] Eight aircraft (four from 171 Squadron and four from 199 Squadron)[15] were prepared for Mandrel Screen operations, with each aircraft also carrying Window[16] and eight 500lb high explosive bombs.[17] 21 aircraft (12 of 171 Squadron and 11 from 199 Squadron) were detailed to form part of a Window/ bombing patrol to Kiel, and a further eight aircraft (two from 171 Squadron and six from 199 Squadron) were to take part in Mandrel / Window/bombing in the Schleswig area.[18]

The air officer commanding RAF 100 Group, Edward Addison, was present at RAF North Creake during the take-off and 'expressed satisfaction at the size of our final effort'.[19] Jim Feasey, along with many crew members, recalls the 'infamous'[20] incident that night, as described by Michael Renaut in his autobiography:

> we invited Lord Leicester and his wife and Mary Harvey and Silvia Combe to come over to the aerodrome to watch the take-off of a 'Maximum Effort' (strictly against the rules to have civilians present!). I remember I was lined up on the runway as the first aircraft to take off when suddenly, as I opened my throttles, I saw a private car driving down the runway towards us! I immediately closed down the power and waited as the car turned off towards the control tower. It turned out to be Mary

Harvey who had got herself lost on the perimeter track and had mistakenly driven straight down the main runway.[A21]

How this incident sat with Edward Addison is not discussed. The first Halifax took off from RAF North Creake at 20:31 hours, and the last at 21:14.[22] One (S H Werner's Halifax, NA275 EX-W) was late taking off due to technical difficulties but left at 21:30 hours.[23] In 45 minutes some 37 aircraft took off – averaging at one aircraft lifting into the air every one minute 20 seconds.[24] Halifax PN378 EX-A (P Brown) discovered that his compass was unserviceable, one hour and 17 minutes into the flight and was replaced by W A Short (Halifax PN385 EX-C) flying a more direct route to catch up.[25]

The Special Window Force flying the feint against Flensburg was made up of aircraft from the RAF 100 Group 'heavy' squadrons that were 'not engaged in other essential duties'.[26] This force was accompanied by four 171 Squadron Halifax, operating a Mandrel Screen to 'lend further credence to the spoof raid and, hopefully, convince the enemy controllers that the main attack that night was mounted against Flensburg'.[27]

In the primary attack on Kiel, the target was almost completely covered in cloud, but the radar systems, H2S and Oboe, were used to help 'see' through it.[28] RAF North Creake aircraft were dropping Window at 12,000 feet to 'create chaos with Würzburg interception and gun laying radar systems',[29] in order to protect other bombers flying towards target. Once complete, they dropped their own bombload. Les Currell, pilot on Halifax RG375 EX-R, known as the 'Jolly Roger' of 199 Squadron, describes the bomb-run:

[we were to] drop our bomb load and immediately commence a 180 degree turn to starboard and drop 200 feet of height. Half way through this turn there was a terrible impact and

A   There is some artistic licence in this tale from Michael Renaut. He was actually the fourth aircraft to take off from RAF North Creake (the second 171 Squadron aircraft; the first took off at 20:31 hours and Michael Renaut took off at 20:33 (199 Squadron & 171 Squadron ORBs)). However, many tell this tale and when I mentioned this to Mary's sister at a memorial fund-raising event, she said 'it sounds like the kind of thing she would have done'.

all control was lost. The order was to abandon the aircraft. Everything was in darkness and I think you would understand the chaos there was. As there did not seem to be anyone else left I released my seat harness and managed to grope my way to the place where the escape hatch was to be located. This was open and I managed to get myself through and out.[30]

Summaries of the operation suggest that little fighter activity had been encountered.[31] However, a number of Ju88 night-fighters had taken off to intercept the bombers. Indeed, Michael Renaut writes that his aircraft was attacked twice by what he believed to be the same Ju88; initially over Kiel and then again 70 miles off the Danish coast. He took violent evasive action on each occasion to escape the night-fighter's clutches.[32] Fritz Brandt of Nachtjagdgeschwader 3 attacked Halifax RG373 EX-T,[B][33] damaging the flying controls.[34] The wireless operator of Halifax NA675 6Y-R, Harry Freegard, remembers his aircraft had to avoid a collision with it by corkscrewing away; it 'made no attempt to change course',[35] indicating he suggests, that it had lost control as a result of enemy night-fighter fire.[36] Halifax EX-T flew on and then collided with EX-R, resulting in the impact that Les Currell describes.[C] The collision was probably witnessed by R Rawsthorn of 162 Squadron, who at debrief reported he witnessed a 'large explosion seen over the target area at 23:26 hours'.[37] Both aircraft, now stricken, plunged earthward. Approximately one hour later, F/Lt Watson of 163 Squadron saw what he thought was 'an aircraft on fire at the target area at 00:21 hrs';[38] what he probably witnessed was the burning remnants of the two Halifaxes. On board were:

Halifax EX-R

B   Fritz Brandt's last Luftwaffe report recorded this incident (http://internationalbcc.co.uk).

C   There are conflicting opinions from the various accounts as to which bomber collided with the other. I have chosen, for the sake of a clear narrative, to accept the statement of the surviving pilot. However, it should be noted that this may be incorrect although it would now be impossible to establish for certain one way or the other. As Philip Croft, Ken Croft's half-brother, observed, 'in my opinion, that's not important, as no blame can be apportioned, or ever should be' (Croft: 9/7/20).

Arthur Andrew Bradley (RAF) Navigator, aged 23
Francis Thomas Chambers (RAF) Bomb Aimer, aged 29
Leslie H Currell (RAAF) Pilot
Desmond Greenwood (RAF) Mid-Upper Gunner, aged 20
R. 'Scot' Hunter (RAF) Rear Gunner
Joseph Loth (RAF) Wireless Operator, aged 21
William Henry Vesey Mackay (RAF) Flight Engineer, aged 29
Reginald Henry Alfred Pool (RAF) Special Operator, aged 28

Halifax EX-T

William Frederick Bolton (RAF) Flight Engineer, aged 23
William Ernest Brooks (RAF) Pilot, aged 23
Kenneth Norman Crane (RAF) Rear Gunner
Keith Alexander Cameron Munro Gavin (RAF) Bomb Aimer, aged 22
Kenneth Norman Joseph Croft (RAF) Wireless Operator, aged 22
Alfred Samuel John Holder (RAF) Mid-Upper Gunner, aged 43
John Roger Lewis (RAF) Navigator, aged 21
Douglas Wilson (RAF) Special Operator, aged 21

Both aircraft crashed at Meimsdorf, approximately four kilometres south-south-west of the centre of Keil.[39] An eyewitness remembers; 'one [crashed] in the field next to the cemetery and the other came down some 3 – 4 fields away. An engine landed in the garden only a yard from the house'. They were 'the last Bomber Command aircraft to be lost in the war'.[40] A dubious honour for RAF North Creake.

Other than Les Currell (pilot EX-R), two further crew members survived the collision; R. 'Jock' Hunter (rear gunner) on Halifax EX-R and Ken Crane (rear gunner) on Halifax EX-T.[41] Les Currell remembers:

the parachute was only open a few moments when I hit the ground with a mighty thump. I knew that I had a fracture in my left ankle because as I tried to turn my foot trying to rise

I felt a grating of bones. I released my parachute and as I had
landed in a small field with a hedge fence I thought that my best
chance was to get to the hedge … I then managed to break off
a longish stick from the hedge and as I could still hear bombs
dropping and they appeared to be quite close I thought that if I
was caught, the people who caught me would not be friendly to
me as I had just been instrumented in bombing their territory,
so I reckoned the best option for me was to get as far away as
possible while it was still dark.[42]

Indeed, this was a very real threat and there is some suggestion that other
crew members did in fact survive the collision, only to be murdered on
the ground. While this assertion is reliant upon one witness account,
with many other examples of such attacks,[D] there is no real reason to
doubt its veracity:

[Ken Crane, rear gunner EX-T] had landed quite near the
plane's wreckage … and others, though badly injured, were still
alive. A group of armed and uniformed people arrived on the
scene, and shot them all. Crane said he was well hidden out of
sight … [this] was only revealed to me, this September [2020],
by Irene [Ken Croft's wife, who spoke to Ken Crane in the
1950s] … if it's true … [they] had to live with that information,
all those years, but thought it best not to share it, until right
near the end.[43]

Ken Croft and Douglas Wilson were found 50 yards from the crash
site[44] and are, if this account is correct, the most likely victims. Officially
it was believed that they had 'unsuccessfully baled out'.[45] However, Ken
Crane's official MI9 Interrogation statement makes no reference to this
shocking incident:

D See Brettingham: 2001: 166-168.

I was suddenly shot through the gun turret and found myself mid-air. I pulled the ripcord and parachuted down.

I landed in open country at about 01:00 hours (3 May) about two miles south of Kiel. I hid in the fields till 05:30 hours when I was picked up by a Dutchman slave worker. He took me to the home of a German merchant service man who sheltered me till 22:00 hours when the Dutchman fetched me and took me to his house. I remained there until 15:43 hours on 6 May when I reported to the British Army who had by that time entered Kiel.[46]

A further statement he made shortly after the war adds more colour:

I have no immediate recollection of what happened when the two aircraft collided and I cannot remember leaving my turret. My first memory of the incident is falling earthwards and, by sheer instinct, pulling the 'D' ring of my parachute and this built-in instinct saved my life. I reached the ground safe and unharmed. I was found by a Dutchman whom I discovered was married to a German lady and they lived in Kiel. I was taken to their apartment and hidden away from prying eyes, particularly those of the authorities. Later we heard a commotion outside their building and when my host had questioned the crowd he was told there was an abandoned train in a nearby siding containing Red Cross parcels. The Dutchman joined the rush outside making their way towards the train in the hope that they could lay their hands on some of the packages. Much later he returned laden with food parcels, which he and his wife proceeded to open as soon as they got them indoors. Among the usual things such as tea, sugar and chocolate they came across a strange white powder, of which they had no knowledge and were baffled by my explanation as to its purpose. For the first time in their lives they had encountered 'powdered milk' and for the rest of the night and into the early hours of the next morning we spent our time reconstituting the dried powder into milk for themselves and their neighbours' benefit.[47]

Ken Crane was officially the last evader of the war.[48] He was liberated by the British 21st Army Group[49] and arrived back in the UK on 9 May 1945;[50] the first day of peace in Europe since 2 September 1939.[E]

Les Currell, the pilot of Halifax EX-R, was, at the same time, struggling with a broken ankle and considering his options. He was officially recorded as a POW, however, increasingly annoyed at seeing statements to this effect, he eventually felt compelled to write his account of that night:

> I walked in a southerly direction hoping that I might meet up with allied troops who I knew were advancing towards Kiel. I crossed a couple of streams one of which I fell into. The water was fresh so I had a drink and filled the little container which is in the escape packs. I crossed a major road somewhere during the night. You will appreciate that by the time daylight came I was in a bad state of despair, I was so worried about so many things.
>
> I hung around the embankment which had a bit of cover on it for the rest of the day … When night came I moved off again and by this time the going was very painful and slow. I was afraid to take off my flying boot because I thought I would lose the support to my ankle which had swollen so much it was awfully tight and I thought I might not get my boot back on. I stumbled along for some time and by this time I was beginning to imagine things … in [a] hedge I saw what I thought was a soldier in uniform. I spoke to him and offered to surrender. There was no answer so I poked at him with a stick but actually there was not anyone there …

E Germany's unconditional surrender came into force at 23:01 hours on 8 May 1945, UK time, which corresponded with 00:01 hours on 9 May in Moscow, in the Soviet Union.

Just before dawn … I found some trees for shelter. There was no chance of sleeping so I just waited until daylight. When daylight came I could see what looked like farm buildings and as by this time I felt I could not go on any further on my own I decided to approach and ask for assistance.

No one came out to arrest me so I continued up to what looked like a farm. There were some fellows in uniform appeared. They did not seem like Germans … Anyway they did not harm me nor did they do anything for me except allowing me to spend the next night on some bags of corn. Anyway in the morning … [5 May 1945] these people in uniform had disappeared. Some other fellows in working clothes came and just picked me up and carried me to another building which was two or three hundred yards away. They were very good to me, they put me in one of their bunks … they told me that they were forced labour prisoners who had been transported up there from their homes in France to work on farms. The other men in uniform were Russians who had defected and became their guards and they told me they intended to hold me as a hostage but had changed their minds and cleared out before the allies got there.[51]

Eventually, the Frenchmen, risking their own lives, managed to get a message to the Allies, and on the 7 May 1945, liberation arrived in the form of a British officer in a jeep.[52] The officer also informed the 'Frenchmen that they were liberated and were free to make their way home as best they could'.[53] Les Currell was then driven to a number of hospitals in a bid to find a working x-ray machine. On one of the excursions the driver asked if he'd like a souvenir to take home; 'he went into one of the few buildings left standing and brought me out a brand new iron cross which I have to this day'.[54] Eventually, he was x-rayed and a temporary plaster cast applied. The following day he was transported back to England, arriving on 9 May 1945, when he was taken to a RAF hospital in Wroughton, Wiltshire.[55]

Very little is known of R 'Jock' Hunter, the second survivor from this aircraft, other than he became a prisoner of war.

On the night of the raid, in spite of the cloud, at 20,000 feet large fires could be seen on the ground over Kiel.[56] Towards morning, 'a large column of military vehicles departed in the direction of Flensburg on the Danish frontier'.[57] Contemporary German accounts describe how there was an 'upsurge in the population's morale'[58] And shortly after, Kiel 'was declared an open, undefended town'[59] and with this the military stores (and some civilian ones) containing rationed goods were thrown open to the public.[60] Four kilometres away at the aircraft crash site, a resident of Meimersdorf, a young boy at the time, remembers 'watching as the aircraft remains were pulled apart and the bodies removed'.[61] All 13 bodies were buried in an adjoining field at the edge of a small village cemetery at Meimersdorf.[62] In 1947 they were moved to Kiel War Graves Cemetery.[63] The Air Ministry informed the families:

> I am directed ... to inform you that the Graves Registration and Enquiry Service have found it necessary to remove your son's grave from Meimersdorf Cemetery to the British Cemetery at Kiel ... I am to explain that it is the practice of the Graves Service to transfer the graves of all British personnel who lost their lives in enemy territory into military cemeteries where facilities are available for their proper care and maintenance, in perpetuity.[64]

In 1994, Cyril Bradley, the brother of Arthur Bradley, the navigator on Halifax RG375 EX-R, went to pay homage to his lost brother. He visited their original resting place commenting that they 'had laid in perfect peace in a beautiful setting for just 2 ½ years'.[65] The acceptance of his brother's death had been an emotionally difficult process and shortly after Arthur was posted 'missing' he had tirelessly attempted to uncover the facts surrounding his loss. In a letter to Les Currell, he writes:

in one communication from the Air Ministry they say your windscreen was frosted over and that Bill was sat beside you in the co-pilot's seat, helping you on the look-out. If this was the case – when the collision took place Bill may have been thrown to the bottom of the kite near to Arthur. When you climbed down to the forward hatch, if the hatch was open and you didn't see Bill, Arthur, Frank or Joe, then they must be out, and believe me Les, till Russia and all the forests around have been searched I will never believe that they aren't out.[66]

The mother of William Mackay, at a similar time, also writes to Les Currell where she explains that 'we are very worried, the Ministry don't give us much help. You did not see him jump and I fear he may have stayed to give a hand, to a pal, do you think this is possible?'.[67] She continues and describes her state of anguish: 'my husband and I are away from our house as I am suffering very much [from] ... the shock I got on hearing the news'.[68] William Mackay, the flight engineer on Halifax RG375 EX-R, was from Glenageary, Co. Dublin, Republic of Ireland.[69] His crewmate, navigator Arthur Bradley, from Wimslow, Cheshire, was on his 37th operation.[70] His brother Cyril, never stopped missing him.[71]

Very little is known of the other crew members killed on this Halifax; the bomb aimer, Francis Chambers was from Redditch, Worcestershire was married to Beryl Chambers; Joseph Loth (wireless operator) hailed from Bitterne, Southampton; Desmond Greenwood (mid-upper gunner) was from Middlesbrough, Yorkshire, and nothing further is known of Reginald Pool, the special operator.[72]

Of the two survivors from the loss of Halifax RG375 EX-R, while nothing is recorded of the rear gunner, R Hunter, other than he became a prisoner of war, more is known of the pilot, Leslie Currell. Always known as 'Pom', no one is sure why,[73] he grew up in Mullewa, Australia. He was married to Elsie Kane in July 1936 and their first child, John, was born in April 1942, five months before Les enlisted in the Royal Australian Air Force. Leaving for overseas duty in August

1943, his twin daughters, Margaret and Lesley, were born in February 1944.[74] A 'quietly spoken, gentlemanly, good natured person',[75] before the war he trained as a cabinet maker 'and a good one too',[76] making all his own bedroom furniture (still in use today by one of his daughters).[77] He settled into a job with the West Australian Government Railways (WAGR) as a wagon builder.[78] After the war he returned to Australia and continued to work for WAGR, until in the late 1950s, he became a cray fisherman.[79]

On Halifax RG373 EX-T, once again, little is known of most of the crew. In the case of the pilot, William Brooks and Douglas Wilson, the special operator, no further details can be found. John Lewis, the Navigator was from Much Wenlock, Shropshire and Keith Gavin, the bomb aimer hailed from Strichen, Aberdeenshire in Scotland. The flight engineer, William Bolton from Plaistow, Newham, London, was married to Edith Bolton. Alfred Holder (mid-upper gunner) from Miserden, Gloucestershire, was awarded the DFC, but for what, is not known. Killed at the age of 43, he was among the oldest to die on Bomber Command operations in the Second World War.[80]

Ken Croft, from Birmingham, married Irene Benton in December 1944, five months before his death. Irene joined the WAAFs in an expression of support for Ken.[81] Philip Croft, Ken's half-brother, remembers that 'he visited us all when on leave, which I remember especially because he would divide all his chocolate issue between me and my three siblings – a rare wartime treat'.[82] In 1948 Irene married Ken's older brother, Stanley. One year older than Ken, Stanley had enlisted in the RAF first. Flying with Coastal Command, he was brought down by anti-aircraft fire when patrolling the Dutch coast on 8 August 1940. He and another crew member managed to bale out and spent the rest of the war as POWs. Two further crew members perished. Irene and Stanley emigrated to Canada in 1952.[83]

Ken Crane was the sole survivor of this aircraft and while good detail exists of his evasion and subsequent return to the UK, there is no record of him in postwar life.

These Halifaxes were two of the three aircraft lost that night.[84] Earlier, a Mosquito of RAF 100 Group 169 Squadron from Great Massingham was lost while carrying out a low-level napalm attack on Jagel airfield.[85] At 22:48 hours, the master bomber called in the aircraft to press home their attack and, 12 minutes later, he saw an aircraft explode mid-air south of the target area.[86] The crew, Robert Catterall and Donald Joshua Beadle, were both killed.[87]

On the journey back to RAF North Creake the Mandrelleros kept their Mandrel equipment switched on until 23:59 hours, affording some protection to returning bombers.[88] Gordon Clarke recalls the journey home:

> it would appear, although, of course, no charts were kept, we were probably the last aircraft (Halifax PN374 EX-N) over enemy territory which would mean that Trevor Molloy, our rear gunner … was most probably the last aircrew member to cross Europe going in … and, of course, going out. We can't confirm that, but it seems very likely[89]

According to the 199 Squadron Operations Book, Gordon Clarke's aircraft (piloted by A W Burley) was the first to return to RAF North Creake at 00:10 hours on 3 May 1945. The last 199 Squadron aircraft to land was C Arkinstall's Halifax RG372 EX-P at 02:13 hours.[90] However, the privilege described probably goes to rear gunner C Lodge of 171 Squadron Halifax NA110 6Y-Z (piloted by W M Dove), that returned at 02:16 hours.[91] There is something wonderfully poetic about the possibility of the last aircraft out of a hostile Europe was piloted by someone called 'Dove'; the very symbol of peace.

The landing aircraft came in two intense waves representing 'a very hectic couple of periods for air traffic control'.[92] Convinced that this must be the last operation of the war, emotions were running high at RAF North Creake, until celebrations were curtailed by the realisation that two aircraft were in fact missing;[93] 'practically all [aircrew on their] second tour … terrible wasn't it?'.[94]

CHAPTER TEN

WHEN ALL'S SAID & DONE

You volunteered for it and that was it, weren't it? There you are, I'm here to tell the tale.

Bernie How, Flight Engineer, RAF North Creake 1944-1945.

In April 1945, 'the pressure of operating began to slacken off considerably'[1] at RAF North Creake, with the Allies overrunning Europe it was becoming 'increasingly difficult to find suitable targets for our type of work'.[2] The same month, Arthur Adcock, a RAF North Creake wireless operator, was coming to the end of his tour. With the end of the war in sight, the crew believed they had got through it, only to be informed that they would need to continue beyond their 30th operation until the cessation of hostilities. He recalls:

> this news shook us to the core. The CO was apologetic and concerned, but there it was we had to go on. As we were not on the Battle Order that day we spent much of the time in the Robin Hood at Walsingham and succeeded in drowning our sorrows.[3]

They may have changed their approach after others had refused to extend their tour;[4] Denis Gill, a 199 Squadron gunner had reached his 30th operation shortly before the end of the war and opted for a mechanics course in Blackpool, rather than signing up for another tour.[5] He recalls the return from his final sortie:

> I lay in my bed staring in the darkness. I found it hard to believe I was a survivor. I also knew my seven months on operations had also had its effect upon me emotionally. Watching other aircraft being shot down, and the civilian victims of our area bombing policy being killed in the flames below, revealed the darker side of human nature. I was, and had been, a participant in a form of nightmare existence. Unknown to me then, the memory of it would stay with me for many years.[6]

By May 1945, the war's imminent end was raising spirits; three airmen at RAF North Creake received a 'penal deduction' from their pay for 'causing a disturbance in the Sergeants' Mess ... [and] wilfully damaging Government and Sergeants' Mess property'.[7] In the officers' mess, Norman Bray hosted a 'big party to ensure the supply of spirits built up in the mess would not pass to other hands'.[8] They did have much to celebrate: between 4 and 5 May 1945, German forces in north-west Germany, Holland and Denmark surrendered, and on 7 May 1945, German forces on all fronts offered their unconditional surrender, effective from 00:01 hours on 8 May.[9] The Operations Record Book (ORB) records that:

> the end of hostilities in Europe was proclaimed today, and that the official V.E. Day would be tomorrow. The general atmosphere on the Squadron was not so much of rejoicing, but one of thankfulness.[10]

On 8 May 1945 'the station went en fete and there was much celebration in all messes'.[11] There was a short service in front of the Control Tower[12] with the Tannoy speakers echoing Norman Bray's voice around the quiet airfield, as he heralded the end of the war.[13] Special 'Victory' meals were provided for the airmen[14] in the Naafi and:[15]

> later in the day, a parade of effigies was held. They included such personalities as Hitler, Mussolini and Dr. Goebbels. These individuals were transported by open lorry to the neighbouring villages, where they were on show to the general public. A large bonfire on camp attracted much interest, and the day came to a close with a grand all-ranks dance in the Station Institute. With the exception of the administrative staff, today and tomorrow were detailed as holidays.[16]

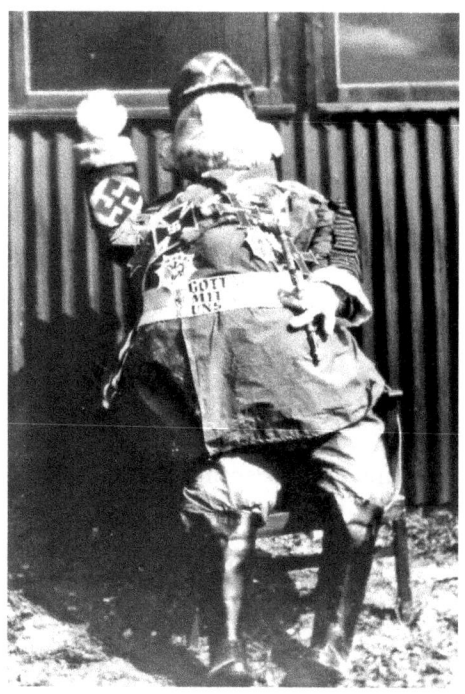

The effigy of Hermann Goering ready to go on tour (John Reid Collection).

Administrative officer, Roy Berrill, working a shift on VE Day in the meteorological office, recalls 'we got a weather report from Scotland saying visibility reduced by flying clods. I think they'd had a drop too much'.[17] Howard Gray, RAF North Creake radar section and orderly officer on VE Day, remembers that it 'passed a lot more quietly than we expected'.[18] Not all stayed on camp; Keith Thompson 'went to Norwich ... had lunch then roamed around. Back to Wells for tea. Went to Picts. Missed both the PM's & George's speeches'.[19] On 9 May 1945, many 'spent a very quiet day – due mainly to the late hour retiring the previous night'.[20] Norman Bray invited all ranks to the 1945 Derby at Newmarket.[21] Harry Lofts, from the Armoury remembers it was 'a great day out. I backed three winners at the meeting'.[22] Les King, special operator with 171 Squadron, recalls, 'Court Martial won [the 2,000 Guineas] ... none of us backed the winner'.[23]

On 13 May 1945, an official thanksgiving service for the whole station was held in east hangar to coincide with Winston Churchill's victory address, which was broadcast over the Tannoy System. About 1,000 personnel attended the Service with a Halifax as a backdrop.[24] The following day, requests were received for the submission, by each squadron, of a 2,000-word essay on their formation and progress.[25] Any organiser knows that a job is not complete until the report is written, and for 171 Squadron, 'as a result of a combined effort ... a very interesting write-up was produced'.[26]

Returning from leave, Arthur Adcock had missed VE Day on the airfield. He noticed that since his departure, the station 'had lost the bustle and sense of urgency',[27] however, Phyllis Willmott, saw it differently. Still working shifts in meteorology, she felt:

> the Peace has made barely a difference ... [we] get some extra time off over weekends, but we just go on as usual. In fact, we just curse the long queue that we find outside the cookhouse because of all these off-duty people. Gradually peace-time systems are being introduced – which really only means one thing – Parade – with a definite capital 'P'. These didn't affect us at all, but before long I expect we shall be waging a battle royal against the authorities to prove that they just aren't for us.[28]

With the end of the war one question remained. Had RAF 100 Group achieved its primary function of reducing Bomber Command casualties?

With, at times, bomber losses far lower than 'even the most sanguine prophet would have forecast',[29] it was generally believed that the Group 'must be seen as a success'.[30] However, with 'both sides constantly adapting',[31] it was an uncertain picture. It wasn't until postwar that a fuller understanding could emerge. Robert Cockburn noted, 'in the last year of the war the enemy's defences were rendered almost completely ineffective by the cumulative effects of our tactical and technical countermeasures'.[32] It was considered that 'in practice, more was achieved than the theoreticians had dared hope for'.[33] On evidence gleaned from the testimony of German POWs,[34] German radar was, at times, unusable in the face of the electronic barrage and the Luftwaffe had found it increasingly difficult to direct its night-fighters to the bombers. Indeed, postwar, the German night-fighter ace Heinz-Wolfgang Schnaufer admitted that 'jamming and concentrated bomber streams rendered AI [Aircraft identification] useless. They would fly to the position where jamming was greatest and then search visually'.[35] In an attempt to quantify the success, Alfred Price postulates that 'if it is accepted that the various jamming tactics and innovations cut the Command's loss rate by just one per cent … then the saving would be more than one thousand bombers and their crews'.[36]

However, what was really needed was a reliable platform on which to test the veracity of the various radio countermeasures. Therefore, in June 1945, an exercise called Operation Post Mortem was scheduled.[37] This operation was to function in two phases. First, using the German early warning defences in Denmark, as they were mostly intact,[38] the exercise would involve RAF 100 Group aircraft flying towards the German early warning system as if for a real raid. Both sides would perform their normal operational functions (except the German side of the exercise would be entirely ground based).[39] Second, there would be an interrogation of Luftwaffe personnel.[40]

After initial examinations of the German equipment, the live exercises followed with German personnel tracking the bomber force with RAF officers watching over their shoulders. In this way they would discover exactly how jamming had felt for the controllers on the ground.[41] There were some limitations in these exercises; for instance, the Denmark sector was not busy during the war and therefore not the most representative of the effectiveness of German defences. Also, in all but two of the trials, the approach of the exercise was the same. Once this was realised by the German controllers, they adopted 'mental dead reckoning', that is, using the experience of earlier trials to fill in any gaps where radar failed to provide reliable data, thereby falsifying the results achieved. Additionally, the short duration of the bomber incursions favoured the RAF, as longer operations would have allowed for a more considered approach from the German operators.[42] Nonetheless, a reasonable picture of the relative effectiveness of the various countermeasures was achieved.

At RAF North Creake, Halifaxes of both squadrons were detailed for Operation Post Mortem between 27 June and 5 July 1945.[43] In advance of the operation the 171 Squadron ORB records:

> the purpose of this exercise ... is to simulate large scale raids upon 'enemy' territory, and, under the observance of our own controllers, to assess the efficiency of the enemy's raid reporting organisation ... the Squadron's part in the operation is exactly the same as that which we practised in giving support to the Main Force during the period 1944/45.[44]

Keith Thompson noted in his diary (26 June 1945): 'bags of panic on Tannoy. Exercise on!'.[45] However, the exercise was scrubbed due to adverse weather conditions. The poor weather persisted until 1 July 1945, when 199 Squadron flew with ten aircraft.[46] 5 July 1945, saw the heaviest commitment from the RAF North Creake squadrons, with 21 aircraft of 171 Squadron and 17 of 199 Squadron taking part.[47] On 6 July 1945, the 171 Squadron ORB concludes:

> information received from our experts in Denmark that the Radio Counter measures employed were so successful that, in nearly every case, the plotting of the Main Force was

incoherent, scattered and unreliable. On the whole it would appear no defence could be put up against the most effective jamming of the Mandrel and Window forces.[48]

This can be considered a slightly optimistic summary of the results of Operation Post Mortem.

Operation Post Mortem had actually concluded that the most effective tactic was the Mosquito intruder raids and that these ultimately defeated the German defences,[49] and that other RCM 'kept losses down to an acceptable level rather than one which soundly defeated the enemy'.[50] Nonetheless, it was agreed that of all these measures 'Window proved to be the most dynamic',[51] with all the German radars affected to a greater or lesser extent. German operators could not 'determine with any accuracy the numbers of aircraft flying when Window was used',[52] and they were also unable to 'distinguish between feint and real forces with any certainty'.[53] Simple in the extreme, it had the 'most devastating effect of any RCM device introduced by the RAF during the Second World War'.[54]

The Mandrel Screen was regarded by RAF 100 Group as 'one of its most effective measures'.[55] However, Operation Post Mortem suggested that it was not as effective as believed, as the trials indicated that there were usually 'sufficient gaps in frequency for at least one radar type to see through',[56] although it should be remembered that some of the German operators had had more than two years' experience of working in an environment of jamming by this point.[57] Nonetheless, even if the jamming was not wholly effective, 'it did make it extremely difficult for them to maintain a steady flow of accurate 'plots' on the bombers'.[58] Moreover, the latter Post Mortem exercises illustrated that when RAF 100 Group 'threw the full weight of electronic measures against the system',[59] in most cases the German radar was 'rendered almost completely useless'. It was only the last German radar development, Wasserman, that proved able to operate with any effectiveness, and even this, when faced with concentrated jamming, 'succumbed to a certain extent'.[60] It is believed, that the effectiveness of Mandrel was ultimately compromised by the constant use of it by USAAF in support of its bomber assemblies; 'simply by giving [Germans] added practice [sic]'.[61] Even so, Arthur Harris concluded in his postwar despatch:

> the Mandrel Screen and Window Diversion were used with telling effect against the enemy's system of mass-controlled night-fighters. The reduction in early warning caused by the Mandrel Screen gave the fighter controllers so much less time to appreciate genuine and feint raids and make their dispositions accordingly.[62]

Edward Addison, the commanding officer of RAF 100 Group, reflected that he was not particularly concerned with the relative merits of any particular countermeasure and was more concerned with 'subduing the enemy by constantly frightening and worrying at him'.[63] Primarily, he saw the campaign as one of attrition.[64] His strategy seems to have paid dividends, with a Luftwaffe officer questioned postwar explaining, that as a result of the RAF 100 Group activities 'in radar jamming and Window-techniques ... [We had] severe problems ... trying to defend Germany in the air'.[65]

Robert Cockburn, from the Telecommunications Research Establishment, believed the programme was a success 'in that it allowed Bomber Command tactical flexibility which it would have otherwise lost through the increasing casualties inflicted on it'.[66] Nonetheless, it was a fast-moving campaign 'in which the victories [were] relative, not absolute'[67] and that given time 'a resolute enemy would always be able to introduce new equipment immune to the form of jamming in use'.[68] An internal appraisal written immediately after the war wrote:

> [the Squadrons of RAF 100 Group] will perhaps remain unknown except in the R.A.F. To them must be given the credit of shielding time and time again the hundreds and thousands of main force bombers that have operated ... it has been their mission to draw off the fighters from the main attack and in this they have succeeded magnificently. When the histories

are written and secrets of the radio and radar night air war are divulged it will be seen how a small and valiant band went out into the unknown and succeeded in achieving what they had intended.[69]

As predicted, with the shield of secrecy concealing the work of RAF 100 Group until the mid-70s, their 'contribution to the success of this offensive has been largely unsung'.[70]

* * *

While we were now content with how the Control Tower looked, there was an outbuilding that looked out of place; worse, it looked derelict. Built as a garage in the 1990s, it was quickly converted into accommodation and rented out. For Laura, who helps with our B&B housekeeping, it was her first place after leaving home. When we moved here it was being used as an office and, shortly after, the roof caved in. We had intended to demolish it, but given it had planning permission as accommodation, we decided to convert it to an extra B&B let. Having just finished the build, we were perpetually short of money; however, we were not ones to let a shortage of cash get in the way of a good plan, so we organised a crowdfund. Crowdfunders paid in advance for B&B accommodation and/or other benefits, but would be asked to wait a year while the work was completed. It took some faith for crowdfunders to invest in us, but it must have hit the right chord, as we successfully over-funded. Lucky really, as it cost more than we estimated. Nonetheless, we were ready for the first guest; just. All except the wall lights; these I'd been trying to finish after a very long day, I was exhausted and I watched myself as I carefully lowered the chop-saw into my thumb. It was a salutary lesson in knowing when to stop.

Injuries aside, the building, now called the Stirling Suite, fits well into the aesthetic of the Control Tower. With the same style bathroom suite and décor, it is presented with its own sitting room which gives a fine view of the garden for nature watching.

Preparation work on the grounds for the Stirling Suite meant entry into some of the corners we had so far failed to reach. I had to dig out three huge tree butts by hand as they couldn't be reached by a digger. My reward was the discovery of a cup base with N.A.A.F.I. written on it; one wonders how it got there and in what circumstances it was thrown. Elsewhere, work in the gardens continued, with more plans coming to fruition; including tackling the roadside bank, clearing it of nettles and brambles; cutting the grass regularly, progressing it from rough ground to reasonable grass.[A] It will never be a bowling green, but neither would we want it to be.

Boundaries were marked; in of front to the Control Tower we placed two Second World War 1000lb bombs to deter reversing lorries from straightening the corner by riding up on our lawn. These were collected from a resident of Wells who asked Claire over the phone: 'do you want to buy some Second World War bombs?'. Claire, although surprised by the question responded, 'I think we possibly do'. They were decommissioned bombs salvaged from a closing museum and they suit their new purpose admirably.

For my 50th birthday I set up a 'hedge fund'. The wonderful generosity of friends ensured enough native hedge whips to plant up the entire perimeter of the garden – 650 hedging plants. This mixed species native hedge now provides us with fruit for jam and cobnuts for the bowl (this is still somewhat theoretical as the squirrels always seem to get there first), but most importantly sloes for the sloe gin. I was also able to purchase a wild service tree at the same time. A beautiful modest sized tree that shows brilliant autumn colours. It is Britain's rarest native tree. I'd first seen one shortly after joining the council in the late 1980s. I promised myself I would plant one once I had a garden. Ironically, the year I planted ours, they were the most popular native tree planted in Britain.

In July 2019, we were in the midst of a reasonably busy summer when we received a phone call from Cillian. He had gone travelling with

A Our then neighbour Ann, always used to joke that she was never sure whether I was cutting grass or shovelling gravel, such was the noise from my constantly grounding mower.

his girlfriend Rosie. Initially in Asia, he had recently flown to Australia, and it was from Melbourne that he was calling. He had news; he had just been diagnosed with testicular cancer.[B] We both reeled from shock.

There is something particularly troubling about such a diagnosis, born from the naive expectation that you will be able to resolve all life's complications for your children. However, with serious illness you are impotent. Powerless. Out of control. It's a horrifying sensation. 'Do you want to come back?', we asked. 'No time', he replied, 'they operate next week to prevent any spread.' Not only were we impotent in the face of a cancer diagnosis, now he was to undergo surgery as far away from us as the earth's geography allows. We felt helpless and remote. Without any hope of offering practical help, we just waited for news.

Very luckily for Cillian, he had Rosie for support. Cillian and Rosie's reasonably recent relationship was severely tested by this diagnosis, but seemingly grew stronger as the challenges mounted. The support Rosie gave Cillian while in Australia having a testicle removed was remarkable. He also had Claire's sister Miriam, who moved there some time ago, and was a huge support to them both and kept us informed when they were otherwise occupied.

One thing of practical use we could do, was to make his return comfortable. We knew that Cillian spending his whole recovery in the Control Tower was not a good option. Even though we had decided to take fewer bookings when Cillian came home (so that there was always room for him and Rosie), the nomadic existence of moving from room to room according to bookings, would be unsettling and we thought could inhibit recovery.

We had an outbuilding; we called it the 'scary chalet' as it looked like something from the opening scenes of *Wallander*. In good time, it was our plan to return it to accommodation for a self-catering arm to our business. Now it was urgent. Nonetheless, if we were doing it, we may as well make it as we wanted it. We therefore found ourselves

---

B   Testicular cancer is the most common cancer in men aged 15 to 35 but it is curable in over 96% of cases as long as it's caught early (itsontheball.org, undated).

in the midst of an unscheduled build. As much as we were struggling with the cost, doing 'something' was a great help, and it felt useful.

After a short period of recovery, Cillian made the arduous journey home to continue his return to health with us. Halifax Lodge, as the chalet was now called, wasn't finished when Cillian returned. I hoped it would be ready for Christmas; another three months.

Cillian looked unwell, but in Australia they had assured him that it was unlikely he'd need any further treatment. While there, he had been referred to Addenbrookes in Cambridgeshire and shortly after his return he went for a check-up, bloods and a scan. He then received a call to come in.

The quietly-spoken sympathetic doctor advised us that the cancer had spread and was now stage four. We were stunned. It was curable, he assured us, but aggressive. The treatment would be tough and it had to start now. Cillian had three months of incredibly intensive chemotherapy; both as an inpatient and an outpatient. We watched helpless as it wracked his body. This period would have been even tougher to get through if it hadn't been for the kindness of friends and family. My brother Greg, driving from Somerset when my car had blown up on the A11 and Cillian's friend, Elliot, who was always on call if we were struggling with an appointment. There was also the understanding of guests, when we were pushed for time, and particularly, Richard and Stacia, who although they were paying guests, insisted on making a breakfast before an outpatient's day, and putting something in the oven for when we returned.

As hard as it was, the chemotherapy did the job. In early December we were shown a scan that suggested the cancer had gone, but we still needed to return for confirmation. On 13 December 2019, we arrived at Addenbrookes and the news was confirmed. The release was immense. Only tempered by the result of the General Election.

Work on Halifax Lodge had been delayed by the constant trips to Cambridge. Cillian and Rosie eventually moved in in time for Valentine's Day 2020. It was theirs for his recovery, and for a period after while they decided next steps. We hoped without the pressure of finding somewhere to live, it would be less likely they would make rash decisions born of haste. We imagined it would be for 12 to 18 months. He must like it; he's still there.

By March 2020, Cillian was feeling more himself, and was beginning to think socialising was, once again, a possibility. And then Covid struck.

* * *

Between 14 and 16 July 1945, 14 crews were posted from RAF North Creake to 192 squadron at RAF Foulsham, 'to form the nucleus of a new Radar Warfare Squadron'.[71] A further seven crews were posted to an Operational Refresher Training Unit.[72] More generally a selection board was established to retrain crews no longer required for flying duties.[73]

In mid-July it was announced that 171 Squadron would be disbanded on 27 July 1945,[74] and 199 Squadron on 29 July.[75] 171 Squadron recorded the occasion in their ORB:

> This is the official day of disbandment. There was no excitement to mark the end of the Squadron's days, and the work of folding up the Unit proceeded quietly and efficiently. To mark the occasion, an impromptu party was held in the mess, where the alcohol produced one or two extremely verbose farewell speeches.[76]

Michael Renaut remembers that for the disbandment of the Squadrons, Norman Bray organised the 'biggest parade of aircrew and groundcrew ever seen at North Creake',[77] although the station chaplain, Bill Peters, claims to have 'arranged and conducted the event'[78] himself. Whoever was responsible, it was a lavish celebration. Held on 8 August 1945, the 171 Squadron ORB records:

> Large crowds of local visitors witnessed the ceremony, including the Earl and Countess of Leicester. The A.O.C. 100 Group

Air Vice Marshal Addison addressed the parade, after which the squadron crests were handed to him by the two squadron commanders. There was a general march past, the Salute being taken by the A.O.C., and appropriate marches played by the R.A.F. Bomber Command Band. A Service was held in one of the hangars conducted by the Bishop of Norwich, the Earl of Leicester reading the Lesson. A running buffet was provided for all in the N.A.A.F.I. and entertainments included a circus on the football pitch and a dance and side shows were held in the number 1 hangar. The dance was later continued in the N.A.A.F.I., officers' and sergeants' messes.[79]

Disbandment Parade, 8 August 1945 (Peter Hill).

Harry Lofts recalls the event with affection; 'my best friend on the camp ... made a beautiful model in Perspex of a Halifax which was won in a raffle by one of our aircrew'.[80] Michael Renaut does not remember it so fondly,[C] 'it was pure "bull" and the speeches went on for hours. I was stuck out there in front, dressed in my Moss Bros best and the awful

---

C   Michael Renaut had been posted to RAF 103 Squadron 24 July 1945 and must have returned for the disbandment (171 Squadron: 1945: ORB).

'cheesecutter'[D] that I hated'.[81] Edward Addison wrote a dedication for the day:

> North Creake and its two Squadrons, Nos 171 and 199, have been second to none in efficiency and aggressiveness. Their task has been a difficult and complicated one. They have been set many and varied problems often of a most intricate, and always unique, nature – all have been solved. The demands made on these units have been heavy and have frequently imposed a severe tax upon the endurance and patience of both flying and ground personnel – all have been met, and satisfied, with a fine spirit of cheerfulness and determination.[82]

On 15 August 1945, Japan surrendered; it was the end of the Second World War. At RAF North Creake the day was marked with 'a general stand down ... a dance was held in the N.A.A.F.I. in the evening'.[83] Roy Berrill remembers, 'I was commissioned by the CO to go to Norwich and get as much beer as I could ... I got one solitary barrel. Everybody else had the same idea'.[84] Four days later the process of removing the Squadrons' Halifax aircraft commenced; it continued until 25 August 1945, involving crews from RAF Foulsham,[85] many of whom, had transferred from RAF North Creake. The best Halifaxes were transferred to RAF Watton and the remainder were scrapped.[86]

Personnel continued to be posted away, Roy Berrill left shortly after VJ Day, and eventually found himself in 'Hiroshima, one year after the atomic bomb had been dropped'.[87] 4 September 1945, marked 'the beginning of a major exodus ... sites, sections and buildings [were] being closed, and the remaining personnel on the station condensed to two domestic sites'.[88] In early October, sports and entertainment were 'strictly limited owing to the removal of cinema equipment and sports gear'.[89]

D A cheese-cutter is generally considered to refer to a flat cap in civilian life, however, in RAF slang it seems to variously mean a forage cap, or in this case, the formal peaked cap.

Resettlement and Release lectures were provided,[90] and also training in areas such as automobile engineering, motor driving, bookkeeping and citizenship.[91] Aircrew Redundancy Boards were also organised.[92] Now for the long-awaited return to civilian life:

> the returning father, particularly, is apt to feel himself surrounded by a jostling and often hostile world which is blind to his new values and his maturity. Equally he feels bereft of the support of his own military group and keenly aware of the lack of satisfaction in his life … the wife is only too likely to suffer from bewilderment arising from her relative lack of insight into her own needs to readjust, and from an irritation, which her children often share, of the multiple changes needed to adjust to someone who is both a ghost and a stranger.[93]

Denis Gill explains why the transition from aircrew, 'without the preparation you were given to learn to kill … overnight … a caring law-abiding citizen',[94] was, for many, so hard:

> when you retire at night, cloaked in darkness, thoughts fend off sleep. What you have done and seen, your less fortunate comrades, the scenes of destruction, your victims, the dead and the dying, return to haunt you and, plagued by your conscience, you find there is no escape from the madness of war.[95]

The RAF dropped 955,000 tons of bombs on Germany, with approaching half the total on populated areas.[96] 593,000 German civilians died and 3.37 million dwellings were destroyed by Allied bombing.[97] Bomber Command also suffered terribly, with 55,573 killed, a further 8,403 wounded and 9,838 prisoners of war.[98] As Britain returned to a peace setting, the process of reflection and analysis commenced. The debate over the relative merits of the offensive began and, even today, no consensus has been achieved.

Controversy surrounds much of the history, aims, success and morality of the area bombing campaign and particularly the

Commander-in-Chief at Bomber Command, Arthur 'Butcher'[E] Harris, who will be forever inextricably linked to the offensive. Its morality has been questioned since the tenets of bombing policy became more widely known; Lewis Mumford, a US historian and philosopher, writing shortly after the dropping of the atomic bomb, captured the concerns in a biting polemic:

> we have dehumanised ourselves and no longer accept any limitations, inner or outer, upon our will-to-annihilation. Within fifteen brief years every restriction has been removed: first in theory by our fascist enemies, then in practice by the same enemies: but finally by ourselves on an even more destructive scale ... this theory held that wars could be won by unlimited aerial attack upon the civilian population ... instead of recoiling against it ... we imitated our enemies. By the practice of obliteration bombing we lost any edge or moral superiority we originally held over the enemy with regard to our methods of fighting (our ends are still measurably more human).[99]

Consequently, it is argued, there has been 'a dreadful chain reaction, which is still with us today. Thousands of innocent men, women and children are still suffering because of it'.[100] And it's hard to dispute; at the turn of the 20th century, nine out of ten war casualties were military, today it is more like one out of ten.[101] It would seem 'death and destruction from the air is with us to stay'.[102] However, at the time, it was perceived that the stakes were critically high. Herbert Morrison, the Home Secretary in the War Cabinet believed, 'we were fighting for our lives and liberties. We had to win'.[103] Behind such assertions, are relived fears of 'national extinction and political subjection, which were taken to be the basis on which total war had to be waged'.[104] The wartime

---

E The nickname 'Butcher Harris' is somewhat contested; its use in this context (see for example Bourke: 2001: 164) is a reasonably recent application of the term which was reputedly coined by aircrews to refer to the indifference of Arthur Harris to the level their losses. It was also the aircrews who shortened it to 'Butch', which, of course, has very different, less pejorative, connotations.

British Secretary of State for Air, Archibald Sinclair believed it was the only option open to them; 'well armed, highly-trained and inflexibly determined ... [Bomber Command were] the only force upon which we can call ... to strike deadly blows at the heart of Germany'.[105] Moreover, 'the nation as a whole demanded revenge for what had happened to Britain's major cities in the early years of the war',[106] and this support seldom wavered.[F] Anecdotally, examples of its popularity abound; Gordon Mercier returning to base after an air crash, remembers, 'we got on the Tube with all our gear, and they had a collection for us on the train ... they gave us a hundred fags'.[107] At the time, 'Harris's men were hailed as heroes':[108]

> the vast majority of ordinary men and women never had doubts at the time ... about the area bombing of German cities. Many people had bitter, direct experience of German air attacks. They also harboured no illusions about the nature of the enemy and what was at stake, for them and for future generations.[109]

While generally the public were comfortable or enthusiastic about the bomber offensive, some did raise objections, including, famously, George Bell, Bishop of Chichester, who made a speech in the House of Lords denouncing the campaign, but supporting those undertaking it.[110] Interestingly, even John Collins, the padre of Bomber Command, raised objections.[111] In the House of Commons, Richard Stokes, the Labour MP for Ipswich,[G] was both strategically and morally opposed to the bombing offensive. On 31 March 1943, he asked in the House, if 'instructions had been given on any occasion to British airmen to engage in area bombing rather than limit their attentions to purely military targets?'.[112] Archibald Sinclair[H] replied that 'targets of

---

F   It should be noted that revenge did not universally motivate calls for retributive action and it would seem the more bombed an area, the less attractive revenge bombing appeared. A letter to the *New Statesman* in 1943 suggests that for many people of Coventry 'very little satisfaction is attained by hearing that Hamburg is suffering in the same way as Coventry has suffered' (Grayling: 2006: 188).

G   Richard Stokes was not a pacifist; he had fought as a gunner on the Western Front in the Great War and won the military medal (Hastings: 1980: 171).

H   Archibald Sinclair was from an aristocratic background. He stood for the Liberals in Caithness (family seat). He was called to the coalition in 1940 but not to the War Cabinet. Loyal to the Air Force, he was

Bomber Command are always military, but night-bombing of military objectives necessarily involves bombing the area in which they are situated'.[113] Unsatisfied, on 27 May 1943, Richard Stokes asked again, with particular reference to indiscriminate bombing. Clement Attlee, the Deputy Prime Minister, responded, 'no there is no indiscriminate bombing'.[114] On both occasions the answers were at best evasive, at worst untrue. When the War Cabinet had agreed to pursue a campaign of area bombing, they had decided there was no need to announce publicly any change of policy.[115] In fact very few, even in the War Cabinet, knew the full details of bombing policy. Indeed, 'it would not be inaccurate to say that bombing policy was settled almost entirely by the Prime Minister in consultation with Portal'.[116] Arthur Harris wanted the public to be told the truth, but the War Cabinet refused, 'the only occasion on which it deliberately deceived the public throughout the war'.[117] Arthur Harris argues, it was this deceit that was a major contributor to the postwar controversy:

> in the House of Commons he [Archibald Sinclair] should have been far more forthright than he was ... I personally thought this was asking for trouble; there was nothing to be ashamed of, except in the sense that everybody might be ashamed of the sort of thing that has to be done in every war, as of war itself.[118]

The fact that the detail of the bombing campaign was unknown to most until postwar, when the levels of devastation in Germany were realised, led to questions and accusations from many. Raymond Williams was part of the occupying force in Hamburg; 'I was quite shaken because I had been told it was military targets and docks that had been bombed, and you could see quite clearly that there had been saturation bombing of the city. That shocked me, however, mainly because I had been lied to'.[119]

---

opposed to 'promiscuous bombing' until it found favour, when he 'swam with the tide' (Longmate: 1983: 151). Seen as a weak minister, he was bullied by both Charles Portal (his junior) and Winston Churchill. As leader of the Liberal Party, he lost his seat in the 1945 General Election to the Conservatives in one of their 14 gains (Longmate: 1983: 152).

While not every British voter would have approved of MPs 'constantly leaping to their feet in Parliament to demand this or that German city be bombed',[120] Frederick Taylor asserts that any withdrawal 'from city bombing would not have been acceptable to Allied public opinion'.[121] Moreover, it's likely that Geoffrey Shakespeare, Liberal MP for Norwich, would have been greeted with general approval when he outlined in Parliament, that he was 'all for the bombing of working-class areas of German cities ... because I do not believe you will ever bring home to the civil population of Germany the horrors of war until they have been tested in this way'.[122] With bitter irony, such widely held perspectives failed to recognise that the very working class areas being bombed were most frequently areas sympathetic to Social Democrats and Communists,[123] and 'contained the greatest chance of opposition to Hitler'.[124] Nonetheless, even the Communist Party of Great Britain (CPGB), after D-Day, urged the Government to 'rain down merciless blows from the sky',[125] and it was left to individual readers of the CPGB organ, the *Daily Worker*, to point out that 'the extermination of defenceless people dragged us down to the level of the Nazis'.[126]

However, what Archibald Sinclair didn't identify in his speeches was the grave inaccuracy of British bombing and that Bomber Command, at this stage of the war (1942), 'could not even guarantee to hit towns, let alone individual factories'.[127] A realisation that led to area bombing,[128] a philosophy that aimed to dislocate the 'industrial, economic and military foundations that lay beneath the German war effort'.[129] Many architects of this philosophy asserted, that 'morale' as a target, was as important as 'war industries and docks':[130]

> I was convinced, having watched the burning of London, that a bomber offensive of adequate weight and the right kind of bombs would, if continued for long enough, be something that no country in the world could endure.[1][131]

German morale didn't collapse; just as it didn't in the Baedeker Raids

---

I It should be noted that the destruction of morale as a campaign 'objective' was disputed by Arthur Harris who claimed that it was always about production and not morale (Hastings: 1980: 132).

on British cities that were intended to 'break the spirit of the British, but in point of fact they had precisely the opposite effect'.[132] Indeed, the bombing of Germany bolstered resilience even with the 'growing awareness that the war must be lost':

> workers everywhere went back to their plants even after the firestorms ... it was a triumph for the courage and determination of the German people in the face of the utmost suffering, paralleling that of the British in 1940 ... In 1943, Dr. Goebbels' department noted a marked stiffening of national morale in the face of raids, matched by the growth of an unprecedented popular hatred for the enemy.[133]

Neither did German industrial output fall. The postwar US Strategic Bombing Survey, records that 'German military and industrial production seemed to increase ... the more bombs were dropped',[134] and while Erhard Milch,[J] admitted postwar, 'the British inflicted grievous and bloody injuries upon us',[135] Albert Speer suggested, 'in reality the losses were not quite so serious'.[136] Nevertheless, Albert Speer argues that such losses are not necessarily the point:

> the real importance of the air war consisted in the fact that it opened a second front long before the invasion of Europe. That front was the skies over Germany ... the unpredictability of the attacks made this front gigantic; every square meter of the territory we controlled was a kind of front line. Defense [sic] against air attacks required the production of thousands of anti-aircraft guns, the stockpiling of tremendous quantities of ammunition all over the country, and holding in readiness hundreds of thousands of soldiers ... this was the greatest lost battle on the German side.[137]

Max Hastings asserts that Albert Speer overstates the case.[138] However,

---

J   The German Minister for Aircraft production.

Reginald Jones identifies that 'we saw many signs of German technical distress as a result of our bombing – for example, delays in getting new electronic equipment developed as the radio war exploded'.[139] Frederick Taylor believes there is 'little doubt that the strategic bombing campaign played a major role in the defeat of Germany ... [and there is] growing evidence that it may have even proved decisive':[140]

> the massive financial and material costs involved for the Reich in creating a complex and sophisticated aircraft tracking and defense [sic] system, in rebuilding and relocating industrial and military installations, and for feeding, housing and caring for victims of the escalating Allied bombing. This not only took weapons and equipment from the frontline land troops, but also vastly reduced the offensive aircraft available on all fronts, especially in Russia ... [while] Hitler demanded more bombers, the constant need for day and night fighters ... meant that fighters were always given priority over a new generation of long-distance bombers ... from 1943, Germany was always ... 'on the back foot' as a result of the strategic bombing campaign.[141]

Moreover, it has been widely asserted that bombing raids, such as Dresden, shifted opinion in Germany from being unable to countenance an unconditional surrender to an acceptance of it; 'better an end to terror than terror without end'.[142] Nonetheless, while the relative strategic merits of the campaign appear inconclusive, there is little moral consideration within these debates, being as they are entirely 'concerned with whether or not it [was] successful'.[143] Many considered the Allied stance in the Second World War as morally justified, some, such as Hugh Jenkins, considered that it was 'the last war in which any gallantry, any nobility, was involved'.[144] Notions of a 'just war' abounded, although, as Donald Soper suggests, 'the concept of a just war is a contradiction in terms – there may be just motives, but they are corrupted immediately in the prosecution of war, and justice flies out the window as soon as you embark on mass destruction and the bombing of innocent civilians';[145] not, as Joanna Bourke pinpoints, 'as a consequence of attacking legitimate military bases, but as an end in itself'.[146] Charles Gutherie and Michael Quinlan discuss how problems arise, even when simply attempting to define the basic terms of a just war:

> 'innocent' means (in line with the Latin from which the word is derived) 'not involved in harming us' … it still leaves open difficult judgements about exactly who is to be regarded as not involved, as non-combatant. By 'deliberate attack' is meant attack to which the harm to the innocent is the direct aim of the attack or essential to achieving its purpose.[147]

The 1961 *Official History of the Strategic Air Offensive Against Germany*, considers that the 'whole development and direction of strategic bombing was a highly and continuously controversial matter'.[148] Nonetheless, as one of the authors of the official history, Noble Frankland, a navigator during the war, later concluded, it had to be considered in the context of the 'German war effort and the need for Britain to find some means of diminishing it'.[149] Like Arthur Harris, he compares the bombing offensive to the naval blockade of Germany and Austria in the Great War,[K] which he points out involved starving civilians rather than bombing but with the same outcome; a terrific loss of life. He concludes, 'if the choice was between letting Hitler's war effort to develop unhindered towards a Nazi victory and undertaking the area-bombing offensive, the moral issue seems clear'.[150] Although, he concedes, opinions did diverge, particularly later in the war but, this 'was not a moral dissention; it was a dispute about what would be most effective in speeding up the defeat of Nazi Germany'.[151] Max Hastings suggests that there was no debate in the cabinet about whether it was morally different to kill civilians incidentally or to directly target them.[152] Indeed, he suggests, attacking whole cities rather than individual installations held no moral terrors for Winston Churchill.[153]

K Arthur Harris argues the blockades were responsible for the deaths of 800,000 (Harris: 1947: 176).

The very concept of a just war is fraught with difficulties, with the term being distorted, confusing, perhaps deliberately, 'just' (behaving according to what is morally right and fair) with 'justifiable' (having, done for, or marked by a good or legitimate reason).[L] Moreover, as Winfreid Sebald suggests, by the point Bomber Command had amassed its phenomenal weapons of war, the momentum was psychologically irresistible, materially and organisationally; 'once the material was manufactured, simply letting the aircraft and their freight stand idle on the airfields of eastern England ran counter to any healthy economic instinct'.[154]

Miles Tripp concedes in his autobiography that doubtless 'mistakes were made but that was war. It is easy in peacetime, and with hindsight, to see what could have been done better or what should have been left undone'.[155]

While the mainstream British press were vocal supporters of the bombing campaign,[156] voices questioning the offensive were becoming audible elsewhere. Disquiet initially arose from a 'small if articulate'[157] group of people, including popular figures such as A A Milne, the creator of Winnie-the-Pooh and a veteran of the Great War; novelist and playwright, Beverley Nichols; and George Bernard Shaw,[158] who wrote of the bombing campaign:

> the mechanization of modern war greatly reduces the power of the human conscience to keep its abuses in check. It would be hard to induce a youth of ordinary good nature to take a woman with a baby in her arms and tear the two to pieces with a Mills bomb in full view of the explosion. But the same youth, thousands of feet up in a war plane, preoccupied with the management of his machine and the accuracy of his aim, will release a bomb that will blow a whole street of family homes into smithereens.[159]

Questions critical of the offensive were also being asked in the House

---

L   See Gutherie & Quinlan: 2007: 5-9.

of Commons, but mostly challenging the tactics and efficiency of the campaign rather than its morality.[160] A challenging tactical question from A V Hill, founding father of radar and Conservative MP for Cambridge University, provoked a cautioning response from Flight Lieutenant Boothby MP:

> in Bomber Command we have fashioned a most formidable weapon of offence ... it is tough to ask these chaps to undergo great dangers and perils, which they do so cheerfully and bravely, unless they are convinced, as they are at present, that it is worth doing.[161]

And these crews, 'in spite of the immense difficulties of their task – quite apart from its appalling hazards',[162] flew night after night. To bomber crews, Germany was a terrifyingly hostile environment, where aircrew were constantly dying. The aircrews were popularly glamourised in the media, generating 'romantic myths of aerial combat',[163] involving brave heroes who were never afraid.[164] The truth was somewhat different. Denis Gill recalls, 'I spent seven months with my operational squadron and every day I was afraid'.[165] The crews did not generally discuss their fear, although most knew that fear was entirely rational and were quite honest about it; but only to themselves. A decorated wing commander once admitted to Victor Tempest, an RAF Medical Officer, 'I am a coward, not because I'm frightened to fly operationally, but because I am frightened to let anybody know that I am frightened'.[166]

Aircrews, who may already be feeling the strain of operational life, 'didn't care about the grand design to smash the enemy; all that concerned us was to fly ten more operations and return safely from the tenth'.[167] This operational strain might be heightened by nearing the end of a tour, or, particularly with the war's end seemingly close, 'each time they were ordered over some particularly well known hot spot'.[168] Towards the end of the war, with daylight bombing for the RAF possible again, the risks literally became more visible; 'when approaching a target ... at night it didn't look so bad. But in day-light, the mass of smoke bursts lingering above the target with more being added all the time, was pretty awe-inspiring'.[169] Tom Sawyer concluded it was a sight they would have preferred not to see.[170] Such pressures could easily affect morale, and morale could prove a difficult emotion:

> it was their [service doctors] job to know the men who were so courageously carrying such tremendous burdens, to husband their energies when the strain on individuals threatened to become unendurable, and to strengthen them physically and psychologically for their tasks.[171]

Assessing morale involved monitoring nervous conditions associated with stress; nightmares, loss of sleep, loss of appetite, loss of power of concentration, and loss of the desire to fly.[172] Milk runs (easy trips), Victor Tempest suggests, could 'lift morale' as could recognition (through medals), successful raids, fair allocation of duties, good entertainment[173] and the company of women.[174] Conversely, frequent scrubs, difficult targets and friction on the station could deplete it.[175] Morale could also be affected by feelings of guilt:

> there were people down there being fried to death in melted asphalt on the roads, they were being burnt up and we were shuffling incendiary bombs into this holocaust ... I felt terribly sorry for the people in that fire I was helping to stoke up.[176]

Arthur Adcock confesses that he always felt uncomfortable about being blessed by the RAF North Creake chaplains; 'I was going out to bomb a city and to kill anyone, regardless of age or sex, serviceman or civilian, who just happened to be unfortunate enough to be in the path of our bombs'.[177] Those that had reason to be on the ground in these bombed cities were often shocked by what they saw and heard. Robert Kee, who became a POW after being shot down, was surprised to hear his German guards discussing bomb damage from British bombers; 'it was a shock to hear the exact tone of bitter resentment that I had heard so often in England and felt so often myself. I had always assumed that this sort of civilized dismay at barbarism was the monopoly of our cause'.[178] Miles Tripp, on finding a bomb hung up in the bomb bay describes the agony of deciding where they should force it out. After managing to dislodge the bomb he relates, 'I lost sight of it before impact but think it fell in a field and although certain slaughter of many German civilians with the other bombs didn't disturb me (any guilt was collective) I very much hoped that this last bomb (my responsibility) hadn't killed or hurt anyone'.[179] George Orwell, writing during the London Blitz of 1940,[180] famously describes this collective responsibility, but relating to German bombers:

> As I write, highly civilized human beings are flying overhead, trying to kill me.
>
> They do not feel any enmity against me as an individual, nor I against them. They are 'only doing their duty', as the saying goes. Most of them, I have no doubt, are kind-hearted law-abiding men who would never dream of committing murder in private life. On the other hand, if one of them succeeds in blowing me to pieces with a well-placed bomb, he will never sleep the worse for it. He is serving his country, which has the power to absolve him from evil.[181]

For aircrew, vocalising concern had its risks; a rear gunner expressing pity for those being bombed below was told by his pilot, 'well if you do, fucking well jump out and join 'em!'[182] Nonetheless, doubts did grow, and the end of the conflict 'provoked a real heart-searching',[183] particularly as the scale of the destruction was realised. This realisation often materialised in the daytime sight-seeing tours organised by squadrons of Bomber Command over battle-scarred Europe. At RAF North Creake, the first flew on the day before armistice.[184] Authorised by Bomber Command and named after the holiday charter company, Cook's tours were an opportunity for ground personnel, and even some civilians living locally,[185] to fly over the devastated areas. At RAF North Creake, they also flew ground personnel from other RAF 100 Group stations where their fighter aircraft lacked the capacity for passengers.[186] Vic Polichek remembers flying with his crew and passengers over the 'continent to several cities to see the horrendous destruction that the air forces and army fighting forces had done'.[187] Keith Thompson recalls flying over 'Brussels, Aachen, Cologne, Dusseldorf, Dortmund, Bochum, Essen, Duisburg & back to Brussels. Also saw "Duren's", heap of rubble'.[188] For many, this was a deeply memorable experience where the abstract concept of bombing became a witnessed reality. For Harry Lofts it would be something he would never forget:

> [A] most stirring memory … we went over the flying bomb sites in France, flying low to see the saturation bomb craters and then we flew along the Rhine ending a day never to be forgotten. All during the flight I had a bird's eye view as we were allowed to stand behind the pilot.[189]

For those that actually visited these devastated areas on the ground, the impact could be far more significant. Percy Bevington, 199 Squadron commander, made a trip with Michael Renaut to Berlin in October 1945, and remembers walking past 'the closed underground entrances where there [was] the most awful stench of dead, practically no clearance has been attempted … and I don't see how they can do much else but level it all over as one huge grave'.[190] Similarly, Leonard Cheshire reported on a trip to Cologne:

> the devastation, the cold and the despair on people's faces helped me to grasp for the first time what Saturation Bombing meant – to the victims. Piloting a bomber was a cold, impersonal game. We were concerned with switches and markers and flak, not with life and death. Now I understand the other side of the problem.[191]

A Canadian navigator with Bomber Command, John Ladbrooke, chatting years later with his rear gunner Donald Bowman, recalled, as tears welled up in his eyes, that he had read a book 'about the damage their mission did to the city and he found it terribly upsetting. "Still, it was war", he said as he tried to regain his composure and blinked back his tears.'[192]

This feeling of guilt, often felt, but seldom acknowledged by serving Bomber Command aircrew, was often regarded by combatants in the other armed forces 'as an endorsement of their essential goodness'.[193] However, such is the criticism of the bombing war, that for those within Bomber Command, any admission of feelings of guilt may be seen to imply that they are in some way 'guilty'. Whereas for most combatants, guilt is simply an accepted symptom of what they have been involved in. For Bomber Command veterans, these feelings can be further complicated as emotions of guilt might also suggest an implied criticism of the offensive, and any criticism has increasingly become viewed by some as disrespectful of the many that died in the pursuit of its aims. However, as Noble Frankland asserts, 'no one writes with first-hand experience of what the dead feel, but from my own experience I can attest that I did not put my life on the line in Bomber Command to sustain a myth'.[194] Further, as Max Hastings observes, 'only a charlatan would seek to entangle the men who flew the aircraft with the strategic controversy'.[195] Generally:

> combatants strongly believed that they *should* feel guilty for killing: it was precisely this emotion that made them 'human', and enabled them to return to civilian life afterwards. Men who did not feel guilt were somehow less than human, or were insane: guiltless killers were immoral.[196]

Raymond Williams, reflecting upon his experience as a tank commander, does not believe 'anyone really gets over it ... the guilt [emerges] once you start recovering your full human perspective, which is radically reduced by the whole experience of fighting'.[197] However, for aircrew, there is argued a 'strong correlation between altitude and guilt';[198] that height reduces feelings of guilt felt by those involved in hand-to-hand combat. Nonetheless, most assert that 'even long-distance killing [can] inspire guilt';[199] Charles Bird, the American psychologist suggests a combatant 'does not question the morality of his acts, he never thinks of it.'[200] Until later.[201]

Guilt is not just the burden of what has happened, but also of what has not. Many aircrew members suffered from 'survivor's guilt'; guilt in men 'who narrowly escaped sharing a death which took the life of a comrade'.[202] Survivor's guilt was easier to articulate for aircrew than any wider feelings of guilt they were commonly experiencing. An unacknowledged collective theme, that forced Ernest Millington, MP and former bomber pilot to ask in the House of Commons:

> we want – that is, the people who served in Bomber Command of the Royal Air Force and their next of kin – a categorical assurance that the work we did was militarily and strategically justified.[203]

Infamously, Winston Churchill failed to mention Bomber Command in his victory address[204] and the crews were allocated only the relatively lowly Defence Medal,[205] perhaps suggesting the level of political unease associated with their activities. On hearing the rumour of this decision Arthur Harris wrote to Archibald Sinclair and Charles Portal, copying in Hugh Trenchard:

> I must tell you as dispassionately as possible that if my Command are to have the Defence Medal and have no 'campaign' medal ... then I too will have the Defence Medal and no other – nothing else whatever, neither decoration, award, rank, preferment or appointment, if any such is contemplated or intended.[206]

In a handwritten postscript on the copy he sent to Hugh Trenchard he wrote, 'I started this war as an air vice-marshall. That is my substantive rank now. With that and the 'Defence' Medal I shall now leave the Service as soon as I can and return to my country – South Africa. I'm off'.[207] He never forgave Winston Churchill for declining to authorise a

Bomber Command medal.[M208] Within weeks the coalition had ended and Winston Churchill was out of power. The new Labour Government compounded the insult by ignoring recommendations to give Arthur Harris a peerage.[209] Winston Churchill conceded to his private secretary postwar, 'of course Harris was under-recognised at the end, so were his gallant men who suffered the heaviest casualties of all'.[210] Herbert Morrison, the Labour Home Secretary in the War Cabinet, wrote to Arthur Harris postwar:

> I was sad to hear your disappointment in certain matters and I wish I had known earlier though the matters you raise are not within my power directly. I need hardly assure you that I wish your desires had been met. It has been a very great pleasure to know you and Lady Harris so well and to have had happy evenings at Bomber Command. I am a great admirer of your work and of the men who served under you, and it was always a real pleasure to come along.[211]

* * *

When Boris Johnson appeared on the television to announce the closure of the economy in response to the Covid crisis, it was a shock to say the least. While there was something surreal about the whole situation, concerns of money and survival rapidly set in. I had recently sold a car, and that paid for a month or so of living, but beyond that, we just didn't know. It was stark, but others had it far worse. And for Cillian it meant a longer pressure-free recovery.

Generally guests were incredibly sympathetic and the support we received during this period was deeply moving. Most waived their deposits until another time, but one guest in particular, started buying

---

M Aircrew were finally honoured for their role in the Second World War in 2013, after a long battle for official recognition. The Bomber Command Clasp (to be attached to the 1939-1945 Star) was granted to crews who served for at least sixty days, or completed a tour of operations, on a Bomber Command operational unit and flew at least one of those operations between 3 September 1939 to 8 May 1945 (ITV News: 28/6/2013: itv.com).

regular vouchers so we would have some income. A mark of generosity we shall never forget.

Eventually, governmental discussions of grants materialised in payments; we were going to be all right. Indeed, the lock-down afforded us time to do all those jobs that we never had time to complete before. We re-rendered the Control Tower, finished fitting-out cupboards and completed the utility room. We did numerous jobs in the garden and even dug a pond. Indeed we became so ambitious about what we could achieve, that by the time restrictions began to ease, we weren't finished and had to continue DIY on the side, in what turned out to be our busiest season ever. When we were locked down for a second time, personally, it was a relief. We were exhausted.

Through all this, Rosie was an extraordinary support to Cillian; as she had been throughout his illness, from when she provided company during his in-patient week-long stays at Addenbrookes, researching and keeping on top of all his treatments when Cillian had his 'chemo-head' on. They were tested in a way a new relationship never should be, and they emerged through his illness stronger and apparently more resilient.

As strong as their relationship was, it didn't survive his recovery; when over the worst, with the all-clear and a cancer-free future ahead of them, they hit the rocks. Claire and I were stunned, but it was their future and they had to sort it out. We were all hurting and Claire and I were smarting from the shock – 'after all they'd been through', we thought. 'Far more common than you'd believe', a cancer researcher who came to stay informed me; 'they survive the worst of it and flounder during the recovery, when the future looks bright'.

* * *

On 13 October 1945, the Naafi at RAF North Creake closed.[212] The station was then passed to Wing Commander Horsfield of RAF 41 Group Maintenance Command,[213] and became the 111 Sub-Storage Site[214] for the RAF Swannington-based RAF 274 Maintenance Unit.[215] Over the next few months the RAF 274 Maintenance Unit received hundreds of aircraft, mostly Mosquitoes.[216] Many of these Mosquitoes arrived at RAF North Creake, for storage, preparation for sale or, mostly, disposal.[217]

An external FIDO fuel tank was moved to RAF North Creake to store fuel from the Mosquitoes. This fuel was often sold on the side to local people.[218] Ammunition was stored on site until removed to Wells-next-the-Sea, where fishermen were commissioned to dump it at sea.[219] Scrap metal was also taken to Wells, loaded onto small cargo ships and taken to a steel works in the north of England to be recycled.[220] Salvageable engines were removed and returned to Rolls Royce.[221] Being wood, the airframes were burnt on site, 'always in the same place',[222] drawing groups of children to watch the flames consume the carcasses of the Mosquitoes.[223] Anything left over was rumoured to have been buried in convenient pits on site.[224]

On 24 June 1946, Mosquito MK. VI RF839, swung on take-off at RAF North Creake; the pilot was unhurt but the aircraft was written off. This was the last flying incident at the station.[N225]

In April 1947, instructions were received that RAF North Creake should be cleared down by 15 September 1947.[226] A subsequent audit of the surplus left on site revealed there was far more than originally reported. As a consequence the clearing of RAF North Creake was made a priority.[227] With approximately 100 tons of equipment and salvage remaining, the majority of 274 Maintenance Unit personnel were deployed to the station working to clear the site.[228] During July 1947, 25 Mosquito aircraft were despatched for further use, 15 aircraft were destroyed and 84 tons of equipment and salvage were moved.[229] Even though one aircraft still remained for repair, the Number 6, WAAF and communal sites were handed over to the Air Ministry Works Directorate (AMWD) on 30 July 1947.[230] In August 'all equipment[O] including serviceable linoleum' was cleared from RAF

N   See appendix one

O   An optimistic appraisal, as those familiar with the airfield relate that there was detritus of one kind or another, including sections of Mosquitoes, lying around the site until the 1980s. Indeed, Teddy Maufe, from Branthill Farm, recalls that growing up his father's farm workshop was equipped with many tools that were 'surplus' to Air Ministry needs (Maufe: 22/2/2024).

North Creake, with the exception of the remaining Mosquito[P] and a small quantity of scrap timber.[231]

All buildings at North Creake were then handed over to the AMWD. Three members of the Air Ministry Constabulary were retained, until bi-weekly inspections of the station by personnel from RAF Bircham Newton could be arranged.[232] The three remaining (Air Ministry) constables departed on 12 October 1947, and the one remaining telephone was recovered by the GPO.[233]

At the point of derequisition, and before the land was returned to the landowner, it was, 'so far as practicable',[234] to be returned to its original purpose or a sum of compensation paid.[235] The absolute meaning of practicable is obviously not defined, and, although the land may have gone through substantial change (in the form of structures, runways etc.) it was, in practice, most often considered not practicable to restore the land 'at all'.[236] It is impossible not to conclude, although unstated, that the reason was the prohibitive cost of restoration. The future financial burden on the State of decommissioning all the unwanted airfields was realised as early as 1943:

> a large proportion of the airfields, constructed for war purposes, cannot be used for either post-war military purposes or for civil aviation. Therefore, so far from representing an asset of abiding value, the British Government upon the termination of hostilities, will be faced with a very considerable liability for the reinstatement of sites and the restoration of land to its former uses.[237]

The end of the war saw the Ministry of Works administering the derequisitioning of numerous redundant airfields with associated claims

---

P This Mosquito (RG176) was finally repaired and despatched from North Creake on 9 September 1947, becoming the last RAF aircraft to leave the station (274 Maintenance Unit: 1947: ORB). However, further aircraft did fly from North Creake; for a while there was a crop-dusting business using light aircraft, there was also a helicopter repair business (whether they were flown in and out is unclear), and in the 1960s and early 1970s night-time flying was once again resumed. This nefarious activity was witnessed by a former resident of the Control Tower with black limousines collected goods from light aircraft that were 'down no longer than three minutes'.

for compensation by landowners.[238] Of the 37 operational RAF stations present in Norfolk at the end of the war, only one, RAF Marham, is still operational today (2024), with a further two having some military use.[239] Most have reverted to 'some form of agricultural use',[240] albeit with many structures persisting in the fields around. Other than agriculture, a number of Norfolk airfields have turned to light industry, four have embraced civil aviation, two have become motor racing circuits and one is a nature reserve.[241] RAF North Creake was initially identified as a permanent station,[242] however, like so many others, the cessation of hostilities was to mark the beginning of the end.

Walsingham Estate Company (WECo) approached the Air Ministry and Ministry of Works in November 1945,[243] to request the provision of both water and electricity from airfield sources for supplying Edgar Farm, situated close by. The first response from the Air Ministry suggested supply from the power line 'erected entirely for Air Ministry purposes',[244] 'will require some investigation'.[245] This was not an exaggeration as some four years later, and with the East Anglian Electricity Supply Company involved, they were still trying to raise an estimate.[246] Similarly with water, having discovered that a sample from the kitchen tap at Edgar Farm was 'unsuitable for drinking',[247] WECo made an approach to the Air Ministry regarding the possibility of connecting to their bore hole.[248] The Air Ministry responded that the 'water supply installation has been taken over by the Ministry of Works',[249] who subsequently replied that, 'it is understood that proposals which this Ministry had for this property have been abandoned and we have now relinquished our interest',[250] and that it was further understood that the main was to come under the control of Walsingham Rural District Council [WRDC]. WRDC outlined that they presently had no interest in adopting the main, although they may do so in the future.[251] However, they warned that any regional scheme will 'not be available for some years'[252] and indicated that the estate should 'make arrangements for an alternative supply as soon as possible'.[253] How this was ultimately resolved is not documented.

WRDC never did adopt the RAF North Creake water supply,[Q] but they did take over the sewage plant at an estimated cost of £34,165 0s 6d;[254] however, the 'scheme did not provide for Egmere [as] ... such extensions would prove very expensive'.[255] Consequently the Control Tower was cut off from the sewage system built to service it. An irony I sit and contemplate most days.

Before derequisitioning, land was allocated to one of three categories: 'A' implied immediate removal of structures and bases as demanded by national or local amenity interests; 'B' indicated that the removal of the airfield structures was considered desirable at some future date;[256] and 'C' denoted that the structures were 'not of a nature calling for removal in the public interest'.[257] These assessments were generally undertaken by county planning officers, and in Norfolk this fell to Harry Hopkins.[258] In July 1949, he inspected sites on WECo land and concluded they were mainly 'unoccupied and in a bad state of repair [with] some of the huts in process of being dismantled'.[259] He visited for a second time in August 1949:

> you will recall in July of this year, Sites 2, 3, Mess, Administrative, and Sick Quarters at North Creake Airfield were referred to me for categorisation and in my letter of July 27th I placed the works in category 'C'. At the time I considered it a 'border-line' case which should have the benefit of the doubt, but revisiting the site and inspecting the further works now under consideration, I am of the opinion that it would be wrong to allow these various buildings of a semi-permanent nature to remain indefinitely, particularly in view of the fact that the majority of the buildings are in a derelict condition and serving no useful purpose. Should they not be removed, they would only deteriorate still further and cause greater injury to the amenities of the district.[260]

Q The opportunity of taking over the RAF North Creake bore holes was ultimately rejected as a result of concerns regarding the cost of maintaining the airfield water tower; instead, WRDC bored their own water supply at Houghton St. Giles. The three airfield bore holes were capped sometime in the late 1950s or early 1960s by the Water Board as they were silting up through non-use (Perryman: 2014: 2).

He consequently changed the categorisation of these WECo sites, and some sites belonging to Holkham Estate, to 'B'.[261] Nonetheless, his decision and the county's recommendation were overruled by the Temporary Defence Works Committee (TDWC). This infuriated Holkham Estates Company's agent, Sydney Turner, who sent a letter to Harry Hopkins, venting his ire:[262]

> If by categorising these works as 'C' it is to be understood that the Ministry of Works are not prepared to recognise our claim based on its original use as agriculture, then we must protest most strongly ... against such categorisation (which shows a lamentable lack of appreciation of the real issues on the part of the individuals concerned) ... From the Town Planning point of view, how can it be stated that the works are 'not of a nature calling for removal in the public interest' when the Norfolk County Council, under the Town and Country Planning (general development) Order 1948, have limited their permission in respect to the huts ... to a period of 15 years, thereby implying at the expiration of that term they will have to be removed. If this applies to complete huts which have been maintained for storage ... surely it must apply even more so to the derelict buildings which have been left by the Ministry on the sites.[263]

Holkham Estates had already started demolishing some of the sites and had instructed a contractor to undertake further clearing work, 'but we must insist on the total clearance of the works and the restoration of the land to agriculture'.[264] TDWC responded to Holkham's appeal:

> [the sites] were referred to this Committee for action prior to derequisition and were accordingly sent to the Ministry of Agriculture and Ministry of Town and Country Planning for their recommendations for a category. Both of these Departments replied with a 'C' category which was accepted by the Committee.[265]

Despite a lengthy dispute and an appeal,[266] there is no suggestion that the TDWC decision was altered, even though the Ministry 'agreed that the buildings were unsightly'.[267] It is perhaps no coincidence that any categorisation other than 'C' would have 'difficult financial implications' for the Ministry of Works.[268] Instead, these serious financial implications were passed to the landowner who would receive no financial assistance for the costs of reinstatement of the land.[269] Unless it could be illustrated that, as a result of damage or work during the period of requisition, the land had diminished in value.[270] Holkham Estates Company contended that the 'works are having and will continue to have, a serious effect, not only on the value of the farm as a whole, but on all future agricultural operations'.[271] Nonetheless, there is no evidence that TDWC softened their line.

Conversely, some attempts were made to clear the land by the Ministry of Works and, they were in the process of clearing the Administrative Site with huts planned to be sold by tender, when WECo asked for first refusal on buildings they considered may be of use.[272] This request was met with a somewhat brusque response from the Ministry of Works, outlining that they had been led to understand in a telephone conversation with WECo, that they were not interested in the hutting; 'arrangements are now in hand for the removal of the buildings, but if you are prepared to make an immediate offer for any of them, I will ascertain whether a sale to you is possible'.[273] Ultimately some hutting was retained, some of which S H Waters at Edgar Farm, had already begun to use,[274] particularly No. 3 Site (nearly opposite Edgar Farm).[275] Having expressed his willingness to pay £60 for retention of all the hutting,[276] he eventually bought two huts for £42.[277]

It does not appear that any land was derequisitioned until late 1949 or early 1950.[R] Once the site was derequisitioned, landowners could mitigate some of their losses by clever use, or disposal, of what was left. Buildings could be reused, and Holkham Estates Company achieved planning approval for a number of 'ex-Air Ministry hutments

---

R   It is clear from correspondence between WECo (5/5/1949) and S H Waters, Edgar Farm, that the land was still not derequisitioned in May 1949 (Walsingham Archive: 5/5/49).

for use for agricultural purposes'.[278] WECo also used many buildings, including S H Waters who rented the standby set house on the Communal Site from WECo for use as a grain store.[279] However there seemed little strategy in WECo's approach to the disposal of items of value left on the land, other than responding to approaches made by companies specialising in reclamation. W G Humphrey of Cromer offered £25 per foot for the Nissen huts on the 'Technical Site north of Edgar Road'. Starting in November 1951, they removed the Nissen hut frames and demolished the end walls. Subsequently, J C & W Jacob bought the rubble for a total of £40.[280]

In June 1951, Jackson-Stops & Staff[281] offered WECo £800 for the buried cabling on the whole airfield, 'divisible in proportion to ownership'.[282] However, the cabling was ultimately removed by M Maclean who had initially offered £200 for WECo's share or £120 per ton if WECo paid all expenses (the same arrangement agreed by Holkham Estates Company).[283] Work started on 31 April 1952,[284] although £90 per ton was finally paid as a consequence of falling copper prices.[285]

In November 1947, the Air Ministry announced that 'they were prepared to revoke the temporary closure order'[286] on the road from Great Walsingham to North Creake, where it crossed the Airfield Site, that had been in force since May 1943.[287] However, while the Norfolk County Council surveyor agreed to the revocation order, he could see no value in reinstatement of the road as it had been 'obliterated'[288] by the construction of the runway. The Regional Land Commissioner agreed.[289] In September 1951, Norfolk County Council applied for an order for permanent closure, as they considered an alternative route served the 'requirements of local inhabitants'.[290] However, WRDC and the local Parish Councils of Walsingham and Wighton, were all of the opinion that the right of way should be maintained for pedestrians and cyclists.[291] The Commons, Open Spaces and Footpaths Preservation Society (now Open Spaces Society), supported them.[292] The Highway Committee of Norfolk County Council disagreed 14 votes to six,[293] with a range of views on both sides of the argument being represented, including that of Bartle Frere, who believed 'it a mistake for strangers to have additional access to an aerodrome in case it was needed again'.[S294] The Chair concluded 'in all my 30 years' experience of public work I have never come across a case where so much local indignation has been aroused'.[295] With no possibility of reconciliation it was referred to the War Works Commission[296] and a public enquiry was set up for 7 July 1955, chaired by Luke Fawcett, former General Secretary of the Amalgamated Union of Building Trade Workers, and Basil Gibson, Justice of the Peace.[297]

Objectors to the proposal included Holkham Estates Company, Tom Hancock (a Holkham tenant farmer)[298] and Great Walsingham Parish Council. The Parish Council believed the road should be reinstated or at least a made-up bridle path and cycle track provided.[299] Whereas, Sydney Turner, representing Holkham Estate, strongly objected to the proposed footpath, believing that it would 'seriously interfere with the cultivation of arable lands',[300] which are already seriously cut up 'by the [30 acres of] airfield runways and perimeter tracks.' He further argued that it was 'an unwarranted expenditure of public money [as] it would be very unlikely that anyone would walk or even cycle along this road'.[301] He concluded that pedestrians and cyclists 'would not be much inconvenienced by having to go the additional seven hundred yards'.[302] Tom Hancock was more worried about people wandering over his crops.[303]

All the land affected by the footpath proposal belonged to Holkham, except that belonging to British Field Products (BFP).[304] BFP purchased the freehold from Holkham Estates Company[305] for 20.75 acres of land and the buildings thereon, including the Control Tower.[306] First rumoured before derequisition, the Air Ministry controlling the buildings was willing to 'release to [BFP] certain buildings at North Creake Aerodrome, including two large hangars'.[307] The plant, intended for the purpose of animal feed production,[308] was seen as part of the

---

S   There were rumours in 1954 that RAF North Creake was to be reopened as a Canadian base with Sabre jets. It is not reported from where these rumours emerged but they were denied by both the RCAF and the Air Ministry. The RCAF stated 'there is no indication of any move of that sort', with the Air Ministry insisting that 'it is most unlikely' as the runways are 'not long enough to allow Sabre jets to take off' (EDP: 28/9/1954: 5).

solution to 'adjust[ing] our economy to postwar conditions'[309] and was primed with a substantial treasury loan of £120,000.[310] By the time of the public enquiry, the plant was well into production and BFP also objected to the proposed footpath. They had been advised by Norfolk County Council that the road would not be reopened and now feared the security of 'valuable stores and equipment which it will be exceedingly difficult to safeguard'.[311]

In support of the proposal were the Commons, Open Spaces and Footpaths Preservation Society.[312] Their secretary, Humphrey Baker, argued that 'Norfolk is a county where there has necessarily been so much invasion of public rights that we hope the Ministry will give every possible weight to the wishes of the local people'.[313] The ultimate outcome of the inquiry is not recorded, but it is safe to conclude that an unmetalled right of way was settled upon, as it still exists today and is marked accordingly on Ordnance Survey maps and is the only public access to the former airfield.

BFP was not the first company to be attracted by the vacant buildings on the former Airfield Site; in 1947, Boome and Co., producers of 'whiting',[T] applied for planning approval.[314] However, this was a contentious product and while planning was granted on 2 August 1947,[315] it was for five years with the strict conditions obliging the company to prevent 'chalk dust, noise and offensive smells'.[316] It is unclear whether production ever commenced, as while Government papers mention a 'hangar let by the Air Ministry to a firm producing chalk products',[317] a contemporary newspaper reports 'the proposals did not materialise'.[318]

The south hangar, the very structure into which BFP was scheduled to locate, was occupied by Grange Brothers, a road haulage company originating from Wells-next-the-Sea, that had been involved in hauling the aggregate for the construction of the airfield.[319] This was causing some difficulty for this 'project of national importance'.[320]

T 'Whiting' is a crushed chalk commonly used for mortar (when mixed with lime putty). However, its planned use in this case, was the manufacture of face powder and other commodities (EDP: 3/9/48: 3).

> we have been asked to try to arrange for possession to be given rather earlier than the date the Notice to Quit by Grange can expire … also [we will] get in touch shortly with the Ministry of Food and/or the Ministry of Transport with a view to them taking over Grange, but clearly it is impossible at very short notice.[321]

Aside from proposing to nationalise a company to circumvent a tenancy arrangement, the Ministry concluded that there was 'little difficulty in providing alternative accommodation',[322] and suggested the Romney sheds across the road, on the Technical Site, belonging to WECo. These huts, even at this early stage, needed substantial repair before relocation was possible as the cladding had 'rusted through at the bottom'.[323] From April 1951, Grange Brothers rented eight huts from WECo,[324] resolving the competing requirements for the south hangar. However, this did not absolve them from state control and in late 1949 or early 1950, they were nationalised, making the owner very wealthy; 'he never really worked again'.[325]

In February 1950, planning permission was granted for the conversion of a number of buildings for BFP,[326] including the Control Tower into two flats (one occupied by Julian Melchett, the primary initiator of the plant).[327] Conversion of the airfield buildings was initially approved for 15 years[328] and thereafter regularised. BFP produced animal feed from the early 1950s, employing a full-time staff of around 80 workers,[329] and contracting local farmers to grow crops (mostly Lucerne grass) which was dried in the south hangar. A fire in 1970 consumed much of the equipment inside the hangar, and it was subsequently decided to abandon Lucerne grass production and concentrate on animal feed.[330] This was the basis for the animal feed plant that still operates on the site today.

Postwar, a number of the RAF North Creake hutments were used as accommodation. The temporary and, at times, informal nature of this encampment has meant little trace remains, but it persists in the memory of local people and in WRDC documents. In September 1945,

WRDC first registered an interest in hutting for temporary housing with the Air Ministry.[331] Initially, Whitehall resisted calls to use the camps as temporary housing for a number of reasons: (1) they were poorly constructed; (2) the sites were badly laid out for domestic use; (3) they were in remote locations; (4) there was little or no transport, shops or amenities; (5) any adaption, particularly of sanitary and cooking facilities from communal to individual was difficult and also diverted materials and labour from the permanent house building programme; (6) the projected other uses for camps (German POWs, emergency training sites for trades/craftsmen for the housing programme and for teachers as a result of the expected demand once the school-leaving age was extended).[332]

In 1945 the future of the airfield was still uncertain,[333] but at the point the Air Ministry decided that it was no longer needed for RAF, it would be first 'hawked around other Ministries who might have an interest in it'.[334] Nonetheless, the Air Ministry assured WRDC that it had noted the council in the 'lists of likely purchasers'.[335] The council sub-committee made an inspection of sites and informed both the Air Ministry and the Ministry of Health that they were interested in WAAF No. 6 Site and the Communal Site (both on Holkham land), to provide accommodation for 17 families.[336] However, they instructed the housing officer to 'defer preparation of plans, specifications and estimates for the conversion ... [until] the hutments [became] available ... it [was] anticipated that no difficulty would be experienced in obtaining tenants'.[337] The WAAF and Communal sites were handed over by 274 Maintenance Unit to the AMWD for transfer to the Ministry of Health on 30 July 1947.[338] WRDC formally took over No. 6 Site in October 1947.[339] The Housing Officer then prepared 'plans and specifications for adapting the various structures for use as temporary houses'.[340] The Housing Committee approved plans for conversion of six Nissen huts and seven brick structures into 25 temporary dwellings on No. 6 Site.[341] Prices for conversions were sought, but by the time quotes had been submitted to the Ministry of Health and were awaiting approval, the Housing Committee:

expressed concern at the large expenditure which would be incurred in the conversion of these hutments, namely £215 each, which were situated on an isolated site and might only be occupied for a limited period.[342]

The scheme was therefore abandoned.[343] However, by now, those in need, had taken matters into their own hands and on 1 October 1947, the clerk of WRDC reported that 'squatters had taken possession of certain hutments on the No 1 Site';[344] some 16 months after the large-scale British squatter movement had emerged.

The RAF North Creake Squatters Camp: Pat Noakes enjoys a bath (Heather Platten).

The Squatters' Movement had been an almost inevitable outcome of the sudden demobilisation of service personnel. By July 1945, 3.5 million people had been demobbed in the UK,[345] and the number of families that wanted a home, exceeded the number of dwellings in Great Britain by 1,170,000.[346] The number of available dwellings fell by 400,000, between 1939 and 1945, with over the same period, the demand increasing from an estimated 12 million to approximately 13.2 million;[347] 'just decent people who wanted a home'.[348] A senior civil servant at the Ministry of Works commented:

> until squatting began nobody in his right senses could believe that families would be content to live in dormitory huts of this nature. The squatting epidemic has shown that large numbers of people are in such desperate need of accommodation that they are only too glad to squat in empty and unpartitioned huts.[349]

The squatters were generally ex-servicemen and women, most of whom had married during the war, and, on being demobilised, 'suddenly found themselves ... having to live with in-laws',[350] often in intolerable and unacceptable housing conditions.[351]

The Labour Government had inherited from the wartime coalition, the hugely ambitious commitment to provide 'a separate dwelling for every family that wishes to have one'.[352] The Government had promised to build 200,000 new houses by the end of 1946[353] and a million over a five-year period.[354] Nonetheless, Aneurin Bevan understood that these needed to be the 'right houses', as 'while we shall be judged for a year or two by the number of houses we build, we shall be judged in ten years' time by the type of homes we build'.[355] Consequently, the aspiration was to build high quality housing.

However, the building industry was among the most severely impacted sectors of the war, 'not only from a diversion of its activities to war work, but from contraction of the skilled labour force on which its efficiency depends'.[356] Moreover, the building industry was very labour-intensive, yet in 1946, the Government was desperate to keep more workers in industries vital for the economy (such as coal or manufacturing); indeed, the Chancellor of the Exchequer, Stafford Cripps, was so concerned with exports, that he argued, that in terms of priority, 'last are the needs, comforts and amenities of the family'.[357] Housebuilding also required lots of timber, almost all of which Britain imported, seriously affecting the British balance of payments.[358] All these issues and more, impacted upon the returning service personnel's ability to have a home.

Even though it was a stated Government priority,[359] by August 1946, the 'majority of local authorities had not completed a single house'.[360] As Aneurin Bevan conceded in 1946, 'how on earth can people be satisfied when the lack of houses is such a fertile source of human misery?'.[361] In November 1940, Frederick Marquis (Lord Woolton), the wartime Minister of Food, wrote a seemingly prophetic note: 'the danger is that if the machine of government which can spend money so recklessly in engaging in war, fails to be equally reckless in rebuilding, there will be both the tendency and the excuse for revolution'.[362]

On 8 May 1946,[U] James Fielding, a cinema projectionist, moved to Scunthorpe for a new job with his wife and four children.[363] Unable to find accommodation, they took over the officers' mess of an abandoned anti-aircraft site. They were joined, in early July, by a further 20 families.[364] Leading on from the first squats in Scunthorpe, military camps were occupied all over the country from Taunton to the West of Scotland.[365] By the end of August 1946, 1,038 camps were occupied by 39,525 squatters. On the 18 August 1946, Aneurin Bevan stated in the House of Commons that he had sanctioned local authorities to supply services where possible. Camps that were suitable and were not needed, were to be offered to local authorities for housing purposes and squatters would not be moved except 'where service need conflicted with occupation, or where the places occupied were unhealthy or unsuitable'.[366]

Whitehall blamed the spread of this 'people's initiative'[367] on the press and particularly 'newsreel coverage'.[368] Indeed, it caused a press storm; initially, at least, sympathetic to the squatters and angry with the Labour Government.[369] Letters to the press suggest the sympathy of the public was similarly placed; 'their action was unusual, unconstitutional, but let no one think they are ruffians. They are ordinary people, they shave every day, eat at tables, go off to earn their own living'.[370] Clementine Churchill, the former Prime Minister's wife, 'dilated on

---

U   Although some suggest it may have started in Edinburgh as early as December 1945 (Branson: 1984: 6).

the sorry plight of those respectable citizens'.[371] At a military camp in Eastcote, West London, a Mass Observation observer discovered that the squatters were made up of a mixture of middle and artisan class:

> one man is a master builder, another a schoolmaster and another a factory worker. All are ex-servicemen ... 2 of them have cars and some could afford to buy a house but have been unable to do so ... There is no sign of any violent political enthusiasm amongst them.[372]

It was no different in Norfolk where many camps were occupied. At Weeting, a village policeman turned a blind eye to the airfield's new occupants; "'I'm supposed to tell you you're not meant to be here,'" he said before cycling away'.[373] Peggy Newton made an appeal to the commanding officer at RAF Feltwell, regarding moving into some vacant buildings. She was told 'he could not encourage her ... yet hearing her plight did not forbid her to do so'.[374] At Ketteringham Hall, 40 to 50 families moved into Nissen huts in the park grounds;[375] Mary Elder, who served with the Americans when stationed at the Hall wrote 'it was a wonderful thought to all of us to know that these barracks, where we shared so much joy and sorrow, laughter and tears were used to give shelter to our British friends'.[376]

At some Norfolk camps the authorities threatened to cut power or nailed doors shut.[377] However, on others the local authority simply charged rent.[378] On camps such as Rackheath, 60 squatters affiliated to the 'National Federation of Squatters'[379] and set their own rent at 7s 6d and put it into a separate account, until asked for it by a 'proper' authority.[380]

There are few records regarding the camp at RAF North Creake, but if it followed the pattern of development of most camps it was run as a 'self-governing democratic'[381] community, with committees established to negotiate with authorities for provision of services, building materials and to set rents.[382] Shared sanitary arrangements and cooking facilities demanded that there was 'a degree of communal organisation'[383] with, most often, cleaning rotas and, possibly, even a nursery for the children.[384] The squatters had settled in, when, in 1948, the hutments on the former RAF North Creake site made headlines in the local press. *The Eastern Daily Press* (EDP) reported that 'a large part of the R.A.F. station at Egmere … is being prepared for [550 Polish dependents] by the Ministry of Works'.[385] The British Government was faced with an urgent need to accommodate 160,000 Polish ex-servicemen (many with families), and they considered the disused military camps a potential solution.[386] There was a depressingly familiar level of opposition to the Polish camp, with the EDP reporting 'great concern on the part of residents in the district'.[387] An editorial in the EDP comments, 'perhaps we do not remember, so clearly as we ought, the Polish share in the Battle of Britain and the Battle of Cassino … when the Government proposes to settle a community of 550 of them in huts on a remote airfield … it does not seem unduly generous to the Poles or hard on homeless Britons'.[388] However, the spectre of 'taking our jobs and homes' was raised by organisations from across the political spectrum. The National Farmers' Union wrote:

> there is already no shortage of agricultural labour in the district … [there is] no other industry situated in the district and there seems no prospect of other employment for these men … it will be to the detriment of the Poles themselves, no less than to the farmers and local population, if large numbers of displaced persons are housed in a remote rural area with no form of regular employment, with insufficient to occupy their time and with no prospect of stability and of leading useful lives.[389]

The remoteness of the site was also raised by the National Union of Agricultural Workers (NUAW); 'how can the authorities possibly expect these people to learn our way of life if they are to be isolated in a place like North Creake?'.[390] Holkham's agent, Sydney Turner's, response was more nuanced: 'while not opposed in principle to housing people who were homeless',[391] he warns, if not properly organised with shopping, recreation and other activities, it would be 'catastrophic for the district and themselves'.[392] Depressingly, both local branches of the NUAW agreed, with the Walsingham Branch warning, 'we shall watch the situation very carefully. If the Poles are employed on the land and any of our men turned off, we shall not wear it'.[393] The Wighton Branch added, '[the Poles] will be coming in, buying what little can be had ... [local villagers] think it most unfair that working people living in Nissen huts adjoining them should have to part off rooms with blankets and sacks, while brought in bricks are being brought in to part off the rooms for Poles'.[394] With accusations flying that, to make room for the Poles, WRDC had overseen the displacement of local families to huts that were inferior,[395] the clerk responded that the council 'had undertaken on behalf of the Air Ministry, to administer a section of the huts occupied by approved squatters and it was to those huts that the families had been moved'.[396] An EDP editorial illustrates a reassuring level of understanding of the situation:

> Not surprisingly ... [the Poles] seem to have had a hostile and prejudiced reception ... it is an unhappy situation ... It is questionable whether the establishment of separate communities is the best way ... but it is all we have the means to do at the moment ... what is needed here ... is an intelligent and sympathetic explanation to the local people beforehand. There should be some understanding of what a tremendous event it is in a rural district to what amounts to a new village ... To establish the new settlement is not just a matter of administration, it is a matter of human relationships. Walsingham ought to be told exactly what is going on – and by Walsingham we mean the men's clubs and the Women's Institutes: not just the local authority. There should be an effort to gain their interest in the project and their friendship for the exiles.[397]

Nonetheless, responding to the overwhelming chorus of objections, WRDC carried the following motion:

> That this Council, whilst deploring the necessity of finding accommodation for 550 Polish Dependants, feel that the selection of North Creake Airfield for such accommodation is ill advised and should be reconsidered in consultation with the Council, particularly in view of the strong opposition to the proposals by the National Farmers' Union and the National Union of Agricultural Workers.[398]

Perhaps predictably, the Ministry of Works responded that 'it had been necessary to abandon the use of RAF North Creake to accommodate 500 Polish dependants'.[399]

In February 1949, the WRDC Housing Committee received another letter from the Walsingham District Committee of the NUAW. This letter drew 'attention to the condition of the hutments on the Airfield occupied by Squatters'.[400] At the same meeting, and possibly because of this letter, WRDC returned to the idea of hutting as temporary housing. The council's architect, F M Dewing, and quantity surveyor, Philip Pank, were instructed to prepare the necessary plans for the Ministry of Health.[401] Within six months plans were submitted for the conversion of 18 hutments on the same site as the squatters (No. 1), at a cost of £3,479, 17s 2d.[402] The scheme was approved by the Ministry of Health in October 1950, on the understanding that the Council was satisfied that the accommodation was required; that conversion costs were unlikely to exceed an average of £200 per dwelling and that they were likely to be acceptable to tenants for a period of five years.[403] The conversions were all completed by February 1952.[404]

It is uncertain whether the squats continued alongside the formalised WRDC camp or whether the squat was 'legitimised' by the use of the local authority rent book. It is reasonable to suspect the latter, and certainly children of parents on the camp remember rents being paid.[405]

Attempts were made to reduce the numbers on the camp as early as 1951, when a tender was accepted for the weatherproofing of huts in Wighton (as the North Creake WAAF Site was now called), as 'it was considered that the time had now come when the Council should seriously consider the future of these huts'.[406] In a letter in 1953, the Principal Officer of the Ministry of Housing and Local Government raised his concerns about the persistence of the camps, and that at the present rate of progress the camps would not close 'in less than four or five years', whereas the life expectancy of most huts was 'eighteen months to two years, and in some cases less'[407] without major repair work.[408]

The camp remained at RAF North Creake until the late 1950s when the last families were moved off.

Without maintenance, the airfield site rapidly declined. The only buildings that survived to any extent were the very well built or those in use. The best chance of survival being if it were both. Where buildings were sold or just removed, pine trees were planted in their place.[409] From the late 1960s through to the late 1970s, parts of the runways at RAF North Creake were grubbed-up for hardcore;[410] a typical runway yielding 100,000 tons, enough to provide hardcore for several miles of modern motorway.[411] Rory Cooke, who still lives in Wells-next-the-Sea, worked removing the concrete. For years he had a pile of old runway lights, although now, he can no longer recall what happened to them. Runway one was almost completely removed, the gouge from Jim Feasey's crashed Halifax along with it.[412] However, the concrete can still be driven along, only underneath the Kings Lynn bypass (opened in 1975[413]). Runways two and three are still full length, but the edges have been nibbled away and they are both a little over a trackway wide. Walking across the airfield site on the public footpath, one of the two T2 hangars can be viewed (the mill surrounds the other). The path then crosses both the peritrack and runway number two (where you can glean a good impression of its length). Crossing the field you reach the primary runway, with the original width evident from the gap in the trees looking west, and the B1 hangar can clearly be seen looking east on the other side of the Dry Road. Near to the B1 hangar is the old pump house, along with a number of other huts on the Communal Site. After the runway, you pick up the old road again, which was used to access the bomb-dump; some concrete of which still remains.

Aerial Photograph from 1946 with the original site plan superimposed. It can be seen that some sites were not built as planned, indeed many changes were made to the location of sites and building during construction. Sadly no post-construction plans exist and it is therefore very difficult to determine the purpose of many buildings. The airfield site is on the left and the two hangars can be clearly seen. The Control Tower is just south of these in front of the copse of trees. The Dry Road runs south to north alongside the Control Tower and the two hangars (Norfolk Historic Environment Record, The Archive Centre/Mark Risborough).

Across the Dry Road from the Control Tower is the former Technical Site; remarkably complete and indicative of the huts finding postwar uses (initially with Grange Brothers). There is now a thriving business community here, involving three motor workshops, an agricultural business, a laundry and so on. Similarly, on North Creake Industrial Park, to the south of the Airfield Site, there are a number of original buildings including the dinghy shed.

Travelling east, the pine woods planted in the early 1950s on the airfield sites have now matured and mark the size and position of the original sites. They also contain concrete bases and the occasional building (cinema, standby set house, etc.) and numerous blast shelters. When veterans returned to see their old airfield in the 1980s and 1990s, there was little left to remind them and their bearings were easily lost. But returning to the Technical Site there was much that was familiar. The Control Tower was still there, although somewhat changed. Julian Melchett, after moving his family out, housed workers for his farm at Ringstead in the Control Tower and 'drove them back and forward in a dormobile'.[414] It was also used for storage, a mess room and lavatories; however, mostly it had been used by workers of the mill in need of temporary housing for one reason or another.

The airfield personnel seldom return now. As time inexorably passes and the Second World War drifts from living memory, it is left to us, those they have shared their recollections with, to maintain it in our collective consciousness. A B&B guest at the Control Tower, on witnessing the arrival of the grandson of a veteran, now long-since dead, realised the responsibility; 'it's still alive for a lot of people', he said.[415]

Former residents of the Control Tower also remember; eager to tell us of their time here. And there are the surprising number that comment, 'I nearly bought the Control Tower', generally followed by, 'but I thought it was too much work', or 'it would cost too much money to do'. They were, of course, correct on both counts. But we didn't see it when we came here, and I'm glad we didn't.

Others did. Cillian recently remarked that when he first saw the Control Tower, he commented to his girlfriend, 'they're fucking mad!'. Although he countered, 'you'd set your mind on it. Everyone says the same, when you start a challenge, you finish … Lewis, Nick, others. Knew you'd finish, even when you didn't have a pot to piss in'. Looking back now, I sometimes wonder why we weren't more terrified than we were. It was probably that we had little idea of how difficult or how expensive it would be. We also had no idea how many hospitality businesses fail. Richard Hughes and Stacia Briggs were early adopters of the B&B and, having since become close friends, Richard, who is a chef and director of the Assembly House in Norwich, confessed to me how stunned he was to learn that we had no hospitality background; 'it so seldom works', he said.

But it has worked. We've created something we love and something we love doing. Furthermore, we enjoyed the process of getting here. It had its challenges, fear and infuriating moments, but was overall, a joy. We have mostly seen the best of people, with very few detractors, and we have been staggered by the generosity of others. On this occasion Vic Godard was correct, 'one big risk in life won't hurt you'; we made the right choice. I remember a rare trip from Norfolk to London to see friends. Hungover, I was dozing on the train on the way home. An announcer woke me with the words 'the next station is Potters Bar'; the station before, I would have alighted when I worked in London. Before I realised the truth, my heart had sunk in anticipation of the day ahead. That never happens now. There is something so much better than that life.

When all's said and done, I realise for all our conscious efforts to discover the history of the Control Tower, we have become inextricably part of it. And also, hopefully, part of its future for some time to come.

CHAPTER ELEVEN

THEY SHALL GROW NOT OLD

Time to leave the ghosts of North
Creake airfield to their whispering
barley and their rusting relics.1

Jack Sinclair, former RAF North Creake Wireless Operator

The Bomber Command aircrew members that were lucky enough to survive the war, returned to civilian life with a greatly increased chance of growing old.[A] Bernie How returned to Suffolk where his parents ran a pub; picking up where he had left off in the building trade, he got married and seldom mentioned the war. When pushed, he would say he 'thoroughly enjoyed it. Yeah. We did really. Because you met different people and that kind of thing'.[2] Another RAF North Creake aircrew member observed, 'great days'[3] and 'the happiest days of my life … comradeship was terrific!'.[4] 'It was sad when we all had to split up'.[5]

A 'They shall grow not old' is from the poem *The Fallen*, by Laurence Benyon, written in 1914 is has become famous through its adoption as the *Exhortation* in the Act of Remembrance:
They shall grow not old, as we that are left grow old:
Age shall not weary them, nor the years condemn.
At the going down of the sun and in the morning
We will remember them.

On returning to civilian life, some managed to get work in similar roles as they had performed in the RAF,[6] although being employed as a pilot was unlikely, as there was a surfeit postwar. Others, such as Les King, retrained in flying control before demobilisation, and subsequently worked as a civilian air traffic controller.[7]

Les King, Special Operator with 171 Squadron (Ray King).

After the war, apart from decisions regarding the preservation of some files and official photographs (and with the disregarding of most), little was done to preserve the memory of RAF North Creake. It was rumoured that the nose section of a record-breaking RAF North Creake Stirling[B] was to be sent to the Australian War Memorial in Canberra for display. The possibility was announced in a press release in 1945, and the story was reported in some Australian newspapers, but by

---

B   LJ514 B-Baker, known as B-Bear, completed 75 operations (330 operational flying hours) from RAF North Creake. It featured a bear holding a beer bottle and a frothing pint jug of beer on the side of the cockpit for each sortie completed (Hines: 2022: 68-69).

1946, the museum seemed to have decided to opt for a Lancaster alone, as space was limited.[8]

The growing interest in Bomber Command in the 1970s, resulted in more artefacts being conserved. At RAF North Creake, the operations board from the Control Tower was still being used for truck departures in the animal feed mill. A volunteer from the Norfolk and Suffolk Aviation Museum pinpointed its importance and the mill subsequently donated it to the museum. It is still on display today. Other items were donated by the mill, such as a Mercury tug used for hauling the bomb trailers during the war[9] and then for moving animal feed around the site.[10] The Mercury tug was delivered in May 1984 to the Lincolnshire Aviation Museum, Tattershall, and photographs exist of it after restoration commenced.[11] However, there is no record of its survival today. A Morris Commercial lorry (JUW 348) was offered to the Fenland Aviation Museum in 1979, but they seem not to have collected it.[12] In 1984, it was offered to Tattershall.[13] Whether they took it is unknown. There was also a hand-operated crane used to remove aircraft propellers, and still used on-site postwar; but no trace of that exists.[14] The greatest act of conservation of an RAF North Creake relic was the removal of the mural of Stirling EX-N. Painted on a wall, it was removed to the RAF Museum in Hendon and dedicated as a memorial to Bomber Command.[C]

There was certainly no discussion of any commemoration or memorial at the former RAF North Creake, until a marker stone was placed on the airfield site in 2011. This was part of a national programme to mark military airfields by the Airfields of Britain Conservation Trust, but this had little involvement of the local community.

When we arrived at the Control Tower in 2011, we adopted a three-stage project strategy. First, we would restore the Control Tower to its original iconic modernist look; second, we would create a business that would sustain our lives here; and finally, we would find a way to commemorate and celebrate those that had served at RAF North Creake.

C   See the chapter 'Missing' above.

During an interview with Roy Berrill, a former RAF North Creake meteorologist, Claire and I explained our plans for a memorial and a book. Afterwards, he asked a friend, 'why are they doing all this work?'.[15] It's a good question. We are not typical participants in this type of endeavour. With Remembrance Sunday, while we had always observed the Silence ourselves, we would never attend a public commemoration. The act of commemoration is a difficult one for us, fraught with emotional and political contradictions that we would be forced to address and reconcile if we were to build a memorial. This internal conflict is best characterised by the wearing of the Royal British Legion (RBL) poppy.

The poppy was first associated with the sacrifice of war after the battle of Waterloo, as they were said to have 'sprung from the blood of the slaughtered soldiers'.[16] A strong association forged as a result of the field poppy's almost exclusive habit of growing where the ground has been disturbed. Having lain dormant in the soil, its germination is triggered by the elimination of competition,[17] after which they are 'as friendly to an unexploded shell as they are to the leg of a garden seat in Surrey'.[18]

> poppy dormancy is legendary ... Europe's earth is full of poppies and bleeds with them when it's cut ... It's been estimated that in the days before chemical weed killers an acre of cornfield may have held up to 100 million dormant seeds. Fallowing, weeding, even the temporary occupation of the ground had absolutely no effect. Come to the next ploughing, or the next war, a myriad seeds-in-waiting came into their moment.[19]

With the publication in 1915 of the poem *In Flanders Fields* by John McCrae, the poppy, as a symbol of commemoration, captured the public imagination. Indeed, Moina Michael, a professor at Georgia University USA and volunteer for the YMCA in the Great War, was so moved after reading the poem that 'she vowed to wear a poppy for the rest of her life'.[20] When the RBL was formed in 1921, she persuaded it to adopt the poppy.[21] Consequently, 1.5 million poppies were purchased by the RBL from France;[22] they sold out almost immediately, raising over £100,000 for the RBL's work supporting veterans.[23]

However, the poppy is not without controversy, and since its introduction as a symbol of 'mourning and regret ... [and] as a pledge that war must never happen again', its symbolism has gradually evolved:[24]

> over the decades, as the memory of both wars began to fade, the poppy began to take on a subtle new meaning. To many people it had become a patriotic duty to wear one, a symbol of pride in the sacrifices of the armed services. Indeed all those who had ever worn a military uniform had become 'heroes', and the dead were described euphemistically as 'having fallen'.[25]

The poppy, the RBL argue 'must be a matter of personal choice. If the poppy became compulsory it would lose its meaning and significance'.[26] However, it is this central idea of whether people feel they volunteer or are compelled to wear one, that has caused much controversy. In 2020 the BBC was forced to deny that there is a policy of compulsory poppy wearing in the week leading up to Remembrance Sunday.[27] However, an examination of poppy wearing on the BBC in Northern Ireland discovered that, in a sample of news and current affairs broadcasts over the past three decades, 'there wasn't one broadcast where a studio-based presenter at BBC NI appeared on screen without a poppy'.[28] Indeed, a BBC insider revealed that 'if a decision by a studio-based presenter not to wear a poppy were to arise they'd be asked to take annual leave'.[29] The footballer James McClean was accused every year of disrespect and reportedly received death threats for refusing to wear shirts sporting poppies, as he considers it would be disrespectful towards the communities in Northern Ireland from where he hails.[30] It is not just a question of Northern Ireland either: Harry Leslie Smith, a Second World War RAF veteran, asserts 'the spirit of my generation has been hijacked ... [to] sell dubious wars'[31] and, as a consequence, he has refused to wear a poppy since 2013.[32]

The former Channel 4 news presenter, Jon Snow, identifies 'a rather unpleasant breed of poppy fascism',[33] after he was the recipient of a torrent of abuse for refusing to wear a poppy on air. He explains he is inundated with requests to wear charity emblems, all of which he refuses, 'and in those terms, and those terms alone, I do not and will not wear a poppy'.[34] Although he felt compelled to clarify 'I do, in my private life'.[35] Dominic Sandbrook, writing in the *Daily Mail,* condemned the poppy fascists' 'culture of bullying ... this behaviour contradicted the message of the poppy and did a disservice to the sacrifice of those who died in the name of democracy and freedom of expression'.[36] Indeed, the very power of the poppy is derived from the fact that it is voluntary; 'respect only counts when it's genuine'.[37] Any accusation of compulsion undermines a genuine considered decision and suggests that individuals are acting on what is 'expected of them, in the same way that politicians appearing in public have a poppy pinned to them by an adviser, or a TV newsreader has one thrust upon them by a production assistant'.[38]

There are also those from among the serving ranks that feel excluded by the poppy. As Zaman Keinath-Esmail explains, 'the red poppy remains staunchly British'[D] and, as Akala asserts in *Natives: Race & Class in the Ruins of Empire,* it commemorates 'dead people when those dead people are truly British ... the implications are clear – some ancestors deserve to be remembered and venerated and others do not'.[E39]

At the outbreak of the Second World War, a previously underlying level of ambivalence towards the poppy was being openly expressed more cynically; 'buy two poppies this year, eh? Why not three,

---

D   It should be noted that officially the red poppy is a symbol of Remembrance in all Commonwealth countries and has also been adopted by Australia, Barbados, Canada, New Zealand, Pakistan, South Africa and South Korea.

E   The introduction of the Black Poppy Rose, founded in 2007, was an attempt to address some of these feelings. It commemorates all African, Black, Caribbean, Pacific Islands and Indigenous Communities (Forces.Net: undated). Its reception has been, predictably, mixed. Some question its necessity when the red poppy commemorates everyone, however there was obviously a significant number of people that do not believe that to be the case, as, surely, if it were, the Black Rose Poppy would not have been introduced. Similarly, the role of gay and lesbian service personnel has been unrecognised and under-represented, which is why, one imagines, a rainbow poppy briefly, and unofficially, appeared. However, the world of commemoration was not ready for it, and it was withdrawn by the seller after online abuse (PinkNews.com: undated).

one for 1914, one for this war and one for the next'.[40] However, in 1939, even though a significant number struggled with the 'farce to celebrate the "war to end war" with the new one started',[41] more people than ever were wearing poppies.[42] Commemoration continued throughout the war; indeed, at RAF North Creake, on the only Remembrance Day when it was operational, the station was 'represented in large numbers at a Parade in Wells'.[43]

Arguments regarding poppies in the 1930s 'lacked the vehemence of the controversy that has attended them in more recent times'.[44] This vehemence has coincided with what Patrick West argues is a wider societal trend of 'conspicuous compassion'.[F] Characterised by 'ostentatious displays of empathy [of] a degree hitherto unknown',[45] it leads to what he has defined as 'compassion inflation'.[46] Citing the example of the poppy, he asserts it is now worn for much longer, and higher donations are illustrated by a poppy range, differentiated by price, where the relative levels of the bearer's empathy can be measured against the poppy purchased.[47] However, this is not, necessarily, a recent phenomenon. When the poppy was launched in Britain, two types were introduced with different prices; silk at one shilling and cotton at thruppence.[48] By the 1930s, this pricing differential had its critics: 'on Armistice Day when high and low, rich and poor are united in thought, it is preposterous that the outward symbol of their unity should vary'.[49] By the time I was at school in the 1970s, a virtue was made of there being, regardless of contribution, no variance in the poppy received.

I do still wear a poppy, particularly at our Remembrance Day event, and we studiously place poppies against the names on the Roll of Honour to mark the anniversary of each aircraft loss. It is the most recognised symbol of Remembrance, a memorial short-cut; nothing further is needed. Nevertheless, for me, it is not a position of comfort for many of the reasons cited above. And, having discovered the white poppy in my late teenage years, I considered wearing it alongside a red. However, the white poppy is perceived to court controversy, in spite

---

F   A play on Thorstein Veblen's 'conspicuous consumption' (illustrating relative power through 'deliberately wasteful displays of wealth') (West: 2004: 4).

of the RBL having 'no objection to the white poppy and see[ing] no conflict in wearing it alongside the red'.[50] With the word 'peace' in the centre, its focus is international rather than national. Initiated by a feminist organisation, the Co-operative Women's Guild (CWG), the first white poppies appeared in 1933. It was then adopted by the Peace Pledge Union (PPU) after its formation in 1934.[51] Today around 100,000 white poppies are sold.[52] The RBL decided in the 1930s that the white poppy was 'a competitor [that] threatened the fund'.[53] This seems surprising, as the CWG claimed that they approached the Legion in 1933 with the idea that RBL produce the white poppy, and take all the proceeds for the Haig Fund.[54] While the RBL denied this assertion, it has a certain ring of authenticity about it,[55] particularly, when a motion at the RBL conference in 1934 demanded 'that Haig poppies should only ever be red',[56] which would make little sense unless an alternative colour had been suggested. Nonetheless, the white poppy is still seen as a threat to the RBL fund today.[57] Many suggest that this misses the point,[58] with some, such as veteran Harry Leslie Smith, while acknowledging RBL's very good work, argues, 'if politicians want war they must be prepared to pay for the consequences and not leave it to charity'.[59]

The Royal Navy characterises the white poppy as being supported by 'hard-left groups ... [who] are effectively politicising remembrance'.[60] Without any sense of irony, they quote the Conservative Party MP, Johnny Mercer, asserting:

> white poppies are attention seeking rubbish. Ignore the wearers of them. If you don't want to wear a poppy don't bother; they fought and died so you could choose. But don't deliberately try and hijack its symbolism for your own ends. [61]

However, from my own perspective, in spite of buying a white poppy in the 1980s and it being more aligned with my feelings, I had not worn it. While I have strong latent pacifist feelings, they have always been suppressed by my conscious belief in the necessity of the Second

World War and the need to defeat such a detestable regime. Despite its shortcomings, the red poppy is more widely recognised as representing the inter-generational solidarity I wish to express, for those that took up the monumental struggle for us.

Fabian Ware held that 'common remembrance of the dead … is the one thing, sometimes the only thing, that never fails to bring our people together'.[62] However, as Martin Evans and Ken Lunn ask, what is the purpose of this remembering? Is it celebratory or commemorative; triumphalist or reflective; based upon international reconciliation or narrowly nationalistic?[63] These are troublesome and difficult questions. Writers such as Jay Winter see commemoration as a society's response to individual grief; a collective release through public mourning, stimulated by the universal desire for 'psychological reparation for loss, in response to the traumatic impact of death in war'.[64] This public mourning is arguably evidenced by the British national focus of commemoration at the Cenotaph[G] in Whitehall, London. In the first such commemoration planned for the end of July 1919, the Prime Minister, Lloyd George, 'opposed any proposals for national rejoicing which did not include "some tribute to the dead"'.[65] Consequently, Edwin Lutyens was asked to design a temporary edifice made of wood and plaster, around which, the commemoration could converge. The structure evoked such popular emotion, that it was decided to make it permanent and it was subsequently rebuilt using Portland stone.[66]

The Cabinet had not considered the anniversary of the armistice a natural point to commemorate the war. However, in wider society the idea was gaining momentum. A proposal for a commemoration and two-minute silence at the Cenotaph was discussed and agreed at a Cabinet meeting on 15 October 1919.[67] It is difficult to exaggerate the impact of the first Silence. For many the 'demonstration of mute solidarity with the bereaved',[68] when the chatter ceased and industry paused, was the first time they had experienced silence in an urban area. On the railways:[69]

G   The literal translation from Greek of Cenotaph is 'empty tomb' (Gregory: 1994: 27).

all over the system … on mainlines and branches, in sheds and yards, passenger trains, goods trains and shunting engines stopped wherever they happened to be. Engine crews stood bareheaded at their footplates, passengers sat silent in their compartments. Great stations fell suddenly silent, travellers froze into immobility.[70]

As powerful as the Silence may have been, it was, in itself, 'a political act; it could not be neutral'.[71] It is argued that such commemorations are inextricably linked with ideas of reverence, obedience, and mythic chivalry: 'the discourse of Big Words'.[72] This lexicon of 'official memory', predicated by prevailing ideology of dominant elites, draws upon the 'sacrifice and loss occasioned by war as a means of preserving and reinforcing'[73] the status quo. Armistice commemorations, it is argued, aim 'to universalise the memory of the war, to make it the property of the nation as a whole'.[74] This universalisation, according to Eric Hobsbawm and Terence Ranger, allows for the 'invention of tradition', where modern societies construct versions of the past, forming continuities between past and present events, as a means of 'establishing social cohesion, legitimizing authority and socializing populations into a common cause',[75] in a 'correct'[76] type of commemoration.

In the development of rituals of remembrance, a distinction cannot be so neatly drawn between the competing ideas of 'invention of tradition' and the 'collective reaction to individual grief'.[77] Both are critical in describing the process of 'official memory' construction within the public domain.[78] This national narrative becomes, for the majority, the prevailing, or conventional 'common sense'; a hegemony adopted through reinforcement by the state, and by constant repetition through other channels (media, church, educational institutions etc.). It is presented as a conventional, universal and uncontroversial response to traumatic war losses, and as an 'act of social solidarity'.[79] Any challenge to this hegemony is most often characterised as outside agitation (anarchists, hard-left etc.) or, as wilful disrespect by a generation of young unpatriotic rebels who lack understanding.

However, such commemorations were not necessarily considered uncontroversial when first proposed. When the Poppy Appeal was introduced in 1921, there were 'doubts as to whether the public would respond favourably to the idea'.[80] When the Silence was first introduced in 1919, a national newspaper, the *Daily Herald,* printed an editorial somewhat divergent from the 'official' national narrative:

> you will remember, mothers, the gay sons you have lost; wives you will think of the husbands who went out in the mist of the winter morning – never to come back. And brothers will think of brothers and friends of friends, all lying dead today under an alien soil ... make the most of this day of official remembrance ... never again ... shall the peace and happiness of the world fall into the murderess hands of a few cynical old men.[81]

Moreover, in 1921, protests revealed active divergence from 'official memory' when, during the two-minute silence, the commemorations around the Cenotaph were disrupted by groups of unemployed ex-servicemen, with placards proclaiming, 'the dead are remembered but we are forgotten'.[82] Further, leading up to the Second World War, 'a very large number of people felt uneasy about the whole performance',[83] with a 'widespread feeling that the ceremony was already out-of-date and should be stopped'.[84] Ideas that seem unthinkable today.

Nonetheless, the 'official narrative' can change with time and shifts in political thinking.[85] The Falklands War serves as a useful illustration. A change in the language employed in the official narrative during the Falklands War – one that embraced a revised memory of the Second World War and, utilising Churchillian tropes of this 'island nation' and 'threats to the British way of life' – successfully led to the marginalisation of 'alternative social-democratic and radical leftist memories of the Second World War', that had been previously common in such discourse.[86] In such a way, some sections of society may become alienated from the public discourse of official memory.

Private memories, the preserve of those that experienced them, may be effectively blocked from official memory by failing to be consonant with the prevailing narrative.[87] It can be cogently argued that the Bomber Command community, outside their own networks (kinship groups, social or interest groups, military/squadron associations[H] etc.), were subject to this blocking, finding it, at times, almost impossible to be heard within the wider articulations of war memory. In Winston Churchill's voluminous history of the Second World War, for example, 'Bomber Command's whole campaign received less space than the sinking of a single German warship'.[88] In this sense, official memory is always a contested narrative,[89] and it is the prevailing narrative at any given time, that governs how people generally respond to a memorial.

Our first proposals for commemoration – museum would be too grand a term, more a small collection of exhibits – had been shaped by a period of intensive acquisition after arriving at the Control Tower. Desperate to find out more about the bombing war and how I felt about it, I acquired anything relating to Bomber Command or the Air Ministry that I stumbled across. Both expensive and unfocused.

However, at a Wedding-Wheels job at the Red Feather Club (former RAF Horham), I was taken on a private tour and my priorities changed. My guide explained that everything on display had to be from RAF Horham, nothing else was accepted. Such focus was impressive and refreshing.

Once home, we disposed of many of my acquisitions, and determined to only accumulate Bomber Command items that were directly related to RAF North Creake. It is a wonderful discipline. Even so, since arriving we have accumulated a good number of items, from fascinating documents and photographs, to uniforms, medals, aircraft dials, flying equipment, bottles and broken crockery. Much of it was dug up in the garden, including, of course, the Window. All of it is precious to us. It is one thing acquiring items, but the difficulty is what

---

H   199 Squadron, unlike 171 Squadron, had an active association that met for several years, starting with 150 members.

to do with them and how best to conserve and display them. Ultimately a museum was not possible due to limited time to dedicate to it, lack of finance and an irascible neighbour. Nonetheless, the items described are on display in the Control Tower for guests to see.

We then considered some form of landscape design commemoration. Nature, gardens and garden design have a longstanding association with commemoration, from the Commonwealth War Graves Commission cemeteries (which were designed to resemble a peaceful English garden[90] that are 'both pretty and bizarre ... projecting an almost unendurably ironic peacefulness'[91]); and the National Arboretum, to numerous peace gardens nationwide.

There are also particular species of flower that play an important role in war memory, the poppy being the obvious example; however, many wildflowers took on huge significance for those serving in the trenches of the Great War. The ravaged, cratered fields of the Western Front, had become highly fertile, fed as they were with the blood and bones of the dead, and nitrates and potash from the explosive shells.[92] As a consequence, wildflowers grew readily on the shell-ruined ground, and in:

> one of the oddest and most poignant attempts to catch an echo of England amidst the horror ... weeds like celandine and cuckoo-pint were transplanted from the surrounding fields and ditches into little plots alongside the trenches, and edged with scraps of battle debris.[93]

In the Second World War, front lines were more mobile and such possibilities did not arise. However, on military camps, such as RAF stations, much time was spent 'beautifying ... especially in regard to gardens'.[94] On bombsites, rosebay willowherb grew in abundance; named by Londoners as 'bombweed', it was 'a reminder, if anybody needed one, of how thinly the veneer of civilisation lay over the wilderness'.[95]

Of the cultivated flowers, the Peace Rose is probably the widest known war-related commemorative bloom. Bred in 1940, in a climate of war, attempts were made to ensure the future of the rose by dispersing plants to three nurseries in Germany, Italy and America, while also continuing to grow them in France.[96] On 29 April 1945, the day Berlin fell, a statement was made at a rose-naming ceremony in San Francisco:[97]

> we are persuaded that this greatest new rose of our time should be named for the world's greatest desire: Peace. We believe that this rose is destined to live on as a classic in our grandchildren's gardens and for generations to come. We would use the word 'Peace' to preserve the knowledge that we have gained the hard way that Peace is increasingly essential to all mankind, to be treasured with greater wisdom, watchfulness, and foresight than the human race has so far been able to maintain for any great length of time.[98]

Within nine years, it was estimated that some 30 million Peace Roses were blooming worldwide[99]. They are still available, and although we are not huge fans of cultivated roses, preferring the simplicity of wild varieties, the story of the Peace Rose seemed appropriate. Now two 'tree' Peace Roses proudly welcome guests to our garden. Not that any guests on a RAF North Creake pilgrimage would necessarily know, and that, in terms of commemoration, was a problem. Consequently, and, with the words of D-Day veteran Philip Burkinshaw, 'thank you for keeping our memory alive', ringing in our ears; we decided any commemoration needed to be something that provided a focus for those on an airfield pilgrimage.

The number of people tracing the steps of a relative on a personal pilgrimage to RAF North Creake has surprised us. However, a little research would have indicated that this is a longstanding pattern of behaviour. With the 20th century's descent into industrial warfare, the desire of bereaved relatives to visit the places where their loved ones served, became insatiable. And it persists into the following generations.

After the Second World War, unlike the Great War,[100] visiting the graves of lost relatives was perceived as an individual endeavour. A mother, writing to the Imperial War Graves Commission (IWGC; now known as the Commonwealth War Graves Commission) requesting information on organised pilgrimages, 'received a brusque circular letter saying that if [she] wanted to see [her] son's grave [she] had better apply to a Tourist Agency'.[101] Such experience was common.[102] Eventually, under public pressure, the Labour Government established a means-tested financial assistance scheme for civilians visiting war graves.[103] Pilgrimages were offered through existing organisations (Royal British Legion, Church Army, Salvation Army etc.). Tens of thousands went,[104] including many of the bereaved of those lost from RAF North Creake.

Rheinberg British Military Cemetery (1948) with unknown girl. Note that Peter Jennings is mistakenly listed as the pilot of Lancaster PB403. There are also other name and rank errors. These would be checked and corrected before the permanent headstones were put in place (Mike Hillier).

These excursions gave succour to the burgeoning war tourism industry, supporting many enterprises both in Britain and abroad and giving rise to what has become known as 'dark tourism'.[105] More recently, this tourism has been boosted by a resurgence of interest, first, in the Great War, as it drifted from living memory,[106] and now, for similar reasons, in the Second World War. An interest that is nurtured on a diet of prolific numbers of anniversary celebrations, television documentaries and feature films on the subject.[107] It is an industry fraught with moral sensitivities:

> the peril of turning the war into spectacle has been threatened as memory of war is appropriated by the heritage industry ... for some commentators, the 'memorialization industry' ... is highly questionable ... for visitors, education and entertainment have been dangerously blurred.[108]

It is an accusation we have always felt sensitive to, and it has tempered some of our more ambitious ideas for our business. It is a fine line between commemoration and commercialisation, and we felt this keenly as we began to consider more seriously how we would mark the historical significance of this site. Few would dispute that the memory of those that served at RAF North Creake deserves to be preserved, but it is a question of approach. We did not want to aggrandize the memory of service personnel, as discussion with veterans very quickly revealed that they hold no truck with the discourse of 'heroes'; ordinary blokes in extraordinary times, Bernie How would say.[109] Or as Mike Hillier explains 'just young men pushed to the front'.[110] We equally did not want to glamourise the war; as Tony Benn observed, 'war is the murder of men, women and children; it's rape; it's torture; it's plunder. That is what war is'.[111] And, even with the essential purpose of defeating fascism, we should not lose sight of this, as Paul Fussell comments 'there has been so much talk about the "Good War", the Justified War, the Necessary War, and the like that the young and the innocent could get the impression that it was really not such a bad thing after all. It's thus necessary to observe that it was a war and nothing else and thus stupid and sadistic'. Citing the British journalist and author, Cyril Connolly, he continues, that it is a war:

of which we are all ashamed ... a war ... which lowers the standard of thinking and feeling ... a war opposed to every reasonable conception of what life is for, every ambition of the mind or delight of the senses.[112]

Monument-raising at its most fundamental level fulfils the desire in society to address the needs of the grieving; 'a monument records the dead, and so gives dignity to their undignified deaths'.[113] However, with so many killed on the battlefields of the Great War, it would be some time before there would be monuments to the dead on the Western Front and beyond. This vacuum was filled at home by the construction of memorials in cities, towns and villages up and down the UK. The number of memorials commemorating the Great War in Britain is not known, but Historic England estimates that there are 'certainly tens of thousands' in England alone.[114] These were mostly paid for by public subscription,[115] some simple, some intricate, in all manner of materials.[I116]

Official memorialisation of the individual war dead was the responsibility of the IWGC.[117] Fabian Ware, who lobbied for the IWGC's formation in advance of its foundation in May 1917, had quickly realised the monumental task of finding and burying the dead in the battlefields of the Great War.[118] He outlined the need for a strategic and uniform approach to their burial and commemoration, a principle rooted in the 1915 War Office decision to prohibit the repatriation of those killed in the war.[119] Fearing that without the IWGC's strong hand, the treatment of the dead would be haphazard, unequal and disordered,[120] and believing that 'only the rich would be able to erect their monuments to their dead',[121] he asserted the burial of the dead could not be left to the bereaved.[122] Moreover, he was sceptical of the merit of any input of relatives in the design of the memorials, being wary of their 'taste and artistic judgment'.[123] Frederic Kenyon (advisor to the IWGC) concurred, 'the public were better off being told what to do by their betters than left to their own unlettered devices'.[124]

I   After 1945 they would be adapted to include the names of the dead from the Second World War.

Three principal architects, Edwin Lutyens, Reginald Bloomfield and Herbert Baker,[125] were appointed.[126] Using Portland stone and in a style of 'stripped-back classicism'[127] they adopted an essentially modernist[128] uniformity, lacking in any distracting ornament.[129] Headstones were identical and arranged in 'ordered ranks ... of a battalion on parade',[130] bearing the rank, name, regiment and date of death of the man commemorated.[131] The relatives were allowed, at their own expense, to add a short 'unforgettable, infinitely pathetic'[132] inscription, subject to the approval of the Commission.[133] Most also featured a religious symbol, 'some – presumably atheist – no religious symbol at all'.[134]

The 1920s have been characterised as the 'monumental phase'[135] of memorial construction with, for example, 4,000 headstones sent to France each week in 1923, and by 1927, some 500 cemeteries having been completed.[136] With the invasion of the low countries by the Nazis early in the Second World War, the workers of the IWGC were forced to flee the 'more or less complete'[137] cemeteries and the 'work of a generation was abandoned to the enemy'.[138] They retreated to prepare for 'a new harvest of death'.[139]

After the Second World War, and the realisation of this harvest, it was agreed that the same style headstones and 'general architectural and horticultural treatment'[140] of the cemeteries should continue. Once again, three principal architects were appointed; Hubert Worthington,[141] Louis de Soissons and Philip Hepworth,[142] who were, despite a strong brief, forced to amend designs in the quest for economy,[143] and it wasn't until 1949 that any significant progress was made.[144]

By the end of 2016 significant progress had been achieved towards restoring the Control Tower and creating a business. We then began to seriously consider what form our 'monumental' memorial endeavour might take. Inspiration came at an unlikely time.

We were viewing a Commer Cob (a small 1960s Rootes commercial 'run-around') of 'original' condition and an 'easy restoration' in south Norfolk. In reality, it had fibre-glass front wings and a lot of rot. We walked away; never to return to the subject. Nevertheless, while in the area we visited Snetterton; another Second World War airfield. The memorial there is fabulous. Fabricated from stainless steel, it is a sculpture of a steeply-climbing B17 bomber that streams vapour trails that reach the ground. Stunning.

We drove home discussing possibilities. We had to be realistic, Snetterton had clearly been a high budget project with plenty of sponsors; for our project, there was Claire and me, plenty of ambition but little idea of how to go about it. After unsuccessfully exploring ideas, we came across the work of Andrew Knighton on social media. When we saw the 22' wide Lancaster sculpted for the Lincolnshire Aviation Heritage Centre at RAF East Kirkby, we were convinced that that was it. While it was made of mild steel, we thought a stainless-steel version of a Stirling with similar proportions would be ideal. We made contact in December 2016.

Using our guest network, we sought advice and made tangible our lofty ideas. The Stirling sculpture, now named 'Home Safe', would, we decided, commemorate everyone who was stationed and worked at RAF North Creake, while the Roll of Honour was dedicated to everyone who lost their life while serving at the airfield. Inspired by the work of the extraordinary International Bomber Command Centre in Lincoln, we designed the Roll of Honour. Made of Corten steel, which is designed to rust, it would record the 73 names of those lost flying from the station. The names, we decided, should be listed in their crews rather than alphabetically; thereby remaining an identifiable community of people, who lived, flew and died together. When fewer than eight names are listed under a date, we hoped this would cause a pause for thought; how can this be? The pursuit of an answer to such a question would potentially reveal them as people, rather than appearing 'solely as names, inscribed on the war memorial'.[145] Information boards would help, with a link to the website where more could be discovered of this person's contribution to the collective endeavour and, a little detail of their life, if it could be found.

However, we still needed to resolve where it was to be situated. We had initially assumed that it would go somewhere on our property, but this presented some difficulties; access when we were not at home and, what would happen when we were no longer resident in the Control Tower. We met with Clovis and Elizabeth of Walsingham Estate in the summer of 2017, and they were happy for it to be sited on their land in a position next to the Dry Road, on the former airfield Technical Site. This also had the advantage of resolving another concern. Ever since we moved here, people, even locals, despite driving past it frequently, had been surprised to discover this was a Second World War airfield. We thought, there is no better way of securing the memory of an airfield than a huge sculpture of an aircraft at the side of the road.

Since the project's inception, we had intended that we would dedicate the memorial in 2020, either on the 75th anniversary of VE day or, as latterly decided, the 75th anniversary of the disbandment of the station. Our immediate goal was to achieve planning consent by Christmas 2017. At a project soft-launch at the Control Tower on a dark evening in October 2017, we sketched-out our plans to a group of Norfolk people most affected by our ideas, and those that could help. It was a well-attended meeting and we were surprised at the enthusiastic reception our plans engendered. We started to pull together a fundraising strategy that was based, mostly, in the local area, using talks, the press and social media to publicise our campaign, now named 'Time to Remember'. With a logo designed by a friend, Marianne, a donations page and a loose strategy we hit the fundraising trail. We thought the bulk of the support would come locally and from grants. We guesstimated we needed £30,000. Tom Coke, (Earl of Leicester), pledged £5,000 immediately after the launch. We were off to a good start. We organised talks and events and approached Beeston Brewery, the producers of Stirling Beer, to produce a fund-raising ale; 'Drink to Remember'. A pun I was very happy with.

We approached local pub owners, Phil and Lena Parker, who ran the Carpenters in Wighton and the Black Lion in Walsingham, in the hope of persuading them to adopt our beer. After we explained our project, Phil not only agreed to take Drink to Remember, but pledged £1,000 and said 'use my pubs'.

The fund was growing. Thankfully, Walsingham Parish Council agreed to run the project account; with them now administering the funds, we were simply left to raise them. We put Andy Knighton on notice that we would soon have sufficient funds for a formal commission but cautioned him that we would first need to secure planning approval. We had hoped that planning consent would be in place in time for a D-Day fundraising event at the Carpenters Arms, but the timetable was slipping.

We benefitted from tremendous goodwill, and the offers of people's time and money were extraordinarily generous. However, it is not always easy for volunteers to find time when the priority must always be to paying clients. Inevitably our plans were delayed. It is difficult to ask someone who is providing a free service to hurry up. Therefore, Claire and I eventually grasped the nettle ourselves and took control of the planning application.

Naively, we thought planning would be relatively straightforward. Of course there are always glitches, but on a project of this sort we expected a level of goodwill on our side. Sadly, national planning portals allow very little room for local goodwill and, indeed, little flexibility. To make a novel planning application fit into the approval process you need some flexibility. Our first attempt at planning was returned needing more information. We answered the request the best we could and waited. The consultation period came and went, an objection from highways was dealt with to everyone's satisfaction, but still no news. I eventually contacted planning to be told correspondence had been sent out but, in a manner reminiscent of Terry Gilliam's *Brazil*, it had been sent to an email address of Porter rather than Morter! The correspondence contained further deeply frustrating requirements: tree survey; waste strategy; light impact statement and contaminated land assessment. As if it were a large development rather than a memorial. I batted away what I could, leaving us with the tree and contaminated land surveys. I pleaded with the goodwill of local service providers, but my pleas fell on deaf ears and their quotes were going to add between £6,000 and £7,000 unbudgeted costs to the project. Ultimately, through on-line provision, our own efforts and the assistance of a sympathetic conservation officer, our surveys were accepted at very little cost. We finally received planning approval on 8 February 2019. While this experience was protracted and not without difficulties, I generally found the planning department obliging, helpful and as flexible as the national planning framework would allow.

We had asked Paul Bishop for a price for the groundworks. With unexpected generosity, he said he would do it for the cost of materials. He was good to his word and did an excellent job. In December 2019, with the concrete base laid, the sculpture and stand arrived. Hung up in our Nissen hut it looked fantastic. Andy had done us proud. It just needed a plinth for the stand to fix to and we'd be ready to erect. We were a little late, but there was still enough time to be ready for August 2020. Little did we know, that before any further work could be done, Britain would go into lockdown. All plans were cancelled and we withdrew to regroup later.

The first person we knew to succumb to Covid was Paul Bishop, the contractor doing our groundworks. Just before the first lock-down he became dangerously ill, and for some time we were unsure he would make it through. Thankfully he did.

When restrictions lifted a little, in the summer of 2020 and with Paul recovering, Andy returned to cast the plinth. With Covid controls preventing a night's stopover, he did it all in a day. It looked fabulous. In September, he returned to put the Stirling up. Socially distanced, several people came up to see the Stirling take to the air.

The Roll of Honour was proving a headache. The company that was to waterjet the letters through the steel plate had quoted a price of just under £5,000. However, they were not responding to my calls. I discovered why; they had gone bankrupt. I then discovered why that might have been; the nearest quote I could get to £5,000 was £25,000. An unaffordable amount. A regular guest, John Pillier, who was familiar with computer-aided design, reduced the cost considerably by completing all the requisite drawings. But it was still unaffordable. We reviewed the plans and reduced the width of the steel, abbreviated the aircrew roles and took out their ranks, punctuation and the word 'age'. The renewed quote was £17,000. We could just do it.

With the names cut, Stephen Lake, the metal fabricator who had restored the external steps to our roof nearly ten years earlier, welded up the Roll of Honour and delivered it. After some fettling and with the help of Ian Foreman, it was put into place using the mill's telehandler. The memorial site was coming together.

Paul had insisted that he wanted to finish the job and, when he was well enough, the polished concrete bench was put in place and a little landscaping done. Despite Paul being in hospital with Covid for months, and with an arduous recovery, he did us proud, and we never received his final bill. The generosity of others.

With Covid restrictions still in place, we now considered plans for a pared-back dedication. We could have delayed further, but we settled on the anniversary of D-Day in June 2021, as we were determined Bernie How should cut the ribbon, if he could. Bernie became our 'go to' veteran, particularly for fundraising events; he would respond to media enquiries and make public appearances. When Tom Coke generously suggested we use the Marble Hall at Holkham Hall for a fundraising talk, Bernie attended with his medals adorning his blazer. He looked the part. We would sometimes worry that he felt ill-used. But I think Bernie liked the attention. When we asked him to cut the ribbon, we told him it would be two years; he looked himself up and down and, in his pragmatic way, said 'I think that will be fine!' We were delighted he agreed, however, Covid isolation had taken its toll and he wasn't as sprightly as he had been.

Planning a dedication was unfamiliar territory for us. Being non-religious and non-military, the trappings of such an event feel alien, and, if I'm honest, uncomfortable. However, this was not about us; the memorial was about the wider community and the dedication had to conform to normal traditions.

Ultimately, Covid restrictions limited the guests to 30. Harri Williams, the vicar of Walsingham, led the dedication at the memorial; he took on board our religious reservations and talked of 'swords into ploughshares'. Stuart Atha, former air marshall of the RAF, dedicated it on behalf of the RAF and Bernie How cut the ribbon on the Roll of Honour. Back at the Control Tower we had a marquee where we served afternoon tea and plenty of 'Drink to Remember', poured straight from a cask in the recently restored Speech Broadcast Building. The three primary landowners on the airfield made speeches, in ascending order of magnitude; me, Clovis Meath Baker and Tom Coke. It was a splendid day which, on reflection, was more powerful on account of its intimacy.

Phil Parker, in effusive mood, wrote on the day of the dedication, 'you have made such an impact in this sleepy corner of Norfolk since arriving. Looking forward to the next project'. So, what of the future? Given the highly dispersed nature of Second World War airfields, the great majority of structures are, in the view of Historic England, effectively precluded 'from being recommended for protection'.[146] Instead, having between 1999 and 2000 conducted a thematic survey of all aviation structures in England,[147] the focus has been on the identification of the 'most complete, historically important and strongly representative sites'.[148] Protection outside these key sites will only apply for structures of 'intrinsic historical or architectural importance'.[149] The Control Tower at RAF North Creake was not among them.[J]

Large-scale sites, a category in which Class A airfields would fall, are not without the additional challenges of competing interests:

> as memories erode it will become increasingly difficult to regard such spaces as designated places of peace or pilgrimage. This is not a new dilemma: mass tourism has long threatened the avowed sanctity of such 'sacred places'. Such ethical issues are especially complex in globally symbolic sites. In Hiroshima the tensions over the preservation of the A-Bomb Dome are ... part of a difficult question which strikes at the very roots of our ability to provide sacred memorials that both honour

---

J   It was felt at the time that the building had changed to such an extent that it did not merit listing (telephone conversation with Historic England 2014).

the past and its dead, while still offering visions towards a peaceful future.[150]

More recent initiatives may indicate another way for memorial sites. The Gallipoli Peninsula, the site of intensive fighting in the Great War,[151] recently promulgated plans involving a proposed network of footpaths that would be created and customised by the individual visitor. Modest and non-interventionist, it gives 'visitors a chance to think or speculate or reflect on what they are seeing',[152] thereby, offering a more abstract understanding of peace, rather than one dominated by commemoration of specific acts of warfare. The plans had an almost non-existent impact on the landscape.[153] Although yet to be realised, they do perhaps offer an alternative vision of how a smaller-scale historical landscape, such as RAF North Creake, may function as combined commemorative, recreational, commercial and environmentally sensitive spaces.

Where competing needs of commemoration and housing (or industry) arise, with a little imagination, they can be reconciled, as with Bicester, in Oxfordshire, that offers an excellent example of airfield preservation for the use of light industry. The same could be applied to airfield sites offered for housing. The potential for housing on former airfields was first recognised in the late 1990s in plans proffered by John Prescott, (then Deputy Prime Minister).[154] However, their approach was one of clearance, rather than preservation. An opportunity missed. Instead, with good planning, the original buildings could have been incorporated into a town plan, constructing a 'rooted' community with a sense of its place in history, rather than just naming a few roads after aircraft that were probably not even based there. The critical point is that for such structures to survive, they must find a relevance or use; preferably both. With their survival we are offered the possibility of remembering and commemorating their past and looking forward to their future.

However, ultimately, we have to ask once again, 'what is the purpose of remembering?'.[155] The American historian, Stephen

Ambrose, suggests that in remembering the war, we can feel proud of what was achieved:

> the most important single result is this: the Nazis were crushed, the militarists in Japan were crushed, the fascists in Italy were crushed and surely justice has never been better served.[156]

Few would disagree with the sentiment, but many may disapprove of the method:

> [for Bomber Command] feuds between various factions were continued in memoires, and the verdict of historians trying to maintain an objective balance swung between admiration for the organization of such a mighty enterprise, and criticism of the futility and atrocity of an operation mercilessly carried through to the end against the dictates of good sense.[157]

Ronald Huzzard, a conscientious objector during the Second World War, considers that 'there was obviously going to come a time when war was a greater evil than the evil it was opposing. I think we've reached that stage. We reached it at Hiroshima and Nagasaki, if not before'.[158] The Archbishop of York, Cyril Forster Garbett, embraces a more nuanced approach; 'often in life ... there is no clear choice between absolute right and wrong; frequently the choice has to be made of the lesser of two evils'.[159] And fascism was certainly evil.

It may be difficult for us as a society to come to a unified view on the moral basis of the bombing war, but we should never forget the contribution and the price paid by *all* those involved; whether on the ground or in the air, whether combatant or non-combatant, whether in death, injury or, as Max Hastings eloquently relates, in 'outstanding young men [that] somehow used themselves up in the Second World War, leaving pathetically little energy and imagination to support them through the balance of their lives'.[160]

Wherever one falls in the controversy, it was a policy promoted by Government[161] and pursued by men in appalling conditions, with death as a constant companion. Whatever the conclusions regarding the ultimate Bomber Command contribution to the defeat of fascism in Europe, these young men lived it, night after night, even when exhausted and even when terrified. We should, and we shall, remember them.

APPENDICES

APPENDIX ONE:

AIRCRAFT LOSSES & INCIDENTS AT RAF NORTH CREAKE

Below is a list of all RAF North Creake recorded aircraft losses and incidents and the occasional summary report, sourced from the Operations Record Book (ORB) of the RAF 100 Group reports. It also contains reference to aircraft diverted to RAF North Creake. The date refers to the date the aircraft took-off from North Creake, or if it involves a visiting aircraft, the date of the actual incident. There are also accounts of aircraft damaged from other sources but not recorded in the ORB, in which case they are referenced separately.

27 April 1944, Mosquito LR329

Flying with RAF 305 (Polish) Squadron, on a night training exercise from RAF Lasham in Hampshire, dived into the ground presumably as a result of catastrophic structural failure in the wing. It crashed into the back garden of a bakery on Wells Road, in the village of North Creake. The crew, John Mathias (pilot) and Thomas Irwin (navigator) were both killed.[1] Despite crashing in the middle of the village, remarkably, no one was injured on the ground. Even without RAF North Creake being fully operational the fire crews attended the crash scene, as John Rees recalls, 'we were first on the scene. It had spun in from 16,000ft'.[2]

16 June 1944, Stirling LJ531 EX-N

The first 'failure to return' from RAF North Creake (see 'Missing' above).

July 1944

'A total of 222 aircraft took off [in July], 220 of which completed successful sorties. All these sorties were completed and the accompanying air tests carried out without a single accident or incident of any description. This accomplishment for a two flight heavy squadron reflects very well on the hard work put in by, and efficiency of, by both ground and aircrews and is certainly cause for much gratification'.[3]

29 July 1944

Six USSAF flying fortresses diverted to RAF North Creake.

29 August 1944, Stirling LJ560

On the night of the 29 August 1944, 'aircraft "H" crashed on take-off having burst a tyre ...The crew got out, one (F/L Hartwright) with serious injury, the remainder with only minor scratches and bruises ... The crashed aircraft 'H' blocked the runway and all were diverted to Foulsham where they landed safely'.[4] The 199 Squadron ORB suggests that the injury was 'a compound fracture of left leg involving knee'.[5] Interestingly, both the Station ORB and the Squadron ORB mention that there was a fire and the aircraft was burnt out. However, the Flight Sergeant in charge of the SSQ witnessed the crash and helped to administer first aid, and specifically says 'no fire'.[6] On board were:

> R Currie
> L Francis
> D H Halliwell (Spec. Op)
> F Hartwright Navigator – Injured
> J R Phipp
> F S G. Robbins

J R Sarjeant

G W Tye

John Rees further describes the injury: 'the Navigator [Frederick Hartwright] had his leg amputated except for the popliteal artery, F/Lt Dyke decided to try and save the limb, I gave anaesthetic gas and air having been taught how to do it in the Western Desert. The bones were lined up and the leg put in plaster and he was then taken to the RAF Hospital at Ely, Luckily, the RAF Consultant in Orthopaedics was there when he arrived and with his expert attention the leg was saved'.[7]

9 September 1944, Stirling LJ578 EX-S

Aircraft swung on take-off, crashed and burst into flames (See page 331).

15 September 1944, Stirling LJ536 EX-P

Failure to return, nothing heard since take-off and remains missing (see 'Missing' above).

16 September 1944, LJ569 EX-C

'Stirling piloted by F/Lt. Harker crashed on take-off at 21:30 hours approximately. The S.M.O. and nursing orderly proceeded to the scene of the crash and the pilot was admitted to Sick Quarters with lacerations of left eye and fracture Os Calcis [the largest of the tarsal bones] of left ankle. He was transferred to R.A.F. Hospital, Ely on 18th September, 1944'[8] (see page 135).

25 September 1944, Stirling LJ518 EX-K

Failure to Return. Crashed at Edgefield, Norfolk, close to the base (see 'Fewer than Five Minutes from Base', above).

23 October 1944, Stirling LJ510 EX-A

Stirling aircraft piloted by G H Simon overshot on landing and went off the runway. 'The Medical Officer and orderly proceeded to the scene but there were no injuries to the crew'.[9]

26 October 1944, Stirling LJ 617 6Y-K

Diverted to RAF Woodbridge in fog (visibility 300 yards), pilot J H Austwick landed on FIDO with port-inner feathered.[10]

29 October 1944

'Fortress of 214 Squadron landed at North Creake. The Navigator, Sgt. Barnfield, was frostbitten on both hands and feet. This was caused by the failure of his electrically heated clothing in a temperature of -45°C. He was transferred to R.A.F. Hospital, Ely, later in the day'.[11]

21 November 1944, Halifax LK874 6Y-C

'Diverted to RAF Woodbridge, the pilot G Cox, swung off runway after landing, hit FIDO pipes, slightly damaged'.[12] This aircraft failed to return from operations on the night of 16/17 April 1945 (see 'Mid-Air Collision').

26 November 1944, Halifax NA108 6Y-V

Failure to return having been abandoned (see 'Abandoned Near Paris' above).

December 1944

'North Creake had a very bad December, returning four accidents – over a quarter of the whole Group total'.[13] Three out of the four accidents were perceived to have involve 'carelessness' with endorsements noted in the logbooks of the pilots concerned.[14]

4 December 1944, Halifax NA695 6Y-D

'Damaged while on ops', and subsequently repaired.[15] It remained with 171 Squadron until 11/8/1945.[16]

4 December 1944, Halifax NA694 6Y-H

Mistakenly identified as Halifax LW471 in the ORB. 'We took a brand new Halifax to Kassel, returning 'with the port inner engine feathered ... we made an unexpected belly landing writing the kite off, an expensive trip'.[17]

5 December 1944, Stirling LJ567 EX-X

Diverted to RAF Woodbridge the night before as a result of the accident above, it was about to land, when R L Todd struck a four-foot high wall in the undershoot area of the runway and damaged the undercarriage.

6 December 1944, Stirling LJ559 EX-Q

Damaged after 450mph out of control dive (see 'Friendly Fire', above).

9 December 1944, Halifax NA674 6Y-Q

Failed to return from Window operation (see 'Nothing Heard Since Take-Off' above).

6 January 1945, Halifax NA687 6Y-A

Aircraft failed to return after crashing at Ambly (see 'Mid-Air Collision').

15 January 1945 Halifax NA111 6Y-Y

Diverted to RAF Woodbridge, pilot W/O Porter 'called Mayday, hydraulics unserviceable and very short of fuel, told to land immediately. Made poor landing probably owing to bad weather conditions'.[18] This aircraft subsequently failed to return on 7/8 March 1945 with a different crew (see 'Nothing Heard of Since Take-Off').

18 January 1945

A North Creake Halifax crashed on the Oulton runway.[19]

18 January 1945, Stirling LJ651 EX-C

Damaged on ground by gale 18/1/45, repaired on site.[20]

3 March 1945, Halifax NA107 6Y-T

Lost to a night-fighter over Britain (see 'Operation Gisela').

5 March 1945, Stirling LJ617 EX-E

Aircraft lost to anti-aircraft fire over France (see 'Friendly Fire').

7 March 1945, Halifax NA111 6Y-Y

Failed to return (see 'Nothing Heard Since Take-Off').

16 March 1945, Halifax NA691 6Y-F

Diverted to RAF Woodbridge 'starboard inner failed – airscrew feathered automatically – cause unknown. Hydraulics U/S – landed O.K. Starboard undercarriage showing unlocked but turned out O.K.'.[21]

4 April 1945, Halifax PN373 EX-Y

Hit obstacle when landing, subsequently repaired.

16 April 1945, Halifax LK874 6Y-C

Failed to return (see 'Mid-Air Collision').

17 April 1945, Halifax PN169 6Y-Q

Crashed on take-off for training flight.

2 May 1945, Halifax RG375 EX-T & Halifax RG373 EX-R

Involved in mid-air collision (see 'Dove Over Europe').

25 June 1945, EX NA259

Crashed at Cromer (see 'Air Test').

24 June 1946, Mosquito RF839

Crashed on take-off.

APPENDIX TWO:

RAF NORTH CREAKE
CHRONOLOGY OF EVENTS

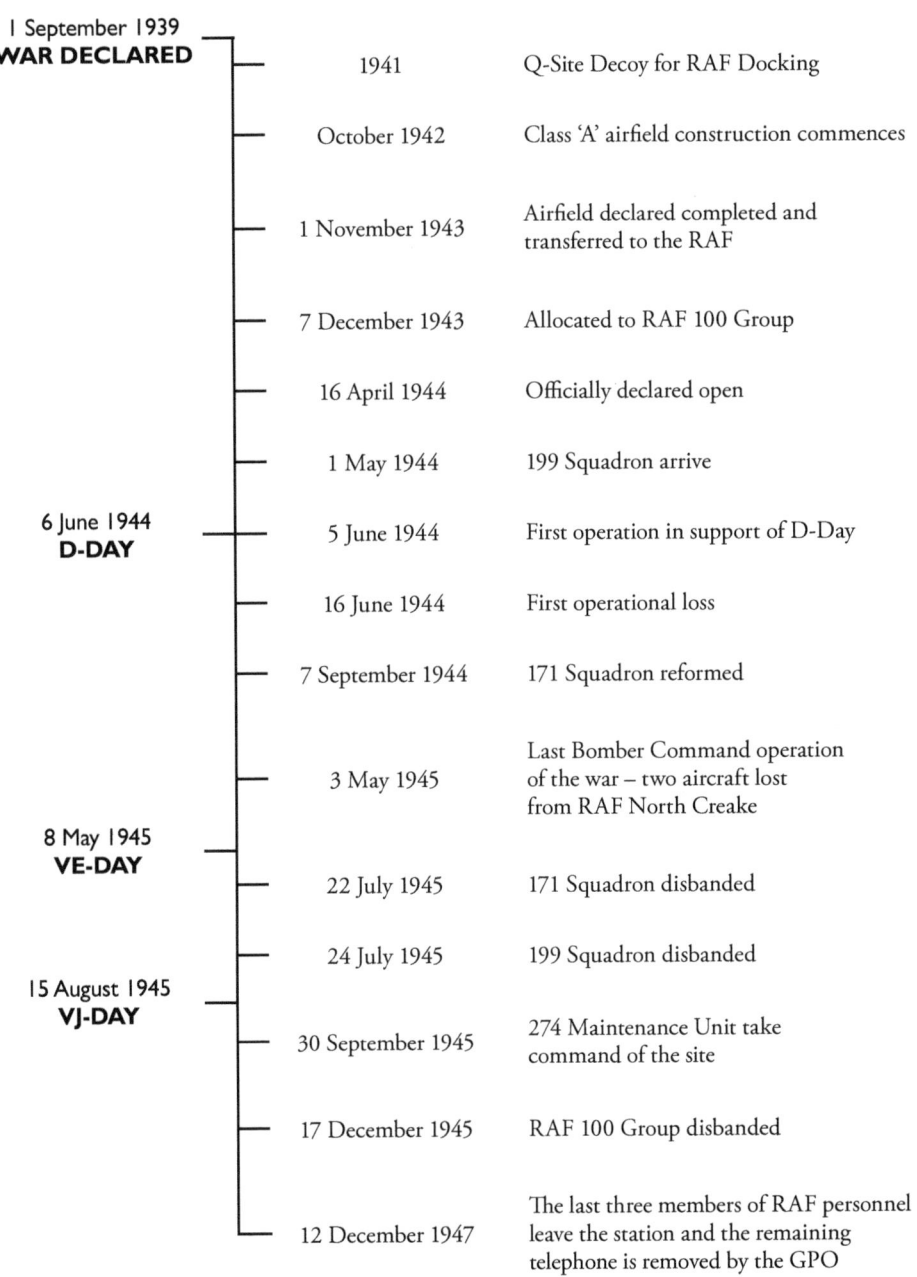

1 September 1939 **WAR DECLARED**	1941	Q-Site Decoy for RAF Docking
	October 1942	Class 'A' airfield construction commences
	1 November 1943	Airfield declared completed and transferred to the RAF
	7 December 1943	Allocated to RAF 100 Group
	16 April 1944	Officially declared open
	1 May 1944	199 Squadron arrive
6 June 1944 **D-DAY**	5 June 1944	First operation in support of D-Day
	16 June 1944	First operational loss
	7 September 1944	171 Squadron reformed
	3 May 1945	Last Bomber Command operation of the war – two aircraft lost from RAF North Creake
8 May 1945 **VE-DAY**	22 July 1945	171 Squadron disbanded
	24 July 1945	199 Squadron disbanded
15 August 1945 **VJ-DAY**	30 September 1945	274 Maintenance Unit take command of the site
	17 December 1945	RAF 100 Group disbanded
	12 December 1947	The last three members of RAF personnel leave the station and the remaining telephone is removed by the GPO

ENDNOTES

Preface

1   Longmate, N. (1983) The Bombers: The RAF Offensive Against Germany 1939-1945.

2   Commonwealth War Grave Commission (undated) cwgc.org.

3   Smith, D. J. (1981) Action Stations 3: Military Airfields of Wales and the North West, p. 29.

Chapter One

1   Plater, A. (1994) Oliver's Travels: A Novel, p. 4.

2   Willis, S. & Holliss, B. (1990) Military Airfields in the British Isles 1939-1945, p. 2.

3   Halpenny, B. B. (1981) Action Stations 2: Military Airfields of Lincolnshire and the East Midlands, p. 25.

4   Bartram, L. (1998) RAF North Creake, Egmere, 1940-1947: A Brief History, p. 2.

5   Eaton, A. E. (undated) RAF Service Log, unpaginated.

6   Brettingham, L. (1997) Royal Air Force Beam Benders: No. 80 (Signals) Wing: 1940-1945, p. 180

7   Brettingham, L. (2002) Even When the Sparrows are Walking: The Origin and Effect of No. 100 (Bomber Support) Group, RAF, 1943-45, p. 291.

8   Brettingham: 1997: 180.

9   Brettingham: (1997): 180-181.

10 Derry, S. (May 2012) in conversation with the author.

11 Bartram: 1998: 5.

12 Bartram: 1998: 5.

13 Bartram: 1998: 5.

14 Halpenny: 1981: 26.

15 Dobinson, C. (2000) Fields of Deception: Britain's Bombing Decoys of World War II, p. 253.

16 Dobinson: 2000: 23.

17 Dobinson: 2000: 68-69.

18 Winter, J. M. (1974) Socialism and the Challenge of War: Ideas and Politics in Britain 1912-18, p. 1.

19 Ambrose, S (1973) 'A Special Presentation: From War to Peace' The World at War.

20 Murphy, R. (1989) Realism and Tinsel: Cinema and Society in Britain 1939-48, p. 219.

21 Priestley, J. B. (1945) 'Britain is in Danger' in Priestley, J. B. (ed.) (1945) Our Nation's Heritage, p. 168.

22 Bates, H. E. (1955) Love for Lydia, p. 129.

23 Guy Anderson (1/11/2021) in conversation with the author.

24 Russell Muirhead, L. (1949) Penguin Guides: Norfolk and the Isle of Ely, p. 8.

25 Willis & Holliss: 1990: 14-210.

26 Bartram: 1998: 2.

27 Jennings J. (9/6/2020) interview with the author.

28 Bowman: 2006: 77.

29 Arbib, R. S. (1947) Here We Are Together: The Notebook of an American Soldier in Britain, pp.18-19.

30 Longmate, N. (1983) The Bombers: The RAF Offensive Against Germany 1939-1945, p. 37.

31 Hastings, M. (1980) Bomber Command, p. 46.

32 Hastings: 1980: 46.

33 Francis, P., Flagg R. & Crisp, G. (2016) Nine Thousand Miles of Concrete: A Review of Second World War Temporary Airfields in England, p. 1.

34 Historic England (undated(a)) historicengland.org.uk.

35 Air Historical Branch (1956) Works: The Second World War 1939-1945, p. 25.

36 Air Historical Branch: 1956: 25.

37 Air Historical Branch: 1956: 28.

38 Air Historical Branch: 1956: 39.

39 Hastings: 1980: 51.

40 Bowman: 2006: 77.

41 Grayling, A. C. (2006) Among the Dead Cities: Was the Allied Bombing of Civilians in WWII a Necessity or a Crime?, p. 106.

42 Hillier, M. (2014) Suitcases, Vultures and Spies, p. 9.

43 Falconer, J. (1998) Bomber Command Handbook: 1939 – 1945, p. 51.

44 Fussell, P. (1989) Wartime, Understanding the Behaviour in the Second World War, p. 49.

45 Gregory, A. (1994) The Silence of Memory, Armistice Day 1919-1946, p. 213.

46 Gregory: 1994: 213.

47 Hastings: 1980: 267.

48 Middlebrook, M. & Everitt, C. (1985) The Bomber Command War Diaries: An Operational Reference Book, 1939-1945, p. 707.

49 Middlebrook & Everitt: 1985: 487.

50 Middlebrook & Everitt: 1985: 707.
51 Hastings: 1980: 167.
52 Parry, S. W. (1987) Intruders Over Britain: The Luftwaffe Night Fighter Offensive 1940-45, p. 126.
53 Brown R. D. (1992) East Anglia: 1944, p. 15.
54 Nunn, S. J. (2019) The impact of the Second World War on the Rural Landscape of Norfolk, ueaeprints.uea.ac.uk, p. 89.
55 Hastings: 1980: 131.
56 Grayling: 2006: 104.
57 Grayling: 2006: 104.
58 Smith, R. (10/4/1945) in correspondence to Robin Neillands.
59 Wainwright, J. (1978) Tail-End Charlie: One Man's Journey Through a War, p. 135.
60 Charlwood, D. (1984) No Moon Tonight, p. 99.
61 Wainwright: 1978: 111-112.
62 Wainwright: 1978: 158.
63 Hastings: 1980: 196.
64 Gill, D. (2006) 'The Skylark' in Abolish War, p. 3.
65 Wainwright: 1978: 158.
66 Wainwright: 1978): 111.
67 Tripp, M. (1985) The Eighth Passenger: A Documentary Account of a World War 2 Bomber Crew, p. 77.
68 Tripp: 1985: 89
69 Dennison, G. J. (11/3/1941) 'Letter to Parents', cited in: Dennison, G. (2007) Memories Are Treasures: The Military career of Pilot Officer Gordon Joshua Dennison, p. 50.
70 Fussell: 1989: 100-101.
71 Hornsey, D. (1943) cited in Hastings: 1980: 222.
72 Winfield, R. (1976) The Sky Belongs to Them, p. 142.
73 Winfield: 1976: 142.
74 Tempest, V. (1946) Near the Sun: Impressions of a Medical Officer of Bomber Command, pp. 50-51.
75 Taylor, E. (1987) Operation Millennium: Bomber Harris's Raid on Cologne, May 1942, pp. 165-166.
76 Renaut, M. (1982) Terror by Night, pp. 82-83.
77 Renaut: 1982: 82-83.
78 Renaut: 1982: 82-83.
79 Gill, D. (2015) My Civilian and RAF Wartime Experiences, unpaginated.
80 Kavanagh, D. (2016) 'Interview with Denis James Gill'.
81 Wainwright: 1978: 134.
82 Winter, J. (2014) Sites of Memory, Sites of Mourning, p. 65.
83 Tripp: 1985: 180.
84 Pedan, M. (1979) A Thousand Shall Fall, p. 414.
85 Thompson, P. (30/9/2023) in correspondence with the author.
86 Thompson, P. (2017) Halifax Bill, 6Y-B Baker, Some Memories of My Father, unpaginated.
87 Fussell: 1989: 50.
88 Allison, J. (1966) Bomber Crew, p. 29.
89 Tripp, M. (1952) Faith is a Windsock, p. 48.
90 Tripp: 1985: 180.
91 Winter: 2014: 65.
92 Calder, A. (1969) The People's War: Britain 1939-45, p. 478.
93 Calder: 1969: 480.
94 Tempest: 1946: 36.
95 Calder: 1969: 481.
96 Berrill, R. (25/3/2023) interview by author.
97 Tripp: 1985: 89.
98 An aircrew veteran (May 2012) in conversation with the author at an RAF 100 Group Association Reunion weekend.
99 Wainwright: 1978: 135.
100 Lorimer, A. (1985) in Hall, A. (1985) We, Also, Were There, p. 188.
101 Renaut: 1982: 161.
102 Wainwright: 1978: 105.
103 An aircrew veteran: May 2012.
104 An aircrew veteran: May 2012.
105 Tempest: 1946: 33.
106 Tempest: 1946: 33.
107 Borthwick, T (17/1/2023) in conversation with the author.
108 Anonymous (28/5/2022) in conversation with the author by telephone.
109 James-Parker, L. (2017) 'Bernie – Unsung Hero', youtube.com.
110 Renaut: 1982: 183.
111 Young, D. (1982) 'Forward' in Renaut: 1982: 13.
112 Tempest: 1946: 44.
113 Wilkinson, E. (1941) 'Social Justice' in, The Fabian Society (1941) Programme for Victory, pp. 119-120.
114 Winter: 2014: 8.
115 Winter: 2014: 8.
116 Blair, J. J. (undated) history.co.uk.
117 History of Ireland (undated) 'The Forgotten Volunteers of World War Two', historyireland.com.
118 Bartlett, H. (21/10/2021) 'Interview with Gordon Mercier'.
119 Mercier, G. (15/2/2017) in correspondence with the author.
120 Tripp: 1985: 165.
121 King, L. (undated) History of Service in RAF, p. 1.
122 James-Parker: 2017.

123 How, B. (27/7/2013) interview with the author.
124 Tempest: 1946: 49.
125 Longmate: 1983: 178.
126 Longmate: 1983: 178.
127 Smith, R. (7/12/2005) 'How I became a Navigator', bbc.co.uk.
128 Gill: 2015: unpaginated.
129 Mitchell, G. (undated) Start and Finish of an Air Gunner, unpaginated.
130 Gill: 2015: unpaginated.
131 Hastings: 1980: 142.
132 Bartlett: 21/10/2021.
133 Mitchell: undated.
134 Kavanagh, D. (16/11/2016) Interview with Bernie How.
135 Knott, S. (undated) cited in, Redding, T. (2005) Flying for Freedom: Life and Death in Bomber Command, p. 23.
136 Tripp: 1952: 27.
137 Sawyer, T. (1981) Only Owls and Bloody Fools Fly at Night, p. 93.
138 Gill, D. (7/6/2014) in conversation with the author.
139 Gill: 2015: unpaginated.
140 Maclaren-Ross, J. (1991) Memoirs of the Forties, p. 104.
141 Moore, B. (1965) The Emperor of Ice Cream, p. 166.

15 Renaut, M. (1982) Terror by Night, p. 171.
16 Renaut: 1982: 171.
17 Rees, J. (undated) in, Bartram, L. (1998) RAF North Creake, Egmere, 1940-1947: A Brief History, p. 14.
18 RAF North Creake (June 1944) Operations Record Book, unpaginated.
19 Chorley, W. H. (2008) Royal Air Force Bomber Command Losses of the Second World War 1945, p. 177.
20 Reid, J. (12/12/2020) in correspondence with the author.
21 RAF 199 Squadron (June 1945) Operations Records Book, unpaginated.
22 Air Ministry (undated) Form 765: NA259.
23 Air Ministry: undated.
24 Air Ministry: undated.
25 Air Ministry (a) (undated) Form 1180 NA259.
26 Poad, R. & Webster, J. (2020) Maidenhead Heritage Centre: The Spiritual Home of ATA (Air Transport Auxiliary) in correspondence with the author.
27 Reid: 12/12/2020.
28 Smithard: 12/8/2004: 42-43.
29 Smithard: 12/8/2004: 42-43.
30 Smithard: 12/8/2004: 42-43.
31 Nolan: 12/3/1995.
32 Smithard: 12/8/2004: 42-43.

Air Test

1 Nolan, F. (12/3/1995) Correspondence with Cromer Museum; Barton, A. (2011) in Poppy Land (2011) Cromer in the Second World War; Eastern Daily Press (26/6/1945) Plane Crash on Cromer Beach, p. 5; Baker, G. (29/09/2020) interview with author; Daily Mirror (26/6/1945) RAF Men go to Death to Save Beach Crowd, p. 1; Smithard, T. (12/8/2004) 'Crash Pilot Saved Our Lives' Eastern Daily Press, pp. 42-43.
2 Barton: 2011.
3 Smithard: 12/8/2004: 42-43.
4 Daily Mirror: 26/6/1945: 1.
5 Daily Mirror: 26/6/1945: 1.
6 Bevington, P. E. (29/6/1945) Letter of Condolence to L. N. Dent, unpaginated.
7 Black, W. B. (27/6/1945) 'To the Editor: Cromer Plane Crash', in Eastern Daily Press, p. 3.
8 Black: 27/6/1945: 3.
9 Black: 27/6/1945: 3.
10 Black: 27/6/1945: 3.
11 Baker: 29/09/2020.
12 Eastern Daily Press: 26/6/1945: 5.
13 Baker: 29/09/2020.
14 Baker: 29/09/2020.

Chapter Two

1 Hoskins, W.G. (1977) The Making of the English Landscape, p. 299.
2 Nunn, S. J. (2019) The impact of the Second World War on the Rural Landscape of Norfolk, p. 70.
3 Nunn: 2019: 83.
4 Nunn: 2019: 81.
5 Nunn: 2019: 83.
6 Nunn: 2019: 83.
7 Nunn: 2019: 81.
8 Air Ministry, (1937) cited in Nunn: 2019: 81.
9 Air Ministry, (1937) cited in Nunn: 2019: 81.
10 Francis, P., Flagg R. & Crisp, G. (2016) Nine Thousand Miles of Concrete: A Review of Second World War Temporary Airfields in England, p. 14.
11 Higham, R. (1998) Bases of Air Strategy: Building Airfields for the RAF 1914-1945, p. 16.
12 Bowyer, M. J. F. (1979) Action Stations: Wartime Military Airfields of East Anglia, 1939-1945, p. 165.
13 Nunn: 2019: 89.

14 Air Historical Branch (1956) Works: The Second World War 1939-1945, p. 79.

15 Francis, Flagg & Crisp: 2016: 7.

16 Kohan, J. M. (1952) History of the Second World War: History and Buildings, p. 279.

17 Air Historical Branch: 1956: 76.

18 Willis, S. & Holliss, B. (1990) Military Airfields in the British Isles 1939-1945, p. 2.

19 Air Historical Branch: 1956: 25.

20 Air Historical Branch: 1956: 164.

21 Air Historical Branch: 1956: 164.

22 Air Historical Branch: 1956: 114-115.

23 Nunn: 2019: 82.

24 Nunn: 2019: 83.

25 Nunn: 2019: 82.

26 Air Historical Branch: 1956: 178-180.

27 Nunn: 2019: 10.

28 Air Historical Branch: 1956: 333.

29 Air Historical Branch: 1956: 331.

30 Alr Historical Branch: 1956: 340.

31 Keesings (1947) Contemporary Archives: Weekly Diary of World Events, p. 8654.

32 Nunn: 2019: 106.

33 Air Ministry (1943) cited in Keesings (1946) Contemporary Archives: Weekly Diary of World Events, p. 6127.

34 Air Ministry (1941) cited in, Nunn: 2019: 91-92.

35 Nunn: 2019: 94.

36 Air Historical Branch: 1956: 81.

37 Air Historical Branch: 1956: 79.

38 Air Historical Branch: 1956: 79.

39 Air Historical Branch: 1956: 169.

40 Kohan: 1952: 280.

41 Air Ministry (1941) cited in Nunn: 2019: 97.

42 Kohan: 1952: 283.

43 Air Historical Branch: 1956: 142.

44 Air Historical Branch: 1956: 462.

45 Air Historical Branch: 1956: 462.

46 Higham: 1998: 23.

47 Kohan: 1952: FN1, p. 284.

48 Berry, P. (1989) Airfield Heyday: Daily Life on and Around Wartime Airfields, p. 84.

49 Nunn: 2019: 92.

50 Bowyer, M. J. F. (2010) Action Stations Revisited: Eastern England, p. 273.

51 Brown R. D. (1990) East Anglia: 1943, p. 5.

52 Halpenny, B. B. (1984) Action Stations 8: Military Airfields of Greater London, p. 21.

53 Jones, J. (undated) in Walsingham History Society (2001) The Walsingham Millennium Book: Interviews and Recollections, p. 4.

54 Maufe, T. (2012) in conversation with the author. Also in: Jones, J. (undated) in Walsingham History Society (2001): 4.

55 Groome, N. (13/4/2020) in conversation with the author.

56 Numerous conversations with locals and the author while at the pub between 2018 and 2020.

57 Rees, J. (undated) in Bartram, L. (1998) RAF North Creake, Egmere, 1940-1947: A Brief History, p. 14.

58 Renaut, M. (1982) Terror by Night, p. 157.

59 Reynolds, A. (12/9/2013) in conversation with the author.

60 Berry: 1989: 84.

61 Berry: 1989: 84.

62 Air Historical Branch: 1956: 253.

63 Air Historical Branch: 1956: 251.

64 Halpenny: 1984: 22.

65 Air Historical Branch: 1956: 121.

66 Francis, Flagg & Crisp: 2016: 5.

67 Francis, Flagg & Crisp: 2016: 17.

68 Air Historical Branch: 1956: 171.

69 Air Historical Branch: 1956: 167.

70 Francis, Flagg & Crisp: 2016: 3.

71 Perryman, D. & Perryman, M. (2014) Some Notes on the Water Supply to North Creake Airfield, p. 2.

72 Air Historical Branch: 1956: 167.

73 Air Historical Branch: 1956: 168.

74 Air Historical Branch: 1956: 168.

75 Cotterell, A. P. I. (1944) Post-War Reconstruction: Water Supplies and Sewage.

76 Francis, Flagg & Crisp: 2016: 3.

77 Air Historical Branch: 1956: 481.

78 Air Historical Branch: 1956: 83.

79 Air Historical Branch: 1956: 94.

80 Bartram: 1998: 17.

81 Air Historical Branch: 1956: 94.

82 Francis, Flagg & Crisp: 2016: 6

83 Francis, Flagg & Crisp: 2016: 2.

84 Air Historical Branch: 1956: 76.

85 Kohan: 1952: 293.

86 Kohan: 1952: 293.

87 Brown: 1990: 3.

88 Tuck, J. (13/02/2017) interview with author.

89 Tuck, J. (2013) John Tuck at Hobbies Ltd, Dereham and Other Wartime Occupations, p. 6.

90 Tuck: 2013: 6.

91 Tuck: 13/02/2017.

92 Kohan: 1952: 139.

93 Tuck: 13/02/2017.

94 Kohan: 1952: 143-144.

95 Tuck: 13/02/2017.

96 McIvor, A. J. (2001) A History of Work in Britain: 1880-1950, 132.

97 Kohan: 1952: 284.

98 Kohan: 1952: 285.

99 Tuck: 13/02/2017.

100 Brown: 1990: 5.

101 Crump, N. (1947) By Rail to Victory, p. 146.

102 Tuck: 13/02/2017.

103 Higham: 1998: 30.

104 Smith, R. (2018) Crossing the Bar: Tales of Wells Harbour, p. 134.

105 Bell, R. (1946) History of the British Railways During the War 1939-1945, pp. 86-87.

106 Bell: 1946: 87.

107 Bartram: 1998: 17.

108 Air Historical Branch: 1956: 76.

109 Kohan: 1952: 282.

110 Brown: 1990: 5.

111 Walsingham History Society: 2001: unpaginated.

112 Brown: 1990: 5.

113 Jennings, J. (9/6/2020) interview with Author.

114 Leach, D. (16/11/2017) interview with author.

115 Skipper, K. (undated) cited in Walsingham History Society: 2001: unpaginated.

116 Skipper: (undated) cited in Walsingham History Society: 2001: unpaginated.

117 Wright, J. (undated) cited in Walsingham History Society: 2001: unpaginated.

118 Boulter, G. (undated) cited in Bridges, E. M. & Baldwin, J. (Eds) (2005) A Conflict & Memories: Fakenham Remembers World War Two, p. 32.

119 Berry: 1989: 84.

120 Mallett, E. (undated) Wartime Memories, unpaginated.

121 Partridge, J. (26/10/2004) Correspondence with John Reid.

122 Smith, D. J. (1981) Action Stations 3: Military Airfields of Wales and the North West, p. 22.

123 Smith: 1981: 22.

124 Francis, P (1996) British Military Airfield Architecture: From Airships to the Jet Age, pp. 131-132.

125 Department of Media, Culture and Sport (2/12/2005) Press Release: Chocks Away! David Lammy Secures a Future for the Aviation Sites that Protected Our Past, unpaginated.

126 Air Historical Branch: 1956: 174.

127 Air Historical Branch: 1956: 132.

128 Harwood, E. (2019) Art Deco Britain: Buildings of the Interwar Years, p. 8.

129 Harwood: 2019: 8.

130 Jencks, C (1973) Architecture 2000: Predictions and Methods, p. 35.

131 Cranfield, I. (2005) Art Deco House Style: An Architectural and Interior Design Source Book, p. 8.

132 Cranfield: 2005: 9.

133 Sassoon, S. (1930) Memoirs of an Infantry Officer, p. 197.

134 Cranfield: 2005: 12.

135 Cranfield: 2005: 9.

136 Tinniswood, A. (2002) The Art Deco House, p. 9.

137 Cranfield: 2005: 13.

138 Cranfield: 2005: 15.

139 Cranfield: 2005: p. 28.

140 Richards, J. M. (1959) An Introduction to Modern Architecture, p. 10.

141 Cranfield: 2005: 27-28.

142 Harwood: 2019: 7.

143 Harwood: 2019: 7.

144 Cranfield: 2005: 13.

145 Harwood: 2019: 7.

146 Rolt, L.T.C. (1946) Narrow Boat, p. 82.

147 Betjeman, J. (1937) 'Antiquarian Prejudice' in, Betjeman, J. (1969) First and Last Loves, p. 60.

148 Cranfield: 2005: 20.

149 Tinniswood: 2002: 18-19.

150 Tinniswood: 2002: 19.

151 Cranfield: 2005: 13.

152 Richards: 1959: 11.

153 Richards: 1959: 12.

154 Cranfield: 2005: 28.

155 Harwood: 2019: 14.

156 Richards: 1959: 101.

157 Harwood: 2019: 16.

158 Kohan: 1952: 139.

159 Kohan: 1952: 140.

160 Kohan: 1952: 140-141.

161 Kohan: 1952: 143.

162 Kohan: 1952: 143.

163 Read, H. (1945) 'The Present State of Design and Its Relation to the Industrial System' in Fry, E. M. (1945) Architects' Year Book, p. 86.

164 Butler, P. (2017) Streamline Worcestershire, p. 63.

165 Pedan, M. (1979) A Thousand Shall Fall, p. 255.

166 Nunn: 2019: 70.

167 Nunn: 2019; 74.

168 Nunn: 2019: 74.

169 Nunn: 2019: 70.

170 Nunn: 2019: 70.

171 Nunn: 2019: 74.

Missing

1 Reid, J. (2014) Let Tyrants Tremble: The War Diary of 199 (Bomber Support) Squadron, November 1942 – July 1945, p. 131.

2   RAF North Creake (1944) Operations Record Book, unpaginated.

3   Reid: 2014: 131.

4   Reid: 2014: 131.

5   Air Council (undated) Flying Control in the Royal Air Force, publication 3024, p. 108.

6   Reid, J. in Conversation with the author on numerous occasions.

7   Hines, M. (2022) Airfields of North Norfolk: RAF North Creake, p. 14.

8   RAF 199 Squadron (1944) Sorties Records N. Creake, unpublished record book, unpaginated.

9   Bourke, J. (1996) Dismembering the Male: Men's Bodies, Britain and the Great War, p. 230.

10 Hope, B. (2014) And in the Morning: RAF Station North Creake, p. 31.

11 Archives New Zealand (undated) 'Royal New Zealand Air Force Biographies of Deceased Personnel 1939-1945', aucklandmuseum. com, unpaginated.

12 Archives New Zealand: undated.

13 Hope: 2014: 34.

14 Hope: 2014: 32.

15 Hope: 2014: 34.

16 Reid: 2014: 137.

17 Reid: 2014: 137.

18 Reid: 2014: 136.

19 Reid: 2014: 137.

20 RAF North Creake: 1944: ORB: unpaginated.

21 Royal Canadian Air Force (6/5/1942) Attestation Paper: Murray Kesselman, p. 1.

22 RCAF: 6/5/1942: 2.

23 Royal Canadian Air Force (9/5/1942) Interview Report: Murray Kesselman, unpaginated.

24 RCAF: 9/5/1942: unpaginated.

25 RCAF: 9/5/1942: unpaginated.

26 RCAF: 9/5/1942: unpaginated.

27 Royal Canadian Air Force (1942) Report on Pupil Pilot -Flying and Ground Training: Murray Kesselman, unpaginated.

28 Royal Canadian Air Force (1942a) Report on Pupil Pilot: Murray Kesselman, unpaginated.

29 RCAF: 1942a: unpaginated.

30 RCAF: 1942a: unpaginated.

31 Royal Canadian Air Force (17/9/1943a) Royal Canadian Air Force: Record of Service Airmen, unpaginated.

32 Toronto Globe and Mail (1944) Truck Langley Officially Listed as Killed in Action.

33 Royal Canadian Air Force (31/12/1941) Attestation Paper: Lloyd George Langley, p. 1.

34 Royal Canadian Air Force (30/12/1941) RCAF Interview Report: Lloyd George Langley, unpaginated.

35 Horner, A. (11/9/1941) Correspondence from Horner (Officer Commanding No. 121 (Technical) Detachment, unpaginated.

36 Royal Canadian Air Force (1943) Record of Airmen: Lloyd George Langley, unpaginated.

37 Royal Canadian Air Force (1942c) Appendix 'A': Progress and Discontinuance Report: Lloyd George Langley, unpaginated.

38 RCAF: 1942c: unpaginated.

39 RCAF: 1942c: unpaginated.

40 Royal Canadian Air Force (20/8/1943) Form 5023: Training Report: Lloyd George Langley, unpaginated.

41 Royal Canadian Air Force (1943a) Part III (Report on Pupil Nav.): Lloyd George Langley, unpaginated.

42 Royal Canadian Air Force (18/11/1942) Attestation Paper: James Duncan Campbell, p. 1.

43 Royal Canadian Air Force (18/3/1943) Occupational History Form: James Duncan Campbell, unpaginated.

44 RCAF: 18/11/1942: 1.

45 Royal Canadian Air Force (26/11/1943) R.C.A.F. Training Report: Wireless Operator (Air Gunner) and Air Gunner, No. 9 Bomber and Gunnery School: James Duncan Campbell, unpaginated.

46 Royal Canadian Air Force (26/11/1943a) R.C.A.F. Training Report: Wireless Operator (Air Gunner) and Air Gunner, No. 9 Bomber and Gunnery School: Gordon Joshua Dennison, RCAF, unpaginated and Royal Canadian Air Force (26/11/1943) R.C.A.F. Training Report: Wireless Operator (Air Gunner) and Air Gunner, No. 9 Bomber and Gunnery School: James Duncan Campbell, unpaginated.

47 Dennison, G. (2007) Memories Are Treasures: The Military Career of Pilot Officer Gordon Joshua Dennison, p. 10.

48 Dennison: 2007: 12.

49 Dennison: 2007: 12.

50 Royal Canadian Air Force (21/1/1943) Interview Report: Gordon Dennison, unpaginated.

51 RCAF: 21/1/1943: unpaginated.

52 Dennison, G. J. (13/7/1943) 'Letter to Parents', cited in: Dennison: 2007: 76.

53 RCAF: 26/11/1943: unpaginated.

54 Dennison: 2007: 14.

55 Dennison: 2007: 15.

56 Royal Air Force (27/7/1944) No. 1653 H.C.U. – Chedburgh Air Gunner's Assessment Chart: Gordon Dennison, unpaginated.

57 Dennison, G. J. (2/7/1944) 'Letter to Winnie, Earl & David (Siblings), cited in, Dennison: 2007: 122.

58 RAF: 27/7/1944: unpaginated.

59 Dennison: 2007: 14.

60   Dennison, G. J. (31/8/1944) 'Letter to Parents', cited in: Dennison, 2007: 117.

61   Dennison: 31/8/1944: cited in, Dennison: 2007: 117.

62   Hadaway, S. (2008) Missing Believed Killed: The Royal Air Force and the Search for Missing Aircrew 1939-1952, p. 25.

63   Royal Canadian Air Force Casualty Officer (22/9/1944), cited in, Dennison: 2007: 135.

64   RCAF Casualty Officer: 22/9/1944, cited in, Dennison: 2007: 135.

65   RCAF Casualty Officer: 22/9/1944, cited in, Dennison: 2007: 135.

66   War Office (1943) Advice to the Relatives of a Man Who is Missing, unpaginated.

67   Hadaway: 2008: 163.

68   Air Ministry (undated) cited in Hadaway: 2008: 163.

69   Hadaway: 2008:163.

70   Renaut, M. (1982) Terror by Night, p. 156.

71   Hadaway: 2008: 26.

72   Air Ministry (1943) Notes for the General Information and Guidance of the Next-of-Kin or other Relatives of Airmen reported Missing, Deceased, Prisoners of War or Interned, p. 1.

73   Air Ministry: 1943: 1.

74   Smith S. (27/2/2022) in conversation with the author.

75   Air Ministry: 1943: 1.

76   Holmes, L. (25/4/2022) in correspondence with the author.

77   Wainwright, J. (1978) Tail-End Charlie: One Man's Journey Through a War, p. 129.

78   Pedan, M. (1979) A Thousand Shall Fall, p. 267.

79   Wainwright: 1978: 130.

80   Wainwright: 1978: 129.

81   Wainwright: 1978: 129.

82   Air Ministry: 1943: 1.

83   Air Ministry: 1943: 1.

84   Air Ministry: 1943: 1.

85   Air Ministry: 1943: 3.

86   Royal Canadian Air Force (undated) Department of National Defence Inventory: Gordon Joshua Dennison, RCAF, unpaginated.

87   Royal Canadian Air Force (undateda) Department of National Defence Inventory: Lloyd George Langley, RCAF, unpaginated.

88   Kesselman, M. (1944) Correspondence Home, unpaginated.

89   Kesselman: 1944: unpaginated.

90   Campbell, L. D. (25/1/1945) Correspondence with RCAF Casualty Officer, unpaginated.

91   Bevington, P. (24/2/1945) 'Letter from the Wing Commander of 199 Squadron RAF North Creake', cited in, Dennison: 2007: 142.

92   Cook, J. W. (9/4/1945) 'Letter form Canadian Red Cross Society', cited in: Dennison: 2007: 143.

93   Campbell: 16/7/1945: unpaginated.

94   Royal Canadian Air Force (22/8/1945) Official Royal Canadian Air Force Casualty Notification Form, unpaginated.

95   Royal Canadian Air Force (15/10/1945) 'Letter from Department of National Defence', cited in: Dennison: 2007: 146.

96   Dennison, H. (3/3/1947) Correspondence between Dennison's Mother and the Secretary, Department of National Defence for All, Ottawa, Ontario, unpaginated.

97   Royal Canadian Air Force Casualty Officer (11/4/1947) Correspondence between RCAF Casualty Officer and Gordon Dennison's Mother, RCAF, unpaginated.

98   Dennison: 2007: 152.

99   Kesselman, L. (2/10/1945) 'Letter from Brother of Murray Kesselman to Dennisons', cited in: Dennison: 2007: 152.

100   Swadling, P. (28/9/2022) in conversation with the author.

101   Swadling: 28/9/2022.

102   Swadling: 28/9/2022.

103   Campbell, M. E. (15/7/1946) Correspondence to RCAF Estates Branch, unpaginated.

104   Director of Estates (18/9/1945) Campbell, M. E. submission on Form P. 64.: Department of National Estates Branch, p. 4.

105   Reid: 2014: 132.

106   Gunn, W. R. (10/6/1952) Letter to Martha Kesselman from RCAF Casualties Officer, unpaginated.

107   Levinson, J. & Granot, H. (2002) cited in Moshenka, G. (2014) 'Token Scraps of Men: Whites Lies, Weighted Coffins, and Second World War Air Crash Casualties', in Cornish, P. & Saunders, N. (eds) (2014) Bodies in Conflict: Corporeality, Materiality & Transformation, p. 136.

108   Moshenka: 2014: 136.

109   Kesselman, M. (11/12/2020) in correspondence with the author.

110   Dennison: 2007: 156.

111   Swadling: 28/9/2022.

112   Franklin, J. (8/2/2020) in conversation with the author.

113   Slater, Bill (undated) Correspondence, via N. Lewis.

Chapter Three

1   Morris, W. cited in Fussell, P. (1975) The Great War and Modern Memory, p. 205.

2 Kee, R. (8/2/1971) 'Mercury on a Fork', The Listener, p. 208.

3 Thomas, M. (2017) The Red Shed: A Topical Tale About the Miners' Strike, p. 31.

4 Hardy, T. (1932) Wessex Tales: Preface, p. VI.

5 Scannell, V. (1971) cited in, Fussell: 1975: 334.

6 Scannell: 1971 cited in, Fussell: 1975: 334.

7 Dyer, G. (1994) The Missing of the Somme, p. 3

8 Bourke, J. (2001) The Second World War: A People's History, p. 221.

9 Fussell: 1975: 327.

10 Fussell: 1975: 327.

11 Priestley, J. B. (1963) Margin Released: Reminiscences & Reflections, p. 188.

12 Delve, K. (2/6/2017) in conversation with the author.

13 Kee: 8/2/1971: 208.

14 Kee: 8/2/1971: 208.

15 Fussell, P. (1989) Wartime, Understanding the Behaviour in the Second World War, p. 145.

16 Hastings, M. (1980) Bomber Command, pp. 343-344.

17 Taylor, F. (2005) Dresden: Tuesday 13 February 1945, p. 432.

18 Webster, C. & Frankland, N. (1961) History of the Second World War: The Strategic Air Offensive: Vol. Victory, p. 112.

19 Webster & Frankland: 1961: Vol III: p. 112.

20 Hastings: 1980: 343-344.

21 Carr, E. H. (1969) What is History? p. 6.

22 Carr: 1969: 16-17.

23 Carr: 1969: 24.

24 Taylor: 2005: 131.

25 Taylor: 2005: 135.

26 Fussell: 1989: 16.

27 Harris, A. (1942) cited in, Whiting, C. (1987) The Three Star Blitz: The Baedeker Raids and the Start of Total War 1942-1943, p. 103.

28 Bourke: 2001: 164.

29 Parton, J. (1986) Air Force Spoken Here: General Ira Eaker & the Command of the Air, p. 140.

30 Hastings: 1980: 135.

31 Bourke: 2001: 164-165.

32 Harris, A. (1947) cited in Hastings: 1980: 11.

33 Hastings: 1980: 135.

34 Pelly-Fry, J. (1994) Heavenly Days: Recollections of a Contented Airman, p. 255.

35 Pelly-Fry: 1994: 255.

36 Calder, A. (1991) The Myth of the Blitz, p. 59.

37 Longmate, N. (1983) The Bombers: The RAF Offensive Against Germany 1939-1945, p. 47.

38 Taylor: 2005: 101.

39 Calder: 1991: 60.

40 Sawyer, T. (1981) Only Owls and Bloody Fools Fly at Night, p. 31.

41 Hastings: 1980: 55.

42 Air Ministry [1940] cited in Hastings:1980: 85.

43 Chamberlain, N. (6/2/1940) 'Bombing of Civil Populations', Hansard.

44 Hastings: 1980: 64.

45 Webster, C. & Frankland, N. (1961) History of the Second World War: The Strategic Air Offensive, Volume 1: Preparation, p. 144.

46 Webster & Frankland: 1961: Vol. 1: 144.

47 Webster & Frankland: 1961: Vol. 1: 144.

48 Hastings: 1980: 107.

49 Churchill, W. (1940) 'Minute to Beaverbrook', cited in, Jones, R. V. (1978) Most Secret War: British Scientific Intelligence 1939-1945, p. 183.

50 Ashworth, C. (1995) RAF Bomber Command 1936-1968, p. 39.

51 Ashworth: 1995: 39.

52 Middlebrook, M. & Everitt, C. (1985) The Bomber Command War Diaries: An Operational Reference Book, 1939-1945, p. 77.

53 Middlebrook & Everitt :1985: 77.

54 Middlebrook & Everitt :1985: 77.

55 Fussell: 1989: 16.

56 Whiting, C. (1987) The Three Star Blitz: The Baedeker Raids and the Start of Total War 1942-1943, p. 105.

57 Hitler, A. (1940) cited in, Whiting: 1987: p. 5.

58 Harris, A. (1947) Bomber Offensive, pp. 51-52.

59 Jones, G. (1942) cited in, Longmate: 1983: 127.

60 Falconer, J. (1998) Bomber Command Handbook 1939-1945, p. 230.

61 Webster, C. & Frankland, N. (1961) History of the Second World War: The Strategic Air Offensive, Volume IV: Victory, p. 205.

62 Webster & Frankland: 1961: Vol. IV: 205.

63 Taylor: 2005: 132.

64 Taylor: 2005: 132.

65 Webster & Frankland: 1961: Vol. I: 178.

66 Hastings: 1980: 48.

67 Hastings: 1980: 94-96.

68 Hastings: 1980: 46

69 Hastings: 1980: 123.

70 Hastings: 1980: 120.

71 Taylor, A.J.P. (1965) English History: 1914-1945, p. 519.

72 Taylor: 1965: 519.

73 Cockburn, R. (1945) The Radio War, Air 20/8953, p. 60.

74 Taylor: 2005: 133.

75 Grayling, A. C. (2006) Among the Dead Cities: Was the Allied Bombing of Civilians in WWII a Necessity or a Crime?, p. 50.

76 Hastings: 1980: 148.

77 Middlebrook & Everitt: 1985: 251.

78 Hastings: 1980: 46.

79 Longmate: 1983: 216.

80 Churchill, W. (10/5/1942) Prime Minister Winston Churchill's Broadcast Report on the War, ibiblio.org.

81 Hastings: 1980: 131.

82 Longmate: 1983: 131.

83 Longmate: 1983: 216.

84 Seversky, A. (1942) Victory Through Air Power, p. 145.

85 Middlebrook & Everitt: 1985: 269.

86 Middlebrook & Everitt: 1985: 270.

87 Longmate: 1983: 223.

88 Sweetman, J. (2004) Bomber Crew: taking on the Reich, p. 80.

89 Middlebrook & Everitt: 1985: 270.

90 Middlebrook & Everitt: 1985: 270.

91 Taylor, E. (1983) Operation Millennium: 'Bomber' Harris's Raid on Cologne, May 1942, p. 159.

92 Bourke: 2001: 163.

93 Taylor: 1965: 528.

94 Taylor: 1965: 529.

95 Taylor, A. J. P. (1977) The War Lords, p. 101.

96 Hastings: 1980: 180.

97 Grayling: 2006: 174.

98 Taylor: 1965: 543.

99 Hastings: 1980: 139-140.

100 Taylor, A. J. P. (1975) The Second World War: An Illustrated History, p. 150.

101 Hastings: 1980: 139-140.

102 Taylor: 1975: 150.

103 Taylor: 1975: 150.

104 Taylor: 1975: 151.

105 Grayling: 2006: 174.

106 Hastings: 1980: 179.

107 Grayling: 2006: 174.

108 Overy, R. (1995) Why the Allies Won, p. 102.

109 Overy: 1995: 102.

110 Overy: 1995: 102.

111 Taylor: 1975: 169.

112 Combined Chiefs of Staff (1943) 'The Casablanca Directive – CCS 166/1/D', cited in Hastings: 1980: 185.

113 Terraine, J. (1985) The Right of the Line: The Royal Air Force in the European War 1939-1945, p. 505.

114 Hastings: 1980: 226.

115 Hastings: 1980: 188.

116 Whiting: 1987: 137-138.

117 Hastings: 185.

118 Middlebrook & Everitt: 1985: 410-414.

119 Overy, R. (2013) The Bombing War in Europe 1939-1945, p. 405.

120 Overy: 2013: 436.

121 Middlebrook & Everitt: 1985: 410-414.

122 Pedan, M. (1979) A Thousand Shall Fall, p. 264.

123 Galbraith, J. (1961) The Affluent Society, p. 126.

124 Galland, A. (undated) cited in, Whiting: 1987: 164.

125 Speer, A. (1970) cited in, Hastings: 1980: 227.

126 Taylor: 2005: 130.

127 Hastings: 1980: 197.

128 Taylor: 2005: 130.

129 Richards, D. (1994) The Hardest Victory: RAF Bomber Command in the Second World War, p. 187.

130 Bartlett, H. (23/11/2021) Interview with Gordon Mercier.

131 Pedan: 1979: 181.

132 Taylor: 2005: 218.

133 Hastings: 1980: 341.

134 Lunghi, H. (1996) cited in, Taylor: 2005: 218.

135 Middlebrook & Everitt: 1985: 663.

136 Middlebrook & Everitt: 1985: 663.

137 Taylor: 2005: 508.

138 Taylor: 2005: 508.

139 Stokes, R. (6/3/1945) Hansard, unpaginated.

140 Stokes: 6/3/1945: unpaginated.

141 Redding, T. (2005) Flying for Freedom: Life and Death in Bomber Command, p. 213.

142 Hastings: 1980: 337.

Fewer Than Five Miles from Base

1 Harley, T. (undated) British Weather in September.

2 Middlebrook, M. & Everitt, C. (1985) The Bomber Command War Diaries: An Operational Reference Book, 1939-1945, p. 589.

3 RAF North Creake (September 1944) Operations Record Book, unpaginated.

4   RAF 171 Squadron (September 1944) Operations Record Book, unpaginated.

5   RAF North Creake: 1944: ORB: unpaginated.

6   RAF North Creake: 1944: ORB: unpaginated.

7   RAF 199 Squadron (September 1944) Operations Records Book, unpaginated.

8   RAF 199 Squadron: September 1944: ORB: unpaginated.

9   RAF 199 Squadron: September 1944: ORB: unpaginated.

10   Archives New Zealand (undated) Royal New Zealand Air Force Biographies of Deceased Personnel 1939-1945, unpaginated.

11   RAF Commands (undated) rafcommands.com.

12   RAF Commands: undated: unpaginated.

13   Heroes of our Time (undated) heroesofourtime.co.uk.

14   Heroes of our Time: undated: unpaginated.

15   RAF Commands: undated: unpaginated.

16   RAF North Creake: 1944: ORB: unpaginated.

17   RAF Commands: undated: unpaginated.

18   RAF North Creake: 1944: ORB: unpaginated.

19   Smithies, E. (2002) Aces, Erks & Backroom Boys, p. 120.

20   RAF Commands: undated: unpaginated.

21   Reid, J. (2014) Let Tyrants Tremble: The War diary of 199 (Bomber Support) Squadron, November 1942 – July 1945, p. 139.

22   Spinks, R. (2013) Transcription of Docking Police Station Call Records, unpaginated.

23   Delve, K. (24/1/2023) in conversation with the author.

24   Rees, J. (undated) in Bartram, L. (1998) RAF North Creake, Egmere, 1940-1947: A Brief History, p. 14.

25   RAF North Creake: 1944: ORB: unpaginated.

26   Noakes, L. (2020) Valuing the Dead: Death, Burial, and the Body in Second World War Britain, p. 8.

27   Noakes: 2020: 8.

28   Berry, P. (1989) Airfield Heyday: Daily Life on and Around Wartime Airfields, p. 66.

29   Moshenka, G. (2014) 'Token Scraps of Men: Whites Lies, Weighted Coffins, and Second World War Air Crash Casualties', in Cornish, P. & Saunders, N. (eds) (2014) Bodies in Conflict: Corporeality, Materiality & Transformation, p. 134.

30   Moshenka: 2014: 134.

31   Moshenka: 2014: 137.

32   Sullivan, E. P. (18/4/2019) Considerable Grief: Dead Bodies, Mortuary Science, and Repatriation after the Great War, unpaginated.

33   Arnold, K. (2005) Green Two: Sgt Dennis Noble: One of Churchill's Few 1940, Southern Counties Aviation Research/Publications, p. 54.

34   Moshenka, G. (2014) 'Token Scraps of Men: Whites Lies, Weighted Coffins, and Second World War Air Crash Casualties', in Cornish, P. & Saunders, N. (eds) (2014) Bodies in Conflict: Corporeality, Materiality & Transformation, Routledge, p. 135.

35   Arnold, K. (2005) Green Two: Sgt Dennis Noble: One of Churchill's Few 1940, p. 52.

36   Arnold: 2005: 52.

37   Moshenka: 2014: 137.

38   Renaut, M. (1982) Terror by Night, pp. 62-63.

39   Pedan, M. (1979) A Thousand Shall Fall, pp. 267-268.

40   Hadaway, S. (2008) Missing Believed Killed: The Royal Air Force and the Search for Missing Aircrew 1939-1952, p. 163.

41   Reid: 2014: 139.

42   Thompson, D. (21/1/2011) No.43 Salvage and Repair Group.

43   Shaw, S. (undated) 54 MU RAF Repair and Salvage (43 Group).

44   Thompson: 21/1/2011: unpaginated.

45   Shaw: undated: unpaginated.

46   Thompson: 21/1/2011: unpaginated.

47   Shaw: undated: unpaginated.

48   Shaw: undated: unpaginated.

49   Shaw: undated: unpaginated.

50   Shaw: undated: unpaginated.

51   Shaw: undated: unpaginated.

52   Shaw: undated: unpaginated.

53   Thompson: 21/1/2011: unpaginated.

54   Shaw: undated: unpaginated.

55   Thompson: 21/1/2011: unpaginated.

56   Thompson: 21/1/2011: unpaginated.

57   Thompson: 21/1/2011: unpaginated.

58   Thompson: 21/1/2011: unpaginated.

59   Thompson: 21/1/2011: unpaginated.

60   Delve: 24/1/2023.

61   Delve: 24/1/2023.

62   Hadaway: 2008: 27.

63   Hadaway: 2008: 164.

64   Hadaway: 2008: 163.

65   Hadaway: 2008: 163.

66   Hadaway: 2008: 164.

67   Hadaway: 2008: 164.

68   Hadaway: 2008: 164.

69   Noakes: 2020: 8.

70   Noakes: 2020: 9.

71   Hadaway: 2008: 164.

72   Hadaway: 2008: 164.

73   Hadaway: 2008: 163.

74 Hadaway: 2008: 164.

75 Hadaway: 2008: 27.

76 Hadaway: 2008: 27.

77 Commonwealth War Graves Commission (undated) cwgc.org.

78 Storr, A. (2006) RAAF Personnel Serving on Attachment in Royal Air Force Squadrons and Support Units in World War Two, p. 307.

79 Heroes of our Time: undated: unpaginated.

80 Archives New Zealand: undated: unpaginated.

81 Hastings and St Leonards Observer (7/10/1944), p. 7.

82 Hastings & St Leonards Observer (30/9/1944) Airman Killed in Action.

83 Hastings and St Leonards Observer: 7/10/1944: 7.

84 Hastings and St Leonards Observer: 7/10/1944: 7.

85 Hastings and St Leonards Observer: 7/10/1944: 7.

86 Brettingham, L. (2002) Even When the Sparrows are Walking: The Origin and Effect of No. 100 (Bomber Support) Group, RAF, 1943-45, p. 155.

87 Rees, J. (undated) in Bartram, L. (1998) RAF North Creake, Egmere, 1940-1947: A Brief History, p. 14.

88 Hillier, M. (15/1/2020) in correspondence with the author.

89 Hillier: 15/1/2020.

90 Heroes of our Time: undated: unpaginated.

91 RAF Commands (undated) rafcommands. com.

92 Brettingham: 2002: 156.

93 RAF Commands (undated) rafcommands. com.

94 RAF Commands (undated) rafcommands. com.

95 RAF Commands (undated) rafcommands. com.

Chapter Four

1 Bowyer, M. J. F. (2010) Action Stations Revisited: Eastern England, Vol. 1, p. 273.

2 Bowyer, M. J. F. (1979) Action Stations: Wartime Military Airfields of East Anglia, 1939-1945, p. 165.

3 Streetly, M. (1978) Confound & Destroy: 100 Group and the Bomber Support Campaign, p. 35.

4 Bowyer: 2010: 273.

5 Bowyer: 1979: 165.

6 Delve, K. (2005) The Military Airfields of Britain: East Anglia: Norfolk & Suffolk, p. 172.

7 Maufe, T. (22/3/2024) interview with the author.

8 Bowyer: 2010: 273.

9 Delve: 2005: 172.

10 Bowyer: 2010: 273.

11 Bartram, L. (1998) RAF North Creake, Egmere, 1940-1947: A Brief History, p. 3.

12 Bartram: 1998: 3.

13 Bowman, M. (2006) 100 Group (Bomber Support) RAF Bomber Command in World War II, p. 78.

14 RAF 100 Group (July 1944) Operations, unpaginated.

15 Bartram: 1998: p. 3.

16 Reid, J. (2014) Let Tyrants Tremble: The War Diary of 199 (Bomber Support) Squadron, November 1942 – July 1945, p. 125.

17 RAF North Creake (June 1944) Operations Record Book, unpaginated.

18 Mackay, R. (1989) Short Stirling in Action, p. 31.

19 How, B. (27/7/2013) in conversation with the author.

20 How: 27/7/2013.

21 RAF North Creake (September 1944) Operations Record Book, Items of Medical Interest, unpaginated.

22 How: 27/7/2013.

23 Mackay: 1989: 31.

24 Bowyer, M. J. F. (2002) The Stirling Story, p. 374.

25 How, B. (1945) Air Ministry Form 1767: Logbook, unpaginated.

26 How, B. (8/3/2017) interview with the author.

27 How: 1945: unpaginated.

28 How: 8/3/2017.

29 How: 27/7/2013.

30 How: 27/7/2013.

31 How: 27/7/2013.

32 Morter, N. (23/11/2021) Transcript of a Dedication to Bernie How: All Saints Church, Worlington, unpaginated.

33 How: 27/7/2013.

34 How: 27/7/2013.

35 Longmate, N. (1983) The Bombers: The RAF Offensive Against Germany 1939-1945, p. 178.

36 Kavanagh, D. (16/11/2016) Interview with Bernie How, unpaginated.

37 Hughes, E. (undated) in Harrington, J. (2015) RAF 100 Group: Kindred Spirits: Voices of RAF & USAAF on Secret Norfolk Airfields During the Second World War, pp. 476-477.

38 Longmate: 1983: 178.

39 Tripp, M. (1952) Faith is a Windsock, p. 42.

40 Smith, R. (undated) Roy Smith – War Years in Bomber Command, p. 7.
41 Bartlett, H. (23/11/2021) Interview with Gordon Mercier.
42 Morter: 23/11/2021: unpaginated.
43 Hawton, H. (1944) The Men Who Fly, p. 8.
44 Kavanagh, D. (16/11/2016) Interview with Bernie How.
45 Flood, M. (undated) My Grandad in World War II 1939-1945, p.5.
46 Pedan, M. (1979) A Thousand Shall Fall, Canada's Wings, pp. 313-314.
47 Hughes: undated: in Harrington: 2015: 476-477.
48 Reid, J. (27/3/2006) correspondence with Roy Smith, unpaginated.
49 Smith, R. (19/12/2005) Life as Part of the Crew of a Stirling Bomber, unpaginated.
50 Smith: 19/12/2005: unpaginated.
51 Sawyer, T. (1981) Only Owls and Bloody Fools Fly at Night, p. 149.
52 Kavanagh, D. (2016) Interview with Denis James Gill.
53 Sawyer: 1981: 149.
54 Redding, T. (2005) Flying for Freedom: Life and Death in Bomber Command, p. 281.
55 Pedan, M. (1979) A Thousand Shall Fall, p. 264.
56 Hawton: 1944: 17.
57 Smith: undated: 6.
58 Taylor, S. (2018) A Day in the Life of Bomber Command Lecture.
59 Tripp, M. (1985) The Eighth Passenger: A Documentary Account of a World War 2 Bomber Crew, p. 26.
60 Smithies, E. (2002) Aces, Erks & Backroom Boys, p. 123.
61 Bartlett: 23/11/2021.
62 Smithies: 2002: 123.
63 Smithies: 2002: 123.
64 Kavanagh: 16/11/2016.
65 Imperial War Museum (undated) iwm.org.uk.
66 Mitchell, G. (undated) Start and Finish of an Air Gunner, unpaginated.
67 Imperial War Museum: undated.
68 Taylor: 2018.
69 RAF North Creake (1944/5) Memo: Firing Air to Sea, unpaginated.
70 RAF North Creake: 1944/5: unpaginated.
71 RAF North Creake: 1944/5: unpaginated.
72 Bartlett: 23/11/2021.
73 Bartlett: 23/11/2021.
74 Bartlett: 23/11/2021.
75 Polichek, V. (3/2/1998) Correspondence.
76 Sawyer: 1981: 138.
77 Philipson, W. J. F. (undated) in Bartram: 1998: 22.
78 Bartlett: 23/11/2021.
79 Bartlett: 23/11/2021.
80 Kavanagh: 2016.
81 Porter, L. (undated) cited in, Smithies: 2002: 132.
82 Gill, D. (2015) My Civilian and RAF Wartime Experiences, unpaginated.
83 Hastings, M. (1980) Bomber Command, p. 45.
84 Hastings: 1980: 155.
85 Redding: 2005: 279.
86 Wainwright, J. (1978) Tail-End Charlie: One Man's Journey Through a War, p. 137.
87 RAF 171 Squadron (4/4/1945) Combat Report, unpaginated.
88 Adcock, A. (2004) Interview.
89 Berry, P. (2018) A Wireless Operator at RAF North Creake, unpaginated.
90 Hughes: undated: in Harrington: 2016: 198-199.
91 Kavanagh: 2016.
92 Kavanagh: 16/11/2016.
93 Pedan: 1979: 383.
94 Smith: 19/12/2005: unpaginated.
95 Pedan: 1979: 381.
96 Smith: 19/12/2005: unpaginated.
97 Bartlett: 23/11/2021.
98 How: 8/3/2017:
99 Gill: 2015: unpaginated.
100 Endersby, J. (12/2/2013) in correspondence with the author.
101 Price, A. (1967) Instruments of darkness: The Struggle for Radar Supremacy, p. 196.
102 Redding: 2005: 280.
103 Pedan: 1979: 261.
104 Feasey, J. (undated) cited in Harrington: 2016: 123.
105 Taylor: 2018.
106 Tempest, V. (1946) Near the Sun: Impressions of a Medical Officer of Bomber Command, p. 77.
107 Adcock: 2004.
108 Polichek: 3/2/1998.
109 Feasey, J. (undated) in Bartram: 1998: 19.
110 Tempest: 1946: 73.
111 Redding: 2005: 74.
112 Tempest: 1946: 73.
113 Tempest: 1946: 74.
114 Feasey: undated: in Bartram: 1998: 19.
115 Polichek: 3/2/1998.
116 Bartlett: 23/11/2021.
117 Bartlett: 23/11/2021.
118 Bartlett: 23/11/2021.
119 Bartlett: 23/11/2021.
120 Sawyer: 1981: 56.
121 Feasey: undated: in Bartram: 1998: 19.
122 Sawyer: 1981: 56-57.

123 Brettingham, L. (2002) Even When the Sparrows are Walking: The Origin and Effect of No. 100 (Bomber Support) Group, RAF, 1943-45, p. 151.

124 Brettingham: 2002: 151-152.

125 Gill: 2015: unpaginated.

126 Sawyer: 1981: 32-33.

127 Cockburn, R. (1945) The Radio War, p. 59.

128 Verrier, A. (1968) The Bomber Offensive, p. 77.

129 National Museum of the United States Air Force (undated) nationalmuseum.af.mil.

130 National Museum of the United States Air Force: undated.

131 Bartlett: 23/11/2021.

132 Winfield, R. (1976) The Sky Belongs to Them, p. 140.

133 Bartlett: 23/11/2021.

134 Gill, D. (2006) 'The Skylark' in Abolish War, p. 3.

135 Tripp: 1952: 128.

136 Bartlett: 23/11/2021.

137 Brettingham: 2002: 145.

138 Gill; 2006: 3.

139 Polichek: 3/2/1998.

140 Wood, C. (2000) Interview with Arthur Gordon Clarke.

141 Price: 1967: 65.

142 Gill: 2006: 3.

143 Sawyer: 1981: 175.

144 Panton, J. (4/9/2022) correspondence to the author.

145 Panton, S. F. (19/10/1944) Air Ministry Form 1767: Logbook.

146 Price: 1967: 104.

147 Price: 1967: 62-63.

148 Cockburn: 1945: 61.

149 Hastings: 1980: 234.

150 Cockburn: 1945: 26.

151 Cockburn: 1945: 26.

152 Cockburn: 1945: 26.

153 Addison, E. (1946) The Radio War lecture', in RUSI (1947) Royal United Services Institute Journal, p. 35.

154 Wainwright: 1978: 97.

155 Addison: 1946: 35.

156 Jones, R. V. (1978) Most Secret War: British Scientific Intelligence 1939-1945, pp. 267-269.

157 Jones: 1978: 267-269.

158 Jones: 1978: 269.

159 Price: 1967: 69.

160 Price: 1967: 69.

161 Price: 1967: 65

162 Price: 1967: 104.

163 Price: 1967: 104.

164 Price: 1967: 104.

165 Price: 1967: 65

166 Streetly: 1978: 187.

167 Price: 1967: 69.

168 Price: 1967: 144.

169 Hinchliffe, P. (1996) The Other Battle: Luftwaffe Night Aces Versus Bomber Command, pp. 129-130.

170 Hinchliffe: 1996: 131.

171 Price: 1967: 146.

172 Pedan: 1979: 408.

173 Redding: 2005: 277.

174 Hastings: 1980: 239.

175 Gill: 2015: unpaginated.

176 Hastings: 1980: 239.

177 Redding: 2005: 277.

178 Price: 1967: 140.

179 Streetly: 1978: 26.

180 Streetly: 1978: 26.

181 Redding: 2005: 278.

182 Wainwright: 1978: 68

183 RAF 199 Squadron (21/10/1944) Combat Report, unpaginated.

184 Pedan: 1979: 265.

185 Feasey: undated: in Bartram: 1998: 18.

186 Master Bomber Craig (undated) masterbombercraig.wordpress.com.

187 Reidy, J. (undated) Unsung Heroes Project.

188 Smith: undated: 5.

189 Pedan: 1979: 259.

190 Bartlett: 23/11/2021.

191 Redding: 2005: 279.

192 Streetly: 1978: 126.

193 Redding: 2005: 278.

194 Redding: 2005: 277.

195 Redding: 2005: 277.

196 Redding: 2005: 278.

197 Woollard, W. (1977) The Secret War: The Complete Original Series.

198 Redding: 2005: 277.

199 Redding: 2005: 278.

200 Longmate: 1983: 181.

201 Redding: 2005: 152.

202 Price: 1967: 70.

203 Bartram: 1998: 12.

204 Bartram, L. in Harrington, J. (2012) RAF North Creake, Egmere 1940-1947: A Brief History, p. 52.

205 Mallett, E. (undated) Wartime Memories, unpaginated.

206 Price: 1967: 112.

207 Price: 1967: 113.

208 Price: 1967: 113.

209 Jones: 1978: 288.

210 Jones: 1978: 291.

211 Cockburn: 1945: 53.

212 Price: 1967: 115.

213 Cockburn: 1945: 24.

214 Price: 1967: 115.

215 Cockburn: 1945: 24.

216 Price: 1967: 115.

217 Price: 1967: 116.

218 Cockburn: 1945: 53.

219 Price: 1967: 149.

220 Price: 1967: 116.

221 Cockburn: 1945: 53.

222 Price: 1967: 116.

223 Price: 1967: 149.

224 Price: 1967: 149.

225 Cockburn: 1945: 53.

226 Jones: 1978: 292.

227 Price: 1967: 116.

228 Jones: 1978: 291.

229 Jones: 1978: 291.

230 Price: 1967: 115.

231 Hastings: 1980: 205.

232 Cockburn: 1945: 55.

233 Price: 1967: 116.

234 Price: 1967: 116-117.

235 Price: 1967: 117.

236 Longmate: 1983: 257.

237 Harris, A. (1943) cited in Price: 1967: 141.

238 Probert, H. (2002) in Royal Air Force Historical Society (2003) Electronic Warfare: Proceeding of a Conference 10 April 2002, 57.

239 Price: 1967: 141.

240 Scott, K. (1993) 'Window of deceit', Army Quarterly and Defence Journal, p. 40.

241 Jones: 1978: 297.

242 Price: 1967: 148.

243 Price: 1967: 149.

244 Price: 1967: 149.

245 Hastings: 1980: 205.

246 Scott: 1993: 40.

247 Longmate: 1983: 261.

248 Scott: 1993: 41.

249 Price: 1967: 152.

250 Price: 1967: 152.

251 Sawyer: 1981: 151.

252 Hastings: 1980: 205.

253 Price: 1967: 153.

254 Longmate: 1983: 264.

255 Price: 1967: 154.

256 Scott: 1993: 41.

257 Longmate: 1983: 264.

258 Longmate: 1983: 264.

259 Scott: 1993: 41.

260 Price: 1967: 154.

261 Price: 1967: 152.

262 Scott: 1993: 41.

263 Longmate: 1983: 264.

264 Price: 1967: 158.

265 Longmate: 1983: 264.

266 Price: 1967: 155.

267 Price: 1967: 156-157.

268 Middlebrook, M. (1980) The Battle of Hamburg: Allied Bomber Forces Against a German City in 1943, p. 128.

269 Scott: 1993: 42.

270 Longmate: 1983: 264.

271 Price: 1967: 159.

272 Scott: 1993: 41.

273 Middlebrook: 1980: 129.

274 Jones: 1978: 300.

275 Redding: 2005: 186.

276 Price: 1967: 158.

277 Cockburn: 1945: 60.

278 Cockburn: 1945: 56.

279 Hastings: 1980: 268.

280 Cockburn: 1945: 60.

281 Cockburn: 1945: 56.

282 Cockburn: 1945: 60.

283 Addison: 1946: 35.

284 Addison: 1946: 35.

285 Price: 1967: 177.

286 Streetly: 1978: 22.

287 Price: 1967: 160.

288 Price: 1967: 193.

289 Furner, J. (2002) in Royal Air Force Historical Society (2003) Electronic Warfare: Proceeding of a Conference 10 April 2002, p. 26.

Abandoned Near Paris

1 Middlebrook, M. & Everitt, C. (1985) The Bomber Command War Diaries: An Operational Reference Book, 1939-1945, p. 622.

2 RAF North Creake (1944) Operations Record Book, unpaginated.

3 RAF North Creake: 1944: ORB: unpaginated.

4 RAF North Creake: 1944: ORB: unpaginated.

5 RAF North Creake: 1944: ORB: unpaginated.

6 Hope, B. (2014) And in the Morning: RAF Station North Creake, p. 23.

7 Chorley, W. R. (2008) Royal Air Force: Bomber Command Losses of the Second World War: Volume 5, 1944, p. 494.

8 Aircrew Remembered (undated) aircrewremembered.com.

9 Chorley: 2008: Vol. 5: 494.

10 RAF 171 Squadron (November 1944) Operations Records Book, unpaginated.

11 Roberts, R. N. (1982) The Halifax File, p. 100.

12 RAF 171 Squadron: 1944: ORB: unpaginated.

13   RAF 171 Squadron: 1944: ORB: unpaginated.

14   Aircrew Remembered: undated.

15   Xtison (14/10/2005) 'Bail Out 25th November 1944', on BBC (undated) WW2 People's War: An Archive of World War Two Memories – Written by the Public, Gathered by the BBC, bbc.co.uk.

16   Chorley: 2008: Vol. 5: 494.

17   Aircrew Remembered: undated.

18   Xtison: 14/10/2005.

19   Chorley: 2008: Vol. 5: 494.

20   Xtison: 14/10/2005.

21   Hope, B. (2014) And in the Morning: RAF Station North Creake, p. 23.

22   Xtison: 14/10/2005.

23   Xtison: 14/10/2005.

24   Xtison: 14/10/2005.

25   Xtison: 14/10/2005.

26   Xtison: 14/10/2005.

27   Xtison: 14/10/2005.

28   Xtison: 14/10/2005.

29   Xtison: 14/10/2005.

30   Xtison: 14/10/2005.

31   Xtison: 14/10/2005.

32   Xtison: 14/10/2005.

33   Xtison: 14/10/2005.

34   Xtison: 14/10/2005.

35   Xtison: 14/10/2005.

36   RAF 171 Squadron: (November 1944) Operations Records Book: Appendix, p. 112.

37   Xtison: 14/10/2005.

38   Aircrew Remembered: undated.

39   Aircrew Remembered: undated.

40   Aircrew Remembered: undated.

41   Aircrew Remembered: undated.

42   Aircrew Remembered: undated.

43   Aircrew Remembered: undated.

44   Aircrew Remembered: undated.

45   Aircrew Remembered: undated.

46   Aircrew Remembered: undated.

47   Aircrew Remembered: undated.

48   Aircrew Remembered: undated.

Chapter Five

1   Nicolson, H. (1941) 'World Government', in Fabian Society (1941) Programme for Victory, p. 48.

2   Streetly, M. (1978) Confound & Destroy: 100 Group and the Bomber Support Campaign, p. 15.

3   Streetly: 1978: 15.

4   Streetly: 1978: 15.

5   Streetly: 1978: 17.

6   Streetly: 1978: 17.

7   Cockburn, R. (1945) The Radio War, p. 10.

8   Streetly: 1978: 19.

9   Streetly: 1978: 19.

10   Streetly: 1978: 19.

11   Cockburn, R. (1945) in Brettingham, L. (2002) Even When the Sparrows are Walking: The Origin and Effect of No. 100 (Bomber Support) Group, RAF, 1943-45, p. 88.

12   Addison, E. B. (1977) cited in, Brettingham: 2002: 86.

13   Air Ministry (5/10/1943) Minutes of a Conference Held on Wednesday 29 September 1943 at the Air Ministry to Discuss Proposals for the Formation of a Combined Radio Countermeasure Organisation for the Support of the Air offensive, p. 1.

14   Air Ministry: 5/10/1943: 2.

15   Cockburn: 1945: 2.

16   The Times (8/7/1987) Air Vice Marshall Edward Baker Addison Obituary.

17   Streetly: 1978: 31.

18   Air Ministry: 5/10/1943: 4.

19   Air Ministry: 5/10/1943: 5.

20   Air Ministry: 5/10/1943: 2.

21   Air Ministry: 5/10/1943: 2.

22   Air Ministry: 5/10/1943: 2.

23   Harris, A. (1943) cited in, Brettingham: 2002: 93.

24   Air Ministry: 5/10/1943: 6.

25   Streetly: 1978: 19.

26   Air Ministry: 5/10/1943: 4.

27   Streetly: 1978: 36.

28   Streetly: 1978: 40.

29   Addison, E. B. (1977) cited in, Brettingham: 2002: 86.

30   Renaut, M. (1982) Terror by Night, p. 155.

31   Addison: 1977: cited in, Brettingham: 2002: 86.

32   Streetly: 1978: 35.

33   Stewart, G. (undated) cited in, Harrington, J. (2016) RAF 100 Group: The Birth of Electronic Warfare, p. 41.

34   Streetly, M. (1984) The Aircraft of the 100 Group: A Historical Guide for the Modeller, p. 7.

35   Delve, K. (2005) The Military Airfields of Britain: East Anglia: Norfolk & Suffolk, p. 172.

36   Addison, E. (1946) The Radio War lecture', in RUSI (1947) Royal United Services Institute Journal, p. 36.

37   Streetly: 1978: 35.

38   Price, A. (1967) Instruments of Darkness: The Struggle for Radar Supremacy, pp. 183-184.

39   Jones, R. V. (1978) Most Secret War: British Scientific Intelligence 1939-1945, p. 387.

40   Air Ministry: 5/10/1943: 6.

41   Air Ministry: 5/10/1943: 6.

42   Cockburn: 1945: 62.

43   Streetly: 1978: 47.

44   Cockburn: 1945: 62.

45   Price: 1967: 189

46   Kammhuber, J. (1959) cited in Pedan, M. (1979) A Thousand Shall Fall, p. 409.

47   Price: 1967: 163.

48   Veteran cited in Harrington, J. (2018) RAF 100 Group: Reasons to Remember, p. 377.

49   Pedan, M. (1979) A Thousand Shall Fall, p. 410.

50   Gill, D. (2015) My Civilian and RAF Wartime Experiences, unpaginated.

51   Harris, A. (1947) 'Bomber Offensive', cited in Taylor, F. (2005) Dresden: Tuesday 13 February 1945, p. 203.

52   Redding, T. (2005) Flying for Freedom: Life and Death in Bomber Command, p. 17.

53   Mitchell, G. (undated) Start and Finish of an Air Gunner, unpaginated.

54   Bartlett, H. (23/11/2021) Interview with Gordon Mercier.

55   Bartlett: 23/11/2021.

56   Berry, P. (2018) A Wireless Operator at RAF North Creake, unpaginated.

57   Bartlett: 23/11/2021.

58   Streetly: 1978: 45.

59   Bartram, L. (1998) RAF North Creake, Egmere, 1940-1947: A Brief History, p. 5.

60   Smith, R. (undated) cited in Harrington: 2016: 189.

61   Smith: undated: cited in Harrington: 2016: 189.

62   Ford, K. S. (1992) Snaith Days: Life With 51 Squadron 1942/45, p. 7.

63   Ford: 1992: 4.

64   How, B. (27/7/2013) in conversation with the author.

65   Ford: 1992: 1.

66   Ford: 1992: 4.

67   Tripp, M. (1952) Faith is a Windsock, p. 12.

68   Tripp: 1952: 12.

69   Ford: 1992: 4.

70   Ford: 1992: 7.

71   Ford: 1992: 12.

72   Ford: 1992: 7.

73   Ford: 1992: 1.

74   Ford: 1992: 7.

75   Willmott, P. (1988) Coming of Age in Wartime, p. 117.

76   Willmott: 1988: 118.

77   Willmott: 1988: 118.

78   Willmott: 1988: 119.

79   Brettingham: 2002: 282.

80   Rees, J. (undated) in Bartram: 1998: 13.

81   Reid, J. (2014) Let Tyrants Tremble: The War Diary of 199 (Bomber Support) Squadron, November 1942 – July 1945, p. 135.

82   RAF 100 Group (May 1944) 'Engineering', in RAF 100 Group (May 1944) Monthly Report of Activities, unpaginated.

83   Polichek, V. (3/2/1998) Correspondence.

84   Thompson K (1945) War Diary.

85   Thompson: 1945.

86   Bartram: 1998: 26.

87   Streetly: 1984: 9

88   Bartram: 1998: 5.

89   Streetly: 1978: 45.

90   Green, W. (1960) Famous Bombers of the Second World War, p.43.

91   Green: 1960: 43.

92   Reidy, J. (undated) Unsung Heroes Project, unsungheroesaustralia.com.au.

93   Green: 1960: 43.

94   Hastings, M. (1980) Bomber Command, p. 155.

95   Renaut: 1982: 41.

96   Falconer, J (2015) Short Stirling; 1939-48 (all marks) Owners' Workshop Manual, pp. 8-9.

97   Falconer: 2015: 8-9.

98   Francis, P (1996) British Military Airfield Architecture: From Airships to the Jet Age, pp. 81-110.

99   Flight (29 Jan. 1942) cited in, flightglobal. com.

100 Clark D. (undated) forum.keypublishing. com.

101 Clark: undated.

102 Clark: undated.

103 Falconer: 2015: 11.

104 Falconer: 2015: 11.

105 Pedan: 1979: 228-229.

106 Longmate, N. (1983) The Bombers: The RAF Offensive Against Germany 1939-1945, p. 157.

107 Longmate: 1983: 144.

108 Kavanagh, D. (16/11/2016) Interview with Bernie How.

109 Wood, C. (2000) Interview with Arthur Gordon Clarke.

110 Wood: 2000.

111 Bowman, M. (2006) 100 Group (Bomber Support) RAF Bomber Command in World War II, p. 80.

112 Wood, D. (29/10/2010) Correspondence.

113 RAF North Creake (September 1944) Operations Record Book, unpaginated.

114 Aircrew Remembered (undated) aircrewremembered.com.

115 Bowyer, M. J. F. (1979) Action Stations: Wartime Military Airfields of East Anglia, 1939-1945, p. 165.

116 Bowyer: 1979: 165.

117 Renaut: 1982: 147.

118 Aircrew Remembered (undated).

119 Renaut: 1982: 147.

120 Brettingham: 2002: 140.

121 Brettingham: 2002: 144.

122 Feasey, J. (11/4/1985) Correspondence with Maurice Hood.

123 Bartlett: 23/11/2021.

124 Brettingham: 2002: 151.

125 Brettingham: 2002: 151.

126 Hughes, E. (undated) in Harrington, J. (2015) RAF 100 Group: Kindred Spirits: Voices of RAF & USAAF on Secret Norfolk Airfields During the Second World War, p. 474.

127 Hughes: undated: in Harrington: 2015: 474.

128 Hughes: undated: in Harrington: 2015: 473-474.

129 Hughes: undated: in Harrington: 2015: 473-474.

130 Aircrew Remembered (undated).

131 Delve, K (17/6/2016) Ken Delve Looks at an Unusual Aspect of one of Norfolk's Wartime RAF Squadrons.

132 Delve: 17/6/2016.

133 Delve: 17/6/2016.

134 Delve: 17/6/2016.

135 Delve: 17/6/2016.

136 Delve: 17/6/2016.

137 Delve: 17/6/2016.

138 Delve: 17/6/2016.

139 Delve: 17/6/2016.

140 Delve: 17/6/2016.

141 Delve: 17/6/2016.

142 Delve: 17/6/2016.

143 Delve: 17/6/2016.

144 Aircrew Remembered (undated).

145 RAF 100 Group (November 1944) Operations, p. 23 & Feasey: 11/4/1985.

146 Berry: 2018: unpaginated.

147 Berry: 2018: unpaginated.

148 Brettingham: 2002: 147.

149 RAF 100 Group: November 1944: 23.

150 Stubbington, J. (undated) 171 Squadron: From the National Archives, p. 24.

151 Renaut: 1982: 147.

152 Reid: 2014: 169.

153 Merrick, K. A. (1980) Halifax: An Illustrated History of a Classic World War II Bomber, p. 14.

154 Falconer, J. (2016) Handley Page Halifax: 1939 Onwards (All Marks): Owners' Workshop Manual, p. 18.

155 Falconer: 2016: 18.

156 Falconer: 2016: 19-29.

157 Feasey: 11/4/1985: Polichek, V. (3/2/1998) Correspondence.

158 Falconer: 2016: 28.

159 Brettingham: 2002: 147.

160 Reid: 2014: 169.

161 Brettingham: 2002: 147.

162 Thompson P. (22/4/2023) in correspondence with the author.

163 Reid: 2014: 164.

164 Streetly: 1978: 104.

165 Kavanagh, D. (16/11/2016) Interview with Bernie How.

166 Air Ministry: 5/10/1943: 3.

167 Pedan: 1979: 402.

168 Addison, E. (1/5/1945) Scapegoats of Bomber Command, p. 3.

169 Bomber Command: 1945: 3.

170 Streetly: 1978: 60.

171 Brettingham: 2002: 146.

172 Price: 1967: 223

173 Price: 1967: 223

174 Streetly: 1978: 60.

175 Price: 1967: 223.

176 Addison: 1946: 36.

177 RAF 171 Squadron (October 1944) Operations Record Book, unpaginated.

178 Hines, M. (2022) Airfields of North Norfolk: RAF North Creake, p. 76.

179 Stubbington: undated: 24.

180 RAF 171 Squadron: October 1944: ORB: unpaginated.

181 Berry: 2018: unpaginated.

182 Hines: 2022: 76.

183 Berry, A. (undated) cited in Brettingham: 2002: 149.

184 Berry: undated: cited in Brettingham: 2002: 149.

185 Berry: undated: cited in Brettingham: 2002: 149.

186 Berry: undated: cited in Brettingham: 2002: 149.

187 Price: 1967: 225.

188 Wainwright, J. (1978) Tail-End Charlie: One Man's Journey Through a War, 136.

189 Brettingham: 2002: 147.

190 Philipson, W. J. F. (undated) in Bartram: 1998: 22.

191 Freegard, H. (9/8/2018) in conversation with the author.

192 Freegard: 9/8/2018.

193 Bowman, M. W. & Cushing, T. (1996) Confounding the Reich: The Operational History of 100 Group (Bomber Support) RAF, p. 107.

194 Cockburn: 1945: 58.

195 RAF 100 Group (March 1945) Operations, p. 1.

196 RAF 100 Group: March 1945: 1.
197 RAF 100 Group: March 1945: 1.
198 RAF 100 Group: March 1945: 1.
199 Cockburn: 1945: 58.
200 RAF 100 Group (December 1944)
     Operations, p. 5.
201 RAF 100 Group (1945) Loose Minute.
202 RAF 100 Group: 1945.
203 RAF 100 Group (October 1944) Operations,
     pp. 1- 2.
204 RAF 100 Group: October 1944: 1- 2.
205 Jones: 1978: 467.
206 Lawson, H. H. (undated) 'Report' in RAF
     100 Group Correspondence.
207 Streetly: 1978: 63.
208 RAF 100 Group: October 1944: 2.
209 RAF 100 Group: October 1944: 1.
210 Streetly: 1978: 73.
211 Streetly: 1978: 73.
212 Jones: 1978: 467-468.
213 Stubbington: undated: 25.
214 RAF 100 Group (January 1945) Operations,
     p. 1 and RAF 100 Group (November 1944)
     Operations, p. 1.
215 Stubbington: undated: 25.
216 Reid: 2014: 164-171.
217 Stubbington: undated: 25.
218 Addison, E. (31/3/1945) Correspondence.
219 Addison, E. (15/11/1944) Correspondence.
220 Addison: 15/11/1944.
221 Stubbington: undated: 25.
222 Addison: 31/3/1945.
223 Bray, N. A. N. (undated) cited in
     Brettingham: 2002: 5.
224 Streetly: 1978: 45.
225 Reid: 2014: 127.

Nothing Heard Since Take-Off

1 Bowyer, M. J. F. (1979) Action Stations:
   Wartime Military Airfields of East Anglia,
   1939-1945, p. 165.
2 RAF 171 Squadron (December 1944)
   Operations Record Book, unpaginated.
3 RAF 171 Squadron: December 1944: ORB:
   unpaginated.
4 Hines, M. (2022) Airfields of North Norfolk:
   RAF North Creake, p. 96.
5 RAF 171 Squadron: December 1944: ORB:
   unpaginated.
6 Royal Australian Air Force (12/12/1944)
   Postal Acknowledgement Delivery,
   unpaginated.
7 RAAF: 12/12/1944: unpaginated.
8 Langslow, M. C. (30/4/1945)
   Correspondence.
9 Powe, J. (undated) Correspondence.
10 Langslow, M. C. (20/11/1945)
    Correspondence.
11 Langslow: 20/11/1945.
12 Langslow, M. C. (18/9/1945) Presumption
    of Death Correspondence, RAAF,
    unpublished, National Archives Australia,
    NAA A705 166/33/265.
13 Hadaway, S. (2008) Missing Believed Killed:
    The Royal Air Force and the Search for
    Missing Aircrew 1939-1952, p. 6.
14 Powe, J. (2/12/1945) Correspondence.
15 Powe: 2/12/1945.
16 Powe: 2/12/1945.
17 Langslow, M. C. (1/1/1946)
    Correspondence.
18 Langslow: 1/1/1946.
19 Langslow: 1/1/1946.
20 RAAF Casualty Section (8/1/1946) Signal to
    RAAF Overseas HQ, RAAF, unpaginated.
21 RAAF Casualty Section: 8/1/1946.
22 Langslow, M. C. (4/2/1946)
    Correspondence, unpaginated.
23 Chorley, W. R. (2008) Royal Air Force:
    Bomber Command Losses of the Second
    World War: Volume 5, 1944, p. 507.
24 Morrissey, B. D. (25/4/1945) Incident
    Report, Headquarters 671st Field Artillery
    Battalion, APO 408, U.S. Army.
25 Chorley: 2008: Vol. 5: 507.
26 Aircrew Remembered (undated)
    aircrewremembered.com.
27 Morrissey: 25/4/1945.
28 Sturch, L. A. (19/10/1945) Casualty
    Enquiry No. G. 155S, p. 1.
29 Clowes, I. C. D. (20/12/1946) Missing
    Research & Enquiry Unit Casualty Enquiry
    Investigation Report, unpaginated.
30 Clowes: 20/12/1946: unpaginated.
31 Clowes: 20/12/1946: unpaginated.
32 Clowes: 20/12/1946: unpaginated.
33 Clowes: 20/12/1946: unpaginated.
34 Morrissey: 25/4/1945.
35 Morrissey: 25/4/1945.
36 Clowes: 20/12/1946: unpaginated.
37 Clowes: 20/12/1946: unpaginated.
38 Clowes: 20/12/1946: unpaginated.
39 Clowes: 20/12/1946: unpaginated.
40 Aircrew Remembered: undated.
41 Missing Research & Enquiry Unit No 4
    (15/6/1948) Correspondence.
42 Aircrew Remembered: undated.
43 Missing Research & Enquiry Unit No 4:
    15/6/1948.
44 Wright, D. A. (9/7/1948) Correspondence.

45   Missing Research & Enquiry Unit No 4: 15/6/1948.

46   Aircrew Remembered: undated.

47   Aircrew Remembered: undated.

48   Aircrew Remembered: undated.

49   Aircrew Remembered: undated.

50   Aircrew Remembered: undated.

51   Hope, B. (2014) And in the Morning: RAF Station North Creake, p. 31.

52   Aircrew Remembered: undated.

53   Hinton, J. H. (9/12/1944) Service Record, unpaginated.

54   Aircrew Remembered: undated.

55   Hinton: 9/12/1944: unpaginated.

56   Burt, J. (23/11/2020) in correspondence with the author.

57   Burt: 23/11/2020.

58   Burt: 23/11/2020.

59   Aircrew Remembered: undated.

60   Aircrew Remembered: undated.

61   Aircrew Remembered: undated.

62   Aircrew Remembered: undated.

63   Aircrew Remembered: undated.

64   Aircrew Remembered: undated.

65   Aircrew Remembered: undated.

66   Aircrew Remembered: undated.

67   Langslow, M. C. (28/2/1945) Correspondence.

68   Langslow: 28/2/1945.

69   Langslow: 28/2/1945.

70   Aircrew Remembered: undated.

71   Aircrew Remembered: undated.

72   Aircrew Remembered: undated.

73   Aircrew Remembered: undated.

74   Aircrew Remembered: undated.

75   Aircrew Remembered: undated.

76   Aircrew Remembered: undated.

77   RAF 171 Squadron (March 1945) Operations Record Book, unpaginated.

78   RAF North Creake (March 1945) Operations Record Book, unpaginated.

79   Aircrew Remembered: undated.

80   Aircrew Remembered: undated.

81   Aircrew Remembered: undated.

82   Hines: 2022: 96.

83   Aircrew Remembered: undated.

84   Aircrew Remembered: undated.

85   Stubbington, J. (undated) 171 Squadron: From the National Archives, p. 26.

86   Stone, J. (undated) March 7/8th 1945: 171 (BS) Squadron – Bomber Support Aircraft NA111:Y, unpublished manuscript, unpaginated.

87   Neale, W (16/10/2023) interview with the author.

88   Neale: 16/10/2023.

89   Heilner, J. (undated) A Dream Came True, unpaginated.

90   Heilner: undated: unpaginated.

91   Heilner: undated: unpaginated.

92   Renaut, M. (1982) Terror by Night, 162.

93   Neale: 16/10/2023.

94   Heilner: undated: unpaginated.

95   Hope: 2014: 41.

96   Stone: undated: unpaginated.

97   Stone, J. (7/3/1945) Target Munster: MI9 Interrogation Report, unpaginated.

98   Renaut: 1982: 161.

99   Department of National Defence (8/11/1945) Estates Branch, Form P. 64, unpaginated.

100 Department of National Defence: 8/11/1945: unpaginated.

101 Harris, J. S. (31/7/1945) Royal Canadian Air Force Overseas Casualty Branch, Correspondence, unpaginated.

102 Harris: 31/7/1945: unpaginated.

103 Department of National Defence: 8/11/1945: unpaginated.

104 Register of Births, Deaths and Marriages (1945).

105 Harris: 31/7/1945: unpaginated.

106 Harris: 31/7/1945: unpaginated.

107 Department of National Defence (3/4/1946) Statement of War Service Gratuity: Kenneth Thomas, unpaginated.

108 Friend, J. (28/6/1946) Missing Research & Enquiry Service No. 20 Investigation Report, unpaginated.

109 Aircrew Remembered: undated.

110 Hope: 2014: 31.

111 Hope: 2014: 31.

112 Royal Canadian Air Force (31/7/1942) Harold Coutts: Attestation Paper, unpaginated.

113 RCAF: 31/7/1942: unpaginated.

114 RCAF: 31/7/1942: unpaginated.

115 Royal Canadian Air Force (17/5/1943) RCAF Training Report, Form 5030, Air Bomber & Navigator: Harold Coutts, unpaginated.

116 Royal Canadian Air Force (17/9/1943) RCAF Training Report, Form 5031, Air Bomber: Harold Coutts, unpaginated.

117 RCAF: 31/7/1942: unpaginated.

118 Medical Officer (29/6/1942) on, RCAF: 31/7/1942: unpaginated.

119 Medical Officer: 29/6/1942: unpaginated.

120 RCAF: 31/7/1942: unpaginated.

121 RCAF: 31/7/1942: unpaginated.

122 Royal Air Force (13/4/1944) RAF Training Report, Form 5034, Air Bomber No 20 OTU: Harold Coutts, unpaginated.

123 RCAF: 31/7/1942: unpaginated.

124 Heilner: undated: unpaginated.
125 Heilner: undated: unpaginated.
126 Heilner: undated: unpaginated.
127 Neale, W. (23/10/2023) in correspondence with the author.
128 Neale: 23/10/2023.
129 Neale: 23/10/2023.
130 Neale: 23/10/2023.
131 RAF 171 Squadron: December 1944: ORB: unpaginated.
132 Neale: 23/10/2023.
133 Neale: 23/10/2023.
134 Stone: undated: unpaginated.
135 Neale: 23/10/2023.
136 Neale: 23/10/2023.
137 Neale: 23/10/2023.
138 Neale: 16/10/2023.
139 Neale: 23/10/2023.

Chapter Six

1 Hastings, M. (1984) Overlord: D-Day and the Battle for Normandy 1944, p. 19.
2 Taylor, A. J. P. (1975) The Second World War, p. 193.
3 Taylor: 1975: 193.
4 Belchem, D. (1981) Victory in Normandy, p. 33.
5 Taylor: 1975: 193-195.
6 Taylor: 1975: 195.
7 Belchem: 1981: 56.
8 Taylor: 1975: 195.
9 Belchem: 1981: 60-62.
10 Belchem: 1981: 56.
11 Longmate, N. (1983) The Bombers: The RAF Offensive Against Germany 1939-1945, pp. 304-305.
12 Harris, A. (13/1/1944) cited in, Longmate: 1983: 305-306.
13 Longmate: 1983: 310.
14 Longmate: 1983: 310.
15 Longmate: 1983: 311.
16 Grayling, A. C. (2006) Among the Dead Cities: Was the Allied Bombing of Civilians in WWII a Necessity or a Crime?, p. 67.
17 Grayling: 2006: 67.
18 Longmate: 1983: 312.
19 Taylor: 1975: 193.
20 Taylor: 1975: 193.
21 Belchem: 1981: 60.
22 Harris, A. (1948) Bomber Offensive, p. 208.
23 Price, A. (1967) Instruments of darkness: The Struggle for Radar Supremacy, p. 200.
24 Price: 1967: 201.
25 Belchem: 1981: 81.
26 Reid, J. (2014) Let Tyrants Tremble: The War Diary of 199 (Bomber Support) Squadron, November 1942 – July 1945, p. 127.
27 Reid: 2014: 127.
28 Belchem: 1981: 81.
29 Pheasant, V. (2003) The Sixtieth Anniversary of Window: 1943 – 2003, unpaginated.
30 Cockburn, R. (1945) The Radio War, p. 72
31 Cockburn: 1945: 73.
32 Addison, E. (1945) No. 80 Wing, Royal Air Force: Historical Report, 1940-1945, Air Ministry, p. 85.
33 Addison: 1945: 85.
34 Cockburn: 1945: 44.
35 Cockburn: 1945: 44.
36 Cockburn: 1945: 5-6.
37 Price: 1967: 111.
38 Price: 1967: 129.
39 Cockburn: 1945: 63.
40 Cockburn: 1945: 63.
41 Streetly, M. (1984) The Aircraft of the 100 Group: A Historical Guide for the Modeller, p. 9.
42 The Guardian (2/6/2008) 'Profile: Peter Melchett', theguardian.com.
43 The Gurdian (20/9/2000) 'Melchett Cleared over GM Crop Damage', theguardian.com.
44 BBC Radio 4 (30/1/2000) Desert Island Discs: Sue Lawley interviewing Peter Melchett.
45 BBC Radio 4: 30/1/2000.
46 Melchett, P. (8/6/2014) Cutting Ribbon Speech at the Control Tower.
47 Streetly: 1984: 9.
48 Streetly: 1984: 23.
49 Cockburn: 1945: 80.
50 Cockburn: 1945: 80.
51 Cockburn: 1945: 80.
52 Streetly, M. (1978) Confound & Destroy: 100 Group and the Bomber Support Campaign, p. 45.
53 Streetly: 1984: 9.
54 Streetly: 1978: 45.
55 Polichek, V. (3/2/1998) Correspondence.
56 Ashworth, C. (1995) RAF Bomber Command: 1936-1968, p. 134.
57 Ashworth: 1995: 135.
58 Bartram, L. (undated) No. 100 Group (Norfolk) R.A.F. Bomber Command: 1943/1945, p. 19.
59 King, L. (undated) History of Service in RAF, p. 4
60 Bocock, F. (2005) 'Norfolk's Secret Airforce', in Bridges, E. M. & Baldwin, J. (Eds) (2005) A Conflict & Memories: Fakenham Remembers World War Two, p. 5.

61   Bocock: 2005: in Bridges & Baldwin: 2005: 5.

62   Brettingham, L. (2002) Even When the Sparrows are Walking: The Origin and Effect of No. 100 (Bomber Support) Group, RAF, 1943-45, pp. 144-145.

63   Berry, P. (2018) A Wireless Operator at RAF North Creake, unpaginated.

64   Smith, S. (17/1/2016) in conversation with the author.

65   How, B. (8/3/2017) interview with the author.

66   Freegard, H. (9/8/2018) in conversation with the author.

67   Streetly: 1978: 45.

68   Pedan, M. (1979) A Thousand Shall Fall, p. 402.

69   Pedan: 1979: 402.

70   Harris, A. (1995) Despatch on War Operations: 23rd February, 1942 to 8th May, 1945, p. 141.

71   Brettingham: 2002: 127.

72   Brettingham: 2002: 127.

73   Docherty, M. (undated) cited in Brettingham: 2002: 129.

74   Streetly: 1978: 54.

75   Streetly: 1978: 9-10.

76   Streetly: 1978: 54.

77   Streetly: 1978: 54.

78   Brettingham: 2002: 125.

79   Streetly: 1978: 53.

80   Streetly: 1978: 50.

81   Webster, C. & Frankland, N. (1961) History of the Second World War: The Strategic Air Offensive, Volume III: Victory, p. 150.

82   Streetly: 1978: 50.

83   Webster & Frankland: 1961: Vol. III: 150.

84   Reid: 2014: 127.

85   Hancock, F. (undated) cited in, Reid: 2014: 130.

86   Hartley, K. (undated) cited in, Reid: 2014: 128.

87   Bartram, L. (1998) RAF North Creake, Egmere, 1940-1947: A Brief History, p. 4.

88   Willmott, P. (1988) Coming of Age in Wartime, p. 122.

89   Wright J. (undated) Walsingham History Society (2001) The Walsingham Millennium Book: Interviews and Recollections, unpaginated.

90   Pedan: 1979: 370.

91   Pedan: 1979: 370.

92   Pedan: 1979: 370.

93   Pringle, J. W. S. (1985) 'The Work of TRE in the Invasion of Europe', in IEE Proceedings: A Special Issue on Historical Radar, p. 350.

94   RAF 199 Squadron (June 1944) Operations Record Book, unpaginated.

95   Reid: 2014: 129.

96   Streetly: 1978: 53.

97   Reid: 2014: 129.

98   Brettingham: 2002: 125.

99   Brettingham: 2002: 125.

100   Brettingham: 2002: 126.

101   Ogden, R. J. (2001) 'Meteorological Services Leading to D-Day', in Royal Meteorological Society (July 2001) Occasional Papers of Meteorological History, No. 3, p. 17.

102   Reid: 2014: 127.

103   Price: 1967: 209.

104   Price: 1967: 210.

105   Belchem: 1981: 81.

106   Price: 1967: 206.

107   Price: 1967: 206.

108   Price: 1967: 210.

109   Addison, E. (1946) The Radio War lecture', in RUSI (1947) Royal United Services Institute Journal, p. 37.

110   Hutton, S. (1999) Squadron of Deception: The 36th Bomb Squadron in World War II, p. 26.

111   Bowman M. & Cushing, T. (1996) Confounding the Reich: The Operational History of 100 Group (Bomber Support) RAF, p. 91.

112   Price: 1967: 204.

113   Price: 1967: 204.

114   Piekalkiewicz, J. (1985) The Air War, 1939-1945, p. 351.

115   Piekalkiewicz: 1985: 351-352.

116   Price: 1967: 210.

117   Streetly: 1984: 10.

118   Reid: 2014: 129.

119   Reid: 2014: 129.

120   Smith, R. (undated) War Memories, unpaginated.

121   Hines, M. (2022) Airfields of North Norfolk: RAF North Creake, p. 13.

122   Reid: 2014: 129.

123   Wood, A, (undated) Interview with Grandson.

124   Melchett: 8/6/2014.

125   Taylor: 1975: 195.

126   Reid: 2014: 129.

127   RAF 199 Squadron (June 1944) Crew Order Book, RAF, unpaginated.

128   RAF 199 Squadron: June 1944: ORB: unpaginated.

129   Addison, E. (6/6/1944) D-Day Signal.

130   Willmott: 1988: 122.

131   Hartsook, L. (12/5/2016) in correspondence with the author.

132   Hartsook: 12/5/2016.

133   Harris, A. (undated) cited in, Bowman & Cushing: 1996: 89.

134   Harris, A. (1947) Bomber Offensive, p. 207.

135   Belchem: 1981: 57.

136   Bowman & Cushing: 1996: 88.
137   Price: 1967: 242.
138   Ogden: 2001: 18.
139   Price: 1967: 210.
140   Cockburn: 1945: 81.
141   Streetly: 1978: 56.
142   RAF 199 Squadron: June 1944: ORB: unpaginated.
143   Webster & Frankland: 1961: Vol. III: 161.
144   Streetly: 1978: 54
145   Streetly: 1978: 54
146   Streetly: 1978: 54
147   Streetly: 1978: 144.
148   Price: 1967: 223.
149   RAF North Creake (September 1944) Operations Record Book, unpaginated.
150   RAF North Creake: October 1944: ORB: unpaginated.
151   RAF North Creake: October 1944: ORB: unpaginated.
152   Jones, R. V. (1978) Most Secret War: British Scientific Intelligence 1939-1945, 468.
153   Jones: 1978: 468.
154   RAF 100 Group (December 1944) Operations, p. 1.
155   RAF 100 Group: December 1944: 5.
156   RAF 100 Group: December 1944: p. 1.
157   Streetly: 1978: 54.
158   Bowman & Cushing: 1996: 91.
159   Bowman & Cushing: 1996: 92.
160   Bartram: 1998: 26.
161   Bowman, M. (2006) 100 Group (Bomber Support) RAF Bomber Command in World War II, Aviation Heritage Trail Series, Pen & Sword, p. 80.
162   Philipson, W. J. F. (undated) in Bartram: 1998: 22.
163   Streetly: 1978: 60.
164   Price: 1967: 224.
165   Cockburn: 1945: 57.
166   RAF 100 Group (11/3/1944) RAF 100 Group Correspondence, unpaginated.
167   Streetly: 1978: 142.
168   Streetly: 1978: 142.
169   RAF 100 Group (July 1944) Operations, unpaginated.
170   RAF 100 Group: July 1944: unpaginated.
171   RAF 100 Group: July 1944: unpaginated.
172   RAF 100 Group: July 1944: unpaginated.
173   RAF 199 Squadron: July 1944: ORB: unpaginated.
174   Streetly: 1978: 63.
175   Streetly: 1978: 62.
176   Streetly: 1978: 62.
177   Streetly: 1978: 62.
178   RAF 100 Group (November 1944) Operations, p. 2.
179   RAF 100 Group (January 1945) Operations, p. 6.
180   Reid: 2014: 159.
181   Brettingham: 2002: 134.
182   RAF 100 Group (March 1945) Operations, p. 5.
183   Price: 1967: 230.
184   Price: 1967: 230.
185   Price: 1967: 231.
186   Price: 1967: 231.
187   Pedan: 1979: 403.
188   Pedan: 1979: 403.
189   Price: 1967: 231.
190   Price: 1967: 231.
191   Price: 1967: 231.
192   Price: 1967: 231.
193   Pedan: 1979: 403.
194   Price: 1967: 231.
195   Price: 1967: 231.
196   Price: 1967: 233.
197   Pedan: 1979: 403.
198   Price: 1967: 233.
199   Price: 1967: 233.
200   Price: 1967: 233.
201   Price: 1967: 233.
202   Price: 1967: 233-234.
203   Price: 1967: 234.
204   Price: 1967: 234.
205   Feasey, J. (11/4/1985) Correspondence with Maurice Hood.
206   RAF 100 Group (March 1945) Operations, p. 1.
207   Middlebrook, M. & Everitt, C. (1985) The Bomber Command War Diaries: An Operational Reference Book, 1939-1945, p. 684.
208   RAF 100 Group (March 1945) Operations Record Book Appendices (ORBA), unpaginated.
209   RAF 100 Group: March 1945: ORBA: unpaginated.
210   RAF 100 Group: March 1945: ORBA: unpaginated.
211   Addison: 1946: 37.
212   Addison: 1946: 37.
213   Chisholm, R. (1953) Cover of Darkness, p. 193.
214   Addison, E. (7/10/1944) Correspondence.
215   Price: 1967: 224.
216   RAF 100 Group: November 1944: 8.
217   Cockburn: 1945: 69.
218   Price: 1967: 224.
219   Webster & Frankland: 1961: Vol. III: 161.
220   Harris: 1995: 120.
221   Hastings, M. (1980) Bomber Command, p. 240.
222   Freegard: 18/8/2018.

223 Price: 1967: 223.
224 Pedan: 1979: 407.
225 Renaut, M. (1982) Terror by Night, p. 158.
226 Brettingham: 2002: 142-143.
227 Brettingham: 2002: 143.
228 Renaut: 1982: 159.
229 Renaut: 1982: 159.
230 Price: 1967: 224.
231 Bomber Command (1945) The Scapegoats – Bomber Command's Feint Forces, p. 3.
232 Price: 1967: 224.
233 Price: 1967: 224.
234 Price: 1967: 226.
235 Chisholm: 1953: 190.
236 Brettingham: 2002: 145.
237 How, B. (8/3/2017) interview with the author.

Operation Gisela

1 Middlebrook, M. & Everitt, C. (1985) The Bomber Command War Diaries: An Operational Reference Book, 1939-1945, p. 674.
2 Luftkrig 1939-1945 (undated) luftkrig1939-45.dk, p. 20.
3 RAF 171 Squadron (March 1945) Operations Record Book, & RAF 199 Squadron (March 1945) Operations Record Book.
4 RAF 171 Squadron: March 1945: ORB: unpaginated & RAF 199 Squadron: March 1945: ORB: unpaginated.
5 RAF North Creake (March 1945) Operations Record Book, unpaginated.
6 RAF 171 Squadron: March 1945: ORB: unpaginated.
7 RAF 171 Squadron: March 1945: ORB: unpaginated.
8 RAF North Creake: March 1945: ORB: unpaginated.
9 RAF North Creake: March 1945: ORB: unpaginated.
10 Luftkrig 1939-1945 (undated): 20.
11 RAF 171 Squadron: March 1945: ORB: unpaginated.
12 RAF North Creake: March 1945: ORB: unpaginated.
13 Hastings, M. (1980) Bomber Command, pp. 235-236.
14 Hastings: 1980: 235-236.
15 Harris, A. (1995) Despatch on War Operations: 23rd February 1942 to 8th May 1945, p. 188.
16 Bowman, M. & Cushing, T. (1996) Confounding the Reich: The Operational History of 100 Group (Bomber Support) RAF, p. 177.
17 Bowman & Cushing: 1996: 177.
18 Bowman, M. (2015) The Night Air War: Voices in Flight, p. 126.
19 Bowman: 2015: 102.
20 Bowman: 2015: 102.
21 Harris: 1995: 188.
22 Harris: 1995: 188.
23 Harris: 1995: 188.
24 Air Council (undated) Flying Control in the Royal Air Force, publication 3024, p. 48.
25 Air Council: undated: 48.
26 Air Council: undated: 36.
27 Air Historical Branch (1956) Works: The Second World War 1939-1945, p. 570.
28 Wilcock, R. (undated) 03/04.03.1945 No 171 Squadron Halifax III NA107 6Y-T Sqn. Ldr. Percy Clifford Procter MiD.
29 Hinchliffe, P. (1996) The Other Battle: Luftwaffe Night Aces Versus Bomber Command, p. 325.
30 Wilcock: undated.
31 RAF North Creake: March 1945: ORB: unpaginated.
32 RAF North Creake: March 1945: ORB: unpaginated.
33 Luftkrig 1939-1945 (undated): 20.
34 Luftkrig 1939-1945 (undated): 20.
35 Luftkrig 1939-1945 (undated): 20.
36 Luftkrig 1939-1945 (undated): 20.
37 Luftkrig 1939-1945 (undated): 20.
38 Luftkrig 1939-1945 (undated): 20.
39 Luftkrig 1939-1945 (undated): 20.
40 RAF 100 Group (July 1944) Operations, unpaginated.
41 RAF 100 Group: July 1944: unpaginated.
42 RAF 100 Group: July 1944: unpaginated.
43 Parry, S. W. (1987) Intruders Over Britain: The Luftwaffe Night Fighter Offensive 1940-45, pp. 126-127.
44 Berrill, R. (27/6/2021) interview with author.
45 RAF 171 Squadron: March 1945: ORB: unpaginated.
46 Wilcock: undated.
47 Renaut, M. (1982) Terror by Night, p. 166.
48 Wilcock: undated.
49 RAF 171 Squadron: March 1945: ORB: unpaginated.
50 Wilcock: undated.
51 Wilcock: undated.
52 Parry: 1987: 128.
53 Parry: 1987: 131.
54 Parry: 1987: 128.
55 Parry: 1987: 131.
56 RAF 171 Squadron: March 1945: ORB: unpaginated.

57   Stubbington, J. (undated) 171 Squadron: From the National Archives, p. 26.
58   Parry: 1987: 128.
59   Hope, B. (2014) And in the Morning: RAF Station North Creake, p. 23.
60   Parry: 1987: 128.
61   Brettingham, L. (2002) Even When the Sparrows are Walking: The Origin and Effect of No. 100 (Bomber Support) Group, RAF, 1943-45, p. 154.
62   Wilcock: undated.
63   Stubbington: undated: 26.
64   Wilcock: undated.
65   Stubbington: undated: 26.
66   Parry: 1987: 128.
67   Wilcock: undated.
68   Wilcock: undated.
69   RAF 199 Squadron: March 1945: ORB: unpaginated.
70   Bartlett, H. (23/11/2021) Interview with Gordon Mercier.
71   Middlebrook & Everitt: 1985:674.
72   Foreman, J. Mathews, J. & Parry, S. (2004) Luftwaffe: Night Fighter Combat Claims 1939-1945, p. 238.
73   Bowman & Cushing: 1996: 179.
74   Harrington, J. (2016) RAF 100 Group: The Birth of Electronic Warfare, pp. 142-143.
75   Foreman, Mathews & Parry: 2004: 238.
76   Chorley, W. R. (2008) Royal Air Force: Bomber Command Losses of the Second World War: Volume 6, 1945, p. 215.
77   Hinchliffe: 1996: 325.
78   Wilcock: undated.
79   Wilcock: undated.
80   Wilcock: undated.
81   Wilcock: undated.
82   Wilcock: undated.
83   RAF North Creake: March 1945: ORB: unpaginated.

Chapter Seven

1   Berry, P. (1989) Airfield Heyday: Daily Life on and Around Wartime Airfields, p. 86.
2   Reid, J. (14/8/2023) in conversation with the author.
3   Reid, J. (2014) Let Tyrants Tremble: The War Diary of 199 (Bomber Support) Squadron, November 1942 – July 1945, pp. 115-116.
4   Halpenny, B. B. (1981) Action Stations 2: Military Airfields of Lincolnshire and the East Midlands, p. 14.
5   Air Council (undated) Flying Control in the Royal Air Force, publication 3024, p. 6.
6   Redding, T. (2005) Flying for Freedom: Life and Death in Bomber Command, p. 223.
7   Air Council: undated: 69.
8   Air Council: undated: 6
9   Air Council: undated: 69-70.
10   Martin, B (1978) cited in Francis, P. (1993) Control Towers: The Development of the Control Tower on RAF Stations in the United Kingdom, p. 18.
11   Air Historical Branch (1956) Works: The Second World War 1939-1945, p. 602.
12   Air Council: undated: 70.
13   Air Council: undated: 70.
14   Air Council: undated: 70.
15   Spear, S. (undated) Interview with Imperial War Museum.
16   Francis, P. (1993) Control Towers: The Development of the Control Tower on RAF Stations in the United Kingdom, p. 116.
17   Berrill, R. (27/6/2021) interview with author.
18   Willmott, P. (1988) Coming of Age in Wartime, p. 119.
19   Air Historical Branch: 1956: 588.
20   Ellin, D. (23/2/2022) Interview with Roy Berrill.
21   Yarham, S. (2012) in conversation with the author.
22   Berrill, R. (25/3/2023) interview by author.
23   Sawyer, T. (1981) Only Owls and Bloody Fools Fly at Night, p. 26.
24   Berrill: 27/6/2021.
25   Berrill: 27/6/2021.
26   Berrill: 27/6/2021.
27   Ellin: 23/2/2022.
28   Ellin: 23/2/2022.
29   Ellin: 23/2/2022.
30   Ellin: 23/2/2022.
31   Spear: undated.
32   Berry, W. (1985) Hall, A. (1985) We Also, Were There, p. 75.
33   Met Office (undated) Remember the Met Office in World War One and World War Two.
34   Berry: 1985: 75.
35   Ellin: 23/2/2022.
36   Berrill: 25/3/2023.
37   Willmott: 1988: 110.
38   Ford, K. S. (1992) Snaith Days: Life With 51 Squadron 1942/45, p. 32.
39   Spear, B. (1988) The Met WAAF Contribution: Talk to the Royal Meteorological Society's Conference, p. 24.
40   Berrill, R. (October 2022) written response to pre-interview paper, p.13.
41   Spear: 1988: 24.
42   Ford: 1992: 32.
43   Spear: 1988: 24.

44 Willmott: 1988: 111.
45 Berrill: 27/6/2021.
46 Berrill: 27/6/2021.
47 Berrill: 27/6/2021.
48 Spear: undated.
49 Berrill: 27/6/2021.
50 Berrill: 27/6/2021.
51 Berrill: 25/3/2023.
52 Berrill: 25/3/2023.
53 Willmott: 1988: 111.
54 Berrill, R. (July 2021) in correspondence with the author.
55 Willmott, P. (1945) Correspondence, WLMT 02001001(20).
56 Willmott, P. (1944) Correspondence, WLMT 02001001(9).
57 Willmott, P. (1944) Correspondence, WLMT 02001001(14)
58 Air Council: undated: 1.
59 Berrill: 27/6/2021.
60 Berrill: 27/6/2021.
61 Spear: undated.
62 Spear: undated.
63 Berrill: 25/3/2023.
64 Skan, L. E. (1990) Half a Penguin: Reminiscences of a Bomber Command Flying Control Officer, p. 7.
65 Willmott: 1988: 120.
66 Willmott: 1988: 120.
67 Willmott: 1988: 111.
68 Willmott, P. (1945) Correspondence, WLMT 02001001(17)
69 Willmott, P. (1944) Correspondence, WLMT 02001002(15).
70 Willmott: 1988: 111.
71 Willmott, P. (1944) Correspondence, WLMT 02001001(12) & 02001001(13).
72 Willmott, P. (1944) Correspondence, WLMT 02001002(2).
73 Willmott, P. (1944) Correspondence, WLMT 02001002(4).
74 Willmott: 1945: WLMT 02001002(20) & Willmott: 1988: 124.
75 Willmott: 1988: 124.
76 Willmott: 1988: 124.
77 Willmott, P. (1945) Correspondence, WLMT 02001002(22)
78 Spear: undated.
79 Morter, E. (1915-1922) Central Military Service Tribunal: Case Number M5306, unpaginated.
80 Allward, M. & Taylor, J. (1996) The De Havilland Aircraft Company, p. 103.
81 Harris, A. (1995) Despatch on War Operations: 23rd February 1942 to 8th May 1945, p. 186.
82 Harris: 1995: 186.
83 Francis: 1993: 125.
84 Maufe, T. (2012) in conversation with the author.
85 Francis: 1993: 125.
86 Francis: 1993: 129.
87 Skan: 1990: 5.
88 Francis: 1993: 129.
89 Air Historical Branch: 1956: 552.
90 Air Historical Branch: 1956: 552.
91 Francis: 1993: 129.
92 Air Historical Branch: 1956: 537.
93 Air Historical Branch: 1956: 543.
94 Francis: 1993: 129.
95 Air Historical Branch: 1956: 545.
96 Air Historical Branch: 1956: 538.
97 Air Historical Branch: 1956: 547.
98 Hawton, H. (1944) The Men Who Fly, p. 149.
99 Acres, D. (1985) in, Hall: 1985: 93.
100 Skan: 1990: 16.
101 BBC (29/12/2006) UK Settles WWII Debt to Allies.
102 Brettingham, L. (2002) Even When the Sparrows are Walking: The Origin and Effect of No. 100 (Bomber Support) Group, RAF, 1943-45, pp. 282-283.
103 Flowers, V. (2016) telephone conversation with the author.
104 Smith, D. J. (1981) Action Stations 3: Military Airfields of Wales and the North West, p. 28.
105 Air Council: undated: 3
106 Air Council: undated: 1.
107 Higham, R. (1998) Bases of Air Strategy: Building Airfields for the RAF 1914-1945, p. 79.
108 Harris: 1995: 186.
109 Harris: 1995: 185.
110 Harris: 1995: 186.
111 Harris: 1995: 186.
112 Harris: 1995: 187.
113 Harris: 1995: 189.
114 Air Council: undated: 68.
115 Air Council: undated: 44.
116 Air Council: undated: 6
117 Air Council: undated: 8-9.
118 Air Council: undated: 8-9.
119 Air Historical Branch: 1956: 83.
120 Chisholm, R. (1953) Cover of Darkness, p. 160.
121 Skan: 1990: 6.
122 Harris: 1995: 186.
123 Harris: 1995: 185.
124 Harris: 1995: 186.
125 Sawyer: 1981: 103.
126 Bowyer, J. F. (1979) Action Stations: Wartime Military Airfields of East Anglia, 1939-1945, p. 6.

127 Air Council: undated: 8.

128 Redding: 2005: 223.

129 Skan: 1990: 5.

130 Air Council: undated: 11.

131 Skan: 1990: 26.

132 Air Council: undated: 44.

133 Redding: 2005: 223.

134 Air Council: undated: 49.

135 Air Council: undated: 50.

136 Cannings, P. (1985) in Hall: 1985: 62.

137 Air Council: undated: 75.

138 Air Council: undated: 50.

139 Air Council: undated: 50.

140 Air Council: undated: 50.

141 Air Council: undated: 44.

142 Air Council: undated: 47.

143 Berrill: 27/6/2021.

144 Air Council: undated: 46.

145 Ford: 1992: 32.

146 Docherty, G. (12/10/1944) Cloud Breaking Procedure, unpaginated.

147 Air Council: undated: 45.

148 Harris: 1995: 185.

149 Harris: 1995: 187.

150 Harris: 1995: 185.

151 Harris: 1995: 187.

152 Harris: 1995: 187.

153 Harris: 1995: 187.

154 Harris: 1995: 187.

155 Harris: 1995: 187.

156 Harris: 1995: 187.

157 Francis: 1993: 125.

158 Taylor, S. (2018) A Day in the Life of Bomber Command, Lecture.

159 Harris: 1995: 189.

160 Harris: 1995: 189.

161 Chisholm, P. N. (2/12/1944) FIDO Landing Precautions, unpaginated.

162 Bartlett, H. (23/11/2021) Interview with Gordon Mercier.

163 Skan: 1990: 35.

164 Harris: 1995: 189.

165 Francis: 1993: 125.

166 Rees, J. (undated) in Bartram, L. (1998) RAF North Creake, Egmere, 1940-1947: A Brief History, p. 13.

167 Hope, B. (2014) And in the Morning: RAF Station North Creake, pp. 23-24.

168 Hope: 2014: 23-24.

169 Bond, S. & Forder, R. (2011) Special Ops Liberators: 225 (Bomber Support) Squadron, 100 Group, and the Electronic War, pp. 111-112.

170 Polichek, V. (3/2/1998) Correspondence.

171 Polichek: 3/2/1998.

172 Philipson, W. J. F. (undated) in Bartram: 1998: 22.

173 Philipson: undated: 22.

174 Philipson: undated: 22.

175 Feasey, J. (1/4/1985) Correspondence with Reg Foreman.

176 Philipson: undated: 22.

177 RAF North Creake (December 1944) Operations Record Book, unpaginated.

178 RAF North Creake: December 1944: ORB: unpaginated.

179 RAF 171 Squadron (December 1944) Operations Record Book, unpaginated.

180 Harris: 1995: 189.

181 Harris: 1995: 189.

182 Willis, S. & Holliss, B. (1990) Military Airfields in the British Isles 1939-1945, p. 218.

183 Harris: 1995: 189.

184 Harris: 1995: 189.

185 Hope: 2014: 23.

186 Hope: 2014: 23.

187 Hines, M. (2022) Airfields of North Norfolk: RAF North Creake, p. 82.

188 Hope: 2014: 23.

189 Feasey, J. (undated) in Bartram: 1998: 18.

190 Brettingham: 2002: 147-148.

191 Brettingham: 2002: 148.

192 Skan: 1990: 7.

193 Reid: 2014: 147.

194 Bartram: 1998: 27.

195 Reid: 2014: 147.

196 Hope: 2014: 23.

197 Air Council: undated: 48.

198 Air Council: undated: 108.

199 Air Council: undated: 108.

200 Flinders, S. & Corns, D. (2019) Stanton: Gone but Not Forgotten: A Derbyshire Ironworks and its People, p. 89.

201 Air Council: undated: 48.

202 Innes, G. B. (1995) British Airfield Buildings of the Second World War: Aviation Pocket Guide 1, p. 120.

203 Air Historical Branch: 1956: 503.

204 Air Historical Branch: 1956: 504.

205 Air Historical Branch: 1956: 503.

206 Air Historical Branch: 1956: 504.

207 Air Historical Branch: 1956: 504.

208 Spear: undated.

209 Spear: undated.

210 Willmott: 1988: 120.

211 Skan: 1990: 24.

212 Skan: 1990: 24.

Friendly Fire

1 RAF North Creake (December 1944) Operations Record Book, unpaginated.

2 Reid, J. (2014) Let Tyrants Tremble: The War Diary of 199 (Bomber Support) Squadron, November 1942 – July 1945, p. 147.

3 Reid: 2014: 147.

4 Reid: 2014: 147.

5 RAF 199 Squadron (December 1944) Operations Record Book, unpaginated.

6 RAF 199 Squadron: December 1944: ORB: unpaginated.

7 Chorley, W. R. (2008) Royal Air Force: Bomber Command Losses of the Second World War: Volume 6, 1945, p. 109.

8 Bowyer, M. J. F. (2002) The Stirling Story, p. 374.

9 Chorley: 2008: Vol. 6: 109.

10 Hope, B. (15/9/2023) in correspondence with the author.

11 Royal Canadian Airforce (12/5/1941) RCAF Medical Board: Form RCAFM2: Jack Thurlow, unpaginated.

12 Royal Canadian Airforce (9/6/1941) Interview Report: Jack Thurlow, unpaginated.

13 RCAF: 12/5/1941: unpaginated.

14 RCAF: 9/6/1941: unpaginated.

15 Thomas Organ & Piano Co. (12/5/1941) Reference: Jack Thurlow, unpaginated.

16 Pearce, W. (10/5/1941) Reference from YMCA, Jack Thurlow, unpaginated.

17 RCAF: 9/6/1941: unpaginated.

18 Royal Canadian Airforce (15/4/1944) Occupational History Form: Jack Thurlow, unpaginated.

19 RCAF: 9/6/1941: unpaginated.

20 RCAF: 9/6/1941: unpaginated.

21 Colgan, G. (7/5/2020) 'VE Day: A Woodstock Pilot's Sacrifice', woodstocksentinelreview.com.

22 Royal Canadian Airforce (11/7/1941) Attestation Paper: Jack Thurlow, p. 2.

23 RCAF: 15/4/1944: unpaginated.

24 Royal Canadian Airforce (10/9/1943) Test: Jack Thurlow, RCAF, unpaginated.

25 Royal Canadian Airforce (undated(b)) Service Record: Jack Thurlow, unpaginated.

26 Colgan: 7/5/2020.

27 Colgan: 7/5/2020.

28 Ellin, D. (23/2/2022) Interview with Roy Berrill.

29 Berrill, R. (27/6/2021) interview with author.

30 Berrill: 27/6/2021.

31 Berrill: 27/6/2021.

32 Reid: 2014: 167.

33 Reid: 2014: 167.

34 RAF North Creake: March 1945: ORB: unpaginated.

35 Colgan: 7/5/2020.

36 Donovan, R. (2009) As for the Canadians: The Remarkable Story of the RCAF's 'Guinea pigs' of World War II, p. 209.

37 Donovan: 2009: 209.

38 Donovan: 2009: 209.

39 Fenning, F. (1945) Statement by F/Lt Fenning (104913) Mid-Upper Gunner in Stirling Aircraft LJ 617 on Night 5.3.45, unpaginated.

40 Donovan: 2009: 209-210.

41 Donovan: 2009: 209-211.

42 Colgan: 7/5/2020.

43 Chorley: 2008: Vol. 6: 109.

44 Donovan: 2009: 210.

45 Donovan: 2009: 209-211.

46 Donovan: 2009: 209-211.

47 Guinea Pig Club Archive (undated) Database.

48 Donovan: 2009: 210.

49 Chorley: 2008: Vol. 6: 109.

50 Bowyer, M. J. F. (2002) The Stirling Story, p. 375.

51 Chorley: 2008: Vol. 6: 109.

52 Chorley: 2008: Vol. 6: 109.

53 Smith, R. (19/12/2005) Life as Part of the Crew of a Stirling Bomber, bbc.co.uk.

54 Bickers, R. T. (1994) Friendly Fire: Accidents in Battle from Ancient Greece to the Gulf War, p. 97.

55 Fussell, P. (1989) Wartime, Understanding the Behaviour in the Second World War, p. 21.

56 Fenning: 1945: unpaginated.

57 Bickers: 1994: 59.

58 Bickers: 1994: 110.

59 Brettingham, L. (2002) Even When the Sparrows are Walking: The Origin and Effect of No. 100 (Bomber Support) Group, RAF, 1943-45, p. 145.

60 Brettingham: 2002: 145.

61 Bickers: 1994: 119.

62 Fenning: 1945: unpaginated.

63 Colgan: 7/5/2020.

64 Colgan: 7/5/2020.

65 Colgan: 7/5/2020.

66 Colgan: 7/5/2020.

67 Royal Canadian Airforce (undated(c)) Registration of Death Certificate: Jack Thurlow, unpaginated.

68 Colgan: 7/5/2020.

69 Colgan: 7/5/2020.

70 Colgan: 7/5/2020.

Chapter Eight

1 Hillier, H. (10/2/2024) in correspondence with the author.

2 Hall, A. (1985) We Also, Were There, p. 31.
3 Ford, K. S. (1992) Snaith Days: Life With 51 Squadron 1942/45, p. 19.
4 Ford: 1992: 21.
5 Phipps, D. (1985) in, Hall, A. (1985) We Also, Were There, p. 59.
6 Ford: 1992: 19.
7 Ford: 1992: 19.
8 Ford: 1992: 19.
9 Ford: 1992: 19.
10 Ford: 1992: 19.
11 Ford: 1992: 19.
12 Sawyer, T. (1981) Only Owls and Bloody Fools Fly at Night, p. 88.
13 Hall: 1985: 31.
14 Hall: 1985: 31.
15 Hall: 1985: 31.
16 Hall: 1985: 31.
17 Thompson, T. (1985) in, Hall: 1985: 48.
18 Air Council (undated) Flying Control in the Royal Air Force, publication 3024, p. 71.
19 Thompson: 1985: 48.
20 Ford: 1992: 26.
21 Met Office (undated) Remember the Met Office in World War One and World War Two,
metoffice.gov.uk.
22 Berry, W. (1985) Hall: 1985: 76.
23 Ford: 1992: 21.
24 Ford: 1992: 21.
25 Tempest, V. (1946) Near the Sun: Impressions of a Medical Officer of Bomber Command, pp. 24-25.
26 Tempest: 1946: 25.
27 Longmate, N. (1983) The Bombers: The RAF Offensive Against Germany, 1939-1945, p. 179.
28 Wainwright, J. (1978) Tail-End Charlie: One Man's Journey Through a War, pp. 92-94.
29 Hastings, M. (1980) Bomber Command, p. 157.
30 Hastings: 1980: 157.
31 Harrington, J. (2012) RAF North Creake, Egmere 1940-1947: A Brief History, p. 33.
32 Ford: 1992: 24.
33 Berrill, R. (25/3/2023) interview with the author.
34 How, B. (8/3/2017) interview with the author
35 Aeroplane (2015) Short Stirling: The RAF's First Four-Engined 'Heavy', p. 43.
36 Storer, I. (1985) in, Hall, A. (1985) We Also, Were There, p. 108.
37 Storer: 1985: 108.
38 Storer: 1985: 109.
39 Ford: 1992: 24.
40 Smithies, E. (2002) Aces, Erks & Backroom Boys, pp. 120-121.
41 Redding, T. (2005) Flying for Freedom: Life and Death in Bomber Command, p. 101.
42 Redding: 2005: 101-102.
43 Nieman, C. (6/4/2021) in correspondence with the author.
44 Pedan, M. (1979) A Thousand Shall Fall, p. 392.
45 Pedan: 1979: 393.
46 Tempest: 1946: 63.
47 Tempest: 1946: 63.
48 Sawyer: 1981: 168.
49 Tripp, M. (1952) Faith is a Windsock, p. 42.
50 Storer: 1985: 111.
51 Longmate: 1983: 157.
52 Storer: 1985: 111.
53 Hughes, H. (15/2/2024) in conversation with the author.
54 Ellin, D. (23/2/2022) Interview with Roy Berrill.
55 Ellin: 23/2/2022.
56 Longmate: 1983: 186.
57 RAF 171 Squadron (3/12/1944) Appendix to RAF Squadron 171 Operations Record Book, p. 196.
58 RAF 171 Squadron: 23/10/1944: ORBA: 79.
59 RAF 171 Squadron (5/2/1945): ORBA: 252.
60 Sant, H. (18/5/2016) RAF Memories: Video Interviews with his Daughter.
61 Sant: (18/5/2016).
62 Wainwright: 1978: 94.
63 Ford: 1992: 21.
64 Taylor, S. (2018) A Day in the Life of Bomber Command Lecture.
65 Ford: 1992: 24.
66 Longmate: 1983: 180.
67 Adcock, A. (2004) 'Interview', Second World War Experience Centre.
68 Parnell, G. cited in, Longmate: 1983: 180.
69 Bartlett, H. (23/11/2021) Interview with Gordon Mercier.
70 Dennison, G. J. (20/8/1944) 'Letter to Lorne & Lillian (Brother & sister-in-Law), cited in: Dennison, G. (2007) Memories Are Treasures: The Military Career of Pilot Officer Gordon Joshua Dennison, p. 119.
71 Stewart, G. (undated) cited in Harrington, J. (2016) RAF 100 Group: The Birth of Electronic Warfare, p. 41.
72 Pedan: 1979: 412.
73 Gill, D. (2015) My Civilian and RAF Wartime Experiences, unpaginated.
74 Tempest: 1946: 45-46.
75 Tempest: 1946: 46-47.
76 Renaut, M. (1982) Terror by Night, p. 152.
77 Renaut, Y. (2015) taped interview.
78 Renaut: 2015.
79 Wainwright: 1978: 94.

80 Madden, M. (1985) in Hall: 1985: 115.

81 Polichek, V. (3/2/1998) correspondence.

82 Bartlett: 23/11/2021.

83 Redding: 2005: 67.

84 Redding: 2005: 67.

85 Ford: 1992: 24.

86 Derbyshire, K. (28/2/1990) Recollections of a 199 Squadron Electrician, unpaginated.

87 How: 8/3/2017.

88 Hyland, S. (29/10/2018) in correspondence with the author.

89 Hastings: 1980: 163.

90 Longmate: 1983: FN: 294.

91 Ford: 1992: 5.

92 Ford: 1992: 24.

93 Ford: 1992: 24.

94 Reid, J. (2014) Let Tyrants Tremble: The War Diary of 199 (Bomber Support) Squadron, November 1942 – July 1945, p. 147.

95 Hastings: 1980: 159.

96 Hastings: 1980: 157.

97 Ford: 1992: 26.

98 Adcock: 2004.

99 Brettingham, L. (2002) Even When the Sparrows are Walking: The Origin and Effect of No. 100 (Bomber Support) Group, RAF, 1943-45, p. 283.

100 Ford: 1992: 28.

101 How: 8/3/17.

102 Reid: 2014: 136.

103 Ford: 1992: 28.

104 Hall: 1985: 31-32.

105 Hall: 1985: 31-32.

106 Skan, L. E. (1990) Half a Penguin: Reminiscences of a Bomber Command Flying Control Officer, p. 22.

107 Berrill: 25/3/2023.

108 Harrington, J. (2016) RAF 100 Group: The Birth of Electronic Warfare, p. 42.

109 Adcock: 2004.

110 Taylor: 2018.

111 Allison, J. (1966) Bomber Crew, p. 12.

112 Tempest: 1946: 25.

113 Adcock: 2004.

114 Reid: 2014: 136.

115 Hughes, E. (undated) in Harrington: 2016: 198.

116 Sawyer: 1981: 137.

117 Adcock: 2004.

118 Ford: 1992: 26.

119 Ford: 1992: 28.

120 Ford: 1992: 26.

121 Gill: 2015: unpaginated.

122 Whiting, C. (1987) The Three Star Blitz: The Baedeker Raids and the Start of Total War 1942-1943, p. 139.

123 Kavanagh, D. (2016) Interview with Denis James Gill.

124 Kee, R. (1947) A Crowd Is Not Company, p. 1.

125 Reid: 2014: 136.

126 RAF North Creake (September 1944) Operations Record Book, unpaginated.

127 Hastings: 1980: 159.

128 Tempest: 1946: 26-27.

129 Hughes: undated: 198.

130 Tempest: 1946: 27.

131 Tempest: 1946: 27.

132 Berrill: 25/3/2023.

133 Ogden, R. J. (2001) 'Meteorological Services Leading to D-Day', in Royal Meteorological Society (July 2001) Occasional Papers of Meteorological History, No. 3, p. 13.

134 Wainwright: 1978: 95-98.

135 Tempest: 1946: 28.

136 Berrill, R. (October 2022) written response to pre-interview paper, p. 6.

137 Berrill, R. (27/6/2021) interview with author.

138 Berrill: 27/6/2021.

139 Adcock: 2004.

140 Tempest: 1946: 28.

141 Ford: 1992: 28.

142 Berrill: October 2022: p. 6.

143 Tempest: 1946: 28.

144 Wainwright: 1978: 95-98.

145 Wood, C. (2000) Interview with Arthur Gordon Clarke.

146 Ford: 1992: 28.

147 Ford: 1992: 28.

148 Ford: 1992: 26.

149 Morgan, M. (undated) Recollections of an MT Driver, unpaginated.

150 Tempest: 1946: 65.

151 Longmate: 1983: 364.

152 Longmate: 1983: 180.

153 Arnett, R. (2014) youtube.com.

154 Bartlett: 23/11/2021.

155 Thompson K (1945) War Diary.

156 Allison: 1966: 12.

157 Longmate: 1983: 180.

158 Lorimer, A. (1985) in, Hall: 1985: 191.

159 Allison: 1966: 14.

160 Bartlett: 23/11/2021.

161 Hall: 1985: 31-32.

162 Rees, J. (undated) in Bartram, L. (1998) RAF North Creake, Egmere, 1940-1947: A Brief History, p. 15.

163 Tempest: 1946: 28-29.

164 Ford: 1992: 29.

165 Wainwright: 1978: 99.

166 Wainwright: 1978: 99.

167 Willmott, P. (1944) Correspondence, WLMT 02001002(12).

168 Wainwright: 1978: 99.

169 Wilson, K. (2010) Journey's End: Bomber Command's Battle from Arnhem to Dresden and Beyond, p. 328.

170 Ford: 1992: 29.

171 Bartlett: 23/11/2021.

172 Bartlett: 23/11/2021.

173 Smithies: 2002: 122.

174 Hastings: 1980: 160.

175 Ford: 1992: 21.

176 Hughes: undated: 198.

177 Bartlett: 23/11/2021.

178 Bartlett: 23/11/2021.

179 Ford: 1992: 21.

180 Hilliard, R. (undated) Nothing on the Clock.

181 Bartlett: 23/11/2021.

182 Renaut, M. (7/3/1945) Escape Kits Memo, unpaginated.

183 Sawyer: 1981: 27.

184 Ford: 1992: 29.

185 Ford: 1992: 29.

186 Lorimer: 1985: 190.

187 Lorimer: 1985: 190.

188 Adcock: 2004.

189 Bartlett: 23/11/2021.

190 Sawyer: 1981: 106.

191 Adcock: 2004.

192 Hastings: 1980: 157.

193 Hughes: undated: 198.

194 Sawyer: 1981: 61.

195 Sawyer: 1981: 61.

196 Sawyer: 1981: 61.

197 Hyland: 29/10/2018.

198 Hyland: 29/10/2018.

199 Hyland: 29/10/2018.

200 Gill, D. (25/8/2018) Correspondence with Sara Hyland.

201 Gill: 25/8/2018.

202 Dennison: 20/8/1944: 120.

203 Thompson: 1945.

204 Thompson: 1945.

205 Ford: 1992: 26.

206 Hay, L. (2002) cited in, Taylor, F. (2005) Dresden: Tuesday 13 February 1945, p. 240.

207 Sawyer: 1981: 138.

208 Ford: 1992: 26.

209 Thompson: 1985: 48.

210 Cannings, P. (1985) in Hall: 1985: 63.

211 Rees: (undated) 15.

212 Rees: (undated) 15.

213 Cannings: 1985: 63.

214 Rees: (undated) 15.

215 Hughes, E. (undated) in Harrington, J. (2015) RAF 100 Group: Kindred Spirits: Voices of RAF & USAAF on Secret Norfolk Airfields During the Second World War, p. 475.

216 Adcock: 2004.

217 Adcock: 2004.

218 Adcock: 2004.

219 Allison: 1966: 16.

220 Hughes: undated: in Harrington: 2015: 475.

221 Hughes: undated: in Harrington: 2015: 475.

222 Hughes: undated: in Harrington: 2015: 475.

223 Ford: 1992: 29.

224 Adcock: 2004.

225 Ford: 1992: 29.

226 Hughes: undated: in Harrington: 2015: 476-477.

227 Bartlett: 23/11/2021.

228 Tempest: 1946: 29.

229 Adcock: 2004.

230 Adcock: 2004.

231 Tripp: 1952: 103.

232 Adcock: 2004.

233 Stockwell, E. M. (undated) Standing Orders for Air and Ground Crews When Operating at Night, unpaginated.

234 Hughes: undated: in Harrington: 2015: 476-477.

235 Hastings: 1980: 161.

236 Gill: 2015: unpaginated.

237 Air Council: undated: 72.

238 Stockwell: (undated), unpaginated.

239 Hastings: 1980: 160.

240 Stockwell: (undated), unpaginated.

241 Air Council: undated: 72.

242 Gill: 2015: unpaginated

243 Hyland, S. (August 2018) in correspondence with the author.

244 Air Council: undated: 72.

245 Adcock: 2004.

246 Philipson, W. J. F. (undated) in Bartram: 1998: 22.

247 Longmate: 1983: 180.

248 Berry, P. (2018a) A NAAFI Girl at RAF North Creake: Jean Kershaw, unpaginated.

249 Philipson: undated: 22.

250 Berry, P. (1989) Airfield Heyday: Daily Life on and Around Wartime Airfields, p. 84.

251 Feasey: undated: 19.

252 Adcock: 2004.

253 Cannings: 1985: 63.

254 Allison: 1966: 17.

255 Air Council: undated: 72.

256 Townroe, P. (2012) Our Three Local World War Two Airfields: Seventy Years On, p. 7.

257 Sawyer: 1981: 112.

258 Adcock: 2004.

259 RAF 199 Squadron (September 1944) Operations Record Book, unpaginated.

260 Skan: 1990: 6.
261 Button, A. H. (1985) 'Introduction', in Hall: 1985: 12
262 Sawyer: 1981: 88.
263 RAF 199 Squadron: September 1944: ORB: unpaginated.
264 Little, S. (30/12/2013) in correspondence with the author.
265 Philipson: undated: 22.
266 Bowman, M. W. (2015) Voices in Flight: The Night Air War, p. 209.
267 Bowyer, J. F. (1979) Action Stations: Wartime Military Airfields of East Anglia, 1939-1945, p. 21.
268 Barrett V. (1985) in, Hall: 1985: 119.
269 Mitchell, G. (undated) Start and Finish of an Air Gunner, unpaginated.
270 Berrill: 25/3/2023.
271 Gill: 2015: unpaginated
272 Mitchell: undated: unpaginated.
273 Gill: 2015: unpaginated
274 Gill: 2015: unpaginated
275 Mitchell: undated: unpaginated.
276 Kavanagh, D. (2016) Interview with Denis James Gill.
277 Gill: 2015: unpaginated
278 Gill: 2015: unpaginated
279 Berrill, R. (July 2021) in correspondence with the author.
280 RAF 199 Squadron (December 1944) Operations Record Book, unpaginated.
281 RAF North Creake (December 1944) Operations Record Book, unpaginated.
282 Pedan: 1979: 389.
283 Mitchell: undated: unpaginated.
284 Mitchell: undated: unpaginated.
285 Gill: 2015: unpaginated
286 Mitchell: undated: unpaginated.
287 Berrill: 25/3/2023.
288 RAF North Creake: September 1944: ORB: unpaginated.
289 Cannings: 1985: 63.
290 Button: 1985: 12
291 Acres, D. (1985) in, Hall: 1985: 90.
292 Cannings: 1985: 62.
293 Dent, P. (1985) in Hall: 1985: 68.
294 Thomas, N. (1985) in Hall: 1985: 165.
295 Morgan: undated: unpaginated.
296 Seal, B. (1985) in, Hall: 1985: 127.
297 Seal: 1985: 127.
298 Berry: 2018a: unpaginated.
299 Renaut: 2015.
300 Renaut: 1982: 152.
301 Tempest: 1946: 31-32.
302 Berrill: October 2022: 10.
303 Thompson: 1945.
304 RAF North Creake: December 1944: ORB: unpaginated.
305 Cannings: 1985: 63.
306 Cannings: 1985: 63.
307 Skan: 1990: 6.
308 Skan: 1990: 6.
309 Skan: 1990: 6.
310 Skan: 1990: 6.
311 Air Council: undated: 72-73.
312 Dent: 1985: 68.
313 Skan: 1990: 7.
314 Skan: 1990: 7.
315 Air Council: undated: 72-73.
316 Allison: 1966: 25.
317 Pedan: 1979: 246.
318 Tempest: 1946: 40.
319 Berrill: 27/6/2021.
320 Redding: 2005: 92.
321 Taylor: 2018.
322 Pedan: 1979: 252.
323 Berrill: October 2022: 11.
324 Pedan: 1979: 247.
325 Rees: (undated) 15.
326 Berrill: October 2022: 11.
327 Rees: (undated) 15.
328 Middlebrook, M. & Everitt, C. (1985) The Bomber Command War Diaries: An Operational Reference Book, 1939-1945, p. 579.
329 Hall: 1985: 32.
330 Hillier: 10/2/2024.
331 Hall: 1985: 32.
332 Spark, S. (2010) The Treatment of the British Military War Dead of the Second World War, p. 172.
333 Berrill: October 2022.
334 Hall: 1985: 32.
335 Hawton, H. (1944) The Men Who Fly, p. 126.
336 Hawton: 1944: 126.
337 Renaut: 1982: 52.
338 Sawyer: 1981: 29.
339 Kavanagh, D. (16/11/2016) Interview with Bernie How.
340 Gill: 2015: unpaginated
341 Brettingham: 2002: 153.
342 Pedan: 1979: 413.
343 Wainwright: 1978: 107.
344 Sinclair, J. (1987) Where's the Old Airfield? – You're Standing on it, unpaginated.
345 Sinclair: 1987: unpaginated.

Mid-Air Collision

1 Maufe, J. (15/8/2023) Memories Related to Jessica Forde.
2 Maufe: 15/8/2023.

3   Ashton, N. (2000) Only Birds and Fools: Flight Engineer, Avro Lancaster, World War II, p. 114.

4   Middlebrook, M. & Everitt, C. (1985) The Bomber Command War Diaries: An Operational Reference Book, 1939-1945, p. 696.

5   RAF 171 Squadron (April 1945) Operations Record Book, unpaginated.

6   Gill, D. (2015) My Civilian and RAF Wartime Experiences, unpaginated.

7   Polichek, V. (3/2/1998) correspondence.

8   Gill: 2015: unpaginated.

9   Gill: 2015: unpaginated.

10   Kavanagh, D. (2016) Interview with Denis James Gill.

11   Polichek: 3/2/1998.

12   Gill: 2015: unpaginated.

13   Bartlett, H. (23/11/2021) Interview with Gordon Mercier.

14   Rankin, K. (1/2/1990) Correspondence with John Reid.

15   Rankin: 1/2/1990.

16   Middlebrook & Everitt: 1985: 649.

17   Lawrence, J. (2007) rafcommands.com.

18   Aldus, R. V. (undated) Graven Halifax NA687 171 Sqn, unpaginated.

19   Hibberd, J. (undated) 462squadron.com.

20   Hibberd: undated.

21   Aldus: undated: unpaginated.

22   Aldus: undated: unpaginated.

23   RodM. (2007) rafcommands.com.

24   Aldus: undated: unpaginated.

25   Aldus: undated: unpaginated.

26   Aldus: undated: unpaginated.

27   RodM: 2007.

28   Hibberd: undated.

29   Hibberd: undated.

30   Lawrence, D. H. (1995) Zebra Five November, p. 5.

31   RodM: 2007.

32   Hibberd: undated.

33   Aldus: undated: unpaginated.

34   Lawrence: 1995: 5.

35   Lawrence: 1995: 6.

36   Hibberd: undated.

37   Aldus: undated: unpaginated.

38   Lawrence: 1995: 6.

39   Topham, K. (4/3/2006) 'Correspondence with Doug Lawrence', Hibberd: undated.

40   Hibberd: undated.

41   Aldus: undated: unpaginated.

42   Aldus: undated: unpaginated.

43   Aldus: undated: unpaginated.

44   Hibberd: undated.

45   Hibberd: undated.

46   Lawrence: 1995: 7.

47   Lawrence: 1995: 7.

48   Aldus: undated: unpaginated.

49   Hibberd: undated.

50   Lawrence: 1995: 8.

51   Lawrence: 1995: 9.

52   Lawrence: 1995: 9.

53   Lawrence: 1995: 2.

54   In Memoriam (undated) inmemoriam.be

55   Parsons, J. W. E. (15/5/1945) Casualty Enquiry No. S82: Halifax MZ469, unpaginated.

56   Parsons: 15/5/1945: unpaginated.

57   Everitt, D. H. (24/2/1945) Report on Investigation for Further Identification of Casualties, unpaginated.

58   Aldus: undated: unpaginated.

59   Everitt: 24/2/1945: unpaginated.

60   Everitt: 24/2/1945: unpaginated.

61   Parsons: 15/5/1945: unpaginated.

62   Hibberd: undated.

63   Everitt: 24/2/1945: unpaginated.

64   Everitt: 24/2/1945: unpaginated.

65   Everitt: 24/2/1945: unpaginated.

66   Casualty Section (14/5/1945) Telegram to the Parents of D. H. Lawrence.

67   Aldus: undated: unpaginated.

68   Sanderson, T. (16/8/1947) Correspondence with the Wife of Mannell.

69   Parsons: 15/5/1945: unpaginated.

70   Everitt: 24/2/1945: unpaginated.

71   Everitt: 24/2/1945: unpaginated.

72   Air Ministry Casualty Branch (3/7/1945) Correspondence, in, Maden, J. (2015) A History of RAF North Creake: Aircraft and Aircrew Losses: 171 Squadron and 199 Squadron, unpaginated.

73   Air Ministry Casualty Branch (24/7/1945) Correspondence, in Maden: 2015: unpaginated.

74   Air Ministry Casualty Branch: 24/7/1945: unpaginated.

75   Cloves, L. D. O. (17/5/1946) Casualty Investigation Report.

76   Cloves: 17/5/1946.

77   Maden: 2015: unpaginated.

78   Thornley, H. E. (11/4/2011) Correspondence with Tom Lewis.

79   Maden: 2015: unpaginated.

80   Maden: 2015: unpaginated.

81   Royal Canadian Air Force (2/11/1942) Charles Mison: Attestation Paper, RCAF, unpaginated.

82   Royal Canadian Air Force (23/4/1942) Charles Mison: RCAF Medical Board, RCAF, unpaginated.

83   RCAF: 2/11/1942: unpaginated.

84 Seddon, R. D. (2/11/1942) Charles Mison Attestation Paper, RCAF, unpaginated, Library and Archive Canada.

85 Royal Canadian Air Force (20/8/1943a) Charles Mison: Training Report: Wireless Operator (Air Gunner) and Air Gunner: Form 5035 unpaginated.

86 Cracknell, D. A. (20/1/1944) Charles Mison: Training Report: Air Gunner, unpaginated.

87 Royal Air Force (26/3/1944) Charles Mison: Training Report: Rear, Mid-Upper Gunner, No. 1651 Conversion Unit, unpaginated.

88 Dicks, W. A. (4/1/1947) Correspondence to Laura Mison from the Office of the Chief of Air Staff.

89 Dunham, H. S. (27/6/1945) Hospital or Sick Record Card: Form 39, unpaginated.

90 Aldus: undated: unpaginated.

91 Mauldon, F. R. C. (22/1/1947) Casualty Enquiry Investigation Report, MRES, unpaginated.

92 Mauldon: 22/1/1947: unpaginated.

93 Mauldon: 22/1/1947: unpaginated.

94 Mauldon: 22/1/1947: unpaginated.

95 McDougall, T. K. (6/12/1945) Memorandum, Minute 1, RCAF Casualties Section.

96 Mauldon: 22/1/1947: unpaginated.

97 McDougall: 6/12/1945.

98 Mauldon: 22/1/1947: unpaginated.

99 Mauldon: 22/1/1947: unpaginated.

100 Casualty Officer (18/10/1945) Correspondence with James Brown, Library and Archive Canada.

101 Casualty Officer: 18/10/1945.

102 Mauldon: 22/1/1947: unpaginated.

103 Mauldon: 22/1/1947: unpaginated.

104 International Bomber Command Centre (undated).

105 Mauldon: 22/1/1947: unpaginated.

106 Gunn, W. R. (24/9/1948) Correspondence to James Brown from the Casualty Section.

107 Maufe, T. (24/9/2023) telephone conversation with the author.

108 Maufe: 24/9/2023.

109 Maufe: 15/8/2023.

110 Maufe: 24/9/2023.

111 Forde, J. (17/8/2023) in correspondence with the author.

112 Maufe: 24/9/2023.

113 Maufe: 24/9/2023.

114 Maufe: 24/9/2023.

115 Forde: 15/8/2023.

116 Archives New Zealand (undated) Royal New Zealand Air Force Biographies of Deceased Personnel 1939-1945.

117 Hillier, M. (3/4/2024) in correspondence with the author.

118 Hillier, M. (11/3/2024) in correspondence with the author.

119 Hillier: 3/4/2024.

120 Hope, B. (2014) And in the Morning: RAF Station North Creake, pp. 31-34.

121 Department of National Defence (Canada) (30/3/1946) Robert Brown: Statement of War Service Gratuities.

122 Royal Canadian Air Force (14/10/1942) Robert Brown: Attestation Paper, unpaginated.

123 Royal Canadian Air Force (14/5/1943) Robert Brown: Report on Pupil Pilot: Flying & Training, unpaginated.

124 RCAF: 14/5/1943: unpaginated.

125 Royal Air Force (28/8/1944) Robert Brown: Training Report: Air Bomber, unpaginated.

126 Royal Canadian Air Force (30/12/1944) Robert Brown: Record of Service: Form R230, unpaginated.

127 Noel, N. I. (24/7/1945) Statement Regarding Sale of Morris 8.

128 Pennington, A. C. (20/6/1945) Correspondence Regarding Sale of Morris 8.

129 Draper, G. C. (4/7/1945) Correspondence Regarding Sale of Morris 8.

130 Overseas HQ (7/5/1946) Correspondence with Director of Estates.

131 Bomber Command Head Quarters (18/4/1946) Correspondence with the RAF Central Depository.

Chapter Nine

1 Rees, J. (undated) in Bartram, L. (1998) RAF North Creake, Egmere, 1940-1947: A Brief History, p. 15.

2 Willmott, P. (1988) Coming of Age in Wartime, p. 119.

3 Willmott: 1988: 112.

4 Willmott, P. (1945) Correspondence, WLMT 02001001(20).

5 Ford, K. S. (1992) Snaith Days: Life With 51 Squadron 1942/45, p. 11.

6 Ford: 1992: 11.

7 Baldwin, A. W. (1967) A Flying Start, p. 45.

8 Beardsell, J. (20/3/23) in correspondence with the author.

9 Sinclair, J. (1987) Where's the Old Airfield? – You're Standing on it, unpaginated.

10 Feasey, J. (undated) in Bartram: 1998: 19.

11 Ford: 1992: 4.

12 Sinclair: 1987: unpaginated.

13 Willmott, P. (1944) Correspondence, WLMT 02001002(16).

14 Ford: 1992: 15-16.

15 RAF North Creake (undated) Mentioned in Despatches, p. 2.
16 Baldwin: 1967: 18.
17 Graham, D. (16/4/2019) in conversation with the author.
18 Starett, A. (1985) in, Hall, A. (1985) We Also, Were There, p. 156.
19 RAF North Creake: undated: 2.
20 Berrill, R. (October 2022) written response to pre-interview paper, p. 12.
21 Lines, P. (23/4/2023) in conversation with the author.
22 Renaut, M. (1982) Terror by Night, p. 147.
23 Renaut: 1982: 147.
24 Renaut: 1982: 149-150.
25 Renaut: 1982: 170.
26 Miller, H. (1971) Service to the Services: The Story of Naafi, p. 29.
27 Miller: 1971: 46.
28 Berry, P. (2018a) A NAAFI Girl at RAF North Creake: Jean Kershaw, unpaginated.
29 Leach, D. (16/11/17) Interview with author.
30 Leach: 16/11/17.
31 Spear, S. (undated) Interview with Imperial War Museum.
32 Willmott: 1988: 120-121.
33 Willmott: 1988: 120.
34 Bray, N. A. N. (4/1/1945) Station Routine Orders, unpaginated.
35 Bray: 4/1/1945: unpaginated.
36 Gill, D. (2015) My Civilian and RAF Wartime Experiences, unpaginated.
37 Brettingham, L. (2002) Even When the Sparrows are Walking: The Origin and Effect of No. 100 (Bomber Support) Group, RAF, 1943-45, p. 153.
38 Hinxman, R. (undated) Recollections of a Radar Mechanic, unpaginated.
39 Hinxman: undated: unpaginated.
40 Ford: 1992: 7.
41 Taylor, L. (undated) Ground Gen for Airmen, p. 22.
42 Bray: 4/1/1945: unpaginated.
43 Bray: 4/1/1945: unpaginated.
44 Hawton, H. (1944) The Men Who Fly, p. 149.
45 Godfrey, G. (1985) in, Hall: 1985: 133.
46 Barrett V. (1985) in, Hall: 1985: 120.
47 Willmott: 1988: 124-125
48 Willmott: 1988: 125.
49 Ford: 1992: 7-11.
50 Ford: 1992: 7.
51 Taylor: undated: 13-14.
52 Ford: 1992: 11.
53 Bayley, D. (1985) in, Hall: 1985: 137.
54 How, B. (8/3/2017) interview with the author
55 Rees: undated: 15.
56 Rees: undated: 15.
57 Rees: undated: 15.
58 Willmott: 1988: 121-122.
59 Willmott: 1988: 147-148.
60 Hartlepool Mail (12/2/1945) Airman's Funeral.
61 RAF North Creake (February 1945) Operations Record Book, unpaginated.
62 RAF North Creake: February 1945: ORB: unpaginated.
63 Rees: undated: 15.
64 Berry, P. (1989) Airfield Heyday: Daily Life on and Around Wartime Airfields, p. 86.
65 American Air Museum (undated) americanairmuseum.com.
66 American Air Museum (undated(a)) americanairmuseum.com.
67 American Air Museum: undated(a).
68 American Air Museum: undated.
69 American Air Museum: undated.
70 American Air Museum: undated.
71 355st Bomb Group (undated) 351st.org.
72 RAF North Creake: July 1944: ORB: unpaginated.
73 Rees: undated: 14.
74 Reid, J. (2014) Let Tyrants Tremble: The War Diary of 199 (Bomber Support) Squadron, November 1942 – July 1945, p. 125.
75 Reid: 2014: 125.
76 355st Bomb Group (undated) 351st.org.
77 Berrill, R. (27/6/2021) interview with author.
78 Polichek, V. (3/2/1998) Correspondence.
79 Berrill, R. (25/3/2023) interview with the author.
80 Berrill: 27/6/2021.
81 Reid: 2014: 115-116.
82 RAF North Creake: January 1945: ORB: unpaginated.
83 RAF North Creake: January 1945: ORB: unpaginated.
84 RAF North Creake: January 1945: ORB: unpaginated.
85 RAF North Creake: June 1944: ORB: unpaginated.
86 RAF North Creake: June 1944: ORB: unpaginated.
87 RAF North Creake: January 1945: ORB: unpaginated.
88 RAF North Creake: January 1945: ORB: unpaginated.
89 RAF 100 Group (March 1945) Operations Record Book Appendices, unpaginated.
90 Berrill: 25/3/2023.
91 Berrill: 25/3/2023.
92 RAF North Creake: December 1944: ORB: unpaginated.

93 RAF North Creake: June 1944: ORB: unpaginated.

94 RAF North Creake: August 1944: ORB: unpaginated.

95 RAF 100 Group (April 1945) Operations Record Book, unpaginated.

96 Hastings, M. (1980) Bomber Command, p. 215.

97 Thompson K (1945) War Diary.

98 Brettingham: 2002: 151-152.

99 Brettingham: 2002: 152.

100 Brettingham: 2002: 152.

101 Brettingham: 2002: 150.

102 Air Council (undated) Flying Control in the Royal Air Force, publication 3024, p. 106.

103 RAF North Creake (April 1945) Operations Record Book, Items of Medical Interest, unpaginated.

104 Feasey, J. (11/4/1985) Correspondence with Maurice Hood.

105 Morgan, M. (undated) Recollections of an MT Driver, unpaginated.

106 Brettingham: 2002: 152.

107 Brettingham: 2002: 152.

108 Brettingham: 2002: 152.

109 Morgan: undated: unpaginated.

110 Hope, B. (2014) And in the Morning: RAF Station North Creake, p. 37.

111 RAF North Creake: April 1945: ORB, unpaginated.

112 Brettingham: 2002: 152.

113 Renaut: 1982: 160.

114 Brettingham: 2002: 153.

115 Brettingham: 2002: 153.

116 Brettingham: 2002: 152.

117 Renaut: 1982: 160.

118 Editor (July 1990) Guinea Pig Club, p. 2.

119 Rees: undated: 13.

120 Tripp, M. (1952) Faith is a Windsock, p. 21.

121 Tripp: 1952: 21.

122 Tripp: 1952: 21.

123 Reid: 2014: 133.

124 Reid: 2014: 133.

125 Baldwin: 1967: 45.

126 Baldwin: 1967: 107.

127 Skan, L. E. (1990) Half a Penguin: Reminiscences of a Bomber Command Flying Control Officer, p. 7.

128 Allison, J. (1966) Bomber Crew, p. 15.

129 Allison: 1966: 14.

130 Allison: 1966: 14.

131 Ford: 1992: 4.

132 Brettingham: 2002: 153.

133 Kavanagh, D. (16/11/2016) Interview with Bernie How.

134 How: 8/3/2017.

135 RAF 171 Squadron: 1944-1945: ORBA: unpaginated

136 How: 8/3/2017.

137 Dennison, G. J. (3/6/1944) 'Letter to Parents', cited in: Dennison, G. (2007) Memories Are Treasures: The Military career of Pilot Officer Gordon Joshua Dennison, p. 107.

138 Caribbean Aircrew (undated) caribbeanaircrew-ww2.com.

139 Thomas, N. (1985) in Hall, A. (1985) We Also, Were There, p. 166.

140 Thomas: 1985: 165.

141 Hastings: 1980: 215.

142 Hastings: 1980: 215.

143 RAF Museum (undated) rafmuseum.org.uk.

144 Thomas: 1985: 166.

145 Thomas: 1985: 166.

146 Wood, I. S. (2002) Ireland During the Second World War, pp. 81-82.

147 Doherty, R. (1999) Irish Men and Women in the Second World War, p. 22.

148 Doherty: 1999: 22.

149 Wood: 2002: 135.

150 Doherty: 1999: 22.

151 Hope: 2014: 33.

152 Wood: 2002: 100.

153 Freeguard, H. (9/8/2018) in conversation with the author.

154 Dennison, G. J. (26/2/1944) 'Letter to Parents', cited in: Dennison: 2007: 94.

155 Dennison, G. J. (7/2/1943) 'Letter to Parents', cited in: Dennison: 2007: 93.

156 Dennison: 26/2/1944: 94-95.

157 Dennison, G. J. (23/4/1944) 'Letter to Parents', cited in: Dennison: 2007: 101.

158 Dennison, G. J. (28/4/1944) 'Letter to Parents', cited in: Dennison: 2007: 103.

159 RAF North Creake: July 1944: ORB: unpaginated.

160 Willmott: 1988: 139

161 Thompson: 1945.

162 Polichek: 3/2/1998.

163 Maden, R. (3/1/1945) 'Last letter Home', in Maden, J. (2015) A History of RAF North Creake: Aircraft and Aircrew Losses: 171 Squadron and 199 Squadron, unpaginated.

164 Willmott: 1988: 138.

165 Dennison, G. J. (2/3/1944) 'Letter to Parents', cited in: Dennison: 2007: 95.

166 Dennison: 22/3/1944: 97.

167 Thompson: 1945

168 Thompson: 1945

169 Thompson: 1945

170 Thompson: 1945

171 Thompson: 1945

172 Willmott, P. (1944) Correspondence,
     WLMT 02001001(3) & WLMT
     02001002(4).
173 Willmott: 1988: 123.
174 Spear (undated).
175 Holmes, L. (2012) My Wartime Story by
     Joan Calvert/Foley/Hollis, p. 8.
176 Holmes: 2012: 8.
177 Maden: 3/1/1945: unpaginated.
178 Dennison, G. J. (14/8/1944) 'Letter to
     Winnie, Earl & David (Siblings), cited in:
     Dennison: 2007: 129.
179 Morgan: undated: unpaginated.
180 Bartram: 1998: 5.
181 Drew, P. (September 2013) in conversation
     with the author.
182 Berrill: 27/6/2021.
183 Renaut: 1982: 151.
184 Renaut: 1982: 151.
185 Renaut: 1982: 151.
186 Thompson: 1945
187 Hawton: 1944: 147.
188 Hammerton, J. (1943) ABC of the RAF:
     Handbook for All Branches of the Air Force,
     p. 13.
189 Berry: 1989: 86.
190 King, R. (2021) Family History – Dad:
     Leslie Henry John King (1921-2002),
     unpaginated.
191 King: 2021: unpaginated.
192 King: 2021: unpaginated.
193 RAF North Creake: July 1944: ORB:
     unpaginated.
194 RAF North Creake: June 1944: ORB:
     unpaginated.
195 RAF North Creake (Christmas 1944)
     Programme of Entertainment, Sports and
     other Festivities for Christmas and the New
     Year, p. 4.
196 RAF North Creake: November 1944: ORB:
     unpaginated.
197 Bridges, E. M. & Baldwin, J. (Eds) (2005)
     A Conflict & Memories: Fakenham
     Remembers World War Two, p. 20.
198 Aldgate, A. & Richards, J. (1986) Britain
     Can Take It: The British Cinema in the
     Second World War, p. 3.
199 Thompson: 1945
200 Thompson: 1945
201 RAF North Creake: December 1944: ORB:
     unpaginated.
202 RAF North Creake: July 1944: ORB:
     unpaginated.
203 RAF North Creake: November 1944: ORB:
     unpaginated.
204 RAF North Creake: August 1944: ORB:
     unpaginated.
205 Polichek: 3/2/1998.

206 RAF North Creake: 1944-1945: ORB:
     unpaginated.
207 RAF North Creake: June 1944: ORB:
     unpaginated.
208 RAF North Creake: 1944-1945: ORB:
     unpaginated.
209 Berry: 1989: 84.
210 Berry: 1989: 86.
211 RAF North Creake: 1944-1945: ORB:
     unpaginated.
212 RAF North Creake: September 1944: ORB:
     unpaginated.
213 RAF North Creake: September 1944: ORB:
     unpaginated.
214 RAF North Creake: April 1945: ORB:
     unpaginated.
215 RAF North Creake: October 1944: ORB:
     unpaginated.
216 RAF North Creake: August 1944: ORB:
     unpaginated.
217 RAF North Creake: August 1944: ORB:
     unpaginated.
218 RAF North Creake: September 1944: ORB:
     unpaginated.
219 RAF North Creake: November 1944: ORB:
     unpaginated.
220 RAF North Creake: 1944-1945: ORB:
     unpaginated.
221 RAF North Creake: April 1945: ORB:
     unpaginated.
222 Bray: 4/1/1945: unpaginated.
223 RAF North Creake: July 1944: ORB:
     unpaginated.
224 Ford: 1992: 16.
225 RAF North Creake: 1944: ORB:
     unpaginated.
226 RAF North Creake: July 1944: ORB:
     unpaginated.
227 RAF North Creake: 1944-945: ORB:
     unpaginated.
228 RAF North Creake: September 1944: ORB:
     unpaginated.
229 How: 8/3/2017.
230 RAF North Creake: September 1944: ORB:
     unpaginated.
231 How: 8/3/2017.
232 RAF North Creake: 1944-1945: ORB:
     unpaginated.
233 RAF North Creake: July 1944: ORB:
     unpaginated.
234 RAF North Creake: 1944-1945: ORB:
     unpaginated.
235 RAF North Creake: September 1944: ORB:
     unpaginated.
236 RAF North Creake: 1944-1945: ORB:
     unpaginated.
237 RAF North Creake: July 1944: ORB:
     unpaginated.

238 RAF North Creake: July 1944: ORB: unpaginated.

239 Willmott, P. (1944) Correspondence, WLMT 02001001(6), WLMT 02001001(7) & WLMT 02001001(8).

240 Bartram: 1998: 5.

241 Rees: undated: 14.

242 RAF North Creake: April 1945: ORB: unpaginated.

243 Rees: undated: 14.

244 Rees: undated: 14.

245 RAF 100 Group: April 1945: ORB: unpaginated.

246 Rees: undated: 14.

247 RAF North Creake: Christmas 1944: 2.

248 RAF North Creake: Christmas 1944: 4.

249 RAF 171 Squadron (December 1944) Operations Record Book, unpaginated.

250 RAF North Creake: Christmas 1944: 4.

251 RAF North Creake: December 1944: ORB: unpaginated.

252 RAF North Creake: Christmas 1944: 4.

253 Bray, N. A. N. (Christmas 1944) Confidential Message from the Station Commander, unpaginated.

254 RAF North Creake: Christmas 1944: 5.

255 RAF 171 Squadron: December 1944: ORB: unpaginated.

256 RAF North Creake: Christmas 1944: 5.

257 RAF North Creake: Christmas 1944: 3.

258 RAF North Creake: Christmas 1944: 3.

259 RAF 171 Squadron: December 1944: ORB: unpaginated.

260 RAF North Creake: Christmas 1944: 5.

261 RAF North Creake: December 1944: ORB: unpaginated.

262 RAF North Creake: Christmas 1944: 6.

263 Willmott: 1988: 126.

264 Spear (undated).

265 RAF North Creake: Christmas 1944: 6.

266 RAF North Creake: December 1944: ORB: unpaginated.

267 RAF North Creake: Christmas 1944: 7.

268 RAF North Creake: Christmas 1944: 7.

269 RAF North Creake: Christmas 1944: 7.

270 RAF North Creake: Christmas 1944: 8.

271 RAF North Creake: December 1944: ORB: unpaginated.

272 Maden: 3/1/1945: unpaginated.

273 Hope: 2014: 33.

274 RAF North Creake: December 1944: ORB: unpaginated.

275 How: 8/3/2017.

276 Thompson: 1945

277 Thompson: 1945

278 King, L. (undated) History of Service in RAF, p. 5.

279 King: undated: 5.

280 Willmott: 1988: 118.

281 Polichek: 3/2/1998.

282 Dennison, G. J. (19/8/1944) 'Letter to Parents', cited in: Dennison: 2007: 115.

283 Dennison, G. J. (21/4/1944) 'Letter to Parents', cited in: Dennison: 2007: 101.

284 Freeguard: 9/8/2018.

285 Berrill, R. (July 2021) in correspondence with the author.

286 Willmott: 1988: 118.

287 Reid: 2014: 133.

288 Thompson, P. (2017a) Some Memories of Wilf Thompson's Time in the RAF.

289 Sinclair: 1987: unpaginated.

290 Willmott: 1988: 119.

291 Partridge, J. (4/11/2004) Correspondence with John Reid.

292 Stones, M. (undated) in Reid: 2014: 125.

293 Willmott: 1988: 121

294 Stones: undated: 125.

295 Sinclair: 1987: unpaginated.

296 Reid: 2014: 133.

297 Willmott: 1988: 134.

298 Willmott: 1988: 128.

299 Hartley, K. (undated) Recollections of a Radar Mechanic, unpaginated.

300 Brettingham: 2002: 153.

301 Rees: undated: 15.

302 Renaut, Y. (2015) taped interview.

303 Thompson: 2017a: unpaginated.

304 Rees: undated: 15.

305 Rees: undated: 15.

306 Kavanagh: 16/11/2016.

307 Bridges & Baldwin: 2005: 17.

308 Delphine Hall, (undated) in Walsingham History Society (2001) The Walsingham Millennium Book: Interviews and Recollections, unpaginated.

309 Bridges & Baldwin: 2005: 17.

310 How: 8/3/2017.

311 Varley, M. (2013) Correspondence Jeanne Endersby.

312 How: 8/3/2017.

313 Brettingham: 2002: 149.

314 Fakenham Men's Probus Club (13/2/2023).

315 Nicholas, C. (undated) Notes on a Life in the RAF, unpaginated.

316 Berrill: 27/6/2021.

317 Ellin, D. (23/2/2022) Interview with Roy Berrill.

318 Berrill, R. (23/11/2021) interview with the author.

319 Hastings: 1980: 156.

320 How: 8/3/2017.

321 Costello, J. (1985) Love Sex & War: Changing Values 1939-45, p. 10.

322   Costello: 1985: 17.

323   Willmott: 1988: 127.

324   Willmott, P. (1944) Correspondence, WLMT 02001002(16).

325   Willmott, P. (1944) Correspondence, WLMT 02001001(22).

326   Willmott: 1988: 124.

327   Willmott: 1988: 125.

328   Longmate, N. (1983) The Bombers: The RAF Offensive Against Germany 1939-1945, 189.

329   Berry: 2018a: unpaginated.

330   Longmate: 1983: 189.

331   Longmate: 1983: 189.

332   Reid: 2014: 135.

333   Longmate: 1983: 189.

334   Willmott: 1988: 126.

335   Willmott: 1988: 127.

336   RAF 171 Squadron: 13/2/1945: ORBA: 266.

337   RAF 171 Squadron: 13/2/1945: ORBA: 266.

338   Willmott, P. (1945) Correspondence, WLMT 02001001(26) & WLMT 02001001(27).

339   Bray: 4/1/1945: unpaginated.

340   Hartley: undated: unpaginated.

341   Polichek: 3/2/1998.

342   Polichek: 3/2/1998.

343   Brettingham: 2002: 153.

344   Willmott, P. (1944) Correspondence, WLMT 02001002(6) & WLMT 02001002(7).

345   Hartley: undated: unpaginated.

346   How: 8/3/2017.

347   Willmott: 1988: 112.

348   Willmott: 1988: 137-138.

349   Berrill: 25/3/2023.

350   Ellin: 23/2/2022.

351   Berrill: 25/3/2023.

352   Willmott: 1988: 138.

353   Willmott, P. (1944) Correspondence, WLMT 02001002(15)

354   Berrill, R. (25/3/2023) interview by author.

355   Berrill, R. (27/6/2021) interview with author.

356   Willmott: 1988: 138.

357   Willmott: 1988: 138.

358   How: 8/3/2017.

Dove Over Europe

1   Thompson K (1945) War Diary.

2   Webley, N. (ed) (2002) Betty's War Diary: 1939-1945, 230.

3   Middlebrook, M. & Everitt, C. (1985) The Bomber Command War Diaries: An Operational Reference Book, 1939-1945, p. 702.

4   Rees, W. J. (2003) The Final Fling, p. VIII.

5   Rees: 2003: VIII.

6   Bradley, C. (1994) Kiel Revisited, unpaginated.

7   Middlebrook & Everitt: 1985: 702.

8   Rees: 2003: 93.

9   Middlebrook & Everitt: 1985: 702.

10   Reid, J. (2014) Let Tyrants Tremble: The War Diary of 199 (Bomber Support) Squadron, November 1942 – July 1945, p. 183.

11   Rees: 2003: 8.

12   Brettingham, L. (2002) Even When the Sparrows are Walking: The Origin and Effect of No. 100 (Bomber Support) Group, RAF, 1943-45, p. 140.

13   RAF North Creake (March 1945) Operations Record Book, unpaginated.

14   Reid: 2014: 183.

15   Brettingham: 2002: 140.

16   Rees: 2003: 8.

17   Rees: 2003: 55.

18   Brettingham: 2002: 140.

19   Stubbington, J. (undated) 171 Squadron: From the National Archives, p. 26.

20   Feasey, J. (undated) in Bartram, L. (1998) RAF North Creake, Egmere, 1940-1947: A Brief History, p. 19.

21   Renaut, M. (1982) Terror by Night, p. 164.

22   Rees: 2003: 55.

23   Reid: 2014: 183.

24   RAF 171 Squadron (May 1945) Operations Record Book, unpaginated & RAF 199 Squadron (May 1945) Operations Record Book, unpaginated.

25   Rees: 2003: 38-39.

26   Rees: 2003: 59.

27   Rees: 2003: 61.

28   Middlebrook & Everitt: 1985: 702.

29   Rees: 2003: 93.

30   Currell, L. (undated) To Whom it May Concern: Memoire of Escape, unpaginated.

31   Brettingham: 2002: 140.

32   Renaut: 1982: 164-165.

33   International Bomber Command (undated(a)) internationalbcc.co.uk.

34   Croft, P. (Spring 2017)'Kenneth Norman Joseph Croft', in Confound & Destroy, RAF 100 Group Association, p. 20.

35   Freegard, H. (9/8/2018) in conversation with the author.

36   Freegard: 9/8/2018.

37   Rees: 2003: 95.

38   Rees: 2003: 95.

39   Chorley, W. R. (2008) Royal Air Force: Bomber Command Losses of the Second World War: Volume 6, 1945, p. 172.

40   Middlebrook & Everitt: 1985: 702-703.

41   Bowman, M. (2006) 100 Group (Bomber Support) RAF Bomber Command in World War II, pp. 81-82.

42   Currell: undated: unpaginated.

43   Croft, P. (29/11/2020) Correspondence.

44   Bradley: 1994: unpaginated.

45   Bradley: 1994: unpaginated.

46   Crane, K. N. (17/9/1945) MI9 Interrogation Report Reid, unpaginated.

47   Reid: 2014: 185.

48   International Bomber Command: undated.

49   Reid: 2014: 185.

50   Crane: 17/9/1945: unpaginated.

51   Currell: undated: unpaginated.

52   Currell: undated: unpaginated.

53   Currell: undated: unpaginated.

54   Currell: undated: unpaginated.

55   Currell: undated: unpaginated.

56   Middlebrook & Everitt: 1985: 702.

57   Middlebrook & Everitt: 1985: 702.

58   Middlebrook & Everitt: 1985: 702.

59   Middlebrook & Everitt: 1985: 702.

60   Middlebrook & Everitt: 1985: 702.

61   Bradley: 1994: unpaginated.

62   Bradley: 1994: unpaginated.

63   Bradley: 1994: unpaginated.

64   Air Ministry (19/12/1947) 'Correspondence', in, Bradley: 1994: unpaginated.

65   Bradley: 1994: unpaginated.

66   Bradley, C. (31/7/1945) Correspondence the brother of A. Bradley with Les Currell.

67   Mackay, F. (July 1945) Correspondence from Mother of W. H. V. Mackay with Les Currell.

68   Mackay: July 1945.

69   Hope, B. (2014) And in the Morning: RAF Station North Creake, p. 33.

70   Harrington, J. (2016) RAF 100 Group: The Birth of Electronic Warfare, p. 153.

71   Bradley: 1994: unpaginated.

72   Hope: 2014: 31-34.

73   Currell, P. (31/8/2006) Correspondence.

74   Currell P. (undated) Biography of Les Currell, unpaginated.

75   Gratte, S. (6/9/2006) Correspondence.

76   Gratte: 6/9/2006.

77   Currell: 31/8/2006.

78   Currell: 31/8/2006.

79   Currell: 31/8/2006.

80   Chorley: 2008: 172.

81   Croft: Spring 2017: 21.

82   Croft: Spring 2017: 20.

83   Croft: 29/11/2020.

84   Rees: 2003: 93.

85   Middlebrook & Everitt: 1985: 702.

86   Rees: 2003: 93.

87   Middlebrook & Everitt: 1985: 702.

88   Rees: 2003: 39.

89   Wood, C. (2000) Interview with Arthur Gordon Clarke.

90   RAF 199 Squadron: May 1945: ORB: unpaginated.

91   RAF 171 Squadron: May 1945: ORB: unpaginated.

92   Reid: 2014: 185.

93   RAF North Creake: May 1945: ORB: unpaginated.

94   Wood: 2000.

Chapter Ten

1   Stubbington, J. (undated) 171 Squadron: From the National Archives, p. 26.

2   Stubbington: undated: 26.

3   Adcock, A. (2004) Interview.

4   Gill, D. (2015) My Civilian and RAF Wartime Experiences, unpaginated.

5   Kavanagh, D. (2016) Interview with Denis James Gill.

6   Gill: 2015: unpaginated.

7   RAF 171 Squadron (5/2/1945) Casualty List: Appendix to RAF Squadron 171 Operations Record Book, p. 449.

8   Gray, H. (undated) cited in Reid, J. (2014) Let Tyrants Tremble: The War Diary of 199 (Bomber Support) Squadron, November 1942 – July 1945, p. 186.

9   National Archives (undated) nationalarchives.gov.uk.

10   RAF 171 Squadron (May 1945) Operations Record Book, unpaginated.

11   RAF North Creake (May 1945) Operations Record Book, unpaginated.

12   RAF North Creake: May 1945: ORB: unpaginated. unpaginated.

13   Berry, P. (1989) Airfield Heyday: Daily Life on and Around Wartime Airfields, pp. 88-89.

14   RAF 171 Squadron: May 1945: ORB: unpaginated.

15   Reid, J. (2014) Let Tyrants Tremble: The War Diary of 199 (Bomber Support) Squadron, November 1942 – July 1945, p. 189.

16   RAF 171 Squadron: May 1945: ORB: unpaginated.

17   Berrill, R. (27/6/2021) interview with author.

18   Reid: 2014: 186.

19   Thompson K (1945) War Diary.

20   RAF 171 Squadron: May 1945: ORB: unpaginated.

21 RAF North Creake: May 1945: ORB: unpaginated.

22 Reid: 2014: 189.

23 King, L. (undated) History of Service in RAF, p. 5.

24 RAF North Creake: May 1945: ORB: unpaginated.

25 RAF 171 Squadron: May 1945: ORB: unpaginated.

26 RAF 171 Squadron: May 1945: ORB: unpaginated.

27 Adcock: 2004.

28 Willmott, P. (1945) Correspondence, WLMT 02001002(29).

29 RAF 100 Group (October 1944) Operations p. 1.

30 Streetly, M. (1978) Confound & Destroy: 100 Group and the Bomber Support Campaign, p. 148.

31 Cockburn, R. (1945) The Radio War, p. 56.

32 Cockburn: 1945: 10.

33 Bowman M. & Cushing, T. (1996) Confounding the Reich: The Operational History of 100 Group (Bomber Support) RAF, p. 91.

34 Addison, E. (1945) No. 80 Wing, Royal Air Force: Historical Report, 1940-1945, p. 89.

35 Redding, T. (2005) Flying for Freedom: Life and Death in Bomber Command, p. 276.

36 Price, A. (1967) Instrument of Darkness: The Struggle for Radar Supremacy, p. 243.

37 Brettingham, L. (2002) Even When the Sparrows are Walking: The Origin and Effect of No. 100 (Bomber Support) Group, RAF, 1943-45, p. 309.

38 Streetly: 1978: 113.

39 Streetly: 1978: 117.

40 Streetly: 1978: 113.

41 Price: 1967: 240.

42 Streetly: 1978: 122.

43 RAF North Creake: June & July: ORB: unpaginated.

44 RAF 171 Squadron (June 1945) Operations Record Book, unpaginated.

45 Thompson: 1945.

46 RAF 199 Squadron (July 1945) Operations Record Book, unpaginated.

47 RAF 171 Squadron (July 1945) Operations Record Book, unpaginated & RAF 199 Squadron: July 1945: ORB: unpaginated.

48 RAF 171 Squadron (July 1945) Operations Record Book, unpaginated.

49 Streetly: 1978: 143.

50 Streetly: 1978: 143.

51 Streetly: 1978: 135.

52 Streetly: 1978: 135.

53 Streetly: 1978: 135.

54 Streetly: 1978: 20.

55 Streetly: 1978: 83.

56 Streetly: 1978: 135.

57 Price: 1967: 241.

58 Price: 1967: 241.

59 Streetly: 1978: 138.

60 Streetly: 1978: 135-138.

61 Streetly: 1978: 83.

62 Harris, A. (1995) Despatch on War Operations: 23rd February, 1942 to 8th May, 1945, p. 142.

63 Streetly: 1978: 143.

64 Streetly: 1978: 143.

65 Galland, A. cited in Pedan, M. (1979) A Thousand Shall Fall, p. 409.

66 Streetly: 1978: 143.

67 Price: 1967: 130.

68 Price: 1967: 130.

69 Bomber Command (1945) The Scapegoats – Bomber Command's Feint Forces, p. 3.

70 Streetly: 1978: 7.

71 RAF 199 Squadron: July 1945: ORB: unpaginated.

72 RAF 199 Squadron: July 1945: ORB: unpaginated.

73 King: undated: 5.

74 RAF 199 Squadron: July 1945: ORB: unpaginated.

75 RAF 199 Squadron: July 1945: ORB: unpaginated.

76 RAF 171 Squadron: July 1945: ORB: unpaginated.

77 Renaut, M. (1982) Terror by Night, p. 155.

78 Reid: 2014: 189.

79 RAF North Creake: August 1945: ORB: unpaginated.

80 Reid: 2014: 189.

81 Renaut: 1982: 155.

82 Addison, E. B. (28/7/1945) 'Message from the Air Officer Commanding', in RAF North Creake (3/8/1945) Programme of Proceedings on the Occasion of the Disbandment of the 171 and 199 Squadrons Bomber Command, unpaginated.

83 RAF North Creake: August 1945: ORB: unpaginated.

84 Berrill: 27/6/2021.

85 RAF North Creake: August 1945: ORB: unpaginated.

86 Parker, D. (6/9/2021) in correspondence with the author.

87 Berrill, R. (July 2021) in correspondence with the author.

88 RAF North Creake: October 1945: ORB: unpaginated.

89 RAF North Creake: October 1945: ORB: unpaginated.

90 Thompson: 1945.

91 RAF North Creake: August 1945: ORB: unpaginated.

92 RAF 171 Squadron: July 1945: ORB: unpaginated.

93 Wilson, A. T. M. (1946) 'The Serviceman Comes Home' in Madge, C. (1946) Pilot Papers: Social Essays and Documents, p.14.

94 Gill: 2015: unpaginated

95 Gill: 2015: unpaginated

96 Bourke, J. (2001) The Second World War: A People's History, p. 168.

97 Hastings, M. (1980) Bomber Command, p. 352.

98 Hillier, M. (2014) Suitcases, Vultures and Spies, p. 9.

99 Mumford, L (1946) Programme for Survival, pp. 15-16.

100 Whiting, C. (1987) The Three Star Blitz: The Baedeker Raids and the Start of Total War 1942-1943, p. 4.

101 Smith, L. (2009) Voices Against War: A Century of Protest, Mainstream Publishing, p. 296.

102 Whiting: 1987: 4.

103 Morrison, H. (1961) cited in Probert, H. (2001) Bomber Harris: His Life and Times, p. 386.

104 Overy, R. (2013) The Bombing War in Europe 1939-1945, p. 631.

105 Sinclair A. (1942) cited in Hastings: 1980: 178.

106 Whiting: 1987: 166.

107 Bartlett, H. (21/10/2021) Interview with Gordon Mercier.

108 Whiting: 1987: 166.

109 Redding: 2005: X.

110 Longmate, N. (1983) The Bombers: The RAF Offensive Against Germany 1939-1945, p. 374.

111 Collins, L. J. (1966) Faith Under Fire, 69.

112 Stokes, R. (1943) cited in Hastings: 1980: 70-171.

113 Stokes: 1943: 171.

114 Stokes: 1943: 171.

115 Hastings: 1980: 123.

116 Hastings: 1980: 115.

117 Longmate, N. (1971) How We Lived Then: A History of Everyday Life During the Second World War, p. 399.

118 Harris, A. (1947) Bomber Offensive, p. 58.

119 Williams, R. (1979) Politics and Letters, p. 59.

120 Taylor, F. (2005) Dresden: Tuesday 13 February 1945, p. 461.

121 Taylor: 2005: 460.

122 Hastings: 1980: 125.

123 Bourke: 2001: 163-164.

124 Whiting: 1987: 157.

125 MacEwen, M. (1991) The Greening of a Red, p. 137.

126 MacEwen: 1991: 137.

127 Jones, R. V. (1978) Most Secret War: British Scientific Intelligence 1939-1945, p. 303.

128 Fussell, P. (1989) Wartime, Understanding the Behaviour in the Second World War, p. 16.

129 Frankland, N. (1998) History at War, p. 33.

130 Bourke: 2001: 163.

131 Harris: 1947: 52-53.

132 Allison, J. (1966) Bomber Crew, p. 50.

133 Hastings: 1980: 232-233.

134 Galbraith, J. K. Cited in: Fussell: 1989: 16.

135 Hastings: 1980: 350.

136 Speer, A. (1976) Spandau: The Secret Diaries, pp. 339-340.

137 Speer: 1976: 339-340.

138 Hastings: 1980: 241.

139 Jones: 1978: 303.

140 Taylor: 2005: 471-472.

141 Taylor: 2005: 472.

142 Taylor: 2005: 471.

143 Jencks, C (1973) Architecture 2000: Predictions and Methods, p. 23.

144 Jenkins, H. (undated) cited in, Smith, L. (2009) Voices against War: A Century of Protest, p. 100.

145 Soper, R. (undated) cited in, Smith: 2009: 110.

146 Bourke: 2001: 168.

147 Gutherie, C. & Quinlan, M. (2007) Just War: The Just War Tradition; Ethics in Modern Warfare, p. 14.

148 Webster, C. & Frankland, N. (1961) History of the Second World War: The Strategic Air Offensive, Volume I: Preparation, Vol 1, p. 10.

149 Frankland: 1998: 33.

150 Frankland: 1998: 33.

151 Frankland: 1998: 33-34.

152 Hastings: 1980: 123-124.

153 Hastings: 1980: 123.

154 Sebald, W. G. (2003) cited in, Taylor: 2005: 461.

155 Tripp, M. (1985) The Eighth Passenger: A Documentary Account of a World War 2 Bomber Crew, p. 139.

156 Hastings: 1980: 173.

157 Hastings: 1980: 125.

158 Hastings: 1980: 42.

159 Shaw, B. (1944) Everybody's Political What's What?, pp. 127-128.

160 Hastings: 1980: 112-114.

161 Hastings: 1980: 112.

162 Tempest, V. (1946) Near the Sun: Impressions of a Medical Officer of Bomber Command, p. 12.

163 Bourke, J. (1999) An Intimate History of Killing: Face to Face Killing in Twentieth-Century Warfare, p. 252.

164 Kavanagh: 2016.
165 Kavanagh: 2016.
166 Tempest: 1946: 51.
167 Tripp: 1985: 77.
168 Sawyer, T. (1981) Only Owls and Bloody Fools Fly at Night, pp. 180-181.
169 Sawyer: 1981: 175.
170 Sawyer: 1981: 175.
171 Tempest: 1946: 8.
172 Tempest: 1946: 37.
173 Tempest: 1946: 38-39.
174 Sawyer: 1981: 168.
175 Tempest: 1946: 38-39.
176 Parnell, G. (undated) Whiting: 1987: 158.
177 Adcock: 2004.
178 Kee, R. (1947) A Crowd Is Not Company, p. 18.
179 Tripp: 1985: 24.
180 Crick, B. (1982) 'introduction' in, Orwell, G. (1986) The Lion and the Unicorn; Socialism and the English Genius, p. 16.
181 Orwell, G. (1941) The Lion and the Unicorn: Socialism and the English Genius, Searchlight Books, p. 9.
182 Whiting: 1987: 62.
183 Taylor: 2005: 461.
184 RAF North Creake: May 1945: ORB: unpaginated.
185 Lines, P. (23/4/2023) in conversation with the author.
186 Freeguard, H. (9/8/2018] in conversation with the author.
187 Polichek, V. (3/2/1998) Correspondence.
188 Thompson: 1945.
189 Reid: 2014: 189.
190 Bevington, P. E. (12/10/1945) Correspondence with his Wife.
191 Cheshire, L. (undated) cited in Whiting: 1987: 167.
192 Toronto Star (2009) cited by Fisk, R. (2009) 'Foreword' in Smith: 2009: 13.
193 Bourke: 1999: 238.
194 Frankland: 1998: 5-6.
195 Hastings: 1980: 12.
196 Bourke: 1999: 238-239.
197 Williams: 1979: 57.
198 Bourke: 1999: 221.
199 Bourke: 1999: 220.
200 Bourke: 1999: 221.
201 Bourke: 1999: 221.
202 Bourke: 1999: 220.
203 Millington, E. (1946) 'Question in House of Commons' cited in Hastings: 1980: 346.
204 Churchill, W. (13/5/1945) 'BBC Radio Victory Broadcast', cited in, Grayling, A. C. (2006) Among the Dead Cities: Was the Allied Bombing of Civilians in WWII A Necessity or a Crime?, p. 176.
205 Bourke: 2001: 164-165.
206 Taylor: 2005: 444.
207 Taylor: 2005: 444.
208 Hastings: 1980: 255.
209 Harris: 1995: IX.
210 Wood, I. S. (2000) British History in Perspective: Churchill, p. 27.
211 Probert: 2001: 362.
212 RAF North Creake: October 1945: ORB: unpaginated.
213 RAF 100 Group (October 1945) Operations Record Book, unpaginated.
214 RAF North Creake: October 1945: ORB: unpaginated.
215 RAF 274 Maintenance Unit (1945-1947) Operations Record Book: RAF Swannington, unpaginated.
216 RAF 274 Maintenance Unit: 1945-1947: ORB: unpaginated.
217 RAF 274 Maintenance Unit: 1945-1947: ORB: unpaginated.
218 Parker: 6/9/2021.
219 Parker: 6/9/2021.
220 Parker: 6/9/2021.
221 RAF 274 Maintenance Unit: 1945-1947: ORB: unpaginated.
222 Parker: 6/9/2021.
223 Tuck, J. (28/7/2016) in conversation with the author.
224 Parker: 6/9/2021.
225 RAF 274 Maintenance Unit: 1945-1947: ORB: unpaginated.
226 RAF 274 Maintenance Unit: 1945-1947: ORB: unpaginated.
227 RAF 274 Maintenance Unit: 1945-1947: ORB: unpaginated.
228 RAF 274 Maintenance Unit: 1945-1947: ORB: unpaginated.
229 RAF 274 Maintenance Unit: 1945-1947: ORB: unpaginated.
230 RAF 274 Maintenance Unit: 1945-1947: ORB: unpaginated.
231 RAF 274 Maintenance Unit: 1945-1947: ORB: unpaginated.
232 RAF 274 Maintenance Unit: 1945-1947: ORB: unpaginated.
233 RAF 274 Maintenance Unit: 1945-1947: ORB: unpaginated.
234 Krusin, S. M. & Thorold Rogers, P. H. (1940) The Solicitors' Handbook of War Legislation, p. 725.
235 Krusin: 1940: 725.
236 Krusin: 1940: 726.
237 Air Ministry (1943) cited in Keesings (1946) Contemporary Archives: Weekly Diary of World Events, Vol. V, p. 6127.
238 Nunn, S. J. (2019) The impact of the Second World War on the Rural Landscape of Norfolk, p. 11.

239   Nunn: 2019: 123.

240   Nunn: 2019: 123.

241   Nunn: 2019: 123.

242   Eastern Daily Press (31/5/1946) Norfolk's 22 Airfields: Permanent Stations Named, p. 1.

243   Air Ministry Works Directorate (9/11/1945) Correspondence with Walsingham Estate Company, unpaginated.

244   Air Ministry Works Directorate (5/12/1945) Correspondence with Walsingham Estate Company, unpaginated.

245   Air Ministry Works Directorate: 9/11/1945: unpaginated.

246   East Anglian Electricity Supply Co. (5/5/1949) Correspondence with Walsingham Estate Company, unpaginated.

247   Walsingham Rural District Council (11/6/1948) Correspondence with S H Waters, Edgar Farm, unpaginated.

248   Walsingham Estate Company (10/11/1948) Correspondence with Walsingham Rural District Council, unpaginated.

249   Air Ministry Works Directorate (20/11/1948) Correspondence with Walsingham Estate Company, unpaginated.

250   Chapman, A. W. (16/12/1948) Correspondence between Ministry of Works and Walsingham Estate Company unpaginated.

251   Walsingham Rural District Council (23/12/1948) Correspondence with Walsingham Estate Company, unpaginated.

252   Walsingham Rural District Council (27/4/1949) Correspondence with Walsingham Estate Company, unpaginated.

253   Walsingham Rural District Council (27/4/1949) Correspondence with Walsingham Estate Company, unpaginated.

254   Walsingham Rural District Council (1/12/1948) Minutes, p. 205.

255   Eastern Daily Press (22/3/1948) Old Sewers at Walsingham, p. 5.

256   Hopkins, H. (11/9/1952) Maintenance of Military Defence Works.

257   Sumsion, E. W. (25/4/1950) Maintenance of Military Defence Works, unpaginated.

258   Hopkins, H. (16/8/1949) Maintenance of Military Defence Works, unpaginated.

259   Hopkins, H. (22/7/1949) Maintenance of Military Defence Works, unpaginated.

260   Hopkins: 16/8/1949: unpaginated.

261   Hopkins: 16/8/1949: unpaginated.

262   Turner, S. (1/5/1950) Maintenance of Military Defence Works, unpaginated.

263   Turner: 1/5/1950: unpaginated.

264   Turner: 1/5/1950: unpaginated.

265   Argent, J. E. (24/7/1950) Maintenance of Military Defence Works, unpaginated.

266   Ministry of Town & Country Planning (26/2/1951) Maintenance of Military Defence Works, unpaginated.

267   Ministry of Town & Country Planning: 26/2/1951: unpaginated.

268   Ministry of Town & Country Planning: 26/2/1951: unpaginated.

269   Krusin: 1940: 706.

270   Krusin: 1940: 723.

271   Turner: 1/5/1950: unpaginated.

272   Walsingham Estate Company (29/9/1949) Correspondence with Ministry of Works, unpaginated.

273   Sumsion, E. W. (5/10/1949) Correspondence between Ministry of Works and Walsingham Estate Company, unpaginated.

274   Waters, S. H. (24/2/1949) Correspondence with Walsingham Estate Company, unpaginated.

275   Waters: 24/2/1949: unpaginated.

276   Waters, S. H. (1/3/1949) Correspondence with Ministry of Works, unpaginated.

277   Waters, S. H. (2/5/1949) Correspondence with Walsingham Estate Company, unpaginated.

278   Walsingham Parish Council (11/1/1950) Minutes, p. 175.

279   Walsingham Estate Company (22/1/1950) Correspondence with S H Waters, Edgar Farm, Walsingham Estate Archive, unpaginated.

280   Jacob, J. C. & Jacob, W. (24/5/1952) Correspondence with Walsingham Estate Company, unpaginated.

281   Jackson-Stops (21/6/1951) Correspondence with Walsingham Estate Company, unpaginated.

282   Jackson-Stops (13/7/1951) Correspondence with Walsingham Estate Company, unpaginated.

283   Maclean, M. (6/11/1951) Correspondence with Walsingham Estate Company, unpaginated.

284   Maclean, M. (30/4/1952) Correspondence with Walsingham Estate Company, unpaginated.

285   Maclean, M. (15/4/1952) Correspondence with Walsingham Estate Company, unpaginated.

286   War Works Commission (7/7/1955) 'Support Document' in Great Walsingham, Norfolk, Closure of Road, unpaginated.

287   War Works Commission: 7/7/1955: unpaginated.

288   War Works Commission: 7/7/1955: unpaginated.

289   War Works Commission: 7/7/1955: unpaginated.

290   War Works Commission: 7/7/1955: unpaginated.

291 War Works Commission: 7/7/1955: unpaginated.

292 War Works Commission: 7/7/1955: unpaginated.

293 War Works Commission: 7/7/1955: unpaginated.

294 War Works Commission: 7/7/1955: unpaginated.

295 War Works Commission: 7/7/1955: unpaginated.

296 War Works Commission: 7/7/1955: unpaginated.

297 Gibson, B. (4/7/1955) 'Letter to War Works Commission' in Great Walsingham, Norfolk, Closure of Road, unpaginated

298 War Works Commission: 7/7/1955: unpaginated.

299 Newcombe, J. A. (5/7/1955) 'Letter to War Works Commission' in Great Walsingham, Norfolk, Closure of Road, unpaginated.

300 Turner, S. (undated) 'Statement of Information' in Great Walsingham, Norfolk, Closure of Road, unpaginated.

301 Turner: undated: unpaginated.

302 Turner: undated: unpaginated.

303 War Works Commission: 7/7/1955: unpaginated.

304 Turner: undated: unpaginated.

305 Valuation Office (6/5/1950) 'Report' in Central Land Board, unpaginated.

306 Hood, M. (undated) 'The Walsingham Mill Site: A Brief History' in, Walsingham History Society (2001) The Walsingham Millennium Book: Interviews and Recollections, unpaginated.

307 Smithies, J. F. (15/6/1949) 'Case Paper' in Crop Drying Project: North Creake, unpaginated.

308 Regional Manager (8/8/1949) 'Valuation Office Regional Report' in Central Land Board, unpaginated.

309 Jewers, D. H. (3/8/1949) 'Statement of Information' in Crop Drying Project: North Creake, unpaginated.

310 Smithies: 15/6/1949: unpaginated.

311 Ward-Walters, L. M. (undated) 'Statement of Information' in Great Walsingham, Norfolk, Closure of Road, unpaginated.

312 Williams, W. H. (4/7/1955) 'Letter to War Works Commission' in Great Walsingham, Norfolk, Closure of Road, unpaginated.

313 War Works Commission: 7/7/1955: unpaginated.

314 Eastern Daily Press (3/9/1948) Poles to Live on Airfield at Great Walsingham, p. 3.

315 Valuation Office: 6/5/1950: unpaginated.

316 Walsingham Parish Council (9/4/1948) Minutes, p. 78.

317 Valuation Office: 6/5/1950: unpaginated.

318 Eastern Daily Press: 3/9/1948: 3.

319 Walsingham Parish Council (4/4/1948) Minutes, p. 100.

320 Regional Manager: 8/8/1949: unpaginated.

321 Tapper, H. C. M. (16/8/1949) 'Letter to Ministry of Agriculture & Fisheries' in Crop Drying Project: North Creake, unpaginated.

322 Smithies, J. F. (16/8/1949) 'Letter to Ministry of Agriculture & Fisheries' in Crop Drying Project: North Creake, unpaginated.

323 Walsingham Estate Company (22/1/1950) State and Condition Report, unpaginated.

324 Grange Brothers (20/3/1951) Correspondence with Walsingham Estate Company, unpaginated.

325 Grange, D. (29/11/2023) in conversation with the author.

326 Valuation Office: 6/5/1950: unpaginated.

327 Valuation Office: 6/5/1950: unpaginated.

328 Walsingham Parish Council (10/3/1950) Minutes, p. 181.

329 Anonymous (undated) 'Case Paper' in Crop Drying Project: North Creake, p. 21.

330 Parker: 6/9/2021.

331 Walsingham Rural District Council (5/9/45) Housing Committee Minutes, p. 9.

332 Hinton, J. (1988) 'Self-Help and Socialism: The Squatters Movement of 1946' in Roper, L & Taylor, B. (eds) (1988) History Workshop: A Journal of Socialist and Feminist Historians, p. 104.

333 Walsingham Rural District Council (10/9/1945) Housing Committee Minutes, p. 12.

334 Hinton: 1988: 104.

335 Walsingham Rural District Council (30/10/1945) Housing Committee Minutes, p. 16.

336 Walsingham Rural District Council (9/7/1947) Housing Committee Minutes, p. 114.

337 Walsingham Rural District Council: 9/7/1947: 115.

338 RAF 274 Maintenance Unit: 1945-1947: ORB: unpaginated.

339 Walsingham Rural District Council (1/10/1947) Housing Committee Minutes, p. 123.

340 Walsingham Rural District Council: 1/10/1947: 123.

341 Walsingham Rural District Council (29/10/1947) Housing Committee Minutes, p. 129.

342 Walsingham Rural District Council (1/9/1948) Housing Committee Minutes, p. 170.

343 Walsingham Rural District Council: 1/9/1948: p. 171.

344 Walsingham Rural District Council: 1/10/1947: 123.

345 Gaster, J. (1984) "London Squatters 1946", in Branson, N. (1984) Our History: Proceedings of a Conference Held by the Communist Party History Group, p. 3.

346 Gaster: 1984: 4.

347 Webster, H. (undated) A Domestic Rebellion: The Squatters Movement of 1946, p. 128.

348 Webster: undated: p. 126.

349 Watson, D. (2016) Squatting in Britain 1945-1955: Housing, Politics and Direct Action, p. 130.

350 Kenton, L. (1984) "London Squatters 1946", in Branson: 1984: 24.

351 Gaster: 1984: 4.

352 Gaster: 1984: 5.

353 Gaster: 1984: 5.

354 Tomlinson, J. (1997) 'The Good War: 1939-1945' in Tiratsoo, N. (ed.) (1997) From Blitz to Blair: A New History of Britain Since 1939, p. 83.

355 Bevan, A. (1946) cited in Foot, M. (1973) Aneurin Bevan: A Biography 1945-1960, p. 82.

356 Cole, G. D. H. (1945) Building and Planning, p. 99.

357 Webster: undated: 128-129.

358 Tomlinson: 1997: 83.

359 Tomlinson: 1997: 83.

360 Webster: undated: 130.

361 Bevan: 1946: 81.

362 Webster: undated: 144.

363 Burnham, P. (2004) 'The Squatters of 1946', in Johnson, J. et al (eds) (2004) Socialist History: Old Social Movements, p. 23.

364 Hinton: 1988: 104.

365 Gaster: 1984: 6.

366 Gaster: 1984: 6.

367 Gaster: 1984: 6.

368 Hinton: 1988: 104.

369 Henderson, S. (1984) "London Squatters 1946", in Branson: 1984: 17.

370 Hinton: 1988: 107.

371 Gaster: 1984: 6.

372 Webster: undated: 136.

373 Berry: 1989: 92.

374 Berry: 1989: 92.

375 American Library: Memorial to the 2nd Air Division (undated) americanlibrary.uk.

376 Elder, M. F. (1987) 2nd Division Headquarters Group, p. 9.

377 Eastern Daily Press (31/8/1946) More Squatters Move In, p. 1.

378 Eastern Daily Press (20/9/1946) RDC Takes Over Brandon Squatters, p. 1.

379 Eastern Daily Press (3/9/1946) Squatters Fix Own Rent, p. 1.

380 Eastern Daily Press: 3/9/1946: 1.

381 Hinton: 1988: 106.

382 Hinton: 1988: 108.

383 Hinton: 1988: 108.

384 Hinton: 1988: 108.

385 Eastern Daily Press: 3/9/1948: 3.

386 Webster: undated: 131.

387 Eastern Daily Press (9/9/1948) Protests Against Housing of Poles on Airfield, p. 3.

388 Eastern Daily Press (3/9/1948) New Village, p. 2.

389 Eastern Daily Press: 9/9/1948: 3.

390 Eastern Daily Press (9/8/1948) Polish Colony Plan to be Raised in Parliament, p. 5.

391 Eastern Daily Press: 9/9/1948: 3.

392 Eastern Daily Press: 9/9/1948: 3.

393 Eastern Daily Press: 3/9/1948: 3.

394 Eastern Daily Press: 9/9/1948: 3.

395 Eastern Daily Press: 3/9/1948: 3.

396 Eastern Daily Press: 3/9/1948: 3.

397 Eastern Daily Press: 3/9/1948: 2.

398 Walsingham Rural District Council (8/8/1948) Minutes, p. 191.

399 Walsingham Rural District Council (6/10/1948) Minutes, p. 199.

400 Walsingham Rural District Council (16/2/1949) Housing Committee Minutes, p. 213.

401 Walsingham Rural District Council (15/2/1950) Housing Committee Minutes, p. 50.

402 Walsingham Rural District Council (27/9/1950) Housing Committee Minutes, p. 101.

403 Walsingham Rural District Council (25/10/1950) Housing Committee Minutes, p. 109.

404 Walsingham Rural District Council (14/2/1951) Housing Committee Minutes, p. 129.

405 Humphrey, S. (21/9/2022) in conversation with the author.

406 Walsingham Rural District Council (11/4/1951) Housing Committee Minutes, pp. 149-150.

407 Walsingham Rural District Council (5/7/1953) Housing Committee Minutes, p. 68.

408 Walsingham Rural District Council: 5/7/1953: 68.

409 Walsingham Estate Company (10/3/1953) Correspondence with British Field Products, unpaginated.

410 Gunn, P. B. (2014) Sculthorpe, Secrecy and Stealth: A Norfolk Airfield in the Cold War, p. 171.

411 Nunn: 2019: 123.

412 Feasey, J. (1/4/1985) Correspondence.

413 roads.org.uk

414 Drew, P. (September 2013) in conversation with the author.

415 Crozier, M. (8/5/2022) in conversation with the author.

Chapter Eleven

1 Sinclair, J. (1987) Where's the Old Airfield? – You're Standing on it, unpaginated.

2 Kavanagh, D. (16/11/2016) Transcript of interview with Bernie How.

3 Feasey, J. (11/4/1985) Correspondence with Maurice Hood.

4 Bartram, L. (1998) RAF North Creake, Egmere, 1940-1947: A Brief History, p. 6.

5 RAF 100 Group Association (2007) Confound & Destroy, p. 16.

6 Gregson, J. (17/9/2013) in correspondence with the author.

7 King, L. (undated) History of Service in RAF, p. 5.

8 Nelmes, M. (18/7/1989) Australian War Memorial Correspondence with John Reid.

9 Hood, M. (9/4/1985) Correspondence with Jim Feasey.

10 Parker (6/9/2021) in correspondence with the author.

11 ABN Ltd Archive.

12 Mulvey, T. (3/1/1979) Correspondence.

13 Taylor, W. J. (21/5/1984) Correspondence.

14 Parker: 6/9/2021.

15 Blyth, J. (20/2/2023) in correspondence with the author.

16 Mabey, R. (2019) Weeds: How Vagabond Plants Gatecrashed Civilisation and Changed the Way We Think About Nature, p. 205.

17 Grimes, J. P., Hodgson, J. G. & Hunt, R. (2007) Comparative Plant Ecology: A Functional Approach to Common British Species, p. 452.

18 McKay: 2011: 79.

19 Mabey: 2019: 33-34.

20 Mabey: 2019: 208.

21 McKay: 2011: 80.

22 Mabey: 2019: 208.

23 McKay: 2011: 79.

24 Harrison, T. (3/11/2016) 'Wearing a Poppy was a Pledge of Peace. Now it Serves to Sanitise War,' theguardian.com.

25 Harrison: 3/11/2016.

26 BBC (9/11/2015) 'Five Reasons People Don't Wear Poppies', bbc.co.uk.

27 Thorpe, V. (31/10/2020) Remembrance 'Poppies Drawn into BBC Row Over 'Virtue Signalling'', theguardian.com.

28 Reilly, C. (undated) cited in, Relatives for Justice (undated) BBC Presenters and the Wearing of the Poppy.

29 Reilly: undated.

30 Hann, M. (1/11/2016) 'Wearing a Poppy is Only Meaningful if it's Voluntary', theguardian.com.

31 BBC: 9/11/2015.

32 BBC: 9/11/2015.

33 Snow, J. (8/11/2006) 'Why I Don't Wear a Poppy on Air', channel4.com.

34 Snow: 8/11/2006.

35 Snow: 8/11/2006.

36 BBC: 9/11/2015.

37 Hann: 1/11/2016.

38 Hann: 1/11/2016.

39 Akala (2019) Natives: Race & Class in the Ruins of Empire, pp. 148-149.

40 Gregory, A. (1994) The Silence of Memory, Armistice Day 1919-1946, p. 173.

41 Gregory: 1994: 173.

42 Gregory: 1994: 173.

43 RAF 171 Squadron (October 1944) Operations Record Book, unpaginated.

44 Gregory: 1994: 155.

45 West, P. (2004) Conspicuous Compassion: Why Sometimes it Really is Cruel to be Kind, p. 1.

46 West: 2004: 25.

47 West: 2004: 25.

48 Gregory: 1994: 100.

49 Gregory: 1994: 108.

50 BBC: 9/11/2015.

51 McKay: 2011: 81.

52 Peace Pledge Union (undated) 'Frequently Asked Questions', ppu.org.uk.

53 Gregory: 1994: 156.

54 Gregory: 1994: 156.

55 Gregory: 1994: 156.

56 Gregory: 1994: 156.

57 Royal Navy (9/11/2018) 'Wear a Poppy or Don't Wear a Poppy. Many Have Died for Your Freedom of Personal Choice', navylookout.com.

58 Harrison: 3/11/2016.

59 BBC: 9/11/2015.

60 Royal Navy: 9/11/2018.

61 Royal Navy: 9/11/2018.

62 Ware, F. (undated) cited in Stanford, P. (2013) How to Read a Graveyard: Journeys in the Company of the Dead, p. 189.

63 Evans, M. & Lunn, K. (eds) (1997) War and Memory in the Twentieth Century, p. XVI.

64 Ashplant, T. G., Dawson, G. & Roper, M. (eds) (2000) The Politics of War Memory and Commemoration, p. 8.

65 Dyer, G. (1994) The Missing of the Somme, p. 19.

66 Dyer: 1994: 19.
67 Gregory: 1994 8-10.
68 Gregory: 1994: 24.
69 Gregory: 1994: 13.
70 Gregory: 1994: 16.
71 Winter J. (2014) Sites of memory, Sites of Mourning, p. 82.
72 Gough, P. (undated) 'From Heroes' Groves to Parks of Peace:
Landscapes of Remembrance, Protest and Peace,' in Places of Peace: Selected Essays, paulgough.org.
73 Ashplant: 2000: 8.
74 Gregory: 1994: 215.
75 Ashplant: 2000: 7.
76 Gregory: 1994: 9-10.
77 Ashplant: 2000: 9.
78 Ashplant:2000: 13.
79 Madge, C. & Harrison, T. (1939) Britain by Mass Observation, p. 200.
80 Gregory: 1994: 99.
81 Gregory: 1994: 12.
82 Dyer: 1994: 51.
83 Madge: 1939: 200.
84 Madge: 1939: 200.
85 Ashplant: 2000: 13.
86 Ashplant: 2000: 13.
87 Ashplant: 2000: 18-19.
88 Longmate, N. (1983) The Bombers: The RAF Offensive Against Germany 1939-1945, p. 366.
89 Ashplant: 2000: 21.
90 Spark, S. (2010) 'The Treatment of the British Military War Dead of the Second World War', p. 239.
91 Fussell, P. (1975) The Great War and Modern Memory, p. 70.
92 Mabey: 2019: 204.
93 Mabey: 2019: 202.
94 RAF North Creake (June 1944) Operations Record Book, unpaginated.
95 Mabey: 2019: 24.
96 Ridge, R. (1965) For love of a Rose: The True Story of the Creation of the Famous Peace Rose, p. 197.
97 Ridge: 1965: 210.
98 Ridge: 1965: 210.
99 Ridge: 1965: 213.
100 Gough: undated.
101 Spark: 2010: 289.
102 Spark: 2010: 284.
103 Spark: 2010: 284.
104 Spark: 2010: 284-294.
105 Murphy, B. (2015) 'Dark Tourism and the Michelin World War 1 Battlefield Guides,' Journal of Franco-Irish Studies, p. 2.
106 Ashplant: 2000: 4.
107 Ashplant: 2000: 4.
108 Bourke, J. (2001) The Second World War: A People's History, pp. 221-222.
109 How: 8/3/2017.
110 Colgan, G. (7/5/2020) 'VE Day: A Woodstock Pilot's Sacrifice', unpaginated.
111 Benn, T. (undated) cited in, Smith, L. (2009) Voices Against War: A Century of Protest, p. 297.
112 Fussell, P. (1989) Wartime, Understanding the Behaviour in the Second World War, pp. 142-143.
113 Hynes, S. (1990) A War Imagined: The First World War and English Culture, p. 270.
114 Historic England (undated) historicengland. org.uk.
115 Moriarty, C. (undated) 'Private grief and Public Remembrance: British First World War Memorials', in Evans, M. & Lunn, K. (eds) (1997) War and Memory in the Twentieth Century, p. 129.
116 Boorman, D. (1988) At the Going Down of the Sun: British First World War Memorials, p. 1.
117 Stanford, P. (2013) How to Read a Graveyard: Journeys in the Company of the Dead, p. 189.
118 Stanford: 2013: 189.
119 Moriarty: undated: 126.
120 Crane, D. (2013) Empires of the Dead: How One Man's Vision Led to the Creation of WWI's War Graves, pp. 123-124.
121 Crane: 2013: 123.
122 Crane: 2013: 124.
123 Crane: 2013: 124.
124 Crane: 2013: 123.
125 Stanford: 2013: 193.
126 Spark: 2010: 239.
127 Stanford: 2013: 193.
128 Bourke, J. (1996) Dismembering the Male: Men's Bodies, Britain and the Great War, p. 227
129 Stanford: 2013: 194.
130 Crane: 2013: 126.
131 Crane: 2013: 129.
132 Fussell: 1975: 70.
133 Crane: 2013: 129.
134 Stanford: 2013: 196-197.
135 Gough: undated.
136 Stanford: 2013: 191.
137 Stanford: 2013: 191.
138 Longworth, P. (1967) cited in Spark: 2010: 242.
139 Spark: 2010: 241.
140 Spark: 2010: 242-243.
141 Spark: 2010: 243.
142 Spark: 2010: 247.
143 Spark: 2010: 248.

144   Spark: 2010: 251.

145   Winter: 2014: 94.

146   Historic England (2/6/2003) 'Conservation Bulletin 44: The Archaeology of Conflict', p. 31.

147   Historic England: 2/6/2003: 29.

148   Historic England: 2/6/2003: 28.

149   Historic England: 2/6/2003: 28.

150   Gough: undated.

151   Gough: undated.

152   Gough: undated.

153   Gough: undated.

154   Hetherington, P. (2/2/1999) 'MoD Putting Rural Policy at Risk', unpaginated.

155   Evans: 1997: XVI.

156   Ambrose, S (1973) 'A Special Presentation: From War to Peace' The World at War.

157   Sebald, W. G. (2003) On the Natural History of Destruction, p. 15.

158   Huzzard, R. (undated) cited in, Smith, L. (2009) Voices against War: A Century of Protest, p. 95.

159   Hastings, M. (1980) Bomber Command, p. 177.

160   Hastings: 1980: 352.

161   Webster, C. & Frankland, N. (1961) History of the Second World War: The Strategic Air Offensive, Volume III: Victory, p. 114.

13   RAF 100 Group (December 1944) Operations Record Book, unpaginated.

14   RAF 100 Group: December 1944: ORB: unpaginated.

15   Bartram: 1998: 27.

16   Hines, M. (23/12/2023) in correspondence with the author.

17   Feasey, J. (undated) in Bartram: 1998: 18.

18   RAF Woodbridge: January 1945: ORB: unpaginated.

19   Bond, S. & Forder, R. (2011) Special Ops Liberators: 225 (Bomber Support) Squadron, 100 Group, and the Electronic War, pp. 111-112.

20   Hines: 23/12/2023.

21   RAF Woodbridge: March 1945: ORB: unpaginated.

Aircraft Losses & Incidents at RAF North Creake

1   Aviation Safety (undated), unpaginated.

2   Rees, J. (undated) in Bartram, L. (1998) RAF North Creake, Egmere, 1940-1947: A Brief History, p. 14.

3   RAF 199 Squadron (July 1944) Operations Record Book, unpaginated.

4   RAF North Creake (August 1944) Operations Record Book, unpaginated.

5   Air Ministry (1944-1945) RAF 199 Squadron Operations Record Book: 29 August 1944, unpaginated.

6   Rees, J. (undated) in Bartram: 1998: 13.

7   Rees: undated: 13.

8   RAF North Creake (September 1944) Operations Record Book, Items of Medical Interest, unpaginated.

9   RAF North Creake: October 1944: ORB Items of Medical Interest: unpaginated.

10   RAF Woodbridge (October 1944) Operations Record Book, unpaginated.

11   RAF North Creake: October 1944: ORB Items of Medical Interest: unpaginated.

12   RAF Woodbridge: November 1944: ORB: unpaginated.

BIBLIOGRAPHY & SOURCE MATERIALS

A Note on Source Materials

The bibliography is divided into three sections: secondary, primary and internet sources. Primary and internet are further subdivided; primary into interviews, correspondence and documents, and internet into data bases and specific on-line page references.

Secondary Sources

Addison, E. (1946) The Radio War lecture', in RUSI (1947) <u>Royal United Services Institute Journal</u>, 565, February.

Addison, P. (1985) <u>Now the War is Over: A Social History of Britain 1945-51</u>, Jonathan Cape.

Air Historical Branch (1956) <u>Works: The Second World War 1939-1945</u>, Air Ministry.

Akala (2019) <u>Natives: Race & Class in the Ruins of Empire</u>, Two Roads.

Aldgate, A. & Richards, J. (1986) <u>Britain Can Take It: The British Cinema in the Second World War</u>, Blackwell.

Allison, J. (1966) <u>Bomber Crew</u>, Thomas Nelson.

Allward, M. & Taylor, J. (1996) <u>The De Havilland Aircraft Company</u>, Chalford.

Arbib, R.S. (1947) <u>Here We Are Together: The Notebook of an American Soldier in Britain</u>, Longmans, Green & Co.

Arnold, K. (2005) <u>Green Two: Sgt Dennis Noble: One of Churchill's Few 1940</u>, Southern Counties Aviation Research/Publications.

Arthur, M. (2005) <u>Lost Voices of the Royal Air Force</u>, Hodder.

Ashplant, T. G., Dawson, G. & Roper, M. (eds) (2000) <u>The Politics of War Memory and Commemoration</u>, Routledge.

Ashton, N. (2000) <u>Only Birds and Fools: Flight Engineer, Avro Lancaster, World War II</u>, Crowood Press.

Ashworth, C. (1995) <u>RAF Bomber Command 1936-1968</u>, PSL.

Baldwin, A. W. (1967) <u>A Flying Start</u>, Peter Davies.

Bartram, L. (1998) <u>RAF North Creake, Egmere, 1940-1947: A Brief History</u>, self-published.

Bartram, L. (undated) <u>No. 100 Group (Norfolk) R.A.F. Bomber Command: 1943/1945</u>, self-published.

Bates, H. E. (1955) <u>Love for Lydia</u>, Mermaid.

Bekker, C. (1967) <u>The Luftwaffe War Diaries</u>, Macdonald.

Belchem, D. (1981) <u>Victory in Normandy</u>, Chato & Windus.

Bell, R. (1946) History of the British Railways During the War 1939-1945, The Railway Gazette.

Berry, P. (1989) Airfield Heyday: Daily Life on and Around Wartime Airfields, Jim Baldwin.

Betjeman, J. (1937) 'Antiquarian Prejudice' in, Betjeman, J. (1969) First and Last Loves, John Murray.

Bickers, R. T. (1994) Friendly Fire: Accidents in Battle from Ancient Greece to the Gulf War, Leo Cooper.

Bond, S. & Forder, R. (2011) Special Ops Liberators: 225 (Bomber Support) Squadron, 100 Group, and the Electronic War, Grub Street.

Boorman, D. (1988) At the Going Down of the Sun: British First World War Memorials, Ebor Press.

Bourke, J. (1996) Dismembering the Male: Men's Bodies, Britain and the Great War, Reaktion.

Bourke, J. (1999) An Intimate History of Killing: Face to Face Killing in Twentieth-Century Warfare, Granta.

Bourke, J. (2001) The Second World War: A People's History, Oxford.

Bourne, S. (2012) The Motherland Calls: Britain's Black Servicemen & Women 1939-45, History Press.

Bowman, M. W. & Cushing, T. (1996) Confounding the Reich: The Operational History of 100 Group (Bomber Support) RAF, Patrick Stephens.

Bowman, M. (2006) 100 Group (Bomber Support) RAF Bomber Command in World War II, Aviation Heritage Trail Series, Pen & Sword.

Bowman, M. (2015) The Night Air War: Voices in Flight, Pen & Sword.

Bowyer, M. J. F. (1979) Action Stations: Wartime Military Airfields of East Anglia, 1939-1945, Patrick Stephens.

Bowyer, M. J. F. (1983) Action Stations 6: Military Airfields of the Cotswolds and the Central Midlands, Patrick Stephens.

Bowyer, M. J. F. (1986) Air Raid: The Enemy Air Offensive Against East Anglia 1939-45, Patrick Stevens.

Bowyer, M. J. F. (2002) The Stirling Story, Crecy.

Bowyer, M. J. F. (2010) Action Stations Revisited: Eastern England, Vol. 1, Crecy.

Branson, N. (1984) Our History: Proceedings of a Conference Held by the Communist Party History Group, May 1984: London Squatters 1946, CPGB.

Brettingham, L. (1997) Royal Air Force Beam Benders: No. 80 (Signals) Wing: 1940-1945, Midland Publishing.

Brettingham, L. (2002) Even When the Sparrows are Walking: The Origin and Effect of No. 100 (Bomber Support) Group, RAF, 1943-45, Librario.

Bridges, E. M. & Baldwin, J. (Eds) (2005) A Conflict & Memories: Fakenham Remembers World War Two, Fakenham Museum of Gas and Local History.

Bridges, J. F. (2023) Doodlebugs and Rockets: Norfolk and Suffolk 1944-1945, Poppyland.

Brown R. D. (1990) East Anglia: 1943, Terence Dalton.

Burnham, P. (2004) 'The Squatters of 1946', in Johnson, J. et al (eds) (2004) Socialist History: Old Social Movements, issue 25, Rivers Oram Press.

Butler, P. (2017) Streamline Worcestershire, Art Deco Magpie.

Calder, A. (1969) The People's War: Britain 1939-1945, Jonathan Cape.

Calder, A. (1991) The Myth of the Blitz, Jonathan Cape.

Carr, E. H. (1969) What is History? MacMillan.

Charlwood, D. (1984) No Moon Tonight, Goodall.

Chisholm, R. (1953) Cover of Darkness, Chatto & Windus.

Chorley, W. R. (2008) Royal Air Force: Bomber Command Losses of the Second World War: Volume 5, 1944, Midland.

Chorley, W. R. (2008) Royal Air Force: Bomber Command Losses of the Second World War: Volume 6, 1945, Midland.

Cole, G. D. H. (1939) War Aims, New Statesman.

Cole, G. D. H. (1945) Building and Planning, Cassel.

Costello, J. (1985) Love Sex & War: Changing Values 1939-45, Collins.

Crane, D. (2013) Empires of the Dead: How One Man's Vision Led to the Creation of WWI's War Graves, William Collins.

Cranfield, I. (2005) Art Deco House Style: An Architectural and Interior Design Source Book, David & Charles.

Crump, N. (1947) By Rail to Victory, LNER.

Daly, H. E. & Cobb, J. B. (1990) For the Common Good: Redirecting the Economy Towards Community, the Environment and a Sustainable Future, Green Print.

Delve, K. (2005) The Military Airfields of Britain: East Anglia: Norfolk & Suffolk, Crowood Press.

Dobinson, C. (2000) Fields of Deception: Britain's Bombing Decoys of World War II, English Heritage/Methuen.

Doherty, R. (1999) Irish Men and Women in the Second World War, Four Courts Press.

Donovan, R. (2009) As for the Canadians: The Remarkable Story of the RCAF's 'Guinea pigs' of World War II, Bushek Books.

Dyer, G. (1994) The Missing of the Somme, Hamish Hamilton.

Evans, M. & Lunn, K. (eds) (1997) War and Memory in the Twentieth Century, Berg.

The Fabian Society (1941) Programme for Victory, Labour Book Service.

Falconer, J. (1998) Bomber Command Handbook 1939-1945, Sutton.

Falconer, J (2015) Short Stirling: 1939-48 (all marks) Owners' Workshop Manual, Haynes.

Falconer, J. (2016) Handley Page Halifax: 1939 Onwards (All Marks): Owners' Workshop Manual, Haynes.

Fielding, S. (1997) 'The Good War: 1939-1945' in Tiratsoo, N. (ed.) (1997) From Blitz to Blair: A New History of Britain Since 1939, Weidenfeld & Nicolson.

Flinders, S. & Corns, D. (2019) Stanton: Gone but Not Forgotten: A Derbyshire Ironworks and its People, Ilkeston and District Local History Society.

Foot, M. (1973) Aneurin Bevan: A Biography 1945-1960, Davis-Poynter.

Ford, K. S. (1992) Snaith Days: Life With 51 Squadron 1942/45, Compaid.

Foreman, J. Mathews, J. & Parry, S. (2004) Luftwaffe: Night Fighter Combat Claims 1939-1945, Red Kite.

Francis, P. (1993) Control Towers: The Development of the Control Tower on RAF Stations in the United Kingdom, Airfield Research Publishing.

Francis, P (1996) British Military Airfield Architecture: From Airships to the Jet Age, PSL.

Francis, P., Flagg R. & Crisp, G. (2016) Nine Thousand Miles of Concrete: A Review of Second World War Temporary Airfields in England, Airfield Research Group/

Historic England.

Frankland, N. (1998) History at War, Giles de la Mare Publishers.

Fussell, P. (1975) The Great War and Modern Memory, Oxford.

Fussell, P. (1989) Wartime, Understanding the Behaviour in the Second World War, Oxford University Press.

Fry, E. M. (1945) Architects' Year Book, Paul Elek.

Galbraith, J. (1961) The Affluent Society, Hamish Hamilton.

Gracchus [Wintringham, T.] (1944) Your M. P., Victor Gollanz.

Grayling, A. C. (2006) Among the Dead Cities: Was the Allied Bombing of Civilians in WWII a Necessity or a Crime?, Bloomsbury.

Green, W. (1960) Famous Bombers of the Second World War, Macdonald.

Gregory, A. (1994) The Silence of Memory, Armistice Day 1919-1946, Berg.

Grimes, J. P., Hodgson, J. G. & Hunt, R. (2007) Comparative Plant Ecology: A Functional Approach to Common British Species, Second Edition, Castlepoint Press.

Gunn, P. B. (2014) Sculthorpe, Secrecy and Stealth: A Norfolk Airfield in the Cold War, History Press.

Gutherie, C. & Quinlan, M. (2007) Just War: The Just War Tradition: Ethics in Modern Warfare, Bloomsbury.

Hadaway, S. (2008) Missing Believed Killed: The Royal Air Force and the Search for Missing Aircrew 1939-1952, Pen & Sword.

Hall, A. (1985) We, Also, Were There, Merlin.

Halpenny, B. B. (1981) Action Stations 2: Military Airfields of Lincolnshire and the East Midlands, Patrick Stephens.

Halpenny, B. B. (1982) Action Stations 4: Military Airfields of Yorkshire, Patrick Stephens.

Halpenny, B. B. (1984) Action Stations 8: Military Airfields of Greater London, Patrick Stephens.

Hammerton, J. (1943) ABC of the RAF: Handbook for All Branches of the Air Force, Amalgamated Press.

Hardy, T. (1932) Wessex Tales: Preface, Macmillan.

Harrington, J. (2012) RAF North Creake, Egmere 1940-1947: A Brief History, self-published.

Harrington, J. (2015) RAF 100 Group: Kindred Spirits: Voices of RAF & USAAF on Secret Norfolk Airfields During the Second World War, Austin Macauley.

Harrington, J. (2016) RAF 100 Group: The Birth of Electronic Warfare, Fonthill.

Harrington, J. (2018) RAF 100 Group: Reasons to Remember, FeedARead.

Harwood, E. (2019) Art Deco Britain: Buildings of the Interwar Years, Batsford.

Harris, A. (1947) Bomber Offensive, Collins.

Harris, A. (1995) Despatch on War Operations: 23rd February 1942 to 8th May 1945, Cass.

Hastings, M. (1980) Bomber Command, Second Impression, Michael Joseph.

Hastings, M. (1984) Overlord: D-Day and the Battle for Normandy 1944, Guild.

Hawton, H. (1944) The Men Who Fly, Nelson.

Higham, R. (1998) Bases of Air Strategy: Building Airfields for the RAF 1914-1945, Airlife.

Hillier, M. (2014) Suitcases, Vultures and Spies, Yellowman.

Hinchliffe, P. (1996) The Other Battle: Luftwaffe Night Aces Versus Bomber Command, Airlife.

Hines, M. (2022) Airfields of North Norfolk: RAF North Creake, Blurb.

Hinton, J. (1988) 'Self-Help and Socialism: The Squatters Movement of 1946' in Roper, L & Taylor, B. (eds) (1988) History Workshop: A Journal of Socialist and Feminist Historians, issue 25, Spring, Routledge.

Hope, B. (2014) And in the Morning: RAF Station North Creake, self-published.

Hoskins, W.G. (1977) The Making of the English Landscape, Book Club Associates.

Hudson, M. (2020) RAF Operational and Flying Accident Casualty Files in the National Archives: Exploring Their Contents, Air World.

Hutton, S. (1999) Squadron of Deception: The 36th Bomb Squadron in World War II, Schiffer Military History.

Hynes, S. (1990) A War Imagined: The First World War and English Culture, Bodley Head.

Innes, G. B. (1995) British Airfield Buildings of the Second World War: Aviation Pocket Guide 1, Midland.

Jencks, C (1973) Architecture 2000: Predictions and Methods, Studio Vista.

Johnson, B. (1978) The Secret War, BBC.

Jones, G. (1978) Raider: The Halifax and its Flyers, William Kimber.

Jones, R. V. (1978) Most Secret War: British Scientific Intelligence 1939-1945, Book Club Associates.

Kee, R. (1947) A Crowd Is Not Company, Eyre & Spottiswoode.

Kee, R. (1972) The Green Flag, Weidenfeld & Nicolson.

Keesings (1946) Contemporary Archives: Weekly Diary of World Events, Vol. V, Keesings.

Keesings (1947) Contemporary Archives: Weekly Diary of World Events, Vol. VI, Keesings.

Keesings (1950) Contemporary Archives: Weekly Diary of World Events, Vol. VII, Keesings.

Kohan, J. M. (1952) History of the Second World War: History and Buildings, HMSO & Longmans.

Krusin, S. M. & Thorold Rogers, P. H. (1940) The Solicitors' Handbook of War Legislation, The Solicitors' Law stationary Society Ltd.

Laird, S. M. (1943) Venereal Disease in Britain, Penguin Special.

Longmate, N. (1971) How We Lived Then: A History of Everyday Life During the Second World War, Hutchinson.

Longmate, N. (1983) The Bombers: The RAF Offensive Against Germany 1939-1945, Hutchinson.

Mabey, R. (2019) Weeds: How Vagabond Plants Gatecrashed Civilisation and Changed the Way We Think About Nature, Profile.

MacEwen, M. (1991) The Greening of a Red, Pluto Press.

Mackenzie, S P. (1992) Politics and Military Morale: Current Affairs and Citizenship Education in the British Army 1914-1950, Oxford Historical Monographs.

Maclaren-Ross, J. (1991) Memoirs of the Forties, Cardinal.

Madge, C. & Harrison, T. (1939) Britain by Mass Observation, Penguin.

Madge, C. (1946) Pilot Papers: Social Essays and Documents, Vol. 1, No. 2, April, Pilot Press.

Mackay, R. (1989) 'Short Stirling in Action', <u>Aircraft</u>, Number 96, Squadron Signal Publications.

Marwick, A. (1980) <u>Class: Image and Reality, in Britain France and the USA Since 1930</u>, Collins.

Maughan, W. Somerset (1953) <u>The Complete Short Stories, Volume Two</u>, William Heinemann.

McIvor, A. J. (2001) <u>A History of Work in Britain, 1880-1950</u>, Palgrave.

McKay, G. (2011) <u>Radical Gardening: Politics, Idealism & Rebellion in the Garden</u>, Frances Lincoln.

Merrick, K. A. (1980) <u>Halifax: An Illustrated History of a Classic World War II Bomber</u>, Ian Allen.

Middlebrook, M. (1980) <u>The Battle of Hamburg: Allied Bomber Forces Against a German City in 1943</u>, Allen Lane.

Middlebrook, M. & Everitt, C. (1985) <u>The Bomber Command War Diaries: An Operational Reference Book, 1939-1945</u>, Viking.

Miliband, R. (1972) <u>Parliamentary Socialism: A Study in the Politics of Labour</u>, Merlin.

Miller, H. (1971) <u>Service to the Services: The Story of Naafi</u>, Newman Neame

Moore, B. (1965) <u>The Emperor of Ice Cream</u>, Andre Deutsch.

Moriarty, C. (undated) 'Private grief and Public Remembrance: British First World War Memorials', in Evans, M. & Lunn, K. (eds) (1997) <u>War and Memory in the Twentieth Century</u>, Berg.

Morrison, H. (1939) <u>What Are We Fighting For?</u>, Labour Party.

Moshenka, G. (2014) 'Token Scraps of Men: Whites Lies, Weighted Coffins, and Second World War Air Crash Casualties', in Cornish, P. & Saunders, N. (eds) (2014) <u>Bodies in Conflict: Corporeality, Materiality & Transformation</u>, Routledge, p. 135.

Mumford, L (1946) <u>Programme for Survival</u>, Secker & Warburg.

Murphy, R. (1989) <u>Realism and Tinsel: Cinema and Society in Britain 1939-48</u>, Routledge.

Nicolson, H. (1941) 'World Government', in Fabian Society (1941) <u>Programme for Victory</u>, Labour Book Service.

Ogden, R. J. (2001) 'Meteorological Services Leading to D-Day', in Royal Meteorological Society (July 2001) <u>Occasional Papers of Meteorological History, No. 3</u>, Royal Meteorological Society.

Orwell, G. (1941) <u>The Lion and the Unicorn: Socialism and the English Genius</u>, Searchlight Books.

Orwell, G. (1986) <u>The Lion and the Unicorn: Socialism and the English Genius</u>, Penguin.

Overy, R. (1995) <u>Why the Allies Won</u>, Jonathan Cape.

Overy, R. (2013) <u>The Bombing War in Europe 1939-1945</u>, Allen Lane/Penguin.

Parry, S. W. (1987) <u>Intruders Over Britain: The Luftwaffe Night Fighter Offensive 1940-45</u>, Air Research Publications.

Pedan, M. (1979) <u>A Thousand Shall Fall</u>, Canada's Wings.

Pelly-Fry, J. (1994) <u>Heavenly Days: Recollections of a Contented Airman</u>, Crecy.

Piekalkiewicz, J. (1985) <u>The Air War, 1939-1945</u>, Blandford Press.

Plater, A. (1994) <u>Oliver's Travels: A Novel</u>, Little Brown.

Price, A. (1967) <u>Instruments of Darkness: The Struggle for Radar Supremacy</u>, William Kimber.

Priestley, J. B. (1945) 'Britain is in Danger' in Priestley, J. B. (ed.) (1945) <u>Our Nation's Heritage</u>, J. M. Dent.

Priestley, J. B. (1963) Margin Released: Reminiscences & Reflections, World Books.

Pringle, J. W. S. (1985) 'The Work of TRE in the Invasion of Europe', in IEE Proceedings: A Special Issue on Historical Radar, Vol. 132, Part A, No. 6, IEE.

Probert, H. (2001) Bomber Harris: His Life and Times, Greenhill Books.

Rapier, B. J. & Bowyer, C. (1994) Halifax & Wellington, The Promotional Reprint Company.

Redding, T. (2005) Flying for Freedom: Life and Death in Bomber Command, Cerberus.

Rees, W. J. (2003) The Final Fling, Compaid Graphics.

Reid, J. (2014) Let Tyrants Tremble: The War Diary of 199 (Bomber Support) Squadron, November 1942 – July 1945, Stenlake.

Renaut, M. (1982) Terror by Night, William Kimber.

Ridge, R. (1965) For love of a Rose: The True Story of the Creation of the Famous Peace Rose, Faber & Faber.

Richards, D. (1994) The Hardest Victory: RAF Bomber Command in the Second World War, Hodder & Stoughton.

Richards, J. M. (1959) An Introduction to Modern Architecture, Pelican.

Roberts, R. N. (1982) The Halifax File, Air-Britain (Historians).

Rogers, C. (1981) The Battle of Stepney: the Sidney Street Siege: Its Causes and Consequences, Hale.

Rolt, L.T.C. (1946) Narrow Boat, Readers Union Eyre & Spottiswode.

Rowe, A. P. (1948) One Story of Radar, Cambridge University Press.

Royal Air Force Historical Society (2003) Electronic Warfare: Proceeding of a Conference 10 April 2002, Journal 28, RAFHS.

Russell Muirhead, L. (1949) Penguin Guides: Norfolk and the Isle of Ely, Penguin.

Ryle, P. (1979) Missing in Action: May – September 1944, W. H. Allen.

Sassoon, S. (1930) Memoirs of an Infantry Officer, Faber & Faber.

Sawyer, T. (1982) Only Owls and Bloody Fools Fly at Night, William Kimber.

Scott, K. (1993) 'Window of deceit', Army Quarterly and Defence Journal (GB), Vol. 123, pp. 39-42.

Sebald, W. G. (2003) On the Natural History of Destruction, Hamish Hamilton.

Seversky, A. (1942) Victory Through Air Power, Simon and Schuster.

Shaw, B. (1944) Everybody's Political What's What?, Constable & Company.

Smith, D. J. (1981) Action Stations 3: Military Airfields of Wales and the North West, Patrick Stephens.

Smith, D. J. (1983) Action Stations 7: Military Airfields of Scotland, the North-East & Northern Ireland, Patrick Stephens.

Smith, L. (2009) Voices Against War: A Century of Protest, Mainstream Publishing.

Smith, R. (2018) Crossing the Bar: Tales of Wells Harbour, Gomer Press.

Smithies, E. (2002) Aces, Erks & Backroom Boys, Past Times.

Speer, A. (1976) Spandau: The Secret Diaries, Collins.

Stanford, P. (2013) How to Read a Graveyard: Journeys in the Company of the Dead, Bloomsbury.

Streetly, M. (1978) Confound & Destroy: 100 Group and the Bomber Support Campaign, Macdonald & Jane's.

Streetly, M. (1984) The Aircraft of the 100 Group: A Historical Guide for the Modeller, Robert Hale.

Sweetman, J. (2004) Bomber Crew: Taking on the Reich, Abacus.

Taylor, A. J. P. (1966) English History: 1914-1945, Oxford Clarendon.

Taylor, A. J. P. (1975) The Second World War: An Illustrated History, Purnell.

Taylor, A. J. P. (1977) The War Lords, Hamish Hamilton.

Taylor, E. (1983) Operation Millennium: 'Bomber' Harris's Raid on Cologne, May 1942, Hale.

Taylor, F. (2005) Dresden: Tuesday 13 February 1945, Bloomsbury.

Taylor, L. (undated) Ground Gen for Airmen, Pitman.

Tawney, R. H (1941) Why Britain Fights, Macmillan War Pamphlets.

Tempest, V. (1946) Near the Sun: Impressions of a Medical Officer of Bomber Command, Crabtree.

Terraine, J. (1985) The Right of the Line: The Royal Air Force in the European War 1939-1945, Hodder and Stoughton.

Thomas, M. (2017) The Red Shed: A Topical Tale About the Miners' Strike, Mr Sands.

Tinniswood, A. (2002) The Art Deco House, Mitchell Beazly.

Tiratsoo, N. (ed.) (1997) From Blitz to Blair: A New History of Britain Since 1939, Weidenfeld & Nicolson.

Tomlinson, J. (1997) 'The Good War: 1939-1945' in Tiratsoo, N. (ed.) (1997) From Blitz to Blair: A New History of Britain Since 1939, Weidenfeld & Nicolson.

Tripp, M. (1952) Faith is a Windsock, Peter Davies.

Tripp, M. (1985) The Eighth Passenger: A Documentary Account of a World War 2 Bomber Crew, Papermac.

Verrier, A. (1968) The Bomber Offensive, Batsford.

Wainwright, J. (1978) Tail-End Charlie: One Man's Journey Through a War, Macmillan.

Wakeman, R. (2020) 'Harris's Scientists: Operational Research in Bomber Command', Canadian Military History, Vol. 29, issue 2.

Walsingham History Society (2001) The Walsingham Millennium Book: Interviews and Recollections, self-published.

Watson, D. (2016) Squatting in Britain 1945-1955: Housing, Politics and Direct Action, Merlin.

Webley, N. (ed) (2002) Betty's War Diary: 1939-1945, Thorogood.

Webster, C. & Frankland, N. (1961) History of the Second World War: The Strategic Air Offensive, Volume I: Preparation, HMSO.

Webster, C. & Frankland, N. (1961) History of the Second World War: The Strategic Air Offensive, Volume III: Victory, HMSO.

Webster, C. & Frankland, N. (1961) History of the Second World War: The Strategic Air Offensive, Volume IV: Victory, HMSO.

West, P. (2004) Conspicuous Compassion: Why Sometimes it Really is Cruel to be Kind, CIVITAS.

Wheeler, M. (Ed.) (1941) Britain at War, The Museum of Modern Art New York.

Whiting, C. (1987) The Three Star Blitz: The Baedeker Raids and the Start of Total War 1942-1943, Leo Cooper.

Williams, R. (1979) Politics and Letters, New Left Review.

Willis, S. & Holliss, B. (1990) Military Airfields in the British Isles 1939-1945 (Omnibus Edition), Enthusiasts Publications.

Willmott, P. (1988) Coming of Age in Wartime, Peter Green.

Wilson, A. T. M. (1946) 'The Serviceman Comes Home' in Madge, C. (1946) <u>Pilot Papers: Social Essays and Documents</u>, Vol. 1, No. 2, April, Pilot Press.

Wilson, K. (2010) <u>Journey's End: Bomber Command's Battle from Arnhem to Dresden and Beyond</u>, Weidenfeld & Nicolson.

Winfield, R. (1976) <u>The Sky Belongs to Them</u>, Parnell Book Services.

Winter, J. M. (1974) <u>Socialism and the Challenge of War: Ideas and Politics in Britain 1912-18</u>, Gregg Revivals.

Winter, J. (2014) <u>Sites of Memory, Sites of Mourning</u>, Cambridge University Press.

Wood, I. S. (2000) <u>British History in Perspective: Churchill</u>, Macmillan.

Wood, I. S. (2002) <u>Ireland During the Second World War</u>, Caxton Editions.

Primary Sources

Interviews, Conversations

Baker, G. (29/09/2020) interview with the author.

Berrill, R. (27/6/2021) interview with the author.

Berrill, R. (23/11/2021) interview with the author.

Berrill, R. (25/3/2023) interview with the author.

Borthwick, T. (17/1/2023) in conversation with the author.

Crozier, M. (8/5/2022) in conversation with the author.

Delve, K. (2/6/2017) interview with the author.

Delve, K. (24/1/2023) in conversation with the author.

Drew, P. (September 2013) in conversation with the author.

Flowers, V. (2016) telephone conversation with the author.

Franklin, J. (8/2/2020) in conversation with the author.

Freegard, H. (9/8/2018) in conversation with the author.

Gill, D. (7/6/2014) in conversation with the author.

Graham, D. (16/4/2019) in conversation with the author.

Grange, D. (29/11/2023) in conversation with the author.

Groome, N. (13/4/2020) in conversation with the author.

How, B. (27/7/2013) in conversation with the author.

How, B. (8/3/2017) interview with the author.

Humphrey, S. (21/9/2022) in conversation with the author.

Jennings, J. (9/6/2020) interview with author.

Leach, D. (16/11/2017) interview with author.

Lines, P. (23/4/2023) in conversation with the author.

Meath Baker, C. & Meath Baker, P. (11/3/2024) interview with the author.

Maufe, T. (2012) in conversation with the author.

Maufe, T. (24/9/2023) telephone conversation with the author.

Maufe, T. (22/2/2024) interview with the author.

Reid, J. (14/8/2023) in conversation with the author.

Renaut, Y. (2015) <u>Taped Interview</u>, via Alison Nilsson.

Reynolds, A. (12/9/2013) in conversation with the author.

Smith, S. (17/1/2016) in conversation with the author.

Smith, S. (27/2/2022) in conversation with the author.

Swadling, P. (28/9/2022) in conversation with the author.

Tuck, J. (28/7/2016) in conversation with the author.

Tuck, J. (13/02/2017) interview with author.

Wood, A, (200?) Interview with Grandson, via Gillian Tewson.

Yarham, S. (2012) in conversation with the author.

Correspondence

Addison, E. (7/10/1944) Correspondence, RAF 100 Group, National Archives, AIR14/2657.

Addison, E. (15/11/1944) Correspondence, RAF 100 Group, National Archives, AIR14/2657.

Addison, E. (31/3/1945) Correspondence, RAF 100 Group, National Archives, AIR14/2657.

Air Ministry Works Directorate (18/10/1945) Correspondence with Walsingham Estates Company, Walsingham Estates Archive.

Air Ministry Works Directorate (9/11/1945) Correspondence with Walsingham Estate Company, Walsingham Estate Archive.

Air Ministry Works Directorate (5/12/1945) Correspondence with Walsingham Estate Company, Walsingham Estate Archive.

Beardsell, J. (20/3/2023) in correspondence with the author.

Berrill, R. (July 2021) in correspondence with the author.

Bevington, P. E. (29/6/1945) Letter of Condolence to L. N. Dent, via Mike Hillier.

Bevington, P. E. (12/10/1945) Correspondence with his Wife, via Russ Bevington.

Blyth, J. (20/2/2023) in correspondence with the author.

Bomber Command Head Quarters (18/4/1946) Correspondence with the RAF Central Depository, Library and Archive Canada.

Bradley, C. (31/7/1945) Correspondence with the Brother of A. Bradley with Les Currell, via Jeff Hudson.

Burt, J. (23/11/2020) in correspondence with the author.

Campbell, L. D. (25/1/1945) Correspondence with RCAF Casualty Officer, RCAF, Library and Archive Canada.

Campbell, M. E. (15/7/1946) Correspondence to RCAF Estates Branch, RCAF, Library and Archive Canada.

Casualty Officer (18/10/1945) Correspondence to James Brown, Library and Archive Canada.

Casualty Section (14/5/1945) Telegram to the Parents of D. H. Lawrence, National Archives of Australia.

Chapman, A. W. (16/12/1948) Correspondence between Ministry of Works and Walsingham Estate Company, Walsingham Estate Archive.

Croft, P. (29/11/2020) Correspondence, via John Reid.

Currell, P. (31/8/2006) Correspondence, via John Reid.

Delve, K. (7/2/2024) in correspondence with the author.

Dennison, H. (3/3/1947) Correspondence between Dennison's Mother and the Secretary,

Department of National Defence for All, Ottawa, Ontario, Library and Archive Canada.

Dicks, W. A. (4/1/1947) Correspondence to Laura Mison from the Office of the Chief of Air Staff, RCAF, Library and Archive Canada.

Draper, G. C. (4/7/1945) Correspondence Regarding Sale of Morris 8, Library and Archive Canada.

East Anglian Electricity Supply Co. (5/5/1949) Correspondence with Walsingham Estate Company, Walsingham Estate Archive.

Endersby, J. (12/2/2013) in correspondence with the author.

Feasey, J. (1/4/1985) Correspondence with Reg Foreman, via ABN Agri.

Feasey, J. (11/4/1985) Correspondence with Maurice Hood, via ABN Agri.

Forde, J. (17/8/2023) in correspondence with the author.

Francis, P. (9/2/2024) in correspondence with the author.

Gill, D. (25/8/2018) Correspondence with Sara Hyland, via Sara Hyland.

Grange Brothers (20/3/1951) Correspondence with Walsingham Estate Company, Walsingham Estate Archive.

Gratte, S. (6/9/2006) Correspondence via John Reid.

Gregson, J. (17/9/2013) in correspondence with the author.

Gunn, W. R. (24/9/1948) Correspondence to James Brown from the Casualty Section, RCAF, Library and Archive Canada.

Gunn, W. R. (10/6/1952) Letter to Martha Kesselman from RCAF Casualties Officer, RCAF, Library and Archive Canada.

Harris, J. S. (31/7/1945) Correspondence, RCAF, Library and Archive Canada.

Hartsook, L. (12/5/2016) in correspondence with the author.

Hillier, M. (15/1/2020) in correspondence with the author.

Hillier, M. (15/3/2020) in correspondence with the author.

Hillier, M. (10/2/2024) in correspondence with the author.

Hillier, M. (14/2/2024) in correspondence with the author.

Hillier, M. (26/2/2024) in correspondence with the author.

Hillier, M. (11/3/2024) in correspondence with the author.

Hillier, M. (3/4/2024) in correspondence with the author.

Hines, M. (23/12/2023) in correspondence with the author.

Holmes, L. (25/4/2022) in correspondence with the author.

Hope, B. (15/9/2023) in correspondence with the author.

Hood, M. (9/4/1985) Correspondence with Jim Feasey, ABN Agri.

Horner, A. (11/9/1941) Correspondence from Horner (Officer Commanding No. 121 (Technical) Detachment, RCAF, Library and Archive Canada.

Hyland, S. (August 2018) in correspondence with the author.

Hyland, S. (29/10/2018) in correspondence with the author.

Jacob, J. C. & Jacob, W. (24/5/1952) Correspondence with Walsingham Estate Company, Walsingham Estate Archive.

Jackson-Stops (21/6/1951) Correspondence with Walsingham Estate Company, Walsingham Estate Archive.

Jackson-Stops (13/7/1951) Correspondence with Walsingham Estate Company, Walsingham Estate Archive.

Kesselman, M. (1944) Correspondence Home, via Murray Kesselman.

Kesselman, M. (11/12/2020) in correspondence with the author.

Langslow, M. C. (28/2/1945) Correspondence, RAAF, National Archives Australia, NAA A705 166/33/265.

Langslow, M. C. (30/4/1945) Correspondence, RAAF, National Archives Australia, NAA A705 166/33/265.

Langslow, M. C. (20/11/1945) Correspondence, RAAF, National Archives Australia, NAA A705 166/33/265.

Langslow, M. C. (18/9/1945) Presumption of Death Correspondence, RAAF, National Archives Australia, NAA A705 166/33/265.

Langslow, M. C. (1/1/1946) Correspondence, RAAF, National Archives Australia, NAA A705 166/33/265.

Langslow, M. C. (4/2/1946) Correspondence, RAAF, National Archives Australia, NAA A705 166/33/265.

Little, S. (30/12/2013) in correspondence with the author.

Mackay, F. (July 1945) Correspondence from Mother of W. H. V. Mackay with Les Currell, via Jeff Hudson.

Maclean, M. (6/11/1951) Correspondence with Walsingham Estate Company, Walsingham Estate Archive.

Maclean, M. (30/4/1952) Correspondence with Walsingham Estate Company, Walsingham Estate Archive.

Maclean, M. (15/4/1952) Correspondence with Walsingham Estate Company, Walsingham Estate Archive.

Maufe, J. (15/8/2023) Memories Related to Jessica Forde, via Jessica Forde.

Mulvey, T. (3/1/1979) Correspondence, ABN Agri.

Mercier, G. (15/2/2017) in correspondence with the author.

Neale, W. (23/10/2023) in correspondence with the author.

Neale, W. (6/2/2024) in correspondence with the author.

Newcombe, J. A. (5/7/1955) 'Letter to War Works Commission' in Great Walsingham, Norfolk, Closure of Road, War Works Commission, National Archives, T180/83.

Nieman, C. (6/4/2021) in correspondence with the author.

Nolan, F. (12/3/1995) Correspondence with Cromer Museum, via Mike Hillier.

Overseas HQ (7/5/1946) Correspondence to Director of Estates, RCAF, Library and Archive Canada.

Panton, J. (4/9/2022) in correspondence to the author.

Parker, D. (6/9/2021) in correspondence with the author.

Partridge, J. (26/10/04) Correspondence with John Reid, via John Reid.

Partridge, J. (4/11/2004) Correspondence with John Reid, via John Reid.

Pennington, A. C. (20/6/1945) Correspondence Regarding Sale of Morris 8, RCAF Overseas HQ, Library and Archive Canada.

Poad, R. & Webster, J. (2020) Maidenhead Heritage Centre: The Spiritual Home of ATA (Air Transport Auxiliary) in correspondence with the author.

Polichek, V. (3/2/1998) Correspondence, via Jayne Jennings.

Powe, J. (2/12/1945) Correspondence, National Archives Australia, NAA A705 166/33/265.

Powe, J. (undated) Correspondence, National Archives Australia, NAA A705 166/33/265.

Rankin, K. (1/2/1990) <u>Correspondence with John Reid</u>, via John Reid.

Reid, J. (27/3/2006) <u>Correspondence with Roy Smith</u>, via Roy Smith.

Reid, J. (12/12/2020) in correspondence with the author.

Reid, J. (16/3/2023) in correspondence with the author.

Royal Canadian Air Force Casualty Officer (11/4/1947) <u>Correspondence between RCAF Casualty Officer and Gordon Dennison's Mother</u>, RCAF, Library and Archive Canada.

Sanderson, T. (16/8/1947) <u>Correspondence with the Wife of Mannell</u>, National Archives of Australia.

Shelley, P. (14/5/2009) <u>Correspondence with J H Moore</u>, via family of Ben Bennet.

Slater, B. (undated) <u>Correspondence</u>, via N. Lewis.

Smith, R. (10/4/1945) <u>Correspondence with Robin Neillands</u>, via Roy Smith.

Smithies, J. F. (16/8/1949) 'Letter to Ministry of Agriculture & Fisheries' in <u>Crop Drying Project: North Creake</u>, National Archives, MAF 105/129.

Sumsion, E. W. (5/10/1949) <u>Correspondence between Ministry of Works and Walsingham Estate Company</u>, Walsingham Estate Archive.

Tapper, H. C. M. (16/8/1949) 'Letter to Ministry of Agriculture & Fisheries' in <u>Crop Drying Project: North Creake</u>, National Archives, MAF 105/129.

Taylor, W. J. (21/5/84) <u>Correspondence</u>, ABN Ltd Archive.

Thompson P. (22/4/2023) in correspondence with the author.

Thompson, P. (30/9/2023) in correspondence with the author.

Thornley, H. E. (11/4/2011) <u>Correspondence with Tom Lewis</u>, via John Maden

Varley, M. (2013) <u>Correspondence Jeanne Endersby</u> via Jeanne Endersby.

Walsingham Estate Company (10/11/1948) <u>Correspondence with Walsingham Rural District Council</u>, Walsingham Estate Archive.

Walsingham Estate Company (29/9/1949) <u>Correspondence with Ministry of Works</u>, Walsingham Estate Archive.

Walsingham Estate Company (22/1/1950) <u>Correspondence with S H Waters, Edgar Farm</u>, Walsingham Estate Archive.

Walsingham Estate Company (10/3/1953) <u>Correspondence with British Field Products</u>, Walsingham Estate Archive.

Walsingham Rural District Council (11/6/1948) <u>Correspondence with S H Waters, Edgar Farm</u>, Walsingham Estate Archive.

Walsingham Rural District Council (23/12/1948) <u>Correspondence with Walsingham Estate Company</u>, Walsingham Estate Archive.

Walsingham Rural District Council (27/4/1949) <u>Correspondence with Walsingham Estate Company</u>, Walsingham Estate Archive.

Walsingham Rural District Council (27/4/1949) <u>Correspondence with Walsingham Estate Company</u>, Walsingham Estate Archive.

Waters, S. H. (24/2/1949) <u>Correspondence with Walsingham Estate Company</u>, Walsingham Estate Archive.

Waters, S. H. (1/3/1949) <u>Correspondence with Ministry of Works</u>, Walsingham Estate Archive.

Waters, S. H. (2/5/1949) <u>Correspondence with Walsingham Estate Company</u>, Walsingham Estate Archive.

Williams, W. H. (4/7/1955) 'Letter to War Works Commission' in <u>Great Walsingham, Norfolk, Closure of Road</u>, War Works Commission, National Archives, T180/83.

Willmott, P. (1944) <u>Correspondence</u>, Churchill College Cambridge Archive, WLMT 02001002(1).

Willmott, P. (1944) <u>Correspondence</u>, Churchill College Cambridge Archive, WLMT 02001001(3).

Willmott, P. (1944) <u>Correspondence</u>, Churchill College Cambridge Archive, WLMT 02001002(4).

Willmott, P. (1944) <u>Correspondence</u>, Churchill College Cambridge Archive, WLMT 02001001(6).

Willmott, P. (1944) <u>Correspondence</u>, Churchill College Cambridge Archive, WLMT 02001001(7).

Willmott, P. (1944) <u>Correspondence</u>, Churchill College Cambridge Archive, WLMT 02001001(8).

Willmott, P. (1944) <u>Correspondence</u>, Churchill College Cambridge Archive, WLMT 02001001(9).

Willmott, P. (1944) <u>Correspondence</u>, Churchill College Cambridge Archive, WLMT 02001001(12).

Willmott, P. (1944) <u>Correspondence</u>, Churchill College Cambridge Archive, WLMT 02001001(13).

Willmott, P. (1944) <u>Correspondence</u>, Churchill College Cambridge Archive, WLMT 02001001(14).

Willmott, P. (1944) <u>Correspondence</u>, Churchill College Cambridge Archive, WLMT 02001002(15).

Willmott, P. (1944) <u>Correspondence</u>, Churchill College Cambridge Archive, WLMT 02001002(16).

Willmott, P. (1945) <u>Correspondence</u>, Churchill College Cambridge Archive, WLMT 02001001(17).

Willmott, P. (1945) <u>Correspondence</u>, Churchill College Cambridge Archive, WLMT 02001001(20).

Willmott, P. (1945) <u>Correspondence</u>, Churchill College Cambridge Archive, WLMT 02001002(22).

Willmott, P. (1945) <u>Correspondence</u>, Churchill College Cambridge Archive, WLMT 02001001(26).

Willmott, P. (1945) <u>Correspondence</u>, Churchill College Cambridge Archive, WLMT 02001001(27).

Willmott, P. (1945) <u>Correspondence</u>, Churchill College Cambridge Archive, WLMT 02001002(29).

Wood, D. (29/10/2010) <u>Correspondence</u>, via Denis Gill.

Wright, D. A. (9/7/1948) <u>Correspondence</u>, RAAF, National Archives Australia, NAA A705 166/33/265.

Documents

Addison, E. (6/6/1944) <u>D-Day Signal</u>, RAF 100 Group Headquarters, Control Tower Archive.

Addison, E. (1/5/1945) <u>Scapegoats of Bomber Command</u>, RAF 100 Group, National Archives, AIR14/2657.

Addison, E. B. (28/7/1945) 'Message from the Air Officer Commanding', in RAF North Creake (3/8/1945), <u>Programme of Proceedings on the Occasion of the Disbandment of the 171 and 199 Squadrons Bomber Command</u>, Air Ministry, Control Tower Archive.

Addison, E. (1945) No. 80 Wing, Royal Air Force: Historical Report, 1940-1945, Air Ministry.

Aeroplane (2015) Short Stirling: The RAF's First Four-Engined 'Heavy', Key Publishing.

Air Council (undated) Flying Control in the Royal Air Force, publication 3024, Air Ministry, Reproduced for Army Air Forces Distribution by Training Aids Division Office of the Assistant Chief of Air Staff, Training headquarters Army Air Forces, New York.

Air Ministry (1943) Notes for the General Information and Guidance of the Next-of-Kin or other Relatives of Airmen reported Missing, Deceased, Prisoners of War or Interned, Air Ministry.

Air Ministry (5/10/1943) Minutes of a Conference Held on Wednesday 29 September 1943 at the Air Ministry to Discuss Proposals for the Formation of a Combined Radio Countermeasure Organisation for the Support of the Air offensive, Air Ministry, National Archives AVIA 7/2303.

Air Ministry Works Directorate (20/11/1948) Correspondence with Walsingham Estate Company, Walsingham Estate Archive.

Aldus, R. V. (undated) Graven Halifax NA687 171 Sqn, translated from Flemish by Hibberd, J. (2017) via Jamie Hibberd.

Ambrose, S (1973) 'A Special Presentation: From War to Peace' The World at War, ITV.

Anonymous (undated) 'Case Paper' in Crop Drying Project: North Creake, National Archives, MAF 105/129.

Argent, J. E. (24/7/1950) Maintenance of Military Defence Works, Norfolk Record Office, C/P8/1/46.

Berrill, R. (October 2022) Written Response to Pre-Interview Paper.

Berry, P. (2018) A Wireless Operator at RAF North Creake, unpublished manuscript.

Berry, P. (2018a) A NAAFI Girl at RAF North Creake: Jean Kershaw, unpublished manuscript.

Bradley, C. (1994) Kiel Revisited, unpublished manuscript.

Bray, N. A. N. (Christmas 1944) Confidential Message from the Station Commander, RAF North Creake.

Bray, N. A. N. (4/1/1945) Station Routine Orders, RAF North Creake, via Peter Hill.

Chisholm, P. N. (2/12/1944) FIDO Landing Precautions, RAF 100 Group Headquarters.

Clowes, I. C. D. (20/12/1946) Missing Research & Enquiry Unit Casualty Enquiry Investigation Report, MRES, RAAF, National Archives Australia, NAA A705 166/33/265.

Cloves, L. D. O. (17/5/1946) Casualty Investigation Report, MRES, Library and Archive Canada.

Cockburn, R. (1945) The Radio War, Telecommunications Research Institute, Air 20/8953.

Cotterell, A. P. I. (1944) Post-War Reconstruction: Water Supplies and Sewage, Walsingham Rural District Council.

Cracknell, D. A. (20/1/1944) Charles Mison: Training Report: Air Gunner, RAF, Library and Archive Canada.

Crane, K. N. (17/9/1945) MI9 Interrogation Report, National Archives WO208/3327.

Croft, P. (Spring 2017) citing a letter, in Confound & Destroy, RAF 100 Group Association.

Currell, L. (undated) To Whom it May Concern: Memoire of Escape, via John Reid.

Currell P. (undated) Biography of Les Currell, via John Reid.

Derbyshire, K. (28/2/1990) Recollections of a 199 Squadron Electrician, via John Reid.

Dennison, G. (2007) Memories Are Treasures: The Military career of Pilot Officer Gordon Joshua Dennison, unpublished manuscript.

Department of Media, Culture and Sport (2/12/2005) Press Release: Chocks Away! David Lammy Secures a Future for the Aviation Sites that Protected Our Past.

Department of National Defence (8/11/1945) Estates Branch, Form P. 64, RCAF, Library and Archives Canada.

Department of National Defence (Canada) (30/3/1946) Robert Brown: Statement of War Service Gratuities, Library and Archive Canada.

Department of National Defence (3/4/1946) Statement of War Service Gratuity, Library and Archives Canada.

Director of Estates (18/9/1945) Campbell, M. E. submission on Form P. 64.: Department of National Estates Branch, Canadian National Defence,

Docherty, G. (12/10/1944) Cloud Breaking Procedure, RAF North Creake.

Dunham, H. S. (27/6/1945) Hospital or Sick Record Card: Form 39, RAF, Library and Archive Canada.

Eastern Daily Press (26/6/1945) Plane Crash on Cromer Beach, EDP.

Eastern Daily Press (31/5/1946) Norfolk's 22 Airfields: Permanent Stations Named, EDP.

Eastern Daily Press (31/8/1946) More Squatters Move In, EDP.

Eastern Daily Press (3/9/1946) Squatters Fix Own Rent, EDP.

Eastern Daily Press (20/9/1946) RDC Takes Over Brandon Squatters, EDP.

Eastern Daily Press (22/3/1948) Old Sewers at Walsingham, EDP.

Eastern Daily Press (9/8/1948) Polish Colony Plan to be Raised in Parliament, EDP.

Eastern Daily Press (3/9/1948) Poles to Live on Airfield at Great Walsingham, EDP.

Eastern Daily Press (3/9/1948) New Village, EDP.

Eastern Daily Press (9/9/1948) Protests Against Housing of Poles on Airfield, EDP.

Guinea Pig Club (July 1990) Guinea Pig Club Journal, self-published.

Elder, M. F. (1987) 2nd Division Headquarters Group, Second Division Association, Vol. 26, No. 3.

Everitt, D. H. (24/2/1945) Report on Investigation for Further Identification of Casualties, Missing Research Enquiry Service, National Archives of Australia.

Fenning, F. (1945) Statement by F/Lt Fenning (104913) Mid-Upper Gunner in Stirling Aircraft LJ 617 on Night 5.3.45, RAF North Creake.

Flood, M. (undated) My Grandad in World War II 1939-1945, school project, via Jean Firth.

Friend, J. (28/6/1946) Missing Research & Enquiry Service No. 20 Investigation Report, RAF, Library and Archive Canada.

Gibson, B. (4/7/1955) 'Letter to War Works Commission' in Great Walsingham, Norfolk, Closure of Road, War Works Commission, National Archives, T180/83.

Gill, D. (2006) 'The Skylark' in Abolish War, No 6, Summer, The Movement for the Abolition of War.

Gill, D. (2015) My Civilian and RAF Wartime Experiences, unpublished manuscript.

Hartlepool Mail (12/2/1945) Airman's Funeral, via Mike Hillier.

Hartley, K. (undated) Recollections of a Radar Mechanic, via John Reid.

Heilner, J. (undated) A Dream Came True, unedited manuscript, an abridged version appeared in Weekend (9-15/12/1981).

Hinton, J. H. (9/12/44) Service Record, Air Ministry, via Jeff Neely.

Hinxman, R. (undated) Recollections of a Radar Mechanic, via John Reid Collection.

Holmes, L. (2012) My Wartime Story by Joan Calvert/Foley/Hollis, unpublished manuscript.

Hopkins, H. (22/7/1949) Maintenance of Military Defence Works, Norfolk Record Office, C/P8/1/46.

Hopkins, H. (16/8/1949) Maintenance of Military Defence Works, Norfolk Record Office, C/P8/1/46.

Hopkins, H. (11/9/1952) Maintenance of Military Defence Works, Norfolk Record Office, C/P8/1/46.

How, B. (1945) Air Ministry Form 1767: Logbook.

Jewers, D. H. (3/8/1949) 'Statement of Information' in Crop Drying Project: North Creake, National Archives, MAF 105/129.

Kee, R. (8/2/1971) 'Mercury on a Fork', The Listener, BBC.

King, L. (undated) History of Service in RAF, unpublished manuscript.

King, R. (2021) Family History – Dad: Leslie Henry John King (1921-2002), unpublished manuscript.

Lawrence, D. H. (1995) Zebra Five November, self-published.

Lawson, H. H. (undated) 'Report' in RAF 100 Group Correspondence, RAF 100 Group, National Archives, AIR 20/4715.

McDougall, T. K. (6/12/1945) Memorandum, Minute 1, RCAF Casualties Section, Library and Archive Canada.

Maden, J. (2015) A History of RAF North Creake: Aircraft and Aircrew Losses: 171 Squadron and 199 Squadron, unpublished manuscript.

Mallett, E. (undated) Wartime Memories, unpublished manuscript.

Mauldon, F. R. C. (22/1/1947) Casualty Enquiry Investigation Report, MRES, Library and Archive Canada.

Melchett, P. (8/6/2014) Cutting Ribbon Speech at the Control Tower, recorded by Richmond, C. (8/6/2014).

Ministry of Information (1942) Front Line: 1940-41: The Official Story of the Civil Defence of Britain, HMSO.

Ministry of Town & Country Planning (26/2/1951) Maintenance of Military Defence Works, Norfolk Record Office, C/P8/1/46.

Daily Mirror (26/6/1945) RAF Men go to Death to Save Beach Crowd.

Missing Research & Enquiry Unit No 4 (15/6/1948) Correspondence, MRES, RAAF, National Archives Australia, NAA A705 166/33/265.

Mitchell, G. (undated) Start and Finish of an Air Gunner, unpublished manuscript.

Morgan, M. (undated) Recollections of an MT Driver, via John Reid Collection.

Morrissey, B. D. (25/4/1945) Incident Report, Headquarters 671st Field Artillery Battalion, APO 408, U.S. Army, RAAF, National Archives Australia, NAA A705 166/33/265.

Morter, E. (1915-1918) Central Military Service Tribunal: Case Number M5306, National Archives, MH 47/49/42.

Morter, N. (23/11/2021) Transcript of a Dedication to Bernie How: All Saints Church, Worlington.

Nicholas, C. (undated) Notes on a Life in the RAF, unpublished.

Nelmes, M. (18/7/1989) Australian War Memorial Correspondence with John Reid, via John Reid.

Noel, N. I. (24/7/1945) Statement Regarding Sale of Morris 8, Library and Archive Canada.

Panton, S. F. (19/10/44) Air Ministry Form 1767: Logbook.

Parsons, J. W. E. (15/5/1945) Casualty Enquiry No. S82: Halifax MZ469, MRES, Library and Archive Canada.

Pearce, W. (10/5/1941) Reference from YMCA, Woodstock, Canada: Jack Thurlow, Library and Archive Canada.

Perryman, D. & Perryman, M. (2014) Some Notes on the Water Supply to North Creake Airfield, unpublished manuscript.

Pheasant, V. (2003) The Sixtieth Anniversary of Window: 1943 – 2003, Chemring Countermeasures.

Poppy Land (2011) Cromer in the Second World War, Film Documentary, Poppy Land Publishing.

Royal Air Force (13/4/1944) RAF Training Report, Form 5034, Air Bomber No 20 OUT: Harold Coutts, RCAF, Library and Archive Canada.

RAF 100 Group (11/3/1944) RAF 100 Group Correspondence, RAF 100 Group, National Archives, AIR 20/4715.

RAF 100 Group (July 1944) Operations, RAF 100 Group.

RAF 100 Group (October 1944) Operations, RAF 100 Group, National Archives, Air 25/782

RAF 100 Group (November 1944) Operations, RAF 100 Group, National Archives, Air 25/782

RAF 100 Group (December 1944) Operations, RAF 100 Group, National Archives, Air 25/783.

RAF 100 Group (January 1945) Operations, RAF 100 Group, National Archives, Air 25/783.

RAF 100 Group (March 1945) Operations, RAF 100 Group, National Archives, Air 25/784,

RAF 100 Group (May 1944) 'Engineering', in Monthly Report of Activities, RAF 100 Group, National Archives, AIR 20/4715.

RAF 100 Group (March 1945) Operations Record Book Appendices, Air Ministry, National Archives, AIR 25/784.

RAF 100 Group (1945) Operations Record Book, Air Ministry, National Archives, AIR 25/777.

RAF 100 Group (1945) Loose Minute, Air 14/2894.

RAF 100 Group Association (2007) Confound & Destroy, Summer, RAF 100 Group Association.

RAF 171 Squadron (1944-1945) Operations Record Book, Air Ministry, National Archive, AIR27/1102.

RAF 171 Squadron: (1944-1945) Operations Records Book: Appendix, Air Ministry, National Archives, AIR 27/1103.

RAF 171 Squadron (4/4/1945) Combat Report, RAF.

RAF 199 Squadron (June 1944) Crew Order Book, RAF.

RAF 199 Squadron (1944-1945) Operations Records Book, Air Ministry, National Archives
AIR 27/1172.

RAF 199 Squadron (1944) Sorties Records N. Creake, unpublished record book.

RAF 199 Squadron (21/10/1944) Combat Report, Air Ministry, National Archive, AIR50/231.

RAF North Creake (1944-1945) Operations Record Book, Air Ministry, National Archives, AIR28/598.

RAF North Creake (Christmas 1944) Programme of Entertainment, Sports and other Festivities for Christmas and the New Year, RAF North Creake.

RAF North Creake (1944/5) Memo: Firing Air to Sea, RAF North Creake.

RAF North Creake (undated) Mentioned in Despatches, via Peter Hill.

RAF Woodbridge Air Ministry (1944-1945) Operations Record Book, Air Ministry, National Archives, AIR28/954.

RAF 274 Maintenance Unit (1945-1947) Operations Record Book: RAF Swannington, National Archives, AIR 29/1554/6.

Renaut, M. (7/3/1945) Escape Kits Memo, RAF.

Royal Australian Air Force (12/12/1944) Postal Acknowledgement Delivery, RAAF, National Archives Australia, NAA A705 166/33/265.

RAAF Overseas HQ (5/12/1945) Signal, RAAF, National Archives Australia, NAA A705 166/33/265.

RAAF Casualty Section (8/1/1946) Signal to RAAF Overseas HQ, RAAF, National Archives Australia, NAA A705 166/33/265.

Regional Manager (8/8/1949) 'Valuation Office Regional Report' in Central Land Board, National Archives, HLG/98/662.

Royal Air Force (26/3/1944) Charles Mison: Training Report: Rear, Mid-Upper Gunner, No. 1651 Conversion Unit, Library and Archive Canada.

Royal Air Force (7/5/1944) Enrolment Form S.1. For R.A.F. Personnel, RAF, via Paul Swadling.

Royal Air Force (27/7/44) No. 1653 H.C.U. – Chedburgh Air Gunner's Assessment Chart, RAF.

Royal Air Force (28/8/1944) Robert Brown: Training Report: Air Bomber, RAF, Library and Archive Canada.

Royal Canadian Airforce (12/5/1941) RCAF Medical Board: Form RCAFM2: Jack Thurlow, RCAF, Library and Archive Canada.

Royal Canadian Airforce (9/6/1941) Interview Report: Jack Thurlow, RCAF, Library and Archive Canada.

Royal Canadian Airforce (11/7/1941) Attestation Paper: Jack Thurlow, RCAF, Library and Archive Canada.

Royal Canadian Air Force (31/12/1941) Attestation Paper: Lloyd George Langley, RCAF, Library and Archive Canada.

Royal Canadian Air Force (30/12/1941) RCAF Interview Report, RCAF, Library and Archive Canada.

Royal Canadian Air Force (6/5/1942) Attestation Paper: Murray Kesselman, RCAF, Library and Archive Canada.

Royal Canadian Air Force (9/5/1942) Interview Report: Murray Kesselman, RCAF Library and Archive Canada.

Medical Officer (29/6/1942) on, Royal Canadian Air Force (31/7/1942) Harold Coutts: Attestation Paper, RCAF, Library and Archive Canada.

Royal Canadian Air Force (31/7/1942) Harold Coutts: Attestation Paper, RCAF, Library and Archive Canada.

Royal Canadian Air Force (14/10/1942) Robert Brown: Attestation Paper, RCAF, Library and Archive Canada.

Royal Canadian Air Force (2/11/1942) Charles Mison: Attestation Paper, RCAF, Library and Archive Canada.

Royal Canadian Air Force (23/4/1942) Charles Mison: RCAF Medical Board, RCAF, Library and Archive Canada.

Royal Canadian Air Force (1942) Report on Pupil Pilot -Flying and Ground Training, RCAF, Library and Archive Canada.

Royal Canadian Air Force (1942a) Report on Pupil Pilot, RCAF, Library and Archive Canada.

Royal Canadian Air Force (1942c) Appendix 'A': Progress and Discontinuance Report, RCAF, Library and Archive Canada.

Royal Canadian Air Force (18/11/1942) Attestation Paper: James Duncan Campbell, RCAF, Library and Archive Canada.

Royal Canadian Air Force (1943) Record of Airmen, RCAF, Library and Archive Canada.

Royal Canadian Air Force (1943a) Part III (Report on Pupil Nav.), RCAF, Library and Archive Canada.

Royal Canadian Air Force (21/1/1943) Interview Report: Gordon Dennison, RCAF, Library and Archive Canada.

Royal Canadian Air Force (18/3/1943) Occupational History Form: James Duncan Campbell, RCAF, Library and Archive Canada.

Royal Canadian Air Force (14/5/1943) Robert Brown: Report on Pupil Pilot: Flying & Training, RCAF, Library and Archive Canada.

Royal Canadian Air Force (17/5/1943) RCAF Training Report, Form 5030, Air Bomber & Navigator: Harold Coutts, RCAF, Library and Archive Canada.

Royal Canadian Airforce (10/9/1943) Test: Jack Thurlow, RCAF.

Royal Canadian Air Force (17/9/1943) RCAF Training Report, Form 5031, Air Bomber: Harold Coutts, RCAF, Library and Archive Canada.

Royal Canadian Air Force (20/8/1943) Form 5023: Training Report, RCAF, Library and Archive Canada.

Royal Canadian Air Force (20/8/1943a) Charles Mison: Training Report: Wireless Operator (Air Gunner) and Air Gunner: Form 5035, RCAF, Library and Archive Canada.

Royal Canadian Air Force (17/9/1943a) Royal Canadian Air Force: Record of Service Airmen: Harold Coutts, RCAF, Library and Archive Canada.

Royal Canadian Air Force (26/11/1943) R.C.A.F. Training Report: Wireless Operator (Air Gunner) and Air Gunner, No. 9 Bomber and Gunnery School, RCAF, Library and Archive Canada.

Royal Canadian Air Force (26/11/1943a) R.C.A.F. Training Report: Wireless Operator (Air Gunner) and Air Gunner, No. 9 Bomber and Gunnery School: Gordon Joshua Dennison, RCAF, Library and Archive Canada.

RCAF, and Royal Canadian Air Force (26/11/1943c) R.C.A.F. Training Report: Wireless Operator (Air Gunner) and Air Gunner, No. 9 Bomber and Gunnery School: James Duncan Campbell, RCAF, Library and Archive Canada.

Royal Canadian Airforce (15/4/1944) Occupational History Form: Jack Thurlow, RCAF, Library and Archive Canada.

Royal Canadian Air Force (30/12/1944) Robert Brown: Record of Service: Form R230, RCAF, Library and Archive Canada.

Royal Canadian Air Force (22/8/1945) Official Royal Canadian Air Force Casualty Notification Form, RCAF.

Royal Canadian Air Force (undated) Department of National Defence Inventory: Gordon

Joshua Dennison, RCAF, Library and Archive Canada.

Royal Canadian Air Force (undated)(a) Department of National Defence Inventory: Lloyd George Langley, RCAF, Library and Archive Canada.

Royal Canadian Airforce (undated)(b) Service Record: Jack Thurlow, RCAF, Library and Archive Canada.

Royal Canadian Airforce (undated)(c) Registration of Death Certificate: Jack Thurlow, RCAF, Library and Archive Canada.

Royal Air Force (6/5/1947) Thomas, K. Exhumation Report, Library and Archives Canada.

Sant, H. (18/5/2016) RAF Memories: Video Interviews with his Daughter, via Diana Sant Angelo.

Seddon, R. D. (2/11/1942) Charles Mison Attestation Paper, RCAF, Library and Archive Canada.

Sinclair, J. (1987) Where's the Old Airfield? – You're Standing on it, newspaper cutting, via Nieman, C.

Skan, L. E. (1990) Half a Penguin: Reminiscences of a Bomber Command Flying Control Officer, unpublished manuscript.

Smith, R. (undated) Roy Smith – War Years in Bomber Command, unpublished manuscript.

Smith, R. (undated) War Memories, unpublished manuscript.

Smithard, T. (12/8/2004) 'Crash Pilot Saved Our Lives' Eastern Daily Press, Archant.

Smithies, J. F. (15/6/1949) 'Case Paper' in Crop Drying Project: North Creake, National Archives, MAF 105/129.

Spinks, R. (2013) Transcription of Docking Police Station Call Records.

Spear, B. (1988) The Met WAAF Contribution: Talk to the Royal Meteorological Society's Conference, School of geography, Birmingham University.

Stockwell, E. M. (undated) Standing Orders for Air and Ground Crews When Operating at Night, RAF North Creake.

Stone, J. (7/3/1945) Target Munster: MI9 Interrogation Report, via Mike Hillier.

Stone, J. (undated) March 7/8th 1945: 171 (BS) Squadron – Bomber Support Aircraft NA111:Y, unpublished manuscript.

Sturch (19/10/1945) Casualty Enquiry No. G. 155S, Nation Australian Archive, NAA A705 166/33/265.

Stubbington, J. (undated) 171 Squadron: From the National Archives, unpublished manuscript.

Sturch, L. A. (19/10/1945) Casualty Enquiry No. G. 155S, Air Ministry, National Archives Australia, NAA A705 166/33/265.

Sumsion, E. W. (25/4/1950) Maintenance of Military Defence Works, Norfolk Record Office, C/P8/1/46.

Thomas Organ & Piano Co. (12/5/1941) Reference: Jack Thurlow, Library and Archives Canada.

Thompson, P. (2017) Halifax Bill, 6Y-B Baker, Some Memories of My Father, unpublished manuscript.

Thompson, P. (2017a) Some Memories of Wilf Thompson's Time in the RAF, unpublished manuscript.

The Times (8/7/1987) Air Vice Marshall Edward Baker Addison Obituary.

Toronto Globe and Mail (1944) Truck Langley Officially Listed as Killed in Action.

Toronto Star (16/11/1945) F.O. Kenneth Thomas Now Presumed Dead, Library and Archives Canada.

Townroe, P. (2012) 'Our Three Local World War Two Airfields: Seventy Years On', Wells Local History Group Members' Newsletter, No. 51, September, WLHG.

Tuck, J. (2013) John Tuck at Hobbies Ltd, Dereham and Other Wartime Occupations, unpublished manuscript.

Turner, S. (1/5/1950) Maintenance of Military Defence Works, Norfolk Record Office, C/P8/1/46.

Turner, S. (undated) 'Statement of Information' in Great Walsingham, Norfolk, Closure of Road, War Works Commission, National Archives, T180/83.

Valuation Office (6/5/1950) 'Report' in Central Land Board, National Archives, HLG/98/662

Walsingham Estate Company (22/1/1950) State and Condition Report, Walsingham Estate Archive

Walsingham Parish Council (1894-1954) Minutes, Norfolk Record Office, PC47/1.

Walsingham Rural District Council (1/12/1948) Minutes, Norfolk Record Office, DC19/6/27

Walsingham Rural District Council (May 1945-May 1949) Housing Committee Minutes, Norfolk Record Office, DC19/6/63.

Walsingham Rural District Council (May 1949-May 1951) Housing Committee Minutes, Norfolk Record Office, DC19/6/64

Walsingham Rural District Council (5/7/1953) Housing Committee Minutes, Norfolk Record Office, DC19/6/66

War Office (1943) Advice to the Relatives of a Man Who is Missing, HMSO.

War Works Commission (7/7/1955) 'Support Document' in Great Walsingham, Norfolk, Closure of Road, War

Works Commission, National Archives, T180/83.

Ward-Walters, L. M. (undated) 'Statement of Information' in Great Walsingham, Norfolk, Closure of Road, War Works Commission, National Archives, T180/83.

Woollard, W. (1977) on BBC (1996) The Secret War: The Complete Original Series, Episode Two, BBC.

Internet sources

Searchable Databases

Aircrew Remembered: https://aircrewremembered.com/allen-robert-francis.html.

Air History: http://www.airhistory.org.uk/dh/_DH98%20prodn%20list.txt.

Archives New Zealand: Royal New Zealand Air Force Biographies of Deceased Personnel 1939-1945, https://www.aucklandmuseum.com/war-memorial/online-cenotaph/record/.

Caribbean Aircrew: https://www.caribbeanaircrew-ww2.com/.

Commonwealth War Grave Commission: https://www.cwgc.org/find-records/find-war-dead.

Guinea Pig Club Archive: https://www.eastgrinsteadmuseum.org.uk/patients/.

International Bomber Command: https://losses.internationalbcc.co.uk/loss.

National Archives: https://webarchive.nationalarchives.gov.uk/

National Archives Australia: https://recordsearch.naa.gov.au/searchNRetrieve/Interface.

Specific Internet Pages

Adcock, A. (2004) 'Interview', Second World War Experience Centre, https://war-experience.org/lives/arthur-adcock-w-o-raf/ retrieved 14/5/2023.

American Air Museum (undated) https://www.americanairmuseum.com/person/212815, retrieved 26/8/2022.

American Air Museum (undated) https://www.americanairmuseum.com/archive/aircraft/43-37705, retrieved 8/2/2023.

American Library: Memorial to the 2nd Air Division (undated) https://www.americanlibrary.uk/second-air-division-history/ketteringham-hall-hq#:~:text=Ketteringham%20Hall%20(Station%20147)%20was,use%20from%20the%20Boileau%20family, retrieved 9/2/2023.

Aviation Safety (undated) https://aviation-safety.net/wikibase/143924, retrieved 18/2/2024.

Bartlett, H. (21/10/2021) 'Interview with Gordon Mercier', IBCC Digital Archive, https://ibccdigitalarchive.lincoln.ac.uk/omeka/collections/document/34735, retrieved, 29/9/2022.

BBC Radio 4 (30/1/2000) Desert Island Discs: Sue Lawley interviewing Peter Melchett, https://www.bbc.co.uk/sounds/play/p0094b85, retrieved 2/6/2023.

BBC (29/12/2006) UK Settles WWII Debt to Allies, http://news.bbc.co.uk/1/hi/uk/6215847.stm, retrieved 28/9/2022.

BBC (9/11/2015) Five Reasons people don't wear poppies, 2015, https://www.bbc.co.uk/news/magazine-34720464, retrieved 21/12/2023.

Blair, J. J (undated) https://www.history.co.uk/article/the-rafs-caribbean-%2520Indian-and-African-pilots-of-ww2, retrieved 2/01/2021.

Brownswood, P. (2019) Ralph Reader and the RAF Gang Shows, https://blogs.lse.ac.uk/lsehistory/2019/08/15/ralph-reader-and-the-raf-gang-shows/, retrieved 28/10/2023.

Chamberlain, N. (6/2/1940) 'Bombing of Civil Populations', Hansard, https://hansard.parliament.uk/commons/1940-02-06/debates/b33adb9d-dbcf-485c-b102-44abd743ab14/BombingOfCivilPopulations, retrieved 24/1/2024.

Church, T: 'Caught Short Aloft' (undated) https://tailendcharlietedchurch.wordpress.com/halifax-bomber/halifax-aircrew/caught-short-aloft/, retrieved 6/3/2023.

Churchill, W. (10/5/1942) Prime Minister Winston Churchill's Broadcast Report on the War, http://www.ibiblio.org/pha/policy/1942/1942-05-10a.html, retrieved 26/04/2017.

Clark D (undated) http://forum.keypublishing.com/showthread.php?119664-Aviation-Myths/page4 , retrieved 11/03/2017.

Colgan, G. (7/5/2020) 'VE Day: A Woodstock Pilot's sacrifice', Woodstock Sentinel Review, https://www.woodstocksentinelreview.com/news/local-news/ve-day-a-woodstock-pilots-sacrifice, retrieved 10/9/2023.

Commercial Aviation Safety Team (undated) Propeller Operation and Malfunctions Basic Familiarization for Flight Crews, https://www.cast-safety.org/pdf/4_propeller_fundamentals.pdf, retrieved 22/3/2023.

Commonwealth War Grave Commission (undated) https://www.cwgc.org/our-work/blog/remembering-the-pilots-of-the-battle-of-britain/#:~:text=544%20RAF%20pilots%20of%20Fighter,a%20result%20of%20the%20battle, retrieved 6/2/2024.

Delve, K (17/6/2016) Ken Delve Looks at an Unusual Aspect of one of Norfolk's Wartime RAF Squadrons, RAF Heraldry Trust, https://www.rafht.co.uk/index. php/2016/06/17/171-sqn-norfolks-secret-squadron/, retrieved 6/8/2016.

Designing Buildings (undated) https://www.designingbuildings.co.uk, retrieved 20/6/2019.

Ellin, D. (23/2/2022) 'Interview with Roy Berrill', IBCC Digital Archive, https:// ibccdigitalarchive.lincoln.ac.uk/omeka/collections/document/36880, retrieved 30/9/2022.

Ex-Mil Recruitment (undated) https://blog.ex-mil.co.uk/2018/05/23/the-british-armed-forces-demystifying-the-military-ranks/, retrieved 20/3/2019.

Flight (29/1/1942) http://www.flightglobal.com/pdfarchi...0-%200248.html, retrieved 16/04/2017.

Foot, M. R. D. (19/12/1997) 'Obituary: R. V. Jones', Independent, https://www. independent.co.uk/news/obituaries/obituary-professor-r-v-jones-1289581.html, retrieved 29/5/2020.

Forces.Net (undated) Why the Black Poppy Matters, www.forces.net/heritage, retrieved 23/12/2023.

462 Squadron (undated) www.462squadron.com/pages/squadron_crews/rohrlach_crew, retrieved 10/5/2023.

Gough, P: 'From Heroes' Groves to Parks of Peace: landscapes of remembrance, protest and peace,' in Places of Peace: Selected Essays, https://www.paulgough.org/places_of_peace/peacepks.htm, retrieved 19/12/2023.

Greenhill, P. & Valentine, P. (undated) Window, https://www.sunprintershistory.com/factwindow.htm, retrieved 3/3/2023.

The Guardian (20/9/2000) 'Melchett Cleared Over GM Crop Damage', https://www. theguardian.com/environment/2000/sep/20/activists.gmcrops, retrieved 2/6/2023.

The Guardian (2/6/2008) 'Profile: Peter Melchett', https://www.theguardian.com/global/2007/jun/02/peter.melchett, retrieved 2/6/2023.

Hann, M. (1/11/2016) 'Wearing a Poppy is Only Meaningful if it's Voluntary', The Guardian, https://www.theguardian.com/commentisfree/2016/nov/01/wearing-poppy-meaningful-voluntary-footballers, retrieved 21/12/2023.

Hansard (6/3/1945) https://api.parliament.uk/historic-hansard/commons/1945/mar/06/air-estimates-1945#S5CV0408P0_19450306_HOC_307, retrieved 30/1/2022.

Harley, T (undated) British Weather in September, https://www.trevorharley.com/weather-september.html, retrieved 16/1/2023.

Harrison, T. (3/11/2016) 'Wearing a Poppy was a Pledge of Peace. Now it Serves to Sanitise War,' The Guardian, https://www.theguardian.com/commentisfree/2016/nov/03/wearing-poppy-pledge-peace-sanitise-war-remembrance, retrieved, 21/12/2023.

Heroes of our Time (undated) https://heroesofourtime.co.uk/stirling-lj518.html, retrieved 19/1/2023.

Hetherington, P. (2/2/1999) 'MoD Putting Rural Policy at Risk', the Guardian, https:// www.theguardian.com/politics/1999/feb/02/uk.politicalnews1, retrieved 24/12/2023.

Hibberd, J: www.462squadron.com/pages/squadron_crews/rohrlach_crew.html, retrieved 10/5/2023.

Hilliard, R: Nothing on the Clock, http://www.rafcommands.com/archive/03038.php retrieved 9/1/2023.

Historic England (2/6/2003) Conservation Bulletin 44: The Archaeology of Conflict, https://historicengland.org.uk/images-books/publications/conservation-bulletin-44/, retrieved 28/12/2023.

Historic England (undated) https://historicengland.org.uk/research/current/discover-and-understand/military/first-world-war-home-front/land/war-memorials/, retrieved 31/12/2023.

Historic England (undated)(a): https://historicengland.org.uk/research/current/discover-and-understand/military/historic-military-airfields/ retrieved 31/12/2020.

History of Ireland (undated) 'The Forgotten Volunteers of World War Two', https://www.historyireland.com/20th-century-contemporary-history/the-forgotten-volunteers-of-world-war-ii/, retrieved 02/01/2021.

Imperial War Museum (undated) https://www.iwm.org.uk/history/whos-who-in-an-raf-bomber-crew, retrieved 17/3/2023.

In Memoriam (undated) https://www.inmemoriam.be/fr/2013-04-23/gerard-marlaire/ , retrieved 28/12/2022.

ITV News (28/6/2013) Growing Controversy over Bomber Command Award, https://www.itv.com/news/anglia/2013-06-28/growing-controversy-over-bomber-command-award, retrieved 5/2/2024.

James-Parker, L. (2017) Bernie – Unsung Hero, https://www.youtube.com/watch?v=lC6sDwOFCd8, retrieved 25/5/2023.

Kavanagh, D. (16/11/2016) 'Interview with Bernie How', IBCC Digital Archive, https://ibccdigitalarchive.lincoln.ac.uk/omeka/collections/document/8856, retrieved 29/09/2022.

Kavanagh, D. (2016) 'Interview with Denis James Gill', IBCC Digital Archive https://ibccdigitalarchive.lincoln.ac.uk/omeka/collections/document/8843, retrieved 29/09/2022.

Lawrence, J. (2007) www.rafcommands.com/archive/10786.php, retrieved 28/3/2020.

Literary Norfolk (undated) 'Norfolk Deserted Villages', http://www.literarynorfolk.co.uk/deserted_villages.htm, retrieved 4/1/2022.

Local Government Association (undated) https://www.local.gov.uk, retrieved 12/12/2023.

Luftkrig 1939-1945 (undated) www.luftkrig1939-45.dk, retrieved, 20/11/2023.

Master Bomber Craig (undated) https://masterbombercraig.wordpress.com/avro-lancaster-bomber/corkscrew-port-go/, retrieved 19/5/2022.

Met Office Fact Sheet (undated) Remember the Met Office in World War One and World War Two,

https://www.metoffice.gov.uk/binaries/content/assets/metofficegovuk/pdf/research/library-and-archive/library/publications/factsheets/remember_world-war-one-and-two.pdf, retrieved 21/9/2022.

Ministry of Justice (26/2/2010) 'Government Response to the 30-Year Rule', https://www.gov.uk/government/publications/government-response-to-the-30-year-rule-review retrieved 29/01/2020.

Monbiot, G. (14/3/2014) How a False Solution to Climate Change is Damaging the Natural World, The Guardian, https://www.theguardian.com/environment/georgemonbiot/2014/mar/14/uk-ban-maize-biogas, retrieved 8/2/2023.

Murphy, B. (2015) 'Dark Tourism and the Michelin World War 1 Battlefield Guides,' Journal of Franco-Irish Studies: Vol. 4: No. 1, https://arrow.tudublin.ie/jofis/vol4/iss1/8, retrieved 23/12/2023.

National Memorial Arboretum (undated) https://www.thenma.org.uk/about-us/who-we-are, retrieved 11/1/2024.

National Museum of the United States Air Force (undated) https://www.nationalmuseum.af.mil/Visit/Museum-Exhibits/Fact-Sheets/Display/Article/196233/flak-36-88mm-multipurpose-gun/#:~:text=The%20versatile%2088mm%20cannon%20 was,cloud%20hanging%20in%20the%20sky, retrieved 10/3/2023.

The NSW Memorials Register (undated) https://www.warmemorialsregister.nsw.gov.au/nsw-stories/charles-joseph-joe-merryfull-mbe, retrieved 12/11/2020.

Noakes, L. (2020) Valuing the Dead: Death, Burial, and the Body in Second World War Britain, University of Essex, http://repository.essex.ac.uk/21751/1/Valuing%20the%20Dead%20Final%20version.pdf, retrieved 16/1/2023.

Norfolk Uncovered (undated) https://www.youtube.com/watch?app=desktop&v=tXWyIyQ5ZJ8

Nunn, S. J. (2019) The Impact of the Second World War on the Rural Landscape of Norfolk: PhD Thesis, University of East Anglia (undated) https://ueaeprints.uea.ac.uk/id/eprint/79294/1/2019NunnSPhD.pdf, retrieved 4/7/2023.

On the Ball (undated) https://itsontheball.org/testicular-cancer-information/, retrieved 2/1/2024.

Peace Pledge Union (undated) Frequently Asked Questions, https://www.ppu.org.uk/remembrance/white-poppies-frequently-asked-questions, retrieved 23/12/2023.

Pink News (undated) '13 Things You Need to Know About the Rainbow Poppy', www.thepinknews.com, retrieved 24/12/2023.

RAF Commands (undated) http://www.rafcommands.com/forum/showthread.php?13128-Aircraft-Crash-in-Norfolk&p=77388#post77388, retrieved 18/1/2023.

RAF Commands (undated)(a) http://www.rafcommands.com/archive/02410.php, retrieved 7/3/2023.

RAF Drem (undated) http://www.rafdrem.co.uk/lighting.html, retrieved, 12/11/2020, retrieved 16/1/2023.

RAF Museum (undated) https://www.rafmuseum.org.uk/research/online-exhibitions/pilots-of-the-caribbean/answering-the-call/the-second-world-war-1939-to-1945-recruitment/, retrieved 6/11/2023.

RAAFA Aviation Heritage Museum (undated) https://staging.aviationmuseumwa.org.au/afcraaf-roll/merryfull-charles-joseph-424778/, retrieved 12/11/2020.

Register of Births, Deaths and Marriages (1945), Bournemouth Vol 2b p. 1065, https://www.freebmd.org.uk/cgi/search.pl, retrieved 8/5/2023.

Reidy, J (undated) Unsung Heroes Project, Temora Aviation Museum, https://unsungheroesaustralia.com.au/unsung-heroes/jeffrey_reidy, retrieved 16/7/2023.

Relatives for Justice (undated) BBC Presenters and the Wearing of the Poppy, https://www.relativesforjustice.com/bbc-presenters-and-the-wearing-of-the-poppy/, retrieved, 20/12/2023.

Roads UK (undated) https://www.roads.org.uk, Retrieved 16/7/2023.

RodM. (2007) www.rafcommands.com/archive/10786.php, retrieved 28/3/2020.

Royal Air Force Benevolent Fund (undated) https://www.rafbf.org/, retrieved 12/12/2023.

Royal Navy (9/11/2018) Wear a Poppy or Don't Wear a Poppy. Many Have Died for Your Freedom of Personal Choice, https://www.navylookout.com/wear-a-poppy-or-dont-wear-a-poppy-many-have-died-for-your-freedom-of-personal-choice/, retrieved 21/12/2023.

Shaw, S (undated) '54 MU RAF Repair and Salvage (43 Group)', IBCC Digital Archive, https://ibccdigitalarchive.lincoln.ac.uk/omeka/collections/document/25991, retrieved 16/1/2023.

Smith, R. (7/12/2005) How I became a Navigator http://www.bbc.co.uk/history/ww2peopleswar/stories/23/a7887423.shtml, retrieved 8/2/2023.

Smith, R. (19/12/2005) Life as Part of the Crew of a Stirling Bomber, https://www.bbc.co.uk/history/ww2peopleswar/user/80/u1424880.shtml, retrieved, 8/2/2023.

Snow, J. (8/11/2006) Why I Don't Wear a Poppy on Air, https://www.channel4.com/news/by/jon-snow/blogs/wear-poppy-air, retrieved 21/12/2023.

Spark, S. (2010) The Treatment of the British Military War Dead of the Second World War, PhD Thesis, University of Edinburgh, https://era.ed.ac.uk/handle/1842/27449, retrieved 17/1/2023.

Spear, S (undated) Interview with Imperial War Museum: iwm.org.uk/collection/item/object/80010432 retrieved 1/10/2022.

Stokes, R. (6/3/1945) Hansard, https://hansard.parliament.uk/Commons/1945-03-06/debates/1de4c059-098d-4e2b-8bb7-3859f7c9ef0d/AirEstimates1945, retrieved, 29/2/2024.

Storr, A. (2006) RAAF Personnel Serving on Attachment in Royal Air Force Squadrons and Support Units in World War Two, https://s3-ap-southeast-2.amazonaws.com/awm-media/collection/RC09125.006/document/6019476.PDF, retrieved 27/09/2022.

Sullivan, E. P. (18/4/2019) Considerable Grief: Dead Bodies, Mortuary Science, and Repatriation after the Great War,

https://nursingclio.org/2019/04/18/considerable-grief-dead-bodies-mortuary-science-and-repatriation-after-the-great-war/, retrieved 16/1/2023.

Taylor, S. (2018) A Day in the Life of Bomber Command Lecture, Duxford, retrieved https://www.youtube.com/watch?v=ZL0T7edGu8E, 17/9/2022.

355st Bomb Group (undated) http://www.351st.org/351stMissions/Mission179/Mission179.html, retrieved 9/2/2023.

Thompson, D. (21/1/2011) No.43 Salvage and Repair Group, https://www.key.aero/forum/historic-aviation/108941-raf-ww2-54-mu, retrieved 16/1/2023.

Thompson K (1945) 'War Diary', IBCC Digital Archive, https://ibccdigitalarchive.lincoln.ac.uk/omeka/collections/document/16887, retrieved 28/9/2022.

Thorpe, V. (31/10/2020) 'Poppies Drawn into BBC Row Over 'Virtue Signalling'', https://www.theguardian.com/media/2020/oct/31/remembrance-poppies-drawn-into-bbc-row-over-virtue-signalling, retrieved, 20/12/2023.

Webster, H: A Domestic Rebellion: The Squatters Movement of 1946, https://humanities.exeter.ac.uk/media/universityofexeter/collegeofhumanities/history/exhistoria/volume4/Webber-Squatters_movement.pdf, retrieved 22/2/2019.

Wilcock, R (undated) 3/04.03.1945 No 171 Squadron Halifax III NA107 6Y-T Sqn. Ldr. Percy Clifford Procter MiD, https://aircrewremembered.com/procter-percy-clifford.html, retrieved 5/9/2023.

Wood, C. (2000) Interview with Arthur Gordon Clarke, IWM 20335 Reel 1, https://www.iwm.org.uk/collections/item/object/80018972

Xtison (14/10/2005) 'Bail Out 25th November 1944', on BBC (undated) WW2 People's War: An Archive of World War Two Memories, http://www.bbc.co.uk/history/ww2peopleswar/stories/68/a6138768.shtml, retrieved 5/1/2021.

INDEX

ABOUT THIS BOOK

In his book, Nigel Morter covers the short but important secret history of RAF North Creake intertwined with the tale of how he and his wife, Claire Nugent, found and fell in love with the airfield's control tower: a superb example of modernist architecture. The story tells of their escape from routine, sensible careers to start a new life running a bed and breakfast on a former Second World War airfield in North Norfolk. In parallel to the story of their escape, Nigel explores the history of the airfield within the context of the bombing war. From construction, operational life, decline and disposal, all life on the airfield is here. As Nigel & Claire restore the Control Tower back to its iconic modernist look, we learn of such things as airfield design priorities, the perils of operational life, the development of air traffic control, wartime socialising and the tragedy of loss.

Based on extensive primary, unpublished and archival research, the book explores the operation of the German's sophisticated early warning radar system that could track, plot and intercept Allied bombers — a radar system that led to a crisis in the bombing campaign when losses reached unsustainable levels. It discusses the formation of the RAF 100 Group and the birth of electronic warfare, revealing the secret yet crucial role RAF North Creake played in jamming German radar through the use of innovative 'Radio Counter Measures'. This book is both an engaging account of a life-changing passion project and also a significant contribution to a neglected area of research in the history of the bombing war.